Hymns to the Silence

Hymns to the Silence

Inside the Words and Music of Van Morrison

by Peter Mills

continuum

2010

The Continuum International Publishing Group Inc
80 Maiden Lane, New York, NY 10038

The Continuum International Publishing Group Ltd
The Tower Building, 11 York Road, London SE1 7NX

www.continuumbooks.com

Library of Congress Cataloging-in-Publication Data
A catalog record for this book is available from the Library of Congress.

ISBN: 978-0-8264-2976-6 (paperback)
ISBN: 978-0-8264-1689-6 (hardback)

Typeset by Pindar NZ, Auckland, New Zealand
Printed in the United States of America

Contents

'Music is spiritual; the music business isn't.'

Van Morrison

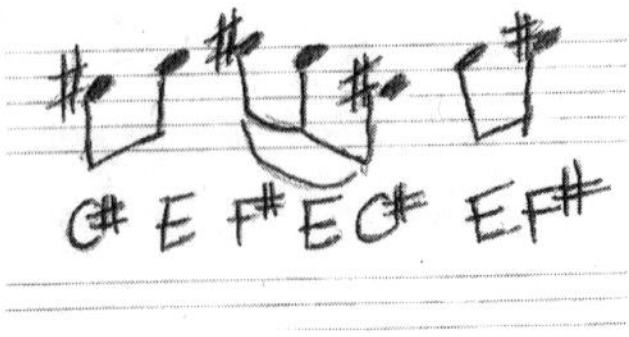

Acknowledgements

This book has taken a long time to write and in truth much longer than the few years since it was commissioned. In fact it has been bubbling up in my mind for over 20 years, ever since a friend mentioned during a pub lunch on the Isle of Portland in Dorset that I should write something, someday about the subject. It's taken a little longer than expected, young man, but here it is.

There have been many kindnesses and courtesies down the road and I am very grateful to everyone who took the time to consider my questions or give pause to reflect or reminisce. I'd like to thank the following very much for their help in the composition of this book, and for giving most generously of their time, insight and experience: Heidi Berry, Phil Coulter, Sid Griffin, Maria McKee, Kevin Rowland, Kate Rusby, Kate St. John, Gary Shearston, Ben Sidran, Bill Staines and Fiachra Trench. What these good people have in common is that they were kind enough to consider and then give full and illuminating responses to my questions on a wild variety of topics.

Many have been kind enough to indulge my interest in the subject, and I'd particularly like to thank those who have been willing to discuss it (and to listen to me expounding on the theme) over the past two decades or so, particularly Jonathan Lynas – who originally encouraged me to think about writing this book in that pub in Dorset way, way back in the 1980s – Jonathan Wolstenholme and John Jackson. Similar thanks go to Chris Hobbs and Heidi Thomas, both of whom, furthermore, were kind enough to read sections of the manuscript and offer insightful and greatly appreciated comments; thanks too to Steve Godrich and our other fellow Innocents Abroad, Stuart Hilton, Martin Malone and David Skidmore. I also owe much to Phil Davis and Brian Nellist in Liverpool, Bob Crossley in Boston, Michael Bott, Mary Bryden, James Knowlson, Anna McMullan and John Pilling in Reading, Peter Eri, Csilla Vago, Istvan Geher, Brigi Jaksa, Beata Palya and Andras Torok in Budapest, Mary Eagleton, David

Pearce and Anne Price in York, and Gordon Johnston, Barry King, Lance Pettitt and Neil Washbourne in Leeds. Thanks and felicitations go to Fiona Talkington at the BBC, Sheila Whiteley and Russ Reising for their friendship and encouragement, to the Duke of Earl ('Mikey's' is *still* playing) and Laura Barton, the best British writer on music currently publishing. Thanks also to Joanna Mills, Jordan Underhill, Sophia Underhill and Rhys Lonnen, while special thanks go to Clare Lynas for the little transcription that graces the front papers.

I'd also like to thank Simon Gee, editor of the now defunct *Wavelength* magazine and website, for his insight and generosity. Anyone who has had more than a passing interest in Van Morrison's work in the past 20 years or so owes Simon a substantial debt. I'd also like to extend my greatest gratitude to David Barker at Continuum for commissioning the book and, thereafter, his kindness, encouragement and saintly patience.

Finally I must thank my family who have tolerated, edited and scribbled every page with me: Charlotte, Bobby and Eva. This book is dedicated to them, for their love and patience, and to my father, Walter William Mills, who played me Ray Charles when I was a child. He wasn't much of a one for books, but I hope he might have quite liked to read this one.

So as we see many people have contributed directly or indirectly to the ideas, thoughts and interpretations within this book – all that is good about it is in no small way thanks to them. The book's faults, however, are all mine.

Peter Mills
January 2010

Author's Note

This book has a long story to tell, but I'll be brief. In October 2005 a version of this book was well on the way to being finished; that same month my father passed away after a protracted illness. In the time that followed I blamed the Morrison project for making me less attentive to his well-being than I might have been, and, consequently, I deleted the computer files and threw away the paper copies of the work. It was finished. Gone, gone, gone.

The next year was spent exclusively sorting out my father's estate and his belongings, which involved clearing the house I grew up in, and dealing with its sale. I barely gave anything else a single thought. Sorting through the clutter of a life, I found a heap of records in the radiogram – 78s, singles, LPs, flexi discs of basic Spanish I remember us listening to as we prepared for the grand adventure of two weeks in Ibiza in 1972, then an almost impossibly remote and exotic destination. Among the records, a George Formby LP I used to love – ukulele, 'When I'm Cleaning Windows'. A CBS compilation, improbably entitled *A Gift From SR Toothpaste*, given to retailers who stocked their products, featuring Simon and Garfunkel hard up against Tony Bennett and Ray Conniff. Jimmy Durante 78s: yellow MGM label, 'Fugitive From Esquire'. I remember looking at that title as a child and wondering what on earth it could mean. Some singles – 'Galveston' by Glen Campbell, duck-egg blue Ember label, an ex-jukebox single, slightly wonky due to the hole being punched out a little off-centre; Nilsson, 'Everybody's Talking', bright orange RCA, a song Dad loved so much we had it played at his funeral. I knew all these discs intimately. But then what are these? A pile of Josh White albums – *Empty Bed Blues*, *Good Morning Blues*. Blues, blues and then some more blues. Here, a stack of Ray Charles – *Modern Sounds In Country And Western*, *Live At Newport*. Singles too: 'In The Heat Of The Night', in its candystripe pale blue and white sleeve, on ABC-Dunhill. I knew he liked Ray but with the exception of the singles I'd never seen these records, and didn't know he had them – where the hell had he been hiding this stuff? Here, some Little Richard. Little Richard! My Dad had some Little Richard records! Suddenly it struck me: all these records, even the Formby, were connected, directly or indirectly, to Van Morrison. Dad was never that interested in him, although he'd say 'Your mate was on the radio' now and then if he'd heard 'Bright Side Of The Road' or 'Precious Time' on the wireless during the day. So I began to think that maybe I should see this book through after all, and that there was a good reason to do so: my Dad might have quite liked to read it. So I sat back down to start all over again. That's the book you are holding.

Introduction

'Have you ever heard *Astral Weeks* by Van Morrison? I think you might like it . . .'

Kevin Rowland in reply to a letter sent by the author, March 1981

This book, we should say straight away, is not a biography. It looks at the music, words and performances of Van Morrison that are in the public domain, and those to which I have been witness. So why did I decide to write it? In comparison to some of his peers, there has been remarkably little written about the work of Van Morrison; where rooms could be filled with the volumes of writing on the Beatles and Bob Dylan, there have been, at most, 17 or so publications taking Morrison as their central subject. This is a mystery, in that Morrison's musical reputation is in many ways the equal of Dylan or Lennon and McCartney. Indeed ever since Kevin Rowland put me on to the case in his kind reply to a fan letter way, way back, I have been waiting for someone to write the book I wanted to read about Van Morrison. In the end, it seemed that if I was ever going to read it, I probably better write it myself.

If this book has any virtue in comparison to the other books on the subject, it is chiefly that it is neither biography nor chronological trawl through the career, nor is it a picture book. Furthermore, with a couple of exceptions, the previous books are over ten years old, so it is able to reflect upon Morrison's later style. Ritchie Yorke's cherishable *Into the Music* (1975) had the substantial advantage of being written with the co-operation of its subject, and the present book seeks to offer a clear-eyed critique of Morrison from a bold and fresh perspective, yet one that firmly acknowledges Yorke's insights. My book also seeks to resist iconoclasm, an approach perhaps embodied by Johnny Rogan's typically audacious *Portrait of the Artist* (1984) and the updated version published as *No Surrender* (2005). Likewise the book does not seek to duplicate the career overviews offered by excellent volumes such as Steve Turner's lavishly illustrated *It's Too Late to Stop Now* (1993), Brian Hinton's thoughtful *Celtic Crossroads* (1997), Patrick Humphries's handy primer (1997) and John Collis's punchy *Inarticulate Speech of the Heart* (1996). Clinton Heylin's biography *Can You Feel the Silence?* (2002) deals well and fully with a version of the life, and in that sense it is hard to imagine it being bettered, but that book by necessity only occasionally touches upon the critical territory the present volume seeks to map. Less widely known volumes have emerged too, such as the delightful *In the Age of Uncertainty* by Katrin Pietzonka (2002) and Pat Kelly's lyrical *More Than a Song to Sing* (1993). We are also promised Howard A. DeWitt's bold multi-volume work, the first part of which arrived in 2005, joining a brace of energetic, late twentieth-century books by Ken Brooks. The works which most closely overlap with the present volume are *Speaking in Tongues: The Songs of Van Morrison* (2005) by Martin Buzacott and Andrew Ford, and a long, insightful essay by Gerald Dawe, 'The Burning Ground', which was first published in 1998. Both display the mix of close musical scrutiny and wider cultural context to which this book aspires.

In some ways books like this one are unnecessary: I could just say, 'Buy these records, they will help you live.' So I will: buy these records, they will help you live. But that's not enough – not for me, anyway, because after the emotion comes the deeper consideration of the art. That's how it works. Initially we have the primary emotional impact and response – 'I love this!' or 'I can't stand this!' or 'So what?' and then, in a secondary but also a more fully conscious way, we experience or move on to the more reasoned response: why do I love it, or loathe it, or why does it leave me cold when others react differently? So this book understands the secondary nature of most of its responses – music is concerned with feeling but in order to unpack, build upon and perhaps even learn from that feeling it is worth stepping back from the emotional (Walt Whitman's 'yawp', perhaps) and allow the analytical voice a say. I'd like to think this book yawps, too, in places, but what I want it to do is be the agent of that second stage, and to try to do that most difficult thing, analyse with words the ideas, feelings, and emotions which flow from the human obsession with music; the truth we feel stemming from sounds. I am interested in the connections between things, be they clear and direct or obscure and hitherto undetected. This book is certainly about Van Morrison and his very distinctive talents as writer, composer, performer and more, but it is not just about that. It is about the music, where it came from and where he took it, how he took tradition and innovated with it, and made it new – sometimes by going back to the ancient source. This book is about connections, and how things carry on.

This is also a very long book and in places it might seem an unnecessarily detailed one. However, it seems to me that it is the tiny detail – the aside in a live performance, the fluffed lyric left on the studio take, the single note which changes the temperature and atmosphere of an entire song – that gives us the key to the bigger themes, and to the impact and resonance of the songs, recordings and performances this book takes as its subject. Some themes are of course so deeply saturated and embedded into the work that they flow the whole way through the book, regardless of the topic at hand: the sense of place and immediate environment, and its obverse, exile; the nature of time; the power, gifts and torments of memory; the centrality of the here and now as a personal and performative imperative; the nature of spirit; the sense of musicality as a matter of feeling, first and foremost. These, among other themes, plot the co-ordinates for this voyage through the work.

The broad structure of the book divides our subject into three major areas: the first being the roots of his work in the music, places and ideas of America and Ireland with an assessment of how they have exerted an influence over his art. In the second we look at him as a writer, via studies of several of his best-known songs, and close scrutiny of key motifs within the work; we then consider him as a singer and a musician, following this with studies of how the realities of working onstage work with and against the practices of the recording studio. The third and final section addresses less worldly and more spiritual matters, first looking at the idea of exile and restlessness, and how the spirit of place is explored and revealed in his work. The book's finale looks at Morrison's periodic technique of through-composition, and examines four albums which seem to me to best illustrate this methodology, which is absolutely central to the works. The individual chapters tend to break down between contextual background, significant theory and close scrutiny of the music, on record and onstage, so that typically there is a theoretically based opening section followed by close analysis of relevant recordings. The book also makes use of original interviews conducted for this book alongside the very many public domain interviews Morrison has given over the decades.

As for the choice of songs upon which the book concentrates, this is I suppose subjective; there is an emphasis upon the recordings which seem to me to best illustrate and exemplify certain creative tendencies that are in my view central to the work overall. I don't try to discuss every song in the catalogue – a tall order, even for a book of this size – and my choices are not necessarily canonical, so that for example 'Linden Arden Stole The Highlights' and 'Song Of Being A Child' are as well examined as, say, 'Madame George' or 'Moondance'. So if your favourite isn't here, I apologize.

The book is divided up thematically, not chronologically. Consequently you will find songs from the first Them album considered alongside material from 2008's *Keep It Simple*, for example. This is not to suggest that there is no difference between the music or the man making it in 1965 and 2008, but to try and seek out connections and continuities over time and circumstance. It is part of my contention that Morrison's work both bears and reveals these continuities even as it clearly, and by necessity, embraces rapid change. The paradox is that here we have music focused intently on the present moment, the 'now', yet a music which frequently draws its strength from the past, from the power of memory. I would characterise this dynamic as a balance between tradition and innovation. In the light of this thought, the book offers close focus on certain songs and albums that seem to best illustrate and illuminate these creative tendencies. Indeed the book opens with a consideration of Morrison as an embracer and utiliser of traditional forms and one who, via such intuitive familiarity with those forms, is able to innovate with and develop them.

Thus we begin with studies of his relationship with American musical forms that have provoked, guided and informed his artistic and creative development – jazz, blues, and country music. Of course, in some senses these terms are only fit for the genre-based marketing of music and the apparent boundaries are spurious. They are however useful for discussing streams of influence and how these have impacted upon his own work later, either in the obvious sense of the 'country albums' or the 'jazz albums', or in the wider and more discreet sense of the way in which these influences have informed his music and how Morrison draws upon these forms even when not necessarily employing their formal musical discourses – *Veedon Fleece*, for example, is arguably a jazz album with no jazz on it. This leads to a consideration of his own first musical genre, which functioned as a composite of these other forms, skiffle, taking time to examine his work with Lonnie Donegan and reflect upon this relatively unexamined area of distinctively British working-class music and how it took deeply American musics and made something unmistakably and indigenously British from them. This section concludes with studies of two key albums that appear to fully illustrate his creative dynamic with the idea of America.

Chapter Two assesses the formative musical influences that constitute the 'Irishness' of Morrison's work. Here we have a puzzle: Van Morrison's music is, in terms of its surface details at least, not very 'Irish' in any generic sense. Yet there is a deep and understated 'Irishness' running throughout his work, even though compared to the work of, say, Christy Moore, or even his *Irish Heartbeat* collaborators the Chieftains it might not seem that way at first glance. Consequently, the chapter looks at how the Irishness of his work has been expressed in other less obvious ways, and also how we can understand

Morrison as an Irish writer. He claims to have read very little of Irish literature until others observed that there was a connection between his work and that of 'literary' figures and has subsequently recorded settings of Yeats and Patrick Kavanagh poems, collaborated with Paul Durcan and dropped quotes from Samuel Beckett into his live performances. We look at his connections with several Irish writers and the theme of literary comparison runs through the book as a whole. This is not to say that Morrison is 'like' Yeats, Beckett or Blake, but rather that somehow and sometimes he seems to be working the same seam as they did, just as he does with Leadbelly, Ray Charles or Mose Allison. We discern a mixture of conscious and unconscious influence, mixed with natural and unforced connection. This chapter also asks what is 'literary' or poetic about his work and what, if anything, is distinctively 'Irish' about these qualities? From which traditions does he come and to which does he belong? How has he redefined these traditions?

Building from this, we consider Morrison as a writer in Chapter Three. He has published a few shards of stand-alone text, such as the short story that adorns the sleeve of *A Sense Of Wonder*, redolent of Flann O'Brien and early Beckett, the tone poem on the sleeve of *Astral Weeks*, which is possibly an unsung verse of 'Ballerina', and its transcendent equivalent on the cover of *Astral Weeks Live*. Yet, as he mentioned to the audience at the University of Coleraine at a remarkable event in April 1988, when he writes a poem they usually end up turning into songs. The audience laughed, but it's true – Morrison is a musician and a songwriter so that is bound to happen. Hence we focus on him as a songwriter and think about how his work fits into the accepted methodologies of popular song via a focus on three of his best-known tunes and a group of his love songs.

Following on from this, in Chapter Four we examine a selection of the key motifs or phrases that seem to have flowed through and also guided his work. Some themes are not spotlit but run throughout all the sections – time, place and memory, for example, course through each and every topic – while some of the key themes do indeed have their own slot, and so I apologise if we sometimes seem to approach a subject more than once, and others only in passing reference. Specifically explored in this book is the theme of the garden, his 'leaf songs', and the theme of healing, alongside scrutiny of specifically 'Morrisonian' vocabularies such as the 'golden autumn day' and the 'ancient highway', leading to a consideration of how he has used the images of the radio and, finally, silence itself.

The second section of the book balances studies of Morrison as creative artist, and the public obligations that the success of that art generates. We begin in Chapter Five by considering the purely creative side of this balance, examining fundamental aspects of Morrison's work, looking at him purely as a singer via key case studies of a wide range of recordings, and also via Roland Barthes' idea of 'the grain of the voice'. Does he, like Bob Dylan, have 'different voices' (cf. Dylan's *Nashville Skyline* voice/'Rolling Thunder' voice) or is he unchanging in his delivery regardless of the musical context? Why does the role of the vocals in jazz differ in function to the job it has in blues, rock or pop? Alongside case studies and contextualising theory, the chapter will also ask direct questions: for example, is Morrison a 'good' jazz singer – does his delivery match his aspiration? Relating to these issues, we also look at Morrison as a musician and consider how tradition and innovation function in his work. We consider how he has attempted to fuse stylistic elements, and how he strives to 'make it new' alongside evocations of 'the beauty of the days gone by'. We consider him as player, bandleader and working musician, paying close attention to the idea of improvisation. We also look closely at two examples of where Morrison has reinterpreted the traditional songs 'Saint James Infirmary' and 'Wild Mountain Thyme' and made them new, one more time again.

We build on this creative dynamic by then looking at how Morrison makes this private work public. Much has been said about Morrison's performative persona but it has never been properly studied. Chapter Six deals with live performance, considering his stage work, via editorialised versions in officially issued live recordings, and the live shows that are, as it were, 'gone in the moment'. This chapter considers the 'liveness' of his performance technique. For example, does he consider his stage work to be an act of definition, re-creation or re-making every night? We look at his insistence on the importance of the concert stage via analysis of his work as a live performer, and scrutinise some key examples from the live recordings that have been issued commercially, on album, single and DVD.

Studying Morrison's style as live performer is balanced by a study of how he endeavours to capture the 'liveness' of moments otherwise heard only in passing on stage in concert performance, 'live in the studio'. He has always aspired to the Sinatra model ('Hey kids, dig the first takes', he sang on 'Hard Nose The Highway'), but the chapter examines in-depth how he takes principles of performance in to the studio. His albums are very 'well made', not full of fluffs or stylised rough edges *à la* Neil Young, so how does this performative element feed into the 'product'?

The final section of the book (Chapters Seven and Eight) gathers in what Morrison once called the more esoteric stuff, looking first at how the lure of eternal movement flows through his work, starting with his youthful interest in Kerouac, and seeing how these ideas move through the themes of exile and restlessness that can be discerned right through the catalogue. This identifies with the wild loneliness of the blues, the musical expression of a covert community of sole and singular people, always in motion, yet somehow connected. This passes on to a very important theme in his work, his sensitivity to the spirit of place. We can read this through songs from 'Cyprus Avenue' right through to perhaps his greatest 'spirit of place' recording, 'Coney Island'.

The book reaches its conclusion via an in-depth study of what I have termed 'through-composition', which is a working through of a distinct and fully recognisable musical mood that can only be found on one particular album. Through-composition as used here represents a kind of creative mining of a seam where the resultant album seems to exemplify this mood, which can only be found on that group of songs. I have written here about *Astral Weeks*, *Veedon Fleece*, *Into The Music* and *Common One*. This is not to suggest that his other recordings have less to recommend them, but it seems to me that in terms of the technique of through-composition and all that it means, these four albums are Morrison's most complete recordings.

The last two chapters bring together the key themes of the book into a consideration of whether the apparent contradictions and tensions identified in the body of work achieve or move towards resolution and wholeness. The spiritual element inherent throughout the book is considered more directly and we consider how the material conflicts of body and soul are reflected in the work. A short postscript examines the return to the landscapes of *Astral Weeks* in the 2008/9 concerts in which Morrison played the album in full, bringing a kind of closure to his relationship with those songs, and those songs' relationship to the rest of his repertoire.

In the period of this book's composition I've been asked many times why I'm not writing a biography – so, why not a biography? First, the previously published volumes on the subject are so thorough that the job seems to be already done. Secondly, my interest is in the work, rather than the life, although of course one is entirely aware that there is a connection between the two. Most pertinently, it seems to me that Van Morrison speaks most eloquently of his experience of the world via his songs and performances, meaning that, in practice, biography in the traditional sense is beside the point. Now Morrison may well be unwilling or simply uninterested in scrutinising his art in the way that, say, Bob Dylan seems to do in his book *Chronicles*, but Morrison's work is full of revelation about his experience of life and the power memory has over his imagination – in very direct and often anti-mythopoeic language – in a way that Dylan's occasionally opaque and perfumed poetics sometimes are not.

Morrison's work has swung between a position of detachment and a more open set of connections, sometimes giving us remarkably candid sketches of Belfast and the world in which he grew up, sometimes mystical and allusive, sometimes bright and direct. This reaches from the churchyard of the semi-improvised lyrics of 'Mystic Eyes', via the trees of 'Cyprus Avenue', on through the spot-of-time of 'Coney Island' to the deep meditations of 'On Hyndford Street' and the Yeatsian contemplations of 'Pagan Streams', or the bright sketches of Belfast childhood and adolescence such as 'Cleaning Windows', and the tender (and almost completely overlooked) reminiscence of his father, 'Choppin' Wood'. So calls for Van Morrison to write autobiographically in the style of Dylan's *Chronicles* are somewhat misplaced, even belated as the songs have recorded and processed aspects of his experience almost since day one. But we need to follow the art, not the artist; the uniqueness of his vision is rooted in experiences that are common ones. He has freely admitted in song and in conversation that he doesn't feel the need to know exactly what he is doing in the moment of creativity, or what the 'meaning' of such work might be, and this book isn't out to force such meaning upon the music. As he once sang, 'Enlightenment, don't know what it is'. Thus he is on a journey of discovery, down the road, and each fresh moment of performance has the potential to unlock another aspect not only of the song but of the experience that feeds and informs any given performance of it. As Morrison said in an interview for the BBC in 2006, 'I don't want to just sing a song . . . anyone can do that . . . something else has got to happen.' He also noted that the moments of achievement or of breakthrough are fleeting glimpses (or we might say 'beautiful visions', revealed then clouded over once more): 'it's momentary release . . . the minute it stops, it's gone.' It is this kind of detail which should give us pause to consider Morrison's work; it is also the ambition of this book to reflect upon that work in such a spirit. Let's take a look.

Chapter One

Imagining America: Jazz, Blues, Country and the Mythologies of the West

> 'When I was growing up in Belfast all I was listening to was American music. Irish music was going on all around me, but that was nowhere. I was looking for something different.'
>
> Van Morrison, 1982

The fact is, as Van Morrison notes above, that if we are talking about twentieth-century popular music, we are for the most part talking about music that is at least in part American. Connections are complex of course – much American music has its roots in that of its migrant populations, and innovations on American forms take place on a global scale – but if we are considering the sound of the pop industry that exploded post-war then we are imagining America.

The interest in America and its uncharted spaces is a youthful, vigorous interest, and one which therefore by definition appeals to the young. Morrison was beguiled by the work of Jack Kerouac, and his work represented both a remapping and rediscovery of what seemed familiar, a revolutionary emotional cartography – a new way of seeing the familiar, of revealing a secret identity of place. This clearly harmonises with Morrison's own evocations of the Northern Irish landscape. For good or ill, America exists as an emotional idea, both within its own people and the wider world. It is also of course one the most heavily mythologized places on earth, and this is in part due to its dominance of the culture industries: American films, music, books and ideas reach further and more deeply than the similar output of any other nation. This mythology has played a strong role in Morrison's art, as this chapter will explore, but this is not to suggest that this is in any way unusual. Arguably all popular culture, as we understand it, indexes the influence of American popular culture on the development of cultures drawn into its slipstream.[1]

There are sound historical reasons for the ubiquity of American influence. In the case of Britain, the BBC depended upon imported American records during the Second World War, there being fewer records issued in the UK due to lack of the raw materials, while the presence of the US soldiery in the UK was another big influence. In the period from the early 40s to the early 60s the flow was from the US to the UK; then in the so-called 'British Invasion' the music was sold back to America, with a UK twist. The British music business absorbed US business practices too – see the plethora of 'British Elvises', such as Cliff Richard, Tommy Steele and Billy Fury.[2] The shift precipitated by the Beatles reversed this flow and provided conspicuous evidence of Anglo-American hegemony in the cultural production, momentum and development of popular music.

Van Morrison was well placed next to Belfast's thriving port to catch the new music, as were the young musicians in Liverpool – port cities throughout the UK emerged as centres of Britain's growing popular music scene. British radio opened up post-war, via the AFN ('American Forces Network') from which Morrison name checks the show 'Stars of Jazz' on 'In The Days Before Rock and Roll', and Radio Luxembourg, similarly cited on the same song and also in the sublime 'On Hyndford Street'. So early British pop was almost entirely in thrall to the US version and sources. Yet the British innovated around the resources of that music, and the collision of Lonnie Donegan and Leadbelly yielded skiffle, a kind of high-spirited musical dandelion, growing up against the odds through the seemingly impassable post-war austerity, and pummelled out on the debris of domestic life – tea chests for drums, broom-handle bass, cheese-grater string cheap guitars. It was pure acoustic music, born out of its immediate circumstances. As Stevie Winwood told Mike Figgis, 'It was purely *British* music'.[3] Morrison was never a full-on teddy boy but skiffle's take on Leadbelly and the rest provided the breakthrough moment for him. This was openly acknowledged on *The Skiffle Sessions*, but is also present in the studied minimalism of 2002's *Down The Road*.

Morrison's father, George, Snr, as the biographies tell us, spent time in the US in the 1950s. This is movingly recounted in the 2002 song, 'Choppin' Wood'. Morrison remembered this sojourn, and also the power of objects charmed by their American source: 'he went to Detroit to sort of check things out. Later he was supposed to bring the rest of the family over but it didn't work out that way. He did send me some American clothes, but the other kids were jealous of them.'[4] The biggest influence, however, were the records sent by his father, and those that circulated in Belfast; jazz, blues, country records, all saturated with the spirit of America, the sound of a far-off new world dream, where even songs of poverty, hard work and harder luck seemed magical. The discs weren't the only sources – there was radio, and an unusually musical neighbourhood within East Belfast – but they were the most accessible, and, as anyone reading this knows, offered the fascinations of potential endless replay. When Morrison repeated his father's journey in 1966, going way up to the New York City, it was not to look for work, but to deliver some to his new mentor Bert Berns. This chapter, then, looks at the three major American forms that Morrison absorbed and how that has influenced his own work. Everything starts with the blues.

SINGING THE BLUES, OR, TALKING TO HUDDIE LEDBETTER

> 'Blues isn't to do with black or white; blues is about the truth, and blues *is* the truth.'
>
> Van Morrison to Mike Figgis in *Red, White and Blues*

'The blues' is understood either as a musical genre that we might seek within the browsers of the record store, real or virtual, or as a quality which can enter into music of various kinds, delivering a kind of cultural penumbra to a lyric, a vocal, a musical arrangement, instrumental timbre or performance. As Steven G. Smith noted, its meaning spreads beyond the musical, into a broader cultural category, being a descriptive signifier employed in a similar manner to, say, 'Romantic' or 'Gothic'.[5] Yet if 'having the blues' is a cultural shorthand for feeling down (and it is strange but true that I find simply thinking of a melancholy mood as 'the blues' somehow makes it better) then 'singing the blues' is surely something else – suggestive of resistance and endurance. This oppositional model is not simply the historically certified sense of 'black man against white enslaver' but also a wider reflection upon the broader human condition, a common experience of the brief details of human life set against the physical and emotional realities of the material world.

The musical patterns of the blues feel direct, simple even, and in their surface details are relatively easy to reproduce – it's a form relatively easily inhabited and democratically configured for wide reinterpretation – and the truncated patterns of ornamentation and sophistication offer a form which, with apparent paradox, opens up a rich matrix of expression. Furthermore, it is both connected to, yet free to distance itself from, tradition. Gospel, the sacred parallel line to the blues' profane link to material realities, is attentive to the promise of the next world while the blues is rooted in the realities of this one. So the archetypal blues opening line of legend and commonplace parody, 'Woke up this morning', is in fact a representational device signifying the growing point of tradition just as it does of experience – it's about now, the current moment, and how the inhabitation of the musical moment is expressive of the human one. Big Joe Turner sings in 'Oke-She-Moke-She-Pop', 'When I get the blues . . .' and then proposes as solution 'I get on the phone and tell my baby I'm coming home' – there are exit strategies implied in the blues, resolutions to the current plight. Even the desolation of Robert Johnson's situation in 'Crossroads' – 'Sun's going down, nightfall gonna catch me here' – carries within it the possibility of movement, of transit, of somehow beating the odds and the natural order of things (represented here by the fading light) which seems to be indicative of being somehow set against nature; as though life were a game of survival. As? Is. The blues acknowledge this and proceed upon that assumption.[6]

Often Van Morrison's music will carry a 'blues influence', rather than be blues in the purist sense; this kind of ghosted influence produces what we might call a hybrid effect. Actual Robert Johnson-style lonesome blues in Van Morrison is rare – more usual is the country blues which characterises his 2006 album *Pay The Devil*, as well the undervalued collaboration with Linda Gail Lewis, *You Win Again*, from 2000, or the big-band swing blues that characterised his live performances from 2001 up to mid-2006. In fact, that distinction between studio and live performance is key; to some extent the essence of blues, despite its apparent simplicities, is beyond the ken of mediating technologies. It makes most of its sense in the moment of performance; the essence of the blues is its 'liveness'.

Now Morrison as a studio artist is more 'live' than most and thus carries the spirit if not always the letter of the blues into almost everything he records, as he does that of jazz, but his shots at blues numbers often complicate their relationships (and thus his) with their source – consider for example, Morrison's mid-70s versions of 'John Henry' and 'Western Plain', two Leadbelly numbers. Leadbelly, or as he is correctly named in 'Astral Weeks', Huddie Ledbetter, was the prison inmate who was famously 'discovered' and freed to sing by John and Alan Lomax, the great American musicologists and collectors. There have been a number of revisionist histories surrounding the Lomaxes' work published in recent years, all well-written and cogently argued, but it is nevertheless them we have to thank for the 'sound photographs' of the great American Library of Congress collection of field recordings from the 30s on and, more broadly, the shapes of our understanding of the blues as an indigenous American form. Their enduring achievement and contribution is clear.[7]

Ledbetter was seen to some extent as the embodiment of the body and soul of the blues; in the absence of Robert Johnson, he had to bear this physical burden in a way that the ghost of Johnson did not. Johnson's story is effectively a modern American creation myth, picked up by, among others, Greil Marcus and the Coen brothers' *O Brother, Where Art Thou?* – the Crossroads, the pact with the devil, the early death, the unmarked grave, all tied in with 'the birth of the blues'. What we really mean is something more prosaic: these voices (Patton, Johnson, Hurt, Leadbelly) were the ones around when recording first captured music in a way that was previously impossible. The link between the significance of these players and the time at which they worked is key; the birth of the blues it may have been but it was effectively facilitated by the record player. After all, that's how the young Van Morrison and his peer group heard this music, while surrounded by the 'live' and local cultural discourses of Irish folk song and church music. As Morrison has often observed, his friends thought the blues was 'like Chinese music or something',[8] confirming its apparent exoticism and bewildering unlikeness to anything else they'd became used to hearing. In some senses the blues taught Morrison to hear and listen differently, just as *Astral Weeks* would later teach its listeners to do.

Listening to Lonnie Donegan's good-natured replications of Leadbelly's spoken word intros we are reminded of how the traditional flow from the margins to the mainstream can both celebrate and modify the original sources, but we also need to acknowledge that this form of essentialism can restrict and stifle as much as protect. Morrison rarely misses the opportunity to remind interviewers that the likes of Leadbelly and John Lee Hooker were also as likely to sing country or mainstream pop tunes for pleasure as they were to stick to their 'authentic blues'. For example, he told *Billboard* that '[Hank Williams] is very important because he influenced not only country people, he influenced a lot of black artists too, which is what a lot of people don't realize',[9] and while publicising *Pay The Devil* he was just as likely to talk about Ray Charles's approach to country music as to laud Williams or Webb Pierce. In this Morrison is completely non-essentialist in his approach to musical styles and who has the 'right' to perform them, while like everyone else, benefiting from the Lomax approach to capturing a notional authenticity via their 'sound photographs'.

Illustrating this are those two Leadbelly covers included on *The Philosopher's Stone*, 'Western Plain' and 'John Henry', the former a cowboy song, the latter a folk ballad telling how a black railway worker, John Henry, tried to 'outwork' a steam hammer in order to prove men were better than machines, and died in the process. They were cut in 1975, went unissued until 1998, and are among the hardest rocking recordings in his catalogue. It is also instructive that Morrison turned to Leadbelly – and to two very tough and hard-handed arrangements of these songs – at a time when he was re-evaluating his whole relationship with music-making and his own place within the industry. There is something both radical and rooted in these songs for Morrison, which allowed him to both shake off his torpor and also force a way forward – just *listen* to the Sisyphean shriek at the climax of 'John Henry' (4.57–5.01). That strength and openness and resolve seems to come to him through the songs and perhaps even the idea of Leadbelly himself; the power and apparent exoticism of the music travelled, via the recording (or 'sound photograph'), between Texas and Belfast.[10]

Both tracks are from the blues songbook but sound nothing like 'the blues'. His vocal performance on 'John Henry' is unrestrained and at the coda frequently extreme, making powerful use of his harmonica which somehow corresponds to the frequently repeated line 'It ain't nothing but my hammer sucking wind', the suck and blow of the harmonica mirroring and evoking the motion of the body at work and also an allusion to the motion of the steam hammer. 'Western Plain' was also recorded in this fierce style, but has also been played live very differently; at the 'In Conversation' event in Coleraine in 1988 it was played with Derek Bell and Clive Culbertson, right there among tunes like 'In The Garden' and 'Raglan Road'. So the blues can *sound* like anything – it is in performance that they become 'truth'. The 'right' of the white man to sing these songs is a long-debated argument, and while not quite redundant it is usually circular. As Morrison said during the *So Hard To Beat* TV show in 2007, 'I wanted to make my *own* blues, my *own* soul music, to do something of my own with it. That's where I was coming from' [my italics].[11]

Barker and Taylor write in their excellent book *Faking It*:

> Blues is said to be a very personal music. There's certainly some truth to this view – blues songs of the first half of the 20th century were generally more personal than other songs, and early autobiographical songs were almost always blues or blues related. Yet it would be a mistake to view the blues as primarily either a confessional mode or a kind of collective autobiography of black Americans, two views that seem prevalent today.[12]

Morrison seems to understand this very well. When Jeremy Marre asked as to whether his interest in the blues was borne out of empathy with the condition of American blacks he replied, 'No, not really . . . if it was anything it was out of empathy with my own culture, white working class culture'.[13] So he wanted to take the tradition, and innovate within and beyond it. The blues offers a framework of expression, be it cries of lamentation or survival, to everybody and so the blues is both heard and felt worldwide. It is also the frequent subject of theoreticised musicological links seeking to uncover the root of the music. In recent years we have heard intriguing arguments connecting it to other musical forms, including the so-called 'Desert Blues' of Mali and Central Western Africa, and the gorgeous, swooningly melancholic Portuguese folk music, Fado, which Morrison sagely cited to a surprised Michelle Rocca in a 1995 promotional interview.[14] In truth, the probable common root is the human heart.

Thus when we listen to Morrison on his 1987 version of the negro spiritual 'Sometimes I Feel Like A Motherless Child', it is not stage-show affectation or simply 'performance'; there is a true connection between the experiences and a kind of natural wisdom in his relaying of it, while never pretending that this is somehow duplicating the details of the source. We also discern the connection between singing and strength, and how singing oneself out of oneself works, as being locked up in the 'sometimes' of the title phrase: sometimes this is how he feels, and by deduction sometimes it isn't. The song and the act of singing it provide both singer and listener with the opportunity to remind themselves that these songs were not necessarily born to be sold, to be 'listened' to for pleasure or 'consumed' by others; other imperatives came to bear upon their coming into being.

The song sports a lush arrangement on *Poetic Champions Compose*, courtesy of Morrison, but with woodwind and strings scored by Fiachra Trench. It features a harp (or a synthesised approximation of one) and conveys a lulling, rocking rhythm, almost evoking the strange and sweet clarities of the final moments before sleep; a sort of lullaby, which, connected to the lyrical pretext ('Sometimes I feel like a motherless child') provides an index of both absences and presences. Morrison augments the traditional lyric by adding the lines:

> Motherless children have a hard time
> Motherless children have-a such a hard time
> Motherless children have such a really hard time
> A long way from home[15]

This brings into play notions of experience and observation; sometimes he feels this way, and why it is difficult when his mood harmonises with this emotional state is both grounded and partially redeemed by the ability *to say what it is like*: to conquer the ineffability of sadness by singing it out. Yet the song also captures a sense of loneliness and of singularity ('Sometimes *I* feel like a motherless child'), and this form of isolation, not wholly redeemed by the articulation of it but tempered through the act of singing of it, is key to the blues. It is the private experience which becomes the public declaration and via which the internal discourse is externalised, and the common experience is acknowledged in the listener. Contrast, for example, Jackson C. Frank's recording of his song

'Blues Run The Game', and the version by Simon and Garfunkel. The loneliness described in the narrative is compounded by the haunted solitude of Frank's voice, whereas in the duo's version, the unforced unity of the voices in harmony somehow draws some of the chill from the lyric; the isolation is broken by the companionship of the two voices.[16]

Morrison's take on the old spiritual was not recorded in a field, or on a porch swing – as Gershwin reimagined it to be, in *Porgy and Bess* – but in the hi-tech comfort of Wool Hall Studios, close by gorgeous and historic Bath. What then does this do to the performance? At the time he recorded this album, Morrison was perhaps at the deepest point of his interest in the metaphysical power of music – music as a healing force. The album contains 'Did Ye Get Healed?' and healing had been a touchstone term for him on record and in performance since 1979's 'And The Healing Has Begun', which led up to 1996's 'The Healing Game' (not unrelated to 'the crying game'), where Morrison declares himself to be 'in the healing game'. This refers to being in the business of investigating and seeking methods of healing – that is, ways and methodologies directed towards fixing, mending, and actively addressing the broken; making things better through process. His performance of 'Sometimes I Feel Like A Motherless Child' can be read as part of that working towards discovery, as part of the spirit of enquiry which moves through so much of Morrison's material (be it overtly or covertly), but also as the thing itself – the theory and the practice in a unified whole. It's not 'about' healing, it *is* healing. That sense of wholeness is very important.

Samuel Floyd wrote about this song:

> The first extended troping of the *tune* of "Sometimes I Feel Like a Motherless Child" was George Gershwin's repetition of it in *Porgy and Bess* . . .. Rhythmically, in other words, "Summertime" is a kind of augmentation of the "Sometimes I Feel Like a Motherless Child" melody . . .. Harmonically, the two tunes follow basically the same harmonic scheme.[17]

George Gershwin, according to Floyd, 'conscientiously attended numerous Black church services'[18] in his researches towards composing *Porgy and Bess* and in doing so in some ways performed a function for the mainstream that the Lomaxes would also do, introducing the 'blue notes' of Black American spiritual music into the mainstream of American popular song, as well as 'authenticating' (in the widest sense) his own composition. So Gershwin mediated between the mainstream and the marginal – the music crosses over. Morrison has sung 'Summertime' in concert only once and that was at Montreux in 1997, as part of a medley, in which it was preceded by 'Help Me' and followed by

– yes – 'Sometimes I Feel Like A Motherless Child'. The route from the diehard r'n'b of Sonny Boy Williamson to the lonesome spiritual plaint of the traditional song, via Gershwin's adaptation of it, is manifest evidence of the connections between these musical discourses and Morrison's intuitive grasp of these links.

Them's take on the blues was indicative of both their own youthful interest in the music and also the processes to which pop music and the musicians who make it are subject once they enter the culture industry. It retains traces of the primal wildness, which draws an audience to it, while it has had some of the edges knocked off in order to make it a good commercial product that can find its niche in the market place. The relentlessness of the 'Gloria' riff is a blues device without question yet the acceleration of the beat, the blameless catchiness of the unmistakably pop melody and chorus hook placed it fully in the beat scene of the time. After all, it started life as the B-side of the theme tune of one of the defining pop shows of the era, *Ready Steady Go!* So there's no doubt that Them brought blues to the pop table in a way that say the Beatles did not – Morrison has noted that for him 'The Beatles were peripheral',[19] and that Them's work had nothing to do with pop, and that he always saw a yawning gap between the music that moved him, and the music he wished to make, and prevailing conventions of 'pop music'. 'Baby Please Don't Go', that theme for *Ready Steady Go!*, was an interesting choice for such a job. It is certainly darker and bluesier than much of what was going on; perhaps the licensing arrangements were favourable, or perhaps the older age range of the show's producers meant they knew the original, and thus welcomed the signs of continuity. Whatever the reason, it gave Them a good push.

So Them got the blues into pop not simply by doing covers but by bringing the influences into their own style and also by incorporating the spirit as well the letter of the blues. This is clear in a late recording, the sly walking blues of 'The Story Of Them', but 'Mystic Eyes' is the key recording for this – the first track on the first album, and a fairly pleasing and definite annunciation. It is a Maritime Hotel-style improvisation, with Morrison delivering a short but remarkably powerful word sketch, in its near-Gothic High Romanticism seemingly distant from the rude sound world the music has conjured up, and then we are invited to reconsider whether these two worlds could be the same, or find a correspondence within each other – the almost Yeatsian image of the girl by the graveyard, the depth of mystery in her eyes, moving swiftly, a 'wild thing' in the most natural sense. The lore has it (like 'Slim Slow Slider') that this number was originally edited down from a very long improvisation and that the vocal came very late in the piece. What possibly caused the engineer to despair that he would never get these boys to settle down and play a two-minute pop song is in fact the thing that turns out to be transformative about this track. It is the blues, but it is also metaphysical – as in all Morrison's best work, it combines the body and the soul, the mind-body problem moving towards a very natural resolution.[20]

Blues in some senses challenges the notions of well-made music. In these terms it is repetitious, harmonically limited, often lyrically impoverished, and definitely going against the notion of the polished and well-made musical work. In truth, claims to virtue in the blues seem to be located strongly in this democratising structure; anyone can sing the blues, the openness of the structural mode permitting any kind of input. As Ray Charles says on Morrison's cherished *Live At Newport*, 'Everybody understands the blues!'[21] They can be understood and used by everybody and anybody. Yet somehow in tandem with this democratic nature, the blues can function like a secret transcript – a hidden language or frame of reference which is lost on the wider audience once the music becomes over-exposed. To illustrate, a book that Morrison has spoken about in approving terms in public more than once is Paul Oliver's *Blues Fell This Morning: Meaning in the Blues*. It contains some excellent images of advertising for 'race records' in the 1920s, 30s and 40s, all of which seemingly wilfully miss the thrust of a song like 'Sugar In My Bowl' or 'Pigmeat Blues'. Morrison pointed this out at a live show in 2006 during his cover of 'Custard Pie', where via a spoken ad lib he pointed out, with a twinkle in his eye, 'I don't think they're talking about a pie'.[22]

Morrison reflected upon how he first encountered this music:

> 'I started out long before Alexis Korner and that movement. It came from the same source but I was already doing it. The first time I ever heard an electric band it was actually Sonny Terry and Brownie McGhee. That was way back. It was called Back Country Blues then but in fact it was urban blues and that was the first Chicago style thing I ever heard. The first thing I ever rehearsed with Them was one of their songs called "Custard Pie". Muddy Waters and Little Walter were on the Pye R'n'B series but it was only the singles. The woman in the shop would tell you what had come in – things like Harmonica Fats. But it was Little Walter who was the master. He was electric but very controlled electric.'[23]

His connection with the blues is wholly bound up with his own life and how he remembers the days before rock and roll. So if the form can belong to everybody, how is it that the music feels and continues to feel so personal? How does one leave one's fingerprints on the blues? Perhaps by bringing one's own distinctive circumstances and touch to the technique, the melodic sensibility, the vocal timbre and the lyrics – in fact, the same criteria broadly speaking that are used to evaluate and critique any other musical form. Yet the openness of the form permits accommodation of mood – so that the young Morrison might give credence to his carnal or his philosophical mood within similar musical contexts – and in the case of 'Mystic Eyes', both. It also provides the image, at least, of being in control of a situation, and of being able to appraise it, and observe it from without.

This is the purpose of what we might call the 'fame blues', the songs about his experience of the music industry and of 'being' Van Morrison and which have divided his listeners. These songs, which reached a kind of critical mass on 2003's *What's Wrong With This Picture?*, have their root way back in the 31 'anti-songs' he recorded to fulfil his contractual obligations to Bang, and on through material like 'The Great Deception', 'Drumshanbo Hustle' and 'Showbusiness', as well as unissued tunes like the ferocious 'I'm Not Working For You' from 1975, all unusually candid despatches from the frontline where art meets commerce. More recent fame blues such as 'Talk Is Cheap', 'Goldfish Bowl' and 'Too Many Myths' may be hard to love for his wider audience but he has an absolute right to sing them. They are evidence of Morrison's understanding of the purposes of the blues and his ability to make them connect truthfully with his own experience. Perhaps tellingly, his most successful fame blues is also his most allusive – 'This Weight' from 1997 could apply equally to love, grief, the weariness of the body, to life itself. That's the blues.

Yet the blues also stands for restlessness and curiosity, moving forward and surviving. So if Morrison reinvents the lyrical modes of the blues to talk about his own life what is really happening is that he is making the ancient form anew and it is that sense of going on, and the spirit of enquiry that has run through his work since the beginning, flowing from the great delta of the blues.

CLOSE ENOUGH FOR JAZZ

Blues, however, is not alone. The other great tributary that has informed the main body of American popular music in the twentieth century is, of course, jazz. I asked Ben Sidran how he saw the fit between Van Morrison and jazz: 'Jazz is not a kind of music, it is an approach, and it applies to how one goes about finding their voice, relating to a tradition, stepping into the unknown and swinging. Clearly, Van is connected to all of these principles.'[24]

Histories of jazz emphasise the development of an American form, and, of course that is not incorrect – jazz is arguably America's greatest musical gift to the world. Van Morrison's take on jazz is manifold: it is musical, conceptual, philosophical. If we listen to his most overtly 'jazz' albums we notice that the first, *How Long Has This Been Going On?*, is most closely allied to the British jazz of the 50s and very early 60s. This is in terms of his collaborators – Chris

Barber, Lonnie Donegan, Ronnie Scott – but also the album's repertoire. The other record, *Tell Me Something*, is a very American affair, being an album of Mose Allison's songs. The use of recognisably 'jazz' music in his repertoire is also spread across individual songs, most obviously 'Moondance'.

As the title track of his second album for Warners, 'Moondance' was the leading point of his effort to make a record that would actually make him some money. Contrasting the stylistic content of *Astral Weeks* with that of *Moondance*, we can see how different the methodology was – short, inclusive and open songs as opposed to the richly personal worlds of *Astral Weeks*' key songs. The album's first track 'And It Stoned Me' opens directly with his voice and the title track is probably the first standard of his post-'Brown Eyed Girl' career, one which any number of singers could take a shot at. Indeed 'Moondance' has become a karaoke favourite, such is its quiet penetration into the repertoire of standards. The point is that by 1970 the free jazz of *Astral Weeks* had been disciplined into a smart, sharp and direct popular song.[25]

Its jazz-pop finger click is irresistible, and Morrison's claim that he could envisage Sinatra singing it, cited below, is not such a vain thought – the chatty vocal, the swaggering horn chart (marked by pleasing puffs of Jack Schroer's unmistakable sound) and the clean arrangement would have sat very nicely on one of Sinatra's 70s albums for Reprise. The title is a neat inversion of a familiar term; the cinemas at the time were playing *Butch Cassidy and the Sundance Kid*, while *Sundance* was the title tune of an album by the Modern Jazz Quartet (featuring *Astral Weeks* drummer Connie Kay) and issued by Atlantic in 1964.[26] It also came less than a year after the first moon landings of July 1969, with the accompanying 'Earthrise' images showing us the planet for the first time. Morrison may well have been mindful of all this, but the term is also his own – a smart, uncomplicated flip of the expected. The romance of the night is not undiscovered by songwriters, of course, and the way the song fits in with an extant tradition of investing the outer darkness with an inner illumination is almost as old as the history of song itself. This in some ways perhaps explains the ease with which it has entered the mainstream. He was undoubtedly pleased with the results, telling Ritchie Yorke:

> 'With "Moondance" I wrote the melody first. I played the melody on a soprano sax and I knew I had a song so I wrote lyrics to go with the melody. That's the way I wrote that one. I don't really have any words to particularly describe the song, sophisticated is probably the word I'm looking for. For me, "Moondance" is a sophisticated song. Frank Sinatra wouldn't be out of place singing that.'[27]

The opening verse is a scene setter and the second is not unlike its album companion 'Caravan' in its seeking to seduce with humour as well as the pleasures of the night: 'Well I wanna make love to you tonight / I can't wait till the morning has come'. That urgency, cogently expressed, is made to run in parallel with the forces of nature – the day and the night, the breezes, the moon and the sun – and is set in a context of complete naturalness and therefore, an irresistibility. The girl is seen as being as much a part of the natural world as the surroundings ('The stars up above in your eyes . . . The soft moonlight seems to shine in your blush') and the autumn setting places the song within Morrison's own group of 'leaf songs', examined later in this book. The song is autumnal in its colour and tone as well as in its lyrical specifics, the arrangement dry and crisp, the vocal tone moving between cloud and sun. The song is in itself more big-band, even jazz-pop than traditional or modern jazz, and Morrison is not 'trying' to sing like a jazz singer. As composer and author of the song, he sings it how he feels it – perhaps exemplified by the very pleasing burbling he drops into the vocal towards the end, resolving itself into dazzling vocal directness and clarity, with a final restatement of the chorus line – and his overall intention – over the final squall of horns.

Morrison's own regard for this song is evidenced by its enduring presence in his live sets, a liking which is both in harmony with and responsive to the song's public reputation – he re-recorded it for his 'jazz' album *How Long Has This Been Going On?* in 1995, and has included it on two of five live albums, various best-of's and themed compilations. This restatement of the song illustrates that he feels there is a world to be explored within the song, as well as acknowledging the plain fact of its popularity. Curiously, given how the 'jazz' methodology functions in his work, the song has never expanded live in the way that 'It's All In The Game', or 'In The Afternoon' have; the closest it came to this was being appended by 'My Funny Valentine' on the San Francisco live album, and by 'Fever' in the live set early in the 90s. The relative 'undevelopment' of a song which has featured almost continuously in his set for nearly four decades is an anomaly, and one which speaks of how satisfied the composer must be with the faithfulness of his initial recording to how he feels the tune. It has often been used almost as a theme tune – the warm-up number before he comes onstage – and it has a hot-valve, 50s TV theme dimension to its runs, and so functions nicely in that context.

'Moondance' is also related to *Astral Weeks*, in a way, in that he has not really attempted another song like it. Strands connect, say, 'I Will Be There' or the swamp-jazz undertow of *A Period Of Transition*, but the song stands as complete and definitive in its original state. The remakes have kept close to the original, the 1995 take being prefixed by the bright, brassy blare of a horn intro that will be familiar to those who have attended his shows over the decades, and has become an integral part of the number. Georgie Fame's off-mike following of the horn line on the *A Night In San Francisco* album (0.01–21) is almost a definitive encapsulation of the spirit of that band; despite its familiarity, it is often the centrepiece of a set, and can provide a turning point. The paradox of the freedom and the discipline at the heart of jazz that this song brings can provide a focus for Morrison's energy and a sluggish set can be transformed by a good and successful 'Moondance'.[28]

His next overtly 'jazz' cut was 'I Will Be There', which sits atypically on *Saint Dominic's Preview*; it loafs between 'Gypsy' and 'Listen To The Lion', sounding nothing like either. Led in by a Big Easy piano, the tune is both brash and lazy in its sound and its swing, of which it has plenty. It locks into a low-riding finger-pop early and stays there, ratcheting up through the horns above and behind the vocal, counterpointing and making richer Doug Messenger's straight Tal Farlow-esque chord-strum on the guitar and the light brush of the drums. Morrison's vocal high-kicks and at the song's close he steps up to deliver one last blurt of the title phrase, drawing out 'there' over four bars, before the song collapses in on itself to good effect with a loving thud on the kit. It's great, and transcends pastiche of the traditions it clearly draws upon – Sinatra, the big bands – but no-one would have bet good money on it having the shelf life it has turned out to have. Yet its dynamics are perfect for the live stage, and it would prove itself to be something of a model for later, more fully realized jazz projects.[29]

Then came a sidestep – his cover of Louis Jordan's 'Caldonia' for a one-off single in 1974, accompanied by the Caledonia Soul Express. Though the cover is straight, on the label and in his pronunciation the title is slyly changed to 'Caledonia'. Morrison's love for this phase of 40s and 50s jazz was, as we have seen, derived in part from his father's record collection. Its energy and verve links it to r'n'b and even early rock and roll, but it really is something different to 'rock' as it was understood at the time Morrison was recording these tracks. Morrison's vocal is unmistakably 'live' and his cover of the song offers illuminating evidence of the root of his conviction that the sound of the vocal, the feeling of it, is more important than exemplary diction, syntax or note-perfect delivery. In fact, on 'What's Up, Crazy Pup?' the single's B-side, the vocal duties are compressed to a rhythmic element, a straight chanting of the title in the mid-section of the number, and a wild, ridiculous and beautiful shout at the track's close. Morrison's 1980s instrumental period, and his interest in non-vocal music, has its roots much further back than a reading of Alice Bailey – it is rooted in his listening to Bechet, Armstrong, Jordan and the rest. Morrison's vocal on 'Caledonia' is one of his toughest and most robust vocal performances, being abrasive and controlled, righteous and good-humoured, and as such is wholly true to the spirit of jazz.[30] Peter Wolf remembered that Jordan was one of Morrison's favourites when they became friends in Boston in 1967:

> 'Over and over we would listen to what he called "the gospel" of Jackie Wilson, Ray Charles, Hank Williams, Louis Jordan, Billy Stewart, Elvis and John Lee Hooker. "They're the real deal," he'd say. He played Gene Chandler's live version of "Rainbow '65" so much, I had to get a new needle for my turntable.'[31]

This intense enthusiasm for the music that moved him way, way back led him to pick up the threads two decades later. That's how long this had been going on.

How Long Has This Been Going On? (1995)

Morrison's brace of 'jazz' albums came together in the mid-90s in rapid succession – *How Long Has This Been Going On?*, and a Mose Allison 'tribute' album, *Tell Me Something*. The records have two distinct sets of ambitions: they are in some respects aspirational, but they are also determinedly bringing the songs to a wider audience. Furthermore it was an attempt to build upon the remarkable togetherness of the band as heard on the *A Night In San Francisco* and let that energy explore and inform another field. Morrison's creative urge is always to go forward, so after the massive James Brown-style review of the early/mid-90s band as recorded on *A Night In San Francisco* had reached its apotheosis, he did as he had done in 1974 and chose to dissolve the group. In 1974 the next step was scaled down and ambient, on *Veedon Fleece*; in 1995 the way forward seemed to be in the direction of jazz.

Befitting the connection between jazz and the idea of 'liveness', *How Long Has This Been Going On?* was recorded in a single live session, on 3 May 1995, at Ronnie Scott's Club on Frith Street in Soho, London. The club was empty of paying guests but the ambience of the 'jazz space' of its interior was present and correct. That a live recording could so closely resemble a painstaking studio endeavour is testament not only to the acoustics of the room but of course the skill of the players, and Morrison had the advantage of some top-drawer British jazz collaborators. The choice of Ronnie Scott's was itself an aspirational gesture, it being the symbolic (arguably the *actual*) home of British jazz, and Morrison was, rightly, clearly delighted to be moving in this company and recording in such a place. The sleeve art makes much of the venue, with Morrison and Fame pictured with Ronnie Scott on the steps outside the club. The emphasis is strongly on this British dimension – a cover shot of Morrison and Fame at a Soho café includes London listings weekly *Time Out* and a copy of the *London Evening Standard*. This, it says, is British music.[32] Yet of course the record is full of American songs; it is the playing of them that belongs specifically to the British jazz methodology. There is a briskness and a conciseness, the sound is snappy and hard-working. The album includes a quartet of Morrison originals and ten from the wider repertoire, drawing in Louis Jordan, Johnny Mercer, Cannonball Adderley, Leo Hickman and Mose Allison among others. This, alongside Morrison's willingness to reinvent or at least test out some of his own 'jazz' numbers under these conditions, offers us a chance to consider his skill as an interpreter.

The album opens with that unexpectedly long-runner from 1972, 'I Will Be There', ushered in with a bowling snare roll and a wide-screen splashy arrangement – this is full-on big-band jazz in the tradition of Rat Pack Sinatra crossed with Lester Young. It finishes, as one knows it will, on a blare of brass. 'Symphony Sid' is Louis Jordan's homage to the DJ at Birdland and on jazz radio in the 40s and 50s, and gives a rare example of Morrison sharing a vocal word for word, 'duetting' with co-pilot Georgie Fame. This is a song reeking of 50s jazz, and Fame's voice fits it like a kid glove; Fame is certainly a more experienced singer of this kind of music than Morrison, maybe even a better one, although he is an inferior vocalist overall – this paradox lies at the at the heart of Morrison's 'explicitly' jazz recordings. Chet Baker, as we shall discover, somewhat grouchily said that Morrison 'shouted' and that which serves him so well in his own work and the blues material – such as the jazzed version of Leo Hickman's 'Early In the Morning' that follows 'Symphony Sid' – somehow limits his fit with some of the (paradoxically for a musical mode that is predicated on self-expression) strict conventions of jazz performance. Yet Morrison manifestly is a jazz performer in his approach – never the same way twice – and thus the paradox lies in this fall-off between his natural creative pattern and the rules that guide jazz. This we see from the (third!) version of his 'All Saint's Day' included here, where Fame's voice clearly reflects the techniques of Mose Allison and Chet Baker, making the human voice hornlike, following the melody of the horn chart – listen to Baker's version of Elvis Costello's 'Almost Blue' for a concise example of how he applied the technique to a song by a pop/rock songwriter.[33] In contrast Morrison vocalises in a natural 'jazz' pattern – there is clear saxophonic phrasing in the way he sings, the bright surges, the slow fallings away. Though unlike the clean lines of Fame or Baker, this vocal technique is still pure jazz.

Morrison's own songs sit comfortably alongside the covers, be they the rhythmic tone poem of 'Sack O'Woe' or the Broadway standard 'Who Can I Turn To', yet the dominant vocal sound of the album is that of collaboration. 'Moondance' and 'I Will Be There' are of course showcases for Morrison's voice, but the ensemble enterprise, according to jazz tradition, prevails. 'Centerpiece' and the title track display this to great effect, vocally and musically. The inclusion of a pair of Mose Allison songs, 'Your Mind Is On Vacation' and 'Don't

Worry About A Thing', is significant beyond being Morrison's first Allison since 1985's 'If You Only Knew'. It shows the enduring influence of the older man's caustic cynicism about the music business on Morrison's own work – both directly (the lyric of the former includes the phrase 'talk is cheap', later to adorn one of Morrison's 'fame blues') and less overtly (the latter reverses the usual pop formula that everything is going to turn out fine, something Morrison later echoed in 2008's 'No Thing'). Mose gave Van a model for articulating his blues about the music industry, and the dry humour of 'If You Only Knew' can easily give way to the more fractious mood of 'Your Mind Is On Vacation'. We can see the conceptual link between the choices of the Allison tune and 'That's Life'; we also see feelingly the debt Morrison's own 'I Will Be There' owes to 'That's Life' once they are in such close proximity. The older song is more restrained on this record than Morrison's own tune but their shared DNA shines through, and it is this mixture of the one-take, high-kicking, big-band Sinatra and the grittier models of British jazz playing, composition and arrangement that characterises Morrison's forays into 'real' jazz music. Morrison also borrowed the promise from 'That's Life', to be back on top in June for the title of 1999's *Back On Top*.

The appearance of 'Heathrow Shuffle', effectively a jump-style instrumental with a scatted vocal line, *à la* 'What's Up Crazy Pup?', bears the influence of Louis Jordan and also the time of its composition, being approximately 1973–74, when Morrison was breaking down his accepted styles and deliberately branching out and away from the Belfast Cowboy role that had been cut out for him. The tune turns up in an audience-confusing form on the DVD of his turning-point show at Montreux in 1974, and very occasionally on set lists thereafter but it is the one surprise guest at this particular table. Undoubtedly it was waiting for the right moment and context to emerge on a 'real' Morrison album; other jazz instrumentals of that era, such as 'Much Binding In The March', have yet to find such a home and, archival projects aside, probably never will. The tune is worn lightly, in the spirit of the jump-jive to which it owes a debt, but also records, in its wry observation of the slow movement through endless airport arrivals and departure lounges, some weariness with the responsibilities ('Gotta go to Heathrow! Gotta go to Heathrow!'[34]) that are the cost of Kerouac's dream of eternal movement, and of the lure of being on the road.

Unlike the hallowed jazz space that hosted its predecessor, 1996's *Tell Me Something: The Songs Of Mose Allison*, was laid down at Morrison's own Wool Hall Studios. The album's subject appears on a brace of the 13 tracks, 'I Don't Want Much' and the closer, 'Perfect Moment'. The band is that of the Ronnie Scott's album, plus the substantial addition of ace jazz pianist and scholar Ben Sidran. Sidran's skilful articulations of the techniques, meanings and purposes of jazz (and music in a wider cultural sense) are well known to readers of his writings on the subject, including the utterly indispensible *Black Talk* and *Talking Jazz*.[35]

I asked Ben Sidran about the experience of making this album.

PM: How did the idea for an album of Mose Allison songs recorded in this way come about? In your sleeve note you allude to Georgie Fame approaching you – do you recall the circumstances?

BS: Georgie was travelling with Van at the time and apparently Van said he wanted to do this tribute to Mose and because I was producing Mose's records, and obviously was a devotee of his music, Van asked Georgie to give me a call and see if I would participate.

PM: How did you decide upon the songs that would be included, and were there any songs recorded that didn't make the final cut for the record?

BS: Originally, the idea was that we would all pick three or four of our favourite Mose songs and bring them to the sessions. In the end, I chose 12 – I couldn't narrow it down any further – and when it came time for the sessions, I was the only one who had a list, so we did all the songs I had picked. With the exception of 'Self Love' which I think was Van's idea. I do not believe there were songs cut but not released. I'm not certain.

What emerges here is that Sidran's precision and expertise really drove the project in terms of content, the exception being 'Self Love' aka 'Benediction', which Morrison had been playing in his live set for some time. How, I wondered, did the 'one take' principles favoured by Morrison play out in the conditions of making a 'real' jazz record, as opposed to one which draws upon the free spirit of jazz?

PM: Your sleeve note mentions the recording being swift. Do you perhaps recall how long it took to record the album, and the 'spirit' in the studio during the sessions?

BS: It took two afternoons. It was just a groove. I had prepared charts of all the songs based on the charts we had used in the original Mose sessions. We just passed them around and ran the songs down. The spirit was very loose and relaxed. All music.

PM: You mention too that the majority of the songs on the record were put down in one or two takes. On Van Morrison's studio recordings there is much emphasis on this idea of 'first takes', with apparent run-throughs ending up on the finished album – is that how the songs for *Tell Me Something* were recorded?

> BS: We were set up 'live' in the studio – that is without baffels so we could hear without ear phones if we wanted to. I think we spent an hour or so running over songs before Van arrived. When he got there, he went to his microphone, pulled out some harps, and off we went. They were all performances, no overdubs, mostly first takes.
>
> PM: Is that in your view the best way for jazz (or indeed music of whatever hue) to be recorded in the studio?
>
> BS: Recording live in the room and going for the feeling is the best way to capture a spirit. It's not necessarily the best way to make a jazz record but I think it was a great way to make this one.[36]

So Ben Sidran's impression of this experience is intriguing: he recalls clearly that the album was made in an open and free-flowing atmosphere – 'the spirit was very loose and relaxed. All music' – but that this wasn't 'necessarily the best way to make a jazz record' although it was right for this one. In this candid and complex answer, Sidran illustrates a masterly and intuitive understanding of how to employ jazz as a creative principle and knowing when and how to apply it – today it's time to lean on the music, tomorrow maybe not.

The album's opener, 'One Of These Days', promises, while never actually committing, to do the sensible and self-preserving thing and the rest of the collection shows how and why that isn't an option, either for the song's author or his younger interpreter. The vocal duties here are shared between Morrison, Fame and Sidran. Morrison takes the solo lead on four tracks, and shares with Fame and Sidran on what is perhaps the album's best-known number (in that it featured in his live set well before and after the album's issue, and also turns up on 2007's *Best Of III*) 'Benediction'. He also duets on two tracks with their author, 'I Don't Want Much' and 'Perfect Moment'. Of the remaining half of the album, Sidran takes four leads, and Fame a trio. What this album does, apart from show us that Morrison can indeed collaborate and create as part of an ensemble, is that it opens up the Mose Allison songbook to show a much wider range and shows the songs are far more humane than his reputation as a prickly cynic would suggest. The closer, 'Perfect Moment', is a kind of jazz manifesto, and bears a lyric which could easily have been from Morrison's own pen, with its sunsets, mountains, crystal clear autumn nights and its connection of the nature of nature to that of music: the 'perfect moment' (outside the nightclub, we note) is 'Never twice th' same'. Allison's repertoire contains a number of these songs, such as 'The Gettin' Paid Waltz', glimpses into the grimly twinkling reality of the jobbing musician, who is hanging on to another of Allison's lines, in 'Your Time Will Come', sung here by Ben Sidran: 'If you live, your time will come'.[37]

The album may well always be seen as a marginal element of the catalogue but this seems to miss the point. It was both an experiment for both Morrison and his audience, a mix of a pleasurable embrace of the one-take philosophy and a respectful, useful acknowledgement of the work of the older, less well-known musician. So how did all these experiments impact upon his live work in the wider sense? Intriguingly, this material received only limited outings – there was no 'jazz tour', and the performances tended to be one-offs or specials, such as the August 1995 show with the BBC Orchestra at the Edinburgh Festival, broadcast live to air as part of the Festival's jazz wing. However in the long run, his work in the decade following showed how these full-on journeys into jazz were absorbed into his own musical language. After the issue of *Tell Me Something* Morrison returned to something bluesier, and closer to his natural *style*. His musical DNA is blues-based, and he tends to write songs which, even when country or pop in outward show, are predicated on the structures of the blues. Yet his natural *approach* seems closer to jazz. So the blend of the two influences sublimate and the music shows aspects of both – the attention to structure, the freedom to wander away from them, while keeping them in mind. It's instructive that he has never made an overt 'blues' album in the way that he made these two jazz collections. Connecting the blues to the jazz of America and American song traditions enables us to arrive at another subgroup of stylistically related albums – the country records.

CALEDONIA SOUL MUSIC?: THE COUNTRY RECORDS

Country music's popularity in Scotland and Northern Ireland is well documented, and rooted in the historic connections between Appalachian and British Celtic music; the original hillbillies were Irish immigrants. It's also been said that country music offers a kind of white man's blues, or white soul music, connecting the music of America and of Morrison's upbringing. Indeed listening to George Jones it is easy to see where the connections are made; the soulful power and emotional force inherent in the voice which does not seem to be trying very hard. So when Morrison sings a song made well known by Jones, such as 'Things Have Gone To Pieces', we have the opportunity to compare the two styles, and see how the younger man's approach locks with the form. Morrison's first effort at a country record, *Tupelo Honey*, ended up feeling more like a superior singer-songwriter album of the time than the pure form, certainly more California than Nashville, while his second, 2000's *You Win Again*, was a mix of country, blues and early rock and roll which – we learn – was effectively a country-blues hybrid. Indeed it seems an echo from a time of wholeness, 'in the days before rock and roll', where the styles were inward-facing and drew from each other freely and with ease, before musical tribalism became embedded. If we accept the premise that modern country music's performative codes and musical shapes are substantially drawn from the work and style of Hank Williams, we can also see how that seminal figure in all his innovative splendour also to some extent laid down rules that were not there formerly. This template has arguably ossified into a kind of conservatism which mitigates against and resists innovation: as Waylon Jennings sang, 'Are you sure Hank done it this way?'[38]

Morrison's interest in country music goes back as far as his taste for the blues, to the records in his father's record collection and the music he heard in the neighbourhood. On the Nashville DVD that came with his *Pay The Devil* album, he recalls that:

> 'When I started out, first started in music, I was singing songs like "Half As Much", "Your Cheatin' Heart", "My Bucket's Got A Hole In It", "More and More" . . . there was Leadbelly, and there was *that*, y'know? I think the first song I learned was "Midnight Special" and the second was "More and More" . . . so it was all part of the same thing. I knew a guy, a neighbour, who had all Hank Williams' stuff, but I seemed to zone in more on Webb Pierce, Ray Price, Faron Young, also Tennessee Ernie Ford, his earlier stuff, which was boogie woogie, a mixture of boogie and country stuff.'[39]

That mixture of the blues and the country is in itself a reflection of the initial undivided nature of the two – so that early rock and roll music came into being on the wings of these rhythms, only later to be divided up and commodified separately. Listen to early Sun Records Jerry Lee Lewis or to Elvis Presley's 'Milk Cow Blues' for the same label and hear how the two styles existed in a single musical entity.[40] As Morrison himself has often remarked, blues musicians would be equally likely to play country songs: in his *Blues: The Basics*, Dick Weissman notes that Robert Johnson, the King of the Delta Blues himself, would play country tunes 'in his spare time'.[41] So the dividing line between country music and blues music is to some extent an artificial one, one devised in order for them to be sold – so we had 'race records' and we had 'country and western', targeted to specific populations, places, and skin tones. Like the blues, country music is in its sensibility attentive to the social function of the music – it tells stories about 'ordinary life'. Morrison:

> 'I think these songs are kind of similar to the blues in the fact that they're the true poetry of everyday life, really . . . a lot different than just pop songs . . . they actually *mean* something. It's the truth! It's something I can relate to, and is very real. The

> lyrics are real, it's about real life experiences, it's very similar to the blues . . . in fact they might be one and the same thing.'[42]

So these unities are historic, and are, as his final comment suggests, very real; but we still recognise the differences between a 'blues' song and a 'country' song when we hear them back to back. So this far-back unity is something which is reached for each time the country blues is played, but the distance is also confirmed in the same moment. Of course, 'country blues' is not simply blues and country music welded together, rather it is the source, and the two distinct forms we recognise are a kind of dual growth away from the shared beginnings.

Morrison's hidden gem 'Foggy Mountain Top' addresses this common root. While it is musically unrelated to the Carter Family song of the same name, Morrison was most likely familiar with that song – he mentioned that his father's record collection included the Carter Family to Paul Jones in 2008. Using the Carter Family's title acknowledges that influence, which is reflected in the lyric itself: 'I've been listening to this music, ever since the age of three'. This is a song he seems to hold a fondness for, giving it a long life on the concert stage regardless of its obscurity in his catalogue (it was unissued until 1998). He included it in the set for the Montreux 1974 gig, in his performance with Derek Bell and Clive Culbertson at the University of Coleraine in 1988, and in live shows as late as 2007. Lyrically, it could be read as little more than a superior improvised blues doodle; in performance it evokes much more. Musically, it is a straight country walking blues and it is perhaps this simplicity and uncomplicated nature that have allowed it to endure. In common with its contemporary 'Twilight Zone' it is a song driven by the vocal, and wheresoever it leads the band follows, with Pete Wingfield particularly skilful in his attentiveness to the nuances of Morrison's performance – responding, reinforcing emphases and echoing the step-downs in tone; listen to Morrison respond to Wingfield's 'sound picture' of the clean glass of water (1.45–50).

The borrowing of the title gives Morrison a mood to explore, an atmosphere to inhabit – while it is a long way from Appalachia to Belfast city, there are correspondences between the landscapes of the Carter Family's song and Morrison's Northern Ireland, where the foggy mountain tops look over the city and the sea. It's not a metaphorical or a mythological mountain; indeed it is an image familiar from Morrison's career-long lexicon, from 'Hey Girl' on *Them* to the epic 'Burning Ground' performances of the late 90s, where he would 'keep going up that mountainside'. Here it is evidence of him seeking to reach for a more straightforwardly realized soundscape than the lush ornamentation of the high state that the Caledonia Soul Orchestra had reached. The song gives us voice, drum, bass and piano and, the cherry on the top, his harmonica, strong and wild and bluesy. The Montreux 1974 take has no harmonica, instead featuring a harder driving blues rhythm and more of the round-backed semi-acoustic that Morrison focused his attention upon so thoroughly throughout the performance. The song has a flexible root to its apparent simplicity and is one that always brings some clear space to any set it is part of, a clean glass of water in itself. Morrison's use of an extant title is both an act of acknowledgement and the carrying forward of tradition via innovation.[43] Morrison's first country album embodies this creative tension.

'I was really trying to make a country and western album', Morrison told Ritchie Yorke in 1974; the country album he wanted to make arrived as *Tupelo Honey*. This is a 'proper' American record, just in advance of the California cowboys who would dominate American popular music and prove extremely successful and exportable, until the arrival of disco in the mid-70s. The album is sepia toned, like its cover art, taking its cue from The Band's 'back to the roots' American music. Thus Morrison mixes the Hank Williams model of country with some Nashville and California cowboy musical touches characteristic of the time, also bringing his tougher blues approach to the table, modifying the singer-songwriter requirement of the time. He quickly saw *Tupelo Honey* and its sister album *His Band And The Street Choir* as products of being placed in a certain position in a certain market, telling Ritchie Yorke in 1974:

> 'I wasn't happy with *Tupelo Honey*. It consisted of songs that were left over from before and that they'd finally gotten round to using. It wasn't really fresh. It was a bunch of songs that had been hanging around for a while. I was really trying to make a country and western album.'[44]

There are only really two survivors from the album that have endured in either the public consciousness or that of their composer, judging by his live sets, and they are 'Wild Night' and 'Tupelo Honey'. It's clear from listening to *Tupelo Honey* as an album that he wanted to make a country and western album, in the traditional sense, but one which stood free of both the centre of country music production – it was recorded in San Francisco, not Nashville – and of its repertoire in that the nine tracks are all Morrison originals. His late turns to the genre in 2000 and 2006, *You Win Again* and *Pay The Devil*, are by contrast heavily loaded in favour of the standard repertoire with merely a trio of Morrison originals between them and only a cover of Rodney Crowell's deathless 'Till I Gain Control Again' deviating from the country blues songbook.

Tupelo Honey makes clear the links between American country music (which is a strand of a bigger American folk music, of course) and the musical roots in

Caledonia that have so intrigued and tugged at Morrison's work almost since the outset. To take an example, the light and lovely 'I Wanna Roo You' has the simplicity of a field song, a charming song of seduction which is also fresh enough to be sung in an innocent spirit almost like a children's rhyme or a skipping game – not unlike the way 'I'll Tell Me Ma' is learnt. This cyclic rhythm and the upturned corners of the melody's smile are emphasised by John McFee's elliptical pedal steel motif. The song, in its subtitle '(Scottish Derivative'), also flags up its own debt to a melody from traditional Scottish folk music – a repertoire which is as powerful an influence in Northern Ireland, as is the more readily recognisable 'Irish' music of the south. The images of domestic contentment in 'I Wanna Roo You' are unusual in a catalogue often distinguished by its sense of movement and restless awareness of the lure of the road, but there is still itchiness here, if good-natured and roguish – 'You know what I'm after, and I'm gonna try it'.[45] While sounding very male in its seductive laying out of his ambitions ('roo' being a saucily ambiguous, rougher cousin of the more chaste 'woo'), the song has been covered by women, notably by Jackie de Shannon and Goldie Hawn, thereby changing the song's perspective and restoring the link between the feminine voice and domestic context which is, perhaps, the cultural norm in popular song.

The tone of the album is undoubtedly upbeat, evoking energetic new vistas for living, intensely felt experience, equally powerful emotion, and love, love, love. 'I Wanna Roo You', 'When That Evening Sun Goes Down' and 'Straight To Your Heart Like A Cannonball' are all 'proper' country songs – they are to do with affairs of the heart, they are connected to the world of weather (snow, setting suns), being out in the open air ('There beneath the stars above' is repeated in the album closer, 'Moonshine Whiskey'), full of trains and railroads and the countryside. All these features and themes recur in Morrison's work of any period or style, we will appreciate, but they are also clearly more closely linked to the country blues of Jimmie Rodgers and Hank Williams than the Nashville of the 1970s. Similarly innovative with form, the bold dual structure of 'Moonshine Whiskey' anticipates his more determined incorporation of distinct movements within a single song that surfaced a decade later on *Common One*.

The title track was the song that most closely allied Morrison to the American singer-songwriter mood of the moment, absorbing both the traditions of the country song and also the modish Californian confessional milieu, and while the songs can seem light, there is a consistency of emotional tone which emphasises the unity of the collection. 'Tupelo Honey' is a slow-dripping declaration of love, free of the murk of the blues – the gentleness and determinedly non-blues tone of Morrison's vocal flags up the coming of the otherworldly falsetto which emerged on 'Warm Love' and *Veedon Fleece*. It feels like a country song, yet if we listen we find no pedal steel, and the languid yet busy drum pattern is closer to a jazz skitter. Vibes settle gently on the offbeat, and Morrison's acoustic guitar runs anticipate his 80s style. Approaching the first climax of the song, an extended improvisation around the chorus, which drops down back into a repetition of the first verse with one of Morrison's characteristic mispronunciations, dropping 'Chyne-aer' from the line, his singing of the line 'She's as sweet as Tupelo Honey' from 5.35–43 is the emotional heart of the song. This is the place the song has been building up to, or earning access to, and the rest of the tune is an exploration of that moment, once reached. Curiously this heady love song was twinned with the acerbic fame blues 'Why Must I Always Explain?' in live sets in the late 1990s. Buzacott and Ford point out that the songs are 'harmonically similar',[46] but the two lyrical discourses make for a deliberately startling juxtaposition. A later studio remake with Bobby Blue Bland – a soul/r'n'b singer, we note, not a 'country singer' – restored the song to its sweet completeness, and Morrison sounds delighted to be singing with one of his inspirations. Especially enjoyable is hearing the way Bland pronounces the title 'Tipelo'. So this song, and album, is a bold innovation upon the traditional form.[47]

For that traditional repertoire, we need to go to the collaboration with Linda Gail Lewis, *You Win Again*. Issued in September 2000, the 13 tracks cover much ground. Befitting the co-billing, the album gathers in several tunes well known in recordings by Linda's brother, Jerry Lee Lewis, including the Hank Williams-penned title track alongside John Lee Hooker's 'Boogie Chillen' and Terry Thompson's 'A Shot Of Rhythm And Blues'. The mix of country, blues and, well, country blues is testament to the source music for much of Morrison's original exposure to American popular music, and harks back to a time 'before rock and roll' where stylistic demarcation was less stringent. That it coincided by and large with Morrison's childhood and youth is both coincidental – he just happened to be born as one of the 'war children' – and absolutely pertinent; this was the age of 'no concepts' as he sings in 'Pagan Streams', and of free and unprejudiced discovery, of being one of the wild children, free to discover.[48]

There is only one Morrison original on *You Win Again*, a song both perfectly tailored for its place and its use: 'No Way Pedro', with its slightly prickly good humour, will probably never be anyone's favourite Van Morrison song, but it is not built to grandstand in the company it keeps on this album. What it does do is show its composer's integral understanding of this music, so that, as Jools Holland says in his sleeve note, it sits alongside the other material here 'as if it were made at the same time'.[49] The record has an uneven reputation. Hardcore fans held wild and wildly differing opinions as to the live shows around the time of its issue, and the working relationship between the co-billed vocalists was not destined to endure, but the album has much that is important for an understanding of how Morrison works and how he brings traditional models to what he is working on in the present moment. The arrangements are constant, and the record has a satisfyingly unified sound, which has been only infrequently the case in Morrison's twenty-first century output.

Of the album, and the experience of making it, Linda Gail Lewis said:

> 'Van is a genius as a vocalist and I didn't know if I would be able to phrase and harmonise with him because his style is so unique. But I did it. I don't totally understand what happened but when we sang together we seemed to know what each other was going to do. People have said he's hard to work with. But he's not. It's a challenge at times but if you're going to be creative you need that. I was amazed at what a good country singer he is. It was incredible. It's like you're listening to Hank Williams.'[50]

She downplays her own role in this project somewhat here, as the blend of their voices is strong and fine, but the close vocal harmonising on this album is unusual for a number of reasons. It's not atypical in country music of course, but the combination of the male and female registers is less common, and frequently complicates the emotional certainties upon which country music is at least in part predicated upon. It is also unusual for Morrison – co-vocalists have functioned as a contrast (Brian Kennedy), a sweet backing voice drawn from established traditions of arrangement (Katie Kissoon), or as a way to give him space for improvisation away from the central task of singing the melody (the trio featured on the Belfast live album). Until this album he had not sung so closely with anyone, in concert or on record, and the album is billed as a vocal collaboration, the only example of this in Morrison's album catalogue. So whatever virtues or failures the record contains, the verdict is to be distributed evenly. In some ways, this record, for all its simplicity, confuses some of the emotional registers of country music by this mix of the male and female voice.

By contrast, the opening seconds of *Pay The Devil*[51] let us know most directly what kind of country music this is: Webb Pierce's 'There Stands The Glass', a hit in 1955, opens with the image of the glass, half empty or half full, which is going to bring succour, comfort, and possibly ruin. Therein lies the appeal and the adventure, as signified by the line 'It's my first one today'. The dominant tone of *Pay The Devil* is just that; the world as a cold and inhospitable place, rendered so by the emotional upset suffered within, turned inside-out and then projected onto the outside world. This is the key to many of these songs – Leon Payne's 'Things Have Gone To Pieces', most famous from George Jones's 1962 version, is a superb example of this technique. The mood is quite different from the bluesy, dusty atmospherics of *You Win Again*, which I think of as outdoor music – *Pay The Devil* is music from interiors, about empty rooms, bottles on bars, rings on women's fingers.

Pay The Devil bristles with the verbal tricks which characterise the best country music writing – the small, telling detail which is proof-positive of a greater, possibly all-encompassing problem. A craftsman-like sleight of hand is also typical of the genre and its writers – a good example here is in Bill Anderson's 'Once A Day', where, building upon but musically distant from Cole Porter's 'I Get Along Without You Very Well', the lyric attests that the singer only thinks of his ex once a day: from dusk till dawn. This kind of linkage of the personal to the general, the finite to the infinite is something at which country music excels, and, perhaps, something which makes it appeal to its audience, including Morrison himself.

'Things Have Gone To Pieces' takes George Jones's version as its model. Composer Leon Payne is also remembered for writing 'Lost Highway', definitively sung by Hank Williams, and also 'Psycho', a song for a character not unlike Lenny in Steinbeck's *Of Mice and Men*, which was covered by Elvis Costello in his 'country' period. The song's premise is to take the details of material breakdown as evidence of the inner turmoil brought on by the disappearance of the singer's lover: 'Things have gone to pieces since you left me'. The domestic chaos is a projection of the subject's inner turmoil. Morrison delivers one of the best vocals on the album, enunciating in the manner that the country lyric needs but bringing to that delivery a blues edge that adds to rather than diminishes the emotional force of that lyric.

'Big Blue Diamonds' is clearly a favourite of Morrison's, as it was chosen for promotional TV appearances around the time of the album's release and has been a frequent feature of the live set since. The arrangement here typifies what Morrison called the 'country and Irish' style that has dominated his live sound for the last two or three years. You can hear it on the *Live At Austin* album, on which 'Big Blue Diamonds' can be heard, and it rests on the clean lines of the arrangement and the pure gospel country of the Crawford Bell Singers, while 'Don't You Get Me High' was known to close listeners to Morrison's live work well before it appeared on *Pay The Devil*, as part of the 'Joe Turner Sings' segment of the lengthy 'In The Afternoon' live version, issued on a CD single in 2002. On there it is one of a sequence of Turner song titles that Morrison declaims, but this tune is picked out for close focus as the lines 'Don't you feel my leg / 'Cos if you feel my leg / You're gonna feel my thigh / And if you feel my thigh / You're gonna get me high'.[52] Big Joe Turner's version of the song belts along on the back of his deep, round soul-shout and he has a laugh in his voice throughout. Morrison, too, evidently enjoyed the adult silliness of the tune, as his laughter at the song's slow dissolution shows.

The best performance on *Pay The Devil* is his version of 'Back Street Affair': this tune, written by Billy Wallace and Jimmy Rule, has been sung by Kitty Wells, Webb Pierce, Loretta Lynn, Conway Twitty and Hank Thompson, to name a few. While clearly part of the deep Nashville songbook, it is unusual in having 'male' and 'female' versions: as it deals with an adulterous relationship, this is good raw material. It also emphasises country music's tussle with marriage and the domestic context, seeking to confirm such values while dealing with wild and free emotions that threaten such stability. This tension is expressed in some of the standards of the repertoire – 'D.I.V.O.R.C.E.', 'Stand By Your Man', 'The Grand Tour' and so on. The title of this song has resonance for Morrison's wider work too; the 'back street' is a key image in his own work from *Astral Weeks* ('Madame George') right up to *Keep It Simple* ('Behind The Ritual'). Morrison seems to inhabit this song in a way that is sometimes missing elsewhere on this album; in 'More And More', for example, he seems to pass by on the other side of the road.

The song deals with the culture of 'shame' within a community, a theme which stretches right back in American culture to the birth of the nation, via Nathaniel Hawthorne's 1850 novel *The Scarlet Letter*, where Hester Prynne, a supposed adulteress, is required to wear a scarlet 'A' on her tunic as a badge of shame in seventeenth-century Puritan Boston. This cultural tendency was later famously satirised in the 60s in Jeannie C. Reilly's hit version of Tom T. Hall's scandalising 'Harper Valley PTA', in which a school council castigates, via a letter, a single mother of a school pupil. The success of this song (the first country song to top both country and pop charts simultaneously) illustrates the note that had been struck by the song's sentiments. 'Back Street Affair' captures a couple caught between the long-suffering stoicism of a Hester Prynne and the gutsy single mother's response to the PTA in Reilly's song: 'This is just a little "Peyton Place" / And you're all Harper Valley hypocrites.' This idea of shame within a community – of the private life being public property – is another of country music's concerns and anxieties: 'everybody knows', and 'Back Street Affair' is a superb example of this tipping-point between self-assertion and the power of public opinion.[53]

Opening with a fiddle flourish, the song tells of a love affair that transgressed marital boundaries and is in support of the song's addressee. Intriguingly this represents a substantial switch from the 'female' version sung by Kitty Wells, in which she lamented that she was the victim, 'paying for that back street affair'. There it is much more a song of remorse and betrayal, where Morrison's version is one of defence and support for a maligned relationship. It's also his best vocal on the album by some distance. This song's lyrical reconfiguration into 'male' and female' versions is an exemplary demonstration of the gender dynamics at work within country music: the two versions call to each other but never meet in the middle: in that, this song is that rare thing, a one-vocal duet. Listen to the purity of the note at 1.36 – the vowel sound in 'judgement' – and how the righteous edge to the tone conveys a kind of urgency to the song itself. Likewise the climb to the title phrase at 1.50–52 (unexpectedly coming off the back of a dipped downturn on the word 'wrong' at 1.49) opens the song up with a sense of tender indignation, made all the more potent by the disciplined articulation of the notes through to 1.57. This finds a correspondence in the final section, where, working towards the emotional resolution of the song (which is expressed lyrically and musically), Morrison draws out 'climb' at 2.15–16, thereby reinforcing the song's sense of purpose. Inverting the lowered note at 'wrong', the song asserts the boldness of this new mood by giving the equivalent note on 'cry' an upward lift, so the face of the song is turned toward, instead of away from, the world. Where the previous mood had been internal and inward-looking, choosing to ignore the world, the final mood is one of resolve to face the judgement of the world down:

> We'll just be brave and strong . . . someday they'll see they're *wrong* [downward modulation]
> So let them call our love a back street affair . . .
> And I'll climb the mountain high . . . and the world will hear me *cry* [upward modulation]
> That our love is not a back street affair.[54]

In this the song conducts that alchemy for which country is so well suited; the matching of the internal state, of the world within, with the demands and condition of the world 'out there'. Thus the local and the universal, the private and the public, the personal and the social selves are entangled but also somehow resolved. Morrison's vocal on this track is clear, steadfast and soulful and both illustrates and embodies this mood in the manner of the great country singers themselves, and 'Back Street Affair' is the one recording on this album that I'd be willing to say that about.

The album's closer, and the cut which draws from a source other than classic Nashville, is Morrison's version of Rodney Crowell's 'Til I Gain Control Again'. The first version of this song to be widely heard was by Crowell's mid-70s employer, Emmylou Harris – Crowell was a member of Harris's 'Hot Band' at the time of her mid-70s breakthrough with *Elite Hotel*. However, it was apparently Willie Nelson's version that Morrison had heard, and this is the template for his take on the tune. Indeed, at first Crowell's song doesn't seem to be a 'country' song at all in the sense that 'There Stands The Glass' is, yet the opening and closing cuts of *Pay The Devil* share a common theme: a figure in some kind of crisis, looking for a way out of it, and a way to steady himself in order for that to happen. In 'There Stands The Glass', the journey is just beginning and heading into the darkness ('It's my first one today'), while in Crowell's song, the light is tentatively glimpsed, illuminating a way forward – it's the light of love and friendship. In this distinction we find encoded information about the social shifts between 1955 and 1975. The lonely drinker of Webb Pierce's song, whose only companion is the drink in the glass, represents a kind of post-war stoical masculinity, which country music of the era was well equipped to articulate, in its spread of topics that, while related to the domestic and work environments, after the manner of the blues, of course, also peeled away the layers of that stoicism to reveal the stifled pain underneath.

Crowell's song is the product of an era of increased emotional candour and articulation; the confessional troubadour, the cowboy with a heart. The mask of toughness of 50s masculinity had slipped and so, while Webb Pierce's song expresses the feeling differently, Crowell's song is a despatch from the same seat at the bar, speaking of the same fundamental and very human feeling. It is concerned with endurance and survival – themes that transcend mere musical genre. The song includes references to a journey's end, and there is very deliberate placing of the song at the end of this album's trip through the emotional range of country music. From here we can see connections to songs of Morrison's own, notably 'Philosopher's Stone', that great, late song of confession and concealment about what it is like to live as he has lived – witness Crowell's lyric, 'Out on the road before me now / There will be times when I will spin.'[55] That spinning would return on 2008's 'Behind The Ritual'.

There are three originals on *Pay The Devil*, all of which step up to the country plate, but 'This Has Got To Stop' and 'Playhouse' (even with its echo of a great country song, Sherrill and Sutton's 'I Don't Wanna Play House') are tiring, unleavened things; only the title cut makes some headway beyond that. In its expression of the bargain with the devil that he is obliged to make, Morrison is reminding us of the nature of his job of work, but also, consciously or not, drawing upon the mythologies which haunt American popular culture, in that we are back to Robert Johnson and the Faustian pact at the crossroads. This modern creation myth has, as we noted earlier, driven some fine writing – Greil Marcus's *Mystery Train* leans heavily on the tale for its sense of an older, wilder America – and also an improbably popular film, the Coen brothers' *O Brother, Where Art Thou?* This film about escaped convict hillbillies is effectively a secret history of twentieth-century American popular song, and features a 'Tommy Johnson' who tells how he sold his soul to the devil at a crossroads, so that he could 'play this guitar real good'.[56] Morrison spoke about 'Pay The Devil':

'A lot of it was from my own life experience, y'know, coloured a bit of course, it's never exactly the same . . . it's walking a fine line between the person and the mythology . . . it's an old expression from way back, I don't know if you've heard it, "you'll have, or you've got the devil to pay".'[57]

Morrison treads that 'fine line' between putting his own life into the songs and adding the drama that sets him free of it in the same moment, and it is the 'mythology' that helps the song succeed in this. So these 'country and Irish' numbers, as he would later refer to them, led him to bring it all back home with distinctly dry and particularly Northern Irish arrangements with his live band as he toured the album and beyond. The songs began increasingly, in their economy and positively parochial formulations, to resemble the music of his youth: the roots of his own art, skiffle.

SKIFFLE, NOT PIFFLE: *THE SKIFFLE SESSIONS* (1999)

When Van Morrison began his association with Lonnie Donegan in the late 1990s, the prevailing critical mood was one of surprise. Yet he had, many times, mentioned the influence of skiffle on his formative musical listening; indeed little traces of the influence of the music in general and Donegan in particular had been evident in the run-up to this period, in the skiffling sway of the rhythm of 'Going Down Geneva' and, most obviously, in the lyrics of 'Philosopher's Stone' ('We were singing, don't you rock me, daddio').[58] Beyond the period of collaboration, the mood of skiffle and its sense of economy would inform a whole album, *Down The Road*, the tight, funky shuffle of which bears its mark strongly. In 2000, he spoke to Ivan Martin about this.

Your first proper band was a DIY skiffle outfit, complete with kitchen washboard and tea-chest bass. How important was skiffle to you in terms of musical development?

For me, skiffle tapped into the Leadbelly thing. When Lonnie Donegan started coming out with versions of Leadbelly songs, that's when it all kicked in for me. See, Donegan never properly received his due. He was a great singer. Also, he's underestimated as a guitarist. He could do more with three chords than most people could do with 50 chords. People tend to dismiss skiffle as DIY music. It can be that. It all depends who's doing it. Skiffle stands on its own. It was never a poor cousin to rock'n'roll. America never produced anything that was close to Donegan. Nothing that I can find.

Was Donegan a bigger influence on you than Elvis?

> Absolutely. Elvis wasn't important to me at all. To me Elvis was peripheral. In my father's record collection I'd heard Chicago blues, country blues, rhythm and blues . . . I liked the energy of rock'n'roll but, y'know, by the time that came along, I felt I'd already heard it. I mean, I liked Little Richard, Big Joe Turner, Fats Domino and Carl Perkins so much more than Elvis. As a singer, I had some admiration for Elvis. But, to me, he was more image than anything.[59]

Skiffle, though hugely influential upon a generation of musicians of the highest calibre, moving them either to sing or to pick up a guitar (Lennon and McCartney, Eric Clapton, and Stevie Winwood among them), its recognisable musical footprint is almost invisible and it is now considered little more than a period piece. Yet while skiffle's great achievement was to facilitate the making of something out of nothing, Morrison was very keen to point out his long-standing admiration for the music but also that the 'anyone can do it' image of the music was a falsehood:

> 'My dad bought the records. Lonnie Donegan was doing Leadbelly and reinterpreting that and coming up with something original. I think it's great the skiffle album is coming out. Donegan is a great singer. I've always thought he was a great singer and he's even better now than he was then. There was this thing when skiffle came out that anybody can play this stuff. It's not true. Anybody can't play it and anybody can't sing it. And so it's great to be able to hook up with Donegan because he influenced me in a big way when I was starting out.'[60]

Morrison sees no discontinuity between the blues and the advent of skiffle – Donegan took the music with which Morrison was already familiar, and had in fact grown up listening to, and turned it into a genuinely fresh, democratic, and very British musical form. Donegan's background as a player in the Chris Barber Band gave him the chops and he then was able to accelerate and emphasise the primal rhythms of the material he enjoyed away from the parameters of the jazz repertoire.

Skiffle grew in part from the confluence of the influence of American music flooding almost undetected into the UK via the GI's and radio and the bohemian seam running through 50s British jazz thanks to the likes of Humphrey Lyttelton, Ken Colyer, George Melly and Chris Barber. The post-war British music scene sat closely alongside the art and comedy scenes – things were yet to split as prismatically as they were later to do. Thus jazz players were art critics (Melly), avuncular hosts (Lyttelton), and the cross-currents of jazz surrealism and post-war gallows humour were embodied in the work of Spike Milligan, a kind of polymath virtually unknown in British popular culture since – a writer, actor, poet, novelist, songwriter and fine trumpet player. There was a fundamental unity to the scene as a whole.

Lonnie Donegan's first hit, 'Rock Island Line', reached the UK charts in January 1956 and kick-started the first wholly British subculture; skiffle represented a seismic shift away from the second-hand glamour of the American hit makers, be they crooners or Bill Haley, and gave the young British some music which belonged to them. Although the music was undoubtedly American in its roots, subjects and repertoire ('Rock Island Line' itself concerns a section of the cross-continental railroad), the sound was undoubtedly British in its echoes of the 'make do and mend' ethic that still pervaded the British way of life. Rationing had finished only a couple of years before Donegan's first hit and a growing sense of relaxation and social freedom was beginning to percolate into daily life and therefore into popular culture itself. Skiffle, perhaps because of rather than in spite of its being a homemade, ration-book facsimile of blues originals, met this very real need for an indigenous music for the young. I recall reading, as a teenager, a justification of the Sex Pistols and their scorched-earth policy towards the pop music that had preceded them – 'This is music for 19 year olds by 19 year olds'.[61] Skiffle was no different, and this was where it acquired its cultural momentum beyond the purely musical discourse, as something that had grown out of previous musical disciplines but broke free with such heat and fervour that it seemed to bear little or no resemblance to them.

George Melly wrote about skiffle in his appraisal of popular culture in Britain, *Revolt into Style*, where he called it 'the first *British* near-pop movement'. His estimation of this 'movement' set the way it has been remembered since: he saw it as 'a bit folksy, it was in no way an anti-social movement. There were no skiffle riots'. Melly saw skiffle's success as being synonymous with Donegan's, although he is stingy with his praise:

> [H]is voice was tinny and harsh, his delivery monotonous, his personality rather prickly . . . in retrospect he sounds more like George Formby than Huddie Ledbetter . . . The world he [Leadbelly] sang of was, in its original, a violent world. Leadbelly, for example, was in prison twice on murder charges and had a near-psychopathic personality. But Donegan's version was, like the traditional jazz it sprang from, safely distanced from that world.[62]

This is of course the voice of the gregarious jazz connoisseur holding his nose just a little, but Melly is also missing the point – the idea was not to sound or live like Leadbelly, but rather to take those songs and make something new of them. As Morrison said, 'Lonnie Donegan was doing Leadbelly and reinterpreting that and coming up with something original'. However, Melly was right in his

George Formby comment in that Donegan was headed for the Summer Seasons rather than the concert stages of the 60s and 70s. Donegan, and thereby skiffle, was very quickly displaced, contained and absorbed into the established tenets of British light entertainment. Listening to the run of Donegan's recordings from 1955 to the Beatles' breakthrough in 1963 is in some ways dispiriting, as the fire and energy seem to drain from his work, even as his playing and singing improve: he gradually drops the stylised American delivery from around 1960, for example. So when Morrison began to work with Donegan, there was a long way to go.[63]

The title track of Donegan's 1999 album, *Muleskinner Blues*,[64] featured their first recorded collaboration and this led to a fuller musical relationship, with Morrison finding space for his revered elder on his own concert bills and at festival events. The 1999 Glastonbury and London Fleadh festivals were particularly effective in introducing Donegan to a new, curious and far less tribal audience than previously – the 19-year-olds of 1999 held no prejudices as far as Donegan was concerned, and just heard the music. This late flowering was very pleasing, as is the recorded evidence of his working relationship with Morrison, a compression of two evenings' worth of shows at Queen's University Belfast and issued as *The Skiffle Sessions*.

Morrison wrote in his sleeve note:

> Although he doesn't get credit for it, Donegan was a major motivator, not just for me, but for many kids with musical ambitions. It wasn't just that anyone could do it, because that would deny Donegan's real skill as a musician and a vocalist.[65]

Such lack of credit yielded the shuffling of feet (but not of the skiffling rhythm) that accompanied the album's release in 1999. It was recorded live and compiled from two evenings in late November 1998 at the Sir William Whitla Hall on the main site of Queen's University Belfast, which had also been the venue for the brace of 'comeback' concerts in Belfast in February 1979 that found their way into Michael Radford's film, *Van Morrison in Ireland*.[66]

The band mixed Morrison's own sidemen of the time – Nicky Scott on bass – with Donegan's men and some stellar guests, including Donegan's old boss Chris Barber, ace sessioneer Big Jim Sullivan and Dr. John, who was in Belfast at the time working on another project and came along to play on Ken Colyer's 'Going Home' and Leadbelly's 'Good Morning Blues'. If proof were needed of skiffle's roots and solid grounding in blues, folk, country and jazz, the composer credits of *The Skiffle Sessions* tell their own tale. Of its 15 tracks, nine are 'trad. arr.'; two are from Leadbelly, one each from Woody Guthrie and Jimmie Rodgers, as well as William Weldon and Roy Jacobs' country blues 'Outskirts Of

Town' and Ken Colyer's take on Dvorak's *New World Symphony*, 'Going Home', which Morrison may well have first heard on a 1957 BBC session by Colyer and his band, where it caused a substantial stir. The song is Colyer's 'theme tune', used as both title for and music on the Ken Colyer Trust's website – the trust is dedicated to preserving and promoting the work of this steadfast true believer in the power and potential of music. This spread shows clearly from where skiffle sprang, while still being, as Stevie Winwood said, purely British music. Morrison writes in the sleeve notes that 'skiffle arrived when and where I needed it. It was too good to be true. What had once been an eccentric taste in American folk-blues was now a popular hit'.[67]

The album opens with a Donegan solo, 'It Takes A Worried Man', which foregrounds the constituent elements of skiffle – the chukka-chukka of the guitar rhythm, the light scuff of the brushed drums and washboard, the walking bass line. Morrison hits the stage for the second tune, 'Lost John', and we can detect how these songs influenced Morrison's later works, with its opening image of the itinerant standing by the railroad track, that key image from *Astral Weeks* and elsewhere: 'Lost John standing by the railroad track / Waiting for the freight train to come back'. That long train running goes right through the landscapes of Morrison's own songs. Thus the connections are made between his the expressive vocabulary of his own highly particularised art and these old, old songs. Morrison expresses this clearly in his sleeve note with a direct summation of his own creative development as an uninterrupted flow from these sources:

> When I formed my first band with my friends, we called ourselves the Sputniks and began playing at youth clubs and school concerts. We had a washboard, guitar, tea-chest bass and a type of kazoo called the zobo. From then on I worked through various beat groups and show bands, through the blues band Them in the mid 60's and on to my solo career spanning the last 30 years.[68]

'Good Morning Blues', 'Outskirts Of Town', 'Midnight Special' and 'Goodnight Irene' crowd around, and Morrison has performed them all 'solo' many times. Perhaps the most famous version of 'Good Morning Blues' in the UK was by Josh White, of whom Morrison always speaks with warmth and enthusiasm. In *Red, White and Blues* he remembers that it was via White that he first heard many songs from the repertoire considered standards: 'I had a single of Josh White singing "House Of The Rising Sun" . . . b-side was "Strange Fruit".'[69] The look of transported pleasure on his face as he remembers that little detail tells us much about the depth of his love for this music. As Donegan points out in his sleeve note to the album, the central part of 'Outskirts Of Town' is given over to a superb acoustic guitar solo by Morrison. Any guitar solo by Morrison is a most unusual thing, but in its manner and execution this one connects this song to some of the 'workshop' moments treasured by close watchers of his live shows.

Donegan, with admirable insight, also identifies a key Morrison technique when he writes of his 'unusual solo guitar technique, somewhere between early Muddy Waters, and, when he adds the unison voice, 1940's Slam Stuart'.[70] Slam Stuart was an innovative jazz bass player, once part of the Sonny Rollins band, who pioneered a technique where he sang an octave higher than he played, in the manner Donegan identifies as 'the unison voice'. This is an important element of Morrison's post-1980 vocalising technique, debuted on record with 1983's 'Irish Heartbeat' and is also familiar from the popular vocal hits of George Benson – with whom Morrison duetted on American TV on a version of 'Misty' in 1977. To add this technique to a song followed by a breakneck take on 'Don't You Rock Me Daddio' makes for a bracing and provocative conjunction of styles and influences. The sense of the freedom to drift was part of the romantic appeal of this music in the austerity of post-war 1950s Britain, a social mood that also added a lustre to the reputation of books like Kerouac's *Dharma Bums* and *On the Road*.

The song in this set most familiar from Morrison's back catalogue is perhaps Leadbelly's 'Midnight Special', a song that exemplifies the crossover of which Morrison's sleeve note speaks, from this music being 'an eccentric interest in American folk-blues' to 'a popular hit' thanks to Donegan and his skiffle peers. *The Skiffle Sessions*' version is, as we would expect, closer to Leadbelly's in terms of its straight-edge directness; combining the acoustic glisten of the original with the big thud of the skiffle beat – and it goes like a train. Miss Rosie is here, as are the railroad and the penitentiary – so that among all the foot-stomping pleasure we retain the sense that somehow the song is both source and evidence of redemption – witness 'Let the midnight special shine its ever lovin' light on me'. Cheek by jowl with Leadbelly is Woody Guthrie, whose 'Dead Or Alive' is shared by the two voices. This tune has featured in Morrison's live sets for over 30 years, while never making it onto any of his albums. The central claim of the lyric that 'It's a hard road, dead or alive' must appeal to Morrison and is of course echoed in his contemporary eulogy for time spent in transit in pursuit of an elusive goal, 'Philosopher's Stone'. The central line, 'It's a hard road, Daddio', combines this feeling with a sly borrowing from the hipster jive of the 50s in general, and Donegan's 'Don't You Rock Me Daddy-O' in particular. Donegan's interest in Woody Guthrie informed his shrug at both Ramblin' Jack Elliott and the young Bob Dylan, as he told Mike Figgis:

> MF: Did you see the likes of Ramblin' Jack Elliott when he came to London?

LD: [tersely] Yes.

MF: Did he make an impact?

LD: [equally tersely] No. (Pause) Next! . . . see, I thought he was a faker. I was a Woody Guthrie man y'see, and doing Woody Guthrie impressions didn't impress me. I can do that![71]

The 50-track *Talking Guitar Blues* anthology seems to prove Donegan's point, containing four Guthrie songs that he recorded in the period 1956–58, several years before Bob Dylan's work made their mutual influence fashionable. By the time Dylan was singing his 'Song To Woody', however, Donegan had been assimilated in British Variety and was recording material like his cover of the Serendipity Singers' 'Beans In My Ears' rather than the ballads of the Dustbowl. The Belfast version has some of the outlaw grit it needs, alongside some of the staginess that saw Donegan take the musical paths he did in the early 60s.

The Leadbelly tune that follows, 'Goodnight Irene', is a song that Morrison has recorded more than once but never issued. In concert, the song was in his set with the Chieftains around the time of *Irish Heartbeat*, usually as part of the encore. That version melded the traditions of Irish music and the blues root of Morrison's muse and deserved to be heard more widely than it was; the fit was so natural and unforced that the connection between the traditions was self-evident and very pleasingly asserted in performance. The version on *The Skiffle Sessions* is undoubtedly Morrison's. Donegan says in his notes that:

> I feel I must mention the extraordinary originality of Van Morrison's version of 'Goodnight Irene'. While I approach this song as a slightly introverted lament, Van's approach is much more 'Macho' and 'in your face'. An intriguing mixture typical of the whole session.[72]

Donegan is perhaps thinking about Morrison's spitting out of the line 'I'll *git* you in my dreams' here, which is certainly neither introverted nor self-pitying. It certainly has an edge of menace to it, which seems somehow closer to the mood of the original blues in itself; a toughness as well as tender melancholy. This is a song which clearly exerts a pull over Morrison's muse and it seems remarkable that this is the first and to date only version of it that he has issued commercially. Leadbelly claimed to have learned the song from his uncle, while the great blues scholar Paul Oliver suggests that the song may have been worked up by Leadbelly around a popular song from the late nineteenth century, 'Irene, Good Night', written by Gussie L. (Lord) Davis, one of the very first African-American songwriters to achieve any kind of commercial standing.[73]

'Railroad Bill' and 'The Ballad Of Jesse James' draw upon American folk myth in the same way as does 'John Henry', but here the protagonists are villainous as opposed to the oppressed heroism of John Henry. Yet both became folk heroes – according to Norm Cohen's fascinating book *Long Steel Rail: The Railroad in American Folksong*, 'Railroad Bill' was in truth Morris Slater, described by state officials as 'a negro desperado, who had been terrorising the country generally throughout the South with his depredations' between 1894 and his death, which occurred while he was trying to rob a grocer's store in Atmore, Alabama on 7 March 1897. Prior to this, fantastic stories had circulated about Slater's/Bill's superhuman powers, and his near-indestructibility had spawned many popular ballads. The song as it stands on *The Skiffle Sessions* is a composite of versions that grew from around 1906, initially as elements in work songs, then into more fully developed folk ballads.[74]

'The Ballad Of Jesse James' fits into the folk-ballad mould of 'Railroad Bill' and tells the story plainly and directly, but unlike 'Railroad Bill', this song is fully sympathetic to its subject. These songs act as a form of alternative social history, and of course are extremely powerful evocations of another age, where the west was indeed 'wild' and freedom was both seductive and frightening. Jesse James has proved very attractive to songwriters and his name has passed into common parlance as shorthand for romantic lawlessness, and popular song has undoubtedly added to this dark glamour. For example John Lee Hooker, Woody Guthrie, Bob Dylan and Warren Zevon have all updated and retold the stories, and Morrison was not immune, telling Richie Yorke: 'There were only two tracks we recorded that did not appear on *Astral Weeks*. One was about Jesse James and the other about trains.'[75] The former may well have become 'Crazy Face' on 1971's *His Band And The Street Choir*, a curious piece that is only one rambling verse long, repeated either side of a lengthy instrumental break and sax solo, telling the tale of how people gathered to see 'Crazy Face' by the church gate, where he appears carrying a gun: 'I got it from Jesse James'. It has the stillness and fabular enigma of a sepia-toned image out of nineteenth-century Missouri, from whence came the real Jesse James.[76] The presence of this song reflects Morrison's fascination with the figures and legends of the Wild West and the songs about them, and is an important creative strand, whether the figures are historical, as is Jesse James or mythic, like John Henry, or direct from Morrison's own creative connection to this kind of storytelling – Linden Arden. The figure of the complex outsider who transgresses yet remains possessed of a kind of challenging moral integrity haunts Morrison's songwriting.

'Muleskinner Blues' is arguably Jimmie Rodgers' most famous song outside of his 'Blue Yodel' sequence and is the only track included here that Donegan and Morrison recorded together elsewhere. Issued on the January 1999 album to which it supplied its title, it is a surprisingly hard-driving piece that is echoed in the force of the Belfast version. The lyric is both celebration and lamentation of hard physical work, with a mixture of enslavement and potential freedom: 'Hey little water boy, bring that water bucket round / If you don't like your job, set that water bucket down.' This seems to characterise so many of the songs in this particular repertoire: these people exist at the margins of society, and are consistently in transit, moving from place to place, where work and the wind carries them. They are often involved with the forefront of 'progress', building the railway lines, but excluded from the benefits that these innovations bring. Morrison also recorded the song for the 1997 Bob Dylan-produced tribute album to Jimmie Rodgers, in a very different version, fat with some delicious high-calorie horns, and lots of space rolling around inside the arrangement set off by some jalapeño-hot piano lines; a New Orleans jazz flavour blended with a rolling Memphis soulfulness. Again, this is a cut that deserves to be more widely heard.[77]

The album's closer was also its single, 'I Wanna Go Home', a song found by Alan Lomax in the Bahamas and perhaps better known as 'Sloop John B', a hit for the Beach Boys in 1966 and the only non-original on their *Pet Sounds* album. It was recorded before them by the Weavers, the Kingston Trio and Donegan himself in 1960. His version is slow and languid, riding on a somewhat over-emphasised but not unpleasingly lazy rhythmic slide. Recorded for Pye, and bearing a full-on orchestral arrangement courtesy of the Wally Stott Orchestra, its borderline kitsch exotica indexes how far Donegan had moved into light entertainment from 'Rock Island Line'.[78] The version on *The Skiffle Sessions* is led by Morrison, with Donegan supplying some high, keening notes behind. 'Sloop John B' is a song I never thought I'd hear Morrison sing, and in the execution he seems to emphasise the deep well of melancholy at the heart of the tune, echoing the wish in Ken Colyer's 'Going Home' earlier in the set, the desire for the wandering and the restless motion to cease. It's a plea for rest – 'I wanna go home'. Such a song with its childlike wishes to return to a place of safety and security is a fitting place for this exploration of childhood inspiration to conclude. The stately pace at which the song proceeds (compare it to the wing-heeled swiftness of the *Pet Sounds* version) connects this simple desire with the material reality of adult corporeality – the drink, the boat, the captain. As in much of Morrison's work, respite and repose are found through memories and reimaginings of home. So this song had, like so much of the material that feeds into this disregarded artefact of Morrison's catalogue, a rich and complex history, and one which, in its choice, reveals much about the root of his art and the traditions from and through which it flows.

Look at the songs on this record: 'Goodnight Irene', 'Railroad Bill', 'I Wanna Go Home', 'Going Home', 'Midnight Special' . . . of course, none of these songs are really 'skiffle' songs at all. Skiffle is, or was, a technique or style or approach to playing which manages to unify and process all these disparate elements – folk and folk ballad, jazz, blues, proto-country, gospel – into a single signifying style. Donegan said as much to Mike Figgis, describing his repertoire as being 'spirituals, gospel, blues, jazz and pop songs of the day'.[79] Donegan observes that in the US it was discovered by a college crowd as 'folk' or indigenous music whereas in the UK it was exotic and filtered through as skiffle. Yet skiffle was not just a copy of these songs – listen to Leadbelly's version of 'Midnight Special' in juxtaposition to Donegan's and you see the distinctions and the invention as well as the appropriation and approximations of pronunciation and chord sequences.

Like punk, which could accommodate versions of 'My Way', 'Walk On By' and 'I Heard It Through The Grapevine' processed through this new music, skiffle was both iconoclastic and reverential in its heat, energy and viral spread, being capable of changing apparently set, or traditional meanings by innovations on, in and around those structures to create something new and distinctively of its time and place. As Morrison said, skiffle arrived when and where he needed it, and *The Skiffle Sessions* is his act of gratitude and homage to that fortuitous, culturally coincidental time and place. American music became British music, became Northern Irish music, became Van Morrison music. And then he took it somewhere else. In *The Skiffle Sessions* we gain a glimpse of this secret map.

TOO LONG IN EXILE?: THE AMERICAN RECORDS

Following our reflection on how the three main American popular musical forms have informed, influenced and been reflected in Van Morrison's work, we now examine how America as a place, idea and feeling worked its way into the songs. It seems to me that while 'America' is a musically guiding root, a sublimated presence deeply embedded throughout Morrison's work, certain records reflect more clearly the impact of that presence upon the music. This seems to be a vexed conjunction of feelings of belonging and the possibility of movement, and the tension between the here and now and the eternal nature of place. Here are case studies of two albums, *His Band And The Street Choir* and *Wavelength*, which seem to capture the alpha and omega of this dynamic most clearly.

His Band And The Street Choir (1970)

Van Morrison's most overtly Americanised record, *His Band And The Street*

Choir, issued in late 1970, represents a late flowering of the hippie idea before it atrophied into the singer-songwriter boom of the 1970s.[80] We can start with the packaging: the double image on the front cover comprises one shot of Morrison in close up, reflective and distracted, ghosting over the main image. Sleeve centre, the singer stands, seemingly growing up from the American earth, in a glade both rocky and verdant. His hair is long but not down his back, the *Moondance* goatee expanding but neatly trimmed, garbed in a full-length tie-dyed kaftan of white and burnt orange. The back cover and the gatefold of the vinyl version feature more shots of smiling, contented lotus-eaters, Morrison, Janet Planet and the band members pictured barefoot, bedenimmed and happy. Yet all these images have a kind of qualification to them; the duality of the image, the hair, the beard, those totems of the free young, are present but controlled. Van Morrison was never a hippie, but this is as close as he came; and why should he not? Living in California, between the earth and sky, making music for a living, married to a beautiful, sensitive and intelligent woman and finding one's place in the world may not be good for the blues but would seem to have its advantages. Janet Planet recalled the time:

> I still think that there is much to love about the songs on this album: Blue Money, Crazy Face, Call Me Up In Dreamland, Domino – these are just great songs in any era, but certainly one important thing to remember about this one in particular was that Van was at his most relaxed and contented in his personal life; this was no small accomplishment after the last few years of struggle and travail. We were finally, really LIVING in a dreamland – believe it or not – it was that magical a time. So for me, *HB&TSC* was a musical manifestation and paean to real happiness, such a fleeting commodity, so hard-won and hung onto about as successfully as a juggler balancing spinning plates on sticks, but precious to me beyond saying and worth noting again, I think.[81]

The sweetness and tenderness of this memoir makes the issue of the music made seem secondary, I'll confess, but as that is our subject, we should take a look. Morrison remembered the record being less satisfying than the context of its making, telling Ritchie Yorke:

> 'First of all there was the title of the album. Somewhere along the line I lost control of that album. Somebody else got control of it and got the cover and all that shit while I was out on the West Coast. I knew what was happening to it, but it was like I couldn't stop it. I'd given my business thing over to someone else and although I had final approval on things, they just went ahead and did the wrong thing. They told the record company it was one way and it wasn't. So that whole thing went wrong.'[82]

So he was disconnected, howsoever slightly, from control of his own work and how it was represented, from the songs to the sleeve shots and the consequence was, in his view, inferior work. Interestingly, being the most relaxed he had been in his career led to the music industry being most able to guide the sound and look of his work. The sleeve is very definitely of its time, and deliberately so, having the Woodstock-nation ambience down to a 't', resembling scores of similar sleeves from the era – look at the Beach Boys' *Sunflower*, or Johnny Rivers's *Slim Slo Slider* for examples of established acts seeking to connect themselves to this new dawn.[83]

Now, if Janet Planet remembers the record as 'a musical manifestation and paean to real happiness' we should take notice of what she says, and listen. Morrison told Yorke that it had its roots in a kind of Marin County recreation of the doo-wop group that he would later eulogise in 'The Healing Game':

> 'It was originally a concept to do an acapella album . . . 'Street Choir' was to be an acapella group. I wanted these certain guys to form an acapella group so that I could cut a lot of songs acapella with maybe just one guitar. But it didn't turn out; it all got weird.[84]

It is odd that Morrison describes the experience as 'weird', when the music is among his most mainstream, yielding two kosher hit singles in the US ('Domino' and 'Blue Money' – although they sank without trace in the UK) and at least one long-running live standard in 'I've Been Working'. So it was perhaps the events surrounding the making of the record rather than the music itself that he found disturbing or disappointing.

The album's sound is an extension of the mood of *Moondance* and it is perhaps this sense of marking time, musically, that Morrison felt stymied by – the music industry's response to a hit, be it in 1952 or 2010, is that they'd like some more of the same, please. If Morrison really did want to make an a cappella record, then his opportunities to do so were probably quietly wrestled away from him, via 'the business thing' residing elsewhere. Commercially, Morrison's appeal was understood as almost exclusively to an American audience: Warners did not even bother issuing the US singles post-'Wild Night' from *Tupelo Honey* in the UK. We need to remember also that 'serious' artists eschewed the charts and therefore the single as well in the UK in the 70s up to the cultural revolution of punk, which brought about the rebirth of the single as a vital and vigorous art form and as the primary format for popular song. Led Zeppelin and Pink Floyd, for example, issued a hatful of singles each in the US and Europe in the period 1970–77, but none in the UK. This of course left the way clear for the likes of Sparks, Queen, Roxy Music and Mott the Hoople to become both genuinely popular and introduce non-mainstream discourses into British pop's bloodstream. Morrison's music was periodically expressing a tussle between these impulses – the softening at the edges required by sustained commercial success alongside his unwillingness to repeat a style as if it were a formula. The deal seems to have been to tailor the music but ensure it had some rough edges left. These include studio chat at a song's tail going unedited – 'I'll Be Your Lover Too' and some seat-of-the-pants (now rather dated sounding) hippie choir vocalising, on the likes of 'Call Me Up In Dreamland' and 'Virgo Clowns'.

Opener 'Domino' is a kind of steam-driven, funky word-game, which opens nicely, via John Platania's spindly folk-funk guitar and drops into the percussive steps supplied by drummer and associate producer Dahuud Elias Shaar. If Warners were looking for singles then he gave them one here: tight, concise and Stax-funky, 'Domino' is a great song, and part of a line running through Morrison's songwriting which would lead on to 'Wild Night' and most famously 'Jackie Wilson Said'. These three-minute marvels, close, catchy, and capricious songs, are seamless blends of pop, soul and r'n'b. They also lead off their respective, and consecutive, albums, illustrating Morrison's awareness of the need to make a good entrance – as he still shows every night on tour. Few of his peers understand the theatre involved in presenting music as well as Morrison does. 'Domino' connects his work not to Woodstock but to Wattstax: Graham Nash it is not. Morrison's vocal is direct and forceful, and eager to foreground some everyday wisdom, and some early hints at discomfort with having a 'public image' rather than starry-eyed mysticism: 'And if you never hear from me / That just means I would rather not'. The chorus is a rolling word-soup of o-sounds – 'Oh, Domino, roll me over Romeo, there you go . . .', while the best musical moments are the stops between chorus-ends and the leap back into the verse: Morrison makes the first with a 'Dig it!' (1.13) and the next at the song's close with 'And the band . . . one more time!' (2.51–58). These ad libs do indeed communicate the 'liveness' of the recording and work every time you listen; it's hard to hear it and not be cheered up. He also favours the swift, unfaded finish that 'Wild Night' and 'Jackie Wilson Said' would also employ: indeed this technique somehow confirms the verisimilitude of the recording – a fade is at least at one level confirmation of artifice, and of editorial intervention. The slam-down, full-volume stop is familiar from live performance: ones as tight as this (3.06) are doubly impressive. The horns are scalding hot, and this cut helped define Morrison's sound in the popular imagination for some time: blue-eyed soul vocal, pop melody and r'n'b scat, piping hot horns, and the importance to the ensemble's sound of Morrison's direction, cueing, leading: 'And the band . . . one more time!' We should remind ourselves that much of the Caledonia Soul Orchestra were working on this album, so that later triumph had long roots.

'Crazy Face' is a song that falls back on Morrison's recurrent interest in the lore of the Wild West, via the references to Jesse James; this is a curious little stump of a narrative not wholly unrelated to Linden Arden in its sepia-toned enigmaticism. It features a lovely throttled sax solo, probably from Jack Schroer. It also suffers a startlingly abrupt truncation, suggesting an unnaturally accelerated end for the figure in the song, courtesy of a violent blow, or a shot from a gun. The mentions of Jesse James also link the song with *Astral Weeks* – as cited in the skiffle section, he told Ritchie Yorke that one of the songs left off that album 'was about Jesse James'. He also says that it was a 'basic blues'. This is not certainly that song, but the connection between his preferred musical language and the imagery of the Wild West is there; as we noted above, he included 'The Ballad Of Jesse James' on *The Skiffle Sessions* nearly three decades later. 'Crazy Face' draws some of that uneasiness and tension into the dappled dell of *His Band And The Street Choir*. Indeed the album has a slew of sunny, good-natured love songs, what the Lovin' Spoonful memorably dubbed 'hums'. 'Give Me A Kiss' is a hum, laid over a chunky pop-blues backbeat; Janet Planet delivers some Linda McCartney-shaky backing vox as the song buzzes from flower to flower. Rarely performed live, the song returned for an unexpected encore alongside album-mate 'Call Me Up In Dreamland' in the late 90s, around *The Philosopher's Stone* and *Back On Top* era. A live version recorded in Berne in 1998 and featuring jazz and funk legend Fred Wesley and Candy Dulfer was issued on a single, where it sounded tight, tight, tight.[85]

The album's best-known non-single tune, 'I've Been Working', is a deep cut of Californian blue funk. It is probably most familiar as track one, side two of *It's Too Late To Stop Now*, and turned up on *A Night In San Francisco*, seemingly double-speed (as was the case with much of that album) and adorned by the buttery sax of Candy Dulfer. It is a superb live number, self-evidently. What do we find in the studio cut? It opens with a nice, dry tick on the snare rim and some pleasingly and uncompromisingly rhythmic riffing from John Platania; it is a superb example of how to keep things simple and make them deep. The arrangement gives a kind of salt pan over which Morrison's tired, thirsty, driven vocal can range freely; his vocal arrives at 0.10, and the vocal follows the blues model of repetition of lines and in its lyric describing work and women in uncomplicated terms. What he does bring into it is what he does with those conventions; listen to what he does from 0.58–1.03 (the 'up . . . down' segment), for example, making a dizzying single syllable out of the sounds – this freedom within a tight structure is what Morrison aims at. The song also permits and accommodates some powerful dynamics; several rises and falls are facilitated by the horn section lifting the body of the song into and down from the 'Woman' chant at the verses' end. This is a song without much of a chorus, but an expansive groove, and after the 'Woman' section the song hangs above a precipitous chasm and sways until the groove corrects itself (1.11–15, for example). It is this tension built into the music that lends the song much of its urgency and drive; it sounds and feels like a working-man's blues. Little wonder then that it became a live favourite, offering a groove to explore and plenty of space for the vocalist to license to explore it. Platania's guitar, John Klingberg's bass and Shaar's drumming lock into a mesmerically dirty groove and the horns throw splashes of colour at it – listen to the heat of the section from 2.11–25.

It's no wonder this song made the cut for the *It's Too Late To Stop Now*, surviving where its album-mates did not – it represents a breakthrough for Morrison in its tight economy matched with wide open spaces for him to explore the possibilities of the voice. It also features a tantalising semi-coda from 3.09 and fades all too swiftly, during which the band back down and we are left with Morrison ruminating over a contemplative Ray Charles-style organ, tambourine and Platania's percussive strum, and the quick fade suggests more to come beyond the limits we have. There's tension and a real physical, sexual energy in this song; that's a rarity on this album and its tough directness has few peers in his catalogue.

'Call Me Up In Dreamland' is a simple, sweet song, featuring what might be a taster of the a cappella style Morrison claimed he had originally picked out for the album, albeit in a full-on denim chorus rather than the slick and sweet vocalising of the street corner doo-wop song of mythology. As Janet Planet recalled, it was a decent description of their life at the time: 'We were finally, really LIVING in a dreamland – believe it or not – it was that magical a time'.[86] The tune's easy, almost Dixie swing is evidence of that sense of well-being, and its first-draft-light lyrics entirely concordant with the musical mood. He is clearly enjoying the song's lightness (listen to his humorous pronunciation of 'saxophone' at 3.43) and the open, sing-along chorus is heavily perfumed with the bouquet of the era. It is a collective, non-competitive, would-be picaresque recreation of the world as it is into what it could be – 'call me up in dreamland' indeed. Morrison, far too much of a realist to fake it, soon lost interest, patience, or both in this kind of dreaming – as he said in 2006: 'We thought we could do something different, and then we found out we couldn't'.[87] So this communal nirvana had a shelf life for sure, but a song like this gives a little glimpse into what it felt like to believe in it, even if just for three-and-a-half minutes: 'never to grow old'.

'Street Choir', a song which was received like a cool drink on a stifling day by the Montreux 1974 audience, has a little of the 'Positively Fourth Street' about it. It is not as acerbic as that song, but is certainly concerned with putting distance between itself and a certain 'other' who is perceived to have abandoned the singer and is now back in light of brighter prospects for the future. Its inclusion in the era-breaking show at Montreux may well have been with this in mind. The crisis on display at that show, and that it came to embody, kick-started the lead in to the 'Period of Transition', where his disillusionment with the industry and his place in it challenged his very reason for being 'Van Morrison' at all. The industry, the audience, even Morrison and his relationship to the music itself became difficult to picture in his 'new world crystal ball'. Back in 1970, it feels like a shoulder turned if not coldly then with some chill to a former ally – the underbelly of the hippie 'cool', of course, was its denial of anger as an energy, polarising the behaviour patterns of the counterculture and thereby admitting psychoses of the sort which led to Altamont and the Manson family. Morrison was aware of this infantilising of human response and this song confronts it.

Musically it could fit on an album like *The Healing Game*, with its Hammond, references to street singing and the importance of doing that 'the old way'; its lyric about being unable to free the 'you' of the song is also a modern (in Morrison's terms) device in its insistence of defending clear space around him. The Street Choir are here, but in a more disciplined form. In an early reference to what would become a later theme, he talks about what constitutes the limits of his 'job'. The mood is far more thoughtful and contemplative than in the more self-consciously free-and-easy 'hippie' numbers on the album; musically that is reflected in the tightness and discipline of the arrangement and the performances. It is this disciplined approach to his work that made it impossible for Morrison to be happy fully indulging in the sloppiness that could be said to characterise the musical mood of the era. In order to get to the free space for improvisation, one needs, as in jazz, to pass through the stage of formal mastering of one's art in order to be able to meaningfully deviate or even depart from it. Untutored raggedness may have had a modish countercultural charm in the Californian canyons but Morrison could never have tolerated dwelling there for long. As Morrison said of his view of his peers in the mid-60s: 'I couldn't believe how lazy these people were . . . it seemed the lazier they were, the more successful they became, somehow.'[88] The tight, disciplined and downbeat mood of 'Street Choir' carries some of this mood, and signals that Morrison has already moved on from this 'dreamland', this American idyll. Thoreau lay in wait for him, with a different reason to be out in the country; one from an older, half-forgotten America, one which connected his love of Leadbelly to his own sense of belonging, and exile. Eight years later Morrison would reimagine these issues, and look back to his roots once more.

Say goodbye, goodbye, goodbye . . . : *Wavelength* (1978)

Wavelength is certainly Morrison's glossiest and in musical terms his most mainstream record, one unusual in sounding absolutely contemporary; this was what high-end pop-rock production sounded like in 1978. It was recorded away from his usual haunts, at the Manor in Oxfordshire, which was Virgin Records 'in-house' studio; this also marked the start of his working relationship with the Manor's producer/engineer Mick Glossop, who was responsible for some of the best post-punk recordings to emerge on Virgin. This shift from the Californian comfort zone ensured a different kind of sound was created; the paradox is of course that because of, rather than in spite of, its contemporary gloss, the album is Morrison's most FM-radio-friendly recording. Garth Hudson of The Band added some accordion and keyboard overdubs at their own Shangri-La Studios in Malibu, but the bulk of this freeway radio-friendly, very American, record was made in England.[89]

The curious fact is that just as he was making this album, full as it is of sunshine, ease and reflection, back in the UK pop music had undergone a set of radical shifts and changes, as punk rattled the industry. *Wavelength*, recorded in spring 1978, is hardly music to shake the foundations, but that is not what it's built to do – Morrison was aware of and did have a view on punk, and he found he liked the spirit more than the matter of it: 'Those punks, I like the attitude, but I don't dig the music.'[90] Lest we forget, an early punk/pub-rock crossover standard was a souped-up version of 'Gloria', played by the likes of Eddie and the Hot Rods and the Count Bishops, among others, not forgetting Patti Smith's art cover, so there was a connection between the new awkwardness and that of the song's composer. Morrison would of course subsequently move even further away from the bursts of raw energy that punk reintroduced to pop's bloodstream, but still somehow the revival of economy, compactness and intense melodicism that punk emphasised informed *Wavelength*; it is stuffed full of great, intense melodies, flab-free arrangements and go-ahead directness. Listen to the blast of sound coming at you from the very first moment of 'Kingdom Hall'; one's lapels are grabbed.

The album is his most complete set of pop writing. From the first notes of 'Kingdom Hall' to the final grandiloquent fade of 'Take It Where You Find It', *Wavelength* impresses with its ability to combine all the key elements of Morrison's art (melody, rhythm, repetition, esoteric motifs of silence, rivers and the radio) with eminently marketable pop music. It is music filled with possibility and good humour. It welcomes attention in a way that other Van Morrison albums perhaps don't; it is no accident that the first lines are 'So glad to see you / So glad you're here' and they are sung in a voice we haven't heard from him before – especially not on the previous album's alluvial muddy flats. It is a rich, high, generous sound that communicates the openness of the music and of the wholeness of this record. It's my contention that the distillation of America into the grooves of this album represents a kind of unconscious valediction: this is his last and most truly American record, even though he continues to record in the States right up to the present day. The tone is of intense celebration and a kind of thanksgiving; the songs bristle with hooks and are infused with the sense of space and light and music that speak of a version of America constructed from experience conjoined with the rich panoply of mythopoeia that wraps the country round. As noted elsewhere in this book, while driving along Route 66 one is not simply driving down a road; one is entering a mythological landscape, one which is somehow key to a collective psyche and the country's understanding of itself. This is partly due, of course, to Bobby Troup's tune (covered by Them on their first album) but is also older than that – the song grew from the idea of the route as an image of free movement and of the possibility of the open road that America itself aspires to represent. Without meaning to, 'Route 66' provided that image with snap-into-focus clarity in a two-minute burst – back to punk – of mythopoeic energy.

'Kingdom Hall' (a meeting place for Jehovah's Witnesses, with whom Morrison's mother had some connection in Belfast) delivers a strong sense of inclusivity and belonging, community and congregation; that is part of the emotional memory that is instilled into this song. Musically, it's a kind of FM gospel and Morrison's vocal is annunciatory – compare the first notes on this record to the more dolorous, lonely holler which opens 'You Gotta Make It Through The World'. If we think that Morrison is an expert sequencer of his records – and I do – then the contrast is instructive. From *A Period Of Transition*'s lone pilgrim beating his own weary path, here the door opens on a benign riot of friendliness and welcome – of arrival and of belonging. This of course is the language and discourse of pop, not of the blues; further evidence that *Wavelength* is a 'pop' record. In its images of getting out from under the weight of inhibition, the song is about casting away what Blake called 'the mind forg'd manacles' and daring to come into the light. It also contains one of my favourite Morrison lines: 'The sugar was tough!' I don't really know why I like this, or even what it means. But I love it, and it sums up the whole album for me – sweet, but with a kickback.

This spirit of openness, discovery and bright curiosity characterises much of the record, and the song 'Checkin' It Out' exemplifies this – an optimistic and clear-sighted proposal of resolution and forward movement through positive thought and exchange of ideas. As overt statements, these are rare in Morrison's work, as is the explicit reference to meditation built-in to the structure of the song (2.38–54), where we are openly invited to use the music, if we are so minded, to join him in checkin' it out. This, although it arrives at the song's close, is the heart of the song. The bringdown comes at 2.27, where he shushes the band and then clears a little room for thought at 2.38, and then, in a moment of dazzling dynamics featuring the vocal cue 'Uh . . .

then you come back!', the rhythm steps up and we are treated to a triumphant fade, which is notable in that it is a fade that seems to get louder the quieter it becomes. Morrison's most impassioned vocal on the track is right at the song's vanishing point: 'Yeahyeahyeahyeah!' (3.23–25). The remarkable thing is that by that point the apparent banality of this line is tied right into the spiritual process of the song. The 'yeah' is a Whitmanesque yawp of pure positivity. It is a good example too of Morrison's studio technique of fading a song at a point where it just seems poised on the cusp of changing into something else. This is a good rhetorical strategy, not unprecedented (consider the fade of 'A Hard Day's Night', for example), but artistically very powerful. Likewise, the lyric and the instrumentation are indivisible here – when he shushes the song, it beds down; when he bids it to come back, it surges up with a benign muscularity.

'Natalia' was possibly the first record by Van Morrison that I ever knowingly heard on British radio. Even though in summer 1978 my head was full of Elvis Costello, XTC and The Jam I noticed it; it matches joy and melancholy so finely that it is almost impossible to discern one from another. Of course the voice is there, audacious in its runs, its repetitions, its grain – listen to how it inhabits and expresses the emotion in the charmed repetitions of the girl's name ('I call out your name') from 1.51–2.17. If Roland Barthes wants the grain of the voice, then here it is – not just in the grit of it, but in the unity of emotion and the means of the expression of that emotion. The use of the apparently banal pop onomatopoeia 'Na na na' is suddenly allowed to flower into the name of the lover, and of desire itself. This is longing, sung.

Following 'Natalia' down the beach boulevard is 'Venice U.S.A', another of Morrison's uses of the spirit of place in order to evoke and capture a moment. Venice is a seafront district in western Los Angeles known for its bohemian nature; the early Beat poets set up home away from the seafront and the likes of Dennis Hopper have lived there in recent years. In Morrison's sketch of it he seems quite at home, living a completely ordinary life, sitting in restaurants with his 'baby', wandering the streets, around the harbour. Yet there is an undertow which connects this to other evocations of place in Morrison's works – the streets are wet with rain as he leaves, he watches the ships come sailing in. The song has a kind of skank which is not quite reggae but is on the way to it – what Johnny Rivers called LA Reggae, perhaps[91] – and is garlanded by Garth Hudson's accordion playing which, perhaps deliberately, evokes the folk music of Venice, Italy. The song is an exploration of rhythm and of vocal experiment and, if you want to grade it, is relatively slight, but it is so catchy as to be practically viral, and evokes a carefree directionlessness which is felt as a kind of freedom: listen to how he hollers 'I'm walking in Venice!' at 5.52. This is Walt Whitman's yawp of life bubbling up.

Side One of the vinyl album concludes with 'Lifetimes', a song which quietly introduces ideas and motifs which would develop in his later work. The opening line considers silence as a language, as an articulation of meaning: 'You sit in silence and the river answers', which is later echoed by 'And I feel the sadness and the river flows' and 'I feel the silence and my doubts are cleared'. This of course would be a rich source for Morrison in his 80s work and beyond, and the references to the river make a connection to 'Old Man River', the Jerome Kern and Oscar Hammerstein II song from *Showboat* best known in the 1936 movie version by Paul Robeson: 'He must know somethin' / He don't say nothin' / He just keeps rollin' along'. To emphasise this, there is a kind of Boatman's Chorus in the second and third verses, from 0.51 to 1.14 and 1.57–2.21 respectively. This features a rare bass voice performance by Morrison (in a tribute, I'd suggest, to Robeson and an effort to link the moods of the two songs) alongside the vocal trio who are so prominent on the whole album, Ginger Blake, Linda Dillard and Laura Creamer. This image of the river would also come to prominence as a key image in the following year's turning point 'You Know What They're Writing About' ('Meet me down by the river') and then beyond into material like 'River Of Time'. Indeed, 'Lifetimes' considers the fluid nature of time and how it might be possible to live many lives within a single one. In its imagery it is poised between the borrowed and the freshly coined, and this speaks of the album as a whole, touching as it does where he has been and where he is going. The sense of grounded physical location (the streets of Venice, in the previous track) is matched with the sense of transportation and the simultaneity of other places – the image of the radio signal as a kind of empathetic telepathy in 'Wavelength' itself. Morrison's vocal is very restrained and thoughtful on this cut, only letting fly towards the fade, while emphasising the simplicity of what he is describing: 'Listen to the music inside / That is all that you have to do'. It is a matter of, as in the title track, tuning in to that music and really being able to hear it. These are the key lines in the song and for emphasis they are accompanied by Peter Bardens's harpsichord-synth, which also suggests that the flow of the river and of the music are one and the same. From the flow of the river to the flow of the unseen airwaves, the album's title song opens with a rare concession to novelty – a synthesiser approximates the sound of tuning in a radio up and down a waveband. Explored in full later in this book, the song celebrates the link between radio and happiness, with the first, falsetto part of the song being the private aspect of the song, and the main part being a public, sunlit affirmation of this happy metaphor between the radio signal and the personal, intuitive signals people pick up from each other. The vocal is, like the rest of the record, a strong, clear, pop-sensitive thing, and is (not accidentally) custom built for America, and for FM radio.

'Santa Fe/Beautiful Obsession' is a song that Morrison had had in the pocket for some time; co-writer Jackie DeShannon recorded it in 1974 alongside 'Sweet Sixteen' and the rest. It is a mellow, reflective melody and this is reflected in its lyric, which poses questions alongside its images of harmony and ease. There is a strong sense of how the surrounding world presents a challenge to the comforts of the present circumstance. In this, 'Santa Fe' – another use of a place name – contains one of my favourite Morrison images, the holding together of the inner and outer, the universal and the local, the world-scale and the human: 'I can feel it from the mountain top, running down to the foamy brine / In a restaurant, 'cross a table top, looking into a glass of wine'. The two rhythms seem to both harmonise and also fly from each other. There is mystery and imminence just out there – 'look around you, it's happening' – as well as continuity – 'the same old way'. It also provides us with a key line with which to deal with Morrison's art: 'It's more than a song to sing', a line we find in DeShannon's original recording too.[92]

Here, however, the line is the cue for the transition into 'Beautiful Obsession', a semi-improvised piece which grows out of its parent song in the manner of his live work further on down the road, where fresh songs would develop from improvisational structures built into and onto songs like 'Rave On John Donne', 'In The Afternoon' and, most spectacularly, 'Burning Ground'. This 'spur' has an ebb and flow in its structure that seems to be pulled from the parent song in a manner almost lunar, drawn from the song like the moon pulls on the tide. The bass-voice chorus we heard on 'Lifetimes' accompanies Morrison's vocal, which emphasises this tidal movement in the relationship between song and singer: 'It goes out . . . and it comes back', characterising such flows as natural and related to the nature of inspiration itself. It is also much like a radio signal fading in and out of clear reception. Its concluding and unexpected break from the repetitions of the title and lines around the idea of feeling and being 'more than a song to sing' comes at 6.35, 'Let the cowboy ride!', repeated three times – it provides the cue for the song to fade, and to become something else again. In this it is not only a comment upon the nature of inspiration but a demonstration of it. With this incongruous image breaking the lyrical pattern which seemed to be set we see the volatile nature of both art and Morrison's approach to it – in 'letting the cowboy ride', he is letting the song go free to develop as it may. In reaching no doubt unconsciously for this image at this moment Morrison is touching again very old (for him) ideas of freedom and unfettered living, as well as how that actually feels – this is indeed a cry for and of freedom – it is of course also drawn from the mythology of the old America.

The intimacies of 'Hungry For Your Love', explored in the Love Songs section of Chapter Four, give way to the album's closer, 'Take It Where You Find It' which embraces chance in its very title. It has been criticised and even mocked for its opening verse, but to me it seems a model of construction, assigning to each talent the proper task in the shared ambition of finding what he would later call the 'philosopher's stone', that is, the right way of saying it that would unlock the mystery at the centre of life. The song seems to work as a reflection on what has been, and the continuities between what has preceded him, where he is now, and what will happen in the 'nows' that follow the present one. In this it boldly connects past, present and future, and ties his own ambition and experience into that sense of discovery. This is part of the appeal of the idea of America for Morrison, in its unification of continuity and change – at least in his imagination, via a mix of his own 'real' experience and multiple received ideas and images.

Here, America seems to function as a great circuit box of dreams where exchange and loss and gain all come to be experienced as aspects of the same thing – the nature of existence itself which the song characterises as 'change'. It also opens itself up to change, happenstance and discovery. The last section of the song is the line 'I'm gonna walk down the street until I see my shining light', ushered in by a forcefully emotive upward surge of Barden's synth (6.07), suggesting a breakthrough into a kind of enlightenment. This is repeated over the next 100 seconds until the finale, a repetition of the line 'Lost dreams and found dreams in America', which then fades and brings us back to source. The song ends on a round of farewell to America and a turn back towards the Old World.

Wavelength is therefore a kind of love letter to, and from, America. It's been reported that Morrison quickly lost interest in the record and it is notable that cuts from it rarely feature in his live sets or on the self-curated best-of's. This may have something to do with the record lacking the anticipated commercial success, but also perhaps the finished sheen of the album. These songs are *there*, and they are so tightly packed and arranged that there is little room for manoeuvre within them; they occupy linear space and this is partly why they are such great driving music – they stretch out ahead to the horizon. But they are also complete; why would Morrison return to them once more? The songs, in my view are fabulous, but they are finished. In this, I suggest, they echo his relationship with America. He was already looking towards Europe, and a different kind of tension. As he told Candy Dulfer in 2007, 'America is too big for me . . . I'm more of an island person',[93] so our next stop is the island of Ireland itself.

Chapter Two

What Makes the Irish Heart Beat?: The Irishness of Van Morrison

This chapter seeks to investigate how 'Irishness' functions as a discourse within Van Morrison's music. But immediately we have a puzzle: if we ask ourselves the question 'How Irish is Van Morrison's music?' then the easy answer is, 'Not very'. The briefest listen reveals that his music is, as we have seen, derived from the great American forms which have both shaped and dominated mainstream popular music without ever being quite fully part of it: jazz, blues, country, folk and soul. Despite the undeniable importance of locality to his key themes ('Cyprus Avenue', 'Coney Island', 'On Hyndford Street' and more), the Irishness of his work has little or nothing to do with the surface details and structures we associate with Irish roots music. Although Morrison grew up in East Belfast hearing and participating in traditional music (his first exposure to live music was via the McPeake Family, who made 'Wild Mountain Thyme' famous, a song which Morrison later covered as 'Purple Heather'), you'll look long and hard for extensive excursions into the traditional Irish songbook or upfront use of traditional Irish arrangements and instrumentation.

Jeremy Marre asked Morrison quite what kind of inspiration Ireland had been to him in terms of his own music and musical tastes:

> VM: I think it's been an inspiration in terms of some of the songs, and some of the lyrics to some of the songs, and the poetry in some of the songs . . . not all of them . . . but music is a broad thing, it can't be just one country . . . music is a whole universe,

> it can't be limited to one thing . . . but the fact that I was born there, and the inspiration is there, at times it comes, at times it goes, depending on what's happening . . . y'know? Come and go.[1]

The 'Irish' in his music is a mixed bag. It first arrived, unexpectedly, via the full-on rediscovery of 'northern life' in *Beautiful Vision*, which was driven in part by his relocation back to Europe and Northern Europe in particular in 1980–81. His songs about Ireland, North or South, rarely sound 'Irish' in the traditional sense. He has rarely engaged with the Irish music business as it now exists, even telling Niall Stokes that there was a good reason for that:

> Niall Stokes: At your induction into the Irish Music Hall of Fame, you spoke about Paul McGuinness and what he brought, as a manager, to music in Ireland.
>
> VM: Well, like I said, I think Paul McGuinness and U2 created the Irish music industry. It certainly wasn't there before that. So that's basically what I'm saying.[2]

Morrison's long journey home, which started on *Beautiful Vision* and *Inarticulate Speech Of The Heart*, with their romanticised images of 'Home' ('Celtic Ray', 'Northern Muse', 'Irish Heartbeat'), got deeper on *A Sense Of Wonder* with the stalled collaboration with Moving Hearts, and flowered most fully on 1988's *Irish Heartbeat* album, recorded with the Chieftains. This feeling periodically surfaced as 'Celtic' but full-on 'Irish' is rare – the references are far more often allusive – and in his song titles, there are only three 'Irish' originals ('One Irish Rover', 'Irish Heartbeat' and 'What Makes The Irish Heart Beat'), but five tunes with 'Celtic' as the first word in the title: 'Celtic Ray', 'Celtic Swing', 'Celtic Excavation', 'Celtic Spring' and 'Celtic New Year'.

So in Morrison's terms there are a complex set of relations between the term 'Celtic' and the term 'Irish', though they may sometimes ostensibly be referring to the same emotion or idea. Ethnographically, 'Celtic' is a term used in the UK to group the people and societies of Ireland, Scotland and Wales, Cornwall and the Isle of Man, as well as various outposts in northern continental Europe, such as Brittany and the Basque region of Northern Spain. This usage is ancient and traditional but has also come to mean a kind of ambience – a browse through any 'New Age' label's catalogue will reveal how the word is used musically, with titles such as 'Celtic Voyage', 'Celtic Relaxation', 'Celtic Moments' suggesting that 'Celtic' is a mood one could drift in and out of.

When Morrison employs it he is referring to fixed, deep-rooted identity, one of place as well as people. The landscape of 'Celtic Ray' is full of people whose movements are governed by their working routine ('When McManus comes around on his early morning round'[3]), or the division of the day described in 'Cleaning Windows' – morning, break, work, lunch, afternoon, finish – an arranging principle which stretches into the future too: 'Number . . . number 136? Ok, we'll be round tomorrow'.[4] 'Celtic Ray' couldn't be more 'realistic' in its depictions of life in a composite 1950s Northern Ireland, yet it is also 'mystical' in that it takes all this as evidence that we are on 'the Celtic ray'. In his coining of the prefix 'Celtic' for the *Beautiful Vision* material and beyond, we see firm evidence of the enduring, if residual, influence of his reading of Alice Bailey. The idea of the Celtic ray matches Morrison's and Bailey's ideas and thus opens a window onto a new way of thinking not just about Irishness but how people and places are connected, and how music can 'feel out' these hidden connections. While the post-*Beautiful Vision* 'Celtic' tunes tend to be more opaque or mystical (often instrumentals, such as 'Celtic Excavation'), or related to the a different way of reading time and understanding the cycle of the year or the movement of the seasons ('Celtic New Year', 'Celtic Spring'), the 'Irish' songs are more specifically localised and as such feel warmer and more parochial, in the best possible sense.

'Irish Heartbeat' doesn't actually use the word 'Irish' in its lyric at all, where the later 'One Irish Rover' and 'What Makes The Irish Heart Beat' do. 'Irish Heartbeat' has a broad and sentimental appeal, which is as much to do with its warmly plaintive melody as its folk-club friendly lyrics. It is an open song, easily sung by all and as such is one of Morrison's best pieces of 'folk' writing. He has written and recorded other material where the instrumentation or arrangements suggest the directness of folk but they could not be described, using Richard Hoggart's term, as 'open chorus' songs – 'Come Here My Love', for example, springs to mind. This is a song which is transferable yet always conjures up a sense of proximity and wholeness. It's been covered a good deal, sometimes rather poorly and sentimentally, and in Morrison's live shows it has had the majority of its outings in Scotland and Ireland, and has not been played in England since the 1980s, but it did appear in a set in Inverness in late 2007, for example.

So although Morrison was part of a reawakening of Irish music from out of its kitsch torpor, he was also, not untypically, standing apart from any determined revivalism. His early 80s experiments with Irish instrumentation (the uilleann pipes on 'Celtic Ray', for example) were easily outdone by the number of tunes on which there were no 'trad.' instruments – for example 'Connswater' sports a wholly local title and is a fresh and recognisably 'folk' Irish melody played entirely on standardised rock instruments of the period. Likewise, his first foray into trad. music was with a folk-rock group, Moving Hearts, rather than diving straight into the traditional songbook. After 'Irish

Heartbeat' there came only two other 'Irish' songs: 'One Irish Rover', which describes the Irish cultural condition of exile, codified as 'roving' here as it is in 'Tá Mo Chleamhnas Déanta' and, more bleakly, in 'Carrickfergus' on *Irish Heartbeat*. In that sense of perpetual displacement it combines the diasporic cultural reflex of 'exile' and the more eagerly embraced sense of movement as characterised by Jack Kerouac's *On the Road*. It is an entirely personal song, the singer of the song being the rover in question, and the anonymity of 'One' in the title suggests a diasporic community of sorts where the narrator is alone but one of a great number. It's a very simple song yet one which, according to Chris Michie, originally bore the line 'one Roman soldier', rather than 'Irish rover'.

> 'When we first recorded "One Irish Rover" the lyrics were ". . . one Roman soldier . . ." I never asked him why the change was made. I feel that the importance of expression is that it's personal and shouldn't be discussed, it should just be experienced. That's the only way that the listener will be able to have their own experience of the music.'[5]

I'd hesitate to attribute the obvious meaning to this – that of the soldier present at Christ's crucifixion who, the synoptics report, on seeing Jesus breathing his last said: 'Truly this man was the son of God.'[6] It may simply be that this phrase spilled out when Morrison was working up the melody, and the rhythm of the phrase and that of the line suggested each other at an unconscious level – that's how songs are written sometimes. But he certainly changed it at some point to what we now know, and in doing so tied the song (and, perhaps, himself) into this long-standing tradition of Irish music and music-making.

The most recent 'Irish' title is 'What Makes The Irish Heart Beat', the title of which echoes 'One Irish Rover' in that it is a conscious addendum to an older and more famous song. From 2002's *Down The Road* album, it is, like much on that record, a tight and deliberately 'small' sound. Furthermore, it is a country blues, far across the waters from a trad. tune in the Irish sense; no wonder it was recorded by Jerry Lee Lewis (in an improbable duet with Eagle Don Henley) on his 2006 album, *Last Man Standing*.[7] It is, however, 'Irish' in its specific references to the experiences of leaving Belfast to come to London with the iconic (and now long-gone) 'Wrigley's sign', an advert for the chewing gum which provided a landmark on Piccadilly Circus, and more generally in its images of wandering:

> I'm far away from home
> But I know I've got to roam . . .
> Like a sailor out on the foam . . .
> That's what makes the Irish heart beat[8]

So, light as it is, it offers a clear and dry-eyed observation of the cultural tradition of emigration, by associating the habit of 'roaming' with the thing that moves the 'Irish heart' most fully. In this way it is an unsentimental riposte to 'Irish Heartbeat' with its pleas to a wanderer to renounce the world 'out there' and remain at home. Of course two decades separated the songs and the good-natured toughness of the later song reflects the mood of Morrison's music at that time just as accurately as 'Irish Heartbeat' did in 1983.

Most of Morrison's 'Irish' songs are identified as such via their references to place rather than drawing upon musical traditions. Here we must be cautious of course, as in one sense we could just as truthfully discuss his 'English' ('Avalon Of The Heart'), 'American' ('Venice USA'), and even his 'Swiss' songs ('Going Down Geneva'), and the centralities of 'Coney Island', 'Cyprus Avenue', 'Orangefield' and the rest are discussed elsewhere in this book, but it's worth saying that these Irish place songs are less easy to define in that they are 'about' Cyprus Avenue or Coney Island but they are also about another world. They are about the spirit of place, and although they are in that sense clearly 'Irish' in derivation, they are not necessarily circumscribed by national identity, be that musical or ideological.

This sense of otherness in the Irish place found expression in 1970's 'Into The Mystic'. Like 'Celtic', we might wonder what and where 'the mystic' is – yet the song describes sailing *into* the mystic, giving it a physical as well as metaphysical locality. 'Into The Mystic' was not his first use of the term – for that, check side one, track one of the first Them album, which says much about the centrality of this idea and its appeal for Morrison. The song refers to a foghorn blowing, and that it is a cue for a kind of homecoming: fellow Belfast boy C. S. Lewis also spoke of the connection between the foghorn and feelings of belonging: 'the sound of a steamer or a foghorn horn at night still conjures up my boyhood.'[9] This is Lewis's idea of joy, and of the spiritual coming out of the apparently mundane; a feeling that he had as a child and then lost, and then, through long and difficult personal and moral struggle, he discovered that he had had 'joy' all along. This is clearly related to Morrison's idea of a 'sense of wonder', and his revelatory discovery detailed in *A Coney Island of the Mind* that the tradition he belonged to was his own: 'I saw what I was . . . an Irish writer.'[10]

This relates too to the idea of the unfound door that leads out of time and space and into – where? When the mood is right and you get the work right you find the door – the most obvious and famous example of this in Lewis's work is in *The Lion, the Witch and the Wardrobe*, a good image of finding the marvellous in and through the ordinary. *Astral Weeks* offers a similar magic door into another world; both works go into the mystic, a kind of nirvana that has to be defended but is never owned, a place built on feeling. As the landscapes of Narnia can very clearly be seen as deriving from those of Northern Ireland, and particularly those of County Down, with its mountains and glens and stunning vistas over the hills, the landscapes of Morrison's work are rooted as firmly in the places in which he spent his childhood – sometimes obviously, sometimes less so. 'Orangefield' typifies the former, 'Hey Girl' the latter. What Morrison and Lewis do have in common is a feeling for the emotional weight of the Northern Irish landscape, and the sensed yet unseen power in its beauty.[11]

So the billowing sail-shapes of 'Into The Mystic' have some concrete links to the real landscapes of Morrison's childhood, and it is these perceptions of the ordinary place as 'ways in' to another world, or another realm – as points of possible transcendence – that we feel at work in 'Cyprus Avenue', for example, and the reference to that 'mystic avenue' years later in 'She Gives Me Religion'. Within Morrison's tune the foghorn mentioned by C. S. Lewis is satisfyingly depicted by the bass sax, and is also cited much later in 'So Quiet In Here' ('Foghorn blowing in the night'[12]), another investigation into the relationship between the present moment and its tantalisingly close yet obscure otherness. There is the sense of being a dweller on the threshold of a breakthrough from this world into another. The song facilitates this, but with frustrating infrequency and unguaranteed intensity.

'Into The Mystic' is a lush song, with a pleasingly spongy horn section providing a buoyancy to its progress, but it is unburdened by strings or choirs to suggest this theme of transcendence. Indeed it is a quiet song, where even the 'foghorn' blasts are discreet and shivery, allowing Morrison's vocal to surge forward and pull back at the key moments, fully inhabiting the chorus from 2.33–50, elsewhere coming down almost to a whisper (1.12–15). The song concludes on a famous line, 'It's too late to stop now', later to provide the emotional climax to the famed early 70s live shows and the title of his 1973 live album. The song is propelled forward by the quietly assertive bass line which pulses beneath the waterline. The maritime image is appropriate as this is a song which, although fully elemental and connected to the open air (the first verse cites the sun, the wind and the sky), is most strongly connected to the sea, with its bonny boats, foghorns, hollering sailors and, most vitally, the *smell* of the sea. It's an invitation to experience oneself and the world about us differently, but is also true: anyone who has stood by the ocean knows what it means, and that directness offers almost complete openness of experience. You don't have to be a 'mystic' to sail into the mystic, you just have to learn to look and listen and feel, and this he somehow learned from the environments of Northern Ireland.[13] Yet, like people, places change and his next home thought from abroad indexed how such continuities are disrupted.

The first post-*Astral Weeks* song to reference Belfast directly, 'Saint Dominic's Preview' is something of an enigma. Melodically undazzling, it still became a favourite with his audience and while it became connected with Northern Ireland via its mention of Belfast, it gives equal measure to the rest of the world. Widely understood as a comment on the state of Northern Ireland in the early 70s, the evocation of Belfast in 'Saint Dominic's Preview' is a purely personal one, and we feel the 'nostalgia', or homesickness implicit in the observation 'It's a long way to Buffalo / It's a long way to Belfast city, too'. It seeks less to 'comment' on Irish life than to connect to his habit of using music to re-enter, re-create or simply invoke time, space and place via memory. Furthermore while the song does cite Belfast, it refuses to settle on a single and distinct locality, sweeping across continents within the space of a line or two, taking in Paris, San Francisco, Buffalo, Belfast and New York.[14]

So just what, I wondered, does this opaque, even runic song – described by Morrison as 'just a stream of consciousness' – really have to do with Northern Ireland? Its supposed link with the Six Counties seems to be predicated on the fact that it mentions Belfast, but its sense of sweeping freedom is key, as Morrison told Donal Corvyn in 1974:

> D.C.: How did you react when you watched broadcasts in the States about the situation in Belfast? Had you felt the violence and antagonism in the air before you left?
>
> V.M.: I felt the antagonism but not only in religion. I felt the antagonism in everything. No matter what you try to do in Belfast they're down on it. Everything I tried to do in Belfast, they put the screws on it immediately. That's just the way people are brought up there. I don't know why. Whew![15]

So the pull towards his home is strong but he is not confined by it; the relief on a personal and creative level not to be subject to the inherent antagonism and having 'the screws' put on everything anymore is palpable in that 'Whew!' So the cinematic sweep of the song is both utterly free of these confines but also shaped in reference to them.

That freedom is expressed in the sound of the song, from the very American opening, the piano stepping down to the recognisable horn sound of Jack Schroer, after which Morrison's vocal comes in at 0.14. The lyric begins surely enough with a reference to his adolescence in Belfast, with its nod to the lot of the window cleaner, making a punning connection between the French name of the leather and the evocations of Frenchness via Edith Piaf and the iconic bulk of the Cathedral Notre Dame. The music and the lyrics are in collusion, however; after Morrison cites Notre Dame, there comes a squirt of *d'orgue eglise*. It is an extraordinarily dense sound, and one which conceals as much as it reveals with each fresh listen. The vocal toughens up at 1.01 with 'And it's a long way to Buffalo . . .', the voice now coming from deeper in the gut, the deep blues shout starting to assert itself as the song, and its singer, find their stride.

The second verse sweeps us giddily, cinematically, to a scene 'back in' (suggesting a home, or grounded place) San Francisco, and personalises the narrative, introducing an 'I' and a 'you, my friend'. Later we get impressions of a showbiz party; these glimpses and fragments are more than the sum of their parts by dint of the unifying reference point – the chorus that repeats the song's title – to which all of the parts are connected. Through it all, Saint Dominic's Preview remains. It is that which holds the song together, and unifies the apparently unconnected, resolving fracture through reimagining what it means to belong: in this, the song is indeed a helpful observation of the situation in Northern Ireland in the early 1970s.

A decade later, Morrison returned an Irishness both direct and esoteric on *Beautiful Vision*. For 'Northern Muse (Solid Ground)' Morrison may or may not have borrowed the first part of the title from a book, edited by John Buchan, author of *The Thirty-Nine Steps*, entitled *The Northern Muse: An Anthology of Scots Vernacular Poetry*.[16] If he did, the muse crossed the Irish Sea first, for in this song the spirit of the Northern Irish landscape is embodied as a woman, moving across the land of the County Down. The sound of the album is a crystal-clear, precise and disciplined one and this track exemplifies it. Dropping in on the off-beat, the melody is picked up immediately by Mark Isham's trumpet and it takes us round the high melody which sits atop the song once before the vocal comes in at 0.12, underpinned again by the sibilant and steadfast hi-hat which is mixed way up on this album. The trio of female singers on this album also have a key role – Bianca Thornton, Annie Stocking and Pauline Lozano contribute much to the mood of the record with their vocals, which are both robustly soulful and sweetly ethereal, like the Northern Muse herself.

The flute of Pee Wee Ellis and John Allair's organ lines, poised between the church and the jazz club (listen to his solo, cued in by Morrison's *sotto voce* 'all right' from 1.58–2.24), sublimate to create the sense of weightlessness which evokes the movement of the subject of the song, almost floating free across and over the landscape, yet still firmly connected to the solid ground, tracing the hills and glens of the County Down. The swift but steady movement of the music delivers this image of her. This is a song without a real chorus, just verses and a bridge, and in the opening two verses every line opens with an 'And', further suggesting openness and continuity. The bridge steps back and is more analytical of the muse's impact on the singer, picked up in the third verse by the suggestion that the Northern Muse was the reason he left home 'when I was young', just as she is now calling him home again to offer refreshment and hope. He slyly quotes from one of Bob Dylan's most remarkable songs, 'If You See Her, Say Hello', to communicate this sense of intimacy and exile expressed as longing and felt simultaneously. Morrison knows where this muse is – on the solid ground, in the County Down – while Dylan's pain came from not knowing: 'She might be in Tangier'.[17] What we know is, thanks to the song's subtitle, that this vision is grounded in a real place, it is not an imaginary 'Happy Valley' somewhere – thus the reality of place and the spiritual nature of it are presented as undivided, via this image of the muse herself. The Celtic nature of the muse is emphasised discreetly just at the fade, where Sean Fulsom's uilleann pipes drift into the mix from 3.36 to the moment the song disappears finally at 3.58.[18]

Morrison went on to explore a high and consciously poetic form of Irishness in the 80s via musical settings of the great Irish poet W. B. Yeats, evoked in the roll calls of 'Summertime In England' and 'Rave On John Donne'. 'Crazy Jane On God' was recorded during the *Sense Of Wonder* sessions and initially barred from release by the Yeats estate, and around the same time came an unissued take on 'Before the World Was Made' entitled 'Your Original Face' – he would later re-record and issue this under its original title on *Too Long In Exile*.[19] With a characteristic body swerve, Morrison's next take on 'Irish' music steered away from the ornamentation of Yeats and dove into the hitherto unexplored roots of Irish traditional music with the help of that repertoire's keenest exponents, the Chieftains.

IRISH HEARTBEAT (1988)

> Niall Stokes: *Irish Heartbeat* led into another area, songs that were familiar from the folk tradition – say a song like 'CarrigFergus'.
>
> Van Morrison: My father loved John McCormack, and he had lots of John McCormack records. So it was always part of the picture. And I always liked those sort of songs anyway. So whether I did it with The Chieftains or not was neither here nor there. I always loved those songs. So basically that's where I came in on that, I was coming from the John McCormack angle, you know, into the Chieftains angle. So it was like marrying the two things.[20]

Flowing out of a period in which Morrison was exploring instrumental music and the ambient nature of musical atmospheres, which reached its apotheosis on *Poetic Champions Compose*, an album of traditional Irish music was something of a surprise. The songs which make up *Irish Heartbeat* are 'All Ireland' songs, from the all-points-of-the-compass sweep of 'Star Of The County Down', ('From Bantry Bay and the Derry Quay / And from Galway to Dublin Town') to the pilgrimage made in search of the beloved in 'Tá Mo Chleamhnas Déanta' ('I walked up and I walked down / I walked Cork, and Dublin, and Belfast towns') and the evocation of a northern place that has also worn a southern title, 'Carrickfergus', also recorded by Dominic Behan as 'The Kerry Boatman'. The whole project reaches past the then troubled present into a more unified and integral past, an identity associated with wholeness as opposed to exile and fragmentation; the songs speak of this unity in their images of free movement from place to place. In comparison, Morrison's own devastating image in 'Madame George' of the train journey from Dublin up to Sandy Row seems both part of this tradition and also to be its endpoint, a final echo before the seismic split which followed mere months after *Astral Weeks*' release. It was no accident that Morrison's music was used as part of the publicity drive for the Peace Process in the early 1990s, as an agent of healing, something that was commented upon by US President Bill Clinton: 'Meanwhile, Van Morrison's music continues to inspire people seeking to end the violence, and, of course, most importantly, in the last year the negotiators did the job with the Good Friday Agreement.'[21]

The Chieftains themselves were as drawn to the sense of experiment with this Northern Irish artist and the traditions he brought to the table, consciously and unconsciously, as Morrison was keen to reconnect with some idea of roots via music. Kevin Conneff noted that he found Morrison 'a very curious person coming obviously from a Protestant background in Belfast but singing in such a broad scope of understanding'.[22] In this little remark, Conneff illustrates an aspect of the Irish conundrum; the perceived distances between next-door neighbours, or fellow Irishmen. The man from up by Sandy Row seems 'curious', even 'obviously' so, and Conneff attributes an 'otherness' to Morrison and how he worked, equating that with his background in Belfast and, by inference, a narrowness of scope. It is the music which permits the contact and the revelation that such 'narrowness' is a delusion. This is part, in David Tame's phrase, of 'the secret power of music'.

Derek Bell recalled that he and Morrison spoke about the use of music in healing and in understanding:

> 'At that time Van was deeply searching for an answer . . . a friend of his had threatened to commit suicide and for two years he'd done no work and just gone into his shell reading and studying theosophy; the rosicrucians, Scientology. Every bloody thing he could think of . . . Van was very interested in my recording of Cyril Scott who had written a treatise on how music could influence future history and how all

the great composers like Handel, Chopin and Schumann had done so. Van knew I must be up to my neck in all this so we became friends . . . Van wanted teachings at the time but he didn't want to do any work. He was in a hurry. He wanted them now and if you didn't have them you could fuck off.'[23]

This bracing appraisal is very pleasing. According to Bell, the *Secret Heart of Music* conference at Loughborough in September 1987 was 'organized' by Morrison to pursue this mutual interest. Paddy Moloney had a more down-to-earth memory of how *Irish Heartbeat* came about: Morrison invited Moloney over from Dublin to London to discuss the possibility of a project and took him not to a grand hotel restaurant but to his favourite cafe in Notting Hill Gate:

'He got stuck in . . . Nobody came near him and that's why he went there because he wasn't pestered. Over lunch we had a bit of a chat about doing the album . . . I think at that time Van was searching for his Irish roots. It was this man of blues, of rock and roll, jazz and more importantly soul, coming home to his Irishness with The Chieftains and the music we'd been playing for so many years. Musically we were going to meet each other half way.'[24]

So which songs made the grade, and why?

We open with 'Star Of The County Down', a proper 'All Ireland' song, and one which would undoubtedly been in the ether as he was growing up in Belfast. The 'hit' version of that time was by Count John McCormack, of whom Morrison's parents were enamoured, and so these songs were perhaps understood by Morrison's generation (that is, the 'war children' of 'Wild Children') as somewhat starchy and of the past. So 'Star' may well have been 'nowhere', the word Morrison used to describe his feelings towards Irish music as a teenager, but by the time he came to work with the Chieftains it was most definitely a 'somewhere', a kind of homecoming. It's worth noting how strong within Irish traditional song is the tradition of the naming of places, and how powerfully this tradition is carried on in Morrison's work, even going right back to his earliest material, be it the London of 'Friday's Child' and 'Slim Slow Slider' through the presence of specific locales of Belfast in 'Cyprus Avenue', 'Madame George', and right through to the reconnection with this tradition via 'Coney Island', 'Orangefield' and, ultimately, Hyndford Street itself 20 years later. It is also interesting to note that the role of place names in titles re-emerged in Morrison's work in the period immediately following his work with the Chieftains.

Martin Lynch asked about *Irish Heartbeat*:

ML: Is it a Van Morrison album backed by The Chieftains?

VM: It comes out 50:50, doesn't it? (to Derek Bell)

D[erek]B[ell]: Yes the sound of our group has to give it its character . . . on the other hand every single Irish song we' ve done Van has done a completely different and a new way. Many of the songs have been sung, and maybe they've been recorded rather too often by both good and bad artists and to hear them done in a completely different way will make them live longer and if you throw new light on a piece of music it will last longer and people will study Van's performance as they won't have heard it done that way before.[25]

Morrison's response recalls Paddy Moloney's estimation of 'meeting halfway'. It is through the work of Derek Bell that Irish trad. music and instrumentation approached the condition of a classical repertoire – attaining an accomplishment and an intuitive sensitivity matched with great technical expertise, so that it has few of the rough edges one might expect from an album of such songs, or after hearing them in a session in a pub. On 'Star', for example, Bell plays an adapted hammered dulcimer, which he called a tiompan, the Irish name for the instrument; this came originally from Eastern Europe as a cimbalom, and the sound is close to that of one of Bell's other favoured instruments, the harp. The percussive nature of the dulcimer adds to the rhythmic nature of the performance of course, as opposed to the more meditative flow of the harp – one that sounds 'Celtic', as explored earlier, in the Alan Stivell sense as opposed to the more grounded, even earthy sense which this track strives for.[26]

Morrison's vocal on this track is a surprise to anyone familiar with his own work – the lyric is verbally very dense, and while we sometimes hear him feeling his way into these songs, the contrast between this and the band's confidence with this material offers a new pleasure as the two distinct elements rub up against one another. Derek Bell said of the album: 'It's a classic . . . In a sense from the purist's point of view it's grotesque.'[27] Bell is defending the project against the 'folk purists' here and the 'grotesque' ornamentations he describes as sure to upset the purists were in fact (as he well knew) developments of that tradition. This is the boldness of the project, with traditional music meeting an input both of itself (the Irishness, the belonging) and the entirely 'other' of the different techniques of singing, which Morrison brings to the songs via the soul and jazz vocalising techniques.

Niall Stokes: You also did a rousing version of 'Star Of The County Down'.

Van Morrison: Well, that was straight off John McCormack, that one. Even his arrangement, you know, the piano with Derek Bell – that's the way John McCormack

> would have done it, but he did it with just piano and voice. That stuff comes from that tradition of those Scottish and Irish type of singers that just sang with piano accompaniment. I always liked that music, so it was just a matter of getting the right songs.[28]

Listening to McCormack's version, which is indeed simply voice and piano, is intriguing in that it is unmistakably Irish, and Northern Irish at that, while sporting no recognisably codified 'Irish' musical signifiers at all – thus suggesting that the 'Irish' trad. arrangement is in some senses a modern creation, after the manner of Yeats's adaptations of folk tales in *The Celtic Twilight* – a reinvention of tradition which stakes a claim to absolute authenticity, in the way that Derek Bell described ('the purists won't like it'), yet it is in itself a confection.[29]

It's also interesting to note that, despite the many, many times that Morrison has alluded to the impact of the music of McCormack and the McPeakes in interviews over the years, they are never represented in analyses of his formative influences. Nor are they included on the unauthorised 'roots' themed compilations, such as *The Roots Of Van Morrison* and *Van Morrison's Jukebox* (both feature exclusively American musics, with the exception of Glaswegian Lonnie Donegan on the latter). This overlooking of the obvious is evidence, I'd suggest, of how certain narratives become fixed in the understanding and interpretation of popular culture: that despite the empirical evidence, the Irish and the American spheres of influence (that is in Morrison's case the recorded music and the 'live' music of his childhood), the division seems absolute. So it is doubly interesting to reflect upon Paddy Moloney's observation that Morrison and the Chieftains were 'meeting halfway', and in doing so uncovered as much as forged links between the two apparently wholly distinct sources.[30]

The version of 'Irish Heartbeat' that follows is a re-recording of the original from 1983's *Inarticulate Speech Of The Heart*. It is distinct from that original in that it is brisker, running to 3.58 where the original reached 4.38, and also in that it foregrounds Irish instrumentation. Where on the original Davy Spillane's pipes were a discreet element of the musical texture, this remake uncovers the adaptability of Morrison's melody, while upping the sentimentality of the song. I do not take this to be a bad thing. The inclusiveness of the lyric is played out in its being a duet with June Boyce, (who features on 'Did Ye Get Healed?' and 'Song Of Being A Child') as opposed to solo voice of the 1983 version. It opens directly with these voices in unison, the first verse appearing right at the top of the song, where on the 1983 version, there is a 25-second instrumental introduction. The percussion is provided by a very loose bass drum rhythm, and a kind of rimshot-sharp percussive strike which may well be Martin Fay using what the sleeve identifies as 'bones'. Whatever the source, it is determinedly not rock and roll percussion. The sound overall is somewhat homogeneous, but as the band climb to the bridge at 1.20 we find the trad. instruments really making themselves felt, and the instrumental break from 2.24 is delightful in its being a completely 'Irish' piece of music. The difficulty of the Morrison originals on this album is that the Chieftains don't know them, in the intuitive or even visceral sense, as well as they do the trad. material here, and the early recording of the album before the material was toured sees them still feeling their way into Morrison's material, just as he was exploring how to sing the trad. songs – 'meeting halfway'.

So on the album versions of 'Irish Heartbeat' and 'Celtic Ray' there is a kind of tentative restraint which the live shows had sloughed off; the band are sometimes heard still looking for their place. This remake retains the vocal scat of the original, somewhat accelerated and emboldened, from 2.59; this is of course important as that original vocal on *Inarticulate Speech Of The Heart* was the source of the seven-note signature motif that has run through Morrison's work ever since and is discussed later in this book. Here the 'unison singing' is less obvious as it does not follow an instrument, as it did the guitar on the 1983 version. Here it stands alone, over a closing section in which the dense swirl of strings and pipe reminds me of nothing less than the final moments of 'Cyprus Avenue', especially when the fiddle goes down into the bass register at 3.16–25.

The record then steps forward into 'Tá Mo Chleamhnas Déanta', perhaps the most explicitly Irish of the songs, being sung in both Irish and English, but not only because of this. The verses mirror each other (i.e. the English sense is a translation of the Irish) although, as we might expect, not completely. For example, the line 'My match it was made last night' in the Irish original refers, more grimly somehow, to this happening on the night *before* last, and there is also a version by Irish folk-rock band Altan which uses a different set of Irish words in which there is less correspondence between the two sets of words. Derek Bell's harpsichord opens the song, adding a courtly ambience to what he called the 'characteristic' nature of the Chieftains' sound, and reminding us that these songs often served first as tunes for dancing: his introduction is the cue to take to the floor. The song's roots in dancing are particularly evident in the middle instrumental section from 1.30–47, and the delicious breakdown from 1.47–52, which leads back into Morrison's second verse. Somewhat uncharacteristically for the group, this track features a singing Chieftain: Kevin Conneff and Morrison trade verses, Conneff leading with the first, third and fifth in Irish, Morrison delivering the English equivalents as the second, fourth and sixth. It is unusual to hear Morrison sing a lyric like this, on record at least, and the contrast between the voices is pleasing – Conneff's is light, stepping delicately across the melody, while Morrison, dealing with the translation, is working harder, the grain of his voice providing an intriguing riposte to the airiness of Conneff. This may have had some influence on the vocal arrangements for the tune, as we note that while Conneff is unaccompanied throughout, Morrison is 'shadowed' by the rain-pure voice of Irish-folk chanteuse Mary Black on the second and fourth verses and the final vocal section, where he is backed by a warm chorus of voices. Hearing Morrison's voice set this way is a rare pleasure.

Providing a gorgeous, green-shaded contrast to roving the wild world over is the melancholy mood of the single, appointed place: 'Raglan Road'. The song provides an interesting correspondence with Morrison's own 'street songs', which are themselves strongly aware of the spirit of place ('Cyprus Avenue', 'On Hyndford Street'); drawn from his own experience and personal meanings for and from such places but via song transformed into universal symbols. In 'Raglan Road' he is coming at the process, and down the road, from the other direction: this is a lyric about someone else's personal experience being etched into the trees, houses and paving stones of a seemingly 'ordinary' street.

The slow tread of Derek Bell's soft synth establishes the pace and tenor of the song at the outset, accompanying Morrison's vocal solo until the band begin to glide effortlessly in at mention of Grafton Street. The hi-hat and low fiddle enter first, then harp (at 'the Queen of Hearts'), then double bass and finally the full band, ushered in by a roll on Bell's piano at 1.42. The track is a model of how a song can build emotionally, from a private thought to a public declaration, and the arrangement (though co-credited, like the rest of the album, with Paddy Moloney) bears the marks of Morrison's deep and intuitive understanding of the internal dynamics of song and performance. The instrumental break, which comes as the band arrive, flooding the private spaces of the song with light and sound, is reined back for the vocal to return at 2.30, for the remarkable stanza detailing the gifts of the mind that the narrator gave to his lover. Morrison particularly relishes the line 'I gave her the secret sign' – in live performances of this song he always seemed particularly attentive to that line. The lover is part of the natural world, and is as present in the now as in his memory; he is haunted, and the place is evidence of that haunting: 'On a quiet street where old ghosts meet / I see her walking out.' The distance between eternal love and human frailty is writ large and amounts to the public declaration of a very private and intensely personal understanding of the nature of place, memory and spirituality. Thus we can clearly see why Morrison would find something of interest in Kavanagh's text.

His vocal here is among the best of his career, swooping up to the top of his most forceful and assertive delivery ('I gave her the gifts of the mind / O Lord, I gave her, I gave her the secret sign' (2.30–38)) then right back down to a whisper ('Shhhh . . . On a quiet street, where old ghosts meet . . . Shhhh . . . I see her I see her walking out' (3.14–27)). His delivery of this final verse is the key to some of his later vocal experiments too: listen to how he sings 'creature' (3.46–47) with its echoes of 'Listen To The Lion' and 'Bulbs' and anticipation of the boldness of his spoken work on *Avalon Sunset, Enlightenment* and *Hymns To The Silence* yet to come. Likewise his 'yawp' (Walt Whitman's word) is given full rein here – the open-throated vowel sounds stretching out like keening thoughts. All the more remarkably, Morrison is the drummer on this track, as he was on the cherishable version performed on a St Patrick's Day show for the BBC in 1988, the giveaway being the same brushed hi-hat pattern which is repeated across the two versions.[31]

The song is set to a melody he would have known well – 'The Dawning Of The Day', a song popular in a version by John McCormack and the melody, thought to have been written by Thomas Conellan in the seventeenth century, has at least four names: 'The Dawning Of The Day', 'The Dawning Of The Day March', 'Fáinne Geal An Lae', and now 'Raglan Road'. It is, as Moloney announced most nights from the stage, 'The Dawning Of The Day' which was the source for this setting of 'Raglan Road'. It was first put to this air by Luke Kelly of the Dubliners, after an encounter with Patrick Kavanagh in The Bailey, a Dublin pub frequented by them both. Kelly, a formidable-looking fellow himself, nonetheless confessed to being terrified of him:

> 'On the one occasion I dared actually to speak to the man, because as Ben [Dublin writer and journalist Benedict Kiely, who had spoken earlier on the subject of Kavanagh's poem] said earlier on, he was a rough sort of man . . . we were in a pub . . . it was The Bailey . . . and he was singing in his own peculiar manner, as was I, and he said "I've got a song for you!" And he said, "You should sing 'Raglan Road'" . . . and I'm very proud that I got the impromata as it were from the man.'[32]

Kelly's version is a dramatic one, with his banjo scrambling and buzzing beneath the impassioned vocal, making the contrast between the beauty of the melody and the torturous emotion of the lyric clear. Benedict Kiely described Kavanagh as 'a rough sort of man but a genius and touched by God', and told of how Kavanagh brought him a rough, pencil manuscript of 'Raglan Road' and asked, 'Could we sing this to "The Dawning Of The Day"?'[33] So Kavanagh clearly had the notion of this being a song-poem from the beginning. This ancient form is something Morrison was interested in around this time, expressing at Coleraine a fondness for Blake's Songs, over Yeats 'more intellectual' excursions into similar territory:

> Bob Welch: Who have you been reading?

> VM: Nature poetry like Wordsworth, some of Blake's stuff, Songs of Innocence and Experience, maybe a tiny bit of Yeats stuff but not so much because he was writing more intellectually but there's a certain tie-in there, so some of his stuff . . . but I'd say mainly Blake, some of his song-poems I connected with.'[34]

Morrison's interpretation is almost completely faithful to the air and to the lyric, embroidering only with the characteristic, purist-bothering technique of sonorous repetition. Yet here Morrison's repetitions assist rather than impede the flow of the lyric and stress the sense, drawing especial attention to crucial moments, such as in the case of the lines 'my reason must allow' and 'away from me', where 'reason' and 'away' are repeated several times. Morrison was perhaps especially drawn to this piece by its evocation of Grafton Street in Dublin as the dividing line between the places of darkness and light, between the angel and the clay; that is, between the body and spirit. Interviewed by Bob Geldof on *The South Bank Show*, Morrison noted that 'Raglan Road and Grafton Street are just ordinary streets, yet you go there and there's this feeling about the places, of lives lived'.[35] The flaws in the relationship between body and mind, and the desire to unify sense and experience – superbly conveyed both in words by Kavanagh and sound by Morrison and the Chieftains – are evocative of both state of mind and spirit of place. They spring from a common source in pure word, pure sound and the explosions of the sung word between them, along the knife-edge between the bright and the shady path.

The album swoons from this dreamscape to a full transfiguration of the external world through the perceptions of the inner mind and emotions in the side's closer, 'And She Moved Through The Fair'. This song is a traditional melody, the original composer of which is unknown; the lyrics sung by Morrison were written for the most part by Padraic Colum, a poet who, like Yeats would sometimes write lyrics for folk melodies. The song was 'collected' by Colum and first published in 1909.[36] Culturally, the melody is a shared one, turning up in Scots Gaelic as well as Irish contexts, but usually accompanying a lyric mysterious and dark. The arrangement by Moloney and Morrison confines it to three verses, and the references in some versions to the lover possibly being dead – that is, making a ghost of her and a ghost story of the song – are excised. A lengthy introductory instrumental section of fiddle, tiompan and abstracted rhythms sets the tone of exquisite melancholia, unnerved but without tension; there is a grace to the movement of the melody, like the 'swan in the evening' cited in the lyric. This is deep Irish trad. Morrison's vocal comes in at 1.31, a third of the way into the song, and there are no breaks between the cyclic verses.

At first, the lover speaks to him, in the second verse she steps away from him, then in the third comes to him again with the promise of their imminent wedding, and all that that will entail for their being together. In this version it is a song of love, desire and counselled patience, and it speaks of an age of fastidiousness and enforced restraint within relationships – desire is intensified by the rules placed upon its expression. Morrison's vocal, both keening and intimate, emphasises the heat of desire in the mind. Really listen to the second verse, for example, and how he sings 'I watched her, move here and move there' from 2.20–27. Count John McCormack is there. The visitation in the third verse may well be in a dream and is an echo of the version in which the lover seems to speak from beyond the grave. So the heat of life and the coldness of the grave co-exist in this deep, dark, river of a song, which functions as both celebration and lament. This is possibly the Chieftains' best performance on the record, and coaxes some incandescent moments from their guest singer, both sustaining and developing upon tradition. Derek Bell told John Glatt:

> 'No purist is going to sing things like "And She Moved Through The Fair" repeating "our wedding day" three times. That's an element of soul music. The repetition and jazz-like style of the words for the sake of emphasis. That belongs to soul. It has nothing to do with our tradition at all.'[37]

Morrison's vocal drifts away from the song via repeating the phrase 'not be long' ten times (3.59–4.16), and then finally out of sight via an almost silent keening drone to the close at 4.45 and Bell's point is both made and built upon thereby: forging links between the two 'types' (soul and folk), this is both tradition and innovation in a single moment. In the old-fashioned sense of a closer to a side of an album, it could hardly be bettered.

In 1989, the year after *Irish Heartbeat* was issued, Maurice Leyden wrote that:

> It may come as a surprise to some people to discover that 'I'll Tell Me Ma' is not a local song peculiar just to Belfast, but a version of a song which also exists in Britain and America. It illustrates the facts that children's street games as we know them are part of a universal folklore and of a self-perpetuating oral tradition that has survived to this day without adult intrusion . . . Many of these street games have disappeared . . . from an early age their [children's] leisure time is programmed by the whim and hype of the media. The era of streets thronged with children entertaining themselves singing and playing their age-old street games has long since passed.[38]

This estimation, both bracingly unsentimental and quietly rueful, is true enough. Yet every child's network of streets, their locality, is effectively their world: think of how John Montague asked Morrison, 'So, what would be Van Morrison's East Belfast?' in reply to which Morrison thought carefully and reeled off the boundaries and inclusions of that imagined territory.[39] So each version of a song like 'I'll Tell Me Ma' – as in all folk tradition – will be specific to the locale, while incorporating variations, even within close-knit communities. Leyden's point is that the song does not belong exclusively to Belfast, not that its role in numberless childhoods there was an illusion. This tune, in its Belfast version, is also sometimes known as 'The Belle of Belfast City', and, as the joyful thud of its skittering cycles of its rhythm suggest, it is best known and remembered as a child's skipping song, adapted to the place in which the children live.

The song is universal, and an evocation of childhood free of the shadow of reflection from the perspective of experience. In this it is a real 'Song Of Innocence', from and of the state of mind that Morrison has called 'the sense of wonder', the unconscious living in the now, that seems to fall from us as we make the transition from childhood to adulthood, or from innocence to experience. It is a rousing and near-riotous performance, the very definition of an 'open' song, impossible not to move or sing along to. Morrison is throughout accompanied vocally by Kevin Conneff, with the latter taking the lead right at the close for some jolly street-scat. It's a fabulous recording, straight as a die, with one curious quirk: the brace of brief snatches of the Northern Irish Protestant marching band tune 'The Sash My Father Wore', right at the song's centre (1.29–33) and at its fade (2.12–27). Why did Morrison and Moloney decide to include this? Despite its adaptability, 'I'll Tell Me Ma' is almost certainly a Belfast song first, and furthermore a children's song – thus, one might hope, free from the burdens of songs which embodied the divisions of communities of Northern Ireland. 'The Sash' is evidence of how those differences are represented culturally, with this and songs like it being a key part of the repertoire of marching bands during the summer season, particularly the marches of 12th July, the anniversary of the Battle of the Boyne, which 'The Sash' celebrates by name. The song commemorates the victory by the Protestant forces of William II ('William of Orange') in 1690 over James II's Catholic invasion, and has served as a kind of rallying tune, a riposte to the Catholic equivalent, 'The Wearing Of The Green'. As Gerald Dawe wrote:

> Band music provided a cultural backdrop to life in Northern Ireland. Its message was double edged: on the one hand it was simply music to be played for its own sake and heartily enjoyed. On the other hand, it was 'protestant' music insofar as it maintained, on particular public and state occasions, cultural distinctions between that community and their fellow Catholic northerners. It was a music played on the streets and in the parks; broadcast on the radio and featured in church. Indeed as Gary Hastings pointed out the role of the church is central in maintaining public interest in ceremonial music. For in one protestant church or church hall after another religion and entertainment met.[40]

So here is a song with lots of what they call 'baggage', a real song of Experience; linking it to a children's skipping game, that song of Innocence, is an interesting move. Both are Northern Irish songs, and this binds them together more strongly, perhaps, than what seems to separate them. Furthermore, it can be read as an attempt, by incorporation into a children's singing game, to free 'The Sash' from its associations, to say 'it's just a tune', and that the meanings it has acquired are nothing to do with the music and everything to do with ossifying tradition. Here they break with such tradition and reimagine the melody as being as positive a part of the Northern sensibility as 'I'll Tell Me Ma' itself. It's a wiping clean of the slate and a reclamation of folk culture, and a bold non-sectarian gesture: a Southern Irish group playing with a Protestant Northern artist, playing a Belfast song, matched with an anthem of militant Protestantism. I am reminded of the Aboriginal proverb: if you want to change your enemy to your friend, sing his song. Music can and should go beyond these barriers.

'Carrickfergus' is another Northern Irish tune, of course, for the town of that name stands on the north shore of Belfast Lough. Now part of County Antrim, the town is actually older than Belfast and the Lough was known as Carrickfergus Bay as late as the seventeenth century. Most notable is the town's Castle and its open waterfront, which has been a blessing and a curse to the town. The sense of the wide expanse of water before one is clear in the song – it's very salty. The Battle of Carrickfergus was fought in 1597 between the Elizabethan English and the Scots clan of MacDonnell. It ended in victory for the Scots, and a strong Ulster-Scots tradition persists in the region to this day. Louis MacNeice spent several childhood years in the town and remembered it as magical: 'I didn't realise, being only two or three, that the water didn't end and that you could sail forever, that the lough never ended.' He also recalled that it was 'the first time I'd ever seen a lot of apple trees in blossom, and it made a tremendous impression upon me . . . a lot of these things I've woven into poems here and there.'[41] This illustrates the powerful pull these landscapes have over the creative imagination, whether we are considering Morrison, MacNeice or the anonymous poet of the song. The exact authorship of the song is disputed, but it is generally thought to be rooted in an Irish ballad called 'The Young Sick Lover', published around 1830 – an extant manuscript is held at Cambridge University Library, published by Haly's in Cork in that year. It had an unexpected renaissance in relatively recent times, in that the actor Peter O'Toole knew the song and taught it to Dominic Behan, who recorded it as 'The Kerry Boatman' on his 1963 album *The Irish Rover*.[42]

The song's contemporary currency can be traced to that unlikely provenance, and since then it has become a standard among aspirational singers of Irish balladry everywhere, pulling together the likes of Behan, Bryan Ferry and

Charlotte Church into an unlikely alliance, and that's to leave aside the countless versions on the folk circuit. The point is, the song's unwillingness to stay in one place, be that geographically or in terms of title or genre, makes it a very Irish song: not a 'Northern' or a 'Southern' one, but an *Irish* one. Had it continued to be sung only as 'The Kerry Boatman' would it have been a 'Southern song'? This was perhaps part of Behan's ambition in dubbing it so, but the song escapes such categorisation. Not only within the parameters of Irish culture but in how it resonates far beyond that context, with its echo of Hero and Leander and archetypes of exile and longing for home, partly embodied in place names, partly in the memory of beauty and love: 'I wish I had you in Carrickfergus'.

Morrison's version of the song opens with a drift of harp from Derek Bell; instrumentally it is one of the sparser cuts on the album, fleshed out by Bell's piano and a gorgeous acoustic double bass part from Ciarán Brennan, who was on loan from Clannad. The technique of slow build is again used to great effect here, with the Chieftains joining one by one until, almost without the listener noticing, the full band is playing, yet with such restraint that the gentle sadness of the melody is never compromised by overstatement. The vocal is shot through with longing, sadness and the sense of being both lost and found at one and the same time; a life of rootlessness, travelling and adventure is shown to be equally one of disconnection, exhaustion and of borderline despair. All his friends and relations are gone, yet he is doomed still to wander, in a stateless purgatory. Morrison conveys this superbly well as he sings these lines from 1.57–2.39: 'But I spend my days in endless roaming, soft is the grass and my bed is free / O, to be home now in Carrickfergus, on the long road down to the salty sea'. Listen to how Morrison sings these lines and feel what MacNeice called 'the rather dull little harbour' of Carrickfergus become transformed into an image of journey's end, paradise and a safe haven. This is a place wherein the curse of being 'a handsome rover, from town to town', made bearable only by the dulling power of drink ('I'm drunk today, and I'm rarely sober'), might be lifted and in which a weary man might 'lay me down'. Morrison's voice, as befitting a song of such a shatteringly personal nature, is solo throughout and, on a record full of choruses, close unison and harmony singing, this emphasises the solitary condition of the song's soul. The weariness of the roving man is channelled into the last note on 'down' from 4.09–18, where, finally, the vocal note and the song's bass home note conjoin, giving some sense of release and relief, at a journey's end.[43]

Refreshing the mood, Morrison's other original on the album, 'Celtic Ray', is a remake of *Beautiful Vision*'s 1982 original. Derek Bell was particularly attuned to the idea of the 'ray', which is drawn from theosophy in general and in Morrison's case from reading Alice Bailey in particular – in John Glatt's book

Bell spoke of how each day of the week has a 'ray' of different colour, and how he would wear a tie of the appropriate colour each day.

> 'It's the red ray today,' explains Bell . . . pointing to his bright red tie. 'It was violet yesterday and it'll be yellow tomorrow. Every day of the week has got a different planet and therefore a different colour and the eighth ray is the diamond Christ ray which is in force every day or we'd be gone.'[44]

Within the exploration of such esoteric and its connections to daily life, the mood of *Beautiful Vision* seems not unconnected to Bell's seeing the hand of the marvellous in the everyday, and that's exactly what 'Celtic Ray' is about, so it is little wonder it was chosen for this album. The song survives the translation to the traditional idiom, and Morrison's drumming, revealing how the melody sits with perhaps unexpected ease therein. So the arrangement draws the song back to its own tradition – that of the Irish song, realising the wish of the lyric, 'I wanna go home', a phrase borrowed from a Lonnie Donegan title, tying traditions closely together: so many of the songs of the trad. Irish repertoire are about wandering, 'roving' and exile. As we have seen 'Carrickfergus' is a song of weariness with living that way, almost unto death, but 'Celtic Ray' is the song of a man who has come through or at least discovered a way that helps him imagine how he might, after all, come 'home'.

As throughout, the recognisable instrumentation of the group is counterpointed by the unexpected glistening presence of Derek Bell's harpsichord – this classical element adds an 'ancient' quality to the sound, almost a kind of stately wisdom. 'What I like about the Chieftains is their integrated style . . . they're like an old music group who play baroque music. Well they play with the same dedication', said James Galway[45] and this dedication is part of the cultural overlap with Morrison's own attitude to his own work. This is simply what he does; it's his job, just as some men make furniture, or build houses, or cure the sick. So Morrison's original stands well among the much older songs, not only in its arrangement but also in its root and ambition, and its sensitivity to the details of the locality it seeks to explore, with the names ('McManus' etc.) being offered as evidence of the magical and the marvellous at work just below the surface. In its brisk and robustly staccato rearranged bridge (2.06–16, for example), Morrison exchanges the 'England' of the 1982 version for the 'Brittany' he had been singing in concert since 1983; a scholarly rather than a nose-thumbing correction which shows he's done some research, as the Breton community are closer to the Celtic than the cultural melting pot of England. Indeed the Chieftains have frequently worked with Breton and Galician musicians, with both being as distinctive (and the subject of just as intense scrutiny) as the Irish.[46]

Morrison's vocal is much changed too; far freer and sure of itself than the calm narrative of the *Beautiful Vision* original, it employs a dizzying array of the vocal tricks, tics, repetitions and rhetorical-emotional techniques he had worked up around this material in the intervening six years. For example, at in the second verse (0.50–1.16), he follows each line with a flat droning note, and as the take proceeds we hear him falling deeper into this mood of expressing the feeling, and, we might somewhat fancifully note, the ray itself through a series of superb vocalisations. The third verse and the lead-in to the instrumental break makes the lines 'On a cold November day / You'll be on the Celtic ray / Are you ready?' a polysyllabic tumble into bliss, buoyed up, after Morrison's cue of 'alright', by the band. Revelling in the dynamic potential of this specifically Irish sound, the second, closing half of the tune sees Morrison bring the vocal back down and finish on a keening scat (2.47–3.12) which echoes his closing vocal on the *Beautiful Vision* version, before calling for 'Billy!' (3.09) as the band picks up the melodic centre of the tune to take it to the close, in a substantial change in arrangement from the long fade of the 1982 recording. Did he mean 'Paddy!' as he used to mean 'Jack!' (for Mr Schroer), or is it some figure stepping forward from the past to greet him? The name, from a Belfast man, may well be simply a sly, local, self-referential joke like the 'Listen Jimmy!' he uses earlier in the song, a figure of speech in the local tongue referring to 'everyman'. This version doesn't have the metaphysical mists or the early morning fog of the *Beautiful Vision* version but has a far more grounded and earthy feel to it, setting it more firmly in the backstreets it describes.

Those backstreets echo again, in 'My Lagan Love'. This is a pure Belfast song, written by Joseph Campbell, a troubled lyric poet much admired by Morrison. The melody, collected in County Donegal by Herbert Hughes and matched to the lyric by Campbell, is a traditional one, also known as 'The Belfast Maid'. The song was first published in *Songs of Uladh*, traditional songs collected by Hughes and published in Belfast by William Mullan & Son and in Dublin by M. H. Gill in 1904, while the Yeats-inspired Celtic Revival was still in full swing. Campbell was born on the Castlereagh Road in East Belfast and as a child he, like Morrison, took delight in the nature of his city, and often took long walks as a child on the banks of the Lagan, the river that rises in the countryside south west of the city then winds through Belfast and into the sea. The 'Lagan streams' that 'sing lullabies' suggest the narrower, quicker flows of the river in the upper reaches of its course as opposed to the latter stages; indeed this is a song that reflects the rhythms of the countryside rather than those of the city. We also note that both Connswater and the section of it known as Beechie River (both referenced elsewhere in original Morrison compositions) eventually flow into the Lagan and Belfast Harbour.[47]

The song was a favourite with John McCormack (who recorded it first in 1922 and several times subsequently) and had also been recorded by Lonnie Donegan in 1959, so it's quite possible Morrison was familiar with these versions as well as hearing it as a folk song within the musical community of Belfast in the 50s. It was initially something of a middle-class parlour song, but Morrison and the Chieftains make something quite different of it, taking it into deeper, wilder resonance and meaning. The song in its original form has been published with five verses; the version here is the most frequently sung, and only comprises two. Like 'And She Moved Through The Fair', this is deep into Irish 'soul music', and the dynamics of the recording show the ensemble's understanding of this. It has the quality of silence, a dichotomy of which Morrison has often pursued. A sense of poised stillness infuses this recording, from Moloney's opening, chilling tin whistle and Bell's harpsichord, which occupy the first 40 seconds until joined by a slow, deep fiddle. Morrison's vocal enters at 1.19, as ever not quite exactly when you expect him to. Under his voice, a keyboard drone provides the lulling hum which enables him to explore the vocal melody. Moloney's tin whistle follows the voice, tracking it but emphasising too the solitariness, as opposed to the choral singing of, say 'Irish Heartbeat'. This requires Morrison to adhere to the melody more closely than he does on, say, the preceding 'Celtic Ray', but the performance is still stunning and full of innovation. The deep-dug notes of 'And often when' (2.47–52) and the emphasised 'n' sounds in 'hor*n*' (2.57) and 'underto*ne*' (3.56) suggest real points of connection between the verbal (lyrical) and emotional (musical) sense of the song. He also has to grapple with the archaic language favoured by Campbell, such as 'lenashee' (a mythical, impish sprite) and 'shieling lorn', a low form of summer house or peasant cottage.[48]

From the song's closing lyric, 'The song of heart's desire' (first heard at 3.58), the remaining 90 seconds or so are extemporisations around the repetition of the phrase, where the unity of voice and tin whistle fades away and, like the close of 'And She Moved Through The Fair', we are reminded of the breakdown of an *Astral Weeks* kind, recalling both the close of 'Cyprus Avenue' and, very briefly, the 'lost' conclusion of 'Slim Slow Slider', which shears away from us on that album. The beautiful chaos we glimpse there is heard again here, I'd say, at 4.53–5.02. The vocal heats up, cools down, stays still, takes unexpected leaps. Derek Bell commented that 'What Van does with "My Lagan Love" is even more grotesque. He virtually makes a Hindu chant out of it in the last note. And the folkies don't like it',[49] and the section from 4.21–5.17 illustrates this perfectly. It is a single utterance of the phrase 'The song of heart's desire' but here it becomes a polysyllabic tumble of dizzying force, tipping over, as Bell rightly notes, into a completely different kind of singing and expression altogether: no wonder he felt that the 'folkies' wouldn't like it. The last minute of the vocal and song is a wordless, mantric keening drone of stunning emotional power. Here again the Irish tradition is stretched and extended into the broader scope Kevin Conneff spoke of, and something new emerges, building upon, while maintaining, the tradition. The vocal overall is one of Morrison's best, reminding me of the high intensity of 'Linden Arden Stole The Highlights', being pushed on by the band and the song to deliver a vocal of real drama, and perhaps the closest thing to an operatic performance he has ever given, establishing the missing link between *Veedon Fleece* and John McCormack.[50]

This mood is roused by the album's final song, 'Marie's Wedding'. This, by comparison with some of the other songs on the record, is a relatively modern and uncomplicated tune; using a traditional Scottish folk tune, it was originally a song composed by Johnny Bannerman for his friend Mary McNiven (Scots Gaelic for 'Mary' being 'Mairi') in 1935, some years in advance of her real wedding, which took place in 1941. It was first sung in Scots Gaelic and then translated by Hugh S. Robertson into the lyric heard on *Irish Heartbeat* the following year, as the song's popularity grew. Mairi is still alive, telling Scotland's *Daily Record* on the occasion of her ninetieth birthday that:

> 'I can't believe it became so popular. But when it was first played to me I found it very catchy – and I still do . . . I still have a clear recollection of that day. Johnny just said the song was for me.'[51]

This is a rousing and uncomplicated way to end the record, recalling the atmospheres of 'I'll Tell Me Ma' with its sense of communal participation and celebration. This is music, both in intention and in effect, which is made for dancing. That is unusual in Morrison's catalogue, and it is very welcome for that reason if no other. The Scottish root of the tune can be detected immediately in the bass pulses under the introductory eight bars, an unmistakably Scottish convention. As the *Daily Record* said, 'millions of people, not only Scots' have danced and sung to this, and it is a great example of how a genuinely popular tune could enter the collective consciousness and become lodged as a key part of folk identity. Vocally Morrison plays this straight, simply delivering the song so that the listener might feel it: the massed whirligig bluster of the final section, a repetition of the chorus from 2.18, is sheer delight, with Morrison joined by 'the company', including Mary Black, June Boyce and Maura O'Connell, as well as the unmistakable, cheerful tones of the Chieftains themselves. It serves as a reminder of the unifying power of song, and of what this music is really for.

The album's success, both in terms of commercial impact and artistic estimation (it was voted by the then all-influential *New Musical Express* as the best album of 1988), whetted the appetite for more. However, within a year Morrison was out of his Phonogram deal and on to other projects, so we have only a handful of occasional pieces post-*Irish Heartbeat* from this pairing. The band appeared on *Hymns To The Silence*, and he guested on a brace of their later albums. There were also two stand-alone cuts, firstly 'High Spirits', the only true original collaboration between Morrison and the Chieftains which turned up as the final cut on *The Philosopher's Stone*. This track is a likeable vocal-trad. hybrid which has a pleasing two-speed structure and a sense of being real modern Irish traditional music. Later came a very grandly arranged version of 'Shenandoah', a key American traditional song that is actually based upon a Scots-Irish melody. This is a song, or at least a melody, that crossed the ocean in order to become wholly evocative of another land, of a new world. It was recorded for Thomas Lennon's US television series about Irish emigration, *The Long Journey Home*.[52]

So we wonder, where is the 'home' that the title of Lennon's film talks about? Much folk music is concerned with establishing links between the present circumstance, perhaps one of peril or uncertainty, and the securities of the days gone by and this can yield a physical effect. It unfolds happiness, and brings comfort, a kind of inner radiance that memory yields from the mental to the physical. 'Shenandoah' does that in the grandeur of its melody and its ability, by its very nature, to hold together the old life and the new – the Irish melody that evokes the American landscape and heartland: the Old World reborn in the New. So again, we ask, where is this 'home'? It's a matter of belonging, and folk music deals with this in a way that, say, jazz perhaps does less directly – the confluence of tradition and its future via a vigorous growing point, which may be a note, a song, a line, a sound. All of this makes one wish that Morrison and the Chieftains had found more time to collaborate on this kind of innovation with tradition, yet these recordings are still not quite the deepest green in Morrison's catalogue. That honour lies with an oddity.

CUCHULAINN (1990)

This curio in Morrison's catalogue was recorded as a fundraiser by and for Moles Club in Bath, a small, funky venue, still going strong.[53] Morrison had just begun living and working in the environs of Bath at the time, working at the Wool Hall Studios owned by local heroes Tears for Fears, who built the studio off the back of their massive commercial success with a string of hit singles and the albums *The Hurting* and *Songs From The Big Chair*. Morrison would later come to own the studio; *Cuchulainn* was recorded, however, in less technologically mediated circumstances, 'as live' in Moles Club itself. What drew Morrison to this esoteric material? The notes on the insert of the cassette offer some context:

> The Cuchulainn saga is a collection of poems from ancient Ireland, written out by monastic scribes in the Middle Ages, but dating from a much earlier pre-Christian Celtic culture. The central theme is the life and death of the hero, and the dispute over the sacred land of Ireland between the royal houses of Ulster and Connaught.[54]

Furthermore, the story's entry into the twentieth century is due primarily to the labours of Lady Augusta Gregory, who published a translation from the ancient Gaelic into English entitled *Cuchulain of Muirthemne*, and her protégé W. B. Yeats, who scattered references to Cuchulainn throughout his works. Yeats completed a series of one-act plays, commonly grouped together under the term 'The Cuchulain Plays' (NB Yeats always spelled the name with a single 'n').[55] So if Morrison was interested in exploring what it meant to be 'an Irish writer', connected up to traditions of storytelling of a kind where the narratives were 'owned' by everybody, his own folk tales are a good place to take a look. The paradox here is that the distributive muscle of the popular music industry facilitates a likeness to the transmission methods of pre-industrial folk cultures: everyone 'knows' 'Gloria' for example. In the way these stories were changed, spun and modified with every telling, we can also see links between Morrison's ideal state for the song – never play it the same way twice – and the much older traditions of storytelling, with it each time being adapted, updated, modified to meet the present moment and its circumstance. In this way this kind of narrative would seem doubly appealing, to the aesthete and to the citizen of these communities, imagined or otherwise. The folk poem also offers a kind of 'nostalgia' as something beyond the romantic shadow of the past colouring the present moment: instead it makes the past live again.

The recording lasts 42 minutes, and is both read and performed by Morrison and Fay Howard. The source of the text used is unnamed, and their animated reading is accompanied by percussion – a drum, some rattles and shakers. Morrison's reading is strongly performative and you can hear him trying this method out as another way of using the voice as means of expressing and exploring communication, of changing the points of contact, delivery and reception. While Fay Howard, with a crystalline voice and diction, reads directly, Morrison's delivery leans on the Northern Irish pronunciation which is his to use, and thereby inhabits the territory of the narrative far more heatedly. His delivery of the line 'Would ye make an *eejit* of me?' is pure East Belfast, and reminds us of the continuities between the ancient and the modern and furthermore that these tales are built to be read in this voice. After all, as part of an oral rather than a written culture, works such as this were originally meant to be *heard*, and *performed*. Morrison's vocal delivery here acknowledges this continuity. *Cuchulainn* came within months of his recording 'Coney Island'

and 'Orangefield', and around the time of *A Coney Island of the Mind*, a TV programme that investigated the nature of the roots of Irishness as expressed via poetry and ideas flowing from that medium. In *A Coney Island of the Mind* Morrison cites the 'Glens poets' of Country Antrim as an influence on 'I'm Tired Joey Boy', which he read as a poem to the assembled 'proper' poets. So Morrison's dramatic vocal performances on *Cuchulainn* and 'Coney island' are as much an experiment in vocal technique as, say, the falsetto of 'Twilight Zone' or the guttural keening of the coda to 'And She Moved Through The Fair'. Thus *Cuchulainn* finds Morrison in a period of heightened sensibilities with regard to the fluctuating, yet ancient and rooted, nature of Irish identity, and also with a burgeoning interest in finding other routes, other outlets for expression beyond the album-tour-album cycle demanded by the music industry as it then stood.

In the key moment of *A Coney Island of the Mind*, Morrison revealed that

> 'I found out that the tradition I belonged to was actually my own tradition. It was like being hit over the head with a baseball bat. You find out that what you've been searching for you already are.'[56]

Thus, after this shock of discovery, Morrison's interests take an esoteric turn; he is more relaxed about his performances, more willing to scrutinise and draw upon his roots, yet always changing the material in the matter of performance. Compare his performances of 'My Lagan Love' with that of 'traditional' Irish singers for an illustration of this. So, the saga of Cuchulainn fell within this deepened interest in the source and core cultural building blocks of Irish identity – and that is, as he had noted, his own.

> 'I started writing songs when I was very young. I didn't have a clue what I was doing. Trying to find a link with my contemporaries . . . I wanted to find out where I stood and what tradition I came from. Why I was writing this kind of poetry and my contemporaries weren't.'[57]

It is this restless curiosity and desire to find out quite why things were the way they were that drove his own response to ideas of identity and towards bold and adventurous projects such as *Cuchulainn* and *A Coney Island of the Mind*, and allowed both to be absorbed by and expressed through his subsequent work. Thus his 'Irishness' is connected to the nature of his creativity and the work's restless exploration of the links between tradition and innovation, as powerfully as it is connected to the realisation, both subconscious and consciously discovered, that the tradition to which he belonged was his own: he is indeed an

Irish writer. Flowing from this, the next section examines how such influences impact upon his wider work, and how the root influences of music and writing operate in his work.

Chapter Three

Get the Words on the Page: Van Morrison as Writer

This part of the book seeks to examine Van Morrison as a writer, doing so via case studies of a trio of his most famous songs (what he calls 'the Hits') and an assessment of Morrison as a writer of love songs. Musical and vocal-performative issues arise throughout of course, but the main focus of this section is the writing itself.

THE HITS

Van Morrison speculated about the status of his catalogue in 2007, suggesting that 'I'm known for, what, seven songs probably?'[1] We might fancy speculating which tunes he means here, but for our purposes we shall scrutinise three which may or may not be on his list, 'Brown Eyed Girl', 'Jackie Wilson Said' and, to begin at the beginning, 'Gloria'.

'Gloria' (1965)

This song was very rapidly assimilated as a standard at the entry level of pop – to the extent that it seemed to acquire a kind of folk song quality, the direct, tough simplicity of its three-chord trick being among the easiest sequences to manage as a beginner on the guitar. It also has the power of the seemingly endless riff – Paul McCartney once described the riff of Ray Charles's 'What'd I Say' as 'the riff of the universe . . . that just keeps going forever',[2] and that seems apposite to 'Gloria' too. This primal, unscripted feel somehow allowed the song to 'belong' to everybody. Hence the idea of a definitive version of the song became problematic; its very ubiquity made the song useful in a wide number of ways, be they those of celebration, unification or subversion. Its appeal, however, is not predicated on appealing melodicism, but in the power of its repetitious three-chord turnarounds. It is a tight, driving, relentless and serious-minded little knot of sound, which has acquired a force well beyond its humble beginnings as a B-side of Them's cover of Big Joe Williams's 'Baby Please Don't Go' and also beyond its garage-band primality; indeed the song has become part of the DNA of post-war popular song itself. Just to illustrate, on 23–24 July 1999, there was a 'Gloriathon' in Austin, Texas, organised by Michael Hall of the alt. country band the Woodpeckers, where the song was played continually for 24 hours by the likes of Joe Ely, Joe 'King' Carrasco and many more. Improbably, Morrison was involved, and contributed by being called up while onstage during a UK live show in Chester (on the evening of the 24th) via mobile phone and, without recourse to pejorative metaphor, phoned in a performance of the song to the event at Austin's 'Liberty Lunch' club.[3]

This delightfully unlikely tale illustrates the centrality of the song to post-Presley rock and roll's sense of itself. The song is totemistic and learning the chord sequence of 'Gloria' is a kind of rite of passage in both its musical sense and in its adolescent theme of desire coming to the boil – a more recent equivalent being the first record by another Northern Irish act, the Undertones' 'Teenage Kicks'. Both are raw, lusty, and fulminating with the energy of frustrated desire; both seem easy to play, but are very difficult to get right. As with 'Mannish Boy', 'Louie, Louie' and 'Wild Thing', this is simplicity of a near-primal kind, but for each the *feel* – that which cannot be transcribed – is everything.

It took some time before I realized that 'Gloria' was actually written by Morrison – I couldn't connect the author of *Into The Music* and *Astral Weeks* with the blazing kid on 'Gloria'. Lester Bangs wrote of this brutal youth and his tune in the sleeve notes for a Them compilation issued by Decca to cash in on Morrison's early-70s success, in a piece called 'Spawn of the Dublin Pubs':

> Opening with the showstopper of them all, "Gloria". This, folks, is the Rock of Ages, sure as "Long Tall Sally" or "Sweet Little Sixteen" or "Let's Spend the Night Together" or maybe even "Are You Ready". It's a demonstrative self contained definition of rock 'n' roll that will have you moving or shrivel you into a Librium puddle of MOR drool. It'll be heard as long as rock 'n' roll endures, and never sound less timely than it did the day they cut it. A paraplegic could dance to it – it has the magic that'll set you free like few songs by the Spoonful or anybody else. Cruising for burgers to it in 1965 was more cosmic than any acid trip, and after even one hearing no one could ever forget those creaming lyrics and how seethingly Van spat them out: "She comes around here/Just about midnight/She makes me feel so good, Lord/Ohh, I wanna

> say she make me feel alright/Cause she walkin' down my street/She knock upon my door/And then she comes to my room/Man, she make me FEEL ALRIGHT!!!!!"[4]

Though geographically off the mark (*Dublin* pubs?), Bangs's style is almost as evocative of era as the music itself. He is right, too, about the riff of 'Gloria' being part of the fundamental make-up of rock and roll, or the 'Rock of Ages' as he calls it. Paul Williams was moved to say that 'here is something so good, so pure, that if no other hint of it but this record existed, there would still be such a thing as rock and roll',[5] while Dave Marsh focused on the adolescent pulse of the song: '[it's] one of the few rock songs that's actually as raunchy as its reputation – unless you think she's going up to his room for a chat'.[6]

Listening to the song, recorded on 5 July 1964 at Decca's West Hampstead studios up in North West London, we are reminded that Them were far from simply being Van Morrison's backing band. This is the sound of a proper group, tight, whip-smart, driving the song forward together, and recorded in their basic form. Drums thud at variable volume, guitars loom in and out of the mix, the bass murmurs, but atop it all is the still-stunningly caustic voice of the 19-year-old Van Morrison. After a cantering opening, he comes in at 0.06, just ahead of the beat, immediately communicating urgency. The famous riff conceals two of its five pulses by pausing on the first chord for two beats, freeing the close oval of the other three to make their way back round to the beginning again – listen to the opening section, up to the vocal's arrival – this lends the tune a sense of steady, even irresistible forward movement while also apparently staying still. Thus we find embodied in the musical structure an image of the growing frustration and levels of feeling which explode out in the cry of the girl's name, which provides both chorus and title, G-L-O-R-I-A. This pressure builds up to the first break into the chorus at 0.48, cued up by a tight scuffle on the snare, which is then reinforced over the 'Gloria' itself by a resounding thump of the floor tom and snare until 1.03, at which point the verse returns. Not that the riff notices – true to McCartney's riff of the universe, it keeps churning away at the song's heart throughout, regardless of the niceties of structure or compositional subdivision. This is so even when the guitar solos (1.06–17, for example), the solo being six trips round the riff played as a lead line.

Morrison's talent for working with musical dynamics, by all accounts already in evidence at Them's Maritime Hotel residencies, is hinted at in the way the arrangement drops back to half-strummed guitar, trimmed quickstep drumming and ready-to-pounce organ in the song's penultimate section (1.18–2.00). The drumming by Ronnie Millings is itself a key part of the build of this mood; later drummers would pick up the humorous 'knock knock' he drops in after the reference to the door. This creates the paradox of lots of space available within a very tight structure; it's marvellous, and a kind of little miracle. The chorus is taken by the rest of the group, hollering 'Gloria!', Harrison's 'lead' in that vocal is as important to the heat of the moment as Morrison's, as the latter details how good it feels; how the very sound of her is 'so good'. The lyric out of the chorus fits snugly, if accidentally, with the pop parlance of the moment: 'Yeah, yeah, yeah, yeah, yeah!', albeit a bluesier Belfast 5 as opposed to Liverpool's 3.

The song's finale is absolutely cacophonous, even in the relatively polite and confining environment of the Decca studio – I always wonder how the Maritime versions must have thundered when I listen to this section. It is cued in after the 'down' section by Morrison's spelling out of the name at 2.00 and then the band go headlong for the finishing line, with a rude vigour undiminished by time, the drums clattering like massed hooves on flagstones, Morrison rasping out until the song closes at 2.34. Bangs was right: this is very close to the pulse beat of popular music itself.[7]

As one of the most covered songs of the post-war era – offering a canvas to punk, both direct (Eddie and the Hot Rods) and performance-theorised (Patti Smith) – it is somehow appropriate that Morrison has reclaimed the song by 'covering' it himself.[8] Victoria Clarke spoke to him about this version, featured on 1993's *Too Long In Exile*:

> VC: "Lonely Avenue" is a cover; "Good Morning Little Schoolgirl" is a cover; "Gloria" is a cover of your own song! Why on earth did you do that?
>
> VM: I thought it was appropriate, seeing as it's a blues album.
>
> VC: But you couldn't top the original.
>
> VM: It's got John Lee Hooker on it. It's different. Blues is improvisation, it's like jazz, so it's always going to be different.[9]

This version seems to be relatively unloved, although commercially it proved to be one of his biggest hits. To echo Victoria Clarke's question, why would he re-record the song? In the first instance, as a Van Morrison recording, it existed only as a closer on *It's Too Late To Stop Now* and the Them recording was nearly 30 years old by 1993. By 1973, the song was already locked into its classic, anthemic status – check the celebratory holler of the title by the audience as well as the band on the live recording. Suddenly here was the primal rock standard rubbing shoulders with string sections, Sam Cooke and 'Madame George'; it was *his song*, and he was taking it back, thank you. Furthermore, Morrison was at that point moving away from r'n'b and this stage of his musical development. So to return to a song nearing its thirtieth birthday does a number of things: it attests to the durability of the song, its continued appeal, and is an acknowledgement of the song's universal resonance. Within the album as a whole we can discern an effort to reclaim the spirit (dare I say soul) of the blues which had undergone its own journey in his work, far from source. So in a sense 'Gloria' is delivered from exile, illustrating the album's title.

The key element of course on the *Too Long In Exile* version is the presence of John Lee Hooker who opens the song: Morrison is not heard until 1.08, when the lyric and the snare and bass drums snap in, moving the tune up a pace. Indeed for a song renowned as a raging celebration of youthful energies, this version opens very tentatively, tiptoeing around Hooker's vocal, the unmistakably blues guitar picking out the riff, the rhythm ticking off on a rimshot. Despite Morrison's obvious delight at having Hooker there on the recording with him, the whole affair seems somewhat muted, and certainly does not blaze in the way the song's history might suggest it would. Occasionally the two great voices seem to be talking at cross purposes, certainly compared to the noirish moods of their collaboration on Hooker's 'comeback' album of 1991, *Mr. Lucky*, 'I Cover The Waterfront'. Notably the song is faster and louder than Hooker's model of the blues, and so the older man's presence confers and confirms status and survival on the song even as the take to some extent recasts it for a more worldly viewpoint. The song itself is remade as an older man's song in terms of its energies (listen to the controlled release of that famous riff at the track's opening), and its internal furniture is rearranged too. The original lyric is housed within a broader, looser and more improvisational structure, more self-consciously bluesy, partly to accommodate its guest performer, and partly because the song, like its author, has grown and changed in the intervening three decades. The running time of 5.19, double the original duration, is telling, and the version bears almost as little relation to the original as any other 'cover' you might hear. To some extent it exists in order for Morrison to reclaim the song as a blues, with the added bonus of the collaboration of one of his (and thereby the song's) original influences to confirm this. The UK single release gave Morrison a No. 28 hit in 1993, testament to the enduring appeal of the song reaching beyond his own fan base and the close connection between the song and a wider audience – after all, everyone knows 'Gloria'.[10]

Come the late 90s, Morrison acknowledged the song's status as a rock and roll chant by leavening the ritual with some humour. This came in the form of an 'elocution' lesson, usually delivered by Kate St. John. It was a self-deprecating novelty to keep it fresh, and was genuinely funny, especially given how well Morrison understands that the 'meaning' of a word is not necessarily located in its 'proper' pronunciation. The slurring and reforming of sounds can create new meanings for them, and the theatrical clarity of enunciation required of and cherished by the standardised lyric somehow belongs to another world, one rooted in theatrical narratives rather than the expression and articulation of less stable and more volatile emotion. The elocution lesson took the comedic possibilities of this disjunction to task, and detained the rock and roll vocabulary, making it stay behind for improving lessons. I asked Kate St. John about this curious role she was assigned:

> PM: How did the elocution lessons in 'Gloria' come about?
>
> KSJ: Just a funny idea of Van's who has always thought that I come from some kind of upper class background. Which I don't![11]

The exaggerated, Joyce Grenfell-style English school-ma'am, over-phoneticising the letters was a deft comic touch, just right for the effect the little point is looking to make, and in performance she swallowed it whole.[12] The journey of 'Gloria' from black-snake moan to rock and roll terrace chant to elocution lesson is a curious one, to say the least, but throughout that riff has been pulsing away, with the ineffable blend of brooding, pulsing desire and dark, sly humour that drives the song through the generations, going on, as McCartney said, forever.

How To Write and Sell a Song Hit: 'Brown Eyed Girl' (1967)

> 'Let's do "Brown Eyed Girl" and get it over with.'
>
> Van Morrison, onstage comment,
> Chester Racecourse show, 21 July 2001

> [Edna Gundersen]: Are there songs you no longer feel an affinity for, songs that no longer ring true or feel comfortable?
>
> [Van Morrison]: There are songs that were written in desperation or in a certain period when you were, like, starving and the ship was going down. Stuff like "Brown Eyed Girl." The reason I wrote it was to get out of handcuffs. It was to get out of being enslaved [by Bang Records]. How can a 51-year-old sing that? I can't relate to it. Why am I expected to, anyway, at 51? I wrote it when I was 20. I was never paid for "Brown Eyed Girl." [Bang] sold it to CBS, and they still aren't paying me record royalties. I don't do the song.[13]

The two quotes above imply a serious breakdown between artist and art. Alongside 'Gloria' this is probably Van Morrison's best-known song, and it is probably one with which he is more readily identified – but is this the same as its being his best loved? Maybe for the member of the audience who thinks of Van Morrison in the way we might think of Rod Stewart – that guy who did 'Sailing' and a few others – it is. In 2001, an official questionnaire was distributed at a series of Van Morrison shows, asking for a few titles the audience would like to hear him play. 'Brown Eyed Girl' came out top of the list, and by coincidence or not, has been a frequent presence in his set since. Let's first examine the song, and then think about its author's relationship with it.

There are two versions of the original recording made for Bang and Bert Berns, and it was issued as a single in May 1967 with Cissy Houston and the Sweet Inspirations on backing vocals.[14] It became a US Top 10 hit in the so-called 'Summer of Love', scooping over 750,000 sales that year. By contrast, and offering a taste of things to come, it did nothing in the UK; as a consequence, as in the case of the Zombies' 'Time Of The Season', it is less associated with that era in Britain. He told Ritchie Yorke:

> 'They put out publicity around that time to the fact that it was written specifically about somebody I knew, but it wasn't. Originally it was called "Brown Skinned Girl" when I wrote the song. I just thought "Brown Eyed Girl" sounded better or something. I guess it really wouldn't have made much difference but "Brown Skinned Girl" was the original title. After we'd recorded it I looked at the tape box and didn't even notice that I'd changed the title. That's how spaced out it was. I looked at the box where I'd lain it down with my guitar and it said "Brown Eyed Girl" on the tape box. It's just one of those things that happen.'[15]

We can find a thematic link with his Them tune, 'One Two Brown Eyes', though Morrison's claim that it was originally 'Brown Skinned Girl' supports his assertion that it was originally a calypso: 'That was just a mistake. It was a kind of Jamaican song. Calypso. It just slipped my mind. I changed the title.'[16] The pleasing live arrangement he employed during 2005–6 hinted at this idea of it being 'a kind of Jamaican song', lending a much warmer, more sensually rhythmic, near-Latinate lope to the tune.

His relationship with the song, as we have seen, has been somewhat troubled, although since the market research exercise of 2001 he seems to have reached some form of rapprochement with the song, making peace with the fact that people 'expect' to hear it as part of his live show. Morrison's attitude to his song was in some ways direct and pragmatic: he told Happy Traum that:

> 'I did "Brown-Eyed Girl" in 1967. One of the guys that produced some of the records for the group, Bert Berns, came over to London to meet the group. He produced one of his songs with the group, and it was a hit. He called me in Belfast from New York and said, how about getting together to do another record. I had a couple of offers, but I thought this was the best one, seeing as I wanted to come to America anyway, so I took him. The two things sort of coincided, so I came over and played him a few songs, and we made the record.'[17]

The story of 'Brown Eyed Girl' is at least in part the bridge between the seemingly wildly diverse tripartite phases of Morrison's mercurial career from 1965 to 1968, via the figure of Bert Berns. He was co-author of a great number of genre-defining pop hits in the early 60s, such as 'Twist And Shout', 'Hang On Sloopy', 'A Little Bit of Soap' and 'I Want Candy'. So he was a writer, and he replaced Lieber and Stoller at Atlantic in 1963 as staff producer, working with Solomon Burke, who covered Berns's 'Goodbye Baby, (Baby Goodbye)' as heard on *Blowin' Your Mind!*. He also produced the Drifters, Wilson Pickett and LaVern Baker. He was one of the few American producers who came to Swinging London and made some hit records with British artists, such as Lulu and, of course, Them, producing and writing 'Here Comes The Night' for the group. Billy Harrison thought he was a 'Helluva producer', adding 'The guy was magic' for his ability to motivate the young band and get the mood of the song going during the sessions for the song.[18] As Lester Bangs noted, his influence could always be spotted in a tune: 'the man never quite got the hot sauce out of his ears after his "Twist & Shout" conquered the world'[19] but he also noted that this led to Berns's own Spanish Harlem musical proclivities as evidenced in Van's later work. By the same token, Charlie Gillett notes in his seminal *Sound of the City* that he was 'able to bring out the best in the singers without imposing himself too demandingly onto the overall sound'.[20] This contrasts of course with Morrison's estimation of how the record sounds.

That Latin touch, musically, signifies *romance*. After all Morrison was the author of 'Spanish Rose', a flower blossoming straight out of 'Spanish Harlem' and which owes a clear debt to the hit model piloted by Jerry Lieber and Phil Spector's hit with Ben E. King in 1961, the latter's first post-Drifters hit. The model here of Spanish guitar, marimba and two-step Latin rhythm embedded itself in pop's vocabulary, especially within the world of the Brill Building, and the song factories liked it – this was Berns's world, and this was one of the reasons Morrison sat uncomfortably within it. Morrison told Jeremy Marre that while Berns 'sabotaged' much of what Morrison was trying to do on the Bang recordings, he liked 'Brown Eyed Girl', 'because he knew that one was a hit!'[21] So unquestioningly, Berns equated a song's worth with its commercial value in the marketplace. This was not unique to him of course – that is the gold standard of the industry. The inhabitants of the Brill Building didn't write the book on pop as industrial product (see also the KLF's ever-more-influential *Manual* of the late 80s[22]), they were all preceded by the likes of Abner Silver and Robert Bruce's 1945 book *How to Write and Sell a Song Hit*, followed up (with perfect music biz logic) with a variant on the winning theme, Bruce's 'solo' work *How to Write a Hit Song and Sell It*. We are reminded of Theodor Adorno's estimation of how pop hits are made in his 1941 essay 'On Popular Music':

> The whole structure of popular music is standardized, even where the attempt is made to circumvent standardization. Standardization extends from the most general features to the most specific ones. Best known is the rule that the chorus consists of thirty two bars and that the range is limited to one octave and one note. The general types of hits are also standardized: not only the dance types, the rigidity of whose pattern is understood, but also the "characters" such as mother songs, home songs, nonsense or "novelty" songs, pseudo-nursery rhymes, laments for a lost girl. Most important of all, the harmonic cornerstones of each hit—the beginning and the end of each part—must beat out the standard scheme. This scheme emphasizes the most primitive harmonic facts no matter what has harmonically intervened. Complications have no consequences. This inexorable device guarantees that regardless of what aberrations occur, the hit will lead back to the same familiar experience, and nothing fundamentally novel will be introduced.[23]

Morrison would recognise this process and how it was, not in any sense uniquely, brought to bear upon him, especially as the author of one such hit:

> Happy Traum: Was there a lot of pressure for you to give in to that kind of thing?
>
> VM: Oh, sure. Bert wanted me to write a song with him that would be a hit, but I just didn't feel that kind of song. I mean, maybe that was his kind of song, but it wasn't my kind of song, so I just told him. I mean, if you want to do that kind of song, man, you should just go in and do it, get yourself a group and sing that song, but I've got my kind of song that's different. I've always been writing the kind of songs I do now, even with Them.[24]

Despite their strained relationship – one which led to him satirising 'a Bert Berns song . . . over and over!' on the Bang contractual obligation squib 'Thirty Two'[25] – Morrison is generous and understanding of why Berns wanted to stick to the formula. He is well aware of the processes, but feels quite remote from them, even when he was their subject. There are clearly links between Scott's formula, Adorno's critique of it and Bert Berns's implementation of it. They are all three approaching the same central 'formula' with different purposes. The writers and producers of the music industry have always clearly related to this idea of establishing a hit formula and then repeating it with enough variation to distinguish it from the previous model already sold, with enough 'novelty' to seem fresh. The emphasis for Bruce and Berns was of course not only how to craft a well-made song according to certain market-led rules, but how then to take that song to the marketplace itself? Here we are at the heart of Van Morrison's famed epigrammatic observation that while music is spiritual, the music business isn't.

In 1945 Robert Bruce wrote:

> It is sometimes difficult to realize that music, despite its nebulous distinction as 'one of the arts' is actually regarded as a commodity and is bought, exploited, distributed and sold in much the same way as other commodities including soap, food, cosmetics, cigarettes and automobiles.[26]

This is of course the dirty secret of the music industry, one which has been 'exposed' over and again, but the industry still runs on as if this were not the case. In fact this is so strong a feeling that we might feel that indeed it is *not* wholly the case, that to assert that it is this way and this way only is to mistake the transaction for the thing itself – food and cars are commodities, it's true, but they still nourish and get you somewhere, regardless of how we come by them. The music industry doesn't employ actual industrial processes until the commodification and distribution stage – rather the industrial element is a code for the process via which music is moulded to suit contemporary tastes. So a pop song may be absolutely the product of industrial manufacture but that doesn't necessarily mean it has no call on our emotions, attention or 'real' feelings. On these terms, 'Brown Eyed Girl', and Bert Berns's production number on it, have given Morrison, and the rest of us, an enduring example of how great a simple popular song can be. Bruce claimed that the writing of a pop song is not unlike baking a cake: 'Almost anyone can do it. On the surface it appears to be merely a matter of selecting the proper ingredients and putting them together according to some prescribed recipe.'[27] Anyone reading this book will feel two things reading this – we know that this is how the industry still works to some extent but we also know that the best pop music that followed Bruce's era has both transcended and frequently simply ignored these rules of the game. Adorno's essay sums this school of thinking up neatly in a single phrase – 'The composition hears for the listener'.[28]

So does 'Brown Eyed Girl' 'hear' for us? As Bill Flanagan says in the notes for the Bang *Masters* CD in 1991, these recordings survive from

> a stormy three-day recording date in which a brilliant, difficult, hungry, 21-year-old musician attempted to record with a bunch of studio pros who didn't know what this crazy Irish kid was up to and for a producer with a great ear for Tin Pan Alley pop at a time when Tin Pan Alley pop was becoming an anachronism.[29]

This forcing together of elements which would naturally push apart – even Bert Berns's own memorial website admits that 'Morrison fought Berns in the studio nearly every step of the way' – is the site of the creative tension in these recordings; the perfect point of overlapping, Venn diagram-shading is 'Brown Eyed Girl', perhaps. Again, Flanagan notes wisely:

> Listen to this session as a tug of war. Sometimes ('Spanish Rose') the Bang side wins . . . other times ('TB Sheets') Van wins . . . occasionally (obviously on 'Brown Eyed Girl') Van, Berns and the musicians find common ground and out comes great music that works both as Top 40 pop and as honest, heartfelt rock and roll.[30]

So 'Brown Eyed Girl' to some extent still fits Bruce's and Adorno's models – using a modish template to offer both the known and a little novelty – while making out of that recipe something entirely distinctive and beyond the musical date-stamping of its own era.

This is in some way evidenced by the song's flexibility as a cover version, adapting itself to a huge range of styles via the likes of Steel Pulse, Ronan Keating, Busted, Ian Matthews, Stevie Ray Vaughan, McFly and even Bob Dylan. So the song is clearly seen as a charm, commercially; yet to scrutinise the bones of Morrison's original – as familiar as they are – shows it to be a more curious proposition than at first seems the case. The first two notes, ascending, are played on the bass – very few of Morrison's songs begin on the bass; I can think of only 'Haunts Of Ancient Peace', which does so by happy accident, and 'When Will I Ever Learn To Live In God?' Then the jazzy guitar skips into the Latin-inflected riff; beyond, the on-beat is met by handclaps and tambourine, the off by tambourine alone. The handclaps keep up throughout – this percussive anomaly (the emphasis on the front beat), for pop at least, marked it as something a little hotter, rhythmically, and lends it the perceptible Latin flavour – this is the default 'hot sauce in the ears' that Lester Bangs noted as being typical of Bert Berns, and it serves the song well. In the bass bridge (1.49–59) the beat is doubled and a tambourine hits you double time. The guitar's meanderings around the melody and the beat give it its jazzy, picaresque figure. What is also unusual is that here is a pop song with a genuine wistful longing for the past – most mid-60s pop was about NOW – 'I Want To Hold Your Hand' or 'I Can't Get No Satisfaction'– yet here a 21-year-old is reminiscing like a man twice his age. The 'Sha la la' hook is central, and connects the song to pop history, while pointing forward to tunes like 'Natalia' and even the provocative 'Blah blah blah' of 'Behind The Ritual'. This last has annoyed some critics – and we can see why – but we need to ask what is the difference between this and the 'Sha la la' of 'Brown Eyed Girl', the 'Be-Bop-A-Lula' of Gene Vincent or Little Richard's 'Awopbopaloobopawopbamboom!', which now resides in the *Oxford Book of Quotations*. Morrison is a skilled user of the onomatopoeia of pop, understanding well how it works as a connection of sound to feeling.

The scat to the fade of 'Brown Eyed Girl' marks it out as having survived the industrial process which, according to the theory, seeks to has squeeze all individuality out of the art. Infamously there were two vocal takes of the song issued, one which included a reference to making love in the green grass, and a 'clean' version, where the couple are laughing and running instead. It's testament to his vocal performance on this track that the two takes are distinct in plenty of other ways too, Morrison's natural way of working pushing against the idea of the standardised model of the popular song and leaning towards the model familiar from jazz, of never singing anything the same way twice. Especially hit records.[31]

'Jackie Wilson Said (I'm In Heaven When You Smile)' (1972)

With its dramatic, high-kicking a cappella scat intro, this is a song built to open an album, doing the job for *Saint Dominic's Preview* and also nominated as opener for 2007's *Still On Top*.[32] This is a street-smart love song which takes its lyrical cue from another, Jackie Wilson's 'Reet Petite'. That song was originally recorded and issued in 1957 and written by the formidable team of a pre-Motown Berry Gordy and 'Tyran Carlo', a song-writing pseudonym used by Gordy's cousin Billy Davis. The success of the song part-funded the launch of Motown just over a year later. Their title was in itself a partial steal, from Louis Jordan's 'Reet, Petite and Gone'. Jordan was of course another Morrison favourite; he covered Jordan's near-Celtic sounding 'Caldonia' in 1974. Now, Jackie Wilson said it was reet petite, it's true, but it was the Bachelors who said 'I'm in heaven when you smile', on their 1964 Decca hit 'Diane'; Morrison will have known the Bachelors, troupers of the Irish show-band circuit as well as Them's labelmates. Thus there is an impressive pedigree of influence and cross-reference at work in this song, before we even arrive at the irresistible spin and twist of Morrison's melody and performance itself.

To say it hits the ground running hardly covers it – it gets out of the blocks at top speed and doesn't quit until its time is up. It's the razor edge between speed and control that gives the song its power as well as its energy. It opens with a run of what we might call pop-soul scatting (somewhere at the intersection of shang-a-lang, a wop bop a loo bop and jazz doodle-bop scat), over a clapped on-beat and a gradual build of sax following the vocal melody before the band launches in to the track at 0.12. The song drapes around this scat hook, the chorus of the song being another run of onomatopoeic rhythm before yielding to 'I'm in heaven'. The song catches itself where the controlled power of the performance makes itself felt in the stops. In the choruses (hear 0.52–1.07), the song pauses, poised for a moment on the tipping point of silence, then joyously see-sawing down again into the thick of the noise. The stop, or silence, is connected to the rest of the song by a brace of tapped beats; they mark time as well as indicating its passing.

The vocal is prime time pop Morrison: tight, melodic, fully vocalised from the centre-back of the throat – open enough to get the distinctive notes out (0.26–29) but also chatty enough to bring the song in unmistakably as a racing pop song (0.32–36). It is almost a textbook illustration of Morrison's ability to sing a closely composed, lyrically rhythmic melody, which also accommodates vocal techniques borrowed from the early and undivided era of r'n'b, pop, jazz and blues, overlapping in the feel and the performance. Listen to his scatting at 2.29–37 and we are directed back to both the 'all the bubbles' section of 'Moonshine Whiskey' and forward to the extraordinary vocal innovations of *Into The Music* and *Common One*, but presented in an immaculate pop song, bundled up into a single side of a 45. Chuck Berry once famously said, 'If you can't say it in three minutes it's probably not worth saying': 'Jackie Wilson Said' lasts exactly three minutes. Kevin Rowland responded to this mix of precision and freedom ('I had a soft spot for that song', he told me) and Dexy's Midnight Runners had a big hit in 1982 with their cover of the tune.[33]

The lyric owes much of its sense to the rhythm built into it, and not only via the scat. The reference to coffee in the cup (or the lack of the need of it) echoes the occasionally puritanical streak that runs through some of his material (think also of 'Turn it up! That's enough' in 'Caravan'), and this connects to remaining in control of oneself, and also knowing thereby whether the mood one is in is real or artificially induced, be that by caffeine, alcohol or narcotics. This may or may not be residua of a Protestant upbringing in 50s Belfast; what we can be sure of is that it sets him apart from the standardised hedonism of much 'rock' music, the mantra of which is more, more, more. There's real humour too. Listen to his live-in-the-studio aside 'Watch this' at 0.38, which cues in the switch to the chorus and for the horns of Jack Schroer and 'Boots' Rolf Houston to drive home the point beneath his vocal, and his 'Uh' at 2.06, grounding the moment during one of the stops. Listening to the song invariably persuades me that the greatest pleasure of it is its completeness, and as such it is a perfect example of the Aristotelian model of creativity: it has a beginning, a middle and an end. It is also such a good-natured, righteous, fine-time song, built to both reflect and capture those fleeing visions of wholeness, glimpsed in ordinary life, when she smiles or walks across the room. It communicates both an unconscious delight in living and a clear-sighted appreciation of those delights, mixing living in the heat of the moment with a cool appreciation of such moments. It is also Morrison's best record to dance to.

THE LOVE SONGS

> 'It's easy to write romantic songs.'
>
> Van Morrison, Cardiff, 2007

> 'I'm a songwriter, I write about men and women,
> I'm a songwriter, and I do it for a living.'
>
> Van Morrison, 'Songwriter'[34]

Van Morrison's love songs frequently make a connection between his more esoteric vocabularies and the traditions of the well-made romantic song – *Poetic Champions Compose*'s 'I Forgot That Love Existed' is a good example of this, connecting personal emotion to the mysteries of the ages. That song shares album space with an unashamedly mainstream example of romantic songwriting in 'Someone Like You': the direct appeal of that song can be indexed via its multiple cover versions and use in a series of Hollywood romantic comedies, even lending its title to one of them. In the rush to praise and explore Morrison's undoubted skill as a kind of aesthetic voyager into the mystic, his skill as a writer of love songs is often overlooked – all the more unfairly because in the sense of his wide and general audience these songs draw at least as many to his work as his more esoteric material does.

Morrison himself has something of an awkward relationship with the love song, as he told Candy Dulfer:

> VM: When you're writing a song there's no audience (laughs). Its a very personal thing. Some of it is real, and some of it isn't. It's all mixed up. So there's no set thing where a song is, for instance, all about me. Some songs might be all about me or my life, most of them aren't, most of them are bits from here and there, different people's lives, it might be something from your life that I put in there.

> CD: Stories that people tell you . . .
>
> VM: Or things that you pick up so you think I'll put that in there . . . that's how you write songs . . . it's easy to write romantic songs . . . it's more difficult to write about the reality of all the crap in life that you have to deal with. It's harder to do that and it's not really acceptable. People don't realise, it isn't that personal what is put into a song . . . and it might be about someone else's life, a fictional character in my imagination.[35]

If it's 'easy to write romantic songs', the inference is that he would more naturally incline towards the fascination of what's difficult – the example he chooses here, the 'fame blues', he feels is 'harder to do', but also 'less acceptable' to the audience at large. As he observes in 'Troubadours', the job of the singer, the minstrel who is on and off the road, travelling from town to town, is to sing 'songs of love, to the lady fair'. There he borrows an image from deep within our shared vocabulary of a romantic cultural unconscious, 'She was standing outside on the balcony, in the clear night air'. Juliet may provide the unwitting cultural model for every 'lady fair' since Shakespeare's *Romeo and Juliet*, but the dynamic is the same – part of the point and purpose of popular song is to declare and propose love.

We need to establish some sort of criteria for a love song, and we can rely on what Smokey Robinson had to say on the subject:

> 'A love song tells the world how it feels inside, without having to find the words yourself! So a song like 'Being With You' is known by everybody, but everybody understands it personally, they put their own lives into the song. That's how a really good love song works!'[36]

Love is almost certainly the central strand and abiding theme of pop composition; indeed it is now a relatively simple matter to do as courtiers did with the troubadours and commission a love song to suit your particular requirements and circumstances. This is in some ways the obverse of Smokey Robinson's view of the generality of the love song being a way in which the song known by all becomes particularised; this is closer to what Adorno called 'pseudo-individualisation' in his essay 'On Popular Music'.[37] In requested and dedicated composition the song is specifically owned in a way that still remains unusual in the era of commodified song. We might cry 'That's just how I feel!' when we hear a lovelorn lyric, but the song is doing half the work for the listener – we bring the meaning and the points of personalised connection. This is a sticky subject for a songwriter – love songs are the easiest to write, perhaps, but they are then subject to scrutiny of a different sort – if the autobiographical is part of a song's perceived value, can a love song succeed if the singer is not 'in love'? That is, if it is 'just a love song', as Morrison once incongruously described the sublime 'Come Here My Love',[38] or as he told Candy Dulfer, 'It might be a something from *your* life I put in there' (my italics). The lazy swing of 'Songwriter' makes a host of claims as to the shape, scale and limits of his work and what might be made of it, and is a self-conscious indexing of the procedures of songwriting itself. As a self-reflexive comment upon his day job it's pleasingly direct and unaffected; it's about how, in the title of his 2008 album, to keep it simple.

This process of reflecting on practice while simultaneously delivering on that reflection was 'discovered' at the close of *Into The Music*, in the 180-degree shift in perspective offered by the move from 'It's All In The Game' to 'You Know What They're Writing About'. Dawes and Sigman's standard is performed, and then Morrison addresses the listener directly through the speaker ('You, *you, you* know what they're writing about'), stepping forward to comment upon and implicate the listener in the art and business of the love song. So there we move from the Smokey Robinson model, in which we imagine ourselves in the moment of the song, to being asked to consider, in an uncomplicated but still sophisticated manner, the nature and appeal of such a song. This device of a narrator stepping out of the art to address the audience directly is not uncommon in theatre but remains unusual, even radical in song. So a less immediately engaging composition like 'Songwriter' exists as a kind of good-humoured manifesto, placing markers down for how he would like the work to be seen and understood. It is his contribution to a long-standing tradition, sometimes for love ('I can even do it when I'm hurtin''), sometimes for money ('my cheque is in the mail'), but always for the song.

This is clearly related to Morrison's strong sense of what he does as being a trade, or an artisan craft ('I'm on the stage doing my job', as he reminds us in 'Peace Of Mind'). The deliberately obvious rhymes and consciously 'unpoetic' plain speaking in 'Songwriter' are, in their artlessness, as well crafted as those of the love song itself – chosen and assembled to do a specific job and meet a specific need. Yet what happens when it's not so easy to do? How do you get round writer's block? As Morrison has said in interviews many times, he frequently finds it difficult to keep going in terms of coming up with fresh ideas and material, and as his most lucid 'writer's block' song, 'Tore Down a la Rimbaud' says, without ambiguity, it's hard sometimes. Morrison's friend Bob Dylan characterised his writer's block from the inside and the outside in the exquisite 'All The Tired Horses', from 1970's critically maligned *Self Portrait*. Morrison's tired horses, for one who has spoken a lot about the difficulty of making music for a living, are in smallish pasture – 'Tore Down a la Rimbaud' and 'I'd Love To Write Another Song'. 'Songwriter' reverses this by describing the craft at which he has some talent. Morrison's 'writer's block' songs both seek and provide a way out. One of the most skilful ways in which Morrison has explored this intriguing connection between the social uses of the love song and the labour that needs to go into its seemingly natural appearance is found in the juxtaposition of 'I'd Love To Write Another Song' and 'Have I Told You Lately' on *Avalon Sunset*. The former is a good-humoured rewrite of the writer's block song, taking the high-art anxieties of 'Tore Down a la Rimbaud' and replacing them with a rolling, bar piano beat and a frank admission of the use of songwriting to the songwriter: 'Make some money, pay the bills, keep me busy too / I'd love to write another love song'.[39]

It's a neat sleight of hand, a strategy for getting out from under writer's block by using it as the subject for a song, and one which, as we have seen, he used to good effect in 'Tore Down a la Rimbaud'. Here the ambition is less lofty in its expression and more grounded in the 'job' of being a songwriter. It seems at this moment that the very possibility of ever being able to write another love song seems remote; he equates writing another song with getting some 'peace of mind', a phrase he would use again as a song title on 1991's *Hymns To The Silence*. Remarkably, this self-effacing little number gives way to the very song the singer has been dreaming of writing: a romantic, sumptuously arranged love song par excellence. In a further twist, 'Have I Told You Lately' has of course become one of Morrison's best known and most popular numbers among his widest audience, garnering attention in his own original version here and via a growing number of cover versions. It has become a standard of the romantic songbook and as such has achieved at least one of Morrison's imagined objectives in 'I'd Love To Write Another Song', in that it has helped 'pay the bills' of the last 20 years or so.

In tenor and arrangement 'Have I Told You Lately' is a near-facsimile of *Poetic Champions Compose*'s 'Someone Like You', almost as if it was a rewrite – that he knew there was a hit in there somewhere and he was going to tease it out as many times as it took. Even the title is borrowed, from Scotty Wiseman's country song, first issued in the year Morrison was born, 1945.[40] 'Someone Like You' had been issued as a single and sold next to nothing, while 'Have I Told You Lately' was granted a luscious-looking promo video – but the song was never a 'hit' in the traditional sense. So why and how did it become so popular, and how does the song make a success of its repertoire of elements?

We have: the piano, the orchestra, the voice, the lyric. The song, stripped of its orchestral arrangement, would still be a romantic proposition, matching a soft and lilting melody with a direct and near-utopian lyric. The one deviation from this model is the reference to the end of the day we should give thanks and pray to 'the one', placing earthly love in the context of it being an echo of a higher one. Morrison's vocal is both generous and tentative enough to suggest both certitude and the possibility of loss and as such strikes an appropriate tone for a love song. The rhymes, as Buzacott and Ford point out,[41] are not complex, but to make them so would be to obscure the point, and blunt the feeling of the song. This is a love song – it is seeking to make a certain and identified impact, and the lyric serves this purpose to very good effect. The song's extensive use of internal as well as line-end rhyming is skilfully employed to suggest an inner as well as an outer concord and harmony: sadness/gladness, for example, ebb and flow around each other in the internal rhymes, first one, then the other taking precedence. This is in itself a kind of wisdom, acknowledging that both lie ahead. But the words don't do it alone; it has an unmistakably lush arrangement, the work of Fiachra Trench, who also arranged 'Someone Like You' and 'Queen Of The Slipstream', the brace of epic love songs on *Poetic Champions Compose*. The appeal of 'Have I Told You Lately', like those, is a combination of the unapologetically romantic lyric with the sensitive mirroring of that mood in Trench's arrangement.[42]

Morrison's own ambiguity to these tunes shows itself in concert – he has only very rarely performed 'Someone Like You' and I heard him chuckle to himself and repeat the title disdainfully when someone called for it at a 2005 gig. While he has played 'Have I Told You Lately' many times, he quickly arranged it as piece of Louis Prima jump jazz, unrecognisable from the album version. Those who appreciate the mix of misty-eyed sentiment and deep soulfulness in the song may rue this, but the song has clearly joined the ranks of those he feels obliged to play rather than wants to. What is undeniable is that it broke through commercially in a way that its near-twin 'Someone Like You' did not.[43] Though not the best known, Morrison's greatest love song, in my view, is the album-mate of 'Someone Like You', 'Queen Of The Slipstream', but that tune could never have become a standard in the way that 'Have I Told You Lately' has, partly because its lyrical and musical symbologies are so closely associated to Morrison himself. Can we imagine Rod Stewart blandly crooning about the slipstream and the poetic champions as he does the lyric to 'Have I Told You Lately'? It seems unlikely.

Fiachra Trench remembers how the arrangement which graces 'Queen Of The Slipstream' came together:

> 'Queen of the Slipstream' is one of the tracks on *Poetic Champions Compose*, the first album on which I collaborated with Van. It was a first for Van also: his previous string sessions in the USA had been for a smaller section than I used; I think we had about 26 players. The string session went very smoothly. Van very content. On 'Queen . . .' I reduced the strings to a chamber group for Van's harmonica solo and the

> second bridge which follows. Otherwise it's the full section. These days Van favours smaller string sections – from string quartet up to, say, 10 or 12. More organic. Less orchestral. There's an epic feel to this track and the strings seem to enhance that feel.
>
> Some of the string lines are derived from Neil Drinkwater's piano lines. I often use that technique when writing string arrangements; it helps to make the strings sound more part of the track, less like an overdub, less pop.[44]

Trench's saturation of sound is key to the mood of high-swoon we feel in the song and the sheer beauty of 'Queen Of The Slipstream' is musically analogous to *Poetic Champions Compose* as a whole, as it is the album's key song, containing the album title. It also references 'Astral Weeks' in its use of a distinctive Morrison term, the slipstream, and 1970's lovely 'Come Running' in 'I see you slipping and sliding in the snow . . . you come running to me, you'll come running to me'.[45] It represents perhaps his best example of the blend between the 'mystic' song and the love song in its fusion of the mystic and the material, the spiritual and the corporeal. The 'innocence/experience' motif which frames the lyric exemplifies this. It also employs some of his key motifs beyond this sensual bipolarity, with the two apparently contradictory or antagonistic states being yoked together and experienced simultaneously.[46] It is certainly used this way in the 1992 movie *Moondance*, where 'Queen Of The Slipstream' is the character Anya's theme, signifying the sensuous tensions between duty and desire in the narrative and cleaving as closely to her as 'Moon River' does to Holly Golightly in *Breakfast at Tiffany's*.[47]

Morrison's voicing of the word 'snow' at 3.55 and his extrapolated 'Queen' at 4.12–14 provide the vocal peak of the song, and this goes close in hand with the musical climax, with the strings at their most abundant and free between 4.15–23. These details link with the beginning too in that Morrison's voice shadows the guitar line in his union-singing style down to the fade, two distinct elements moving in agreement, creating an entirely fresh and 'other' element which still maintains and establishes an new wholeness within itself. This mix of smooth surfaces and complex emotional memory – exemplified by the blend of harmonica and strings – is indicative of the album's whole sonic mood and perhaps the nature of love itself.

Going back in time, 'Crazy Love' was part of his deliberate attempt to make more of a commercial mark with the *Moondance* album: as Sam Cooke told Dick Clark on *American Bandstand* with only a little shuffle of embarrassment, he had made a deliberate decision to come over from gospel to pop because of '. . . my financial situation, Dick!'[48] If Morrison wished to improve his 'financial situation', then writing a love song or two must have seemed like a smart move.

This is not of course to denigrate the tune or Morrison's sincerity in writing it; but he had to eat, and many of the greatest love songs, as Smokey Robinson taught us, are written with a clear-sighted focus on the market. 'Crazy Love' debuts his gentle falsetto, a voice only infrequently used in his output; this adds to the tenderness, depth and vulnerability of the vocal and the lyric it carries. What is 'crazy' about this love? The irrationality of it? The intensity of it? The natural gentleness of it? All of this and more. That's why the song exists the way it does. The close-miked intimacy of the performance illustrates how the singer is in the position of the receiver – 'She give me love' – a kind of blissful passivity which is in some ways a feminised position, perhaps emphasised by the falsetto vocal, and in this the received binaries of gender are broken down.[49]

The song also stands as the only commercially issued duet between Van Morrison and Ray Charles, being recorded live at the Songwriter's Hall of Fame ceremony at New York's Marriott Hotel in June 2003, after Ray had 'inducted' Morrison, and presented him with the award. As a formal duet it doesn't really happen – both men are singing the same song at the same time – but there are some cherishable moments, most notably when Charles gets sufficiently inside the song to utter an 'Alright' at 2.03, in response to which Morrison laughs to himself (2.05) and sings the next line, 'So far away', in a tone poised between delight at his idol's owning of his song and also a kind of recognition of the older man's influence. Charles's spontaneous utterance is exactly the kind of thing Morrison does while singing a song that moves and interests him. In this tiny moment of recognition is registered a whole lifetime's admiration and influence which has informed Morrison's own creativity as singer, writer and performer, making it a love song of a different order, perhaps.[50]

It is not until *Wavelength* – a long way from the mood of the early 70s records – that we get another of what we might call unambiguously romantic songs. 'Hungry For Your Love' is, however, neither a hippie love song nor a 'Brown Eyed Girl' rewrite (which, for all its joyous sound, album-mate 'Natalia' is); it's a proper, grown-up love song, cognisant of the physical as well as the metaphysical meanings of love. In its context it is a gorgeous, understated piece of work, immaculately produced and played and sung. It is borne from and expresses with a sensual deftness physical intimacy and tenderness, and the feeling of love from within the centre of it. 'Queen Of The Slipstream' is Morrison's most complete wedding of his own vocabularies to that of the love song, but 'Hungry For Your Love' is perhaps his most sensual work. I'd suggest this stems from the quiet anticipation and the control of emotion that is exerted:

> I'm hungry for your love
> But I can wait now . . .

And after all the years
And after all the tears
And after all the tears
There's just the truth now[51]

This feeling of having broken through to a kind of completeness and wisdom of sorts may well have lasted only as long as it took to write and sing the song but the recording nonetheless catches it and we can hear and feel it anew each time. The electric guitar, working on the bass strings, carries the riff as it flows into and builds upon the sensuality of the song; the structure is slightly odd in that the verses carry the song, while the chorus, such as it is, feels more like a bridge which leads back into the slowly circulating centre of the song.

The last minute of the song forgoes the structure altogether, allowing the vocal to explore feelingly the space, the wildly evocative and sensual 'I love you in buckskin' is surrendered, giving way to a direct 'I love you', an admission that the final veil has dropped. The potential banality of 'I love you' repeated over and over in a song is triumphed over by the nature of those repetitions, rolling and tumbling over each other into a final, liberatingly candid confession of feeling as the title is repeated a single time at the song's close; a kind of open question as much as a statement. In its duelling complexities and simplicity the song is a powerful and adult evocation of how it feels to be in the middle of love and desire. The unabashed sensuality of 'Hungry For Your Love' guaranteed an appeal to filmmakers and it soundtracked a memorable scene in *An Officer and a Gentleman*, thereby qualifying it for inclusion on 2007's themed compilation *Van Morrison At The Movies*.

'She's My Baby' (1990) is gorgeous, uncomplicated and deep. Driven by a sweet acoustic guitar motif from Bernie Holland, this is a love song in which echoes of other songs swirl around: there are fore-echoes of 'In The Midnight' and reminders of 'Queen Of The Slipstream' in Fiachra Trench's delicious string arrangement. Yet the song to which it owes most is not one of Morrison's own compositions, but 'Be-Bop-A-Lula' – the title itself is of course the second half of that song's opening and most famous line. 'Be-Bop-A-Lula', credited as being written by Gene Vincent and his manager Bill 'Sherriff Tex' Davis (who allegedly bought out the rights of the original lyricist, Donald Graves, an army friend of Vincent, for $50), was one of the biggest hits of the 50s, reaching high into both US and UK charts in 1956 and quickly becoming a standard for other acts and skiffle/garage bands of the sort the young Morrison played in Belfast. Vincent gave a famous performance of the song, seen on a TV set, in *The Girl Can't Help It*, which Morrison almost certainly saw – indeed he covered Little Richard's title song for the one and only time in concert in an epic show in

Utrecht in February 1991, on the tour to promote *Enlightenment*, the parent album of 'She's My Baby'.[52]

So his familiarity with Vincent's song seems assured. On an album dealing with the nature of memory and the significance of music in the formation and renewal of such memories, 'Be-Bop-A-Lula' looms large – it is of course mentioned by name earlier in the same album as part of 'In The Days Before Rock And Roll', so it was clearly in Morrison's mind at the time. It found its way into his live set at this time, being almost ever present between 1991 and 1995, either standing alone or being attached to 'Cleaning Windows'. 'She's My Baby' doesn't resemble Vincent's song in any way in terms of arrangement but the continuity is strong, and it has some fun with the lyrical conventions that the older song introduced to pop too. In the second and third choruses 'She's my baby' is shamelessly rhymed with 'don't mean maybe' (2.24–27 and 4.26–28, for example), a gift from the lyric to 'Be-Bop-A-Lula' of course, as is the 'Well well well' that precedes this chorus at 2.18–20, and the third at 4.18–20.

Making use of the connection to what Morrison calls 'the days before rock and roll' that all this conjures up, where his world was the street, the song grounds the love affair in real life, and that is nicely exemplified by the locale of the song. Here he isn't going into the mystic, but into the 'caff', where he 'won't get egg on [his] face'. This is a bad pun, but a sweet image of how relaxed and uncomplicated such a life might be for him, free of the need to keep up a public image. This is the meaning of 'the street', an image of liberty, one which finds its metaphysical correspondence in the 'slipstream', of which his baby may also simultaneously be the Queen. So this plain and direct love song finds echoes across to his more consciously allusive constructions of the ideal.[53]

'Reminds Me Of You' (1999) is perhaps his latest truly great love song; although albums subsequent to *Back On Top* have had their contenders, songs like 'Once In A Blue Moon' (another borrowed Count John McCormack title) and 'Steal My Heart Away' are definitively minor works. 'Reminds Me Of You' has a biographical context, well covered elsewhere. As a performance of the bittersweet confusion of desire it is almost without peer in his songbook. Opening on a lonely circular acoustic guitar riff and pushed along by a shuffling rhythm under the vocal, the song drips rainy afternoon melancholia. So intense is the feeling of loneliness that when Brian Kennedy's vocal chimes in at 1.52 with a pleasingly irregular harmony it is a startling, almost supernatural moment – especially after the line 'Sometimes it feels like I'm going to Hell'. This arrival of a second voice is an almost Beckettian moment, offering a glimmer of hope in its evidence of something beyond the encircling gloaming. It also represents Brian Kennedy's best contribution to Morrison's work, culminating in the harmony to 'stand it' at 4.41, a stunning moment that always leaves me breathless.

Morrison's vocal is wracked but supple, lacking all affectation, pretence or conscious performative gesture. He may well have asserted to Candy Dulfer that it was 'easy' to write love songs but here is a song that, we feel from the performance, cost the writer something more than the time it took to compose it. When he sings 'Everything I do, reminds me of you', we believe it. This is the sound of a troubled soul poured into 5 minutes 40. Rarely performed live, I was lucky enough to catch only its fourteenth ever outing in a decade at Harrogate in late 2007, and the song retains its haunted quality. Unlike 'Have I Told You Lately', it is unlikely to become an easy-listening or karaoke favourite, and this is at least in part due to the emotional saturation of the song. I'd suggest that it is almost uncoverable; it exists entirely of itself, a kind of confirmation of the loneliness that stalks the song's inner space.[54]

It is interesting too that for a writer who places such store by and draws so fully upon memory and its power to reanimate and reclaim emotion, in this song we see how that is not always a pleasant thing. Here the memory keeps wounds open and functions as a source of torment – 'Everything I do reminds me of you' – and as a possible gateway to damnation rather than salvation. The dreamy wish for 'Someone Like You' has a dark consequence. The opening line, although printed as 'I miss you so much, I can't stand it', sounds to me very much like 'Now it's the summer, I can't stand it' and if that's correct we have another example of Morrison's knack for deft and skilful sequencing, following as it does 'High Summer', a time which in that song seems oppressive and depressive. Pop has always loved the summer, and loved love – think of early Beach Boys, or Jerry Keller's 'Here Comes Summer' – but here are two songs that find the darkness under the brightness, and in doing so cast fresh light upon both, shadow and light co-mingling.[55]

Keep It Simple's 'Lover Come Back' is that album's only song to directly address the matters of the heart, and is a strong addition to Morrison's catalogue of love songs. In its cry of loss we are at the well of loneliness – love here is no longer the warm and sensual closeness of 'Hungry For Your Love', nor the high eulogy of 'Queen Of The Slipstream', but is closer in kind to the wracked plea and painful emotional openness of 'Reminds Me Of You'. Again, the song records a kind of exile – calling the lover home, out of exile and into the arms of love once more, a pleasure desired and denied in the moment of longing captured and consumed by the love song itself.[56] This is the complex root of Morrison's ambiguous relationship with the ease and difficulty of writing a love song. From his dealings with universally recognised songwriting duties – hits and love songs – we can now turn to deeper and more particular aspects of his own style as a songwriter, what we might call his specific and particular themes.

Chapter Four

Caught One More Time: Themes and Thematics

Throughout Morrison's catalogue run a number of key themes or motifs, which ebb and flow, pulsing through the work and becoming both quite central, and yet always somehow evasive of definitive statement. Some come from the wider fields of cultural practice such as the garden or the radio, some are particular coinages of phrase such as the 'golden autumn day' or the 'ancient highway', while others are almost reflex images, such as the falling leaf or silence itself. In this chapter, I investigate what seem to me the most telling and significant recurrent themes in his work and how they seem to work towards what I call the 'summative song' in which the phrase or image is fully spotlit and foregrounded. The key phrases function as a kind of covert through-composition, a 'micro' version of the 'macro' of the through-composed album. Here we examine a selection of themes that seem to me to be the most characteristic of Morrison's work as a whole.

IN THE GARDEN

Evocations of the garden, misty wet with rain or otherwise, stretch right back to Morrison's earliest recordings, with the siting of 'Mystic Eyes' in the early morning fog, down by the old graveyard, introducing the importance of this kind of place, man-made but susceptible to the rhythms of the natural world – in that case, the fog and the memento mori of the graveyard. This fascination with the borderline between the natural world and man's engagement with it runs through Morrison's work and these are special, charmed places. In 'Sweet Thing' we find the first reference to the 'garden misty wet with rain' and this sets a benchmark image for Morrison's work – we find in this song that it is analogous to youth, vigour and the delight of discovery. The promises cradled within the lyric ('And we will walk and talk in gardens all misty wet with rain'[1]) offer a kind of anticipatory delight with bejewelled, dew-hung imagery, heavy with romance, whereas the standpoint of 'In The Garden' ('wet with rain') is retrospective. In both cases, the garden provides both the image, already culturally loaded, and the physical space in which things are permitted to happen. So the garden is an image both local and universal.

In literary terms, the garden has a tradition of use that stretches right back to the root of the Old Testament, to Eden (the Hebrew word for 'delight') and the creation myths in the book of Genesis itself.[2] Of course the Garden in this sense is a place of ambiguity, a place called Paradise, but one from which Man was cast out – so it can be a place of myth and memory, prompting a longing to return to a state of innocence. The memory of it is both a thorn in the side, a reminder of the Fall, but also a spur on to working towards a kind of return. The parallels with some of Morrison's evocations of time and place via memory find a plain and resonant correspondence here – think of the last line of 'Coney Island' and its Edenic wish: 'Wouldn't it be great if it were like this all the time?' Even if we think of his choice of covers, a song like 'Sometimes I Feel Like A Motherless Child', with its central motif of being 'a long way from my home', addresses this feeling, as if being 'on the road' is part of the price paid and part of the journey back. John Milton's *Paradise Lost*[3] retold the story of the Fall as an epic poem, with some sympathy for the devil – borrowed by Morrison for a song called 'High Summer' – and Milton's friend Andrew Marvell provided metaphysical poetry with one of its central texts with his delicious evocation of spiritual and sensual abundance, in 'The Garden' – the place where all pleasures are laid open.[4] Thus the appeal of the garden as a place of potential discovery and loss is clear.

In the Bible, though, there are two significant gardens: Eden for the Old Testament, and, in the New, Gethsemane. Bob Dylan's 'In The Garden' from *Saved* represents a New Testament use of the image, unambiguous in its references to that latter garden. As a piece of writing it combines the technique of the cumulative open question that Dylan had earlier employed to such effect on songs like 'Blowin' In The Wind' with memorable directness and openness of melody. It meets the criteria of music built for a specific purpose, to achieve a certain effect on its listeners. It's congregational music, for public performance. It's out *there*.[5]

Morrison's garden, by contrast, feels like a private place; it's in *here*. Morrison told Mick Brown something about the intended purpose of this song:

> MB: Can we talk a little about the latest record? The latest Van Morrison record's called *No Guru, No Method, No Teacher*. What is the meaning behind the title?

VM: Well – it's actually in one of the songs . . . 'In the Garden' where I actually take you through the meditation programme. From about half way through the song until the end . . . if you listen to the thing carefully, you should have gotten yourself some sort of tranquillity by the time you get to the end. So when this happens in the song, I say, "And I turn to you and I said, 'No Guru, No Method, No Teacher. Just you and I and nature, and the Father and the Son, and the Holy Ghost'". So really – you have to do the whole line to know what it means . . . on another level what it says is that . . . due to what popular opinion says it's been implied that this guy and that guy and the other organization was my guru . . . that's all speculative and its not real. So you know this is a statement. You know you could call this a press statement. It's making it quite clear that I'm not affiliated with anyone or organization. I don't have a guru. I don't have any teacher. And there's no method that I subscribe to. And that's really what its saying as well. So that's what it saying in the song.

MB: So it was rejecting dogma, in a word.

VM: You could put it like that, yeah.[6]

'In The Garden' clearly has a substantial weight of communicative ambition to bear. What is remarkable is how the song matches this intensely personal set of meanings to the universally potent image of the garden as a kind of charmed place in a way that connects it to other more localised and specific 'special places' elsewhere in Morrison's catalogue.[7]

The musical dynamics of this track are intriguing, the volume and intensity ebbing and flowing and surging around the repetitions of the title phrase. It has its mood set from the off, the dominant tone being that of the piano, and the track opens with long-time string arranger Jeff Labes's pealing piano cascading, but at a tempo temperate enough for him to drop back to the 'home notes' which ground and moderate the forward motion of the music. At 0.08 it drops into the main body of the track, when acoustic guitar enters and a metronomic click, cut with a little swing hi-hat, marks the time. The song swells and subsides, rises and falls, the surges coming at the end of each verse, as the bass of David Hayes pushes the song up onto the next time round, the next level up.

By the time Morrison's vocal comes in at 0.35, a musical feel has already been deftly established, one that is both measured and possessed of an urgency, of pressing on. The sound of that vocal is of interest in itself, aside from the lyric; sounding somewhat muffled, it recalls the onstage moments where Morrison has sung through a harmonica mike or has wrapped his hand around the ball of the mike to focus the sound, shutting out residual resonance. The impact of this close-miking (which is more a convention of the live stage than the studio) is that it conveys an intimacy and a proximity to the listener – it sounds like the voice is being poured into your ear, and, while feeling physically closer, is also less intelligible. We are responding to the feel as much as to the sense of what is being said. Lyrically, it employs and renews some of Van Morrison's key lyrical vocabularies and distils the image of the wet garden into a moment of crystalline clarity. The juxtaposition of the image of the garden seems key, for preceding the title phrase in the lyric come moments of change, continuity, danger, safety, ambiguity, certitude. The lyric carries eight verses which index this see-sawing that later reveals itself to be both linear and circular in motion. The final section of the lyric takes the song on to the meditative stage, giving some kind of breakthrough into wisdom and vision where the polarities of the verses are superseded, yet also somehow retained in a wholeness, and held together within a bigger vision of how things are. That insight, contained powerfully within the 'No Guru' phrase which gives the album its title, can only be arrived at via the journey which it takes to arrive at it – that is, a straight road which leads you back to where you started, arriving quite changed by the journey.

The sound of the track contributes to this – the ambient sound-spaces between the instruments are not incidental. They are constructive elements in building the mood, and the state of mind represented by the track; it takes and costs something to get to the 'No Guru' moment. Yet within this conclusive section it seems there is a paradox – 'No Guru, No Method, No Teacher' but not 'No Father, No Son, No Holy Ghost'. Rather, the Holy Trinity seem part of this new level of consciousness, and he seeks to try to keep the scene clear of the obstacles in the way, in an apparent reduction that is actually a distillation. As he later points out in 'Thanks For The Information', this doesn't always work, and he has often been vexed and frustrated after a promising start – 'I don't wanna quibble over insignificant details / And I've tried every trick in the book . . . Every time I'm ready for a major breakthrough / I always have to think in terms of better or worse'.[8] This entrapment within these polarities, binaries which are both antagonistic and mimetic, is a source of frustration – like seeing the sky above but not being able to get the roof open, or being trapped under the ice. It seems the image of the garden provides Morrison with a metaphor that becomes the thing itself – the 'place' in which such a breakthrough can be facilitated, and can actually occur. So the garden can represent a moment, as envisaged in 'Coney Island' or 'Country Fair', in which one can move around and have one's being, but one in which the 'meaning' of everything, every gesture, every movement has changed. This is something like allegorical landscapes in paintings, such as Bosch's *Garden of Earthly Delights* (1503), the triptych structure of which emphasises the three-part unity to which Morrison alludes to in his Father-Son-Holy Ghost trinity here.

In theological terms the song is making a strong distinction between the pathways of getting to the 'Garden' and the actual place itself. Whatever names or methods we might concoct are human stabs in the dark – the failure or indeed success of any of these does not alter the fact of the Father, Son and Holy Ghost; these are in themselves non-denominational allusions, because it is the spirit rather than the 'brand' that endures. Yet this is not easy. Speaking at Coleraine with Morrison in 1988, Derek Bell said:

> 'Van says there's no guru, no method, no path . . . that would send me to chaos as I'm not as clever as him . . . I prefer to have a Guru, to have a path, to have a method so at least I can fail at something and know I've failed, whereas if I have no method I'll be in chaos, I won't know if I'm getting anywhere or not!'[9]

Morrison, and the audience, laughed very fondly at Bell's sense of amused outrage; he pursues that from which Morrison apparently flies, yet the two shared an ambition towards the same eventual insight. Morrison then went over to his music stand and played 'In The Garden' accompanied by Bell on piano and Clive Culbertson on bass. This most hushed and seemingly studio-bound number was getting into its stride as an unexpectedly central part of Morrison's live performances. It became one of the key numbers in his set over the next decade, a set-closer in the manner of 'Summertime In England' or 'Cyprus Avenue', and while on *A Night In San Francisco* it retained some the melodic and ambient space of the studio version (finding room for a nod to 'Danny Boy', courtesy of Kate St. John 0.05–25), it was taken at a breathtaking full-pelt. This dual identity for the song connects with both senses of the actual and metaphorical meanings of the garden as a space – an intensely personal image of creation, and a theatre of expression and contemplation, but one which is entirely manifest and public, occupying real, material space.

What distinguishes the recorded version's finale is the last few seconds, where the track takes on a remarkable, physical aspect. The final segment stretches out, like limbs in afternoon sunshine, like a body which has been still, asleep, dreaming or in meditation, now stretching, waking up, coming back to the world of manifest physical reality; the sense of the body awakened yet transformed is remarkable and almost visible to the mind's eye. Effectively this is the close of the meditative process through which Morrison has tried to guide the song, and the listener; it is time to return to the real world, subtly changed by the memory of this experience.

There is a comparable transposition in 'Alan Watts Blues', another song that describes what the process of meditation actually feels like, and what happens after:

Well I'm waiting in the clearing, with my motor on
Well it's time to get back to the town again
Where the air is sweet and fresh in the countryside
Well it won't be long till I'll be back here again[10]

Yet 'In The Garden' seems a more powerful and potent piece in the sense that the foggy mountain top, which provides the setting for 'Alan Watts Blues' ('Cloud hidden / Whereabouts unknown'), is more remote, and harder to picture, in every sense. Human drama plays itself out in the garden, as a balance between natural and man-made worlds. The garden is an image of both allegorical gravity and absolute free space, symbolic of both exile and return, betrothal and betrayal, openness and closure, and Morrison's quietly powerful evocations of the garden introduce these rich moods into his work.

WHEN THE LEAVES COME FALLING DOWN: THE 'LEAF SONGS'

Morrison's symbolic methodologies, such as that of the garden, are not self-conscious song cycles in the manner of Jimmie Rodgers' 'Blue Yodels' (13 songs all dealing with more risqué subjects than his mainstream material). They are closer to a natural and naturalised outflow of imagery that speaks to him through the channelling cipher of the image itself, and a key example of this is the falling leaf. There is a strong tradition of the 'leaf song' within all popular song, of course: think of a well-known example such as Joseph Kosma and Johnny Mercer's 'Autumn Leaves', recorded by everyone from Louis Prima to Eva Cassidy: 'I miss you most my darling when autumn leaves start to fall'.[11] Mercer's 1947 lyric was actually a translation from a French original, 'Les feuilles mortes' ('Dead Leaves'), composed by Kosma and Jacques Prévert for the 1946 film *Les Ports de la Nuit* starring Yves Montand, and then featured in *Hey Boy! Hey Girl!*, eventually, like 'White Christmas', getting a film to itself, 1956's *Autumn Leaves*. Prima's version with Keely Smith would almost certainly have been known to Morrison. Indeed, 'I Need Your Kind Of Loving', a sweet, overlooked song (originally demoed in the late 60s) that closes *Hymns To The Silence*, almost directly quotes from Mercer's lyric:

Well I love you in the wintertime
Baby when the snow is on the ground
Well I love you in the autumn most of all
When the leaves come tumbling down
When the leaves come tumbling down[12]

Morrison's work is, appropriately, littered with leaf songs, and they are both related to his own intuitive interest in the cycle of the year, and connected to a long-standing poetic motif. The most famous example in English literature is probably provided by John Keats in his ode 'To Autumn' of 1819, and Morrison described his own 'Autumn Song' as 'just an ode to autumn'[13], clearly tying his own work to the older tradition. Whether we choose to contemplate John Keats or John Mercer is a matter of mood I suppose, but in Morrison's leaf songs we find evidence of his interest in both: distinctions between the high cultural standing of Romantic poetry and the relatively low cultural status of the popular song are dissolved, entirely unforcedly, by Morrison's connection to both traditions.

So the leaf songs are both the growing points of certain artistic responses to the world and also innovative in their newness and recontextualisations of both that tradition and the possibilities of the popular song. The mix of the blues and traditions of nature poetry from a culture where, in September, the leaves come falling down is something which comes from him, while he is describing what everyone, were they so minded, could describe. As he says himself in 'A Sense Of Wonder', 'It's easy to describe the leaves in the autumn'.[14] Keats wondered out loud 'where are the songs of Spring? Ay, where are they?',[15] and they can indeed be found on *Hard Nose The Highway*, in a neat balancing act in the tender, hopeful and elegiac 'Wild Children', where Morrison's childhood is connected with a time and place 'Where the springtime rivers flow'.[16] This comes alongside 'Autumn Song', the warm-hearted jazz five-step which initially seeks to do for that season what Mel Torme and Bob Wells's 'The Christmas Song' does for Yuletide, and then stretches out into a remarkable improvised section which occupies over half the track, eventually reaching a state of blissful peace and stillness, expressed as 'I'm transcending myself, child', a phrase which would unexpectedly reappear in the poetic sleeve note of 2009's *Astral Weeks Live*.[17]

Indeed the days of leaves seem to enable Morrison to better connect with his key theme of memory, particularly in *A Sense Of Wonder*, the cover art for which is strewn with leaves, and in the title track's lyric, set in 'the days of the leaves'. In the lyric he says he could describe the leaves, and promptly does it, the vision emphasised by the autumnal colours detailed: 'Rich, red browney, half burnt orange and green'.[18] There is a sly joke for Northern Irish listeners here – the painterly 'burnt orange' is also a reference to the delicious, warming and strangely exotic pudding of Burnt Oranges, a wintertime warmer in Belfast kitchens, and as redolent of home as the barmbrack mentioned in the same song's recitation. Orange and green are also, of course, Ireland's colours. Thus the registers of memory, time and identity sublimate in the image of the leaves, both bearing and representing this sense of wonder.

The summative leaf song emerged on 1999's *Back On Top*, in the shape of 'When The Leaves Come Falling Down'. The album art again foregrounds the autumnal theme, with insert and photography being presented in russet shades resembling a glossier version of the *Sense of Wonder* design. This song directly and explicitly centres the image of the falling leaf, and the sense that it is in the open air where life is experienced most intensely.

> I saw you standing with the wind and the rain in your face
> And you were thinking 'bout the wisdom of the leaves and their grace
> When the leaves come falling down
> In September, when the leaves come falling down[19]

The song pulls together forces of nature (the wind and the rain) but also human projective reasoning (the wisdom of the leaves): as in his version of Patrick Kavanagh's 'Raglan Road', the environment both reflects and is transformed by the interpretative encounter with it that the song represents. Instead of being part of a broader pattern of allusion, this song foregrounds the image of the falling leaf. Here they are a sign not only that a season cycle has come to its close, but also that the time has come for these things to happen – a kind of imaginative cue for living in a more awakened state. While the references to the moon connect the theme to 'Moondance' ('And the leaves on the trees are falling / To the sound of the breezes that blow) the leaves here are considered both as prompts to understanding ('the wisdom of the leaves') and as elements within a still life: 'And as I'm looking at the colour of the leaves in your hand'. There are appeals to all the senses: 'I'm thinking, I'm looking, I'm listening' all occur in response to a contemplation of the leaves. The song's bridges echo the deliberately pastoral setting of 'Haunts Of Ancient Peace' ('beside the garden wall' being reimagined as 'the place between the garden and the wall . . . the space between the twilight and the dawn'), but here the setting shifts, from the garden to (in an unexpected leap) the beach. The song, suddenly dislocated from the leafy glade, seems at least to have located itself. The sheer abundance of references to leaves in this song of course suggests the autumnal fall in composite, leaves falling like rain. The final dislocation to the beach is like the disturbance of a waking dream – the final dream-logic image of regarding the colour of the leaves is supplanted by listening to Chet Baker on the beach.

Baker didn't rate Morrison as a singer, as it happens, but Morrison clearly didn't bear a grudge, as far as the music went. The song itself bears some of Baker's influence, being a slow, spacious jazz ballad, missing a trumpet, it's true, but possessed of a high and melancholic melody, driven by the mellifluous piano of Fiachra Trench, whose string arrangement also brings much grace to the song, and the imperceptibly consistent notes from Geraint Watkins on the Hammond. The quiet determination of these elements characterises the song and this mix of resolve and melancholia reflects the image of the falling leaf perfectly; faced with the evidence what we do is to go on; here we hear Beckett's 'I can't go on, I'll go on'.[20] On this album, 'Reminds Me Of You' represents the 'I can't go on' (as summer often does in Morrison: 'Now it's the summer, I can't stand it') whereas this song represents the 'I'll go on', with autumn representing a toughening up of the will and the resolve to survive. The repetition of 'follow me down' with the modal uplift on the final 'down' of the three suggests continuity and redemption, something that persists beyond its apparent demise, in the ambiguous image of the falling leaf. Kavavagh said 'let grief be a falling leaf' but here Morrison is not surrounded by grief, he is crowded round by possibility, and the leaves are contemplative prompts to action, each and every one.

THE HEALING GAME

A time to kill and a time to heal.

Ecclesiastes 3.3; Pete Seeger/
The Byrds: 'Turn! Turn! Turn!'[21]

What does Van Morrison mean when he is writing and singing about healing? It is by no means a subject limited to Morrison's personalised expressive vocabulary: we can find examples in any CD store discs designed to relax, the use of Mozart in therapy sessions or ante-natal clinics is commonplace and the ritual and shamanistic use of music in medicine has been well documented. So there is this literal use of the term to consider, and it is certainly part of Morrison's deeper interest in music, its nature and its 'secret power'.[22] Alongside this is a less esoteric meaning, one which draws directly on the plain fact that listening to music can act as a restorative, or as a tonic, and as a resource for the survival of dark times: music can make you feel *better*. Indeed, it is arguable that much music is borne out of those very circumstances, as a response to them – an act of life and of energy and of persistence. This is both the root and use of the blues, for example. This is a very old idea: Morrison has simply found his way to the same seam of understanding via his own path, represented by his work. Morrison has put 'healing' into the title of four songs: 1979's 'And The Healing Has Begun', 1987's 'Did Ye Get Healed?', 1993's less successful 'Till We Get The Healing Done', and finally on to the summative song of this theme, 1997's 'The Healing Game'. In 1979 Morrison spoke to Chris Welch:

> 'Music is like a healing thing, and we're all being healed. I'm being healed. That's what I know, what I feel. It's what I'm going through and we all go through. Any kind of art or music is involved in healing, whether it's rock 'n' roll or classical music, it's all healing. People go to a rock and roll show and they come away feeling better. All this is just the foreground, but the background is something else.'[23]

Clearly this idea of the use of music, of 'feeling better', was central to Morrison's methodology, at least in 1979, and his willingness to ignore the business-driven issues of genre and classification ('Any kind of art or music is involved in healing') opens the subject up and places his interest in it into a much wider context.

Once foregrounded, healing became a coherent and conscious strand in Morrison's work and his ambitions for it – the idea clearly has significance for his view of the meaning and uses of music. Arguably, his remarkable creative run from 1979 to 1988 drew very strongly on this idea of music as physic. *Irish Heartbeat*, Morrison's 1988 album with the Chieftains, can be seen to bring this run to an end, and evidence in itself of a kind of healing, of his art going back to its preconscious source, in the collective unconscious of the folk tune. The album before this, *Poetic Champions Compose*, carried the next explicit foregrounding of the theme, this time asking a retrospective question, 'Did Ye Get Healed?', in contrast to the annunciatory, epic pastoral of 'And The Healing Has Begun'.[24] This is a very compact, managed and concise sound, its brightly metronomic rhythm allowing all the elements – voice, sax, brass (featuring some lovely Bacharach/Alpert trumpet at the close), piano, organ – to stand clean and clear of each other while forming a very satisfyingly unified thought. The song exists as a series of questions, addressed by the singer to the listener, but also to himself, with the song functioning as a tool of self-analysis. Morrison is always looking for some indication of how the 'spirit moves him', not out of narcissism but out of a sense that it is himself that he is best qualified to judge. So the set of enquires in the lyric of 'Did Ye Get Healed?' are matched with the urgency and buoyancy of the recent convert, a zealous energy and need to share what has been found. The musical directness and focus of the song and its arrangement is testament to this desire for clarity. The lyric suggests that when you get it down in your soul 'it makes you feel good / And it makes you feel whole'. It is connecting the sensual ('feel') with the spiritual ('in your soul'), yoking the physical with the metaphysical in a single, simple, direct musical image. It's a remarkable achievement in such an apparently modest song.[25]

Too Long In Exile (1993) featured his least well-known 'healing' song, 'Till We Get The Healing Done', a disappointing mid-point delivering little of Morrison's 'background'. It opens with words he will later employ in 'The Healing Game': 'Down those old ancient streets / Down those old ancient roads',[26] suggesting that this song is evidence of a struggle towards expression which was evasive. It's on the road. So when 1997's 'The Healing Game' arrived we feel how it builds on this failure, establishing from the start where he is, and where he needs to be in order to get the healing done – on the corner, in the backstreet. The video clip for the song makes the point in a manner both clear and curious – Morrison is shown on the streets of East Belfast, but they are strangely empty, almost like a film set. He is dressed in the *Godfather* garb seen on the sleeve of the parent album, back where he belongs, but he appears there as something of an exotic, like one of the late Guy Peellaert's *Rock Dreams*.

Opening with the righteous Hammond, the vocal attests the main point of the song: that the author is back on the corner again, but what is key is the assertion that these places are a kind of eternal now: 'Everything's the same . . . It'll never change . . . Where I've always been . . . Never been away / From the healing game.'[27] This is in direct contravention of one of the rules of rock culture, which is about restlessness, the flight from the source, and about leaving home. Morrison of course was wholly beguiled by these possibilities when he was right to be – leaving Ireland to go to Germany, then to London, then to America. The healing comes from the completion of the circle; after all that, he's back on the corner again – it hasn't changed but he has, and in those changes he has discovered his roots and his way of belonging. 'The Healing Game' is very deliberately constructed to suggest both his roots and the roots of the music in the way it incorporates elements of blues and doo-wop (street music, redolent of creativity beyond the strictures of the music industry), alongside an acknowledgement of the role of church music in both traditions, via the church-organ ambience of the Hammond and references to the church choir. The lyrics refer to both when 'the choir boys sing' and when 'the home boys sing', and this lyrical correspondence finds a musical match too: Brian Kennedy is at his most resonantly angelic from 1.18 to the drum-break at 1.48, while there is a doo-wop choir (again featuring Kennedy) from 2.35–50. Mixing the two types of choir – that of the church and, in his own phrase, the street choir of the doo-wop chorus – makes explicit the twin forms of praise, and also thereby the duality of the road to healing here. After all, the repeated line as it builds to its brassy climax is '*Sing* the healing game' (my italics) – he couldn't really be clearer. It is in the singing that the healing comes. Holding the two traditions together in this way – street music and church music – both reveals their common root and Morrison's rich delight in both.

Morrison's restless relationship with the song – he has recorded the tune several times over, with John Lee Hooker and the Chieftains – suggests that the song has never quite assumed the right shape to properly express itself. In the latter version the uilleann pipes of Paddy Maloney ground the song in

Irish traditions, its acoustic surfaces connecting it strongly to street tradition which extends back beyond the 1950s or doo-wop and into a deeper shared past, invoked and reinvigorated here. It seemed right that this version should appear on the benefit album for the victims of the Omagh bombing, *Across The Bridge Of Hope*, to somehow aid the healing how it could.[28]

ON A GOLDEN AUTUMN DAY

'On a golden autumn day', unlike 'healing' or 'silence', is a coinage quite specific to Morrison's terminology. It is heard in 'Tir Na Nog', 'Orangefield', 'The Waiting Game', 'Raincheck', and the summative song 'Golden Autumn Day' itself, as well as cropping up in the call-and-response section of live versions of 'Summertime In England' in the 80s and 90s. It's a key image in Morrison's creative, emotional and stylistic vocabulary, unlocking the door to creativity and to the inner space which then opens up beyond the self-reflexive terminologies into the realm of art – that is, the inner space made public by being remade, connected to traditional models of creativity while simultaneously confounding and refreshing those methods.

This phrase seems so integrated into Morrison's symbolic vocabulary that it sounds and feels as though it is a phrase that has informed his work almost since the very beginning, but its first studio incarnation is in a verse deep into 'Tir Na Nog', on 1986's *No Guru, No Method, No Teacher*: 'We made a big connection / On a golden autumn day'.[29] 'Orangefield' begins with the phrase and by 1989 it had acquired the status of a mood-setter, as a kind of intensified signifier or shorthand for a certain kind of journey that the song is going to undertake with and on behalf of both its author and the listener: we pick up the signal and listen accordingly. The song begins with a single note plucked on an electric guitar set to an acoustic mute, giving the singer the note. He picks it up and runs with it: 'On a golden autumn day'.[30] The glow from this opening image colours the whole of the landscape, both emotional and physical, that the song traverses.

The summative song arrived on 1999's *Back On Top*, and is a vexatious creature: if we imagined that it would function after the fashion of 'In The Garden' in drawing together the multiple strands of the image into a single dazzling beam of light, we are brought up short, for it is among the strangest songs in Morrison's repertoire. It begins as a dead ringer for the same album's 'Philosopher's Stone', and Morrison's vocal has the clarity as well as the nervous tightness of someone approaching a self-confession, a man gearing himself up to look in the mirror and anticipating a flinch at what he sees. This honesty sets the tone. In the first verse he speaks of having fallen very publicly from grace, but the consequence of that is that he wants to get back in the game, the game of the human race, and also to 'get on with the show', a phrase that re-emerged as a song title at the close of 2003's pugnacious *What's Wrong With This Picture?*[31] The mood thus swings from shame to tentative optimism within the first verse and as it tips into the chorus, the melody releases the tight knot of tension built up by the sinewy verse. The title phrase seems, as we might expect, to provide the final moment of release. Later, images of being assaulted by thugs in a dimly lit town sit beside allusions to Blake (the town has 'dark satanic mills') – there is nothing 'golden' or even faintly illuminated about the world as presented here.

The break from 2.51, with its anxiously pitched harmonica solo up to 3.32 where it yields to Pee Wee Ellis's stout sax solo, matches these two musical voices with the uncertainties of the lyric in a way which both grounds the tune but allows it to proceed along this path of uncertainty – pools of light between the spots of darkness. The real musical innovation in the track, which suggests the victory of the imagined ('pretended') version of the world over the 'real' as it is presented to us, is the fade-out of all other instruments, leaving only Fiachra Trench's string arrangement, present throughout but here uncovered and revealed in all its thoughtful beauty. It is a simple melodic line of only seven strokes but its persistence beyond the fade of the rest of the track concludes the track in a mood appropriate to the rest of it – cautiously, realistically optimistic. Trench told me that this was the only time in their working relationship that Morrison had asked him to change what he had arranged for the strings: 'he wanted a darker sound from the strings, so we augmented the cellos',[32] and that darkening colours and reflects the mood of the song in every sense. The co-present duality in the song lyrically played out through the contrast between the 'dimly lit town' and the 'golden autumn day' is illustrated musically by the bright darkness of the cellos in Trench's coda.

The song is undoubtedly bizarre, and a wholly unpredictable shape for a summative song for one of his most evocative phrases, but it shows levelheaded, fearless realism about his own work and his relationship to it and in that sense the use of the phrase to frame this song is wholly appropriate. The musical echo of 'Philosopher's Stone', that self-portrait of the artist as itinerant worker as well as seeker of answers to deep mysteries, is appropriate because this song presents the other side of that dynamic: an image of dealing with the world as it is, rather than how we would prefer to see it being.[33]

ALL ON DOWN THE ANCIENT HIGHWAY

Another phrase Morrison has continually returned to, and which like 'the golden autumn day' is quite particular to him, is 'the ancient highway', hinted at in the 'The Healing Game', which talks of ancient streets and ancient roads.

Somewhat surprisingly, the first mention of this phrase comes not in one of his late songs but instead via Bert Berns's sleeve note for 1967's *Blowin' Your Mind!*:

> Van Morrison . . . turbulent . . . today . . . inside . . . a multi-coloured window through which one views at times himself and his counterself. Van Morrison . . . erratic and painful . . . whose music expresses the now!! The right now of his own road, his ancient highway.[34]

Even in the giddiness of 1967, that phrase 'ancient highway' must have struck the purchaser of *Blowin' Your Mind!* as an unusual one. It's an odd, remarkable piece of writing, and one composed, we must remember, if not before rock and roll, then certainly before *Astral Weeks*, *Moondance* and all the rest, showing at the very least an impressive, even uncanny prescience. So what does Berns mean by 'ancient highway' and where did the phrase come from – from Morrison himself or from some shared source?

In terms of prosaic application, the term is an established and non-poetic one in the descriptive terminology of local governance in the UK: it refers to a track, trail or a known route which has been in existence prior to 1835. That's not so long ago. For example, Pall Mall in London follows the line of an ancient highway that stretched from Charing Cross to St. James's Palace.[35] The point being, the ancient streets and the ancient roads are under our feet, criss-crossing what appear to be our fixed navigational material realities, hidden but perceptible. Thus the ancient highway becomes an image of an emotional remapping of territory, one which reconnects with the spirit of place implicit in the present moment and state of affairs. Berns's note implies that Morrison is attentive to this hidden reality and is minded to track, follow and explore it.

Whatever the source, the phrase has become a key part of Morrison's symbolic vocabulary. Michelle Rocca asked him about the key song 'Ancient Highway' in the 1995 *Days Like This* promotional interview:

> MR: Your song "Ancient Highway" . . . What mood were you trying to evoke in this song?
>
> VM: It was getting out of the rat race. It's sort of like . . . It relates to one of my . . . Well another song I wrote, you see, it keeps coming back to patterns again. I wrote a song called "Alan Watts Blues" and it's sort of relatable to that song. It's about just trying to get out of the rat race, basically.
>
> MR: There's a Ray Charles feel to it.
>
> VM: Yeah, well the closest I can get, there's a picture in, oddly enough, in a book

called, um, I hate the term, but "Rock Dreams." It's paintings of . . . loads of people. There's a painting of Ray Charles in a car, driving through the desert. And it's called "The Fugitive's Dream" or something like this.[36]

Morrison may not like the title of Guy Peellaert's famed book, but it connects to the dominant theme of motion, of being on the road, and in transit. Morrison's habitual deflection up towards Ray Charles is charmingly manifest here – 'well the closest I can get' – yet of course Brother Ray never sang of the ancient highway or the mystic or the garden in the way that Morrison has. The younger man has developed this signature lexicon to approach 'the Ray Charles feel' it seems, so that the spirit of the inspiration is running through everything, even when the musical surfaces seem to have little direct correspondence.

The ancient highway may be a road that many have taken before him but it is also near-allegorical in its particular references, a road which is universal but also of one's own making. It appeared first as an integral phrase two decades after Berns's use of it on the *Blowin' Your Mind!* sleeve notes, in 1986's 'A Town Called Paradise', a song which very deliberately uses the recognisable rhythmic tug of the song 'Astral Weeks', suggesting kinship between the two songs and the moods they represent. The listener is drawn into the allegorical landscape of the song after the fashion of Florentine painting, realistic depictions which are also a metaphorical remapping of the familiar. Thus the hills and roads and plains and towns become images of what lies beyond their structures and material realities, even while they are faithfully representing those realities. This is the role of the ancient highway, to provide a link between the 'forgotten' reality and the present material circumstances, which of course are much harder to read as representative. 'A Town Called Paradise' describes and proposes a journey, and the ancient highway leads both to and from the town called paradise. The song's closing section is where this idea seems to approach a partial fulfilment, if not full resolution: at 4.18–23, comes the line 'All along the ancient highway', almost swallowed up in the growing harmonic clamour of the song's finale. At 4.37, he sings 'By the river, we will linger', and directly at 4.42 the horn section's upward movement through the chart pauses for the first time, lingering as the forward motion of the song's narrative lingers. As he cries 'paradise!' at 5.37, trumpets cascade down to the fade, the song disappearing over the backlit hills of this transfigured landscape.[37]

By the time 'Ancient Highway' itself arrived in 1995, it was a phrase easily recognised by the frequent concert-goer: indeed the song is a working summation of a whole slew of his touchstone phrases and images. The piece – a single take improvisation in Wool Hall – pulls us back to the town called paradise, matching the mythologized landscape with that of the real in East Belfast:

In a town called Paradise near the ancient highway
When the train whistle blows
All the sadness that Hank Williams knows
And the river flows
Call them pagan streams and it spins and turns
In a factory in a street called Bread in East Belfast
Where Georgie knows best
What it's like to be Daniel in the lion's den
Got so many friends only most of the time[38]

This single verse contains references to at least four other Morrison songs yet no-one could criticise this song for the lack of something new to say. Indeed novelty is not the point; like Beckett, Morrison periodically returns to his touchstone images to try and restate them in his new circumstance. 'Ancient Highway' provides then not only the 'summative' song, as per our sequence, but a kind of condensed gathering together of central yet elusive images, filing past our field of vision like the ghosts in Macbeth's vision on the heath.[39] Somehow, it seems, they are all connected to this image of the ancient highway. The song sees the mythological landscape and the real one almost as one and the same, akin to the connection between body and soul, the material world and the spiritual. One is implicit in the other, and the image of the ancient highway connects them. The musical mood, flowing from the 40 seconds of Miles-style trumpet that opens the song, expresses this feeling of high perception, with a tone both grounded and direct but also fragmented and dreamlike in its connective structures. In this sense, 'Ancient Highway' is perhaps Morrison's most successful summative song, by dint of its retaining a kind of runic, unresolved mystery.

So while images like the ancient highway are highly rarefied compressions of very personalised references which admit and transmit meaning via associative means within the wider symbolic system that Morrison employs, the very nature of the widely commodified and distributed nature of his recordings means that they become shared with and part of the expressive vocabularies of the audience, as well as the artist. Thus the intensely personal image – the ancient highway, the garden wet with rain, the golden autumn day – becomes part of a public system of understanding and mapping of realities.

YA RADIO

In Morrison's work, the radio is always a positive presence. In comparison, other mediating technologies are regarded with suspicion – computers, mobile phones and the internet have been scorned, and television, even when he is appearing on it, seems particularly deceptive: 'You see me baby, up there on the screen' he laments in 'I'm Not Feeling It Anymore', inferring that almost by definition television misrepresents and is not to be trusted. Likewise his rap in 'See Me Through Part II (Just A Closer Walk With Thee)', suggests that life was somehow 'better' when there was 'no television'. Hence when on the *Saturday Night Live* NBC special on 4 November 1978 Van Morrison added 'coming out of Frankfurt-am-Main' to the 'Voice of America' line in 'Wavelength', the title track of his then-current album, he was dropping radio into the TV, connecting to his memory of the 'Voice of America' as the 'real' radio station he had in mind, rather than any more metaphorical interpretation, and flagging up a familiarity with the roll call of the faraway and exotic locations of the dial-tuning plate on vintage radio sets.

In her book *Glamour: A World Problem*, Alice Bailey writes the following about telepathy:

> It is necessary for all those isolated disciples working in every country in the world to become aware of each other and then to enter into telepathic rapport. This may seem to you a beautiful but impractical vision. I assure you that this is not so.[40]

Morrison found his way to Bailey's work in the late 70s and early 80s, as the several borrowings or 'rub-offs' from her work into his on the *Beautiful Vision* album of 1981 show – indeed one is contained in the short paragraph quoted above. Morrison's interest in, and the importance of, radio to his childhood and absorption of music, and his later interest in esoteric spiritual theory, are not as far apart as they would at first seem.

Morrison's first exposures to popular song were distinctive in that (in post-war Britain at least) the era seemed the cultural tipping-point between music being something people played with and for each other – in Theodor Adorno's phrase, 'a form of social cement'[41] – and the coming deluge of music pouring into the home in recorded form, be it on discs by an identified artist with whom one could develop a form of relationship, or over the airwaves via the radio. The development of popular music radio was key to the widening distribution of and familiarity with popular musics from a vast range of sources. The bulk of pop music radio, of course, played American music, and the young enthusiasts on the receiving end picked up on the signal, and took what they heard, or thought they'd heard, and made something fresh from it, eventually finding like-minded fellow-listeners.

Radio Luxembourg is cited in two Van Morrison songs but the ghost of the influence of this and other such precious resources is spread far more widely across his work than this. The station began in 1933, and was immediately notable for its wide-ranging musical selections, juxtaposing supposedly high and low styles to great effect. Silenced under Nazi occupation of the Grand Duchy, it began broadcasting again in 1946, to the war children. It proved to be central to the musical development of that generation, and the explosion of British popular music in the 60s. Mo Foster's brilliant book *Play Like Elvis!: How British Musicians Bought the American Dream* explains a little more:

> By the mid 1950's, Radio Luxembourg was transmitting on medium wave, on its now famous 208-metre wavelength, and started the first ever Top 20 chart show, which was then based solely on the sales of sheet music rather than records . . . Listeners would suffer frustration at the constant fading and phasing, which seemed to permeate at least a couple of verses' worth of each record . . . nevertheless, most listeners found the compression and fading quite magical, certainly in hindsight.[42]

Foster is spot-on; part of the pleasure of listening to Radio Luxembourg was indeed the fading away and the coming back, and the sense of connection that gave. As he says, the eccentric reception most small radios gave brought a character to the broadcasts and 'certainly in hindsight' this effect is a great part of how the station is recalled. These are the swooshing noises that Morrison recreates on 'Wavelength' and 'In The Days Before Rock And Roll', giving perfect examples of Foster's 'hindsight'. As Jeff Beck has said:

> 'Radio Luxembourg was one of those stations that you could just tune into, as if it was coming from the far-flung regions of Africa or something, but it was only in Luxembourg. And it was all muffled and indistinct, and you had to strain your ears so much to hear the guitar.'[43]

Beck's observation about it being 'only in Luxembourg' shows us something of how the world shrank between 1955 and 2000, for him, at the very least, but here there is still that mystery, the obscurity of source and that hard-won pleasure in actually *listening* ('you had to strain your ears so much') to the sounds coming through the radio set.

The frequency with which Morrison alludes to the radio in his work as an agent of communication, of information and of deliverance is if nothing else an index of its importance to him and its formative influence in how he understood the world and the nature of relations. It is of course an excellent metaphor, attentive to an unseen system of connections between apparently dispersed and wholly unconnected individuals. It stands for a world we cannot see, but one which is plainly manifest at the listening point of the loudspeaker, and hints at possibilities of communication and contact even under conditions of physical separation.

Paul Durcan's recitation of a list of place names during 'In The Days Before Rock And Roll', familiar from an old radio tuning panel dial, is read as a roll of honour, or as a much-cherished catechism, a mantra for the imagination when the places, distant from each other as well as from the listener, were gathered together by the mediating technology: Hilversum, Budapest, Athlone, Helvetia. These names ring with evocations of mystery, of other ways of living and being, coming over the airwaves, fading in and out, going away and coming back – rhythms that find emotional equivalence in the lyrical pulses of Morrison's songs: they go out, and they come back. The opening sound effects on 'Wavelength' itself seek to recreate the beauty and internal logic of this white noise, from which music and voices would emerge and into which they would once again fade. That ebb and flow, impossible (in every sense) on a DAB radio, brought something other than irritation to the listener; it taught the listener to *listen*. Morrison clearly remembered that static very well; in live performances of the song at the time when this intro was retained (it was later dropped, kicking straight into the up-tempo main body of the song) he did the fizzing himself. The intro's structure reflected the experience of listening to the radio in this way – the slow section or the static gives way, gradually, like a signal surging through more strongly again, to the main song. The full-on up-tempo melody reflects the signal being locked on to, and fully tuned in; these terms are now deeply entrenched in common parlance for general understanding and communication but stem from the popular common experience of early radio listening. As the lyric says, happily developing the metaphor: 'And I can get your station / When I need rejuvenation'.[44]

There is also the sense that the radio/other is a source of pleasure that does not fail or tire – 'You never let me down, no' – and in that sense 'Wavelength' is something more than a song about the wireless, with a metaphoric twist. It is more a hymn of praise for the support and tireless succour given by the radio: is the 'you' of the song a lover or the radio set? Yet it also stands as a love song to the medium itself – read it without recourse to metaphor with this in mind and the importance and centrality of radio is revealed. The ethereal nature of the radio signal ('You are everywhere you're supposed to be') can also of course be read as being directed to a lover or to a creative spirit, omniscient and benign.

After the faded-in sound effect suggestive of the noises heard when tuning an analogue radio set, moving up and down the wavebands, the purpose of the song is announced unambiguously and immediately: 'This is a song about your wavelength / And my wavelength, baby'. We note the emphasis on the shared subject. The self-consciousness of process here is a soft surprise, and is delightful. The focus then switches to the nature of the relationship between the narrator and the subject, and the transmitter/receiver roles are purposely overlapping and unascribed. He employs a light pun, echoing Joni Mitchell's own glance at this dynamic, 'You Turn Me On, I'm A Radio', a hit in 1972,[45] in the following line: 'You turn me on / When you get me on your wavelength'. Later in live performance Morrison changed this to the more successful 'My heart is strong / When you get me on your wavelength', as can be heard on the 1980 Montreux DVD.

The vigour described, and melodically reinforced, suggests that it is the flow between the two 'points' that is the source of the heart's strength – the dynamic between them is what makes it work, receiving and transmitting being sublimated into something like what Olaf Stapledon called 'radio-bliss'.[46] This 'bliss', blame for which is placed squarely at the feet of 'your wavelength', is then articulated in a rhetorical articulation entirely characteristic of Morrison's most intuitive work, with a form of improvised scatting which doesn't just 'describe' the feeling, but somehow also *is* the feeling. The repetitions 'Oh mama, oh mama, oh mama, oh mama' render the potentially banal deeply expressive. Morrison's falsetto carries the song over this intro, and its unusual, light and 'other-worldly' quality gives this segment much of its ethereal buoyancy. As the song surges into its more up-tempo main body, its weightlessness passes into something more physically present and responsive to gravity – yet the feeling keeps him up there – the double meaning of 'You never let me down, no, no' keeps this feeling of lightness afloat. When the rhythm section kicks in and grounds the sound, as noted, it's like the signal from a far off transmitter gradually acquiring full clarity once again. For the corpus of the song Morrison drops back down to his normal, 'earthly' register.

The radio often accompanies such moments of happiness in Morrison's catalogue – in 'Brown Eyed Girl', 'Going down the old mine with a transistor radio', or in 'Caravan', 'Turn up your radio, and letta me hear the song', with the added intuitive caveat that volume is not placed before feeling: 'Turn it up! That's enough – so you know it's got soul'. 'Wavelength' explores this soulful connection, and Morrison's interest in the radio as an object and also as metaphor for communications and a medium for transmission as well as reception. Likewise the listener hears, actively. It is rarely a passive relationship between signal and receiver, as in 'I can get your station / When I need rejuvenation'.

The radio also provides mediation for the environment in which it's used – a room, a moment, a mood is established or changed by its presence. For example, in 'TB Sheets' the world outside the cool room is admitted via the turning on of a radio and, more happily, in 'Real Real Gone', Sam Cooke is *on the radio*, not on the turntable or the tape deck. That is, Sam Cooke is on the air, in the ether, all around us, in the air we breathe, surrounding and filling the room, and we are suddenly made aware of this – 'And the night is filled with space' – via a sublime cause and effect. The fact of the radio transforms the meaning and perception of the music flowing through it. Morrison's tribute to the power of the radio as metaphor in 'Wavelength' found a correspondence in his remarkable 1990 collaboration with Paul Durcan, 'In The Days Before Rock And Roll'.

Paul Durcan is a poet of the Dublin sort – urbane, dry and acerbic – and in 1988 he published a lengthy appreciation of Van Morrison entitled 'The Drumshanbo Hustler', in which he eulogised the work and argued, not completely unseriously, that it should be taught in schools.[47] He is particularly moved by Morrison's version of Patrick Kavanagh's 'Raglan Road', part of his album with the Chieftains *Irish Heartbeat*. Indeed, he argues that Morrison and Kavanagh are Ireland's foremost poets:

> Van Morrison's rendition of Patrick Kavanagh's "On Raglan Road" is fitting because it brings together the two finest poets in Ireland in my lifetime. No other Irish poets – writing either in verse or in music – have come within a Honda's roar of Kavanagh and Morrison.[48]

He describes how life as a travelling poet is not unlike that of a touring musician and how their work finds echoes in each other – imagining how he'd argue for the value of Morrison's work to the makers of the curriculum, he hazards that:

> Maybe I'd tell them also that I like Morrison because I know that his work comes from the same level as my own poetry – the level of daydreaming; that he's out to annihilate ego; that he's after the same "nothingness" as Kavanagh was after. In this sense, he's really not a poet at all, no more than I am. He's after the musical technique of how to live.[49]

This is a fine and righteous piece of writing but his essay reads partly like a rarefied fan letter and partly like a courting of the musician, slyly proposing collaboration. He finishes the piece by observing that 'I have never met him and I am glad to say that I know little or nothing about his personal life – an achievement in anonymity which is as refreshing as it is inspiring', but within two years he was co-writing with the object of his interest and they were exploring their mutual interests over the extraordinary 8.13 of 'In The Days Before Rock And Roll'.

The track opens on a looping bass line and skipping conga, swooping around the dainty piano playing. Durcan's high, wiry voice comes as a shock, a sinuous texture added to this mellifluous musical mix. I like it; plenty don't. It is curious how often it is revealed that great poets are poor readers – a Dylan Thomas, renowned for his reading almost as much as for his writing, is a rare beast. In a 1946 recording for a set of six 78 rpm discs for HMV, T. S. Eliot made a likeable and self-deprecating remark on his lack of vocal abilities ('I apologise for the lack of drama; I'm working on my delivery'[50]) before reading in a steady, constricted, nasal oratory, thereby drawing attention to the phenomenon of how writing and reading are separate arts, and how their relationship has changed since the advent of print cultures. Durcan very consciously and deliberately 'performs' this piece, his voice swooping up and down, testifying, proclaiming and offering praise via pitch, tone and technique – that is, poetry as it has always truly been sung. It's a vocal performance but it isn't a singer's performance, nor does it need to be – it's a rare thing, a piece of performed poetry, rather than performance poetry.

The narrator finds himself in a position of worship before the radio ('I am down on my knees / At the wireless knobs') seeking a message, seeking some kind of affirmation via the radio signal. The device of 'Justin' seems to me to be an imaginative projection of the younger self, a composite figure who dwells eternally in this 'previous' moment: 'Where's Justin now? / What's Justin doing now? / Justin . . . '. This is a powerful meditation on lost, shed versions of the self, working towards a kind of wholeness where completeness is restored, and this song is somehow a vessel which permits such a journey – hence Morrison's final encouragement and exhortation, to 'Come aboard!' There is a poet's relish for the *sound* of words – 'Telefunken' is rolled around the palate and spat out, likewise the place names, which are actually radio stations (we note the inclusion of AFN (American Forces Network) in the list), and the poem makes the point that the success and distribution of American popular song was both a glorious thing and also one that changed the world. So for Fats, Buddy, Elvis, Lightnin' and the rest to 'come in' (the radio terminology, again) was heavily dependent upon the radio for its impact – it led to the creation of a new kind of community, sharing experiences though separated over time and space. That the singular experience is also a shared one is confirmed by Durcan's unedited remark at the tune's conclusion, 'You've certainly got some beautiful things in there, Van'.[51]

As the song starts to lift towards its finale Morrison begins to extemporise around the theme we recall from 'Wavelength', of the sheer physical pleasure of tuning the radio and listening in to all the sounds it made, be they musical or the crackle of static in the night-time air. Delivering the line 'And we went over the wavebands', he then provides an approximation of the fizzing static familiar from old radio sets, tuning the dial, before settling with delicious satisfaction upon the charmed word 'Luxembourg', repeated twice followed by the next name on the plate, 'and Athlone' (5.00–28). I am reminded of the moment in Chekhov's *Three Sisters* where the youngest, Irina, recites the names of all the names of the metro stations in Moscow, as she dreams of the glamorous life there, far from her pinched provincial life. Morrison's recalled litany of the faraway stations transmitting into the night has a similar lustre: this is a world of promise and possibility, and it is brought into his room by the radio. Yet it is not disruptive in its presence; indeed, in 'On Hyndford Street' the radio seems part of the fabric of the heart of silence itself.

HYMNS TO THE SILENCE

From a platform of large, raised stones
Lines appear to lead us along the hillside . . .
Bog tuft softening beneath each step
Bracken and briar restraining our march
Clawing us back
Slowing us to perception's pace . . .
This is the slope of loneliness
This is the hill of silence . . .
This is the wind's fortress
Our world's Pole Star
A stony patience . . .
Let us also lay ourselves down in the silence
Let us also be healed

John Montague, 'The Hill of Silence'[52]

In the television programme *A Coney Island of the Mind*, John Montague reads this poem to Van Morrison by a lake under the Wicklow mountains, prefacing it by saying:

> 'In ancient Ireland there were four ways of achieving supreme knowledge, and one was the Way of Loneliness, and the second was called the Hill of Silence . . . and I won't tell you about the other two, just to keep you on your toes! . . . the Hill of Silence was a path followed by some of the old Gaelic poets, and it's a way of being healed by nature.'[53]

Montague's connection of silence and healing to the central, 'ancient' themes of Irish poetry connects to the traditions and themes running through Morrison's own work, a link which Morrison was shocked to discover, as he says in the introduction to the programme:

> 'When I started writing songs at a very early age, I didn't have a clue what I was doing. Later on, I tried to connect what I was doing with my contemporaries. I discovered

> however that I was writing what some people call transcendental poetry, others people call it mysticism in poetry, other people call it nature poetry. Why was I writing this kind of material when my contemporaries weren't? So I wanted to find out where I stood and which tradition I came from. Well eventually I found out that the tradition I belonged to was actually my own tradition. It was like being hit over the head with a baseball bat. You find out that what you've been searching for you already are. This writing comes from the places I used to go, for example when I was a kid, the area I was brought up in. The thread took me from there to research poets like Yeats, Keats, Wordsworth and Coleridge, eventually to the Glens Poets of Northern Ireland, for example.'[54]

This candid and detailed exposition of a critical moment in his artistic work is a little miracle, one which illuminates so much of what preceded this moment, in all its revelation, and the work that flowed, changed, from it. Within months of meeting and talking with Montague and his fellow Northern Irish poets Michael Longley and Seamus Deane at a house owned by Garech de Brun, proprietor of Claddagh Records, in the Wicklow mountains south of Dublin, Morrison was writing and recording the material that would become his next album, the startling *Hymns To The Silence*.

In 'Just A Closer Walk With Thee (See Me Through Part II)' on that album, Morrison testifies as to the essential nature of 'the way it was': 'Music and no music . . . silence.'[55] In music, silence is as essential to the recognition of sound as the white of paper is to the identification of print. Throughout the history of music there have been significant silences incorporated into the structures of sound, but they generally appeared at the end of sections and had a separating function. In some music of the near-modern period pauses occurred in the middle of sections and took on a more constitutive function. In France the most striking user or 'composer' of silences was Debussy (mentioned by Morrison in 'On Hyndford Street'), who attempted to suggest the silent communication of lovers in *La Démoiselle Élue* and again in *Pelléas et Mélisande*. In a letter of 1893 Debussy explained his intentions: 'Quite spontaneously, I used a method which seemed rather exceptional. I refer to silence (don't laugh) used like a mode of expression and perhaps the only way of getting the most emotion out of a phrase.'[56] Within music silence functions both as this universal framework, almost as an absolute antithesis – there is sound, and there is silence – and the space between the notes, recreated by the proximity to 'meaningful' noise. Thus what was once thought secondary and 'background' was foregrounded.

Silence thus became a central feature of late twentieth-century 'classical' music, employed as an explicit musical discourse in itself. The work of American avant-garde composer John Cage was driven by his interest in this relationship between sound and not-sound, as a kind of enquiry into the dynamics of being and not-being. In this his work has something in common with the characters of Samuel Beckett, who are found waiting, passing time, and in the words of the song, stuck in a moment that they can't get out of. Cage's *4'33"* is a formalised, performed silence lasting 4 minutes and 33 seconds, and is the most famous (and also infamous) example of this technique. Indeed Cage effectively managed to 'corner' silence as his own compositional and conceptual field, which is something of an achievement in itself. Silence as a musical texture is to be found in pop too, of course, be it the stops which provide the 'hook' of Cockney Rebel's 'Make Me Smile (Come Up And See Me'), the experiments in amplified silence on Talk Talk's *Laughing Stock*, or the daring pauses in something as deceptively light as the Beach Boys' early single 'The Little Girl I Once Knew'.[57]

Within literary traditions, among the nineteenth-century Romantics silence meant melancholy, separation and loneliness, a reminder of the futility of verbal communication. Among the symbolists silence suggested mystery, the infinite, the unknown. Morrison's use of silence places him somewhere between these apparent oppositions. The interdependence of sound and its absence is a kind of koan riddle: at the heart of music lies silence. This is the root of the mystery of music and how it moves us, how it reminds us that we are alive and that we will not always be so. So any performance of song, or music of any kind, involves a series of negotiations with silence; music, like any language, is a set of agreed disruptions of the silence, whether it is the immediate one which might pass between two people in a moment of love, or the final silence that awaits us all. Samuel Beckett said that the most he could dare to hope for was to make or leave 'a stain on the silence', as some evidence of having been here at all. That is everyone's lot, and hope. Beckett's ambition was to create what he called 'a literature of the unword'. His problem was that, perhaps in the way of musical notes, words signify in a way beyond the author's control. His ambition was not to destroy language but to reconnect it to the well of expression, or perhaps the hill of silence, from which it originally flowed. Beckett was paring down language in a way not unlike how Morrison uses the blues – to express a lot in a little.[58]

I am put in mind of Beckett's conversations with George Duthuit about the purpose and uses of art, where the Irishman tabled a now-famous explanation of his relationship to his own work:

> The expression that there is nothing to express, nothing with which to express, nothing from which to express, no power to express, no desire to express, together with the obligation to express.[59]

This in turn reminds me of the anecdote regarding a meeting in a hotel restaurant between Bob Dylan and Van Morrison, during which the pair were silent throughout. Dylan left, and Morrison supposedly commented, quite pleased, 'He was on good form today, don't you think?' It's a funny story, and quite possibly a true one, but it shows us something too: communication and survival are not merely matters of how much we stir up the waters. As Morrison sang on the album *Enlightenment*, 'It's so quiet in here' – an unusual state of affairs to be celebrated (and created) within pop or rock music, which at first glance seems to depend upon volume: come on feel the noise, suggested Slade. Morrison asks us if we can feel the silence. That's the point; Morrison's work is about feeling before it is about ideas and the ideas flow from the experience of encountering the work and taking something from it. Distrust the artist who tells you they know exactly what their work is 'about'.[60]

Morrison's 'hymns to the silence' are evidence of existence, of creativity, of feeling – of life. His uses of the term veer from the unconscious and unattributed through a phase where it begins to develop as a symbol and then into a third, 'high' phase where it is centralized as a carrier of meaning and feeling in his work. The word turns up within seconds of the opening of 'Astral Weeks' itself: '[L]ay me down / In silence easy / To be born again', and this of course is what amounts, simply through repetition, to a chorus for the song, but it is also the verse to which the song returns at its finale, emphasising the paradoxical centrality of the sections which bookend the song. Although not loaded in its use as it would be in the 1980s, post-*Common One*, the term in 1967–68 clearly has some seductive, organic potency for Morrison, associated with repose, renewal and happy change. 'Astral Weeks' also begins at an end point – 'In the ditch, where the back roads stop', and the rest of his musical sojourn begins to spool out from here too, including this effort to incorporate the feeling of silence into musical form.[61] A strange goal, perhaps, but an intriguing one, and one that matches this idea of finding beginnings in places for endings. In Beckett's *Waiting for Godot*, Vladimir's early question to Estragon echoes Leadbelly's 'Where Did You Sleep Last Night?'

> VLADIMIR:
> Get up till I embrace you
> ESTRAGON: (*irritably*)
> Not now, not now
> VLADIMIR:
> (*hurt, coldly*). May one inquire where His Highness spent the night?
> ESTRAGON:
> In a ditch.

VLADIMIR:
(*admiringly*). A ditch! Where?
ESTRAGON:
(*without gesture*). Over there.[62]

The vagueness of 'over there', without formal identification of the spot, confers (if that's an apposite term) anonymity on the place; this is the very quality cherished by Morrison in his 'ditch, where the back roads stop'.

The most direct and unhurried uses of silence as both an idea and a feeling come on 1991's audacious, sprawling *Hymns To The Silence*. Broadly speaking, this album is an exercise in old-school thematics: each of the four vinyl sides has a strong musical and thematic coherence. Side One is a brisk address towards the nature of the artist's engagement with the music industry while Side Two dovetails this theme into the beginning of some musical metaphysics, and an exploration of memory. The third side digs deeper and more boldly into this, while the final group of songs on Side Four connect this intensely personalised mode of expression with equally candid, if more widely accessible emotional expression, through a series of love songs. The rocks in the stream are, for example, 'Pagan Streams' a kind of 'Afterwards' to the 'In the Beginning' of 'On Hyndford Street', and the tender, Beckettian sketch of an outsider who also belongs, 'Village Idiot'. The restlessness and silence which mark out this character – 'he must know something / But he's just not saying' – is analogous to that of 'Old Man River': 'He must know somethin' / He don't say nothin' / He just keeps rollin' along', almost as if this life was a more natural one. The 'simple mind' is not then necessarily a pejorative term: it certainly seems less so when held against the frustrating obfuscations which make everything 'So Complicated' in Side One's suite of 'music business' songs.

The virtue and desirability of keeping silent is of course an irony not lost on Morrison, and the internal paradox of *Hymns To The Silence* is that while it displays acutely his unease at being obliged to reveal himself as a private individual, this is by far his most thoroughly candid and revealing record, with his mind being spoken very directly and as clearly as will fit into a three-and-a-half-minute song. So 'Why Must I Always Explain?' comments directly upon his role as 'star', and performer, and following it with 'Village Idiot', a portrait of someone who is free of such pressures and such obligations to explain himself, is deliberate. He can be read other ways: 'you can see it in his eyes, sometimes he looks so happy when he goes walking by'. There is definite tender admiration in Morrison's tone toward this character, almost a soft envy for his anonymity and freedom from the complex social negotiations which mark out Morrison's day, detailed thus: 'I get up in the morning and I get my brief / Stare at the world in complete disbelief'. The village idiot seems to know something he doesn't.[63]

Employing the shared language of a community through the use of a 'real' hymn, 'Just a Closer Walk With Thee', the track 'See Me Through Part II' breaks down into high, spoken-word testimony:

> 'Before, yes, before, this was the way it was, more silence, more being together, not rushing, being, before rock and roll, before television, previous, previous, previous, see me through, just a closer walk with thee.'[64]

Here silence is synonymous with a kind of real community, which mediated entertainments have somehow fragmented and dispersed. Related to this is the use of a 'real' hymn (the first of two such melodies on this album) which emphasises the communal root to his singing, and to the social uses of song. 'More silence' seems to be a defining strand of this apparently lost world, from which Morrison's remarkable testifying (1.19–2.09) seeks to shake the dust, if not completely reanimate: 'music and no music, silence and then voice'. A chain of images which suggest the life force itself, almost, being poised somewhere between music and silence, between 'music and no music'.

Hymns To The Silence represents the strongest connection between the idea of silence and the feelings associated with memory in his work; indeed in the title track we approach the heart of Morrison's view of his own work and his ambition for it. The song is addressed to another, in their absence, and represents a kind of devised company: 'When I'm away from you, I have to sing my hymns to the silence'. So the song is in part a way to break down time and space and bring two physically distant individuals together through the power of the imagination: the silence becomes a palpable presence which stands for the 'other', the 'dear sweet love' of the lyric. The second verse deals with the realities of an itinerant life, away from the place of calm and of rootedness, and of silence, in a place of interrupted sleep, day and night turned upside-down. The third finds release from these intensely 'present' pressures by removing itself from them and imagining the landscapes of repose and silence in which, like the silence on summer nights on Hyndford Street, he seems to find a feeling almost Holy to him. The song concludes with the key question, first heard on 'Summertime In England', 'Can you feel the silence?', and here the distinctions between pure perception and pure feeling are broken down and reconfigured; the key phrase is the cue for the song to dissolve slowly, via a remarkable long fade on a repetition of the song's title, sung not by Morrison but by Carol Kenyon and Katie Kissoon. They are accompanied only by the spiralling organ lines of Eddie Friel and Georgie Fame; it's a remarkable, weightless moment of pure realisation, of the themes of the song and the wider ambition of the record. Indeed this is the kind of alchemy Morrison speaks of in 'Philosopher's Stone', where the themes of the song have earned meditative space, drifting out into the darkness, like watching the light of a boat disappear imperceptibly slowly from view over the horizon. This mesmerising incantation is surely related to the meditative structures Morrison seeks to explore in his music. The slow drifting outro leads us into the mood of 'On Hyndford Street', perhaps his most intensely realized exploration and inhabitation of memory. What is the role of silence in this? It brings stillness, a sense of focus and of concentration.[65]

'On Hyndford Street' is a not quite free-form stream of consciousness flow of memory; it does after all have enough to do with the blues to finish, not unlike 'Astral Weeks', with a repetition of the first section, which moves from 'On Hyndford Street' to 'God'. Flowing through this piece is the power of silence, with six references to silence itself, the 'quietness' of 'restful slumber' (echoing the mood of 'Haunts Of Ancient Peace'), which expands the idea of the influence of those periods of quiet, including early mornings 'when contemplation was best'. The mood of this reminds me of that of Wordsworth's *The Prelude*, with its keen emphasis on hearing, and the feeling of the memory of sound – listening to Radio Luxembourg, the voices whispering across Beechie River, the laughter, the jazz and blues records, Debussy on the radio, the internalised voices of Mezz Mezzrow and Jack Kerouac. This clamour of voices feeds into the sense of contentment and calmness; harmony is achieved through the bringing together of apparent cross-currents of sound, meaning and feeling. The endpoint of all this sound is silence, but a silence which is rich and full, pendulous with experience, rather than one which is empty and indicative of loneliness. That fullness is expressed by a sense of inhabiting the moment in a state of complete fullness and awakedness, even at the edge of sleep.

It is here that the purpose of the pursuit of these moments of stillness, and of silence, is made manifest: 'And it's always being now . . . It's always now'. This is satisfying metaphysically, as a place seems to have been discovered, or created, in which the clocks are stopped and a different understanding of time and eternity moves towards our understanding, achieved not in a laboratory or via complex thought processes but simply through thinking about ordinary life in a particular way. It's some discovery. It is also satisfying as a listener because we are drawn into this mood, either by the cumulative effect of this track following the title song, or simply via listening to the blend of Morrison's rich, close-miked voice, which feels like the truth, and the unobtrusive yet absolutely integral synthesiser playing of the late, great Derek Bell. Indeed the discovery of profundity through the uncomplicated details of a life in the lyric is mirrored by the simplicity of Bell's synth lines which also suggest the richness of the mood: slow, warm, on the brink of dreams but fully awake to feeling and meaning. There is also meaning and pleasure in Morrison's pronunciation of the word 'now' in the Belfast manner, as 'noy'. It has the same impact as the 'face' in 'Coney Island', in that the very sound of this locates the thought culturally and topographically, as unmistakably Northern Irish and furthermore specifically East Belfast. This is the most important word in the piece, and it is both related to, and the endpoint of, the idea of the feeling of silence.[66]

David Steindl-Rast wrote in his fascinating book *The Music of Silence* of how time was experienced in the Benedictine monastery he was part of:

> The hours are the inner structure for living consciously and responsively through the stages of the day. The monastic relationship to time through the canonical hours sensitizes us to the nuances of time. And as this sensitivity deepens, we become more available to the present moment.[67]

He also speaks of the way the day is charged with different emphases at different times. Vigils are 'time outside the practical demands of the day'; Lauds is 'an opportunity for the spiritual practice of attention'; Prime is 'an important teacher of intention'; Terce is a 'gateway to openness'; Sext is an occasion to 'exercise perseverance'; None is a moment to face 'the little death of each passing day'; Vespers is an invitation to acknowledge 'the quiet beauty of the evening'; and Compline is a time 'to examine our conscience and ask forgiveness, and thereby make a clean transition into night and sleep'.[68]

The dividing of the day thus finds a kind of corresponding structure in the idealised and compacted 'day' represented by the litany of 'On Hyndford Street', with its emphasis on the quiet beauty of the evening and the moments before sleep being the point at which experience and conduct are considered and examined in pursuit of ending the day with a quiet mind, and by its ending with the line 'And [we] carried on dreaming, in God'. So the 'real' and the dream or spiritual worlds are sublimated in this more secular setting, as they are in the demarcated processes of Steindl-Rast's monastery. In his book, a chapter is devoted to each of 'the hours' around which the day is structured, just as 'On Hyndford Street' speaks of early morning as a time 'when contemplation was best'. Thus Fusco's, Abetta Parade, the Castlereagh Hills and the rest function as symbolic 'hours' within the piece, as elements of a movement towards the fullness and quietness pursued through the day, up to the drift into restful slumber, or in Steindl-Rast's term 'a clean transition into night and sleep'. Running through Morrison's work and intensely focused in these works is his desire and struggle to live in the moment, again corresponding to Steindl-Rast's mindfulness of the present.

Music that evokes silence is, then, both a paradox and a goal in the connection between creativity and spirituality. A work like Miles Davis's *In A Silent Way* foregrounds this, via a kind of autodescriptive terminology – the title suggests the ambition for the music, or even an instruction from Davis to his musicians as to how to play.[69] Morrison's understanding and use of the dynamics which run between 'the word' and 'silence' and what lies between those twin poles is at the root of his understanding of how music works and the effect it has on the mind and on the emotions. Consider too the use of silence in concert: in the central part of the live version of 'In The Afternoon', issued in 2002, he steps right to the back of the stage, by the drum riser, still singing forward but some distance from his mike. The audience, as well as the group, are required to focus, to concentrate and to really *listen* in order to follow him. It's no coincidence that at this stage he is outlining the 'Level One' meditation, stepping back up to the mike for 'Level Two'.[70]

This is a high-risk strategy – sometimes the audience let him down, as in a late 2007 show in Amsterdam's cavernous Heineken Hall where the audience kept clapping the beat while he was trying to work this section. After a minute or so trying to let the crowd settle he gave it up and brought his arm down to signal to the band that they should close the song out. This shows that an audience is as much part of the formula for success of a live concert as the performers on stage, and also that to work with silence as a creative raw material via the dynamics of popular song is a very difficult thing to do. After all, isn't pop and rock about noise, about sound, an amplified celebration of theatricalised escapism? Well yes it is, sometimes, and is often very welcome as that, but not always. In Morrison's art, silence is at the centre, and sometimes when he approaches that centre on a good night onstage – when something is about to happen – the conditions need to be absolutely right or else it *won't* happen. This is the alchemic process he references in 'Philosopher's Stone', where the commonplace can become the marvellous. He also, we note, has the good grace and integrity to admit when it isn't happening – the arm came down in Amsterdam – because as he said in 'Sometimes We Cry', 'I ain't gonna fake it, like Johnnie Ray'.[71]

Thus these moments are actual experiences of this powerful dynamic between the word and silence; in other songs within Morrison's catalogue he will report on experiences, in a manner which suggests that the encounters are not, for him, limited to good nights on stage before a paying audience. In 2003's gorgeous 'Little Village' he sings of having 'Heard the voice of the silence, in the evening / On the long cool summer nights', telling him 'not to worry / Everything's gonna be alright'. Once again this key paradox of the silence being given articulation beats at the heart of Morrison's urgent art and offers not emptiness or despair, but tender comfort, almost like that offered by redemptive religious creeds – everything is going to be alright.[72]

The song itself shows the manner in which Morrison's art holds together its influences – the title and part of the lyrical conceit are lifted directly from Sonny Boy Williamson's song of the same name, and in borrowing the title Morrison is both referencing this Williamson track and transposing the idea to the landscape with which he, and his listeners, are more familiar – that of the tight community in which life is a shared experience, and where settlements huddle in the sight of the natural world, with the mountains looming above the village. There is a sense of the human and the natural worlds being heard by each other, as they were in Morrison's childhood Belfast, where the mountains and the sea and the city are in a kind of visible, rhythmic harmony. As John Montague notes in *A Coney Island of the Mind*, this led to a kind of emphasised countryside, as a buffer between the city and the untamed landscape beyond. This informs the use of silence as an image or agent of healing in 'I'm Tired Joey Boy', a close kin of 'Coney Island', a song of substantial economy and clarity, which concludes its business with the lines 'Go up to the mountain, go up to the Glen / When silence will touch you and heartbreak will mend'.[73] This is an unmistakably Northern Irish landscape, made allegorical through the device of it being employed as a source of healing, but still completely 'realistic' nonetheless. It is also evidence of Morrison being influenced by the Glen poets of his home. It emphasises the fact that silence is a positive presence, rather than a vacuum, or an absence: it is an aspect of being, rather than non-being.

So Morrison presents silence in various contexts, for our contemplation at the end of 'Summertime In England', as an agent of healing and an object of praise in *Hymns To The Silence* and, most exquisitely, set like a jewel in a ring in 'Piper At The Gates Of Dawn'; hard won in the first instance, rich and complex in the second, apparently utterly natural in the third. Silence is not represented 'literally' post-'Summertime In England' but more in the sense suggested by French symbolist poet Stéphane Mallarmé; he said that the artist's eye should be on 'places and people away from the great men and the grand parade of events: do not paint the thing, but the feeling it creates'.[74] This is of course our paradox: sound invoking silence is painting not the thing but the feeling it creates. So Derek Bell's synthesiser in 'On Hyndford Street' showcases silence, and in the step-back from the vocal we are being bidden to behold the silence. We are also asked the famous question again, a decade down the road from *Common One*, here in a much more intimate and deliberately scaled-down world – can you feel the silence?

It is interesting that the Chieftains were involved in both 'On Hyndford Street' and 'Piper At The Gates Of Dawn'; the latter was written for possible inclusion in Terry Jones's film of *The Wind in the Willows* released in 1996, but the tune went unused.[75] It sits well in the opening salvo of *The Healing Game*, musically being a late flowering of the spirit of *Veedon Fleece* alongside an unapologetically imaginative retelling of parts of Kenneth Grahame's novel. The silence here is 'heard' from 2.18–26 ('and we listened to the silence [. . .] Of the wind in the willows'[76]), and in using this signature device he makes the tale his own, via the retelling of it. This is the nature not only of folk or collective art but of creativity itself – the taking on of an extant element and making something new with and out of it. The silence in the song is not entire of itself; it is 'of' the wind in the willows, and the piper at the gates of dawn. These few seconds are Morrison's best use and most effective evocation of silence. Again we get the feeling created rather than the thing itself: we understand more of the scene by the absence of formal description of it. Music, like painting, is well equipped to perform such a feat, being both sensual and spatial, occupying both time and space. In this sense, Morrison's placing of 'silence' within the music of the song is his most refined and evocative employment of the effect. Samuel Beckett said of his most famous play *Waiting for Godot* that 'silence is pouring into this play like water into a sinking ship'.[77] Silence blows through Morrison's music, an active, positive and animating presence, as does the wind through the willows.

Chapter Five

Listening to the Lion: Van Morrison as Singer and Musician

> R.D. Laing: All the times that I've listened to your voice, you seem to sing somewhere between your throat and your heart. Sometimes it's right in your heart, sometimes it's more up in your throat. When you do that now, is that the zone that you want to both come from and resonate in other people, the heart . . .
>
> Van Morrison: Eventually it'll get into the heart. That's what the eventual goal is – Exactly.[1]

What kind of singer is Van Morrison? The first few years of my interest in his work roughly coincided with a period during which I was the singer in a band called Innocents Abroad – we played live, we made records, we went on the road: we did it. Over that period I also saw so many Van Morrison live shows and internalised the recorded works so completely that almost without meaning to I came to pay very close attention to his singing technique. At the time I was just loving the sound but from this distance I see what he taught me – where does he breathe? Does he come in on, before or behind the beat? Does he draw out certain sounds and truncate others? Where does he sing, and where does he choose to not sing? Which lines did he always sing straight, which were always open to variation, and which were up for grabs? All this and more. I didn't try to sound like him – chance would be a fine thing – but being attentive to his technique certainly made me a better singer, and gave me some insight into how the voice can be used as a mode of expression in itself, not simply delivering a lyric. So in this chapter we'll try to pay close attention to how, as well as what,

Van Morrison sings.

'LEAD VOCALS: VAN MORRISON' (SLEEVE CREDIT ON THE FIRST THEM ALBUM, 1965)

On the *Live at Austin City Limits Festival* album Morrison introduces the somewhat unexpected 'Don't Start Crying Now' as 'The first song I recorded as a vocalist'.[2] His memory didn't deceive him, for Them's take on this James Moore and Jerry West r'n'b tune was recorded in their first two studio sessions, according to Clinton Heylin, in Coromac Studios in Belfast in early June 1964, and then remade as heard on the first Them album in Decca's West Hampstead studios in London the following month. The sound that Morrison makes on this track, especially in the unaccompanied first few moments, still startles me – a bad-pup snarl, full of juice and r'n'b kickback.[3] Even in 1964, no-one sounded like him; his illustrious peers (Jagger, Winwood, Burdon, et al.) couldn't match that attack and indeed Gordon Thompson has suggested that Decca labelmate Mick Jagger toughened up his singing style by borrowing very heavily from Morrison, describing his vocal as 'an authentically aggressive style of singing that Jagger soon personalised'.[4] The tightened throat on 'Don't Start Crying Now' delivers a pure stream of vocalised energy, spuming out with such force and drive that he barely has the time to pronounce the words. This natural knack of running sounds together to make their collective meaning far outweigh the sum of their parts would remain a central feature of Morrison's style and development as a singer.

By the time a year had passed, Morrison's singing had evolved as an instrument and his ability to use it as such had grown too. Consider his performance on 'My Lonely Sad Eyes', recorded in summer 1965. Here the caustic, Belfast-born edge is still part of the story, but there is greater openness of tone, and haste is less readily taken for verisimilitude. More care is taken with clarity, and, as lyricist for this song, it shouldn't surprise us that that is the case. The melody too, has more ornate twists and turns, highs and lows through which the lyric is led. Morrison's vocal swallows them whole into a single sound, which is direct and candid, yet multi-faceted and mindful of the impressionistic tones of the lyric itself: 'Throw me a kiss / Across a crowded room / Some sunny windswept afternoon / Is none too soon to miss / My sad eyes'.[5] The inner and outer modes here (crowded room/sunny windswept afternoon) anticipate the metaphysical balances that distinguish the territory into which he was headed, and which first blossomed on *Astral Weeks*. This gorgeous little song is desperately under-rated and underplayed. No record of Morrison ever playing it post-1968 exists. It is both a glimpse forward to the places and soundscapes of *Astral Weeks* and a look back to a youth spent close to the sea, memories flashing across the field of vision with great speed and clarity.

Maria McKee covered this song in 1993 and told me why she loved the vocal on Them's original so much:

> MM: Well I guess it was because it is such a great example of his pacing and timing in delivery . . . the melody just runs on and sounds natural, but it also goes places you would not expect it to – that's the vocal line, I mean –
>
> PM: So it always seems to be ahead of itself and also catching itself up?
>
> MM: [laughs] Exactly! And the tune is so pure and uncomplicated at the same time. You get a real sense of freedom from that song, sadness and happiness too.[6]

The lyric is indeed both celebratory and cautionary at one and the same time: the toasting of the good times over sparkling wine is met by the image of the sad eyes of the title while the crowded room at a party and the flirtatious kiss is matched with the image of a sunny windswept afternoon outside. The furious carpe diem of the fast, bright young life ('Fortunate and free') is set against the thought that life is fragile, lived 'Between the earth and sky', while 'The moon in all its glory / The song that I sing and everything' infers this complex sensation of loss and completeness. The final lines repeat the first, suggesting an eternal cycle, yoking happiness and sadness, earth and sky, even life and death in a single image of sensation; this is real wisdom, and furthermore wisdom which comes in at 2.31. McKee's version is absolutely faithful to the *Them Again* arrangement and her unmistakable voice gives the tune a powerful restatement, while guitar, drum and keyboard are closely attentive to the spirit as well as the letter of this then 30-year-old song, sung in the original by a 20-year-old boy.[7]

Now, where Bob Dylan's early vocal stylings strongly reflected the influence of Woody Guthrie, Morrison's early heroes – people like Leadbelly, Webb Pierce and Lonnie Donegan – were less easily encapsulated or compressed into a vocal tone or a style of dress. To some extent it was the filter of skiffle that gave a shape to his interest in blues, country and jazz singing, unifying these apparently disparate approaches into something new – something which, according to Morrison, ended up diluted as Them were obliged to fit into the pop frameworks of the time. As Morrison notes on the sleeve of *The Skiffle Sessions*, 'skiffle arrived when and where I needed it'.[8] Donegan in some ways aped Leadbelly's recordings but the sum total was something quite unlike those originals. Indeed Morrison has frequently remarked that the versions of his own songs he enjoys most are those where the singer makes the tune their own: think of his approval of Johnny Rivers's version of 'Slim Slow Slider', saying 'I dig it because he does it like himself'.[9] So Morrison's *recognisable* voice has always been absolutely central to the appeal and the understanding of his work in a way that Dylan's, with all its vexing shifts and changes, hasn't.

We can identify distinct phases in Morrison's vocal development; sometimes they are obvious, sometimes they start very quietly and developing over time. These changes represent natural as well as artistic development, of course. I would also suggest that we can take Morrison's vocal styles and classify them via his influences and the styles themselves; jazz, blues, soul, country, folk and pop. First, we have the Them records, in their adolescent fury. Then the Bang recordings which, for all their troubled genesis, represent a mid-point between the raw power of the Them voice and the *Astral Weeks* voice. Morrison's troubled and obscure view of his own direction informs the vocal ambiguities of these recordings yet *Astral Weeks* itself does little less than invent a new way of singing, of pacing delivery, of *breathing*. This breakthrough led to the singer-songwriter voice that stretches from *Moondance* to *Tupelo Honey*. A restless, malcontent spirit informs his voice on *Saint Dominic's Preview* and *Hard Nose The Highway*, and on *It's Too Late To Stop Now* these vocal approaches reach a kind of confluence, and thereby an ultimate realisation – which of course is exactly why Morrison broke up this world-beating band immediately on the release of the live album. *Veedon Fleece*, as we shall discover, represents a multiplicity of possible ways forward for his voice. His 'American' voice reaches a kind of apotheosis on *A Period Of Transition* and *Wavelength*, albeit in very different kinds of singing and material, before a European (if not obviously Irish) tone re-emerges on *Into The Music*, leading into the stunning cauldron of audacious experiment represented by the vocal performances on *Common One*.

These in turn gave way to the telescopic precision of his style on *Beautiful Vision* through to *A Sense Of Wonder*. It is worth noting too that in this period his singing was deliberately de-emphasised, as instrumentals became increasingly important in the work. Alongside there was the growing use of 'unison singing' – a technique where the vocal follows an instrumental line – heard first on the closing section of 1983's recording of 'Irish Heartbeat' as a kind of language for the 'inarticulate speech of the heart', emotionally expressive but not formally linguistic. This feels 'mystic' but is not unprecedented – as we have noted, George Benson used this technique on many million-sellers, such as 'Give Me The Night'. Coming out of this run of records, what we might call his mid-period style exhibits a very characteristic extended vowel sound, heard to best effect on 1988's 'Raglan Road' and what Paddy Moloney called 'his traditional West of Ireland keening'.[10] This gave way to his jazz and blues voice, which dominated the 90s live work up until his unexpected vocal relationships with Brian Kennedy and Linda Gail Lewis. This was then creatively reduced to the dry, tight British jazz and 'country-and-Irish' voice we hear on the albums up to 2006, and finally the open, more revealing and plaintive voice on *Keep It Simple*.

So, let's ask again, what kind of singer is Van Morrison? In technical terms, he's a rich tenor, yet also one capable of reaching deep down into the visceral bass notes, or way up into the falsetto range. As for the aesthetic and artistic quality of his singing, estimations vary, of course. Kevin Rowland told me that 'the sound of his voice changed my life . . . it showed me what was possible', while Maria McKee revealed to me that his voice 'has something very free and wild about it. It's all out there . . . it makes me want to go and *do something*, live some more', and no lesser man than B.B. King said that 'His voice is pure yet bitter'.[11] In contrast, according to his biographer, Chet Baker was not so impressed when they met in London in 1984:

> [Elvis] Costello showed up for rehearsal with Van Morrison, the raspy-voiced Irish singer-songwriter of such 'blue-eyed-soul' hits as 'Gloria' and 'Domino'. When Morrison asked if he could sing too, the producers were thrilled. As the cameras rolled he snapped his fingers and bungled his way through 'Send In The Clowns', making numerous gaffes even as he held the sheet music in front of him. Baker had never heard of Morrison and couldn't believe he was a professional singer. 'He's not singing, he's shouting!' Baker told [Riccardo] Del Fra. But Costello's reedy, nasal voice had a lot of feeling, and Baker respected him. 'He's a very talented man, Elvis', the trumpeter told interviewer Ib Skovgaard.[12]

These variable estimations are of course wholly subjective – do we like the sound or not? Yet the musics of Rowland, McKee, King and Baker are wildly distinct from each other, while sharing an essential soulfulness. If Morrison's output has crossed boundaries and covered all sorts of genres, we can think about how his voice has adapted to the requirements and demands of each new type of singing, often where the significance of the voice shifts – the emphases are different in country or pop, say, from the demands of jazz.

In this sense changes in Morrison's singing and vocalising have been discreet and almost imperceptible, but that isn't to say his voice has not developed and been integral to how his work has grown and flowered as he has passed through life, recording his experience in the grain of the voice. The road from the r'n'b squall of 'Don't Start Crying Now' to the near-operatic power of 'Linden Arden Stole The Highlights' took only ten years. Morrison has not, with a couple of exceptions, made the kind of gesture that Dylan made in moving from what

Philip Larkin called the 'cawing, mocking voice' of *Blonde On Blonde* to the honeyed lilt (which was understood, paradoxically, as an act of confrontation and refutation) we hear on *Nashville Skyline* and *Self Portrait*, the sound of which prompted an ace Dylanologist to infamously ask: 'What is this shit?'[13] Greil Marcus's sense of betrayal when he opened his *Rolling Stone* review of *Self Portrait* with this question was in part derived from a recoil from the *sound* of Dylan's voice as much as the nature of the material included. So what does Van Morrison's voice tell us?

Listening to the voice on early Them recordings and then to anything from 2008's *Keep It Simple* shows, of course, the difference between a 20-year-old and a 62-year-old. It is the miraculous but illusory nature of recorded sound that enables and perhaps obliges us to compare the two; otherwise who would be able to recall how the younger man sounded at the expense of the elder? The four decades between the recording of 'Don't Start Crying Now' and 'Keep It Simple' encompass vocal changes that are consistent with the passage of time and the effect it has on both the matter and substance of singing, but there's more than this at work. Morrison's use of the grain of the voice is less concerned with concealing, evading and masking in this sense. It does, indeed, strive to keep it simple in how it explores the moment and expresses feeling as much as ideas. If Morrison seeks to confound or simply play with expectation, he does it lyrically and musically rather than via the sound of his voice. In truth, he has probably expended little energy over these 40-plus years on 'confounding expectation'. He has sung what and how he wants to sing.

The title cut of *Keep It Simple* is a reflective piece – where 'Don't Start Crying Now' is in Maria McKee's phrase, all out there, this is at the other end of the line, reflecting upon practice as well as pursuing it. In the style of the delivery we feel everything that preceded it – it's full and rich with all this history as well as directly of the now. A key feature of Morrison's late style is the directness and clarity of the voice and the frequent flinty lack of ambiguity in both lyric and delivery, and in this he has indeed come to resemble Sinatra more closely than the blues singers he has so frequently eulogised. Sinatra was channelled on 'Moondance' of course, but even earlier than this, on the Bang recordings, Morrison was marking out his territory in terms of how his vocal performances would be fringed with techniques drawn from jazz and free movement across genres that he had absorbed at a young age. Listen to the scatted outro of 'Send Your Mind', matching his vocal with a hard driving bluesy pop groove, hinting at Bo Diddley while keeping firmly in the Beat idiom. This finds a kind of correspondence in the more famous sha la la's of its album-mate 'Brown Eyed Girl' as part of the rhythmic vocabulary at the heart of pop as opposed to jazz or blues.

In his singing Morrison has employed for the most part a 'chest voice', singing from the belly and the gut and as such the voice has a rich, visceral quality, but he has also explored the corresponding 'head voice', which we might also call the falsetto – a voice which, although initially much more striking (think of 'Who Was That Masked Man' or 'Try For Sleep'), is less varied in its range and tone. In 2009 he observed how he had tried to manage and maintain his voice:

> Chris Neal: How has your approach to singing changed since you recorded *Astral Weeks?*
>
> VM: I have practised just about every genre of singing since 1968. Picking up a little from classical, a little from jazz, and a lot from blues has made my singing technique what it is. I think they call it my own. The approach now is to sing from lower down [the diaphragm] so I do not ruin my voice. Before, I sang in the upper area of my throat, which tends to wreck the vocal cords over time. Singing from lower in the belly allows my resonance to carry far. I can stand four feet from a mic and be heard quite resonantly.[14]

This mixture of the creative and the physical is key for us – unlike the piano or guitar, the voice comes from within. We can hear how he has developed this 'lower down' style post-*Wavelength*, as his music flowered into his remarkable run of records in the 1980s. The deep scat section of 2003's 'Blue and Green' (4.21–5.14) offers a superb late example of the opportunities this approach gives him. As listed here, his vocal influences are multiple and manifold – the tale is well known of how his early years were spent soaking up the blues, jazz, folk, country and classical of his parents' record collection, as well as the wider musical scene in 50s Belfast. He has credited the obvious – John Lee Hooker, Ray Charles, Hank Williams – and the less obvious – the McPeakes, Count John McCormack, and Louis Prima.

Prima, in particular, has come into the frame since Morrison's music took on a big-band brassy flair from the mid-90s. While his singing is not obviously internally vivacious enough for him to really be heard as 'after' Louis Prima, his more recent music can sometimes carry that kind of 50s fizz, from the days before rock and roll. This is caught well, for example, on the good-natured rumble of 'Whinin' Boy Moan' from 2003. Indeed, he has covered several Prima numbers live and on disc, and this has enabled us to detect influences retrospectively – hear, for example, his duet with daughter Shana on 'That Old Black Magic', a Prima favourite shared with his wife Keely Smith. In a 2007 interview he claimed that his vocal style was 'more like a Louis Prima thing', and such a description, while less obviously true in the majority of his earlier work, is accurate in regard of his post-2000 singing.[15] As a mainstream entertainer in the 1940s and 50s with a sly and roguish style, Prima's vocals were shot through with humour and a keen sense of the ridiculous – Morrison's technique is outwardly more obviously 'serious' but there are definitely links. Prima was thoroughly professional and worked very hard on his vocal stylings, perhaps especially so in the case of the apparently 'lighter' vocal trickery. For an earlier example of how this style has blended in with Morrison's more regular vocalising, listen to the 'all the bubbles' section (4.00–20) on 'Moonshine Whiskey' (note the Irish 'e' in whiskey) that closes *Tupelo Honey*. Prime Prima. His style has borrowed from the vocabulary of Prima and his peers who used these techniques, such as 'vocalese' and scat. He has frequently remarked on the influence of these techniques on his style, particularly vocalese: so what is it?

In his illuminating book *A New History of Jazz*, Alyn Shipton offers some enlightenment. He recounts how Eddie Jefferson

> struck upon the idea of taking solos by the likes of Lester Young and Coleman Hawkins and writing lyrics to them . . . His lyrics for 'Moody's Mood For Love' (based on James Moody's solo improvisation on the Fields/McHugh song 'I'm In The Mood For Love) were recorded by King Pleasure, and became a minor hit. Pleasure himself (whose real name was Clarence Beeks) had also tried his hand at writing lyrics to some of Young's solos in the 1940's, and so could claim some measure of joint responsibility for the innovation.

So vocalese is in part born out of vocal riffing around pleasing horn melodies, writing rhythmic verbal correspondences to wordless solos:

> The most successful vocalese works in the first instance as poetry, challenging the lyricist to fit rhyme schemes and comprehensible words to the spontaneous twists and turns of a recorded solo . . . equally it stands as a test of a singer's skill in negotiating the nuances of the instrumental solo to which the lyrics have been set. Jefferson's efforts were mainly applied to swing-style solos and even 'Moody's Mood For Love' was only mildly influenced by bebop.[16]

Morrison's own cover of 'Moody's Mood For Love' is one of his more startling vocal performances, being both respectful of the techniques and traditions of vocalese, but also picking those methods up and running free with them. In this he is surely close to the spirit if not the letter of King Pleasure. He would also surely relish what Shipton calls the 'test' of matching voice and instrument in a fresh and pleasurably risky performance of this sort. Shipton emphasises that vocalese is a technique that flows from and with, and not against, the original melody, and Morrison's take on the tune fits smartly with that ambitious requirement; it is a tricky technique for a singer to use or to follow. We see here too how Morrison's use of the voice in his unison singing or his saxophonic phrasing dovetails with this method.[17]

> Whereas vocalese is about a skilled combination of transcription, poetry, vocal and verbal dexterity, it can impede new and spontaneous improvisation, not least because most vocalese pieces are themselves based on somebody else's extant instrumental improvisations.[18]

Morrison is of course a lyricist as well as a singer, so that 'skilled combination' of verbal and vocal dexterity is very important to him; indeed vocalese in some ways began the process of the word being as important as the sound in the process of building popular song. The sound and shape of words grow out of the sound and shape of the music, as opposed to the well-made song and lyric merged in an arranged marriage between words and music; this is clearly close kin to scat. Commonly assumed to have been 'invented' by Louis Armstrong, scat is the verbal equivalent of pure rhythm. Morrison uses scat to carve out some free space for the voice within the structures of a song beyond the 'fixed' lyric. Intriguingly, the only song that Morrison has ever completely scatted live was 'Into The Mystic' at a San Anselmo club gig in 1973 – an unlikely contender, but it is a song which is an experiment in matching language to feeling. In this performance he broke down into laughter several times, as he perhaps heard the echoes of Spike Milligan's high nonsense rubbing shoulders with Satchmo.

Singing, no less than playing an instrument, is to some extent genre-specific: a classical piano virtuoso is not necessarily a great ragtime player, and a great blues singer is not by default a great jazz one. Yet the majority of jazz singers have employed techniques drawn from blues singing; indeed vocal jazz tends to blur these distinctions anyway, with the vocal traditions of one informing those of the other at the root, so it is difficult, and arguably unnecessary, to try and separate them. In the kind of vocal jazz that Morrison necessarily works with (he is a vocalist first, an instrumentalist after, of course), this is the case, where the voice is always to some extent guesting within an instrumental form. In Miles Davis's phrase, the vocal in jazz is *kind of* blue. Likewise, Morrison has married the vocal streams of blues, country, soul and pop to create what is quite distinctively his own, as he told Chris Neal. Yet, to restate, the voice is a physical thing – it comes from inside, and thus involves the body in a way that, say, playing the piano does not. Let's seek some reflection through theory upon practice.

Roland Barthes' famous essay 'The Grain of the Voice' explores this set of connections between sound and meaning via the mediating form of the body.

Barthes writes particularly about German Baritone Dietrich Fischer-Dieskau, a very well-regarded opera singer, but is unpersuaded by his work, however:

> His art – expressive, dramatic, *sentimentally clear*, borne by a voice lacking in any 'grain' in signifying weight, fits well with the demands of an *average* culture . . . with Fischer-Dieskau, I only seem to hear the lungs, never the tongue, the glottis, the teeth, the mucous membranes, the nose.[19]

Barthes hears only sound, and not the body. Reading what he finds missing from the Fischer-Dieskau's performative lexicon, I am strongly reminded of Morrison's vocal performance in 'TB Sheets', and all its claustrophobic physicality. Barthes later suggests that vowels should bear all the emotional gravity, 'which is meaning in all its potential voluptuousness' in a performance of a song, connecting his idea to Morrison's late 80s vocal style of extending the vowel sounds as he sang them, heard to good effect on 'Raglan Road', for example. Barthes sees the end-product of this process as being what he calls 'the sung writing of language', the product of a kind of positive friction between music and words, both aural carriers of expression, emotion and information, which might seem opposed but also are in cahoots in pursuit of a higher form of expression than either might achieve alone. Interestingly for Morrison listeners, Barthes equates this mix of languages, this 'sung writing of language', with the French tradition of the troubadour – the title of a song on Morrison's watershed album, 1979's *Into The Music*. He notes that romantic poetry in France is 'more oratorical than textual', and we think of the Montreux DVD version of 'Troubadours' where, alongside the musical signifiers of the 'ancient' in the final section, the voice exhorts us to 'Listen!' to the sax, surrendering centrality and definition of effect to the non-verbal, one language deferring to another.[20] So, as Barthes argues, what the voice cannot achieve on its own might be available to it alongside the melody, working at the language, through the shared space of the song in what he calls 'the sung writing of language'. He also proposed that the true story might be told by a less well-known voice.

Indeed, one of Morrison's less well-known albums seems to me in particular to display this intriguing cultural meld of music, voice and culture, this 'sung writing of language'.

LOOKING FOR THE VEEDON FLEECE

Veedon Fleece, issued in 1974, represents a search: on this record we hear a voice looking for a fresh way to express itself. It is also a search for a new musical language, which would both support and develop the sung one. It is also perhaps an exercise in myth creation, a set of short stories which seek through the telling to reveal a truth rather than the image of a truth. The bulk of the songs derive from Morrison's journey around Ireland in late 1973 and that lends the songs a beguiling mix of the real and the fantastic, the physical and metaphysical – connecting with the spirit of place while remaining soundly earthed, whether describing Killarney's lakes ('so blue'), or walking the streets of Arklow. These are real places, but become revealed in their mythic, transcendental meaning via this 'sung writing of language' in the sound of the music, in collusion with the grain of Morrison's voice. Let's look at *Veedon Fleece* as a kind of case study of this sort of process in action.[21]

What sort of singing do we find on this record? It reveals a wide palette of styles, tones and performance applied to a remarkable set of lyrics. In album opener 'Fair Play', he uses a strange, back-of-the-throat style, which brings a kind of watery, melancholic smile to the tone of his voice. The key lyrics in this song are, unexpectedly, 'architecture', 'Geronimo' and the line 'only one meadow's way to go'. That 'o' sound is central to the slow wisdom of this performance, the voice possessed of sensual openness which is also at one remove from the appetites and rhythmic diktats of the body. The voice does not simply suggest or reflect this state of temperate bliss, it somehow *is* it. Thus the appeal to the mind offered and requested by 'Tell me of Poe / Oscar Wilde and Thoreau' is also physically slow and sensuous. He doubles 'mystery' (2.12) and at 2.38–45 allows the word 'dream' to slide into a soft mist of sound, as he does on the 'love that loves to love' section of 'Madame George'. The repeated line 'Hi ho silver, tit for tat and I love you for that' doesn't really 'mean' anything – its meaning lies in the sound, the place it occupies, and how he moulds the sounds. He laughs, and repeats himself. There is time and space in this music and the instrumentation works round it, framing his musings and mutterings. As with the 1980s live vocal-echo technique, we feel how repetition increases significance. It is a rhetorical device but there is deep musicality to it, especially in the ''ronimo' repetitions towards the song's end (5.14–20). The voice on 'Fair Play', coming from the back of throat and halfway up the chest, is perfectly expressive of the music and the body in sounding somehow both constricted and free.

In 'Linden Arden Stole The Highlights' we hear a deep, chest voice: it is visceral and guttural. This is what Roland Barthes wanted from Fischer-Dieskau, as we hear the whole body: 'teeth, glottis, tongue, mucous membranes'.[22] The song itself is centrally concerned with the burdens of the body, and is corporeal in both sound and subject: Linden Arden stole the highlights 'With one hand tied behind his back', and also 'Cleaved their heads off with a hatchet'. The body in all its force and weakness is present here. The voice is as close as Morrison has come to operatic, and the piano playing is appropriate: as with the illustrative function of music in opera, the strings slip in as his voice modulates upwards at 1.45. It is fabulous. He delivers the vocal in a grandly enunciated recitative style, almost in the spirit of Schubertian lieder, finding connections to Count John McCormack (who once described opera singing as 'too much effort for too little reward'[23]) or an English equivalent, Benjamin Britten and Peter Pears's then-revolutionary recordings of English folk songs in the 1950s. The lyric is, like the outlaw/Jesse James songs he grew up listening to and would eventually record with Lonnie Donegan, a sympathetic portrayal of a renegade who chose to live outside the law, but who struggled with his conscience as he did so. As a kind of morality tale, this is a clear and direct telling, almost like a piece of reportage, without the window-dressing and evasiveness of, say, 'Crazy Face', and the vocal delivery facilitates this.

'Who Was That Masked Man?' provides an operatic continuity, picking up on the last line of the previous number for its opener. The other side of Linden Arden, the song is delivered in a high and lonely-sounding falsetto, the better to communicate the isolation of the central character. This is Morrison's most extreme use of the 'head voice' of the falsetto – the strangeness of which repeated listening does nothing to diminish – and it teeters between something quite marvellous and something unintentionally comical. Yet Morrison pulls it off, perhaps precisely because of the high-wire risks that he takes with the performance. The striking pitch at which the song is delivered meets and captures the tremulous sense of absolute vulnerability identified within the apparent securities of the lyric, where the subject of the song is well protected, but pinned and on show like a butterfly under glass. He is free but only within the confines of a goldfish bowl, swinging from a star but, courtesy of the flimsiest and most incongruous of connections, wishing upon a toilet roll, in a place where one's only company is a gun and a spectre. The falsetto emphasises this mixing of the secure and the vulnerable. It's worth noting that he has used a lower register on the rare live performances of the song. The enigmatic ambiguities of the lyric, the instrumentation and even the arrangement are all deepened and troublingly emphasised by that falsetto voice. The unresolved concluding chord is a kind of emotional correspondence to the curiousness of the vocal, sending the listener back into the song to reconsider it and try to come to terms with what they have just heard.

The recitative style of 'Linden Arden' finds a less austere outlet on 'Streets Of Arklow', a vocal which we recognise as being close kin to some of Morrison's best 80s work, balancing power with texture and including advance notice of the characteristic extended vowel sound which ruled in that decade, being heard to good effect on '*gay* profusion'(1.36–40) and 'raging beauty' (2.29–34). This is a fuller and more rounded sound than we hear on, say, 'Astral Weeks' in '*here* I am' and '*there* you go', where the wire in his voice, uncoiling since that first blast on 'Don't Start Crying Now', full of Belfast salt and vim, is still winding round the sound he makes. In that sound we also find an unconscious mythologisation of landscape. In this most played of *Veedon Fleece* numbers we find signification of Irishness via pipes, but the piano is playing in a minor register more familiar from American funeral blues, bringing melancholia and moral ambiguity to the song's undertow. Again, the strings echo the upward movement of the voice – hear how they are triggered by his unexpected modulation during 'walked' at 2.19. This moment is a superb example of the radical unity of this album, is explored further in the final chapter of this book. The song is sung straight from the centre of the chest, and brings the most recognisably 'Van Morrison' vocal on this album. His delivery of the last line (a repetition of the first) invites us to see the song as circular but also progressive. The vocal tone is steady, central and solid, the voice direct, clear, and unencumbered.

'You Don't Pull No Punches (But You Don't Push The River)' is the album's vocal high point, with extended vowel sounds, off-mikes and embellishments. Yet even these swiftly passing moments endure. For example, the lines 'Talking about the real soul . . . going out in the country', which fly past when one is listening, are used by arch Morrison fan David Gray in live versions of his song 'Nightblindness'. Gray has also adopted, in part, Morrison's extended vowel sound as a key element of his own vocalising technique, heard to good effect on his hit single 'Babylon'.[24] The passing detail can also be the long-running motif: the lines 'Going out to the West coast / Shining our light into the days of blooming wonder' make use of, in 'blooming wonder', a phrase which reaches forward to 'A Sense Of Wonder' and also back to his pre-*Astral Weeks* cast-off 'Hey Where Are You?'[25] 'You Don't Pull No Punches' draws in Morrison's whole armoury of vocal stylings from that period, and offers a kind of map of possible routes his singing could take: the bass voice, the falsetto voice, the folk voice, the whisper, the soul shout, the pop melodicist, the scat, and the blues growl are all encompassed in this remarkable, unrepeatable piece of work. To illustrate, listen to how he cascades from falsetto through a gruff blues voice down into the bass register from 6.33–37 in a single phrase:

> '. . . [falsetto] but you do [blues] n't push [bass] the river . . .'

We feel particularly the sense of free movement, sometimes urgent, sometimes tentative, sometimes swooping, sometimes, in Yeats's phrase, dropping slow, which characterises the song and indeed the mood of the whole album in the way he sings that single word 'don't', divided between vocal registers. Likewise, we hear again the extended vowel sound he developed and favoured in the 80s deployed on '*out* in the west' at 4.49–53. The song functions as a complete and unified piece of labour and inspiration, but also offers that series of opening doors, into different voices he might adopt or pursue. In common with its album-mates, on its very infrequent and fragmentary concert outings, this song has been performed at least an octave lower, in Morrison's 'normal' singing voice, the wild and daring variations smoothed out.

Flipping the album, 'Bulbs' was recovered from the bottom drawer as an extra and as a single, and is somewhat out of character with the rest of the record stylistically, but in terms of vocal fits the pattern of experimentation, in its employment of range, 'non-verbal' vocalisations of the middle section, and haywire vowel extrapolations at the song's close. The vocal, on such an 'Irish' record is pure Americana; the first four lines containing 'centerfield', 'being down for the game', 'one shot deal don't matter'. She's also 'leaving Pan American'. The vocal is a remarkable assemblage of experimental vocalising, with 'heh-heh' noises after 'Pan American' (1.01), and the startling vulpine low growl of the middle eight (2.03–23), straight from the throat in a manner which recalls 'Listen To The Lion'. The voice comes clear of this tangle of dark sound occasionally, soaring into clarity, as on 'the batteries are corroded'. The 'Lalalala' section carries the song's hook throughout: the percussive vocal rhetoric of pop reasserts itself here, as it does in say, 'Brown Eyed Girl', 'Natalia', and 'Kingdom Hall'. At the song's close comes a wild and unexpected address to the listener as the voice leaps up at 3.28–30, with the way he sings 'screaming' forcing new vigour upon the performance and also working as a kind of autodescriptive challenge to the listener. Asked if we can hear the lonely cry, and if not, why not, we are sent back into the song to hear it encoded into the way he sings 'screaming'.

The vocal on 'Cul de Sac' is more measured than the startling flights of 'Bulbs', and this somehow suits the suburban mood of the title; an elegant dead-end but one actively pursued ('You will double back to a cul de sac') in balance with great and unlimited adventure 'Oh I travel far the nearest star'. The voice is pitched between the croon of 'Fair Play' and the shouty bark of 'Bulbs', and the key vocal hook is a tightly concertina'd vowel sound heard to good effect on the 'e' sound in 'relax' (0.27–32), the 'a' in 'lay' from 0.58–1.02 and the 'o' in the 'you' of the first chorus at 1.56–59. The 'and this is it' ad lib at 2.02 builds upon the sense of forward motion inferred in the long vowel sound of 'travel' and 'nearest star', and is very astute in its connection to the 'who you know' repetitions which flow into 'really are'. In the final section the voice becomes more engaged with its task; repetitions build, ad libs supply the matrix for the main lines, and a remarkable scream comes before 'It's not as far as a country mile', inferring Hank Williams distances. Barthes' wished-for guttural element is distilled into the 'Dohn-dohn-dohn' slow scat that follows (4.38–48), building into an expressive scream (4.55–5.01) that precipitates a loosening up of the arrangement: cymbals start to splash more, guitar slides up and down the scale somewhat more readily, leading 'you got it' (5.18–19) into the final section. The song offers no final resolution, rather a bear-like, hunched and deep-gut growl, making one last unexpected turn at 5.46, down into the depths of the fade. This inconclusive conclusion feels as if it is in agreement with the ambient mood of the song – the prickly frustration of the closed exit, and of the cul-de-sac.

The voice on 'Comfort You' comes again from the middle of the throat; in some senses this album represents the desire to sing from another place, in the physical sense, neither the head nor the gut. In seeking expression of emotion via physically produced sound, it is working towards Blake's unity of body and soul. By employing the head, throat and the gut Morrison produces a sound both sonically and emotionally resonant, and one which on this tune is lucid in its emotional clarity but also vexing in its multiplicity of sources and levels of pitch. D. H. Lawrence wrote about what he called, in a little, Nietzschean grumble, the 'greed of giving', in the sense that in acts of kindness one is 'buying' or 'stealing' a reaction, a response, a connection, and incurring a debt, with another.[26] The evocation of empathy of 'Comfort You' and the tough-tenderness of such a relationship both evades this trap and shames Lawrence. The voice carries this promise and hope that things can be different, and also bring a return to a state of grace, 'like when you were a child', as the lyric puts it. The voice is steady, temperate and strong, just like the support and comfort being offered.

'Come Here My Love' is not the sexual invitation the title might infer, as in a blues song; this is a metaphysical unspooling of care. It has at its heart a purple strangeness. The song contains a vocal both fragmented and whole, with slight malapropisms, yet rendered poetically as 'fathoms of my inner mind'. Melancholy is rejected, and the proposed closeness is a solution: 'I will raise my spirits high for you'. The two are contemplating fields and leaves, 'talking about nothing', working to point of stillness. The vocal performance makes the song, despite the desire of the title, almost entirely free of sexual connotation, and the voice is free of the guttural, visceral physicality of say, 'Bulbs'. Instead we have an intimate take on the distinctive mid-throat sound employed on the album, and we hear the sound being gently, physically extruded from the throat, giving sense of both muscularity and strength but also of measure and a kind of wisdom which accommodates both physical (worldly) and metaphysical (spiritual) knowledge and understanding. The line 'Come along with me and take it all in' is not indiscriminate in its scope but able to see the connections between 'it all'. The only moment of 'performance' in the vocal comes as he relishes and repeats 'effervescent' (1.30–33), the repetition illustrating the slow and natural reaction inferred in the word. This and the album's final song are very closely connected, and there is a kind of meditative movement between levels: 'Come Here My Love' proposes the state in which 'Country Fair' simultaneously inhabits and recalls as a lost Eden.

'Country Fair's' lyric is a metaphysical paradox, as the idyll it inhabits is consigned to memory and described retrospectively; indeed they are lying in the grass as the previous song suggested they would, but the voice recalls this, from eternity's distance. It is like a held gaze, up to a star one has the vague memory of having once happily visited. The song itself is beauteous, yet it sounds painful for the singer to recall, with its Blakean warnings: 'We were too young to really know . . . And never thought that it would pass'. It is a painful memory but also one to which the narrator is drawn, over and over again. Dissonance creeps in towards the end, to suggest the closure of something and the vaguely perceived presence of something about to begin. The voice here is closest to realising the blend of the three elements which characterise the voice on this selection of songs as head, gut and throat meet and are in accord in the delivery. The role of memory is important – this is the voice of experience reflecting upon that of the condition of innocence, which is always, necessarily, a retrospective and 'coloured' one. It seems to exist in the state of a dream: the falling asleep at the end of 'Come Here My Love', that lover's lullaby, and the sweetness follows, like the visions of Dante in *The Divine Comedy* and Olaf Stapledon in *Star Maker*,[27] both glimpsed between the strokes of a midnight bell. Yet the dream itself is also a memory of a fleeting moment, kissed as it flies, but also eternal, both freeing and entrapping the mind that remembers the body experiencing it.

The river picks up image form 'Punches' and the different voice we hear on this song – tired and seeking rest where the Punches voice was relentlessly driving forward – makes us feel this change, which is also a remaining the same. Like the river, it is flowing, ever changing, but always remaining the same. The meditative process is deeply engaged here, and it is best expressed through the grain of the voice on these songs; endlessly flowing, changing, remaining the same. How does one produce a definitive version of a river? The same question might be asked of Morrison's voicing of his songs.

Veedon Fleece also operates a kind of synaesthesia – that is, the relationship between colour, sound and feeling – the most famous example of this of course being the 'blue note'. Morrison discussed this with R. D. Laing, and claimed he had yet to investigate the subject, consciously at least:

> RDL: In your own musical imagination, do you see these zones with specific colours?
>
> VM: Colours? No I've never seen them as colours.

RDL: Eisenstein. He was very attracted to the whole idea of the chromatic, colour of the different notes. The Tibetans?

VM: No I haven't explored colour yet.

RDL: The idea of a trumpet is red.

VM: I think some at Lighthouse teach that. What Chakra are they related to, all that. That's part of my research programme, that one. That's on that tape I was telling you about, it's all on that tape about that. Not the colours but the instruments. It talks a lot about the violet flame in the heart, so they relate violet to the heart.[28]

He is intrigued, as well he might be, by this system of understanding and this new order of perception – 'The idea of a trumpet is red' – but the intriguing detail for us is that he had already woven this kind of sensitivity into his work, sometimes obviously (with his cover of 'Bein' Green'), and less overtly via his use of synaesthesia in the sound of an album like *Veedon Fleece*, which is, in the title of one of his later songs, blue and green.

So *Veedon Fleece* offers and uncovers a mix of the metaphysical (synaesthesia, the image of the Veedon Fleece itself) and the determinedly physical realms – there is an emphasis on the life of the body, in the songs and in their lyrical concerns. The voice is poised between these two modes: the physical response to the metaphysical dimension, a wise, weightless and inscrutable extrusion from the gut, chest and head – the bridge and meeting point of the body and soul, made real through Morrison's voice. The album is, I'd suggest, Morrison's most remarkable in terms of his singing. In order to provide a balance to the scrutiny of a single album, we might now usefully explore a handful of songs that seem to be expressive of moments of change, development and discovery in his singing.

'FRIDAY'S CHILD' (1966)

'Friday's Child' is the vocal bridge between the 'old' Van Morrison, the r'n'b-beat boom pop star, and the reborn child of 1968 and *Astral Weeks*. As a late Them recording, it reveals how his early squalling style had been sloughed off and a more supple, worldly tone had begun to emerge, and as such stands apart, if not alone, in his catalogue. The song's obscurity is in part no doubt due to its very limited release, being first issued on an EP in the Netherlands in 1967, well after Morrison had quit the band. It was unavailable in the UK until Decca's commendable and pioneering *Rock Roots* series got round to Them in 1976, and finally emerged in digital form on 1997's *The Story Of Them* double CD. So its obscurity is less of a mystery than it might be, yet it is a key song in the development of Morrison's art and vocal style, and deserves to be more widely known.[29]

The vocal and lyric of the song introduces a range of feelings and themes which previous work had hinted at and which would become more sharply focused and important in later work; consider its motifs of north and south, images of movement, evocation of place, leaving home and entering into exile, and references to folk tradition. It is a celebration of youth and adventure, but one which is melancholic in cast, both lyrically and musically. The vocal timbre, caught between adolescence and adulthood, is both a confirmation of and a challenge to this mood. Lyrically, the line 'From the north to the south' anticipates the sweep in the opposite direction in 'Madame George', on the train from Dublin up to Sandy Row, a cross between the compass point chorus of 'The Star Of The County Down' and the emotional sweep across the continent offered by Woody Guthrie's image, 'From California to the New York island' in 'This Land Is Your Land'. The sense of exile and leaving home, the need to go, whether one wishes to or not, is clear: 'you left your home, left your home for good to stay'. The mix of yearning and warning in the vocal with its twists and turns, by turns grave and light, wise and passionate, philosophically detached and carpe diem direct, is powerful. The extended vowel sound on 'Friday' bears all this bright hope and trembling fear for the girl's destiny, inevitable and yet uncertain: 'You can't stop now'.

The song's title, which had also been used in a 1966 hit song for Nancy Sinatra, stems from the children's singing game:

> Monday's child is fair of face
> Tuesday's child is full of grace
> Wednesday's child is full of woe
> Thursday's child has far to go
> Friday's child is loving and giving
> Saturday's child works for its living
> And a child that's born on the Sabbath day
> Is fair and wise and good and gay.[30]

It is no doubt entirely coincidental, but we can note that Morrison was born on a Friday, 31 August 1945. The girl in the song seems open to life, eager to give and to love, even when that ends up costing her something; it is about the delicate balance, the poise, the tipping-point between innocence and experience; something he would explore much more deeply on *Astral Weeks* and beyond. This is where the song's potent blend of excited anticipation and jaded melancholia is rooted.

Musically, the song opens on determinedly minor guitar chords, suggesting ambiguity, lending an almost elegiac atmosphere. This is not a rock and roll celebration of youth; the tone is one of unease and moral fable. Its tone is of sadness. The lyrical reference to Notting Hill Gate links it with 'Slim Slow Slider', and we can read the song as a kind of fore-echo of it, both in terms of location and its wider sense of hopeful melancholy. Indeed, the girl in both songs could perhaps be the same person, at first in a state of innocence (or 'Before' in *Astral Weeks*'s terms) and then in a state of experience (the 'Afterwards' of that album's second side, which 'Slim Slow Slider' closes). The song is about the building up of dreams in a state of innocence, with 'rainbows hanging round [her] feet', even when the girl is 'making out with everyone that [she] meets', and how those dreams are brought back down to earth not by the actions of others but by the dreamer, awakening: 'I watched you knock 'em down, each and every one', into a condition of realism. This dichotomy of dream and reality, of innocence and experience, is of course a familiar one in Morrison's work, but it is in 'Friday's Child' that he first begins to find the lyrical and musical vocabulary to express it properly.

That opening line, moving from the north to the south, does of course have a resonance for an Irish musician, yet to confine it to that would be reductive. This emotional mapping and the energy of curiosity as a creative impulse towards the compassing of the self that, as we shall see, surfaced much later in the live incarnation of 'Summertime In England': 'We're gonna go from north to south we're gonna go from east to west we're gonna go right through the middle of the land'.[31] Furthermore, the movement is from north to south – that is towards the warmth and away from the cold – Samuel Beckett noted that he changed a line in his play *Footfalls* where May talks of entering a church from by the south door to by the north door as 'south was too warm'.[32] In 'Friday's Child', the girl heads towards the warmth.

The song possesses glistening acoustic surfaces matched with a folk-rock rhythm, not unlike that of 'My Lonely Sad Eyes', but, paradoxically, much lonelier and sadder sounding. It is haunting and haunted. It has attracted only a couple of covers, one being a straight and robust reading by Morrison's old comrade Herbie Armstrong, and the other appeared on the 'tribute' album *No Prima Donna*, sung by Lisa Stansfield. Sensual stylist as she is, she adds little vocally, pointing up how intricate and rich Morrison's vocal is on the Decca original. Stansfield's vocal feels as though she couldn't quite cope with the song, de-emphasising its key elements until there was little left, but it is interesting in its very inclusion. Here is a ten-track covers album that concludes, with perhaps typical perversity, with an obscure song that was never really given a proper release neither in the lifetime of the group that recorded it nor subsequently as the fame of its composer grew.[33] In its melancholic, reflective, troubled beauty it stands as one of the overlooked classics in his repertoire – this is the earliest song to truly suggest the melancholy ecstasies of *Astral Weeks* and I'd argue the song is at least the equal of much that followed it. It is as powerful an evocation of innocence under pressure as Brian Wilson's 'Caroline, No', while being tougher and more accepting of change than that wonderful song.

'Friday's Child', then, while it is tentatively, even strangely recorded, with its acoustic folk-rock textures underpinned by a very heavy bass sound, offers a turning point in Morrison's work. The key feature is how Morrison's vocal is poised between the Belfast of the Maritime Hotel and that taken out into the world via 'Cyprus Avenue' and beyond, the more sophisticated instrument that emerged on 'TB Sheets', and of course *Astral Weeks* in the two years that followed. This vocal balancing point is reflected in the song's themes of standing on the threshold of great change, of transformation through experience and exile, even if that which one undergoes is fearful – it's too late to stop now. This sense of obligation to experience and to the present moment is undoubtedly a key theme throughout Morrison's work, and it is feverishly sketched in his vocal performance on this song.

'TB SHEETS' (1967)

That sense of fever in the voice leads us to the greatest vocal performance from the Bang sessions. 'TB Sheets' is 9.36 of pure performed claustrophobia and clammy, cold, white-hot panic.[34] Randy Newman referred to this song as one of his favourite vocal performances, referring to the 'early great acting job he [Morrison] did on that song'.[35] In this Newman opens up a question as to the nature of performance itself, live or in the studio, but it is beyond dispute that 'acting job' or not Morrison's performance on and of 'TB Sheets' here is something unlike almost anything else you'll hear. It's hard to believe that it once shared vinyl space with 'Spanish Rose', and the co-presence of the pair on one LP is evidence of the very fine balance in the battle for control within the studio on these Bang sessions.

The content, as well as the form, of 'TB Sheets' illustrates this further. Berns was a pop businessman who knew a hit when he heard it, or wrote it. Morrison was coming from, and going to, somewhere else. There is a strong tradition of TB songs in blues and country music, exemplified by Victoria Spivey ('TB Blues', 'Dirty TB Blues' and 'TB Got Me') in the former, and by Jimmie Rodgers ('TB Blues'), who died from the disease, in the latter. Morrison would certainly have known these songs. Indeed, according to PRONI, TB was still at large in the Ireland of the 1950s.[36] So the daily realities connected with the roots of the music he loved, and these tensions inform the remarkable vocal he delivers on this track. In Spivey's TB songs, for example, the singer is the sufferer and this is the view of 'Julie baby', who is, like the figure in Spivey's 'Dirty TB Blues', 'cryin' in the midnight'. 'TB Sheets' comes from the perspective of the visitor, trying to do the right thing and counteract the loneliness of the sufferer, but always aware of the risk he is taking.

Musically, the song's structure reflects the lyrical mode of entrapment; it opens with a blustering squall of arhythmic drums and organ before settling back into a relentless and unrelieved cycle of chords, rolling and tumbling in circles around itself. This is a progression that never progresses. Only two bursts of almost impossibly high-end harmonica playing cut across this mesmerising sequence, and they are shrill, tight and alarming, as if they were struggling for breath, notes wheezing from the instrument like short breaths – a musical suggestion of air squeezing in and out of the lungs. We feel the tension in the studio in the extremity of the vocal performance, caught up in this chord cycle, an eternal moment of paralysis between staying and leaving, never quite managing to do either. The song is a kind of 'mono-dialogue' drama; like a stereo record with only one speaker working, it is a dialogue we only hear one side of and Morrison's vocal skilfully responds to the unheard voice: hear how he responds to a rebuke – 'It ain't funny, baby, it ain't funny at *all*'. In this we hear and feel the closeness of the cool room.

Importantly for understanding the ambiguously sympathetic and anxious mood of 'TB Sheets' is the fact of transmission: it can be spread by close proximity via coughing, spitting, sneezing or speaking. Anyone visiting a TB sufferer was taking a real chance of being infected in some way and this emotional ambivalence is in the dark balance of the line 'Your little starstruck innuendoes, inadequacies and . . . foreign bodies'. This draws an explicit and direct link between Julie's apparently unwanted infatuation with the narrator and the illness that keeps her housebound: 'I see the way you jumped at me, from behind the door, and look into my eyes'. Both are uncomfortable for him to be in close proximity with. The narrator is deeply uneasy, and Morrison's skill at indentifying mood via sense of place serves him well here – 'And the sunlight shining through the crack in the windowpane, numbs my brain'. The light does not blaze rich vitamin D into this room, it steals in via a crack, suggesting the room is dark, or that the window itself is filthy – a window cleaner's eye perhaps? – adding to the sense of discomfort and claustrophobia, which is forced home, with some fury, in the next line 'Open up the window, let me breathe / Open up the window, *let me breathe!*' (my italics).

The lyrical structure of the repeated line places it in a blues tradition, but also emphasises the double nature of the narrator's feelings at being there – the duality of duty and disgust, each emotion pulling equally hard upon him. All this is borne by the sound of the voice in this startling vocal performance. The claustrophobic panic is made uncomfortably real for the listener (3.15–24), where 'Open up the window . . .' is followed by seven choked and stifled attempts at a breath, an extraordinary illustration of the physical experience. This is hard to listen to, because it is almost *too* real, even though we recall that it is a performance of the sort he outlined to Spike Milligan in 1989:

> SM: Listening to your singing, Van, you have a sense of excitement. Not many singers have this. That's what you convey.
>
> VM: It's drama isn't it? The blues are drama, that's what I picked up from it. You make things more than they really are, to get it across, I find. It's fantasy, illusion.[37]

Illusion, fantasy, drama, or not, it is strong stuff and Milligan is right to locate that 'excitement' in the voice.

The song sounds like a single take, but according to Bill Flanagan it took two, and as he says in the notes to *Bang Masters*, 'here rock was taken as far as it's ever dared go – rock talks tough but "TB Sheets" is about disease . . . it's a wrenching scene. Lyrically, emotionally extreme.'[38] That extremity makes it remarkable that the song was ever issued at all, and Berns's inclusion of the song on *Blowin' Your Mind!* shows that he was not without insight into Morrison's deeper strengths. The struggle for creative control in those New York studios in 1967, expressed through the extremity of the vocal performance set against that steady, deadly, unchanging chord map, provided Morrison, paradoxically, with a way forward.

'YOU'VE GOT THE POWER' (1972)

Tucked away on the B-side of the single of 'Jackie Wilson Said', and uncollected ever since, lies a remarkable recording. The ensemble performance on 'You've Got The Power' is a mighty-sounding thing, righteous and powerful in its proclamation. It is so far ahead of plenty of other cuts that have become live favourites that, like 'Friday's Child', its obscurity is puzzling to me. The vocal is right at the funky forefront of the stereo picture here and combines both the raw soul attack for which Morrison was by 1972 well known with the deft skill of withholding and withdrawing from such directness when the tune demands it. This is one of the best examples we have of Morrison's voice working in a fully integrated way with the superb band that blasted on to the concert stages of the early 70s, leading up to the summative documenting of *It's Too Late To Stop Now*.

From the opening terpsichorean tumble of the drums, the band moves like a single entity, using hot stabs of organ amid a sensual, climbing progression, while the horn section is sinuous, muscular and jalapeño hot. The band grabs this track by the scruff of its neck, delivering a platform seemingly miles wide for Morrison's vocal to explore the upper and lower limits of the tune. The horns and the voice in particular drive the track, and refuse to yield to each other for the 3.36 duration: even the two vocal-only bridges ('Baby . . . baby . . . baby . . . baby') are like breathing spaces in which the horns are resonating around the track and preparing for the next blast. It is somewhat unusual in the way that the horns and voice take each other into the ring in this way, horn surges punctuating and emphasising shifts or reinforcements of the melody, pushing the voice on to further heights. Like all great ensembles, the band makes the song sound as if it had just fallen from the tree, entirely unforced and natural. Morrison even has time to play with 'fire' on the fade, rolling the word around and exploring its sensual, soulful possibilities.

The track is, in the absence of any other evidence, a leftover from the *Saint Dominic's Preview*, although it sounds more like the tight, warm horn sound of *His Band And The Street Choir* era than the diversity of the later record. Not a note is wasted and it is lean, sleek and apparently effortless. It sounds like the song is asserting its right to exist and has at last found the right conduit, and the song gives us a great early example of Morrison's voice as integral part of a full-force ensemble sound.[39]

'TWILIGHT ZONE' (1974)

This song, recorded on 9 April 1974 just on the cusp of the so-called 'Period of Transition', is a kind of experimental canvas on which he was able to experiment and play around with different, new tones and methodologies. Morrison had just released the Caledonia Soul Orchestra from his employment, having taken that project to the fullest of realisations via *It's Too Late To Stop Now*. In this studio take – a live version at the infamous Montreux 1974 show, with different lyrics, is available via DVD – he employs up to four distinct vocal timbres and techniques, which we might classify as:

- 'Falsetto'
- 'Mechanical Bliss'
- 'Growl'
- 'Off-mike'

Tom Donohue mentioned the singing in a November 1974 radio interview:

> TD: I like that. ['It's not the 'Twilight Zone'] I like the voice effects you're getting.
>
> VM: Yeah, that's singing up an octave. Falsetto. In the key of C in that one.[40]

The falsetto vocal dominates the performance but it also features other key elements; what we might call his 'Bulbs' growl, involving dropping down from the high register to a bluesy rasp, is heard from 6.08–14, which then quickly yields to his 'Mechanical Bliss' voice from 6.19–33. This stagey approximation of the received version of an English 'upper-class twit' voice via Spike Milligan and childhood memories of hearing the BBC's radio comedy of the 50s is heard in full cry on 'Mechanical Bliss', recorded at the same sessions in Hilversum. We get only a sliver here, which would be barely believable if we hadn't heard 'Mechanical Bliss' itself. Soaring back to falsetto at 6.35, the track begins to very slowly wind down as a song – he is back to the 'Bulbs' growl at 7.08–14, then into what we might refer to as an 'off-mike stage voice'. This is a kind of rhetorical technique Morrison favours when minded to do so during live shows; it's something he has often done and is frequently evidence that it might be a good night. In some ways it is definitively a live technique as, paradoxically, it conveys and connotes intimacy and a kind of authenticity, even though the voice seems much more 'far off'. Singing without direct amplification makes an audience become far more deeply attentive, requiring them to listen harder, and we feel the sense of risk and of 'liveness', and thus the atmospherics within a hall step up, becoming more charged and of the moment. He will step away from the mike and stand somewhere just below the drum riser, his voice still drifting into the live mikes onstage but not directly into any. Listen to 7.02–8.12 in the live version of 'In The Afternoon' for a good example of this technique and the positive tension it creates, as well as the space it can open up. It is also a superb example of Morrison's instinctive understanding of the internal dynamics crucial to musical performance. In the studio, however, it is usually a kind of leaning *into* the mike that conveys this level of intimacy – think of the last minutes of 'You Know What They're Writing About' – and to hear his stage method at work in a studio recording is rare. It's here, though – listen to the section 7.15–42, until the vocal turns back to its falsetto hum and finishes on a low, gruff finale riff around the word 'honeycomb'.

An additional aspect of the cut's watershed nature is the dialogue between voice and piano. Opening with Pete Wingfield's classical flourish on the piano and some expansive, rolling ride cymbal from Peter Van Hooke, the tune slips into a groove of gentle resolution. Morrison's vocal is given light-years of room in which to feel the space of the melody; entering at 29 seconds, behind the beat, and lending the track a languid and unhurried mood. It dictates the ebbs and flows of this mood: listen to how the piano works to follow the vocal's rising and falling, for example at 1.34 when the line 'And they tried to freak me!' is echoed by the piano delivering some splintered notes worthy of Ben Sidran himself. Later at 4.32–38 voice and piano engage in a light-footed conversation over the phrase 'Didn't you get', which stands as a fore-echo of the great sax and vocal live experiments in the performances of 'Summertime In England' with Pee Wee Ellis in the 1980s. Wingfield's airy solo from 2.46–3.44 likewise meets with gruff off-mike approval from the composer, communicating both the 'liveness' of the recording and also Morrison's understanding of the rhetorical force of such a role for his voice in setting the atmospheres of a track.[41]

'SONG OF BEING A CHILD' (1986)

This is perhaps a curious choice for a study of Morrison's singing – a cut that is mostly spoken word. Yet the spoken word recordings that stud the 1980s catalogue are key to the development of the sound of his voice, and how he chose to use that sound. They mark a distinction in terms of both performance and his approach to a song as a 'text', to use Roland Barthes' term from 'The Grain of the Voice'. For these reasons and more, 'Song Of Being A Child' seems to me one of the best and most important vocal performances in Morrison's catalogue. There is an unusual backstory to the recording; in the opening sequence of Wim Wenders' *Wings of Desire* we see a hand writing and hear a voice languidly reciting a poem which periodically resurfaces throughout the narrative.[42] This German text is the original of 'Song Of Being A Child', which emerged, beautifully and unexpectedly, on Morrison's 1998 anthology, *The Philosopher's Stone: The Unreleased Tapes Volume One.* Written by co-writer of the *Wings of Desire* screenplay, Peter Handke, the poem was recorded, with musical accompaniment and in Handke's English translation, by Morrison alongside Northern Irish folk/session singer and actress June Boyce, who was in his band at that time. Hers is the voice one can hear asking 'Did ye get healed?' at the close of the song of that title. The piece didn't make the movie cut, arguably because their mutually coaxing Ulster intonation lends this Central European poem an unmistakable linguistic locale, so much so that it's progressively difficult to think of it as a 'German' text: indeed it is one of Morrison's most 'Northern Irish' vocal performances. We can compare too the development of the spoken word voice in his work from the staginess of 'Mechanical Bliss' and the self-consciousness of the recitation in 'Summertime In England', through to the unapologetic Ulsterisms of this track. Helping in this was his co-vocalist,

June Boyce, who was working live and in the studio with him at the time – she is on *No Guru, No Method, No Teacher*, *Poetic Champions Compose* and *Irish Heartbeat*, subsequently going on to a whole range of top-drawer work. But it is surely these four minutes and nine seconds that represent the most startlingly original work in which she has been directly involved.

The two voices work together to introduce two levels of understanding and perception: first, the loneliness inherent in the poem is qualified by the bouncing back and forth between the two voices which, in their companionship, stand against isolation. Further, the male and female voices make a further claim upon completeness or at least a more rounded understanding of the meaning of memory; for of course that is what the poem is exploring – the relationship between the child we all once were and the adult perspective upon that childhood. This is the Mississippi Delta of Morrison's methodologies: the view from Experience of the state and time of Innocence. I'd suggest that these themes are more fully realized in this track than might at first seem the case. Musically it is simple: a buoyant, mesmerising keyboard motif played and played, against the Chronos-click of a rimshot snare, some rattles of semi-acoustic guitar and the two unmistakably Northern Irish voices. It fades in, on the keyboard, a trick of the studio which nevertheless lends an metaphysical gloss to the sound – that is, this music is already playing, and we have just and only now tuned into it – and the rhythm comes in with the voices at 0.10. This association of time being marked and the arrival of the human voice deliver a sense of humanity and mortality – time begins to be marked and begins to slip away when the human voices appear. Boyce reads a little more self-consciously than Morrison, but her voice is a beautiful sound.

The text of Handke's poem ends at 2.48, and in the booklet accompanying the CD it notes 'additional words by Van Morrison'. Immediately these 'additional words' are recognisable as being from the heart of his very own distinctive lexicon, as he begins to riff and improvise around the word 'child'. He proceeds to remake the poem in his own image, with 'a sense of wonder . . . up on the highest hill . . . Are you there? Are you there?', invoking 'A Sense Of Wonder', and 'You Know What They're Writing About' and its extended live performances. Morrison asserts the primacy of the words and the voice by rhetorically shushing the keyboard and rhythm at 3.23 (with no noticeable impact, it must be said), the better to explore the forceful *sotto voce* technique he is employing. This is what Sinéad O'Connor described as his style of 'animated speaking'.[43] June Boyce comes back in at 3.45, joining him in the scatting over the word 'child', and there is a little break of laughter in Morrison's delivery at 3.43, just as she joins him, and she responds with a little, fond smile in her voice at 3.54–55. This passing of the ball back and forth between the two is the secret heart of this recording's beauty; it is formal and connected to a written text, but that text is simply the framework around the seesawing exchange between the two voices. The track ends absolutely, finally and perfectly at 4.04, on an optimistic note in both the musical and the philosophical senses. I would suggest that this is one of Morrison's greatest vocal recordings that, in its apparent simplicity, speaks of deep, wide resonant complexity, the small sketch which captures the whole.[44]

'I DON'T WANT TO GO ON WITHOUT YOU' (1995)

In all of Morrison's catalogue, there are few true duets: shared vocal recordings are more likely to be two voices circling a common centre within a song, be that his version of 'Tupelo Honey' with Bobby 'Blue' Bland or 'Song Of Being A Child' itself. Why is this? Perhaps the discipline required to hit the note at the same time every time works against his natural gifts and preferred techniques of vocalising? Phil Everly had something to say on the matter:

> 'By singing harmony, and singing the way I sing it, I had to listen to every little variable that Donald did; each time he sang 'Bye Bye Love', he may have felt he was singing it in the same way, but he never did, because you can't say a word the same way twice, and to harmonise with someone is rather like talking in unison. To do it is a fine art and I guess I was always busy on stage and I never had the feeling, 'I'm tired of doing this'. There were times when I didn't enjoy performing – it depended. But I was so busy trying to blend or hold a note for the same time or get the same vibrato or keep on pitch or whatever, that was the difference – it didn't bore me.'[45]

Everly, perhaps the greatest natural harmony singer of the pop era, displays both the ease and labour of his craft here. We can certainly imagine Morrison having some trouble with being expected to sing the same way each time – yet we note that so did Don Everly and that therefore in fact Phil's greatest skill was to do precisely what Morrison does – sing it differently, but correctly, every time. So how does this 'fine art', as Everly calls it, inform his rare duet recordings? An obscure example reveals much.

'I Don't Want To Go On Without You', most widely available on *Best Of Vol. Three*, is a song written by Morrison's mentor of old, Bert Berns, and Jerry Wexler, and I knew it via the beautiful recording by Patti Labelle in her girl-group days with the Bluebells. Morrison's version, we learn, was recorded in 1994 at the Wool Hall, and mixed by Mick Glossop. The credits on the single of 'Days Like This', where the song received its first release, don't reveal the identity of the co-vocalist but it is James Hunter, a British bluesman much admired by Morrison – he has praised Hunter's work in interviews and even provided glowing praise for a promo campaign for Hunter's 2006 album *People Gonna Talk*. Hunter's superb and smoky vocal on this track had me fooled for a long time; I thought the voice must belong to a Bobby Bland or a Solomon Burke quietly guesting on a song with their admirer. The two singers are co-vocalising from the outset, and most unusually for Morrison the guest voice is not there to echo (Brian Kennedy) or be traditional back-up (Katie Kissoon and others) but actually takes the lion's share of the vocal in terms of solo spots.

The song begins with a shared vocal: not quite a harmony in the sense that Phil Everly describes but close listening shows us that Hunter is playing the Phil role to Van's Don on the shared sections. The song breaks down into distinct vocalised sections which we can tabulate:

Acoustic guitar intro: 0.00–03.

First Verse: 0.03–0.35. Harmony 0.03–14; Hunter punctuates pause with ad lib at 0.15, back to harmony for brief bridge 0.16–20 ('baby, come home') then back to verse melody to bridge, with Hunter coming in before the beat at 0.31, 'trailing' his harmonic spot behind Morrison which continues up to 0.34.

Instrumental segment: 0.35–0.42. Hunter hum-improvising a counterpoint to the melody up to his 'solo' spot, between 42 and 58 seconds, at which point Morrison rejoins and Hunter goes back up to the harmony role. It's quite a leap, and one which he facilitates both for the listener and for himself by stepping up to a higher 'whoa' sound at 56 seconds so that he is in the right place when Morrison rejoins at 58.

Second verse: 0.58–1.29. Harmony 0.58–1.06 when Morrison unexpectedly takes the lines 'Oh my darlin' hear my plea / Come runnin' back to me' as a solo, with Hunter dipping in with an echo, *à la* Brian Kennedy, of 'hear my plea' in Morrison's pause at 1.10 between the two lines. The harmony returns from 1.14–1.23 until Hunter drops out on the words 'your face', leaving Morrison to sing them solo, only to echo them back into the song at 1.25. The effect of this is to powerfully convey the interplay of isolation and togetherness which complicates the apparent emotional directness of the song. The two voices re-merge for the clincher line 'every place'.

Hunter's second solo section: 1.31–52. This solo is trailed by a high, lonely soulful improvised vocal run from 1.31–36. (This was the part which persuaded me most completely that this other voice belonged to a soul legend of an earlier generation, so moving and effortless is it.) The lyrics are the same in both of Hunter's solo sections but, like all great singers, he sings it quite differently second time around: we can refer back to Phil Everly's observation of the virtues and problems of such an approach. This time his vocal leads up to a high, almost falsetto blue note which allows him to step right back into his harmony part as Morrison rejoins at 1.52. Responding to this, Morrison's opening note rocks a little on its axis and communicates the unsettled undertow of the measured lyric.

Third verse: 1.52–2.22. Harmony is added to by a couple of moments; at 2.05, in the breathing pause between the first and second segments of the verse, Hunter delivers an echo/aside which, unlike the Kennedy technique, eschews a straight mirroring of the vocal, instead providing a fore-echo of what Morrison is about to sing, packing itself into a half-beat just before the main vocal returns. Furthermore, it is a phrase of significance in Morrison's catalogue, 'come running'. The emphasis may well be accidental but it is certainly serendipitous. Morrison then takes the line 'Come running back to me' as a solo at 2.06–07. The section 2.08–14 is distinguished by Hunter's harmony modulating up and therefore becoming much clearer to the ear, adding to the emotional climb of the song, as the harmonies become both more overt and less tightly packed.

Finale: 2.22–3.24. This then paves the way for the song's finale, a kind of loosening and winding down which is also an emotional climax – Morrison and Hunter cross-weave their contributions from here to the fade but abandon the tight harmonies of the opening sections. Hunter takes most of this space with his high, lonesome tones swooping around the melody, while Morrison delivers a low, almost mantric 'Come running on back, running on back' from 2.52–57 as Hunter riffs around 'I don't wanna', and at 2.58 Morrison begins to blow his harmonica which ebbs and flows alongside his voice until the very final fade at 3.24.

This is a stunning vocal performance by both men, particularly in the playing off of the two vocal styles and deliveries; these are not voices born for harmony but in the first half of the song their common purpose carries the day. Their more natural inclination towards improvisation and 'liveness' in performance is deployed in measured terms, yet ones which tread the very fine line between the restrictive obligations of an arrangement and the freedom to pursue a mood central to the music they make. This is not to say that close-harmony singing as a matter of course is less creative, far from it – see Phil Everly's account of how 'busy' he felt onstage – but this cut is a rare example of how the two techniques can be made to spin off and benefit each other.

The warmth and soulful melancholia of the arrangement is of course the other 'voice' which we should acknowledge and take account of in this; the horns, the piano and the just-on-the-button drumming all enable the vocal to move and flow and develop in the manner it does. The spirit of the ensemble moves through this song, and that a performance as free and considered as this was devoted to a Bert Berns number in some way seems, to me at least, appropriate as a gesture of reconciliation and appreciation. Furthermore, it is easily Morrison's best vocal collaboration.[46]

'LISTEN TO THE LION' (1972)

Standing at the close of one of Morrison's most musically diverse collections, 1972's *Saint Dominic's Preview*, 'Listen To The Lion' provides us with a sprawling, 11.08 spread shot of Morrison's vocalising characteristics, techniques and tendencies. On this cut, the voice becomes the absolute centre of endeavour and the song's focus – after all, in the title we are asked to *listen* to the lion. Yet what does the lyric mean? How is the way it is sung related to any such meaning? Let's start by looking at the lion. The lion is a culturally available symbol of courage, strength and boldness, yet one also mixed with gentleness – drawing upon this, C. S. Lewis used the Lion to represent Christ in his children's myth *The Lion, the Witch and the Wardrobe*. We can only speculate as to whether Morrison knew the story by his fellow Ulsterman, but there is a correspondence between the capacity for discovering the marvellous via the mundane and everyday (in Lewis's case, the wardrobe) in both men's work. Furthermore, ask any child to describe the sound they would hear if they listened to a lion and they will give an extravagant roar. So these primal and culturally complex associations inform this final case study song.[47]

'Listen To The Lion' is a song upon which all those who have written about Morrison's work seem to concur: it has been dubbed variously as 'a considerable achievement . . . which ranks amongst Morrison's greatest work', 'breathtaking', and 'a tour de force'.[48] A return, it seemed, to the free expansiveness of *Astral Weeks* at the close of each side of *Saint Dominic's Preview*, with its near-twin 'Almost Independence Day' (a song more concerned with stillness than the pushing forward of 'Lion') reflecting back, like two lighthouses either side of a promontory, winking at each other out of the darkness. The subject of 'Listen To The Lion' is an interior journey, one of self-discovery. We hear echoes of this throughout his work of course – in the spoken interlude of 'Angeliou' ('About a search and a journey . . . just like mine'[49]), for example. The song builds like a wave, rising and falling, ebbing and flowing, threatening to break and overwhelm itself, then pulling back. Ritchie Yorke described it brilliantly:

> It was a soaring exercise in effective rock dynamics. Chunky rhythm guitar, brushes whisking across the drum kit, trembling bongos, flat fat bass, chattering piano, dipping chords, topped off with a stunning vocal.[50]

Yorke has it. Yet while the recording may well be a master class in musical dynamics, what it is most fully, it seems to me, is an exploration of the expressive possibilities of the human voice. The lyrics themselves do not occupy much space on paper; it is in the manner of their being sung that they are charged with meaning and purpose. The opening stroke of brightly gleaming acoustic guitar strings lifts the veil and the soundscape of brushed drum, plashy cymbal, wandering bass and Morrison's own characteristic guitar picking exists to provide not only the setting for the vocal but a context via which the connection between the voice and the backing can be better understood as interdependent elements.

The vocal performance can be divided into distinct sections:

0.19–5.05: main lyric/chorus-verse structure

5.05–6.10: unaccompanied growling

6.11–8.08: 'Listen To The Lion'

6.11: chorus joins in; brings structure and measure back in: every eighth beat

7.37: last chorus. Morrison has by now joined the chorus of 'Listen To The lion'; chorus fades here

8.09–10.23: 'And we sailed and we sailed'

So from the bright and dramatic annunciation of the song via a strong opening chord, we are very soon into the main body of the song, some 19 seconds later, as Morrison's vocal enters. In this opening section, his vocal is clear and he enunciates the words unmistakably, but still flags up the mood we are exploring with a sequence of eruptive notes and unexpected punctuations of the melodic structure. Contrast this with the opening take on the title phrase, from 1.07–17, careful, cautious and measured, and then hear him from 1.20–30, where on the repetition of the title his vocal suddenly leans back and soars upward; the musical backing follows him, rising commensurately and in a kind of empathy. Here the voice does not fade into a murky muddle of sound; rather it brings the band forward, voice and instruments unified, bouncing and playing off each other. Listen to his 'In!' at 1.32 and later at 2.59, a sharp pinpoint of sound, almost completely free of its 'literal' meaning, and equally deeply enmeshed in the articulation of pure feeling.

The blues basis of this song is clear in the repetitions within the verse structures: they are effectively a single line repeated, manipulated and sung into meaning:

1 All my love come down . . .
2 I shall search my soul . . .
3 All my tears have flowed . . .

It is at the close of the third verse that we first feel the coming force of the vocal excursion which comes to dominate the song and its reputation: 'for the lion-uuuhhh' at 4.37–45 trawls the depth of his register before springing up anew at the final assertion of the lion inside, from 4.47–5.03. This rise and fall, the voice swooping between the bass and lung-bursting tenor registers, between the earth and sky, expands the emotional scope of the performance by incorporating within it a kind of primal volatility – we never quite know where it is going to do or where it is going to go next. In this, the boldness of Morrison's image of the lion is justified and earned. Furthermore, the musical backing is the natural habitat for such a 'creature' of sound and feeling.

Once 'released' in this way – by an act of attention, we note, by *listening* – the lion prowls. The second distinct segment of the song runs from 5.05–8.08 (that is, about the fabled, prescribed length of the well-made pop song – the length of 'Jackie Wilson Said', on the same side of the same album, for example) and the vocal consists completely of Morrison exploring a range of improvised vocalising. Some of this we might truthfully call scat, some a development on the vocalese he heard from King Pleasure (Morrison would cover his 'Moody's Mood For Love' in 1993), but all of it unlike anything heard in mainstream pop or rock before and far from frequently since. While great artists like Björk, Jane Siberry and Kate Bush have used some similar techniques, they have not tended to work on this concentrated scale.

The vocal improvisation moves through recognisable phases: beginning with a low-level throaty rasping reminiscent of a kind of whispered version of James Brown's guttural and lusty shouts, before surging skyward at 5.33 with a loud and strong scat, following, building upon, and eventually guiding where the guitar is going, drawing the band up there with him. The drums splash around the counter-rhythm of the voice (5.42–6.10), giving way to the first imposed structural device in this section, the overdubbed 'chorus' of Morrison, sax player 'Boots' Rolf Houston and guitarist Ronnie Montrose, which repeats the title phrase every eighth beat between 6.11 and 7.37. The effect of this is to both discreetly bequeath structure on the piece (as we have seen, improvisation without structure is self-defeating), but also serves as a chorus in the sense of the Greek drama – a comment on the action directed out towards the receiver, mediating between the events and the audience. So it is both part of the music and a comment upon it, and the processes at work. This is a technique he would use again in 'You Know What They're Writing About', being part of a love song that is about a love song.

While the chorus is directing us towards our subject, the voice is raging, snarling, soothing, exploring, exploring its own moods and limits – it is a controlled experiment, certainly, but one which has no fixed outcome or expected destination. This is why and how the lyrical image of the voyage, away from somewhere, to a destination as yet unknown, harmonises so closely with the performance of it, even with, and especially because of, these determinedly non-linguistic verbalisations. Within this frame the voice bubbles (6.17–22), drawls like a drunken grizzly bear (6.30–40) and falls back into formal language, echoing the chorus in repeating song's title at 6.43–53. Using this pause as a launching pad, the vocal then takes off again into an expansive and audacious exploration of the real meaning of this idea of the 'lion', manipulating, mouthing and mauling the notes from 7.01–27 in an autodescriptive manner both sensual and disturbing, predatory and erotic. The section winds down with a more contemplative section, a kind of 'afterwards'. Pushing on through from this consummation, the song moves into its final phase around 8.09, into the 'And we sailed and we sailed' section. Here the song turns back to formal language for its expression, alluding to a voyage by boat in which 'we sailed . . . Looking for a brand new start'. The song is evocative of the voyages of the Norse sagas and of Celtic heroes, of course, with the Vikings moving from Denmark, to Caledonia, and then across the vast oceans to the US. It's worth noting that the last words of this song of the Old World and of discovery are 'New York City'.

Morrison's mentions of Denmark, Caledonia and New York City give us a map of a kind, but he also mentions sailing 'all around the world', and going 'back home again', so we might be disappointed if we tried to follow the cartographies too literally. The point is that as a consequence of 'listening to the lion', this journey becomes possible: it's a very particular mythopoesy of course, but one that reveals something which is open to all who can and do take notice. The last section is sung in an animated blues-folk whisper, confidential and intimate while retaining the sense of wonder and surprise of the earlier, more directly dramatic vocalising. The 11-plus minutes of the song both demonstrate and discover a deep and wide palette of voices within a single mood and performance – so that 'the lion' is no more located in the roar and bellow than it is in the tender whisper in the ear. Rather it is a spirit that moves across the song, which informs and inhabits all the voices we hear within it.[51]

The live version on *It's Too Late To Stop Now* collapses the wholly improvised segment into the song, and this live take focuses on the verses which open the album version. As we might expect, it is more closely attentive to the dynamics of the live stage – which, however free we feel to be in the studio, are a different set of rules – but still leaves plenty of room for Morrison to explore the space the song opens up to us. The verses give the structure, or the frame, to use Alan Watts's term, and this more demarcated structure makes improvisation within it more effective. By the time this live performance was recorded, of course, the song was at least a year old, and had been played in enough for the ensemble to know it well but not so well that they ceased to really inhabit the song while they played it. It is this measure of discovery alongside the feeling for the song that gives it its near-physical presence and power; it occupies a near-perfect moment between knowing and unknowing, between discovery and foreknowledge. As Morrison told Candy Dulfer, when a band is working right 'It's almost like telepathy'.[52] We can hear that on this live recording, and this enable Morrison's vocal to make some bold moves. Listen, for example, to how in the closing couple of minutes he begins to hint at and suggest the extended improvisations of the studio cut, eventually bringing the song down to a partially disclosed silence in which we can hear the squeak of bow on string, scrape of mike stand on stage boards, and Morrison's breathing as his whisper of 'Looking for a brand new start' deliquesces down into ambient, amplified silence. It is a remarkable, high-wire moment and the crowd commendably maintain a pin-drop quiet until someone's nerve breaks at 8.32 with a rather anxious 'Alright!', and the door closes again with the onset of applause.[53]

By the time the song was given a rare live outing in November 2003, during a free-to-air BBC radio concert recorded at Malvern, and broadcast in support of *What's Wrong With This Picture?*, the vocal mining had been replaced by another exploratory sound; Morrison's harmonica playing. Giving it plenty of space and time in a lengthy solo, he used it to both echo and build on the human voice, playing right down in the bass notes, and in this modal sucking and blowing it delivered a wheezy vocalese of its own. A gorgeous, light and unexpected horn part, which in its ease and poise would not have shamed a Burt Bacharach arrangement, counterpointed this soul mining. That this version has never been issued commercially is a pity, but 2009's *Astral Weeks* live album closes with the song, signalling its significance to its composer. He told the *Los Angeles Times* that 'I think "Lion" is a song that is all me, I guess about me . . . probably the only one about me'.[54]

AD LIB TO FADE

The Wire, a very well-regarded British jazz and avant-garde music monthly, noted that 'The most registered complaint about Morrison's later music concerns his singing: the unchained wildness throttled by age into a congested, slobbish instrument'.[55] This is true in that the voice has certainly become thicker in its textures and enunciations over the years; yet how would a 60-plus-year-old man continue to sound like a 30-year-old? Johnny Rogan pulled out daily-newspaper pop writer and Spice Girls biographer David Sinclair's thoughts on *How Long Has This Been Going On?*: 'Morrison's . . . ragged diction, approximate phrasing and often wildly suspect pitch fail to meet the exacting technical standards required in the world of straight jazz.'[56] He's right, in one way, at least. Morrison is not a 'straight' jazz singer in the way that younger, modern jazzers such as Michael Buble or Claire Martin are – if we want 'clean jazz' of this sort, with crystalline diction and stage-school pronunciation then we are looking to the wrong singer. As Morrison admits ruefully in 'No Religion', 'When I cleaned up my diction, I had nothing left to say'.[57] The meaning is in the sound, rather than the words.

I asked Ben Sidran, jazz pianist, author and collaborator and co-producer of the Mose Allison tribute album *Tell Me Something*, about this:

> PM: In the wider sense, what is your view of Van Morrison as a singer? Is he a 'good' jazz singer? What do you think makes a good jazz singer – is it possible to define or describe?
>
> BS: Like most everybody, I love listening to Van sing . . . [at the recording of *Tell Me Something*] he just stepped up to the microphone and sang. There was no pretence or artifice, just pure delivery of the message of the lyrics. I think singing is singing, and whatever names you put on it are after the fact and often beside the fact as well.[58]

The musician and the critics clearly have different observations to make. As we have seen, Morrison spoke in 2009 about how he feels his voice has changed over the years, answering Chris Neal's question: 'The approach now is to sing from lower down [the diaphragm] so I do not ruin my voice.'[59] Here Morrison unsentimentally describes how he manages and protects his greatest asset, and in doing so returns to the basic physical realities of the dynamic between the human body as instrument, and the human voice as expression of feeling.

So the point is that rather than hankering after where Morrison was as a singer in 1972 when he originally recorded 'Listen To The Lion', and finding the present voice in our view wanting by comparison, the wise approach is to understand and truly listen to what he is doing now, today, and judge how that moves us or not. If we want the Van Morrison of 1972, we are fortunate enough to have him immortalised on CD, vinyl, tape or MP3 file: it is a form of nostalgia, I suppose, to wish the 'old' voice was back, or had never changed on us, like we might wish old friends to be close by at certain times. Yet as Morrison told Candy Dulfer:

> 'I'm just like where I am now, really, I just relate to where I am . . . I don't remember [CD: no, you don't like looking back] . . . I don't remember *Astral Weeks*, y'know, all I remember is I was getting no money, it was really hard to keep going, I was playing for $75, everything, the band, by the time you'd paid the taxi there was nothing left. I just remember things like that: I don't remember "Oh, that changed my life" or did this or did that . . . I just know what I'm doing now . . . I don't live my life in the past or other people's nostalgia. I've got my own nostalgia, which is before that, my nostalgia's from the 50's, not the 60's or 70's, my nostalgia's from the 50's, . . . singing country and western songs with my friends, cos that's really where I got the source of the music, during that period, so the stuff I've developed since then, that's the foundation, it's been built on that, that's the source . . . also I don't mind nostalgia, I've nothing against it, so long as it's mine! Obviously I can't relate to other people's nostalgia, maybe some of my records for other people are nostalgia, that's fine; but it's not mine.'[60]

The young man who sang *Astral Weeks*, about the reputation of which Morrison is here vexed and somewhat tetchy, is immortal in the sense of his being 'caught' on magnetic tape, but the real man is not, and is subject to the same changes as everyone else. So, wishing that our artists could remain undiminished by time in the way that we are ourselves reduced is a complex response to the passage of time and its effect upon our own lives, and as such is an intimation of mortality. We don't necessarily welcome or even particularly want to acknowledge such thoughts; so we blame the singer, and the erosion of vocal power we detect. In such diminishments we see a reflection of our own: so we turn the record over.

TRADITION AND INNOVATION: VAN MORRISON AS MUSICIAN

In this section we examine the work of Van Morrison as a musician. We consider his working practices in regard of his characteristic playing style, his uses of improvisation, his periodic interest in instrumental composition and explore how these recognisable aspects of his style have very long roots, via a case study of two standards which he has remade in that personal style, mixing tradition and innovation to create something new.

In some senses this entire book is concerned with Morrison as a musician – so much information is contained within the way his music *sounds*, from the guitar style or the sax style, to the inherent understanding of the dynamics of the ensemble and the music it makes – how the many make the one. Although he sometimes plays keyboard live or in the studio, his main instruments are the saxophone, harmonica and guitar. Technically speaking, jazz buffs have told me, Morrison's saxophone technique leaves much to be desired – one can hear the buttons clacking on the horn, the note being approached, the flow between the notes not being as it should be, and so on. These experts may be right, but my own – wholly subjective, naturally – view of the matter is that he is a great player, and I can get at least as much from 'Celtic Swing' as I do from, say, John Coltrane's magnificent *Giant Steps*. It seems to me that what counts is not the technique, but the sound, mood and emotional gravity of the final performance. Further, I'd suggest that Morrison's style is closer to players like Stan Getz and Gerry Mulligan than it is to the 'deeper' (according to the received wisdoms) jazz players like Coltrane or Bird. Indeed, Morrison is not necessarily 'playing jazz', although he is a jazz *player* – that is, he plays according to the spirit if not the letter of jazz. Likewise, Morrison is a superb harmonica player, whether digging deep into the blues spaces offered by the curious technique known as 'chugging' he learned from the likes of Sonny Boy Williamson, Little Walter or Clarence 'Gatemouth' Brown, or the gleaming, high-pop gaiety his Hohner brings to 'Bright Side Of The Road' or 'Perfect Fit', both worthy of John Sebastian at his most optimistic.

As for the guitar, Morrison is not an especially technically gifted player – I think of Elvis Costello's self-deprecating name for his own style, 'The Little Hands of Concrete'[61] – but once Morrison starts playing one understands immediately that it is him, and not one of the many – undeniably brilliant – players he has hired over the decades. When picking, he will usually play a semi-acoustic (though he uses the classic solid-bodied Fender too), the better to add the glissando shower to his picking. He rarely, if ever solos – he's strictly rhythm – but the key characteristic of his style is to pick out very distinctive clusters of notes, strands picked from a tight, tough ball of yarn, grouped together, usually at the bass end of the fretboard. These quick little bundles of notes, flowing yet staccato bursts over the rhythm, owe something to John Lee Hooker's playing – check the trading of such playing on the reworked 'Gloria' from 1993 – but are not simply lifts from the master's notebook, or indeed the blues style in the wider sense.

Morrison is quite willing to let others take the lead, so to speak, with the guitar – Mick Green's contributions from *Back On Top* onwards spring to mind – but Morrison's music, *Wavelength* era excepted, tends not to be driven by the six string. It is the horns that most closely describe the arc of his art. Yet even here, he has been willing to delegate, with such first-rate players as Richie Buckley, Jack Schroer or the peerless Pee Wee Ellis. Even at the mike – as *A Night In San Francisco* records – he has periodically permitted the notional 'backing singer' to step forward, with the voices of Brian Kennedy and the sublime Katie Kissoon showcased particularly down the years.

So the foregrounding of 'Van Morrison' also accommodates the substantive presence and input of his fellow musicians. Yet he is undoubtedly the bandleader onstage and all take their direction from him – watch their faces, following him in a live show – and this is of course after the working practices of not only the likes of Ray Charles or James Brown but also the big bands he grew up listening to, to which the style of much of his post-2000 work, both live and in the studio, is indebted. Morrison struggles with this also of course: he admired Sinatra's ability to lead and guide how a performance sounded in his merely fleeting presence or sometimes even in his absence (see 'Hard Nose The Highway'), but wishes too to leave that mark, to communicate that vision in sound by his own centrality and direction, which requires presence. In some ways one is reminded of a definition offered by drummer Bill Bruford of being a member of the band King Crimson, led always by Robert Fripp: 'King Crimson is not a band, it's a way of doing things.'[62] One might make the same claim for 'Van Morrison'.

So that 'way of doing things' must necessarily inform how his work approaches what preceded it as strongly as it inhabits the present, and influences how that present develops into what is to come. In this section we will consider his musicianship as both philosophy and practise, examine his non-vocal recordings and, finally, consider two songs, one from the jazz tradition, one from the folk repertoire, which seem to demonstrate the link between tradition and innovation that seems so central to Morrison's musicianship. The jazz tradition is by definition an American one, and the folk tradition, in this case, a northern British one, yet these two songs are, research reveals, more closely related than at first it might appear – Morrison's performance and reimagining of them uncover these connections, and their related, if not quite shared sources.

'TAKE IT BACK UP TO THE OTHER THING': THE ROLE OF IMPROVISATION, THEMES AND TURNAROUNDS

In 2007, Jeremy Marre asked Van Morrison about the role of improvisation in his work:

> Marre: I was going to ask you if improvisation was really important to you, responding to the spirit of the moment, the spirit of a piece . . . if you feel that improvisation is a really important element in your music.
>
> VM: Oh it's very important, it's the only thing . . . I wouldn't do it otherwise, and I couldn't perform live . . . if I didn't have that choice . . . the freedom of that, that is it, it's the whole thing for me.

> JM: So you're responding to a different moment, a different audience a different place, to a different time every time you perform?
>
> VM: Yeah, to a different vibration, a different . . . ambience, whatever you wanna call it . . . different sounds, every place is different, different playing, different interplay . . . everything. But the main thing is being able to improvise vocally, because if I couldn't improvise vocally then that's it, y'know, I just don't wanna sing a song . . . anyone can do that. It's really not worth doing it if you're just going through the motions in singing a song, something else has got to happen. You have to make something else happen, well for me anyway.
>
> JM: Is it a cathartic experience in a way?
>
> VM: It can be; it can be. A momentary release . . . momentary . . . when you're doing it for that period you're doing it, it *is*. The minute it stops and you walk out the door, it's gone.[63]

Morrison is not unique in his habit of being attentive to the sounds that he hears, or feels, in his mind, but he is perhaps unusual in the manner in which he foregrounds the meeting between feeling and musical realisation, which we might call improvisation. In that sense, any performance you care to select is effectively an offshoot of improvisation, in that it is all made in the here and now. There he stands, centre stage, directing in the spirit of Tubby Hayes as much as James Brown, driving the band on, beating out the rhythms on his thigh that he wants the drummer to pick up, leaning off mike to tell the keyboard player that he wants him to 'play the fills' or 'shuffle', standing down from the mike and directing the band through a succession of solos, some acknowledged, some not. In this he is very generous to the players he hires, giving them the chance to play, to stretch out, to impress. Some can, some cannot; but they get the chance. In Morrison's case, the approach tends to be one of freedom of manoeuvre within a recognisable and familiar set of structures. Intriguingly, this could also serve as a working definition of the blues.

Joachim Berendt offers a view of how the composed and the improvised connect:

> The jazz musician places new melodic lines over the given harmonies of the song or the blues. This is done by embellishing or making slight alterations (Andre Hodeir calls this manner of improvising 'paraphrasing') . . . or by creating entirely new melodic lines over the given harmonies (a manner of improvising that Hodeir calls the 'chorus-phrase').[64]

So well-known themes become the root of improvisation, and one feeds into the other – consider where John Coltrane took 'My Favourite Things', for example. Furthermore, the 'author' of a theme, be it improvised or otherwise, becomes identified with that theme – a signature element in every sense. In Morrison's case, I'd suggest that his 'signature theme' is not the acoustic undertow that tugs the sleeve of *Astral Weeks*, nor the brassy blast that heralds the post-1970 recordings and performances of 'Moondance', but rather the seven-note motif which is first heard on the 1983 original studio recording of the song 'Irish Heartbeat' (3.50–4.38):

C# E F# E C# E F#[65]

This little run has become part of the DNA of his music, alongside the unison singing that frequently parallels it, and this mix of voice and guitar emphasises the blending of textures in his music – nothing, arguably not even the voice, is permanently privileged. The motif has cropped up as a free-floating element within other tunes and it has come to represent the secret heart of Morrison's music, a kind of musical code which will flame up in the right place at the right moment – for example, it featured frequently in wild and beautiful live versions of 'Summertime In England' in the 1980s. Furthermore, it has been heard from voice, guitar, sax and keyboard, sometimes providing a kind of musical language that the instruments can use to speak to each other during performance – the motif echoing back and forth between instruments.

As well as such characteristic features, he has his limits: Morrison's musical style is by no means radical in its structures and he could never be mistaken for, say, Don Van Vliet or Cecil Taylor in that sense. As Mick Cox has noted 'a lot of his numbers start the same so it can be hard to tell which one it is before he starts singing'.[66] Morrison is instinctively a bluesman and much of his work, even when not apparently a blues, makes use of blues structures. One way in which these structures underpin the roots of his songs is via the 'turnaround'; these are cycles of chords which, while in themselves are not excessively melodic or demonstrative, are tight, clean, cyclic clusters which provide a bedrock upon and over which may be lain the other elements of a song. This discreet formality has at least as much to do with the techniques of jazz as it does the blues. As we have seen, improvisation, even for the hardcore jazz player, necessitates a structure at the centre from which to depart and to which it can return.

These cycles can be heard to good effect in, to select two at random, the neat and tightly arranged 'She Gives Me Religion' and the much more expansive and open-ended 'And The Healing Has Begun'. The four chords at work in each provide this firm basis for the developments that the songs require, and could, theoretically, go on forever – this is felt especially powerfully in 'And The Healing Has Begun', the untiring openness of which seems to suggest and even briefly capture the eternal renewal inferred in the song's lyric and performance. Indeed, something like the secret power of music, in David Tame's phrase, seems to be held in the cyclic nature of those four chords. All the contributory elements agree within the song – things just seem to fit into place with the feel of a force of nature – and it is a extremely potent effect. Improvisation needs a structure – this is the great dynamic paradox at the heart of jazz – and Morrison's use of these tight yet free turnarounds exemplifies this. His method and philosophy of creativity is close kin to that which prevails in the best jazz music: go with the moment, with its mood and the work that's being done. Sometimes it works, and sometimes it doesn't. His non-vocal tracks afford us a view into this process.

THE INSTRUMENTALS

> '*SING*!!'
>
> Audience member, Manchester Palace Theatre, 14 June 1982, after the second consecutive instrumental at the opening of Van Morrison's set

Morrison's work in the 1980s frequently foregrounded non-vocal composition – instrumentals. These, by definition, make different demands upon players and playing; they also, it might seem, offer a broader scope for improvisation than the song with a demarcated lyrical framework. Yet is this truly the case?

Stephen Davis asked Morrison about his interest in the instrumental as a form:

> SD: Have you ever thought of doing an album of only instrumental compositions?
>
> VM: Yeah, I have. I've been developing some piano pieces out of my own piano meditational music. I'd like to do an album of just piano tunes alone.[67]

Within Morrison's music, the instrumental is fixed to a very specific period, on record at least. He has recorded many over his career but they only found their way onto albums between 1981 and 1987. The instrumental mode provided a new musical vocabulary for him, best described in the title of his 1983 album *Inarticulate Speech Of The Heart*. For a singer, the instrumental functions as an aspect of silence – that is, using absence to communicate presence in a different way. The preponderance of the instrumental in this period indexes the enduring impact of meditation, as well as his readings of Alice Bailey, David Tame and Cyril Scott. This phase we can detect fading into his work, through the experiments in musical and spatial dynamics on *Into The Music* and, especially, *Common One*. Here, silence proves an eloquent tongue.

The notion of music existing without words is hardly controversial; indeed before rock and roll, this was often the way it was. However, Van Morrison's purpose for these instrumentals is intriguing. They represent a very definite and deliberate phase where he was trying out the idea of *not singing*, and of conveying mood or emotion, light and shade, in purely musical terms – what he dubbed, rhetorically and purposefully, as 'inarticulate speech of the heart'. The oxymoronic twist in the cheek-to-cheek of inarticulacy and speech in this phrase is an effort to reconfigure the dynamic between apparently absolutely distinct categories of human expression. This is echoed in the way Vladimir Jankelevitch wrote about Debussy, who is of course cited in the catalogue of stillness in 'On Hyndford Street':

> Musical silence is not nothingness; and indeed it is not only 'cessation' but attenuation. As with reticence or interrupted exposition, it expresses a will to return as soon as possible to silence; as an attenuated intensity it toys with near-nothingness, on the threshold of inaudibility . . . Singing dispenses you from speaking! Singing is a way of being silent.[68]

In live performance, the place of the instrumentals tends to be less provocative and confrontational nowadays, coming either as part of the opening warm-up blow before he comes on – as noted elsewhere, Morrison rarely comes on or goes offstage without music playing him in or out. In the early 80s, however, as in the Manchester show I saw, he was in the centre of his explorations of the possibilities of non-vocal music, and so my first memories of him as a live performer are of shows in which he would indeed often *not* sing, parked behind a keyboard sometimes centre stage, often far left or right, sometimes part-obscured from the audience's view. I'd argue that this was a deliberate act, obliging or encouraging the audience to focus less on the charismatic individual figure centre stage, which pop performance traditionally requires, and more upon the sound that the ensemble was making. That ensemble was still following his lead, of course, even though he was visually marginal, and so even though he was not occupying centre stage in the conventional manner, he was still the 'central' presence in the hall, his music filling the space. This is difficult for an audience raised on the stage traditions and conventions of show business. We paid for the person whose name is on the ticket, so let's *see* and *hear* him. Sing!!

The instrumental music reinforced this radicalisation of presentation. It also enabled him to explore pure sound as expression of mood, seeking to articulate a dimension of perception and experience which moves beyond the structures of spoken language and also what was possible within the structures and strictures of the popular song. His interest in the looser clothes of jazz was another way to help him to find a way through this. The infamous Montreux 1974 show featured three instrumentals, and it is my feeling that there he used the act of not singing more confrontationally than in the 80s; the difference being that in 1974 he was an artist at the end of his tether, while in the 80s he was looking for a way through, rather than a way out.

The first commercially released instrumental track on a Van Morrison album was 'Scandinavia', the last cut on Side Two of 1981's *Beautiful Vision*, but perhaps the best example for us came on the following album in the shape of 'Celtic Swing'. The titles of these instrumentals take on great significance – like captions at an art gallery, we are strongly guided in our responses by the titles: 'Connswater', 'Evening Meditation', 'Yo', and indeed 'Celtic Swing' itself. The track opens with a soft sonic indistinctness mixed with precision playing, which feels like the key to the Morrison's instrumentals – indeed the tune's very title connects indigenous musical tones and colours to an apparently unrelated American form. It is also precisely autodescriptive – this track *swings*. It is something of a curio in that live versions were always, literally, a different tune; shows from 1983/84 featured this variant version. The recorded version opens with some mood tones from Mark Isham's synthesiser, fading in just before Morrison takes up the sax, which does not blow in immediately – rather it runs together with the synthesised notes and deliberately blurs the edges of the mutual contribution – we cannot tell where one sound ends and another begins. Morrison seems more interested in the penumbral, impressionistic resonances around the note as much as the note itself, and the intro to 'Celtic Swing' is a good example of this technique. After ten seconds of Isham, the sax comes surging up alongside. As in 'Connswater', Chris Michie picks out the guitar motif he will be playing throughout the piece, but loosely, deconstructedly; it gathers itself together for the momentary invigorations of the track, then as the track dissolves, it 'lies down again'. Thus this has something of the cosmic music of John Coltrane about it – music that never truly starts or finishes, just comes and goes and we might, occasionally, be able to tune into it for ourselves.

The ambience is of a kind of musical 'Brigadoon', awakening gently, living fully, then softly disappearing again. The track records this cycle. At 1.15, the drums start to chip out a regular beat, and therefore lend a firm internal structure to this cloudlike piece. The piece finds its second speed, and right on cue the sax line snaps into focus and starts to deliver the melody line. The drums at 1.32 take on a more integrated shuffle. The sax cuts out at 2.19 and the guitar and organ lead into the middle section, bright, sunlit; the sax lands again at

2.51, leading to a satisfying first use of the cymbal at 3.04, which releases the tension that has been gently building. The sax responds by punching out half a dozen clear and bell-ringing tones and this signals the beginning of the end of the 'swing'; like a child's swinging game in a park, it starts slowly, builds up, reaches a peak, then, slowly but surely, slows down and returns to stillness again. This has echoes of Blake's 'Echoing Green', with the children playing wildly and then going home, tired out, at dusk.[69] Thus the track describes the nature of movement in the material world. Michie's guitar figure remains as it has been throughout the main body of the song, and the metronomic rimshot of Tom Dollinger records the memory of the 'swing' until we are left with, as at the opening, the slow fade (out this time) of the synth and the sax, now being blown across the note once again. The live versions of 1983/84 were necessarily less 'ambient' and more direct, and while the internal structures of the tune were identical, though accelerated, the main melody was changed, and not simply sped up. The dual identity of 'Celtic Swing' stands as a strong example of Morrison's adapting his studio work for the stage, and his adhering to the notion of never playing anything the same twice; it is also something that an instrumental makes more possible than a song with a vocal-based structure.[70]

By the time he issued *Poetic Champions Compose* in 1987, Morrison was immersed in an interest in how music can be used for good and for healing. The album harbours three instrumental cuts, all of which fall into the piano-sax-meditation mode: 'Spanish Steps' again evokes time place and space with its title and its soft, effortlessly positive assertions; 'Celtic Excavation' doesn't follow 'Celtic Swing' in delivering a dance beat, offering instead a subtly unfolding mood of warm intensity, and as its title suggests invites some work within the relaxation – we might call that meditation; and 'Allow Me' makes its well-tempered case, its title again setting the mood alongside its musical fluidity, a hint at the form of help that music can offer. Fiachra Trench remembers that the album was initially envisaged as an album of these meditative jazz pieces; in some ways, this is a better term than 'instrumentals', which suggests lyrics as a kind of absence or negative presence. This throws up the shift in definitions we find across distinct genres: pop seems more focused on the lyric, jazz on the music – does anybody, for instance, call *In A Silent Way* an 'instrumental' record? Trench recalled that lyrics started pouring into these melodies, and by the time the record was issued in September 1987 only a trio remained. They are very much of a mood – the record as a whole has a very pleasing unity and the 'instrumentals' fit seamlessly with the vocal tracks. Indeed, the fit is so natural and unforced that *Poetic Champions Compose* represents the high-water mark of the integration of lyrical and non-lyrical elements in Morrison's recorded output.[71]

So it seems fitting that shortly after recording the album, over the weekend of

18–20 September 1987, Van Morrison attended and performed at a conference held at the University of Loughborough, organised by Sir George Trevelyan and his Wrekin Trust, entitled 'The Secret Heart of Music: An Exploration into the Power of Music to Change Consciousness'. A reading of Sir George's work reveals quickly why a person interested in matters of the spirit and mysticism, and how they function in the real world of work, would find something of significance therein. In his essay 'Meditation and Its Purpose', he writes:

> Essentially, meditation is the art and practice of creating an inner centre of quiet and stillness within the self and then allowing this to be flooded with light from the higher planes. It is the way to inner contact with the realm of eternal being. In our hurried and anxious world where everything is on the rush it is not easy to be innerly still. Emotions and thoughts and the concerns of our day crowd in and fill any vacuum of quiet. Yet how precious it is when we can achieve a spell of time in which we are quite freed from the inroads of active thoughts. How shall we achieve this?[72]

One way Trevelyan's semi-rhetorical closing question may be answered is via Morrison's instrumentals on *Poetic Champions Compose* – they are the summation of his journey towards shaping a musical vocabulary that helps facilitate and 'achieve' this state. As noted regarding 'Celtic Excavation', while these pieces might sound merely relaxing, like refined easy listening, they are also a kind of work song. It is interesting that Morrison's next move was into traditional Irish music and folk song, and this may well coincide with the fact that *Poetic Champions Compose* was the fullest realisation of this kind of music for him – where could he go next? It is helpful here to note that this style developed out of his instrumental phase.

Post-1987, Morrison's instrumentals became less frequent and took on a jazzier turn. *Too Long In Exile*'s 'Instrumental' typifies this style, even down to its functional title. Despite this, it features a vocal of sorts, fading up, and is clearly part of a much longer jamming session which then 'drifts' into 'Tell Me What You Want'. His vocal utterances from 1.12–32 are heard off-mike following the melody line of the sax before the vibes come in; effectively he is vocalising at the same time as blowing. It's a remarkable sound, and could be the work of no-one else. The first two minutes of 'Tell Me What You Want' contain his voice, but no lyrics – what Paddy Moloney called his 'guttural keening' is used to great effect here, and when the mood has been explored, he moves on. We hear the instruction 'Take it back up to the other thing . . . make the change' at 3.02 and the modal brightening that follows a beat later is musically very satisfying, providing a fleeting glimpse into the 'liveness' that Morrison dares to accommodate into his work. Indeed this cut arguably has more of the spirit of jazz about it than his brace of 'real' jazz albums which followed in the next couple of years. Whenever this track happens to be playing, I end up stopping what I'm doing, and find myself standing and listening; it always fades too soon. It's superb. The album's second instrumental piece, 'Close Enough For Jazz', is bright enough in its mood and textures to recall the original 1981 take on 'All Saints Day'; it also features and centralizes the signature seven-note motif identified earlier, picked out on the acoustic guitar. In a pleasing paradox this is one of the less consciously aspirational 'jazz' pieces, and as such perhaps is more successfully connected to the spirit rather than the practice of the form.[73]

So clearly the sphere of the non-vocal interested Morrison in parallel with his own esoteric interests in music and its possibilities beyond entertainment and marketing. Yet could Morrison have ever abandoned singing altogether? In 1985, Al Jones asked him the question:

> AJ: I've noticed that on the last few albums there have been several instrumental tracks. Would you like to move into that direction of pure music, without singing and without lyrics?
>
> VM: No, I don't think so. No – no, I wouldn't, no![74]

No; Morrison is a *singer*, even when he is remaining silent.

TRADITION AND INNOVATION

What is tradition? This is a question wanting a single answer – tradition flourishes, dies, is reborn, never goes away, is always changing. Tradition is rooted continuity, and perpetual change. Music is in its very core an exemplification of the tension between tradition and innovation, and, given Morrison's instinctive adherence to the idea that a song should never be sung the same way twice, his music provides a fascinating window into these natural processes. At the root of Morrison's music, and indeed, if you dig deep enough, of all twentieth-century popular song, are traditional forms – that is, forms of music which have arisen not out of market demand or show business, but out of the innate human tendency towards making meaningful, organised sound, which we call music.

Morrison's work determinedly draws freely upon a wide range of musical genres and traditions, yet these sources have their own distinct roots in and of themselves. A jazz tune like 'Saint James Infirmary' and a folk song such as 'Wild Mountain Thyme' are standards of their individual repertoires. The jazz tradition is by definition an American one, and the folk tradition, in this case, a northern British one, yet these two songs are, research reveals, more closely related than at first it might appear – Morrison's performance and reimagining of them uncover these connections, and their related if not quite shared sources. In a 2003 interview, Morrison was asked about this connection between tradition and innovation:

> NW: Is there also a sense of the covers creating a sense of continuity and illustrating how your music is part of a greater tradition?
>
> VM: Absolutely – the r&b tradition and going back even before that to Louis Armstrong. I've been into Armstrong since the first time I heard him in the '50s and I still listen to him today. And Louis Prima reinvented Louis Armstrong in an r&b version, so it's in that kind of lineage. I was brought up on traditional jazz. My father had all these records and he just played them all the time, so I absorbed that kind of music very early on. British trad as well – Ken Colyer, Chris Barber, Acker Bilk. All of that. On the previous record, *What's Wrong With This Picture?*, we did 'Saint James Infirmary', which was based on the version Armstrong recorded. So yes. That music has always been in the background for me, along with rhythm and blues, blues, folk blues, country, gospel . . .
>
> NW: But that sense of tradition is also very important in your own songwriting, isn't it? You use these phrases like 'further on up the road' and hearing 'that lonesome whistle blow' on the new record and you're taking this language and vocabulary which is so evocative and redolent of the music that inspired you and you're reinventing it anew . . .
>
> VM: Yes, that's the lineage again. You have to understand a bit about the poetry of the blues to know where the references are coming from – whether it's Sonny Boy Williamson, or Lightnin' Hopkins or Bobby Bland. It's all part of the songwriting process for me because the first poetry I ever connected with was actually the poetry of the blues, via a book by Paul Oliver called *Blues Fell This Morning*.[75]

It is interesting to see that Morrison cites such a scholarly source as Oliver's book, one which provides much socio-cultural context to the tableaux behind the gritty foregrounds of what he calls 'the poetry of the blues'. So the connections to tradition can be conscious in the first instance – you are moved by the sounds, the lyrical and vocal gestures, and you take them on, adding them into your own efforts, thereby effecting a mutual transformation. Later, once the influences are properly absorbed, they become part of one's being, as in the difference between reading from a phrase book and being fluent in another language, using the vocabularies of expression naturally and without self-consciousness; one just does it. This is in part how tradition and innovation flow, one to the other, and back again. Morrison talks of a lineage – and he is right of course – but there is also a less strictly defined set of connections, less sharply drawn but equally powerful, so fully are they absorbed. So when, as I saw him once do, he suddenly steps away from the mike after the first line of 'It's All In The Game' and calls out 'O baby!' up to the Gods, it is an entirely unscripted and unplanned punctuation, yet one which draws as fully on the traditions he has absorbed as the more consciously derived lyrical devices identified by Nigel Williamson.[76] Tradition is not merely the craft of the curator, nor is innovation an iconoclastic sweeping aside of the old for the new; they are intrinsically linked, and both flow with a vigorous heat through Morrison's work. Let's look at two songs which illustrate this: 'Wild Mountain Thyme' and, first, 'Saint James Infirmary'. Morrison spoke about his history with this song:

> 'I'll give you an example, like in those days [the 1970's] 'Saint James Infirmary' is a song I wanted to record – but there was no way that they were going to let me record that song then. No. It was a joke. So now I'm in a situation I can do what I want.'[77]

It seems that Morrison's recording of 'Saint James Infirmary' represents liberation from the strictures of the music industry: 'I can do what I want.' This song seems to be associated with changes in direction, or breaks for freedom. Humphrey Lyttelton, doyen of the 1950s British jazz scene, was asked for advice by Jonny Greenwood of British rock aristocrats Radiohead as to how they could develop their sound in a new direction, and replied that the best tip he could give him was to listen to Louis Armstrong's version of 'Saint James Infirmary'.[78] What's interesting is that this song shows folk and jazz to be at root indivisible. Indeed this is a folk song as much as a jazz song – it was made famous by Louis Armstrong and his All Stars and therefore became rapidly assimilated into the jazz repertoire, but it is much older than that, being a New Orleans tune that must really count as a *folk* tune, one which by dint of location was absorbed into the jazz tradition which sprung from there. To illustrate, the late, great Scottish-Jamaican folk-blues guitarist Davy Graham sang the tune at one of his rare shows, in Leeds in October 2007, with lyrics different to the Armstrong and Morrison versions. These variant versions are a key signifier of pre-recording, 'folk' tradition, before copyright and the recording technologies 'fixed' lyrics and melodies.

The history of 'Saint James Infirmary' is traced back by Rob Walker in his excellent book *Letters from New Orleans* and associated website, and I refer you to them both. He suggests that the song may have originated as part of a group of songs known as 'The Unfortunate Rake' song cycle, and observes that sleeve notes to a collection of related songs issued in 1960 speculate that the original source song may have been collected in 1848 in County Cork, 'from a singer who had learned it in Dublin in 1790'. As Walker observes, the song may have been 'in tradition' for years prior to that, but it's impossible to say, and he points out that the history of this song is a murky one, full of variant versions evolving over time and space, and of copyright loopholes so wide the Mississippi could flow through them.[79]

This tracking back to source is a kind of pre-Fall, pre-Babel creation myth, that there was a time when wholeness prevailed and everyone spoke and sang a musical language that satisfied all moods within itself, before fragmentation and generic distinction. We hear an echo of this desire in Morrison's own 'In The Days Before Rock And Roll', suggested as a pre-Fall era, where wholeness reigned. It also turns up as part of his rap in 'See Me Through Part Two (Just A Closer Walk With Thee)' on *Hymns To The Silence*:

> Before, yes before it was the way it was
> More silence, more breathing together
> Not rushing, being
> Before rock 'n' roll, before television
> Previous, previous, previous[80]

It is this imagining of a Golden Age of wholeness which both hankers after healing as if it is lost but is also proof of its persistence, via memory. This is precisely the kind of thing that has Morrison's detractors referring to his obsessive nostalgia, but as he freely admits in 'Magic Time', 'Call it nostalgia, I don't mind'[81] – if that's how it seems then he's fine with that, because it has done what he wanted it to do for him. Yet the singing of the song picks up and refreshes this obscure tradition, and connects the singer to it at the same time. So Morrison's feeling on recording the song for *What's Wrong With This Picture?* – his album for jazz label Blue Note, and all the kudos that goes with that – is one of *freedom*: 'now I'm in a situation I can do what I want' . How does he use that hard-won freedom?

First he takes the Louis Armstrong version as his model, and follows it very closely, so that we hear the direct, first-person experience of the narrator. In this version of the lyric the encounter with the song's central tragedy is raw and intimate – it is '*my* baby' (my italics) who is stretched out on the long, white table in St. James Infirmary. Armstrong doesn't use the story-within-a-story motif; his version begins with a New Orleans funeral jazz slow shuffle, picking up the tempo at 0.08, led by Armstrong's trumpet, trailed by the unmistakably wildly wandering New Orleans clarinet, skeletal barrelhouse piano, downstruck banjo and the ragged-shoed chuf-chuf-chuf of the melancholic New Orleans swing. At 57 seconds, Armstrong's vocal comes in and he is already in the hospital: 'I went down to St. James Infirmary'; by 1.26, the girl is history, and he is planning his own funeral. The vocal is done by 1.44, ending far short of other takes on the song, with 'So the boys will know I died standing pat', and the rest of the 3.11 is an instrumental restatement of the mournful melody.[82]

While Morrison is clearly mindful of Armstrong's version, he develops the song and adds his own signature to it: most directly by laying his alto sax over the intro, a sound both characteristic and distinctive. This version takes much more of its own time, and retains a smoother, blues-based time signature; to his credit he does not try to recreate the New Orleans swing beat. He also matches Armstrong's abbreviated version of the lyric, but the song lasts well over five minutes, a good two more than the 1928 recording. What he does add are the uncanny backing vocals, which usher the song from opening into verse: where Armstrong used a brief piano interlude, Morrison uses this otherworldly chorus to ease the song towards its vocal. Where Satchmo nods at the New Orleans 'Second Line' structure, where the mournful is followed by the more upbeat, Morrison's version makes no effort to counterfeit or gesture towards the authentic, instead pulling the song into line with the version of jazz that Morrison has been developing almost since his first solo recordings – a rich and complex hybrid of jazz, blues, folk and pop traditions, and it is this that unites the 1928 recording with his performances, studio and live, of the same song.[83]

Morrison's vocal resists over-performance: a trap for the ambitious vocalist tackling the standard. His only inclination into embellishment comes with the 'Let her go, let her go' section, and the final demand for his funeral regalia, particularly on 'black box coat' and '20 dollar gold piece'. His delivery of these lines puts me in mind of a question asked of Morrison in an interview promoting the release of the album in 2003:

> *You do Saint James Infirmary on the album. Is death something that you think about much?*
>
> It's a song I always liked. I grew up with this music, this is what I listened to when I was a kid. It's as simple as that. It's a good blues vehicle. Even before I recorded it, it was a hit live – so it's natural to put it on a record.
>
> *But presumably, as you get on, death becomes more of a concern, in the sense that there's only so much time left.*
>
> Well, I think I said that in some other song I put on the previous record. Which was

'I have to watch my back when I'm running out of time'. I said that in there. Yeah, to answer your question, that's in that song. That is a thing for anybody over 50.[84]

The break in Morrison's voice on these two lines is indicative indeed of the passage of time, and every time I hear him sing the song onstage or on the Austin live version, the tightening of his throat and the deep reach needed to get the note is certainly a 'thing' for anybody over 50. The Austin version uses a lonesome violin and a very discreet pedal steel to take it into the main section of the song, where a trumpet, sounding much more Satchmo than the album version, accompanies Morrison's superb sax break; there is a deep noir-chill about the song. Morrison is also using this ancient tune to give us something new; a different voice, high, vulnerable and capable of swooping down into the visceral bass notes when it needs to. The querulousness and vulnerability in his voice at, say, 2.37–45 on 'wherever', is a new sound for the singer.

When Morrison was performing 'Saint James Infirmary' in late 2005, the song functioned as homage to the city of New Orleans. At 3.53–56 on the Austin version he announces the kick for the end of the song like this 'And we go back down to New Orleans and the drummer does a roll on the snare'. He is bringing together the physical, mechanistic dimension of the music and the metaphysical urge behind that same music – evoking some aspect of the spirit of the place that evoked that music in the first place. It is also a kind of love song to the city and its musicality – especially in the wake of Hurricane Katrina that struck the city in August 2005 – in recognition of its role in the birth of so much of central importance to the development of popular song in general, and the styles that interest Morrison in particular. Its brew of musical styles is in some way indexical of the alchemic blend that Morrison himself claims to be in search of in 'Philosopher's Stone'.[85]

Nigel Williamson asked him in 2003 about his version of the song:

I often wonder about the songs, covers specifically, that you choose to perform or record. I know that you know literally thousands of songs by other people, I mean it must be thousands and you have this strange ability to know the words of all these songs. And here on the album you have a cover on here of Saint James Infirmary – a great song but why single that one when you could have picked any of thousands of songs to record . . .?

Well, there's a reason, there's two reasons behind that. You know one is it's a song I've always liked that I grew up with and those are the types of songs that I used to hear when my father played those records when I was a kid so I've kind of got this stuff ingrained, you know it's ingrained in me and the other reason is that we'd been doing it live for actually several years live and it's actually a hit live without even being on a record so that's another reason. And plus the same thing, it's what do you like to do stuff like that you know?[86]

So recording the song spun the circle in terms both personal – 'my father played those records' – and professional – 'it's actually a hit live' – and in doing so tradition and innovation are conjoined. Our second case study examines a song which carries similar connections, but seems a world away from New Orleans.

'Wild Mountain Thyme' is a song which has long fascinated me, not least because when I was young I could not understand how a single song could go under several titles and still be the same tune. The melancholy beauty and longing in the melody alongside the bittersweetness I discerned within the lover's prayer in the lyric drew me closer to the song and as I grew up and heard more and more versions my understanding and interest grew. By the time I discovered Van Morrison in my late teens the fact that he had recorded a version of the song made me all the more certain I had stumbled upon something important. The song came up in an interview with Donal Corvin in 1974:

DC: Do you reckon that Bert Berns was much of an influence on you?

VM: He was an influence on me in a way. So was Ray Charles. So was John Lee Hooker. After a while you do what you want with the influences. Like 'Purple Heather' – I don't do that like anybody else does it. I don't do it like an Irish song. Generally people who hear it won't even click on it. If you're not from Ireland you're not going to click on it.[87]

So it is not the supposed 'Irishness' of the song that interested him – and we see how deftly Morrison gets out from under the biographically specific question to a wider, wiser view of the nature of musical influence and the role of tradition: 'After a while you do what you want with the influences.' Later in the same interview he is asked about this song, and his source is revealed as one both very specifically local to him and his backstreet, and yet also one much more widely known.

DC: When you have so many of your own songs unreleased how come you did 'Purple Heather'?

VM: I heard the McPeakes do it at a party in Belfast a long, long time ago. I'd probably heard it first from my mother but the McPeakes sold me on it. I just thought it was one of the greatest things I'd ever heard. Period. On record or off record. And I had an album of Dolly McMahon's with the uileann pipes and all that stuff. I liked it too.[88]

The McPeakes are now considered the first family of Northern Irish folk music and it was Morrison's great good fortune to be so local and familiar with them and the music they made. Yet we need to remind ourselves that in 1974, Irish music was in his term 'nowhere', most unfashionable and almost invisible commercially. So his citation of the McPeakes as a formative influence was nothing to do with allying himself to a fashionable source or tradition.

The rootedness of the song in his musical upbringing is clear. But how does a song like this develop in the living with it? As with very many folk songs that have survived substantially into the era of recording, copyright and commodification, the song is a site of dispute over authorship and arrangement. While not quite matching the infamous schism between Martin Carthy and Paul Simon over 'Scarborough Fair', the song has moved and shifted enough for its roots to be obscure. This in a way is of course a consequence of it being exactly what it is – a folk song, from a folk tradition in which songs were not 'owned' or copyrighted in the modern sense. They belonged to everybody, in that anyone so minded could develop their own versions of a melody or a lyric, specific to their own gifts or their own community. This is how folk music worked for the centuries before recording technologies arrived in the late nineteenth century – untranscribed, and without definitive authors.

'Wild Mountain Thyme' first became more widely known via a performance of it in 1957 by Francis McPeake on a BBC Home Service programme called 'As I Roved Out'.[89] Such mediation can tend to imply authorship, and this is what happened – it was the first such exposure the song had received and thus the assumption was that McPeake was responsible for the song. The family certainly popularised the song beyond the world of the session and the folk club, but the song is much older than this arrangement of it. Francis McPeake himself learned the song from his uncle, linking the song to Ulster for a generation back at least, but the song's presence there is evidence of a much older connection between Ulster and Scotland. The earliest back the song has been traced (and this of course is limited by printed or written records, and is therefore by no means necessarily definitive: the song is quite possibly much older than the first written record of it) is the mid-nineteenth century. 'Wild Mountain Thyme' appears to be a developed variation of a song attributed in an 1850 collection, *Songs of Scotland*, to one Robert Tannahill. His song was known as 'The Braes of Balquhidder'. That volume contains some background on Tannahill and his song: 'This song was written by Robert Tannahill, a Paisley weaver, born in that town 3d June 1774. His death occured [sic] on 17th May 1810, by suicide.' His biographers assure us that this lamentable act arose from no pressure of poverty: 'his means were always above his wants . . . His constitution was delicate; his temperament shy and morbidly sensitive.'[90]

So the Ulster song turns out to be a Scottish song. Yet 'The Braes of Balquidder' has also caused some disputes over location: some maintain it was named after the braes, or hills, of Balquidder in Dumbartonshire, others that the hills are near Lochearnhead adjacent to Loch Earn in Perthshire, in Central Scotland. Those whom Kate Rusby has called 'the folk police' may dispute such matters; we can respect such scholarship but also reflect that, for example, while the route in Van Morrison's 'Coney Island' is geographically jumbled, it is the music that is the real point. Wherever we see the Braes, Tannahill's lyrics are unmistakably Scots in their lilt and take us there; we note too how similar the scansion is to that of 'Wild Mountain Thyme'. For example, the first two verses of this song are:

Let us go, lassie, go
Tae the braes o' Balquhidder
Where the blaeberries grow
'Mang the bonnie bloomin' heather
Whar the deer and the rae
Lichtly bounding thegither
Sport the lang summer day
On the braes o' Balquhidder
I will twine thee a bower
By the clear silver fountain
And I'll cover it o'er
Wi' the flowers o' the mountain
I will range through the wilds
And the deep glens sae dreary
And return wi' their spoils
To the bower o' my dearie

We compare this with the more familiar lyric:

Oh the summer time is comin'
And the trees are sweetly bloomin'
And the wild mountain thyme
Grows around the bloomin' heather
Will ye go, lassie, go
And we'll all go together
To pull wild mountain thyme
All around the bloomin' heather
Will ye go, lassie, go
I will build my love a bower

By yon clear crystal fountain
And on it I will pile
All the flowers of the mountain
Will ye go, lassie, go[91]

The bower, the fountain and the flowers of the mountain survive while the blueberries are supplanted by thyme in the move across the 23 miles of the Irish Channel between Scotland and Northern Ireland. The melody changes too: the well-known McPeake melody is quite different from the one attached to the Tannahill song in *Songs of Scotland*. This, too, is no mystery – music changes as well as survives and ideas of what constitutes mellifluous melody change too. Listen to nineteenth-century melodies and aspects inevitably strike one as archaic or as belonging very strongly to their time. The McPeakes' version allows the ghost of Tannahill's tune to weave around the bones of their own.

So all versions of the song post-1957 are consciously 'after' McPeake, and unconsciously after Tannahill. The family tree of a tune is as rich complex and as open to disputed readings as any dynastic genealogy. If Van Morrison 'heard the McPeakes do it at a party a long, long time ago' then he was still entering the story late, but the point about a song such as this is that it grows and changes while still taking with it something of its root DNA. Thus it can accommodate, even welcome the variant version that is so central to the way folk song (as opposed to music produced by and for the rock and pop industry, say) functions. So in changing the title and turning the spring tune into an autumn song, as he does with 'Purple Heather', Morrison is not working contrary to the spirit of the song, but, instead, is with such innovations contributing to a long and complex tradition. This reflects both a local issue – it suited his mood on that particular album at that particular time, as the closer to a triptych of tunes that bathe in natural light – and the broader notion of how songs develop over time and distance, thereby resisting the ossification of the definitive version. *Hard Nose The Highway*'s credit is merely 'Arranged by Van Morrison', although he has never failed to credit the McPeakes as the source of the song as far as he is concerned. This is not to say that in the 1950s this folk culture was cherished or even acknowledged as significant by the powers that were. In his foreword to Maurice Leyden's *Belfast: City of Song*, David Hammond related a tale that reveals much about the 'underground' status of this music at that time:

I remember twenty odd years ago when that notable Belfast singing family, the McPeakes, won a Gold Medal at a Berlin festival for their performance of Belfast music and song. The master of ceremonies remarked, 'Your Burgomaster in Belfast

> will be much pleased with your prize'. Francis McPeake truthfully replied, 'Our Burgomaster in Belfast doesn't even know we're here'.[92]

This is funny, and melancholic, all at once. The McPeakes recorded a version of their arrangement of the tune that was issued on an album called *The McPeake Family Of Belfast*, under the title 'Will You Go Lassie Go'. The very detailed sleeve note mentions the song only in passing, suggesting that the song's status as a folk standard had not yet come to pass. It does however paint an intriguing picture of Belfast in the 1950s:

> It is difficult to think of Belfast as a city of singing and music. It is a bleak, grimy city, windswept and cheerless in the winters and wet and cloudhung in the summers . . . The surrounding countryside is a a beautiful landscape of small farms and rolling hills, with the coast and mountains not far away, but Belfast itself seems itself apart from the beauty, as it huddles against its riverside tangle of shipyard building cranes . . . Its only picturesque neighbourhoods are the slums behind Sandy Row. If it were not for Belfast's people, both Irish and Scottish, there would be as little music in its streets as there is in Birmingham or Liverpool.[93]

This is a powerful sketch, and one which would surely never be countenanced on a record sleeve today, but within the gloomy prospect we recognise very clearly Van Morrison's Belfast, the place of rain, coast, mountains, the back-street, Sandy Row, shipbuilding and rolling hills. It also notes that while harmony singing was 'not traditional' in uilleann pipe arrangements of folk tunes, 'Will You Go Lassie Go' is sung 'in full harmony': this is one of the ways the McPeakes carried tradition forward.

To listen to it is to hear a remarkable thing: it is a querulous, elemental sound, the sensation of which is not unlike hearing the recordings of Charley Patton or Son House. The harmonies are wild and free and live, and nothing is quite where one expects it to be, seemingly simultaneously before and behind the steadily spinning rhythmic centre that ghosts through the performance. The uilleann pipes are both melodic and a kind of refined white noise, their drone providing a primal, adaptable frame for the voices, the family likeness and the generational tonalities of which make the listening a most moving experience. This is ancient music, both dark and light, the sound of tradition making itself new.

Recorded less than a decade later, but sounding like a century so, The Byrds' version is lush, sporting a swirling string arrangement by Allan Stanton which, while some distance from the Ulster drone of the McPeakes' version, does not swamp the melody. The three-part harmonies of McGuinn, Crosby and Hillman again smooth the song out somewhat but create their own shimmering, understated loveliness. This was the version of this song I heard first, when as a child I would sneak into my sister's room to play *Fifth Dimension* on her Dansette; duplicating the assumptions surrounding Francis McPeake's 'ownership' of the song, I assumed it must be a Californian song. With its generous open guitar tunings and unmistakably 'Byrdsian' Rickenbacker solo (1.22–52) it still sounds like one, while retaining much of the windblown toughness of its source. It is credited as 'Traditional'.[94]

The version by the great Australian singer-songwriter Gary Shearston, best known for his hit cover of 'I Get A Kick Out Of You', pitches somewhere between the folk club and the Byrds, with a distinctly Antipodean twist. It sports a luscious arrangement showcasing Shearston's rich, very Australian vocal, the sweet Aussie vowels staking a claim to the song's relocation among the traditions of the generations of the displaced and diasporic communities who moved from Scotland and Ireland to that particular New World.[95] If we needed evidence of the viral potential of the folk song to effect a global spread here we have it.

I asked Shearston about his connection with 'Wild Mountain Thyme' and what he took to be the song's root:

> 'Though the McPeakes were based in Northern Ireland, I considered the song Scottish in origin due to traditional connotations with heather. It sounded traditional to me, with all the associated connotations of hand-me-down. I'd always wanted to attempt a version that moved to an 'Aussie blues' feel. I don't think I got there but enjoyed trying.'

Shearston is modest: his version is very fine. I wondered what his thoughts were on how an Irish-Scottish song like 'Wild Mountain Thyme' fits into the Australian folk tradition and culture:

> 'You hear a song (from whatever source), decide you'd like to sing it, and work up your own version, and channel it through your own soul. The Australian folk music traditional, as with the American, is firmly rooted in the traditional music of Britain and Ireland. The words and music from that tradition simply took on different dimensions in the land of their import where, so often, the tunes were used to relate new tales of a new land. In Australia, because of its vast landscape, many of the tunes got stretched to maximum storytelling width. It was something of this I was aiming for with "Wild Mountain Thyme".'[96]

This is a singer's and a musician's response, connecting that very local thing – the folk tune – to what Shearston calls 'the vast landscape' of another place, becoming part of the 'new tales of a new land'. The song travels and adapts, because people do. In his estimation of the need to 'channel [a song] through your own soul' we must also feel an echo from singer to singer and think of Morrison's own thoughts on channelling music through one's own 'higher self'.

Extending and developing living tradition is that which Kate Rusby presently does like no-one else. In my view by far the greatest living English singer, she placed a version of the song, which she called 'Blooming Heather', as the final track on her 2007 album *Awkward Annie*. Morrison also made it his album closer. This version builds an arrangement around an unusually dense vocal pattern, as she is joined by her fellow Barnsley-born English National Opera singer John Hudson and Scottish pop-folk singer Eddi Reader. I asked Kate Rusby how she first became aware of the song:

> 'I can't remember a specific time, because this song has been around me since I was born. My parents both sing and play, so I'm sure they would have sung it, also we were taken to various sessions and festivals through out childhood so I would have heard it then too. I can remember it being the last thing sung every year at Whitby Folk Week. They would parade in a garland made of heather and everyone in the room would stand and sing it, before taking a piece of the garland . . . I never actually learned it. I know it sounds a bit strange, but I just knew it, just like I can't remember learning nursery rhymes, as soon as I was aware of what they were I already knew them because I heard them so many times already.'

This connects interestingly with Morrison's memory of how he first came by the song, 'a long, long time ago', and hearing it from his mother. This is a song which in its modern version exemplifies this process of songs being handed down: remember, Francis McPeake heard it from his uncle who had probably in turn received it from his elders and so on. Like Morrison's memory of the party at which he heard it, Kate Rusby has a specific memory attached to the song, although not a particular moment of acquisition. She told me something of why in her view the song has such an enduring appeal:

> 'It is easily accessible, both to people already involved in folk music, and to those who aren't. It's an easy song to like, again due to the simple repetitive tune, and chorus. Also I can't really explain this one, but as a singer, it's a very lovely song to sing physically, where the notes fall in relation to each other, make it a pleasure to sing.'

That physical, visceral response to the melody – 'where the notes fall in relation to each other' – is a beautiful evocation of the centrality of feeling to the appeal of a song, either in its melody or lyric. The open, shared chorus of Rusby's version is typical of folk music in its communal function, illustrating the collectivity of 'And we'll all go together'; in Morrison's version it is less open in its delivery, more idiosyncratic, perhaps even introspective in its form. There are no other voices on 'Purple Heather'. This is in some way indexical of Morrison's own relationship to harmony and the rules of performance that go with that – these rules work against his natural inclination towards improvisation, which places him naturally on the side of jazz as an approach rather than as a genre.

There is, as we have noted, a melancholy air to the song and the unexpected operatic textures of John Hudson's voice playing off against the pop tones of Eddi Reader provide a wholly unpredictable setting for Rusby's own steady sweetness of tone. The voices, despite their differences, come together to serve the song's steadfast wistfulness. The steady pulse on the guitar helps develop this addressing of mood, as it opens the song and endures throughout the 4.51 running time; it provides the basis around which the arrangement is built. Intriguingly, Kate Rusby and I found different moods at work here:

> PM: The song on paper is a youthful, happy song for lovers, but the melody seems to me melancholic (autumnal, even): what do you think about this strange fit between the lyrical mood and the musical one?
>
> KR: I find the melody quite uplifting, just because it's slow doesn't make it melancholic for me. I think the tune fits the lyrics perfectly, but that's just my opinion!

It may well be that my familiarity with the Van Morrison version has influenced the way in which I hear all and any versions of the song – Kate Rusby, like Gary Shearston, finds the song buoyantly uplifting where some (for instance me, baby) find a warm melancholia. I asked her about such variant readings and how they fit into this pattern of tradition and innovation:

> PM: Van Morrison's version of the song ['Purple Heather'] makes it an autumn song [the first lines are 'Well the summertime has gone / And the leaves are sweetly turning']: do you know of such seasonal variations of the lyric or do you know it and feel it purely as a springtime song?
>
> KR: I only know the version I sing. That said, I haven't done any research into the song, so there could be many. I do know that singers alter words and tune of most traditional songs, to make them their own, that's why there are so many versions of songs.[97]

In her final comment, Kate Rusby sums up the dynamic that drives folk song: the combination of tradition and innovation that causes both tension and fracture but also ensures that a repertoire does not become fit only for the museum cabinet or the archive. As she said to me, 'I want to get the song off the page of the songbook and back out into the world'. This is the motivation of the musician who experiences a kind of personal relationship with songs, which does not simply mean ownership and copyright. Morrison is one of these too, but he, like Kate Rusby and Gary Shearston, understands that that is a dynamic and ongoing process, and, in an age of commodification, one which is harder to negotiate without taint. All are pragmatic idealists, and 'Wild Mountain Thyme' is a song that allows them to confirm and renew tradition while contributing to it. As noted, Morrison's setting of the tune is an autumnal one, developing tradition by changing the lyric from its usual springtime context. His arrangement of the song pleased him, telling Yorke that '"Purple Heather" is really "Wild Mountain Thyme" . . . just my interpretation of that. I like the arrangement of that. I really dig the way we did it: it worked out well I thought.'[98]

'Purple Heather' begins quietly, with a low-key on-beat and with the fourth beat emphasised by guitar, piano and snare, giving the song's progress a catch, like a benign scratch on a record. The vocal enters at 0.16, immediately inverting the seasonal setting usual to this tune, setting it in the autumn: 'Well the summertime has gone / And the leaves are sweetly turning'. This is of course entirely in keeping with the mood of *Hard Nose The Highway*'s second side on vinyl (Tracks Six–Eight on the CD), following as it does 'Autumn Song'. It also matches the broader tendency within Morrison's work to favour the unfashionable season, be it autumn as here, winter (in 'A Sense Of Wonder') or spring ('Celtic Spring') over summer (whose dog days are lamented in 'High Summer'). Thus there is a sense of loss but also of fullness. He weaves and improvises around the lyric, changing and retaining as he goes, making it more opaque but also more like his own images ('the place . . where heart is yearning'). The piano of Jeff Labes is given free rein to extemporise around the main chord structures (e.g. at 28–32 seconds, or in his lengthy, flowing run from 2.42–3.15), drawing down other musical registers to this old, old song. But Morrison's cleaving to the spirit if not the letter of the song he heard as a boy sustains and carries it forward. The first chorus cues an upward modulation in the voice, from the mellow tone of the opening up to the full richness of his deep chest voice at 55 seconds, stepping up to it at 54, with the 'And' before 'we'll all go together', the vowel sounds in 'all' and 'wild' drawn out with pure feeling. It is as if Morrison has his hands down on the good earth of Ulster, feeling the grass beneath his fingers, as Rob Springett's cover art shows him doing: indeed Morrison told Springett, 'that's exactly how I felt' on seeing the sketches for the sleeve.[99] The Caledonia Strings ease into the frame at 1.26, at the promise of the tower, giving the very emotional blend familiar from 'Cyprus Avenue' on *Its Too Late To Stop Now* its most effective studio outing. Indeed Morrison regularly included a sublime version of this in his live show at the time, vocally riffing around the line 'The banks of the river' and making the song far more impressionistic and languid. However, it was dropped from the album at the acetate stage and, most regrettably in my view, was not restored to the 2008 reissue.

The emotional resonances of the song are most capably caught and communicated by the musical mix here, with voice, piano and strings melding into a blissful whole which lifts the song into a sweetly soulful reimagination of this venerable melody. The strings hover above the melody (e.g. 2.10–19), occasionally swooping down to follow and reinforce the structure (2.20), but eventually the voice comes up to greet the strings and the two elements deliver a tough and elegant terpsichore, anticipated at 2.34–44 but fully realized on the slow fade. The song builds from its quiet opening through to a peak at 3.15, and then drops back in order for it to build again towards the climactic waltz between the rhythmic pulse of the song, the elysian strings and the vocal as it breaks down – or reaches up – into the pure emoting of the scat of the finale. 'Go!' at 3.46–47 heralds a step up in the vocal performance – listen to his 'And we'll all go together' from 3.54–58 – and the last two minutes are a head-spinning kaleidoscope of piano, string and voice, ebbing and flowing towards and away from each other, yet still remaining within the whole. It is like watching the movements of a flock of birds darkening the sky at dusk. Morrison's scat, hinted at at 2.34, meets the strings full on at the song's climax, starting at 4.28 and running up until the song's remarkable moment of restraint, pulling back from the brink at 4.47. This section brings the dynamics of soul music to the folk tune, building back up to a controlled climax at 5.15 and then a final sustained, radiant fade over which Morrison scats with rare tender eloquence, the piano, strings and voice agreeing, poised between the earth and sky. This performance is the nature of tradition made new.[100] In this it is perfectly illustrative of the dynamic flows between tradition and innovation which course through Van Morrison's art, and his natural musicianship.

Thus Morrison's musicianship is both distinct from and unbreakably connected to his singing and to his roots, as well as his work which grows beyond and innovates both with and away from the sources. In our next section we examine his combination of the instrumental and the vocal as a live performer and in the technological environment of the recording studio.

Chapter Six

On the Burning Ground: 'Liveness' and the Recording Studio

> [Rick McGrath]: You don't perform the songs live the same as the album, or indeed the same way every time.
>
> [Van Morrison]: I seldom play the same thing twice. If we do play the same thing twice I usually say 'why?'
>
> Van Morrison interviewed by Rick McGrath, 24 February 1971[1]

Filing out of a Bob Dylan arena show in 2005 I found myself behind a group of friends discussing the show – one was disappointed: 'It wasn't like the records', she said. She was quite right; it wasn't at all like the records. But why would we expect it to be? In this chapter we look at Morrison's relationship with the stage and with the idea of live performance as expressed through his live work and recordings made public. He has asserted many times that he feels most comfortable working with live music, and that it is there where he feels his best work is done.

Van Morrison's reputation is founded strongly upon his ability as a live act yet he has made few concessions to traditions of theatricality and stagecraft in the conventional sense. In fact the tension between 'rehearsal' and 'liveness' is at the centre of the act of creativity itself, the need to know what you are doing but not exactly knowing how you are going to do it at any given time, or how it's going to turn out. This is the creative dynamic: the tussle between the way you've done it before, which we might call tradition, and the way you're doing it now, which we might call innovation – the future can abide with itself. This is now.

The issue with popular music as it is widely consumed and understood is that the reproduction has to some extent overtaken the live performance of it: this is the root of 'It wasn't like the records'. In comparison, it is instructive that so many of the 'great' jazz albums were recorded live, because that's how, when and where jazz 'happens'. As Ben Sidran told me, 'Jazz is not a type of music, it is an approach',[2] and that approach incorporates 'liveness' as a matter of course. If we think of the great jazz names, we are often thinking of bandleaders, almost by definition: Duke Ellington, Louis Armstrong, Count Basie, Miles Davis and so on. Morrison may not as yet have the presence of those names as a bandleader but he is undoubtedly mining some of the same seams, mixing this directorial lightness of touch with the more didactic techniques of someone like James Brown, about whom Morrison said: 'He wasn't just the Godfather of Soul and Funk, he was the Godfather of *dynamics*.'[3] So it is clear that a big part of Morrison's live performative methodology is to do with having good people with him: when he asks his audience to give a 'big hand for the band' at each show's close this isn't lip service or stage convention, it's his acknowledgement of what's just happened. He is also, like James Brown, capable of castigating his musicians in public for perceived errors, flaws, or slackness. At a performance which I won't identify, he subjected his drummer to a fairly humiliating in-song tutorial after a number of missed cues. It wasn't comfortable to watch or listen to, but there was a reason for it – going on stage is going to work, and in the ensemble each player needs to be able to rely on all the others. Something is happening there before your eyes – it's not choreographed or staged in its delivery. It's alive.

As a stage performer, Morrison is a curious hybrid: simultaneously revelatory and present in the moment, yet also shielding something via performance itself, perhaps made manifest nowadays by the shades and hat he sports on his public appearances. It is a private exploration, made public. His career has been marked out with remarkable performances and often these have shown how his work has evolved, while remaining connected to the sources from which it originally sprang. The film of Them that survives (notably that of the *NME* Poll Winners Concert at Wembley in 1965) shows a young man already directing the music amid an array of gestures still familiar to the Morrison concert-goer – the nods, the arm sawing down to signal a cut, the off-mike shouts, all showing his own spin on the blues artists he revered alongside his years of experience in showbands such as the Monarchs and the Sputniks, working hard in the clubs and dancehalls of Ireland and Germany.[4] That ability to cross musical boundaries, absolutely essential in the world of the Irish showband, would serve him very well later in his working life. Maria McKee told me that she found something of the showband in Morrison's approach to stagecraft, in its humour, its quicksilver ability to move from genre to genre, and what she called 'the inherent musicality and soulfulness of the Irish'. I asked her what she meant by this:

> 'Well, Van, and any band he has had with him, seems to have that innate ability to play in any style, maybe even several styles in an evening, and do them all really well and really soulfully! I think he got that, or some of that ability anyway, from the showband scene . You know, playing and loving it, but also working hard, giving what's needed in the moment.'[5]

So it seems that this ability to both inhabit and be at a distance from the live moment has deep roots in Van Morrison's approach to 'liveness'.

Even the name of the band 'Them' was a kind of performative, demarcated gesture. Borrowed from a 1954 sci-fi movie[6] that drew upon and exploited the Cold War paranoia of US popular culture and cinema in particular – specifically fears of invasion, of otherness, and of the outsider arriving and changing the way things are – the fear of 'Them'. In this 'Them' is one of the great band names in pop history, with a claimed 'outsiderhood' that is both real and good business sense – pop culture facilitates and celebrates the outsider, usually by absorbing it and making their innovations part of mainstream discourse. So, for example, 'Gloria' becomes part of pop's DNA, as we discovered earlier in this book. Their outsider status was thus incorporated into their public image from the outset. In this sense, the self-mythologising, seven-minute talking blues of 'The Story Of Them' is as powerfully performative of identity as any visual document. The very sound of it conveys the outsiderhood that feels like a breaking free, as the passers-by gawp at them, and at *Them*: 'Look, look, LOOK'.[7] Gerry McKervey said of Morrison at this time that 'he was able to project onstage what he couldn't project in social company. He would sing things that maybe he thought, but he couldn't have sat and said the same things'.[8] His claim to be a working man becomes less and less petulant with each consideration of this. He is a man in the right job.

We can identify significant points in his performative development after Them. For example, the Byronic singer-poet figure heading up the Caledonia Soul Orchestra, caught live on record and also on film by the BBC is, thanks to the widely seen TV show and the success of *It's Too Late To Stop Now*, very strongly fixed in his audience's mind, with the frock-coat and flowing red hair serving as a kind of cipher of Morrison in the way that the *Don't Look Back* image does for Bob Dylan. Morrison's 'look' and performance of 'Caravan' in Martin Scorsese's film of The Band's 1976 farewell show, *The Last Waltz*, was also a key moment. He was by all accounts very nervous and his clothing compensates for this in a way, being a remarkably 'showbizzy' outfit for him – a sparkly jacket, maroon waistcoat and trousers. Here we are back to Maria McKee's showband idea. His physical performance in that movie was effectively a career-restarting one: a new generation who knew only his name could suddenly see and hear this dynamic performer. It was certainly the first time I ever saw him, on the screen at the Bluecoat Chambers in Liverpool, and I'm not entirely sure that I have got over it yet.[9] In some ways this is the definitive Morrison performance, with the vocal blazing and sweeping across the words and melody, taking it way up there, bringing it right down here, the repetitions, the vocal asides and, unforgettably, the showmanship of the high kicks as he sidles off the stage at the finale. Scorsese's camera doesn't know where to look – the delighted, joyous surprise on the faces of Robbie Robertson and Garth Hudson? The thrilled and roaring crowd? Morrison himself, legs kicking high and eyes closed in relieved rapture before taking a bow stage-side? The high kicks would be familiar to anyone who had seen the shows with the Caledonia Soul Orchestra three years earlier, but undoubtedly this is a superb performance, both in terms of musicianship and stagecraft, by someone who understands the dynamics of 'liveness' and the theatre of the stage very well indeed. This is a feeling confirmed by his acknowledgement of how something true may be revealed by something rehearsed in his 2008 song 'Behind The Ritual': 'behind the ritual, you'll find the spiritual'.[10]

In the 80s, his live performances became more and more possessed of their own internal logic and frames of reference, particularly in the case of 'Summertime In England's increasingly epic extrapolations. Eventually in the late 90s, his performances of 'Burning Ground' – often running to over 15 minutes – reached a kind of dramatic apotheosis for this kind of stagecraft, ending with him dashing his microphone stand to the ground in a kind of ritualised despatch and renunciation of his stage persona that was extraordinarily powerful. This recalled nothing less than Prospero's breaking of his staff in Shakespeare's final play *The Tempest*, destroying the symbol of his 'so potent art'.[11] Yet it wasn't just a great spectacle, or good theatre – it was the kind of gesture that changes everything that follows it. Morrison's officially released live documents offer some insights into how live performance can capture such rare moments of 'liveness', and of art existing at the brink of change. Yet how can a live recording address such complex and ambient concerns? Let us begin our examination of the live recordings with an important exception that perhaps proves the rule.

MONTREUX 1974

The commercial DVD issue in 2007 of two Montreux shows, *Van Morrison Live At Montreux 1980/1974*, was a genuine delight and surprise. Morrison appeared at Claude Nobs's famed festival by the shores of Lake Geneva a startling 17 times between 1974 and 2007. His very first visit on 30 June 1974 is twinned on the DVD with his second, on 10 July 1980. In the lengthy gap between appearances lies a tale, one not completely told by the visual document. Morrison, having broken up the Caledonia Soul Orchestra the year before, had come to Montreux in 1974 without a band, as Claude Nobs explains in the sleeve note:

> Van called me from California telling me that he was coming alone and needed a band. I found two musicians from the Olympic Studio: Pete Wingfield and Jerome Rimson. And since Dallas Taylor was around, we were able to put a band together for a very jazzy set . . . There was none of the big hits but the set was very torching and left the audience in a different world![12]

Of this hastily assembled band, Taylor was used to the big gig, being CSNY's drummer, Pete Wingfield was already a highly regarded session player, and Chicago-born Jerome Rimson, a superb, flexible and melodically funky bassist who would in 1975 produce and arrange for, in my view, the best soul group to come out of the UK, The Real Thing. Putting such a strong band put together at short notice was an achievement in itself. As Nobs notes, the set did indeed offer a different kind of live experience to the epic shows with the Caledonia Soul Orchestra in the previous two years: it was 'very torching' indeed. This difference is wilfully emphasised by the set list: of the ten numbers performed (the DVD is missing the 'encore', 'Since I Fell For You'), three were unreleased vocal originals, three unreleased instrumentals, two were covers and the remaining two were the then brand-new 'Bulbs' and an oldie, 'Street Choir'. The latter is greeted with rapture from the by then somewhat vexed audience.

The music throughout, however, chugs beautifully; it's a dry, solid four-piece sound, fresh and alert, with Wingfield, Rimson and Taylor watching for their cues with consummate professionalism and skill, and building on them just enough to relax into the material. Bespectacled and dressed in plaid shirt and brown corduroy trousers, Morrison looks very different from the gypsy-poet figure of the *It's Too Late To Stop Now* sleeve of the previous year. There are no theatrics of the sort associated with that set either – how could there be at such short notice? – but this was also, I would suggest, a very deliberate break with the expectations that those shows had inculcated in his audience. The smallness of the sound is very refreshing in comparison to the aural mosaics of his work onstage with the Caledonia Soul Orchestra. He chops away for the most part on a round backed six-string acoustic, adding a skiffly skid to the sound. Wingfield's Wurlitzer piano is the main melodic texture in the mix while Rimson and Taylor's jam-solid rhythm section underpin this selection of obscure and unlikely numbers. Morrison's voice also explores places unfamiliar to his audience: hear the gruff blues voice let loose on 'I Like It Like That', the country-blues swagger exploring the musical dynamics of 'Foggy Mountain Top', the sheer visceral attack of his screams on 'Naked In The Jungle', the Joe South-style southern swamp pop-shout of 'Bulbs', the still-startling falsetto of 'Twilight Zone'.

The set has a curious dynamic, in some ways designed to provoke its audience, refusing to give them what Nobs calls the 'hits' but at the same time offering them a peek into where he might be going next with his work. The mixed signals of the set reflect Morrison's own growing disillusionment with the music business and his place in it but also his own work – how to take it forward, and keep it developing when the industry, and perhaps the audience, want more of what they already know of him? These big issues underpin this 50 minutes of fragile, pithy, tense, muscular, disputed music. 'Naked In The Jungle' is itself a cry out against the industry and how vulnerable he feels in his dealings with it, and the version caught on the DVD is blisteringly caustic, all the more so for the dignified disgust in the singer's voice, rather than his performance, expressing a kind of refined yet venomous contempt for the industry. Of course he is well aware that he is part of that industry and so some of the tension stems from his own vexation with his own complicity. It is worth noting that this show, and its chaotic finale, effectively ushered in his extended break from the album/tour slog he had been working at since the early 60s, which tends to be referred to (though not by Morrison) as the 'Period of Transition'.

The strange finale to this show has been edited from the DVD release. If you want a transcript you could consult one of the biographies, but the exchange between Morrison and an audience member after 'Harmonica Boogie' coalesced Morrison's sense of dissatisfaction and disillusionment with himself and the business as a whole into an unpleasant verbal dispute. This was a rare transgression by Morrison, who for the most part has been a respecter of the 'fourth wall' in terms of audience interaction; in his live career, only the wild and outrageous monologues at New York's Supper Club in April 1996 rival this. I would suggest that as an example of such transgressions, it is as startling and as pivotal as Roger Waters' spitting in the face of a fan at a Pink Floyd show in Montreal in 1977 on the *Animals* tour (history does not record whether it was during a performance of 'Dogs', the lyric of which tells of a young boy told not to spit *in* rather than *at* the fan). As gestures they both run remarkably counter to the codes not only of pop and rock but of performance itself. By contrast, Sid

Vicious's shooting into the crowd at the end of his version of 'My Way' in *The Great Rock 'n' Roll Swindle* was merely a staged, kitsch fantasy.[13]

Morrison and Waters handled the fall-out from these turning points differently of course. The former responded in part by 'disappearing' for three years, while the latter conceived, wrote and actually built 'The Wall' as an image of his perceived inability to communicate meaningfully with, and escape the scrutiny of, his ever-growing audience. Both events scandalised their wider audiences, but there in the Casino in 1974 the audience clapped determinedly for an encore, almost on a point of principle. Morrison obliged, incongruously, with a slow and rapt take on 'Since I Fell For You', which is not included on the DVD.

It's my opinion that this concert, short and under-rehearsed as it was, proved one of the most significant Morrison has ever given in the effect that it had upon the development of his art. Had the audience member not abused him he would perhaps still have fallen back from the frontline of the business but the matter was crystallised by this strange encounter. This connects us back to the volatile and two-way dynamic of live performance, as opposed to the slick representations required by show business. Let's look at how that work has been taken to the marketplace.

THE LIVE ALBUMS

It's Too Late To Stop Now (1973)

What is the point of a live album? Prior to the issue of *It's Too Late To Stop Now*, the live album had frequently been simply a souvenir – either 'I was there' or 'I wish I had been there'. The Woodstock albums are a prime example. There were the indifferently recorded cash-ins, and the barrel scrapings: the Hendrix catalogue groans with them. The Rolling Stones had issued a live album in the US only in 1966, while Bob Dylan had a handful of tracks recorded at the Isle of Wight Festival, 31 August 1969, on the reviled (though I rather like it) *Self Portrait* to mark the low-key debut of the live Bob. The Beatles steered clear altogether, with only a patched together album, *Live At The Hollywood Bowl*, emerging in 1977, EMI hoping to catch the coat-tails of the new market for the live record in the wake of the first huge-seller, 1976's *Frampton Comes Alive*. Pink Floyd had devoted half of *Ummagumma* to live remakes of old tunes as they cast about for a new direction. The Allman Brothers had issued *Live At The Fillmore*, closely followed by The Band's *Rock Of Ages*, while the Who's *Live At Leeds* demonstrated that the new medium of the live rock concert could perhaps capture something which went beyond the limits of the souvenir.

The mediating technologies of amplification and recording had changed the nature of the live experience for pop and rock music by the early 70s. In the era of the dawn of 'hi-fi' and music as a luxury product with high cultural status post-Woodstock, things moved quickly, and the industry was trying to keep up. Morrison didn't invent the live album of course– jazz acts had been recorded live for a long time, and B.B. King's *Live At The Regal* is a classic of its kind – but I'd argue that *It's Too Late To Stop Now* was the first recording from his peer group to stand alone as an integral work of art, and a document of a truly distinctive live experience. In this he effectively invented a new art form with this record. The added twist came from Morrison's reputation as a live performer; he was supposedly erratic, yet here was a document of something truly remarkable happening on the concert platform. While no-one was looking, Morrison had snuck up on the field, and delivered something unprecedented.

He was characteristically sober about it when talking to Ritchie Yorke, and displayed an often unacknowledged sensitivity to what an audience might want from a Van Morrison show, even then, only five years in from *Astral Weeks*:

> 'I do the mellow stuff and I do the harder stuff and I do a lot of other stuff. It doesn't throw the audience off, but it's kind of hard to please everybody. That's what I've been finding out in the performances . . . they [the audience] get off and all that but there's so many different types of people who dig my music, so it's hard to make a record. Some people want to hear this album, some people want to hear another album.'[14]

The album, which takes its title from the closing line of 1970's 'Into The Mystic', appropriately embraces a range of his own material, stretching back to 'Gloria' and 'Brown Eyed Girl' – and that's perhaps what he means when he speaks about 'the mellow stuff'. The fistful of formative influences that surface in his choice of covers are, along with the lengthy takes on 'Listen To The Lion', 'Caravan' and 'Cyprus Avenue', a then radical, now familiar run of the key names: Bobby 'Blue' Bland ('Aint Nothing You Can Do'), Ray Charles ('I Believe To My Soul'), Sonny Boy Williamson ('Help Me' and 'Take Your Hand Out Of My Pocket'), alongside Sam Cooke ('Bring It On Home To Me') and Willie Dixon (the well-known 'I Just Wanna Make Love To You'). With the exception of Dixon, Morrison has namechecked each one of these artists in his own songs. It's worth reminding ourselves that if the names above now seem 'legendary' or 'classic', in 1973 they were perhaps less well known, and the subsequent reputation of the songs and their composers is perhaps due in some small part to the success, commercial and artistic, of Morrison's live album.

The album also introduced an idea to which he has remained faithful in terms of live recordings – that is, no overdubs. This policy has given us such 'live' moments as *Live At The Grand Opera House Belfast*'s 'O what swine . . . sweet wine we drink' on 'Rave On John Donne', and Crawford Bell's (single and most uncharacteristic) shaky vocal on 'In The Midnight' on the *Austin City Limits* album. The faithfulness to the uniqueness of each live performance of each song is tied into the philosophy, if not the practice, of jazz – one take, forget it, it's gone, next number, next moment. The live album is a way of showing that philosophy in action, captured forever. This is a paradox, of course, but one which the idea can withstand and survive.

What needs to be remembered on listening to *It's Too Late To Stop Now* is that not only were some of these songs being played for the first time in this form, there was among them brand new material – such as 'Wild Children', of which Morrison observed:

> 'The 'Wild Children' track that we recorded is a killer, it's much better than the version on *Hard Nose The Highway*. When we recorded that song, we weren't really into it. I'd just written the tune then we went straight in and recorded it. Ideally you should take a song on the road for a couple of months and live with it a while. That would be the best time to record it, I believe.'[15]

The album was drawn from three shows, at the Troubadour in LA, the Rainbow in Finsbury Park, London, and the Santa Monica Civic Auditorium. It's noteworthy that the edits between the trio of sources are almost undetectable. As we have seen there were precedents for live albums, but not necessarily on this scale – these 18 songs serve as the only record of a remarkable band of musicians and of both potential realized and a glimpse of what might have been. But as Morrison has said, he felt that the band had gone as far as it could, and to go on would have let that freshness become staid. Phil Coulter observed that 'in Van's book, the way to react to that success [Caledonia Soul Orchestra] was to dismantle it'.[16] Coulter knows that of which he speaks, of course, but I'd perhaps argue that the restlessness he very rightly identifies is more to do with the pursuit of a creative and aesthetic agenda rather than a commercially inclined one. While it might seem self-defeating, it is rooted in the need to avoid creative stasis, mixed with a little pinch of unwillingness to continue to deliver that which is expected of him. Kevin Rowland, that erring disciple of Morrison, shares something of the same spirit – consider how he dismantled the hugely successful *Too Rye Aye* version of Dexy's Midnight Runners at the height of their success – they were No. 1 in the UK, the US and worldwide – and took three years to make the utterly unalike follow-up *Don't Stand Me Down*. The same maverick spirit of creative restlessness informed the decisions of both men in the face of standing on the threshold of massive mainstream success. Rowland told me that his favourite Morrison album was *It's Too Late To Stop Now*, and how he had first heard it:

> I didn't pay too much attention [to Morrison's music] to begin with. I had loads of other music. Then I was asked to go and pick something up for the hairdressing salon I worked at. The owner lent me his car. There was a tape of *It's Too Late To Stop Now* already in the machine, it was set on either 'Caravan' or 'Cypress Avenue'. I couldn't believe it. This I got almost immediately. When I got back to the shop, my employer said: 'How did you like driving the E Type?' I said 'It's great, thank you, that Van Morrison tape is amazing'. He agreed. I bought it, and from then on I discovered a wealth of riches.[17]

He also spoke of the album to Swedish music journalist Andres Lokko:

> 'It has a feeling and a musical flow which has never been captured in a studio. I tried to capture it on "Don't Stand Me Down" but I didn't quite succeed. On the other hand, no one else has managed either.'[18]

Kevin Rowland's response to hearing this music – 'I couldn't believe it' – is tempered with the recognition one feels when one hears the previously unheard but somehow recognises it: 'This I got almost immediately.' He also recalled to me that he 'liked the cover, where he is looking down . . . that showed me what was possible onstage, somehow, the drama of it . . . was really important for me.'[19] Likewise, his comment to Lokko is testament to the enduring impact of the music upon him – it effectively set him on the road he is still travelling down. The power of it is perhaps one of the reasons Morrison dissolved the band – he had reached the end of his road with that sound, while it provided the 'ditch where the back roads stop' for Kevin Rowland, that place from which he could begin.

What's remarkable is how closely the dynamics of Morrison's live performances, right up to the present day, adhere to the model laid out on *It's Too Late To Stop Now*. The bluesy cover to open, the mercurial exchanges between his own songs and favoured covers, segments of one song slipped into the performance of another and, most of all, the tightrope-daring extrapolations of studio tracks which in the process of performance are changed utterly, drawing together strands of inference from outside themselves and thereby changing their nature, these songs often standing at the far end of the set. Morrison has a superbly developed sense of how to raise, maintain and build upon the temperature of a show, so that it climaxes at its climactic moment, as it were. Today the technique is not quite as dramatic as the key moment of the 70s set (his dramatic 'collapse' at 'It's too late to stop now!'), but still can reach a place to which the set has been carefully, discreetly building.[20]

Opening on Malone and Scott's 'Ain't Nothing You Can Do' (also writers of barnstorming Them live favourite 'Turn On Your Love Light'), the record ebbs and flows between a set of songs via which he pays tribute to the influences that have brought him here, and a selection of his own numbers, mainly post-Them but also including 'Gloria' and Bert Berns's 'Here Comes The Night', which are discharged as prelude to the climactic brace at the album's closing height, being both summative and pointing beyond the record – 'Caravan' and 'Cyprus Avenue'.

It's Too Late To Stop Now also includes a long-enduring feature of his live sets that he has never recorded in the studio, Sonny Boy Williamson's 'Help Me'. The song itself bears that famous riff which was later reworked into 'Green Onions' by Booker T. & the MG's but Morrison has played it as big-band jazz, dirty r'n'b, shuffling country blues, and as a straight blues, with scorching harmonica, sax or guitar solos punctuating its verses. It seems infinitely adaptable to his mood. Sometimes the beat drives the song on, accentuating the undisguised carnality of the lyric, sometimes Morrison holds that energy back, drawing the song down almost to a whisper, holding the mike close to his mouth and enfolding it within his fist in order to deliver a vocal sound of almost suffocating intimacy. The most memorable take on the song to which I have been witness was a 1986 performance in Hanley's Victoria Hall, where he sang/spoke the 'nightshirt' verse as a blisteringly loud whisper actually through the harmonica, packed tight between lip and mike. It may well be a borrowing of Williamson's famed 'chugging' technique, but as far as Morrison's repertoire of rhetorical performative tricks goes, this is one of my favourites, and this was a fabulous example of both the technique and its power. On this album, it is a swaggering, muscular performance designed to showcase both the power and control over their material which the singer and his band had at this moment – it is full of light and shade, great surges forward and sensual holdings back, connecting the old song to the very present moment. This capacity for variation within a structure offers the player who understands the blues as deeply as Morrison an almost infinite range of expression within a relatively simple musical framework; this perhaps is part of the truth offered by the blues to Morrison.

This influence informs material on this album which at first listen seems to owe little to such traditions, but the musical dynamics of 'Caravan' are an example of how Morrison works up tradition into innovation. The internal shapes of this performance are so attuned to the song's mood and also the sheer *sound* of the Caledonia Soul Orchestra that it is no surprise that it developed onstage from being 'one of a dozen' to it being among the dramatic highpoints of his live sets in this period. This version was caught superbly on this album. Sequenced on the album, as in the show, as the penultimate track, it functions symbiotically with 'Cyprus Avenue', which follows it to allow the band and the singer to really explore the possibilities offered by the freedoms (and the rules) of these songs. It spanks along and Morrison makes good use of his burgeoning repetition method, on 'mama', 'gypsy', and 'really wrong', and introduces the 'that's enough' into the first 'turn it up' segment. At approximately 4.15 Jack Schroer takes up the sax line before something quite marvellous happens at 4.30 as the string section comes in with a part and melody unheard on the studio recording. The song lifts, and is taken up to another plane altogether. The strings interweave and wind ribbons of melody around the song's central pulse, emphasising as they do so the balletic pastorale of the song's core. Doing his job, Morrison talks over much of it but it does far more for the song than provide a pleasing backdrop for his introductions, bringing the song right down to a languid whisper until then at 7.05 it explodes back, as Morrison's instruction 'Turn it up!' is for once not metaphorical and it blasts back, driving towards its climax.

The album and show's closer is 'Cyprus Avenue', which by this time had expanded to a ten-minute exploration of the tune; the album version provided a starting point but in terms of dynamics the song undergoes a dramatic transformation. Here we can identify a sequence of discreet but related sections. The opening section takes the lyric up to the half-quote from 'All Shook Up' at 2.14, where he has some serious fun with the vocal, frequently barely singing at all, and occasionally bordering on the absurd: listen to the section 1.33–2.02. This is followed (and indeed cued in by Morrison as such) by the 'Railroad' section, the driving six-note sequence that provides a fore-echo of the unstoppable rhythms which the later part of the song delivers. Morrison still sometimes uses 'Railroad' as a distinct segment to drop into live performances of more recent tunes. This is supplanted at 2.57, as Morrison cues the next change with 'Catch up!' and ushers in the very beautiful 'Yonder Come My Lady' section, string section and all. This runs to 4.21, when the strings drop out, leaving the solo viola of Nancy Ellis to deliver the slow and mesmerising line that accompanies the 'Nobody' section which leads, via the absurdist interlude of 'You Say France' (an old Bang 'anti-song' which somehow survived as a bit of rhythmic nonsense in the live set) to the 'Revelation' section. This builds very slowly out of the 'Nobody' section until he brings the band back on-stream at 7.14, through which the famous four-note horn riff starts to build, giving way at 7.36 to the pounding 'Babybabybaby' section which stops at 8.02. Morrison allows 11 seconds to pass, the crowd cheering, perhaps thinking the song is over, before he returns to the mike with 'I said . . .' The band issues a single hard chord. The crowd continue to cheer. At 8.18, he calls out 'Baby!', leaving eight seconds before the next one, followed by the band's plummeting chord at 8.26. At 8.37, he calls again 'I said . . . Mama!', the band hard at his heels. After 22 seconds of silence from the stage comes an 'Alright!', and we feel the arm come down, the band following his lead. A shout from the audience, 'Let's turn it on', is batted back by the singer at 9.11: 'It's turned on already'. At 9.14, 'I said' is followed by a longer and more ragged band blast. At 9.19 he says 'Over there?', meaning shall I do my line over that side, or over that side? It is a remarkable piece of stage rhetoric, and one that is made all the more powerful by its essentially improvised nature, free to 'happen' around an agreed structure. The audience is transfixed. At 9.23 he finally lets out the anticipated climax: 'It's too late to stop now!' and the band are free to let fly with that driving four-note riff which concludes at 9.43, as Morrison takes his bow and slips from the stage. What is remarkable is that the greater percentage of the last two-and-a-half minutes of the performance is given over to silence.[21]

As Phil Coulter said, there were two possible responses to success – artistic and commercial – on the scale of *It's Too Late To Stop Now* you either develop it, or start all over again. Morrison chose the latter and broke up the band. Much later he was asked about such moments of 'release':

> Michelle Rocca: When you do an album it must feel special at the moment of creation. But once it's released, do you feel you've let it go?
>
> Van Morrison: This minute you put it on tape and you think it's as close as you can get it, then you move on. If you don't let go, you'll get stuck there—it's like giving birth. You must go on. The whole thing about creativity is to go on. Movement![22]

This movement is heard on these live documents: each of his live albums has proven to be a record, in every sense, of a certain band and a certain sound that had come to fully characterise his live shows. After this album there would emerge a pattern of live recordings in Morrison's discography, roughly one every decade: *It's Too Late To Stop Now* (1974), *Live At The Grand Opera House Belfast* (1984), *A Night In San Francisco* (1994) and *Live At Austin City Limits Festival* (2006). The four live albums together provide a not wholly inaccurate set of snapshots as to where Morrison was at a given moment every ten years or so. The decade separation/cycle of the albums cannot be coincidence, and it serves to mark the growth of the artist. Furthermore one can chart one's own relationship with the work – my favourite live album is the 1984 one, probably because I had just discovered his work, was going to see him regularly (this sound was like nothing I'd ever heard), and every show was a discovery. The album reminds me of why I liked him in the first place. If anyone ever asks me why I am so interested and care so much about Van Morrison's work, I give them that album to listen to. So let's listen to it.

Rave On: *Live At The Grand Opera House, Belfast* (1984)

This album is routinely overlooked in career summaries, and previous books on the subject have paid it scant attention, but *Live At The Grand Opera House Belfast* is the record of a band in its own way the equal of the *It's Too Late To Stop Now* ensemble.[23] It is a document of a very specific sound, produced at and faithful to a particular time in Morrison's career and the product of a distinctive and particular group of players. It was recorded over two nights out of a four-night run at the Grand Opera House, Belfast, on 11 and 12 March 1983, under Mick Glossop's careful tutelage. It differs from its predecessor a decade earlier in that it contains no covers – yet in this it is faithful to the set at the time, which contained Morrison originals almost completely, the one regular exception being Ray Charles's 'What'd I Say' and, occasionally, Sonny Boy Williamson's stalwart 'Help Me'. Both, spiritual though they are in one sense, stand out in the company they kept in Morrison's set around this time. Indeed the sets were at their most integral in this period, as evidenced by the fact that over the 11 tracks on this album only a brief fragment of 'Into The Mystic' goes back further than 1979's *Into The Music*, while the actual live sets from which the album was culled only offered one extra trip back beyond then, via 'Tupelo Honey'. Morrison's mind and energy was clearly on the present moment. The album is far from workaday, moving from its intro directly into a bold brassy take on 'Dweller On The Threshold', at something approaching twice the speed of the *Beautiful Vision* version.

This band, with the curiosity of two drummers, Peter Van Hooke and Tom Dollinger, at its heart, thunders with great restraint, a kind of rolling-thunder sound (the force of nature, not Dylan's rag-rock revue) which lends a magmatic rumble to much of the material. Yet it can also tread lightly, as it does in the take on 'It's All In The Game', the only officially issued example of Pee Wee Ellis's echo-vocal relationship with Morrison, which was so central to the great live performances of the 1980s. This 'Game' is one of the quartet of versions on the album which I would argue are as good as anything else he has issued – the song developed far beyond this version in subsequent performances, but the tightness of it here is testament to the power and strength of this ensemble. Chris Michie's guitar, audible on *Beautiful Vision* and *Inarticulate Speech Of The Heart*, here really steps forward and makes an indelible impression upon the songs and the listener. That ringing, resonant tone added to the philosophical, questioning ambience of the material, and also contributed to the sense of weightless engagement with the non-corporeal realm, and a leaning towards the cerebral and spiritual dimension, higher than the world.

The relationship between Morrison and David Hayes on bass, deep here and deeper still to the present day, is evident in the intuitive contributions that the bass registers throughout this record. It locks in with the unusual set-up of double drummers to produce a deep, resonant yet nimble and supple bass grounding for the material, from which the upper register of Michie's guitar, the vocals of Katie Kissoon, Bianca Thornton and Carol Kenyon can spring. The mood tones of Mark Isham's synth and John Allair's keyboards find their place between the bass and treble registers, touching both. The two-drummers idea seemed odd at first; it had antecedents in pop of course, with the clatter and dull crunch of the Glitter beat, the unexpected nimbleness and force of Adam Ant's near-contemporary twin set, and I saw Robert Palmer in 1983 with his band sporting two hefty kits too. Yet this is the pop end of a lengthy spectrum – Morrison was just as likely to have been looking at the possibilities offered by double drummers in jazz innovation too, with John Coltrane's plan for using two kits being stymied by Elvin Bishop's unwillingness to double up, leaving Rashid Ali as Coltrane's last drummer. Like late Coltrane, Morrison has periodically employed a separate percussionist – his 2008 band featured Bobby Ruggiero, who in 2004–5 had been his drummer, in this role – to augment, deepen and leaven the rhythmic element. So this band tackles half a dozen numbers from *Beautiful Vision*, only one from the then-new *Inarticulate Speech Of The Heart* plus a fragment of the title tune, one from *Common One*, two from *Into The Music*. Let's look at a quartet of indicative tracks: 'Dweller On The Threshold', 'It's All In The Game', 'Vanlose Stairway' and 'Rave On John Donne'.

'Dweller On The Threshold' develops out of a intro medley combining the theme of 'Into The Mystic' with a snatch of 'Inarticulate Speech of the Heart No. 2'. Morrison thereby manages to combine a reference to where he has been with what was at the time the title track of his brand new album, emphasising the continuities as well as the progressions. This little bit of superior walk-on music tips over very pleasingly into an up-tempo, frenzied-heeled version of 'Dweller', which scampers along at twice the speed of the studio version. The misty, laid-back ambience and mellow swing of the album version are swallowed by this bold rush at the song that is supercharged by the clattering double drum sets, the strident voices of the backing singers and the bright trumpet playing of Mark Isham. The album take has something of a medieval feel, with the horn lines following determinedly non-modernist patterns. Here that mood is overtaken by the busyness of a song which speaks of the here and now, while looking to the future: 'I'm a dweller on the threshold / Someday I'll cross the burning ground'. Borrowed from his readings of Alice Bailey, that latter image would return with unexpected force to the live stage in the 90s. Understanding the dynamics of the live context as well as he does, this is a strong opener, and the move from the medley to the song delivers an exciting shift of gear.

March 1983 was perhaps a little too early for the take on *Into The Music*'s pivotal cut, 'It's All In The Game', to be recorded live. Over the next couple of years it developed and grew into a site for what Morrison would later call, on another live album, 'the workshop' – that is, the part of the live show where he could stretch out and explore (and sometimes extend) the furthest reaches of a song in performance. But this is not to say that this version lacks anything. Experience has taught me that a barometer of Morrison's mood in the live moment are the *sotto voce*/off-mike grunts and humphs of approval that he utters, and in the opening minute of this cut he declares 'Yeah . . . this is hip!', simultaneously assenting to what is happening (and his band will brighten and focus noticeably whenever he does this kind of thing) and bringing the influence of John Lee Hooker to the table, making connections hitherto unperceived.

It also contains the first example of the echo-vocal technique, caught in the brief conversation between Morrison and Pee Wee Ellis: Ellis seems not to catch Morrison's words exactly, answering in both the negative and affirmative – 'I wanna lose myself / I don't wanna lose myself'. It captures the dynamics of the live performance well, and what strikes one is how frequently Morrison *infers* notes as opposed to actually *singing* them – he has a big band on here (as evidenced on 'Dweller', they could make a righteous and forceful noise), but what is remarkable on this take is the level of restraint the whole ensemble displays. This is so much so that Morrison chuckles to himself when introducing John Allair after the shimmering calmness of his organ solo (2.55–3.50), half in admiration of technique, half in delight at what he's just heard. When a member of his group satisfies and delivers, Morrison will always unostentatiously direct praise towards them. Years later, in a 2003 concert for the BBC, he would spontaneously comment on Geraint Watkins's take on the solo in the same song as 'A bit too Reginald Dixon', referring to the famed organ player whose fulsomely kitsch style became synonymous with British seaside resort Blackpool through his 50s residency at the town's Tower Theatre. Morrison is right, too – it does sound like Dixon. The humour that he finds in Allair's 1983 solo is partly admiration of how these limits can be skirted and exceeded. This recording is indicative of the period as a whole precisely because of this interplay of quiet finesse and surging waves of volume, powerful yet controlled. I also like it because you can hear, at 1.20–26, the splendidly sausage-fingered stabs at the Wurlitzer electric piano Morrison played much of the time during these concerts. These staccato punctuations of the smooth surfaces are the musical equivalent of his ad lib that 'this is hip!', in that they bring some of the rawness of the blues to the well-made song, reinvented here way beyond the composer's original imaginings.

These rough notes feature too on the version of 'Vanlose Stairway'. The song has a metaphysical depth and richness, while being deeply indebted to Little Richard's 'Send Me Some Lovin' and named after the flight of stairs in a block of flats in Vanlose, a suburb of Copenhagen, where Morrison would visit a friend. That balance of the complex and the direct gives us another illustration of the function of live performance. On *Beautiful Vision* the song seems somewhat under-realized, yet in performance, almost from its debut appearance at a show at San Francisco's Palace of Fine Arts on 22 October 1981, it flourished and grew in a manner entirely beyond prediction, becoming one of the touchstones of Morrison's set well into the 1990s, and still turning up periodically to the present day. Indeed if the stats are to be believed, it is the fourth most played song by him in his entire live career, behind only 'Moondance', 'Gloria' and 'It's All In The Game', clocking up over 700 appearances. What does the Belfast 1983 version reveal about this dark horse of a song, to account for such a status? Coming in at 5.30, a good 80 seconds longer than the album version, the song here takes on a languid muscularity, slow moving but darkly powerful. Ushered in via a rolling note on the bass from David Hayes, it begins with a solid plod that is initially unpromising, but one which quickly takes on a mesmerising pulse. Morrison's ad libs are at their height in this take, as are his keyboard punches. When the horns come in at 33 seconds, Morrison's vocal mimics them for a moment and then delivers the first line at 0.40 – at which point the audience get a positive ID on the song and a ripple of applause swells up, acknowledged in a gabbled 'Thangyyouvermuch' between lines of the verse.

The secret of this song as a live favourite is its imperceptibly slow build, from little more than a slow drumbeat into a crescendo of voices, horns, organ and crashing drumbeats, alongside the space that the staggered vocal part gives the singer. The lines are some distance from each other in the musical space, and Morrison' s engagement with the song is, I'd argue, related to its value as a vehicle for his exploration of the possibilities for each line each time. As such it is a perfect construct for his type of singing, and also the spirit of it – the same song, assuredly, but delivered freshly and under reconsideration each time. This live take is definitive in that recording confers a kind of immortality upon it, but in truth it stands as a representative example of what might (or might not) happen in this song at any given time. This 'jazz' methodology extends to the specifics of this performance of course, that is, the practice as well as the theoretical approaches to a song. Allair's organ winds around the intro, as Morrison's electric piano picks out stabbed notes. The addition of the vocal backing takes some of the burden of the vocal and Morrison is free to explore around the lines and the notes – if you transcribe the lyric there is remarkably little to appraise. He develops and improvises around the album lyric, slurring the syllables for effect, adding off-mike ad libs and offering substantial evidence that this song offers him a chance to find a space to work and explore. Indeed the song can almost feel like it is hardly there – check the section 3.30–40, where it falls right back to just the drumbeat, a low vocal hum and Chris Michie's pacifically twisting guitar line – before it surges forward into the full power of the band again.

Morrison's electric piano playing on this cut has been a consistent source of delight to me ever since I bought this album. In some senses, the playing is ham-fisted and inept, but it brings so much to the performance that worrying about technique becomes redundant. The only way I can describe his run up the keyboard from 3.40–47 is to ask you to imagine a badger tap-dancing across the keys, getting away with a pirouette for a moment or two and then collapsing onto the centre of the board at 3.58. And yet I cherish it, and find it central to the soul of the performance, and to the emotional meaning of it. This is proven by how Morrison's vocal up to the song's end is propelled to new heights after this 'solo', providing one of the highlights of his live recordings from 4.25 onwards, the emotional climax coming with the eruptive 'Leave it!' at 4.39. So despite the roughness of some of the playing and the ragged edges of the arrangement, this is in my view one of the most important tracks on the officially released live albums.

Now that, in the words of Norman Whitfield, is really saying something when it is followed directly by 'Rave On John Donne' and its live spur 'Rave On Part Two', from which 'Did Ye Get Healed?' surely grew. Playing once again to the strengths of his line-up, the song opens to a slow tick, plenty of space around the rhythm for Ellis's flute to float and Allair's frill of organ before the vocal. The live version of the song always delivered a compressed précis of the opening narrated litany and this version arrives at the sung section by 2.05, and is through by 2.42. Morrison's picking up the sax gives the rhythm its cue, and at 3.08 it doubles to lead into the climactic 'Part Two'; the drums slowly build behind Morrison's sax solo and crash cymbals sound at 4.03, 4.11 and 4.18, heralding the shift from this bridge section into the second part.

Pee Wee Ellis's flute takes the synth part and the absence of Isham's swirling backdrop gives it a more earthy feel – the recitation is complete, if admirably undubbed (Morrison mangles a line: 'O what swine . . . sweet wine we drink'), and the tone is far more unabashed, especially on the sung section, punctuated as it is by the asides ('Aaaah', 'Yeah', 'It's alright') which signal that something good is afoot. The doubling of the tempo to the fade on the studio version proves to be more crucial than we could have predicted. It provides the springboard for the sublime and wholly unexpected beauty of 'Rave On Part Two', where the insistent chords of the keyboards are made robust by the double drum kits, and the lyric makes the most of the hard work of mood-setting which 'Rave On John Donne' has provided, describing the kind of moment he espies in 'Coney Island': 'Wouldn't it be great if it was like this all the time?' Here he is free to move around and explore this moment in the music, holding together stillness and free flight, contemplation and great forward momentum. There is a startlingly illuminating emphasis on the 'now': 'Tonight, let it all begin tonight', but at the same time he is invoking past moment. The vibe of being fully alive is strong, and deeply human and moving – 'The leaves shaking on the trees / In the cool evening breeze / And the people passing in the street / And everybody that you meet, tonight' are gathered into 'the oneness'. If this isn't wisdom, show me what is. Something has happened; something has been discovered: 'Ain't it true, what you sing about in your song?'

So the great bulk of the track's 9.09 duration (as final number, it provided the emotional climax of the performance) is taken up not by 'Rave On John Donne' but by the instrumental section and the semi-improvised, rawly affecting 'Part Two'. The latter seems to build and build, and eventually to represent and encompass and contain the full emotional range of the set as a whole, expressed in distilled and concentrated form, somehow all contained in the repetitions of 'Knowknowknowknowknow . . . tonight' from 6.55–7.12. On the far side of this, Morrison's vocal uses this repetition as a springboard for further exploration, as he so often does; he delivers one more line at this pitch and then pulls the arrangement back down in an exemplary illustration of how the power is deployed, under control and then pulled back into shape. The moment in 'Caravan', a former live moment of similar emotional force, is also a kind of performative manifesto for Morrison: 'Turn it up! That's enough; so you know it's got soul.'[24] Once the steady, running-on-the-spot moment is regained, Morrison shows that the work is done by introducing his band. There is not a moment nor a note wasted on this track, and it is this spirit of economy and sense of purpose which in my view characterises the whole album and marks it out as very special. While the music on the Belfast live album is the most limited of the four in its temporal range, it is also the most concentrated representation of Morrison's work at the particular moment of its recording.

A Night In San Francisco (And One in Petaluma) (1994)

A Night In San Francisco is, like the Belfast record, the product of two nights worth of recordings, made at the Masonic Auditorium San Francisco on Saturday 18 December 1993 and, less truthfully for the title, at the Mystic Theatre, Petaluma, California, on Sunday 12 December. Of the 22 tracks, 18 come from the SF show, with the Petaluma takes being confined to the encore section of Disc Two. These are 'It Fills You Up', 'I'll Take Care Of You', 'Lonely Avenue' and' So Quiet In Here'. So the two discs do have a kind of integrity, and a flow which you really catch on Disc One; the speed of the show is effectively the speed of the disc, and as such it feels like a 'proper' live album.[25]

The whole idea of a live record – alongside a good deal else – changed in the decade that separated Belfast from San Francisco. By 1993 the CD was well established and the format's running time was just about accommodating enough to capture the epic dimensions of Morrison's live shows of this era. Guest vocalists drop in and out, songs are handed over to them and the choice of material, unlike the Belfast album, casts the net far and wide, backward and forward, hauling in some well-known and some hitherto uncelebrated numbers. Although it's a lot to take in, the uneven nature of the event is befitting of a revue style show, which was clearly Morrison's model for this era. It is an accurate record of the show at the time and of the culmination of a certain kind of ensemble playing which at times does indeed rival the integrity and individuality of the Caledonia Soul Orchestra and sure enough, after this album Morrison dissolved this somewhat unwieldy set-up. Where could it go? He had to take it back down and move somewhere else. Interestingly, the album features only one track from *Too Long In Exile*, his then 'current' album, which was less than six months old when this set was recorded – compare that to the close focus on his current material that characterises the Belfast record. Yet *A Night In San Francisco* never quite satisfies – just as it seems to be heading somewhere, there will be an abrupt change in direction, as another vocalist will step up to the mike and howsoever well they sing (and they all do well) the mood cannot help but be interrupted. Thus this album doesn't really have a 'Caravan' or a 'Rave On Part Two' – that is, a track which never fails to reveal more about itself and the group that played it. The playing on *A Night In San Francisco* is almost flawless, providing evidence of an almost psychic bond between the players – but I still wish they'd take 'In The Garden' at a slower lick, for example.

The standout track is the single survivor from *Too Long In Exile*, Doc Pomus's 'Lonely Avenue', after Ray Charles, which trails after it, according to the CD booklet notes, seven or eight fragments from related works, bringing Gene Vincent, Sly Stone, Mike Vernon and Roy Orbison to the table for a sublime conference on the nature and locality of the Lonely Avenue itself. The track lasts just shy of quarter of an hour, features the vocals of Jimmy Witherspoon, and listening to it we feel that at last time is being taken, and something 'live' is happening, as opposed to the professional, slick gallop which marks out much of the rest of this album. Morrison's choice of Mike Vernon, Bob Ross and Gary Shaw's 'Sooner Or Later' (recorded by Witherspoon in 1992) as part of this exploration down the Lonely Avenue is surely indicative of what his feelings were at this time of culmination for this particular band:

> Sooner or later the good thing's gonna end
> Sooner or later the good thing is gonna end
> But who knows the answer to where, how or when?[26]

The answer was, soon. Morrison broke up this big-band soul revue and his next records were tight, radio-friendly pop and hardcore British jazz. The purpose of the band was to draw in and not only accommodate but also authentically refresh the inputs that the sleeve boasts the two discs contain – ballads, blues, soul funk and jazz. This was the opening salvo in a campaign which made explicit what he and his music had covertly been asserting for years – that Morrison's music had little or nothing to do with 'rock music'. Even as far back as Ritchie Yorke's book he had been voicing confusion as to exactly why his music was lumped in with all that 'rock'. The takes of 'It's All In The Game' and 'Vanlose Stairway', surviving in the set a good decade down the line, signpost the past and the future from the present moment. The dominant mode of the songs which had survived was by now *speed*, and while that's not the case on this record, if you listen to live recordings of 'Summertime In England' from the very late 80s and early 90s you'll note the rapidity of them in comparison to, say, the version featured on the 1980 Montreux DVD. Indeed in comparison to that version, the model sported ten years later functions almost as an abbreviated summary, a kind of medley of its own sections. This acceleration of the long-standing numbers in the set extended to 'Game', too: the San Francisco version runs along hard on the heels of the opener, 'Did Ye Get Healed?', piling in straight behind it. With a running time of 4.20, it takes just short of three minutes less to conduct its business and be off than does the Belfast take, at 7.09. This is not necessarily a bad thing, but what it does mean is that there is less space within the tune for expansion and for getting the feel of the music from within; moving with such swiftness, the song can simply present itself in the time it has and be done. Now there is no direct link belong lengthy duration and aesthetic value of course – 90 seconds of the Ramones beats 40 minutes of Emerson, Lake and Palmer, for example – but listening to the calm space of John Allair's solo in the Belfast version against the seen-from-a-moving-train flash of beauty that the 1993 version conveys, I can't help but note that speed, while evidence of a band motoring full-on together to dazzling effect, compromises some of the potential musical depth of the players and of the playing.

Looking forward, the version of 'Vanlose Stairway' offers a sound example of how songs develop in live performance over time. The Belfast version (5.30) is entire of itself, while on *A Night In San Francisco* (6.55) a line which was grafted onto the song from 'Aryan Mist' (another song on its parent album, *Beautiful Vision*) – 'You got railway carriage charm' – develops into the spur known as 'Trans Euro Train', via Ray Charles's 'Fool For You', the melancholic closer to *Ray Charles Live At Newport*. 'Trans Euro Train' is lyrically little more than the phrase repeated over and over, but the mood it creates is one of longing, of melancholy, and one of perpetual movement, which is consistent both with the theme in Morrison's work as a whole, as explored elsewhere in this book, but also specifically with this recording and this band, in that the propulsive nature of the sound and the arrangements catapults the songs through time and space. So the simple line 'I'm on a trans-Euro train', picking up (no doubt unwittingly) the image from Kraftwerk's hugely influential homage to perpetual motion 'Trans Europe Express', conveys this sense of a stillness which is also forever in transit.[27] He also makes it real in the time and space he is in, on 18 December, customising the line 'Sign it with kisses . . . Do it before Christmas!' to the occasion. So I am not arguing that *A Night In San Francisco* is a somehow a flawed document, or that it contains indifferent performances; instead my sense is that it is the document of a dazzlingly adept ensemble, recorded at a point where they were just slightly overcooked. As Pee Wee Ellis says at the album's close – 'How 'bout this band, huh?!' That's the point: this album is about that band.

Country and Irish: *Live At The Austin City Limits Festival* (2006)

Morrison felt happy enough to let another decade, plus three years, to elapse before issuing another live document: 2006's *Live at the Austin City Limits Festival* is again a faithful document of an era. It was recorded on a single evening, 15 September 2006, at the Austin City Limits Music Festival, Texas.[28] It is worth noting, of course, that Austin is the centre for both 'western' music, as in 'country and western', and also the centre for 'alt. country'. My point is, it is not Nashville. Having just issued a straight country album, *Pay The Devil*, it was an interesting choice of show to record and issue; maybe it was simple coincidence, maybe not. Either way, the set is as performed that evening, with no omissions. This double CD has never been given a mainstream release, being available only via the Van Morrison website. This album goes back to, as he says, 'the first vocal I ever recorded', on the version of 'Don't Start Cryin' Now', and progresses thence up to a trio from *Pay The Devil*. There is a definite dynamic to this album which the others do not have – the whole show, famously 90 minutes' worth, fits nicely onto a double CD of course, and acts as a career-spanning résumé which offers, in the dread phrase, something for everybody. Those who want 'the hits' ('Days Like This', 'Bright Side Of The Road'), the old stuff ('Brown Eyed Girl',

'Gloria'), the historian ('Don't Start Cryin' Now'), and the connoisseur (via the 'workshop' of 'It's All In The Game') are all catered for. The jazz stretches out and rearranged classics ('Saint James Infirmary', 'Moondance') allow a bit of muscle-flexing, alongside promoting the new album with a band well equipped to show it off and so on. The set is truly democratic in this sense and carefully tailored to meet the various constituencies within his audience. The questionnaire undertaken at shows which led to the restoration of 'Brown Eyed Girl' to the set lists some years ago suggests that he does actually pay attention to what his audience wants and he is, via a careful structuring which still leaves room for experiment and for things to happen if they happen, prepared to deliver that.

This album was also novel in that it captured a group at the start of its tenure as opposed to its culminating moment. The Belfast album recorded a group still evolving, while *It's Too Late To Stop Now* and *A Night In San Francisco* recorded ensembles at the top of their powers – and, in Morrison's own salty phrase, what do you find out when you reach the top? That there's nowhere to go. So Morrison broke the bands up. The Austin album has more in common with the Belfast record than the other two – it is a document of a work in progress rather than the finished article. The collection is coloured by its participants – Morrison rarely hires anonymous sidemen, rather he seeks those who can not only give him the sound he is looking for but also take that sound and develop it and take it somewhere that, perhaps, he couldn't have taken it without them. Think of the influence that the likes of Pee Wee Ellis, Chris Michie, John Platania, Jack Schroer and the like have brought to Morrison's songs over the years, and witness this:

> Candy Dulfer: Whenever I play with you the guys bring me the list and its already 30 songs but I always notice that when you're feeling in a great groove or feeling things after the third song we'll be going somewhere totally different . . . do you like that, the impromptu thing?
>
> VM: Well it all depends what they know . . . there's so many levels to this, first of all they have to have a groove together, so they have to know this material not just from the point of view of learning the songs, the chords . . . that's just very basic stuff . . . in my bands learning the chords is below zero . . . to get above zero you have to be able to do something with the chords, develop having a groove, a foundation of a groove to start with, playing on that, spontaneity, following me, and all these other layers on top of that.[29]

Taking these requirements into account, what strikes one on listening to the Austin album is the lightness of the sound. The line-up features well-known names from his live and studio past: John Platania, David Hayes and John Allair, alongside a new touch – the apparently pure Nashville sound of the Crawford Bell Singers, who are – we should note –actually from Northern Ireland. Bell, equally adept as a vocalist, trumpet player and producer, is a stalwart of the British country scene, and specifically records country gospel; a typical example being his cassette-only album *The Master's Hand*, and he has recorded songs called 'Precious Memories' and 'In The Garden'. We see from those titles how he and Morrison could be said to be drawing upon similar sources. Texan Cindy Cashdollar's pedal steel and dobro playing completes this Northern Irish country music sound, owing as much to Ray Charles's country albums as it does to Nashville. Another British country player, Sarah Jory, later took over from Cashdollar, adding perhaps a grittier musicality but the style remained ostensibly similar.

The material does not draw excessively strongly upon country materials in the strict sense, however, with only three cuts from *Pay The Devil* making the set, only the un-country 'Wild Night' making the cut from *Tupelo Honey*, and nothing at all from *You Win Again*. Rather it is the players themselves who do the work; for example, the occasionally flat-footed 'Back On Top' becomes nimble and lithe, thanks to the pedal steel and fiddle which confer a skirl upon the solid r'n'b thud of the tune as originally recorded. Likewise, 'Playhouse' is much perkier in this environment, outdoing its studio incarnation especially when the Crawford Bell Singers join in on the 'All that money' sections to powerful effect. The set, to which the album is faithful but for one flip of the running order, is more deliberately attentive to the whole span of the career, and the sense of a review, as opposed to a revue, permeates proceedings. The format enables him to reinvent the well-known and best-loved songs such as 'Days Like This', on which the Crawford Bell Singers take the title line; it's good. Morrison can then do more with the lines between the repetitions of the title phrase and thus lends something else to the spaces between the days, which is where we need to be looking. It's good rhetorically and it's good for the sense of the ensemble in performance.

'Muleskinner Blues' is here, partly as a connection to the departed Lonnie Donegan, with whom he had recorded it in 1999, and also because it unexpectedly sports a very pleasing, 'I've Been Working'-style, good-natured swagger and enables the band to cut loose somewhat, with something approaching Ulster country-funk. One of Morrison's finest songs of longing, 'In The Midnight', sits very well with the sparse melancholia available to this ensemble, the mix of the pedal steel and fiddle, frequently accused of being lachrymose in country music, here feeding into the deep soulfulness of the song, and bringing refreshment to its lovesick weariness. The trio of falsetto love calls at the song's close sound, in this context, like something which somehow missed the cut for *Pet Sounds*, and although Crawford Bell doesn't hit the vocal mark as squarely and directly as Brian Kennedy did, there's soul in it, still. The version of 'I Can't Stop Loving You' shows in plain sight where at least part of the inspiration for this line-up/sound came from – the brace of Ray Charles's *Modern Sounds In Country and Western* albums. This arrangement takes the song much more directly back to source – that is, Charles's groundbreaking mix of 'black' and 'white' musical discourses – than does the 1991 studio version with the Chieftains that emerged on *Hymns To The Silence*. The music is clean, articulated, and possessed of a kind of robust Puritanism that makes the sensual pleasure of the sound a happy confusion. In acknowledgement of this fit of song to style, Morrison hands a verse to the Crawford Bell Singers, which they execute with perfect diction and – until Morrison unaccountably talks across them – rapt focus. This is both the minimum requirement and the height that a live show can reach, and these live albums make a public record of how and when such moments are touched, and when they are missed.

Postscript: 'Oke-She-Moke-She-Pop'

Morrison's greatest single live number has been, in my view, 'Summertime in England' from *Common One*, and the only officially released live performance of that tune is discussed in this book's final chapter. Running it unexpectedly close however is the live arrangement of a much later number, 'In The Afternoon'. When it developed into a major 'workshop' piece in the late 90s, the song became one of the late highlights of this technique, developing from a relatively unlikely source: the closing tune on *Days Like This*. It is part of the meditative sequence which closes what begins as his most perky and poppy of his albums. The paradox of the album is that while in its periodic pop focus and bright, tight production it is a kind of 90s equivalent of *Wavelength*, its lyrical concerns are frequently the obverse of that mood in songs like 'Underlying Depression', 'Melancholia', and 'Russian Roulette'. The album takes a long, strange journey from the daring-to-hope optimism of 'Perfect Fit', to the ruminative triumvirate at the end of the album, 'Melancholia', 'Ancient Highway', and the closer 'In The Afternoon'. The last of the three presents a summation of the themes of the record overall: that is, matters of the heart fused with matters metaphysical – the attractions and repulsions involved in the dynamic between body and soul.

On the studio take, what strikes first is Morrison's vocal – a low, primal mutter deep-trawled from the belly of the blues, sung like one half lost in a waking dream. Instrumentally it echoes the album's first cut, the impossibly bright 'Perfect Fit', opening with a harmonica run backed by piano and the tick of a snare, but used very differently, while the vocal is akin to that of 'Melancholia', slow and confidential. Indeed the setting is the same as in that song, with the first line of 'Melancholia' being 'In the afternoon, baby in my room' and 'In The Afternoon' beginning with 'The light is fading in the afternoon / Won't you see me baby in-a my room', making plain the links between the two songs, and showing a darkened, experience-heavy version of the mood and setting of 'Gloria' itself.

The state has changed too: where 'Melancholia' is appropriately blue in mood, here the dominant tone is of a kind of slow-limbed longing and of seeing love as the way out of the blues, the presence of another being the way to break down the loneliness. So while the time and place are the same, all is changed, and the two places lean into the 'Ancient Highway' that stands between and also connects them. The symbols of nature mark the mood – the fading light, the wind blowing outside, the moon rising behind the fields – and are familiar motifs in Morrison's lexicon, while the combination of the outer and inner modes (the wild wind, the close and claustrophobic room, the world at large, the fevered imagination) emphasises this duality in the bringing together of the two modes of experience. The apparently voyeuristic element ('I can see my baby but she can't see me') emphasises the power of the imagination – he can see her in his mind's eye – and also the frustration of being set apart from her, and having to fall back upon the image rather than the physical reality of the object of desire. It is a song of longing above all else, and the slow pulse of the melody communicates this with some power.[30]

That such an interior monologue became such a key element of Morrison's live performances in the late 90s is on paper surprising, yet on stage it became clear what it offered – a kind of open-ended starting point for a slowly building flow of improvised developments, aggregating over time until it reached a state of pleasingly paradoxical ever-changing completeness. The version issued in 2002, recorded at Newcastle City Hall in March of that year, stands, as I write, as the last truly great live recording he has made public.[31] Using the *Days Like This* version as its basis, the song becomes a 10.40 trip through ideas and developed vocal and musical riffs, establishing and breaking down musical connections. For example, instead of picking up the substantial bundle of threads that link this song with 'Melancholia', the song is twinned in live performance with 'Raincheck', the latter being employed as a fragment in the build towards the 'workshop' section. It stands, I'd argue, with 'See Me Through/ Burning Ground', 'Summertime In England', and 'It's All In The Game' as indisputable evidence of Morrison's power as a live performer, and of how his work can exist in a continuous state of creative flux. Sometimes these songs fly and establish connections spattered across the heavens, sometimes they are walked through and emerge unchanged. On this particular recording, we are shown something remarkable, which signposts both back to where his music has been, and forward to where it might be going – thus all these states are held together concurrently, in what he has called the 'eternal present'. This takes some doing, and is probably only rarely done consciously; we are all the richer then for hearing or seeing it happen before us.

This live take sticks closely to the studio plan at first, albeit with a more supple snap to the marking of its time. Accompanied by Pee Wee Ellis (taking Brian Kennedy's place), Morrison's vocal is strong and takes flight quickly, scattered with direct and muscular repetitions of the percussive phrases such as 'the light' and 'see you running'. The flute employed gives it a lighter feel too, lifting the woodwind above the languorous weight of the brass tones. In one of the delightful touches, which only happen when a group is working together sublimely well, the brief steal from Burt Bacharach and Hal David's 'Alfie', cued in by Morrison's 'What's it all about?' at 3.50 and carried on obliquely by the horns until 4.00, is evidence of how a these 'workshops' can take a song far beyond itself. At 5.08 the horns change direction, growing slowly towards a change and at 5.12 Morrison begins to summarize 'Ancient Highway', and its section describing 'the lights from the cars on the overpass', and despite the epic quality of that cut on the parent album, by 6.02 he is onto 'Raincheck', the lyrics flowing unimpeded.

Proving his mastery of stage dynamics, on the repetitions of the line 'I won't fade away' he makes a steady retreat to the rear of the stage leaving his voice virtually unamplified (from 7.05). By paying close attention, we just hear him call out 'Level One! Meditation . . .' (7.19–24). By now it is clear that we are being taken somewhere by this performance; the audience, to their great credit, do not applaud, laugh or assume the song is over, nor do they allow the tension and energy of the moment to be dispersed; these are the moments in a Van Morrison show which are to be cherished. The silence from the singer, therefore, is a kind of active device to deflect the attention of the listener to the music, and what is happening there, rather than the 'star' of the show, centre stage – hence his retreat to the back of the platform. Yet very little is happening musically – there is a rhythm ticking over, a rising-falling organ riff, a low guitar strum and not much else – but the way we have been prepared for this lets meaning flood in; the music represents a kind of discovered, achieved space for contemplation and release. The inarticulate expression of the brief keening scat (7.55–8.09) as he moves back towards the mike bridges between silence and language as modes of expression, and when he cues 'Level Two . . . Meditation' at 8.12 he draws the music back towards a more focused centre, and the climb continues. When he says, on the studio version of 'Raincheck', 'Gotta keep movin' on up toward that higher ground', he is not only citing Curtis Mayfield and Stevie Wonder, he is also describing the process that this live performance is exploring. He returns to the 'not fade away' image from 'Raincheck' and snapshots of the 'Ancient Highway' before calling the band back in for what has been christened, among his audience at least, as 'Joe Turner Sings'.

Big Joe Turner was one of the major influences, alongside Louis Jordan (whose 'Caldonia' and 'Symphony Sid' Morrison was to cover) on post-war r'n'b, via the jump blues, which proved central to the development of early rock and roll. He often sang in clubs without PA systems, and so developed a deep, rich and indisputably loud holler. He actually began in the pre-Second World War era, coming to New York via the tutelage of John Hammond in the late 30s and riding the boogie-woogie craze of the early 40s, but it wasn't until the key figure of Ahmet Ertegun signed him to Atlantic in 1951 that he really broke through. His material came from Ertegun, from Doc Pomus (author of another Morrison favourite, 'Lonely Avenue', of course), Lieber and Stoller and the rest, even sneaking his own material in under the nom de plume 'Lou Willie Turner'. Come the 60s, the star of acts like Turner began to fall as a new generation took the stage but, as with those bundled back into the spotlight via the blues boom of the post-psychedelic era, he found an audience with those seeking the roots as well as the flower of the music which was by then a worldwide phenomenon, until his death in November 1985.

Turner was clearly of interest to Morrison, both as a young man hearing that voice in 50s Belfast and later as he returned to the days before rock and roll for liberation and inspiration from the late 80s on. Coincidentally, Turner's first million-seller, 1951's 'Chains Of Love', was co-written with Van 'Piano Man' Walls, whose name may have rubbed off on the young Morrison. Turner's recordings for Atlantic – which include all the songs name checked in 'Joe Turner Sings' – swing as much as rock, jump as much as funk, and furthermore his older recordings for Decca and smaller independent labels from the 30s and 40s are not wildly dissimilar, adding fuel to the thought that Turner was one of the very first 'modern' soul singers, and as such preceded the likes of bigger names, even Ray Charles himself. 'Joe Turner Sings', which occupies 9.16–10.30 of this live track, has a lyric which consists entirely of Big Joe Turner song titles. Despite this unpromising expedient, it is extraordinarily moving and exciting – the titles are so resonant and Morrison takes such sensual pleasure in their recitation that we cannot fail to be moved and intrigued by them. So there is a missionary zeal in this – 'Check these songs out, they're great' – but the titles themselves are like storehouses of memory, little explosions of another age bursting into the present moment, their force undimmed by the passage of time:

> 'TV Mama! Boogie Woogie Country Girl! Oke She Moke She Pop! Honey Hush! Flip Flop And Fly! Shake Rattle and Roll! and Don't You Get Me Hiiiiiggh . . .'[32]

This septet of sides from Turner's catalogue are slapped down on the counter before us, the sheer joyous force of assertion in Morrison's delivery of them being irresistible as the dusty 45s are laid out as incontrovertible evidence of their greatness and enduring beauty. The theme is developed as, at the end of the list, Morrison picks up the last title and begins to sing it for us: 'Don't you feel my leg / Cos if you feel my leg / You'll wanna feel my thigh / And if you touch my thigh / You're gonna get me high'.[33] The full version of the song as covered on 2006's *Pay The Devil*, as robust as it is, seems a shade flat after hearing this take on the spirit if not the letter of the song. Morrison's gruff and throaty extrapolation of 'high' (10.00–27) draws the themes of the song – desire, memory, the condition of the soul as expressed in musical terms – together and forces them up into a brilliantly sharp and illuminated conclusion, at the very last moment inviting aboard another soul legend, James Brown, by swiping a sample from one his best-known and fleshiest songs at 10.28: 'Get on up!' The song screeches to an abrupt and wholly unexpected halt right there, on the third beat of 'Sex Machine''s exhortation to movement. In this abrupt conclusion we are given an image of both freedom and control within the music and how the players deliver it, and these few moments communicate directly the power of 'liveness'; musicians play, and an audience listens.

So Morrison's stage craft is a potent, volatile mix of what is rehearsed and expected, what flows in and from the moment, shared cross-references between musicians and audiences, confirmations and subversions of expectations,the stage as either a clock-in, clock-out workplace where a shift might be turned in, or an open, creative space via which magic is turned on, and tuned into. It is in the tension between these apparent poles that Morrison's 'liveness' thrives. How is this captured outside of the concert platform?

LIVE IN THE STUDIO: VAN MORRISON AND THE ART OF THE RECORDING STUDIO

In Van Morrison's case we find an intriguing collision between the meaning of music as a 'live' performance art and as something which is also required to be 'captured' in the studio. Telling an interviewer in 2005 that 'I was a performer long before I got into recording music. I didn't get into this to put albums out. That was always more of a secondary thing', he makes clear his natural inclinations.[34]

Morrison's desire to have his own hand on the tiller also perhaps stems from his experiences way back with Them and Bang, where he had very little say in how the songs were recorded and issued. So if the recording of the popular song is somehow a by-product of a successful career in writing and singing it, it is artistically and financially smart to be master of its destiny. That is the situation that Morrison has been moving towards and has fairly well achieved by 2010. He has owned his own studios on and off since the early 1970s and this brings both artistic freedom and a potential income stream if the studio is deemed successful. His first studio was the Caledonia Studios in Fairfax, California; in the early 90s he bought the Wool Hall near Bath and more recently bought the famous Windmill Lane Studios in Dublin (see Appendix Two).

While Morrison sees live performance and record making as entirely distinct processes, the record isn't negligible; it provides the point from which performance can begin and the reference point to which it comes back, so people will say, like that lady in Sheffield, 'It's not as good as the record' or 'It's better than the record'. For example, it's my view (it may not be yours) that the 1988 live shows with the Chieftains were 'better than the record', while live performances of *Veedon Fleece* tracks, infrequent and cherishable as they have been, were 'not as good as the record'. So the recorded work is very important in terms of money and reputation: the catalogue is built and allows distribution and repetition. The songs are recorded in every sense – rather than the Blakean model of the live work, emphasising the moment of creation that passes as it occurs. For example, the songs on Side Two of *Into The Music* all feel absolutely freshly minted, even improvised on the record, yet live versions of these songs have frequently stuck very closely to the recorded versions.

Morrison seems almost as a matter of principle to practise a culture of first takes in the studio and I asked Fiachra Trench about this aspect of his studio methodology:

> PM: How does his 'first take' ethos fit with the notion of score and arrangement?
>
> FT: Session orchestras play wonderfully from first reading/rehearsal, so our overdubs are often 'first takes' following that rehearsal. And once or twice I have asked the engineer to put the light on straight away, that is to say: to record the rehearsal; that was the case with 'Coney Island'.[35]

This is risky, in that you might catch something, or you might not. As Ted Templeman observed, not all studio staff are primed to work this way: 'I've had to change engineers who couldn't keep up with him.'[36] In the case of 'Coney Island', they clearly *did* catch something. Either way, what happens is what happens. This is perhaps partly to do with cultural certification, and that it is not a 'special event' to be in the studio. In that environment you have to stop and start, get levels right, the flow of a song and a performance may be arrested and fragmented in a way that would be disastrous in live performance. Similarly, the performance is not 'gone' in the moment – one might have to live with it. His long-time engineer Mick Glossop spoke to *Resolution* magazine about his experience of working in the studio with Morrison, sometimes with good-natured weariness: 'having done it before you know what you're up against'. But he also sees this methodology as virtuous: 'you have to recognise what the job is, and then be capable of doing it . . . if that's him being demanding then I think everybody should be like that.'[37]

So how does Morrison adapt to the conditions of recording? The progressions in his music are often fairly straightforward so accomplished musicians in the forms he employs will be able to follow him without too much difficulty here, as live. I asked Trench about this:

> PM: How does the art of the studio affect his music in your experience?
>
> FT: Over the years I've sometimes played piano or organ as part of the band on recording sessions for Van. I've experienced how he performs in the studio with the same intensity as he exhibits on stage. So everybody is on their toes and it's almost invariably a 'first take' every track.[38]

Morrison has in the past eulogised the Sinatra model of coming in, delivering one take and sweeping out again. It was of course much easier for Sinatra: he wasn't a writer or an arranger, he did the vocals and that was that – Nelson Riddle and co. did the rest. Trench's observation suggests something similar, with the musicians 'on their toes' for something special to happen. Morrison is more engaged with the musical processes than Sinatra, of course, and willingly, but would perhaps be interested in an idea Bob Dylan details in *Chronicles*, where the ideal would be that his music would be performed and 'I wouldn't even have to be there'.[39] There's something of this idea in Morrison's periodic use of the expansive revue format in his live shows, as caught on *A Night In San Francisco*. He was absent from a goodly number of the songs, but the show as a whole was undeniably centred around him and his work, even when he wasn't there, and the evening's performance was bookended by his first entry and final bow.

The interesting fact is that while accommodating the principles of one take and 'liveness' into his studio work, his albums always sound very well 'produced' and recorded. There are none of the signifiers of 'liveness' or stylised rough edges that we find on a Neil Young album, for example – fluffed lines or notes, P's popping, mike leakage or bleeding, missed cues – all the practical difficulties of the studio recording are also the stuff of performance, and of 'liveness' itself.

Yet Morrison doesn't really leave these in, incorporating this 'liveness' instead via vocal asides, ad libs, off-mike blues shouts, and the also occasional, visceral performative elements. Listen to the spluttering, keening, 'fffffffffind my feet' (6.02–5) on 'Haunts Of Ancient Peace'; it is still unusual to hear these devices on a record. This sort of idiosyncratic gesture is central to how Morrison's work in the studio differs from but also connects up to the live work.

We might consider then how and where this aspect of control and guidance is relaxed, in areas where he has less expertise, such as the string arrangements he has commissioned from Jeff Labes and latterly Fiachra Trench.

> PM: Do you work with him in the studio, as you have done with, say, Paul Brady, or does he send material for you to score and arrange for via CD/DAT etc.?
>
> FT: Various scenarios here: in the case of *Poetic Champions Compose* (the first of the albums in which I was involved) and one or two other albums, Van and I listened together to all the tracks, decided together which tracks might benefit from sweetening and whether it should be strings or brass or both, and I went away and wrote. 'See you at the recording session.' For others, Van has sent me a tape or CD; I have listened and then suggested which tracks could have sweetening. And for yet others, Van has already ear-marked the tracks he wants me to work on.[40]

The fact that in his lengthy career Morrison has only employed two arrangers, Trench and Labes, is evidence both of their professionalism and his sense that they know what he means:

> PM: Is it straightforward material to score for? Does he say what he wants or do you find you have a relatively free hand with the arrangements?
>
> FT: The latter – I have a free hand with the arrangements, but we do seem to have a mutual, unspoken understanding as to what is appropriate.
>
> PM: What sort of right of approval operates in your professional relationship? Has he ever turned anything down or asked for changes?
>
> FT: Van, as writer, performer and producer, has ultimate right of approval, but in 18 years of working together, there has never been a problem. Van has never rejected anything I have written. And I can only recall two occasions when he asked for a change: he wanted a darker sound from the strings, so we augmented the cellos [this refers to the cello coda for 'Golden Autumn Day'].[41]

This 'mutual, unspoken understanding' is plain when you listen to the arrangements Trench has delivered to Morrison's work, which he modestly calls 'sweetening': listen to 'Orangefield', the single version of 'Meet Me In The Indian Summer' or, perhaps most successfully of all, 'Queen Of The Slipstream'.

Yet how do a slick production and sumptuous strings square with the jazz-blues ethos? Though it is 'live' in feel, there is no reason why the music has to be roughly made, or deliberately flaunt self-consciously rough edges. Indeed jazz production values are high: within the form, there is a canonical repertoire alongside the periodic shifts in reputation, the players sport smart suits and expertise is lauded and applauded in venues like the Royal Festival Hall. So while the sound of jazz is key to its meaning, where that music has travelled is evidence of its appeal – from the bordello to the classical concert stage. I asked Trench about this apparent conundrum:

> PM: Does a tight orchestral arrangement work against the freedoms supposedly offered by jazz and the blues?
>
> FT: No doubt about it. I can well understand that such conjunctions are not to everybody's taste, but personally I'm very partial to a smooth string 'pad' behind jazz instrumentals or vocals.[42]

Trench acknowledges that these juxtapositions can be uneasy but his 'unspoken understanding' with Morrison over how to best serve his work in this way has, on the recorded evidence, evaded such ill-fitting conjunctions.

What Morrison has done less frequently in recent years is to record an album as a whole: for example both *Magic Time* and *Pay The Devil* were recorded in patches over lengthy periods, with tracks laid down and then picked up for release at an appropriate moment. The former was not recorded at the Wool Hall, as Morrison was unwell for much of the period of recording and was domiciled in Ireland – Dublin's Westland Road was used instead for much of it. What difference does this make? It was a different environment, with different musicians, and Morrison was the client, not the proprietor. Can we put a hair between them? Walter Samuel commented upon Morrison's studio methodologies:

> 'Van's not one to sit in the control room and peer over your shoulder . . . The way it works is that I'm in the control room by myself for most of the time, then Van will come down to listen to a mix, say, 'take this out . . . I don't like that' then he will take a cassette and say yes or no. But he wants to hear the thing pretty well finished and then he'll decide whether it's good enough.'[43]

Here we see that Morrison is not over-interested in the processes of recording from a technological point of view – he is interested in the outcome, and whether or not what he wanted has been captured: 'he'll decide whether it's good enough.' That final arbitration is important, of course, as Trench notes above: 'Van, as writer, performer and producer, has ultimate right of approval'. That apparently self-evident truth masks a whole web of complex negotiations within studio recording: how hard has Morrison had to work to win this assumption?

It would be some years into his career before he could truly be said to have achieved this, but it was his long-standing goal, as he told Jeremy Marre:

> I noticed that the guy who did the singing got next to nothing, and it was the producer who had the control, the power of what happened. So I thought that's what I have to be, a producer. And that's what I set out to do, to have control over my own work, y'know?[44]

After the Bert Berns productions for Bang, Morrison understood the importance of driving the studio performance. Lewis Merenstein produced *Astral Weeks* and was 'Executive Producer' over Morrison's own control of *Moondance*, but since then he's been in charge. Morrison has shared production credits only four times, co-producing with Ted Templeman on *Tupelo Honey* and the lion's share of *Saint Dominic's Preview*, on *Irish Heartbeat* with Paddy Moloney, and with Phil Coulter on *No Prima Donna*; it is interesting that, listening to these albums, we can tell the difference – it clearly does effect the sound. *Saint Dominic's Preview* illustrates this well, bringing the unalike sounds of the Morrison-only 'I Will Be There' and the shared 'Almost Independence Day' to the table. Walter Samuel spoke of how Morrison's studio method had changed and also remained the same:

> 'Van's method of recording hasn't changed over all these years . . . if anything he's working more live than he was in the eighties – live vocals and backing vocals – although I think he's a lot more disciplined now, certainly than he was in the early seventies. We wanted ten songs for *Back On Top* and ten songs were recorded – and he had them pretty well sorted before he comes into the studio. It was very quick, mind you, he would go in and cut three or four songs a day. Short and sharp, really. I think during the seventies he was doing a lot more experimentation.'[45]

Samuel's point at first seems contradictory: although the methodology 'hasn't changed over all these years', he is less experimental than he was in the 70s. The bridge is the idea of discipline, and of being 'short and sharp'. That informs the music, as any listen to his post-1999 albums will prove. So although no-one could mistake *Down The Road* for *Veedon Fleece*, both share an approach to 'liveness' in the studio which, earlier in his career, accommodated more deliberate, formal experiment. That experimentation is illustrated by our first case study.

'Almost Independence Day' (1972)

Produced by Morrison and Ted Templeman, this cut, alongside its more famous companion piece on *Saint Dominic's Preview*, 'Listen To The Lion', is a pointer towards Morrison's most audacious work of the early 80s. That shared producer credit seems somehow an echo of the song's title; this was the last time Morrison would give over editorial control in the studio to another. Described by some as 'an 11 minute jam' which is 'filler',[46] it seems to me rather the genesis or crossroads point of one of his methods of performative composition, that is, a discovery via actual performance of what he wants to say, and the nature of a song itself – which reveals itself and is revealed via performance and recording rather than meticulous rehearsal, drafting and redrafting. This song is a prime example of the stage workshop brought into the studio.

A contemporary write-up catches some of the atmosphere of the time, and some fore-echoes of later observations of his studio technique:

> In the studios, Morrison approaches his work with the same admixture of spontaneity, intensity and impatience. Ted Templeman, his producer at Warner Bros.: 'Van's ability as a musician, arranger and producer is the scariest thing I've seen. When he's got something together, he wants to put it down right away with no overdubbing. He'll play guitar and sing at the same time. He works fast and demands the same of everyone there. I've had to change engineers who couldn't keep up with him. He hates to do re-takes on vocals so when he's recording we let a lot of little mistakes go by which we can go back and correct later. Afterwards I usually do the rough mix-down because Van can't stand doing it.[47]

This technique is clearly discernible in the soundscape of 'Almost Independence Day' and the 'one take' approach mentioned by Fiachra Trench is here too. The song itself is a development of the sort of thing he first tried in 1970, with the lengthy, unreleased studio cut 'Caledonia Soul Music', but this tune is more supple in its internal dynamics, and the song brings the album to a climax that is both stunning and entirely temperate. The measured release of energies makes for a feeling of slow-limbed wheeling, and a strange awareness of the movement of the planet, and of the stars in the sky – after all, this is a song about time, space and distance, and yet also nearness. This is somehow appropriate and certainly harmonises with other work by Morrison in that it is poised on the cusp of something happening, with some change about to come over – 'You can't stop now' ('Friday's Child'), 'It's too late to stop now' ('Into The Mystic' and after), and 'Dweller On The Threshold' itself. It is also part of the pattern within Morrison's work of citation of significant dates and times of the season ('Celtic New Year', 'All Saints Day', 'Autumn Song', 'A Sense Of Wonder' and more).

The track opens with steel-stringed acoustic and a good early example of Morrison's 'unison singing' technique, twinning notes on the 12-string guitar with an off-mike wordless vocalisation. This is also evidence of authorship – had another player been playing the guitar, in this live-in-the-studio context, then Morrison could not have followed the notes with such accuracy. After this opening the last five seconds of this section find the guitar doubled, and the song changes at 0.51 into the hazy still point from which the rest of the song will make its observations of the scene.

The band was assembled for this track alone, featuring jazzman Leroy Vinnegar on bass, ex-Beau Brummel Ron Elliott on guitar and Bernie Krause on Moog; indeed the track was pioneering in its use of a Moog synthesiser, which comes in at 0.55. The world premiere of the instrument in live performance had taken place at the Monterey Pop Festival in 1967, and the Minimoog, launched in 1971, made the instrument more widely available and accessible. The album sleeve notes only 'Moog' so it may well have been the full size model used here, well before it had been really assimilated into the lexicon of pop, rock or jazz, and before most pop listeners had heard it as a dramatic novelty on hits like the Osmonds' storming 'Crazy Horses' or the fabulous 'Popcorn' by Hot Butter. Here it shows its ability to lend shade and tone, expressing mood as opposed to carrying a melody. The Moog was played in the studio by two players – the high part in the middle section by Bernie Krause and the low by Mark Naftalin. Krause had been a member of the Weavers after the departure of Pete Seeger, and it is fitting somehow that a doyen of American folk music should add a very *moderne* touch to this meditation upon the eve of the most emotionally charged date in American tradition. While there is only a three-note range on the track, within that limited range it delivers much and it carries a deep bass texture which is free of the grounding thud of an actual bass instrument. In fact, the synthetic nature of the note contributes strongly to the feeling of weightlessness in this track, accentuating the feeling of suspension and of looking down from a vantage point where all is visible and audible. In this it is a kind of device to defeat the physical limitations of the body and also the dimensions of time and space. So when the vocal begins at 1.17, 'I can hear them calling, way from Oregon', the source of the line may well be, as Morrison told Ritchie Yorke, some people calling him on the phone from that state,[48] but as far as the world within the song is concerned, the effect is more of a kind of metaphysical calling, the senses heightened, attuned, listening, hearing all, seeing all. The emphasis in the song is very strongly on heightened senses, almost supernaturally keen, with a great flood of visual and aural stimuli and data flowing in, registered at the line openings: 'I can hear . . . I can see . . . I can feel'.

Musically, the acoustic/humming intro yields to a synth note and a drum pattern which could not be further from the traditional use of the drum in pop and rock. Instead of banging out a beat, it drops fragments of fractured rhythm into the deep and wide stretches of the song, never falling into what might be described as a recognisable beat and therefore keeping the song as it were in the ether, not grounded by or locked into a rhythmic pattern. The atmospherics of the track and indeed the opening, rolling steel-stringed acoustic guitar line have always been suggestive to me of the riff used three years later by David Gilmour on the opening section of 1975's *Wish You Were Here* title track. As part of a hidden pattern of correspondences between Morrison and Pink Floyd, it is intriguing to wonder as to whether there was some borrowing here.[49] The wholly unexpected thrashing of the guitar at 1.43–47 is both startling and violent and always takes me by surprise, no matter how often I hear this song. It is, satisfyingly and appropriately in this song which delivers both a lulling and a very broad range of internal dynamics, an asymmetrical device, being nine sweeps long, across the full set of the strings.

With its mix of piano, drum, the sound of two guitars and the Moog synth, the track builds on what 'Caledonia Soul Music' began, employing the experiments in internal dynamics in which Morrison was becoming expert – check the next record, *It's Too Late To Stop Now* for the proof. We have the blues humming intro, the slow build into the song, the crashing of the guitar, the drop back in the mid-section, the rebuild back up to the release of the break back into the 'chorus' (such as it is) at 6.18. The emotional centre of the song seems to be the stunning and unexpected modulation at 6.17 – and each time the line 'And it's almost Independence Day' is sung, the music responds, before we are led back into the detail and the observation. The unison singing with the guitar and the percussive abuse to which the guitar strings are subject all tug at the song's hem (8.59–9.04, for example). This song creates an entire world through which you can pass, if you are listening properly, for the 10.05 minutes of its duration. For the *Astral Weeks* enthusiasts the slow spiral to the close reprises the 'way up' motif which closes the title track; he even shushes the band as he does on 'Astral Weeks'.

The band assembled in the studio for this tune were undoubtedly capable of catching and following what Morrison was looking for, their credentials reaching back to post-war jazz and forward to the future sound of pop. In 'Almost Independence Day' these traditions and innovations meet and create a new model of possible musical textures. Morrison's use of the 12-string is unusual in itself, the clanging, resonant chiming notes and chords of the song more closely associated with folk and pop than Morrison's musical spheres. The violent thrashing of the 12-string in this track shows him delighting in exploring the possibilities of an instrument for both musical and dramatic effect.

Ritchie Yorke called the track 'an extended essay in the stream-of-consciousness style',[50] and notes that several reviewers were moved to refer to the song as a form of sequel to 'Madame George' – a salty observation, but one perhaps more based upon the use of the 'way up and down the line' phrase towards the close of the tracks. The last notes of the song, and the album, are, intriguingly, given to the Moog. That 'Ssshhh' we hear Morrison give to the band is not studio artifice, however:

> 'It wasn't my concept to write a sequel to Madame George [paradoxically, that song already existed, as 'Madame Joy' – a parallel text rather than a sequel] . . . I like the song though. It was just contemplating organ and the Moog synthesiser. Everything was recorded live except that one high part on the synthesiser. I asked Bernie Krause to do this thing of China Town and then come in with the high part because I was thinking of dragons and fireworks. It reminded me of that.'[51]

Morrison's highly visual imagination seeks to find the sounds to both accompany and animate/characterise the images of which he was thinking. The slow drag of the bass Moog part enables the rhythm to pulse slowly through the track, and frees up Lee Charlton to drop drum snaps into the mix as and when he feels it. The track itself is undoubtedly a fully integrated part of the album, and provides its climactic moment, but also stands alone from it in that we hear Elliott, Vinnegar, Charlton and Krause on this track alone. Hardly evidence of 'jam' or 'filler'. The high synth part which Morrison reveals as the only overdub (3.40–4.40) has the feel of a whistle or a small pipe, but also of a kind of radio white noise or static – the clash of the acoustic and synthetic, the made and the found, is key to the soul of this track, born in the studio. It is the synth that has the last of it, the machine singing to itself yet wholly consistent with the pure acoustic of the song overall. In this we see and feel the complex, organic coming together of the technological advantages of the studio with the principles of musicianly 'liveness', and of never playing something the same way twice. Morrison here is allowing the technologies of the studio to sublimate with and therefore influence the textures of his song: 'Almost Independence Day' both depends upon and floats free of the circumstances of its performed composition. This is a technique he would continue to allow to develop through subsequent albums, and we now consider one of his most pristine studio recordings.

'Rave On John Donne' (1983)

This tune first appeared on *Inarticulate Speech Of The Heart*, supposedly coming out of a studio improvisation described by Peter Van Hooke as 'some session . . . it was like being in church'.[52] The song has an unusual tripartite structure, opening with a recitation, leading to a sung section then a sax-led instrumental part to the fade after the vocal concludes, with Van Hooke's clicking rimshots signalling the final stage of the triptych. As Van Hooke said, 'The reason that it worked was that by then we knew each other so instinctively'.[53] That kind of communication in the studio is to some extent the purpose of the project, and once it is achieved it is time to move on.

There is a deliberate fusion of the language of rock and roll and a figure from another era – making connections where formerly there were none, a link between the blues, a key form of the popular song, and 'the blues' as sung by the metaphysical poets. The combination in John Donne's work of the sanctified and the secular, the sacred and the profane, the spiritual and the bodily appetites, piety and worldly wit, links him to the development of soul music – that is, music which attempted to fuse these elements – and Ray Charles is the conduit and the key element, bringing the two traditions of the sanctified and the wordly together. Many have struggled with it, like Donne did – Marvin Gaye, Little Richard, Prince, Al Green and the rest.

The song itself is effectively an exploration (again, like 1970's unreleased 'Caledonia Soul Music') into the possibilities of a supple two-chord see-saw; the basic chordal heart of the piece is very simple but it seems infinitely renewable. This in itself is a spiritual exercise, for as Morrison once observed:

> 'What I'm dealing with is repetition . . . two chords played over and over again, ad nauseam. Now that's really what I do . . . to transmit this to people and take this repetition through stages of boredom and run that whole range . . . from boredom to serenity.'[54]

This is a fascinating insight into the purposes of his music and his ambition for it. 'Rave On John Donne' corresponds to this, with its two-chord root, taking the listener through the spoken/sung/sax structure, up to serenity without particularly subjecting the listener to the boredom stage. Indeed its success as a recorded piece is testament to the success of this ambition overall, and this band in particular, in realising both the richness and the directness Morrison was looking for – the album title, after all, seems to suggest a reaching for a complexity which, in its directness of delivery, supersedes the limits of spoken language. Listening to it as part of the album sequence, it arrives after the slow fade of 'Celtic Swing', and the impact of the first notes is modified because of the aural memory of what we've just heard, and furthermore it is some time since we heard Morrison's voice.

The song opens with a spread of the characteristic contributions from this band; the bright, moonbeam guitar chord from Chris Michie, where each note is wholly distinct within the strummed chord but the effect of the chord is whole and complete. The wash of synthesiser from Mark Isham – a steady synthesiser tone, shimmering, fog-like – is typically ambient, playing around the note, shrouding the note in this 'fog' which makes it shimmer and move while staying 'still' on the note. The organ notes seem almost viscous, bringing a sense of contentment and unhurried wisdom, indeed of having 'come through' – and they drop like the peace in Yeats's 'Lake Isle of Innisfree': 'for peace comes dropping slow'.[55] The 'dropping' notes from Morrison on his Fender Rhodes piano (0.09–25) echo this feeling. Beneath this, Peter Van Hooke's lulling, low thud on the kick drum grounds the shapeshifting ambience, giving the dropping notes a place to rest, and Isham's 'fog' a place to hover over. The notes from Morrison, totally recognisable as his touch, describe a kind of slow, dreamlike drift over this ground, appearing, descending, then rising again. Morrison's choice of the Fender Rhodes is intriguing in itself – the instrument was originally created as a mobile piano for the US armed forces and was used by Ray Charles and his contemporaries, and is therefore a sound Morrison would have grown up listening to in the 1950s.

The vocal comes in at 0.27, revealing how his voice was de-Americanising itself. We are some way from the '*face*' of 'Coney Island', which is so determinedly Northern Irish it is effectively a declaration of intent ('your original face', indeed), but his voice is not that heard in radio interviews of the 1970s. The mid-Atlanticisms have shifted back east – listen, for example, to the characteristically Northern Irish pronunciation of 'down' at 0.33. Accidentally or by design, this significant word for an Ulsterman (see 'Northern Muse (Solid Ground)' on the previous album, *Beautiful Vision*) illustrates how his increasing attentiveness to the source is being registered in his work: 'Down through the ages'. The recitation is at first somewhat self-conscious in delivery, but becomes bolder as the take goes on, with the Ulster vowel sounds coming and going – 'space' is pronounced like a naturalised Californian, 'page', seconds later, like a resident of East Belfast. Likewise, citing 'empiricism' links these sounds and ideas to Morrison's own methods, and his interest in what can be explained and what cannot. Thus the ebb and flow of the accents functions as a live index of how his art was being located unconsciously, how the centre was shifting, and this was reflected even in the personnel of his group. The American line-up was giving way to a more British-dominated one – although of course he had always, appropriately, mixed the two traditions in his choice of musicians.

Witness Herbie Armstrong and Peter Bardens playing alongside John Platania and David Hayes in the *Wavelength*-era band, for example.

The recitation continues to 2.09, his voice rising as he locks into the mood more firmly, and he evokes Yeats as 'Mr Yeats', a form of address familiar to those who have, like us, been attentive to the development of 'Summertime In England' throughout the 80s, with its 'Mr Heaney', 'Mr Thomas' and 'Mr Lawrence' section. As a studio moment, it is the consequence of the structures of meditative repetition that the wide experimental spaces make available; here is the creative tension between potentially endless takes and the precision of the finished, edited recording we hear as a seamless whole. His voice raises and the track draws towards the moment where it has to become song. Thus at 2.11 it does, with Morrison singing an abbreviated version of the recitation, repeating the first section relating to Donne – but of course it is now transformed by song and its resonance is much broader, calling in all those he has cited. There are only 42 seconds of Morrison actually singing on this track; the vocal concludes at 2.53, superseded by his sax, his signature style unmistakable. Van Hooke's drum tick-tock goes to double time at 3.10 and drops out completely at 4.01, allowing the synth, guitar and sax to spiral slowly down to the (faded) conclusion. The nebula-drift of this suggests that the music does not stop, ever, rather that we have simply run out of time to hear it – a metaphysical proposal if there ever was one. The sax outro takes up the speaking role. We note that the instrumental basis for this track – synth, guitar, drum-tick – has not varied at all during this song, which feels, paradoxically, incredibly rich and complex.[56]

The Buddy Holly root of the phrase 'rave on' (Holly's 'Rave On' was a hit in 1958 when Morrison had just hit his teenage listening years[57]) is part of the vocabulary of rock and roll. His yoking together of the language of his own youth and of the youth of post-war popular song (that is, 'low' culture) with the discourses and signifiers of deathless art (that is, 'high culture') is a shift away from such binaries, into an area where these ideas of entirely and utterly distinct eras and times are placed cheek by jowl, and are seen to correspond. The 'rave on' of 'Mr Yeats' in relation to the whole album is, we might feel, appropriate, as that work does have the quality of an inspired and entirely singular line of thought drawn down, but it is also, like this song, a wholly controlled and programmatised model, seeking to, as Yeats said, 'hammer thoughts into unity'.[58] The tripartite structure of 'Rave On John Donne' – spoken word, singing, instrument – is as programmatic within itself as any more ambitious through-composed body of work. It involves a deploying and sorting, and a controlled release of ideas, live in the studio, the right to do so at each stage won by the work done in the preceding section. Yet even though the six minutes we have are edited, this is not mere process – the spirit of creativity, that which 'raves', passes through the track in an uninterrupted seam. Rave on.

A Dream Where the Contents are Visible: *Poetic Champions Compose* (1987)

Recorded over summer 1987 at the Wool Hall Studios, Beckington and London's Townhouse, *Poetic Champions Compose* offers an interesting case study in how Morrison constructs and fashions an album in the studio, pulling together aspects cherished from live performances and placing them into the very different environment of the large, comfortable multi-track studio. The risks taken in live performance can be attempted in the studio, for sure, but there is the safety net of the retake or the overdub to make good any fluffs or over-reaching. How much use of this advantage does Morrison make?[59]

Initially, Morrison intended the album to be the instrumental disc he had been planning for some time and the environment helped him relax into such non-mainstream ideas – indeed the album features three substantial instrumentals very much developing the mood and model set down by 'Scandinavia' and 'Evening Meditation', among others, in the preceding five years. As he noted to Martin Lynch the following April in Coleraine, when asked about using 'different forms':

> Lynch: Are you looking to develop different forms for your work . . . like instrumentals?
>
> Morrison: Oh, yeah, I'm still developing instrumentals . . . I cut three on my most recent album [*Poetic Champions Compose*].[60]

The album begins and closes with sax and piano instrumental pieces (as did the second vinyl side), very clearly shaped from the same raw material in the room at Wool Hall, but in the end these pieces, placed at key positions in the sequence, guide the tone of the album; they don't dominate it. This is in no small part down to the quality of the songs and the vocal performances that occupy the other eight berths on the record. In Clinton Heylin's book, trumpet player Martin Drover remembered that:

> '[I]t was a jam, that album . . . we went to the Wool House [Hall] and we sat there, looked at one another. "What do you fancy, Van?" "Sod it, let's just have a play." You don't usually do that – you've usually got some dots in front of you. The first couple of days Van was just playing alto, we were just busking, playing over things . . . stuff evolved out of that, and that's how that album was made . . . he was fairly relaxed.'[61]

The professional session musician's fear of the empty page seeps through here ('we sat there, looked at one another . . . You don't usually do that – you've usually got some dots in front of you'), but clearly Drover soon relaxed into the process.

Roy Jones, drummer on the sessions, recalled that once the songs had evolved in the way the Drover describes, 'it was mostly only one take, perhaps two takes, no more, then repairs'.[62] This methodology is familiar in its adhering to the 'one take' philosophy Morrison used and also aspired to – think of the eulogy to Sinatra's technique in 'Hard Nose The Highway', described later by Morrison: 'The first verse is an image of Frank Sinatra going into the studio and saying "Let's do it." He makes an album then takes a vacation. It's an image of professionalism.'[63] This idea holds a strong appeal for Morrison in terms of how he views the art and/or labour of making *records*, by their very nature definitive to an extent that a live show is not. So while we see that he to some extent treats the recording studio as an extension of the live stage, the most casual listen to an album like *Poetic Champions Compose* reveals recordings that are not rough and ready, but sophisticated and carefully constructed pieces of work, functioning at a highly refined level. The trick, if we may call it that, is for the song to be subject to such processing while retaining the kick of the new. It takes an expert touch, both in composition and arrangement.

Neil Drinkwater's piano and Van's sax, along with Fiachra Trench's string arrangements, are the dominant elements of the instrumentals on *Poetic Champions Compose*, and provide a draped soundscape for the vocal cuts on the album too. The sound is mellow contemplation made musical – it facilitates the thing that it also embodies, and in this is remarkable in itself. The strings on these pieces both dress and release them from their moorings – listen to how the strings on 'Spanish Steps' keep the weightlessness of the piece right up to the concluding instant (4.40–5.20), a superb example of how less can be more, the cinematic focus showing why Trench is in such demand for his film and TV scores. The sound is typical of the album – spacious, each instrument heard in the round, matched with airiness, giving a dual sense of fullness and lightness. This matching of the heavy and the light matches the metaphysical mood of the material, grounded in material and earthly concerns (or should we say *blues* concerns) – love, loneliness, unhappiness – while having its gaze also turned upward to spiritual matters and sources. A song like 'Did Ye Get Healed?' is in all its simplicity directly metaphysical, as it addresses the impact of the spiritual upon the physical. The sound of the tracks laid down at the Wool Hall by this band is fully expressive of and in harmony with this kind of ambition for the music.

Picking this up, 'I Forgot That Love Existed' is a tale of redemption through love, which extends right back to the roots of Western civilisation to make the point that love is a universal presence and we need to tune into it. Furthermore, it presents love as a leveller as well as a step up from ordinary life, with no-one particularly privileged or favoured – Socrates and Plato are brought to the table but directly on their heels comes 'Anyone who's ever loved, everyone who's ever tried'. It is almost a perfect late-80s-period Van Morrison song, especially in how the clean studio lines of the music illuminate the lyrical point – it seems like a summation of what his work had been aiming for over the preceding five years or so. Yet what we notice too is its simplicity and directness – like the rest of the record, it bears a 'small' and compact sound, yet one also full of space. It flowers from a tight little knot of bass notes that are quickly joined by tentative shots of piano, their refusal of the major, and the chord communicating a wise and cautious optimism. The beat is picked up by a light hi-hat at 0.20, and is awarded an affirmative 'Yeah' by the singer at 0.23 and 0.29 as he locks into the moment. It is not that love does not exist, but that he forgot that it did: we feel a parallel here with Hamm's challenge to the sky in Beckett's *Endgame*: 'God, the bastard! He doesn't exist!'[64] That memory is experienced emotionally – memory is such a theme in Morrison, particularly so in his work from the 80s on, that it is worth noting that here he is working from a position of having forgotten ('I forgot that love existed'), and then the present is redeemed ('but now it's alright') by the act of remembering. The song has at its centre a metaphysical conundrum worthy of John Donne himself: 'If my heart could do the thinking / And my heart begin to feel'. We have an inversion of traditional models of understanding human perception – head for ideas, heart for emotion – and the song imagines what difference that would make: 'Would I look upon the world anew / And see what's truly real?' The element and admission of doubt is a properly philosophical mood, and the musical hue of robust caution matches this. It's a wise song which is prepared to countenance the dissipation of that wisdom, if that proves necessary.

This studio-made atmospheric is concise and spacious yet presents a whole emotional landscape in which we are free to move. The switch to a stronger and more assertive beat, signalled by the entry of Neil Drinkwater's synth at 0.52, beneath a far firmer repetition of the title phrase, makes the song step up a gear. This controlled rise and fall is a 'live' sound, well tempered for the pristine clarities offered by the studio, the technology providing an outlet rather than an obstruction to his ambition for the material. The gorgeous fade (that most studio-bound of rhetorical devices for a musician), featuring Morrison's sax, is both ideally measured and frustratingly abrupt.

The sound of this album and its correspondence to its emotional and philosophical content take another turn in 'Alan Watts Blues'. Watts was a beat philosopher who ended up harmonising, without ever quite intending to, with the hippie ethos of free love and alternative social programming. Dick Hebdige wrote about Watts in his essay 'Even Unto Death: Improvisation, Edging and Enframement',[65] pointing out how Watts had understood the difference between the 'genuine expansion of the frame of any art form and its conscious, stagey demolition in "experimental" work'. Watts identified one incursion of Zen into creativity as the allowing of the accidental detail in his essay 'Zen and the Art of the Controlled Accident', a title which on its own clearly has some connection to Morrison's own willingness to allow music to flow and develop according to its own energies and principles, rather than to force it here or there. Yet Watts also argues for the importance of what he calls 'the frame':

> A frame of some kind is precisely what distinguishes a painting, a poem, a musical composition, a play, a dance, or a piece of sculpture from the rest of the world. Some artists may argue that they do not want their works to be distinguishable from the total universe, but if this be so they should not frame them in galleries or concert halls. Above all they should not sign or sell them.[66]

Morrison's whole career has been poised on this very fine line of division between the making of music and the framing of it – that is, the signing and the selling of it. Morrison has never been opaque about the nature of the music industry ('Let's not kid ourselves, the music industry is all about money', as he told Jeremy Marre in 2006[67]) and this has been his salvation as well as the source of trouble for him. The puzzle is how to reconcile the organic internal logic of improvisation with the apparent paradox of deliberate spontaneity. Watts related this to what he called 'the law of reversed effort', not unconnected to the saying 'Whosoever would save his soul shall lose it'.[68] In nature, according to Watts, the accidental is always recognised in relation to what is ordered and controlled. This serves as a decent annotation to Morrison's working methodology, and as such draws together his techniques on the live stage and in the studio – the accidental moment is a function of arrangement and controlled structure. It is fitting then that one of his most 'controlled' and formally gorgeous albums contains 'Alan Watts Blues', a song which doesn't mention the man by name beyond its title, but whose influence is felt on almost everything else about it. Remarkably, it's also the only Van Morrison original to include the word 'Blues' in the title.[69]

As a studio production it is a gorgeous sound, bright and crisp, and the Zen-funk overdubs of Mick Cox add curlicues of lightness to its dizzy heels. It opens with thoughtful and tentative picking on a semi-acoustic guitar, before the beat ticks in at 0.19, beaten in by the vocal a second earlier. It clicks in on the space which opens between 'I'm' and 'taking', anticipating the tap of the 't' in 'taking'. The song draws in this busy but unobtrusive guitar, bright patches of piano and a determinedly metronomic rhythm into what, against the odds, is a very catchy pop song. The chorus line is the title of one of Watts's best-known books, *Cloud Hidden, Whereabouts Unknown*, itself borrowed from an aphorism from the Chia Tao.[70] In this the title flags up and acknowledges the influence of Watts, while the song builds upon that set of connections and inspirations. The melody is almost jaunty, the piano solo at the centre of the song sounding remarkably like Bob Andrew's deliberately fragmented solo in Nick Lowe's 'I Love The Sound Of Breaking Glass', reassembled and restored like a brightly hued stained-glass window.[71] There is a gorgeous and significant lift towards the song's close at 3.59, when the chorus spills over into the verse and bridge structure in a manner which not only suggests an underlying unity of its constituent parts but actually delivers and reveals that unity, down to the eventual fade 20 seconds later. The mystery is retained and respected, but it also has a frame put around it, as Watts argued that it should. The 'frame' that the smooth, beautiful, studio-even surfaces of *Poetic Champions Compose* places around the complex music and lyrics within its 11 tracks illustrates how well Morrison can employ those textures when it serves his greater purposes. This is his smoothest album, while also being among his most experimental.

At the Wool Hall on *Poetic Champions Compose* Morrison achieved a kind of perfect fit between his ambition for the sound of a record and the lyrical, even philosophical ambition of the same songs; a delicate, responsive balance between smooth and rough textures, word and music, planning and improvisation, and between body and soul. Given his career-long habit of reaching a kind of perfected endpoint and then flying off in a wholly unpredictable direction, we should recall that his next record was not a further refinement of this sound, but a dive into the traditional songbook, in his collaborations with the Chieftains. This tells us something of how successful he deemed the sonic fidelities of *Poetic Champions Compose*.

'Meet Me In The Indian Summer' (2002)

Our final case study is a scrutiny of one of the few Morrison tunes to exist in two very distinct versions. Some, such as 'The Healing Game', 'Flamingos Fly' and 'Full Force Gale' have been returned to and remade, but none of these is as unalike as the two versions we have of 'Meet Me In The Indian Summer'. The two versions are quite distinct, capturing a studio mood which is also the artistic temperature – the single version is gorgeously arranged by Fiachra Trench, *à la* 'Orangefield', while the other version agrees with its parent album in being a smoky, 1950s British jazz-r'n'b tune. The latter is a tight, lean chewy little fist of a song, chinning the listener with the double sucker punch of its 'Meet me!', whereas the open spaces of the single sweetly seduce.

I asked Fiachra Trench how and why these two very different arrangements of the song came to be:

> PM: I'm very interested how 'Indian Summer' in album and single (your arrangement) versions are almost different songs. Do you feel all his work has such 'parallel existences', i.e. could be arranged fruitfully in a number of ways or styles? If so, where does this flexibility come from within the songs themselves do you think?
>
> FT: I'm sure many of Van's songs could be arranged in a number of ways or styles, as evinced by the two very different versions (album and single) of 'Indian Summer' and by Van's current live version of 'Have I Told You Lately', which is radically different to the recorded version on *Avalon Sunset*. But in these instances, and where other artists have covered Van's songs, the songs endure. I put that down to inner strength.[72]

Trench suggests that the songs have potentially multiple musical identities, and in doing so harks back, interestingly, to a pre-studio era of popular song, where songs were able to develop free of the idea of the definitive version, which recording technologies tend to provide.

Why make the two versions? Fiachra Trench told me that the *Down The Road* arrangement is the latter of the two, and that the bed of the single is taken from the abandoned *Choppin' Wood* sessions. The 'earlier' version, as we hear on the single, belongs to another strand of Morrison's work – the wide-open, 'calendar' songs of place and of the tension between memory and the necessities of the now. It also demonstrates the possibilities for a dual existence for a song, that metaphysic being better served perhaps by a wide-screen and more deliberately emotional arrangement. This however does not reduce the flinty British jazz-blues of the *Down The Road* take, indeed its tight, valve-driven monochrome serves as a refreshing counterpoint to the wide-screen Technicolor of the single version. Morrison clearly felt there was mileage in both approaches and his use of the studio to create two very distinct existences for the same song is instructive as to how he is able to express and explore the personalities of his material according to mood and moment within that environment.[73]

Morrison's studio work always expresses a balance between the live moment and the score that stands on the stave – Alan Watts's frame, if you like – and the dual identity of 'Meet Me In The Indian Summer' illustrates how this plays out in practice. Just as the live extrapolations require the frame of shared understanding of where the performance might lead, so the definitive tendencies of working in the studio are informed by the pursuit of the possibility that this time need not be like the last time. All else follows from this understanding.

Chapter Seven

Down the Road: Exile, Place and the Idea of Eternal Movement

[Candy Dulfer]: You were in bands from such a young age . . .

[Van Morrison]: Yeah but I was working before I was famous, I was in bands before I was famous. Some of the musicians I was working with very early on were very good, but they didn't want to leave home, so they didn't go any further . . . but I did [want to leave home] or I felt like I had to.[1]

When Van Morrison sings about exile, what does he mean? Exile from what, and from where? It's not just a matter of 'nation' or place: it feels more complex than this. Throughout his work we can detect aspects of exile and liminality (think of 2005's 'Stranded': 'I'm stranded at the edge of the world'[2]), feelings of displacement and of not belonging, and the burdens, as well as the freedoms, of being perpetually in motion, moving down the road. If we look up the definition of exile in the *OED* it offers 'Penal banishment: long absence from one's country',[3] tying the idea of exile to that of retribution, or punishment: exile as a form of judgement. How we understand it culturally is a different matter. Yet it is a state towards which Morrison seems drawn – not only is it a key theme in his work, but he also named his production and recording company 'Exile'. So we must wonder what kind of exile does Van Morrison experience, and what does he mean when he uses the term? After all, he has liberty of movement; he often has a private plane that waits for him at the nearest airfield to his UK gigs to fly him home to Belfast, the place where he grew up. What kind of matrices of complex belonging and wandering inform his work, and why does the idea or perpetual movement, of restlessness as a spiritual condition, spin so centrally in his work?

Morrison's foremost song of exile provided the title for his bluesy 1993 double album. 'Too Long In Exile' is a song that asserts his sense of belonging and also his distance from the certainties and comforts that that idea of belonging should or could entail. He also connects himself to a non-user-friendly element of Irish culture – in the early 90s the Celtic Tiger was awakening and 'Irishness' was being marketed very heavily as a virtue and as an acceptable alternative to other versions of national identity. The idea was, as far as marketing an tourism went, to appeal to the Irish in all of us – so that somehow we all felt some connection to the place, and felt at home there. That was the gloss. Yet of course 'Irishness' has historically also involved suspicion of creativity, leading to judgement and exile. At the song's tail Morrison lists what he perhaps saw as good examples of this, if not likenesses to himself – the circumstances were different but the net result was the same, and this is what links the names used: Oscar Wilde and Hurricane Higgins, Samuel Beckett and George Best, James Joyce.

There is a relevant epigram in another language, another culture which has a strong tradition of exile – Hungarian. It runs:

> Kivándorolni – szomorúság! [To emigrate is sad]
> Visszavándorlni – nem öröm! [To return is no joy, either][4]

There is something of this sense of being at one remove wherever one is, an outsider everywhere, in the way Morrison uses the idea of exile – we can think back as far as 'Astral Weeks' for evidence of this, with its feeling that the singer 'Ain't nothin' but a stranger in this world'.[5] There is no great homecoming or return to the motherland in a blaze of redemptive glory. What there is is a slow creep towards some kind of rapprochement between ambition and reality. When Morrison began to delve into his Irish roots, we recall, he made a startling discovery – 'I saw what I was, an Irish writer. The tradition I belonged to was my own'.[6] This was, however, only the beginning of a lengthy process, not the instantaneous resolution of a set of problems and puzzles.

'Too Long In Exile' is by definition an acknowledgement of the condition of the self; once that realisation has been made, in Yeats's phrase, what then? Announcing itself via fade-up on a snare beat, the song opens with a chorus of backing vox, in which Georgie Fame's is the most obvious. The song taps along on the off-beat aided by deftly delivered slices of Hammond and, with the exception of Candy Dulfer's sax solo, that's how the song moves, providing a steady bed for Morrison's voice and lyric. In that lyric, the condition of 'exile' is rendered analogous to being stranded in a place where one feels both crowded and quite alone, where one feels overworked and also at a loose end: 'Too long just grinding at the mill'. The key to this are the lines 'Too long in exile / You can never go home again': there is a connection forged between place and being, so that although one might be able to return to the same place in which one grew up, for example, both place and person change and hence one can indeed never go back home again – because everything has changed. It is not only space but time too that separates the past and the present in terms of place.[7]

With its images of the mainland and isolation, this song is about physical exile; it is also about living, in the specific parlance of the blues, too long like a rolling stone, rootless and without connection to one's environment. This is one reason, perhaps, that Morrison first considered abandoning the idea of the album/tour cycle in the early 80s – it took him another ten to get his way, however, around the time of *Too Long In Exile*, as a matter of fact. The song is also concerned with the psychological nature of exile – of becoming a stranger in one's own backyard. This is not an exclusively 'Irish' phenomenon – anyone who has left home and returned in changed circumstances knows this feeling – but it is culturally centralized for the Irish via historical and socio-cultural precedents of migration and exile. So, as exile has clearly provoked some extraordinary lives and works, does he view exile as a cathartic, even necessary, preparation for redemption?

In the 2002 song 'Whatever Happened To PJ Proby?', we find this verse:

> All the cards fell so many rounds
> Down the road a piece Jack
> I saw a bus coming and I had to get on it
> I'm still trying to find my way back[8]

The tone of this suggests that what has happened to the young man since is purely a product of luck, the fall of the cards which began accumulating a shape and a destiny. In this it draws upon one of the dominant motifs of Morrison's lyrical modes, that of movement, and of being in transit. It repeats the title phrase of its parent album, *Down The Road*, and makes it clear that the 'I' of the song was somehow colluding with, but also out of control of, their own destiny – 'I saw a bus coming and I had to get on it' – but now he is 'Still making my way down the highway'. This is close to what Nick Lowe called the 'endless grey ribbon', which leads not only to the next gig but into the existential condition of eternal movement.[9] That condition found its first and perhaps purest expression for Morrison's generation in Jack Kerouac's *On the Road*.

Jack Kerouac and Route 66

First published in 1957, *On the Road* is full of dreamy, poetry-soaked evocations of the pleasures of eternal movement. Try this: 'The purity of the road. The white line in the middle of the highway unrolled and hugged our left front tyre as if glued to our groove.'[10] In 2003, Morrison told Niall Stokes that:

> 'For me, it was Kerouac. I was working with this geezer who was reading all this stuff so he gave me a few books by Kerouac and then Sartre, *Nausea*. Things like that. Initially you go – woh! – when you're 58 it's a different take but I suppose I still have the same influences. Even now, I can still see the direct line back to those kind of things.'[11]

Kerouac's book is at once more readable and more juvenile than its reputation suggests. Its impact upon a generation's speech patterns and frames of cultural reference – indeed, a whole post-war generation's view of what was possible in one's lifetime – is discernible upon every page. Likewise, if you read the novel with an eye on its effect on Morrison's work, there are innumerable points of contact. The language of the novel, in its seamless blend of the fictional and autobiographical, also pre-empted the lyrical discourses of the popular music that was to follow it. It has the drama of youth, an innocence tempered with the analytical, even rueful candour of the more experienced eye. William Burroughs observed that the book 'sent countless kids on the road . . . the alienation, the restlessness, the dissatisfaction were already there waiting when Kerouac pointed out the road.'[12] We refer back to Morrison's memory of the real need to 'get on the bus': Kerouac's narrator ('Sal Paradise') begins his journey on a series of Greyhound buses, before the adventures truly begin.

We can also detect little points of connection between Kerouac's book and Morrison's work that he himself is perhaps unaware of: the breathless, gusting description of an evening scene in San Francisco is initially evocative of the street scene in 'Wild Night' and moves into 'The Back Room' via Jerry Lee Lewis:

> Out we jumped in the warm, mad night, hearing a wild tenorman bawling horn across the way, going 'EE-YAH! EE-YAH! EE-YAH!' and hands clapping to the beat and folks yelling 'Go, go go!' Dean was already racing across the street with his thumb in the air, yelling, 'Blow, man, blow!' A bunch of coloured men in Saturday-night suits were whooping it up in front . . . In the back of the joint in a dark corridor beyond the splattered toilet scores of men and women stood against the wall drinking wine–spodiodi and spitting at the stars.[13]

This mix of gleaming sleaze and metaphysical intimations of mortality ('spitting at the stars') with a lyric from a song which echoes both (Jerry Lee's 'Drinking Wine Spodeeodee') is bracing, and so fast-paced that we barely have time to take in one detail before it is replaced by another. In this sense it is very 'live' living, almost like listening to a piece of music being played live – the detail has to be assimilated immediately and directly, and cannot perhaps be analysed beyond the crude descriptive stab – 'EE-YAH!' Yet the speed of things 'on the road' somehow increases and intensifies their impact, rather than reducing it.

Kerouac's influence on Van Morrison is a matter of record in more than a conversational sense. Morrison has made explicit and direct references to his books in a brace of his more directly biographical recordings, the meditative dream-drift of 'On Hyndford Street' and the bright sketch of Belfast adolescence 'Cleaning Windows', where the twin impulses of living contentedly in the real world and imagining the world beyond the physical and metaphysical horizons of that world harmonize for three-and-a-half minutes. Such influences thus catalogued make up triangulation points for a remapping of the familiar, so that the street where he was born becomes as one with the new, outside influences and smoke signals from other worlds. In the fourth, six-line verse there are a fistful of five blues singers, two writers and four books, showing the benign crowding in of these voices and influences upon the young, open mind – the working man in his prime – welcomed and pursued, and co-present with the details of (in a phrase from another Morrison song) ordinary life.[14]

This eye for the small local detail which somehow both relates to and begets the grander, universal picture that is inherent to Morrison's work is also to be found in Kerouac, where a rainstorm is indicative of an older, wilder America, or a sunset and a spat grape skin reflect and involve each other. The language Morrison picked up from Kerouac has informed his lyrics, and his delivery of them, throughout his songbook. The argot is employed consciously in a song like 'Real Real Gone' – *On The Road* makes frequent reference to someone being 'real gone', meaning that they are brilliant, or wholly lost in a moment. For example Sal announces that 'I have found the gonest little girl in the world', proving that Kerouac was a conduit for, rather than the sole source of, this language as Nellie Lutcher had a hit in 1947 with a song called 'He's A Real Gone Guy'. His other direct lyrical reference to Kerouac is as part of another roll call of the formative influences, names that belong to a very specific point in memory, if not time.[15] In 'On Hyndford Street' he mentions books, but they are books by jazz musicians: ' . . . reading Mr. Jelly Roll and Big Bill Broonzy / And "Really The Blues" by Mezz Mezzrow [and then in the same breath] / And "Dharma Bums" by Jack Kerouac / Over and over again'.[16] So the influences sublimate: the jazz music, the jazz book, the jazz *life*. Furthermore, these are existing cheek by jowl with the 'Sunday six bells' (resonating across the decades from 'Beside You', of course) and 'Debussy on the Third Programme', connecting up to the importance of the radio once again. Thus these disparate elements find a unity in their recollection; this is the nature of memory, revealed via art.

Kerouac's work seemed to speak to Morrison's past, contextualise the details of his present, and exert a transformative influence over his future. Not only Morrison's of course: the impact on his peer group was strong and direct. Paul Simon's 'America' describes a similar journey, covering terrain both physical and metaphysical. The lines 'Kathy, I'm lost, I said, though I knew she was sleeping' (is he lost in his physical location, or in a more spiritual sense – the next line is 'I'm empty and aching and I don't know why'?), and most pertinently, 'Counting the cars on the New Jersey turnpike' – a very Kerouacian observation – reveal that everyone is the same: 'They've all gone to look for America'. Free to wander, but whither? Another child of Kerouac, Bruce Springsteen, noted optimistically that his peer group were born to run, but, as he concluded in his other natal album title track, 'Born In The U.S.A', he found that this dream of eternal movement left him 'ten years burning down the road / Nowhere to run, ain't got nowhere to go'. Clearly movement as an end in itself has a limit, and Morrison scrutinised this in one of his greatest late numbers, 'Philosopher's Stone'.[17]

The correlation of Kerouac and popular song finds its apotheosis in Bobby Troup's song, 'Route 66'. Them's version of the song shows it to be as much a standard of the tough young r'n'b/garage band then as 'Gloria' would prove to be later, and the song has a more interesting history than might be expected.[18] It belongs to a previous era, certainly, but importantly the post-war surge of optimism and freedom, where restructuring of society had yet to begin and suddenly the possibility of unrestricted movement offered itself to a new generation. The song was originally recorded by Nat King Cole in his jazz trio days, shortly after its composition in 1946. Route 66 was laid down in the mid-1920s and opened on 11 November 1926, although it remained unmarked until the following year. Of course, Bobby Troup's song turned Route 66 into *Route 66*, the symbol of freedom, possibility and the American love affair with the motor car. Before the song, it was, well, just a road. Thereafter, it was Route 66. This is the power of the popular song, to change the meaning of place, and of the journey – to travel down Route 66 today is to undertake a kind of pilgrimage, just as it is to follow Morrison's scrambled travelogue/itinerary as laid out in 'Coney Island'.[19]

As Morrison sang in 'Cleaning Windows', he read Kerouac alongside modish books on philosophy, and the idea of motion and movement, of rootlessness being both a blessing and a curse, has never left him. This is the obverse of his idea of still points in time within which one might dwell for ever, yet the two are inextricably linked – experience creates memory, memory processes experience into image, which can then be held for consideration, scrutiny and contemplation: 'Wouldn't it be great if it was like this all the time?' Yet a later song like 'Philosopher's Stone' scrutinises an eternal moment which is purgatorial rather than paradisal. This mixed blessing also surfaces in the figure of the gypsy which emerges in 'Caravan', then fully in 'Gypsy' and, after a gap of 33 years, 'Gypsy In My Soul', with its vexed assessment of living in a 'permanent restless state'.[20] Aside from the cultural archetype of the wandering gypsy, Morrison has clearly adapted the idea of eternal movement to take account not only of his own condition but of those who fall by the side of the road. Precisely because of this *derive* ('drift') element (see the next section), Morrison has identified some unexpected fellow travellers, down the road apiece. Thus his work also considers evocative, and frequently obscure figures such as P.J. Proby and Vince Taylor, the brilliant pop-bluesman who became a huge star in France, provided alleged inspiration for David Bowie's Ziggy Stardust persona, and ended up working for many years as a baggage handler at Geneva Airport. Morrison references this via name checking Taylor in 'Going Down Geneva'.[21] Morrison's concern is not simply for those 'out there' but, like the road which always returns home, is focused on himself too – as he says after all the rhetorical questions of 'Whatever Happened To PJ Proby?', 'whatever happened to me?' The most concerted effort to answer that question lies in our next case study song.[22]

THE PHILOSOPHER'S STONE

The idea of perpetual movement is clearly a seductive and alluring one, and one which Morrison has accepted with a mix of weary resignation – the road having a meaning both powerfully mythic and very specific and non-mythic for a musician like him – and also acceptance of how life is going to be. This mixed feeling was expressed in 1973's 'Hard Nose The Highway', an lyric which overtly links movement and work, and the bejewelled wisdom of 1986's 'Foreign Window', a song which suggests the existential compulsions, burdens and rewards of a live lived in transit, looking out on an unknown landscape, trying to find your way back home. A refined view of this duality became the focus of one of his greatest late songs, 'Philosopher's Stone'.[23] The song dramatises perhaps better than any other in his songbook the mix of weariness and compulsion to move on that lies at the heart of his work: 'it's a hard road, it's a hard road, daddy-o'. The engine droning through the song is that of the car, the coach, the train, the aircraft – it is the ambient signifier of transit, always there in the background. 'Up in the morning, out on the job', he sings – it's a working man's blues and it is not an affectation. The sense we get from the song is one of loneliness and a wintry landscape that expresses the long hard winter of work and the looking for evidence of change and redemption. What is striking about the song is how it gathers together snapshot shards of images which collectively mosaic into a natural refutation of the glamour of the 'the road' as lifestyle and as socio-cultural mythic construct. He is moving because that is what he does, not because it is bright or gorgeous or sexy to do so – as he told Candy Dulfer, 'by the time I was 18 I was already completely jaded with the whole thing!'[24] They both laugh, but he is telling the truth; when he wrote this song he was well into his 50s. He is on the road here with a purpose, unlike the permanent restless state of 'Gypsy In My Soul', his goal it seems characterised as searching for the philosopher's stone.

This steadfastness of purpose is communicated in the slow tick of the rhythm and Fiachra Trench's ground-floor piano which opens the song, soon joined by Geraint Watkins's Hammond and Mick Green's muted and syncopated downward guitar strokes, and all of these contribute to this melancholic air that blows, like a sharp winter bora, through this song. The blast of harmonica (from 2.51) unexpectedly connects the song to the boxcars of Woody Guthrie's *Bound for Glory* and the idea of endless, perpetual movement planted in his garden by Kerouac – as the characters of *On the Road* discover, sometimes one needs to go backwards to go forward.

The song is about eternal movement, and also eternal stasis; a kind of running to stand still, which also alludes to a kind of movement which does not involve the body at all, and complicates our relationship to time and space. In his book *The Philosopher's Stone*, Peter Marshall attempted to define the search for the stone:

> Alchemists refer to their work as the *Magnum Opus*, usually translated as 'The Great Work' or simply 'The Work'. It involves the 'outer work' of making experiments in their laboratories and the 'inner work' of perfecting themselves. No alchemical experiment in the laboratory is devoid of a moral or spiritual dimension. Alchemists agree with the ancient principles: 'As above, so below' and 'As within, so without'. The transmutation of external matter mirrors the inward transformation of the soul. Indeed the discovery of the Philosopher's Stone is an outward sign of the alchemist's inner self-realization.[25]

To be so bold as to translate these into terms relating to our subject, we have here a programme for connecting the inner and outer experiences, and in the image of the stone a symbol of the final resolution of these distinctions. It is an image of unity and of wholeness, and as such harmonises with the primal human urge towards a return to the centre, to the source. This may be expressed in an interest in religion, science, love, art or the furthest reaches of the cosmos, but all are in pursuit of an image of this wholeness. This is the root of Morrison's pursuit of what he calls 'the philosopher's stone' as an image or metaphor. It provides a way of thinking about his perpetual movement as being in pursuit of something, something that is not guaranteed to exist, and it provides the summative image for a long-running set of references to such searches. He has alluded to the pursuit of such elusive yet compelling quests before, in 'Haunts Of Ancient Peace' ('The Holy Grail we seek') and, via his own self-authored terminology, when he described 'Looking for the Veedon Fleece'.[26]

So Morrison's use of the image links back to his view of a hard-working life, from the base elements of which he is both obliged and compelled to make something marvellous. Despite the tedium, the restlessness, the hard labour (or perhaps because of them) he is in pursuit of 'the work', which may be grasped fully, or only seen in glimpses. That much is uncertain: sometimes it happens, sometimes it doesn't. The much older songs that Morrison has appended to the song in live performance flow into this mood – Louis Armstrong's 'Didn't He Ramble' is the tale of an itinerant who is perpetually on the road but is stymied by the consequences of his actions, and the force of law brought to bear upon him: 'Didn't he ramble, all around . . . until the vultures cut him down'.[27]

Armstrong often performed the tune without the lyric, but Morrison, as a singer, alights upon this connection between ideas of freedom and confinement and the enigma of liberty and restriction co-existing in a single life and set of circumstances. The song has also been connected to the traditional 'White Lilies', a tale of a funeral on a pale winter's afternoon, and the road's inevitable, final end.

CONCLUSION: SONGS OF HOME AND EXILE

1986's 'Foreign Window' seems directly concerned with these ideas of exile. The protagonist is a wandering, scholarly, suffering spirit, someone obliged somehow to be continually in transit, driven to experience and to learn, and far away from home in the process. The very title of the song suggests this kind of dislocation: far from being the window of 'number 136', the locality and the street of 'Cleaning Windows', it has become a *foreign* window, a portal into the unknown and the unpredictable, and the street has become the 'suffering road'. Morrison's vocal on this song is a perfectly balanced mix of blues gravity and metaphysical lightness, both adhering to the plaintive melody and soaring above and around the notes the better to communicate the empathetic urge of the performance. It is a song about, to paraphrase 'Saint Dominic's Preview', feeling somebody else's pain. The stately opening of Morrison's song, subtly suggestive via the horn part of splendour and spectacle, gives way to a steady blues rhythm, suggesting the unending road, and is overlaid by sweeping acoustic guitar chords and arpeggio picking. Rooting the tune in the musical discourses of the blues, a bass harmonica is blended into the mix, giving the breaks some grit and gravity.[28] Key too is the cor anglais, adding its empathetic tone to the picture. I asked Kate St. John about her contribution to this tune:

> '[It was done] quickly and spontaneously . . . Van produced it. I improvised, first or second takes and he seemed happy with what I did . . . [Working in the studio with Morrison] was on the inspirational, improvisational end of the spectrum. Van liked what I contributed and didn't feel the need to mess with it or put his own imprint on it like others do sometimes.'[29]

Morrison's respect for Kate St. John's contributions is instructive: firstly, it's testament to their languid, intuitive soulfulness – who would want to 'mess with' what she plays on 'Foreign Window'? – but it is also illustrative of how Morrison can trust his fellow musicians to follow their best instincts and deliver what is right at that moment, so that the music is fully of itself in the moment of its making. The song also seems to suggest that the return home can come only via hard work and suffering, in an ambience of scholarship and study as well as an embrace of experience, as opposed to the traditional separation of these two spheres into the mind and the body. The road viewed from the foreign window leads to a unity and wholeness that we might call 'home', via a community of exile. 'Down the Road' is a case in point. Originally demoed in the *Beautiful Vision* sessions in 1981 as 'Down the Road I Go' (melody and lyric scattered and sketchy but recognisably the same song), the 2002 version is a blend of melancholy and optimism and closes by asserting that the endpoint of the journey is its starting point – 'trying to find my way back home'. The song in all its modesty of form and melody still manages to evoke both the physicality of the road – the tiredness, the miles covered, the years passing – and the metaphysical spaces that it also maps:

> And I got to be so far away
> Oh don't you see
> All our memories, dreams and reflections
> That keep haunting me
> Down the road[30]

So in this little song, set aside for 20 years, we find a way of bringing together these ideas of movement and homesickness, exile and memory, that run throughout his work, expressed through open and direct terms. The simplicity here and of which he sings on *Keep It Simple* is hard-earned, like the clean lines of late Miles Davis. The road is circular, and linear: the song of the road leading back to the song of home.

'Song Of Home' and 'End Of The Land', both from 2008, are songs of exile, seemingly both internal and external in their form and realisation, drawn from the same well as 'Little Village'. In 'End Of The Land' Morrison sings about wanting to drive as far as he can, to reach the edge of things (maybe a willing surrender to the feeling described in 2005's 'Stranded': 'I'm stranded, at the edge of the world'[31]) and reach the sea – the extremity of the place offers some sort of healing possibilities, and some possible peace of mind. It is a song of flight, and of escape, while 'Song Of Home' is a song of, well, home. It is also a specific landscape that is recognisable from other songs – the foghorn blowing in the night we know from 'So Quiet In Here', and the use of 'lough' sets it in a very particular, Northern Irish landscape. In an unusually romantic image, the singer reflects upon the similarities between his life and that of the seemingly endless flight of the bird – indeed it is the bird who hears the song of home, endlessly.

These two songs represent a romanticised notion of exile, fit for poetry. This is realized particularly well in 'Song Of Home', via a melody which in its melodic progress is sailing close to the Irish trad. repertoire but in its arrangement is approaching a Nashville-Appalachia hybrid, uniting the Irish and American sensibilities to seamless effect. The four-step descent after the chorus, and on which the song closes is pure country, but with a whiff of the eastern Atlantic breaking saltily on the Irish shore. 'Song Of Home' is harmonically close kin to 2002's 'What Makes The Irish Heart Beat', linking these chordal structures and progressions with a musical idea of Irishness.[32] This leads us into a consideration of how the spirit of place, Irish or otherwise, fits into the creative schema of Morrison's work. So if this first section has dwelt upon notions of rootlessness and displacement, then the next examines the complex nature of belonging, and how Morrison's work accommodates and reflects his own musical and cultural roots, even in exile, via the spirit of place.

GOT TO GO BACK: 'PSYCHOGEOGRAPHY', MEMORY AND THE SPIRIT OF PLACE

In the past few years the idea of 'psychogeography' has come under a certain degree of cultural scrutiny and, as we shall see, it has some rarefied intellectual credentials. Yet it is effectively another way of describing what has been referred to as the 'spirit of place', something which anyone with a feeling for a certain space or locale will acknowledge and recognise. D. H. Lawrence employed the term in a cultural sense – it is a chapter title in his book on American literature – but it is a primal human response to environment.[33] It connects to when people were more dependent upon and therefore more sensitive to changes within their immediate environment – that is, whether a place was sheltered from the wind, protected from the rain, near possible supplies of water or food, or by land that could produce crops and be farmed. All these responses are compromised by modern living – not lost because they still function in less overt ways – and as such we are today probably far less connected with, aware of and sensitive to our immediate environment than previous generations. We have demarcated special places, of course – the church, the library, the garden, for example – which hold ritual or personal significance, while certain natural places – the mountains, the rolling hills, the coast – also impress themselves upon our minds by their beauty and grandeur, but our daily environment is more likely to be overlooked or to simply become visually too familiar to be noticed as we fill our time with other business. The term 'psychogeography' was coined by French situationist Guy Debord, and he described it as 'the study of precise laws and specific effects of the geographical environment, consciously organized or not, on the emotions and behaviour of individuals'.[34]

All this finds an answering bell in Van Morrison's work; he is closely attentive to the small detail of local life that reveals unexpected depth and significance, and which somehow connects the present moment with a kind of eternal moment, a secret identity of place that is unfading. He is caught one more time up on Cyprus Avenue, for example: a recurring cycle in which he is obliged to become part: 'nothing that I can do'. The key tenet of psychogeography as suggested by Guy Debord is the *derive* ('drift'), the apparently aimless movement which allows things to happen. Morrison is a natural *deriviste* in that sense, and his generation – born after the Second World War – were in part looking for a freer world, shaking off the physical and social constraints of the 'realities' of the post-war world. They were for a deeper freedom, something reaching further back than the immediate circumstances, a kind of remembering of a lost meaning to place. This may well be part of the appeal of a book like *On the Road* or *Dharma Bums* to young people growing up in the 1950s, offering images of apparently limitless movement and possibility.

Morrison has rarely written about Belfast in the wider sense, focusing instead upon specific places of significance, as in 'On Hyndford Street', which acts as a kind of psychogeographical gazetteer to the topographies of East Belfast as it existed in his emotional memory at the moment he was recording that particular track. Ditto 'Coney Island', as we will see. These details represent a mapping of memory as well as landscape, and this is a key part of Morrison's muse. Think of the first lyric he sings on the first Them album. It's a very evocative image of place: 'One Sunday morning / We went walking / Down by the old graveyard', and how that place is connected to intense feeling: 'The morning fog

/ I looked into / Those mystic eyes'.[35] The two could not be separated without one or other or both being diminished. The 'mystic' in the eyes of the girl is connected to the place, the brightness of youth and life and desire amidst the nameless dead, shrouded in fog. This is intensely Romantic, Gothic even, and the juxtapositions of place and experience of course became less overt as he developed as an artist and as a writer.

'I kinda like just walk about': The *Derive*

A key aspect of the situationist idea of psychogeography is the *derive*, which we can translate as 'drift'. It involves setting aside one's usual, consciously pursued goals in movement and action and instead walking with a view to being absorbed by the place in which one is walking, and being completely open to what might happen and to any encounters that might occur. It is an openness to environment which simply allows the unexpected and the unplanned to happen. This involves a letting go (of safety, security, time itself) as well as an acquisition of possibility. Morrison seems to have something of the natural *deriviste* about him, as we saw in 'Philosopher's Stone' which depicts his work as a kind of extrapolated *derive*, and one which both costs and rewards the drifter. He also looked at place this way as a very young man, as shown by his amusing-to-watch encounter with Dick Clark on *American Bandstand* in 1967. After Morrison has mimed to 'Brown Eyed Girl', Dick Clark comes over to speak to the young man in the candystripe jacket:

> Dick Clark: Nice to have you with us today. How old are you sir?
>
> VM: Twenty two.
>
> DC: Do you ever have any spare time to yourself?
>
> VM: Ermm . . . not much.
>
> DC: What do you do when you have a moment off – do you work?
>
> VM: No, I kinda like just walk about . . . y'know, parts of cities, in the rain, and things like that.
>
> DC: And compose in your spare time?
>
> VM: Yeah!

DC: Did you write this next song ['Ro Ro Rosey']?

VM: Yeah, I wrote this next one.

DC: Let's try it on for size . . . ladies and gentlemen, Mr Van Morrison!

['Ro Ro Rosey' starts to play][36]

In this exchange Morrison comes over as somewhat evasive, although polite – and certainly not as confrontational as Syd Barrett was on the same show a few weeks later – but that's only because pop singers, even in 1967, weren't supposed to talk like this. Dick Clark, the consummate pro, copes perfectly well with it but even at this age Morrison shows himself to be a natural *deriviste*, with his description of walking through 'parts of cities', and in his casual responses somehow indicates where his ideas are leading him musically – the 'parts of cities, in the rain' map the terrain of *Astral Weeks*, which he would be recording within a year of this conversation.

Debord of course simply coined a new term to describe a very old, very human set of responses, and writers have always responded to the spirit of place. Obvious examples in the Morrison sphere being William Blake, with 'London' and 'America' being two such epic examples of poetry of place, while almost the entire written work of James Joyce is an effort to enquire after the quintessential nature of Dublin City. Debord described this sensory perception thus:

> The sudden change of ambiance in a street within the space of a few meters; the evident division of a city into zones of distinct psychic atmospheres; the path of least resistance which is automatically followed in aimless strolls (and which has no relation to the physical contour of the ground); the appealing or repelling character of certain places – all this seems to be neglected.[37]

Let us scrutinise some of Morrison's work which is clearly attentive to psychogeography, or the spirit of place, and quite how it reveals that which, as Debord says, seems to have been neglected.

'Oh yeah, I got Orangefield' (1989)

Growing up in Northern Ireland, Morrison was quite awake to the spirit of place as it functioned there. Seamus Heaney suggested that the Northern Irish landscape was a manuscript that we have forgotten how to read, and in the television programme *A Coney Island of the Mind*, John Montague and Seamus Deane discuss with Morrison about how in the 1960s and 70s the 'Northern mouth' was almost 'hermetically sealed', and that the ancient names for places in the six counties were being lost.[38] 'Orangefield' functions on Side Two of *Avalon Sunset* as an urban correspondence to the rural reverie of 'Coney Island' and the vexed exile midpoint of 'I'm Tired Joey Boy' on the album's first side. The song begins with a single note plucked on an electric guitar set to an acoustic mute, giving the singer the note. He picks it up and runs with it: 'On a golden autumn day'. This line has surfaced periodically throughout Morrison's work, as we explore elsewhere, and the song's events take place by the riverside, linking the song to numerous others in his own repertoire ('You Know What They're Writing About' ('Meet me down by the river'), 'River of Time', 'Country Fair' and 'Take Me Back', to name just a few), as well as 'trad. arr.' songs he has recorded such as 'Down By The Riverside'. The riverside is a place where things *happen*; it is the site of change in these songs.

The sound of the track also does much work, and this is a great example of how lyric and melody and arrangement can collude to bring into flower something which could not be achieved by one or other element alone. It has been called over-orchestrated, but it sounds to me that it is not wasteful of a single note – everything we hear contributes towards the power and impact of the song and its resonance, and the song would be diminished by the addition or removal of any of its elements. The presence of Fiachra Trench and Katie Kissoon, two of Morrison's most enduringly successful and empathetic collaborators, is a factor in this. The guitar solo picks out the vocal melody on the bass strings, adding just enough and carefully adhering to the structure of the mood before the song sweeps back into the bridge.

Lyrically the song is, as Buzacott and Ford pejoratively suggested, 'simple', in its rhyming and metric formulations, yet it is also complex – each line actually has two rhyming elements, one which changes (e.g. day/way), and one which remains constant – Orangefield itself. This device illustrates how the place and its meaning is surrounded by change and flux but remains in itself and of itself uncorrupted. Witness the first verse:

> On a golden autumn day
> You came my way in Orangefield
> Saw you standing by the riverside in Orangefield
> How I love you then in Orangefield
> Like I love you now in Orangefield[39]

Here we find sets of sounds which agree ('day'/'way'), and agreed binaries ('then'/'now'), but these internal correspondences are signifiers of change which emphasise the enduring nature of Orangefield itself. There is a meeting by the river and we have of course been well met down there before in Morrison's work – not least in the turning point of his output from the 70s transatlantic singer-songwriter to the 80s European/Irish mood, 'You Know What They're Writing About'. The first two verses of 'Orangefield' change their front end – the second makes rhyming reference to the subject's hair, 'When I saw you there', again in Orangefield. The major rhyme is an extension of the line – an extrapolation of it which confirms the importance but also the jutting, just-out-of-reachness of the idea. The repetition of it is a kind of attempted invocation – say the name and make the connection. After the bridge, the verses lengthen, into six lines (the third) and finally into seven (the seventh) which rhetorically brings the song up into a kind of sustained crescendo, especially riding as it does upon Fiachra Trench's dazzling arrangement for strings. Indeed, the song has the distinction of being the only one that Morrison has performed with a full orchestra, using Trench's arrangement, in 1990. The power of the body of musicians behind the song pushes Morrison on to a very strong vocal performance. This came up in my conversation with Fiachra Trench:

> PM: Would he ever play live with an orchestra playing your arrangements? If not, why do you think not?
>
> FT: He has done. Van performed 'Orangefield' at a Prince's Trust concert in Birmingham with the strings of the City of Birmingham Symphony Orchestra, conducted by George Martin. They used the same arrangement that I had provided for the album [*Avalon Sunset*].[40]

So part of the blazing, majestic power of the recording and its evocation of the undivided states of feeling and place is clearly located in that arrangement, which somehow harmonises with and emphasises the emotional weight of the song. The lyrical references within the song to the throne of Ulster, attached to the historical resonance of the place and its name, site it in a very specific locality and historical-geographical context, but one from which the song also rises free via the mythopoeic power of the performance. The 'Throne of Ulster day' is no less than a Blakean image a kind of visionary citation, a lifting of the veil so the secret identity and power of a place and the feelings which have passed there are intimately revealed and interrelated. It is not however specified by the calendar as in 'Celtic New Year' itself, and the live references to 'July 12th bonfires'. Within 'Orangefield' there is finally an insistence, confirming what the lyric has been asserting throughout, that the past and the present exist together in a kind of eternal now, a realisation of the nature of love and the meaning of place within that set of perceptions. This realisation couldn't have happened just anywhere – it seems to depend upon the place for its existence or at least the perception of its existence: 'How I loved you then in Orangefield / Like I love you now in Orangefield'. The brace of bridges are equally apposite – describing continuity but also recording the subtle differences of light and shade that the passage of time forces upon us, and how we understand experience. They are alike, but not the same. The first describes the moment from a closer perspective, telling the girl she was the apple of his eye, as a kind of revelation, using 50s pop vocabulary ('Baby it's true'), while the second describes the same set of relations from a more distant prospect, reminding the object of his affection that is was indeed her he adored ('Baby (it) was you'). The difference we can discern between the two takes on this single state is encoded in the first two lines of each bridge – the first refers to the sun lighting up 'all our days' – that is, that which is countable and measurable on a calendar. It is almost the transition from a summer romance to an eternal connection, yet one that does not seek to find fault with either state, rather to hold the energy of one and the reflective wisdom of the other together to evoke and to re-enter both states simultaneously. This I would argue is what the place of Orangefield allows to happen, and what the song 'Orangefield' does.

Orangefield Park itself featured in the *A Coney Island of the Mind* programme, in a section where Morrison and the poet Gerald Dawe are shown walking through the park, reminiscing about their shared experiences at Orangefield School and also demonstrating that the place gives one a powerful vantage point over the city:

> VM: There's Harland and Wolf – who's afraid of Harland and Wolf?
>
> Dawe: So have you got songs from round here, Van?
>
> VM: Oh yeah I got songs, I got Orangefield.[41]

A natural, modest and anecdotal exchange which reveals a good deal about Morrison's own sense of ease here and also the importance of the place to him as a creative soul. The very name is delicious to contemplate, and to say, suggestive as it is of the exotic, the heat and spice of the orange grove clinging to the ash-slopes of Sicily. Of course this is not the historical derivation of the name, but that does not block or reduce the sensual or aesthetic response to it, or its rhetorical use in Morrison's own songs which connects it to his own narrative – changing the meaning of the word by the way it is used. The significance of the colour orange is not a trivial one – it competes with the green as the signifier of national identity in the island of Ireland. Mercifully these debates are not as volatile as they once were and the green and the orange – which, we recall, bookend the Irish tricolour, kept apart by the neutral sweep of the white stripe – are less semiotically loaded than during the last quarter of the twentieth century. Van Morrison, we note, has never 'worn' either colour, and again we see how his work came to be seen as a sign of a future Belfast even as it evoked a past one.

The song contains the word 'Orangefield' 17 times and this out-of-the-round repetition reinforces the special nature of the place, via the charmed word; indeed, it is the final word of the song. In the manner of the blues, the fifth line of the final chorus does much the same, finding a way to draw the structure down towards a purposeful, and musically satisfying, conclusion. It is the power of the place and of the word that opens up all these evocations, connected and animated by the performance itself, so that 'Orangefield' is at once both the real place and the setting for an imaginative recreation of experience which permits reconnection over time and space.

Down by Avalon

Morrison's sensitivity to place is not confined to Northern Ireland; a key theme in his 80s work was the idea of 'Avalon'. Having grown up aware of the significance and frequently 'hidden' meaning of place, it shouldn't surprise us that Morrison was attentive to such a spirit elsewhere too, and he found it in a variety of locales – in San Anselmo, Geneva or Notting Hill Gate, for example. Particularly significantly he found it in the area of Somerset between Bristol and Bath, an area colloquially known as 'Avalon', occupying the Somerset Levels and the fields of Glastonbury. The myths about the meaning of the landscape here and the undeniably potent sense of place are hard to resist; the stories and events of the past seem very close 'down by Avalon', and they find both an echo and a sustained impact in the present. Put like that, the appeal of the area to Morrison is easy to understand. After his works concerning very personalised 'psychogeographies', Morrison's interest in Avalon is connected but also more widely contextualised: here was a landscape about the specialness of which there was a much wider consensus, and a lengthy history. The very name Avalon is something which is intrinsically linked to an ancient idea of Englishness, and it is interesting that it has been so artfully and emotionally explored as an idea and an image by an Irishman.

Morrison first mentioned Avalon in 1980's 'Summertime In England', that cornerstone and benchmark of his definitively post-*Wavelength* sound. Indeed it is arguable that *Common One* is a musical exploration of the idea or feeling of Avalon itself. The landscape is thick with rich, berried legend and stories with meaning both physical and metaphysical. Most famously, we have the tale of the Holy Grail arriving at Glastonbury, the cup in which Joseph of Arimathea is said to have caught drops of Christ's blood beneath the cross, which was also reputed to be the drinking cup at the Last Supper. The Grail is thought by some to be buried under Chalice Hill, close to Glastonbury. The appeal to the imagination and the eye of this part of England is not mysterious; it is beautiful at any time of the year and the light has a remarkable soft brilliance, blushing the land at dawn and sunset. Its impact upon him is heard plainly in the lines 'Can you feel the light in England?' and this image gives way to the key image 'Can you feel the silence?', which is explored elsewhere in this book. The album title, *Avalon Sunset*, also records this impact, of course. This was not the England of motorways, hotels and packed theatres Morrison usually saw on the road and it seemed to appeal as strongly and directly to his intuitive sense of the spirit of place as did the streets of Belfast and Arklow, the 'God's green land' of *Veedon Fleece*. He may also have been amused and intrigued by a connection with blues lore: Mississippi John Hurt's hometown was Avalon, Mississippi, and one of his best-known tunes was 'Avalon Blues'. So the early working up of his own mythopoeic terminology (the coining of mythological systems) was further developed around the time of *Common One* into a reimagining of previously extant systems of myth and symbol, where he took the mythologies of the area and built upon them, working them into his own music.[42]

The link between these two methodologies is of course Blake: he was a mythopoeist *in excelsis*, yet he is perhaps best and most popularly known for his foregrounding of the mythologies surrounding Christ's possible visit to England, and specifically to the environs of Avalon, with Joseph of Arimathea, via his poem 'Jerusalem'. This poem was later to become a great English patriotic song, set to music in 1916 during the Great War by C. Hubert Parry.[43] Parry's turning to Blake's poem during the deepest and darkest period of the Great War was not accidental – it was an attempt to draw upon the mythological energy of the spirit of England as embodied by the atmospheres down by Avalon. Connecting with Blake and Parry, the supposed grave of King Arthur lies somewhere amidst the ruins of Glastonbury Abbey, alongside the Glastonbury Thorn with its supposed magical powers of regeneration. There is also the beauty and mystery of Glastonbury Tor on the Isle of Avalon itself, which is a rare elevated feature amidst the fenny flatness of the Somerset levels and visible for miles around. Much later, and perhaps in acknowledgement of a relaxation of creative intensities such as this, Morrison addressed the beauty of the place more directly through his lilting, lovely, cider-sipping arrangement of Acker Bilk's famous tune 'Summer Set', providing his own lyrics and unravelling Bilk's punning wordplay by restoring the county's name to his title, 'Somerset'.[44]

The opening line of 1989's 'When Will I Ever Learn To Live In God?' echoes the title of its parent album, *Avalon Sunset*. 'The sun was setting over Avalon'. This provides the physical setting which, as we have seen, is also an establishing detail for the spiritual terrain we are about to enter and explore, and the landscape and the unhurriable rhythms of nature are here taken as incontrovertible evidence of the hand of God in the shaping of the Earth. The presence is inferred even when unremarked upon – this external evidence finds an internal echo, as the song precedes 'Orangefield', which explores a landscape internally charmed by intensely personal symbols. Reading the landscape of 'Orangefield' in such a way suggests that Morrison sometimes *does* know how to 'live in God', holding together the physical and spiritual desires after the manner of Blake, and for that matter, Ray Charles. The latter yoked together the sacred and profane traditions of church music and r'n'b to 'create' soul music via the likes of 'I Got a Woman', in which he used a gospel melody (shared by 'Jesus Is All The World To Me' and 'I Got Heaven', among others) to express very worldly urges. In Avalon, these intensely physical desires are not subjugated but the energy they generate is redirected towards a longer-term – we might say 'higher' – goal, that of the 'higher self' of which Morrison speaks in 'Ancient Highway'.

The song also offers a contemplative space for both singer and listener: I repeat, the question in the title is not rhetorical. The sense of a man coming to the end of his capacity for self-rationalisation is powerful, and he is starting to see a bigger picture, a broader panorama – like that offered of the Somerset Levels from the geologically anomalous Tor at Glastonbury, once you make the effort to climb it. This song is one of Morrison's most directly Christian tunes, which would sit unproblematically in the repertoire of any of the acts who use the pop-rock-soul model to construct modern songs of praise. A song like 'Dweller On The Threshold', for example, would be less easily assimilated into such a songbook on account of its esoteric imagery and whiff of spiritual wildness, even amidst its images of abiding patience. This is a song almost unregarded by Morrison's wider audience, and rarely played in concert, but Morrison clearly holds it in high regard, as it has featured on two self-curated 'best-of' albums.[45]

The following year, on the *Enlightenment* album, came something of a conundrum. Recorded post-*Avalon Sunset*, so not a leftover from those sessions, 'Avalon Of The Heart' is Morrison's most explicit homage to the inspiration and insight brought to him by his relationship with the idea of Avalon.[46] It features a gusty performance from London vocal choral group the Ambrosian Singers. This was only the second time he had called upon an operatic chorus for his songs, the first being the Oakland Chorus's crisp and glacial contribution to 1973's 'Snow In San Anselmo'.

Perhaps aware of its summative nature, Morrison certainly throws everything into, and at, the song. While it captures one of his best studio vocal performances of the period, perhaps spurred on by the great surging wave of sound always just coming to its crest behind him, the experience of listening to song is somehow, with topographic appropriateness, flat. It is a very noisy song, especially for one that starts out with engaging sparseness of arrangement, and in this case one is left to speculate what the sound and elegantly restrained fury signify. In the lyric, Avalon is unambiguously located in the internal realm (the heart) as firmly as a landscape through which one might go riding. The landscape is thus appropriately a mix of mythological elements, some of which are universal or public in that they are drawn from the lore of Glastonbury – the enchanted ancient vale, Camelot – some from the intersection of Arthurian and Christian fable – the Holy Grail, 'the upper room' – and some are local or personal to Morrison, most notably the unexpected reintroduction of a detail of the emotional architecture of 'Astral Weeks', in the reference to 'the viaducts of my [as opposed to 'your' in the older song] dreams'. The landscape seems to represent the opportunity to begin again and this holding together of the inner and outer realms establishes a symbiosis between the experient and that which is experienced, be that an emotion or the world as it is; one transformation facilitates the other. The lyrical integrity of the piece is clear to the point of overstatement, and, as in the précis version of 'Summertime In England' that Morrison was playing live by the end of the 80s when this song was written and recorded, it feels as if the symbols are beginning to fall in on themselves – their mercurial nimbleness replaced by dramatic, over-robust assertion. This is a weakness of the technique of repetition, but as Morrison always says, there are no guarantees: he does what he does and sometimes it works and sometimes it doesn't. In its widescreen incarnation, 'Avalon Of The Heart' falls short of less ostentatious settings of the same thought. In aiming for a summative use of this important term, something slips away from it. A far less conscious use of the naming of place provides his most powerful, successful and natural piece of psychogeography.

'Coney Island' (1989)

> **Rebirth for village Van made famous**
> A Co. Down mill village that Van Morrison fell in love with as a schoolboy – and later immortalised in song – is to be rebuilt. Morrison was so taken with his childhood visits to the Lecale coast and the former mill village of Shrigley that he referred to it in one of his most popular 'songs', the narrative Coney Island. In the 1989 hit, Morrison recalled trips to the seaside with his mother, passing through Shrigley near

> Downpatrick, on their way to the beach at Coney Island. Van spoke on his *Avalon Sunset* album of taking photographs in Shrigley on those schoolday visits.[47]

The name Coney Island is most famous worldwide for being the resort close to New York, on a peninsula at the southern tip of Brooklyn, which Lou Reed's 1975 album *Coney Island Baby* paid tribute. Beat writer Lawrence Ferlinghetti published his book of verse, *A Coney Island of the Mind*, in 1958. In Belfast, the young Van Morrison may well have been intrigued by the unexpectedly specific connection between the world of the Beats and his own childhood haunts – 'his' Coney Island is to the south of Ardglass in County Down, and was a frequent day-trip destination for him as a boy.[48] To visit Coney Island is to find a small, quiet stony beach, fringed by low, pale houses and a sense of remoteness, freedom and possibility. In this it is no different from any other undeveloped coastal spot one might visit but, like Route 66 or Penny Lane, it has been in some ways transformed by the music associated with it. This is at the root of the relationship between music and place – music has the power to completely transform the meaning of place, and therefore the psychogeographical gravity of that place. The above newspaper report shows this force in action. The arrangement of 'Coney Island' is rich and complex and contributes much to the emotional force of the recording: we recall how – remarkably, given its depth and unforced sophistication – Fiachra Trench remembered it as being recorded as quickly as one of Morrison's one-take blues offerings: 'once or twice I have asked the engineer to put the light on straight away, that is to say: to record the rehearsal; that was the case with 'Coney Island'.[49]

The track opens to a lush, slow wave-sizzle on the ride cymbal, alongside vibes and those gull-swooping strings. There is no instrumentation here that belongs to jazz, blues, rock, or pop. The arrangement's thoughtfully heroic melancholia might recall the likes of Jim Webb's work with Glen Campbell, but this is in no sense a pop record – it is a performed poem. Morrison does not sing. The exclusively spoken word track had its day in his work in this era (1989–93), although he had experimented previously, and successfully, with spoken interludes on tracks in the early 80s. Thus, perhaps ironically, the music is there in a supporting role to the voice, confirming, building upon, reinforcing it in both its timbre and its verbal and emotional sense, even more than when he sings. The helter skeltering string line, best heard at 1.29–34, exemplifies the slow gentle burn of these images on the mind, slowly coming forward like images on a Polaroid picture, and then another assumes its place, like the place names piling up as the tune proceeds, the images seen clearly but fleetingly from a window. The string line here heralds one of the performance's key moments: 'I look at the side of your face', and that 'face' is pronounced with an Ulster tang so strong it stings like sea spray, afresh, every time I hear it. This is the most obvious example of something the voice is doing throughout this track. It is so overtly Northern Irish in both accent, vocabulary and internal rhythms of speech that I'd suggest it is clearly done with a purpose, and a central part of that purpose is to evoke place through sound.

'Coney Island' is introduced formally by the voice, in the poetic tradition; Coney Island is the destination but its two words are also the first words of the piece. The text is full of sensual references: the food, the light, the appetite: 'The light comes streaming through the window', 'I look at the side of your face', 'In case we get famished before dinner'. Fascinatingly the lyric slips from the past tense 'And the crack *was* good' to 'and the crack *is* good' (my italics), like the final line of 'Orangefield' which hauls the emotion into the here and now. It has the nature of a travelogue but the landmarks and place names are cinematically employed, for their semiotic and sensual richness, even in the relish with which he says the place names. The piece takes place in 'Autumn sunshine' (mentioned twice) and there is a sense of fullness, richness, a connection to the land. Here the harvest is in, the sun is setting, displaying a connection between a sense of the rhythm of the seasons, but also of time. It is an awareness which is both wide awake and intuitive but also dreamlike and melancholic; a melancholic intuition, which is both enjoyed and visually realized: 'I look at the side of your face, as the sunlight comes / Streaming through the window, autumn sunshine'. The payoff line opens the piece up to us, inviting us to go back and dig deeper in its details, inviting us to revise our understanding of this curious memoir of adolescence: 'Wouldn't it be great if it was like this all the time?' In some ways, this provides the key to all Morrison's techniques of evocation of sight, sound and sense via place: a point of contact between the present fleeting moment and the repossession of that lost moment by the future reimagining of it, an awareness that even as the joy is kissed it flies. There is some sense of loss accompanying the fullness. Here is the autumnal resonance that has reoccurred throughout Morrison's catalogue. In his lyrical cinematic evocations of place we feel a sense of both fullness and loss, of recalled wholeness and perceived fragmentation which is closely and undeniably related to issues of Irish creativity and cultural identity. In the last line of 'Coney Island' the two are held together briefly, so completely that the song has to stop immediately after he has made the observation. Once stated, once encapsulated, the track cannot go on: yet, like Beckett, he goes on.[50]

'I'm Tired Joey Boy', the following track on *Avalon Sunset*, offers a twin piece to 'Coney Island', positing urban constriction as opposed to rural liberty.[51] The running order is cinematic too, switching from rural scene to urban enclosure via the images of wild nature in the former, an urban park in the latter. There is barely a beat between the end of one and the opening of the other, yet there is all the difference in the world between the two cuts: one describes the freedom, the other describes the partially compromised reimagining of it. Both songs lay open the mutual impact of music and place, and show how spirituality effectively mediates between these two elements. As with James Joyce's imaginative remapping of Dublin in *Ulysses* or *Exiles*, we have the spirit of place mapped out for us in 'Coney Island' as surely as we have the happily jumbled road map of one man's memories.

Chapter Eight

A Three-cornered Quartet: Van Morrison and the Art of Through-composition

INTRODUCTION

What is through-composition? This is a term I use to mean how a collection of songs, or album, possesses a unity which runs more deeply than the fact of their being gathered together under one title. The connections may be musical or thematic or both. I should say straight away that I am *not* talking about 'concept albums', where a pseudo-operatic narrative framework might be fixed in advance of completion or composition.

Through-composition refers instead to a group of songs which can be compared to the view from the top of a hill: from the same point, the landscape reveals different aspects of itself. So the term refers to an exploration, a working discovery of a seam, and as the work continues, fresh discoveries are made. A sound is discovered, explored, and while subsequent live performances of the songs may be faithful, they will not be able to fully recreate it: if you want that sound, you have to go to that record. That's what the albums examined in this chapter – *Astral Weeks*, *Veedon Fleece*, *Into the Music* and *Common One* – have in common, a three-cornered quartet (I take the last two to be sister albums, two stages of the same exploration) which reveals much that is deep and fundamental to Morrison's work and creativity.

Now, most acts who make any kind of impression in the music industry have a distinctive sound, so that as soon as a number starts, you know it's them whether you actually 'like it' or not – be it Prince, U2, or James Brown – but through-composition concerns itself with individual and finite works. I'm proposing that Van Morrison's best and most coherent works display strong evidence of this compositional and performative methodology. The technique is also strongly present, if less fully realized, on other albums – *A Period Of Transition*, *No Guru, No Method, No Teacher*, *Poetic Champions Compose* and, as an atypical template, *Hymns To The Silence*. There are arguments to be made in favour of other albums of course – perhaps even the almost forgotten collaboration with Linda Gail Lewis, *You Win Again* – and certain songs, such as the complete sound world of 'Into The Mystic' or the bluebeat metaphysics of 'Precious Time', but I am going to confine my application of this theory to our three-cornered quartet.

THE DITCH WHERE THE BACK ROADS STOP: *ASTRAL WEEKS* (1968)

By late 1967 expectations for Morrison's work were low, and he was free to do, it seemed, anything he wanted to. He had shaken himself free of the Bang enterprise, delivering a kiss-off in the shape of the 31 contractual obligation tracks which belied his own frustration and disillusionment with the music industry as much as his own work. Them, as a proper, creative working unit, was already three years behind him – a long time in pop, especially in the 60s, and certainly a long time for a 22-year-old.

It's worth noting too that the reputation of *Astral Weeks* grew slowly. As Morrison notes frequently, the album wasn't a great commercial success at the time and indeed has never troubled the chart statisticians. The reputation that it has acquired must be rooted in some other set of values, not just the fact that, in Morrison's sweetly disengaged comment, 'it wasn't a big record . . . I think it was critically acclaimed'.[1] But of course that doesn't put food on the table. Warner Bros. has retained the rights to the album since day one and Morrison has made little from its sales, which have remained steady throughout the years. This is perhaps partly why Morrison assembled as many of the original players as he could – showing his grasp of the importance of through-composition – for what were effectively 40th anniversary concerts in Hollywood and New York in Autumn 2008, shows later issued commercially: he was reclaiming ownership in the artistic as well as the commercial sense.

So what binds these songs together into eight aspects of the same thing? First, the music: it was played by a hastily assembled ensemble, being Connie Kay on drums, Jay Berliner on guitar, Richard Davis on bass, Warren Smith, Jr. on percussion and John Payne on flute and soprano sax. Morrison has not stinted in his praise of these players, telling Ritchie Yorke: 'The musicians were really together. Those type of guys play what you're gonna do before you do it, that's how good they are.'[2] We should also note that while through-composition is not the same as song order, we may, via force of feeling or sheer repetition, perceive internal dialectics at work within the running order. The sequencing of *Astral Weeks* is key to this: the two vinyl sides of the record were subtitled on the sleeve (but not on the record label) as 'In The Beginning' (Side One) and 'Afterwards' (Side Two). This plain fact makes us, whether we consciously try to or not, read the groups of songs differently. Yet this is not necessarily any form of clue or guide to how we should listen – *Astral Weeks* flautist John Payne remembered that:

> 'Van I know has been quoted as saying that he had the order different, he didn't like the order they put it in, and he listed the order he liked . . . but . . . I know the album so well now after all these years, I don't want to hear it any other way than – the next song I'm hearing in my head before the previous song ends. It's too late, yeah, I think it works. I think it flows nicely cut to cut, they were probably just thinking how it would work musically, or just the amount of things you can get on a side, too, might have had something to do with it.'[3]

So all these considerations, from the philosophical to the mechanical, are brought to bear upon the selection of a running order for any given record. As Payne notes, it is the familiarity of certain connections between songs ('the next song I'm hearing in my head before the previous song ends') that establishes these connections, that makes the songs feel as though they belong to each other. Yet in the case of *Astral Weeks* we move deeper into this puzzling economy of proximity by way of the songs being grouped into two, for want of a better term, conceptual and thematic subsets – were the four and four always envisaged this way or is it, as Payne says, just to do with 'the amount of things you can get on a side'? The running time of the album as a whole is fairly evenly split between the two sides (times according to the sleeve are 46:05 for the album, 23:10 for Side One, 22:55 Side Two. The CD indexing muddies the waters somewhat by including silences and run off times, giving a screened running time of 47.16, and while certainly outstripping the 27.01 minutes of *Nashville Skyline* or the 39.42 of *Sgt. Pepper*, the running times would not have been too much of a challenge for the shiny new stereos or dusty Dansettes of early 1969. Thus, as the music fits snugly into what a side of 12" vinyl can comfortably accommodate and reproduce with some fidelity, we need to acknowledge that the running order we know is the product of both aesthetic and pragmatic decision.

The division of the record into two conceptual groups also illustrates an understanding of the psychology of listening to recorded music on disc: songs follow and flow, and come to be seen, as in John Payne's aside, to belong together. Morrison, as a listener to and player of records since childhood understood this intuitively; the act of a side finishing, of flipping the record over and going back to the start, which is a *different* start, is key. For an album concerned (among other things) with beginnings, experience and rebirth, the sheer mechanical organisation of the material into a certain order must interest us. This has an effect on its impact – think of the attention Dylan Thomas paid to how his poems looked on the page for an interesting comparison (the remarkable 'Vision and Prayer' is perhaps the best example).[4] The possibilities of 'the other side' are enticing and almost without end. If this sounds far-fetched, which it well might, just consider how much internal logic you attribute to the running order of one of the sides of your favourite vinyl album. The CD and MP3 file have of course complicated this habit of delineation and subdivision, but it is still culturally significant, and fully relevant to an album like *Astral Weeks*. If one broke the order, and transposed 'Beside You' to Track Seven, 'Young Lovers Do' to Track Four and 'Slim Slow Slider' to the album's opener, would *Astral Weeks* be a different record? This is a rhetorical question: the answer is yes. Morrison acknowledges as much by the subtle shift in song order on 2009's *Astral Weeks Live*. Yet track order undoubtedly delivers coherence and allows meaning to gather and settle upon it.

When it was first issued, the album received a mixture of perplexed shrugs and tentative eulogy, one of the best-known being by Nick Logan in the *New Musical Express*:

> The album is as far removed from Them as possible, Morrison sounding for all the world like Jose Feliciano's stand-in on eight of his own compositions. The comparison rather deadens the impact of the album because Morrison can't better Feliciano's distinctive style. The songs themselves aren't particularly distinguished apart from the title track, and suffer from being stuck in one groove throughout.[5]

Feliciano's name was no doubt meant reductively, but I take it as a positive, and furthermore the observation is not too wide of the mark. The thin, high reed of Morrison's voice mingling with the flamboyant Latin jazz of his acoustic guitar playing on 'Beside You', with its lurches into unexpected flamenco-bunched notes and tight explosions of Spanish guitar chords, notes splintering off them at the top and low ends, does indeed resemble the atmospherics of Feliciano's best work, both in its virtuosity on the guitar and also its infusion of a storytelling urge into song, a narrative that makes best sense once sung.

Feliciano, remember, was very big news in 1968 and had hit worldwide with his version of the Doors' 'Light My Fire', a cover I much prefer to the original, and its Spanish guitar and wisps of flute do indeed have a more than passing resemblance to the *Astral Weeks* sound.[6] So, perversely, Logan identifies that the musical textures of *Astral Weeks* not only had a currency but one which was, potentially, commercially successful at that time. His confusion comes from his expectations – 'as far removed from Them as possible'. We note too that the very thing for which *Astral Weeks* is celebrated, the singularity of its mood, was initially read as problematic: 'The songs themselves . . . suffer from being stuck in one groove throughout.' That is where Logan lets the record down.

Equally well-known is Lester Bangs's review, published in a collection called *Stranded*, a title which would later grace one of Morrison's best post-Millennium tunes. That book was edited by Greil Marcus, who also wrote a review of the album for the young *Rolling Stone*. Marcus's review was contemporary, while Bangs's was composed as he says 'ten years, almost to the day', after the album was released. Bangs's review is thick with rich phrasemaking, perhaps one of the best-known being his assertion that:

> [It sounded] like the man who made *Astral Weeks* was in terrible pain, pain most of Van Morrison's previous works had only suggested; but like the later albums by the Velvet Underground, there was a redemptive element in the blackness, ultimate compassion for the suffering of others, and a swath of pure beauty and mystical awe that cut right through the heart of the work.[7]

Bangs, seeing how the 60s dream had soured, reads the album retrospectively in that sense as a lament for the lost fleeting dream of the counterculture; this is understandable. Each of us who is moved by the record is somehow obliged to index our own lives alongside it, the contexts in which we heard and understood it first, and how far things have moved from there. Morrison meanwhile was already planning his next move, which would be the wholly unalike pop-soul breakthrough represented by *Moondance*. Morrison has since asserted, characteristically, that the division of the sides via subtitles was meaningless: for him, maybe, although the division is maintained on 2009's live album of the songs. For the rest of those drawn into the world the record creates, I'd suggest not. This is the conundrum: an artist cannot create the meanings generated by their own work once it is out in the world. They can only describe their own relationship to it, not everyone else's. It is free of them.

Greil Marcus's *Rolling Stone* review reads as if – with the judicious excision of a few archaisms – it could have been written in the light of *Astral Weeks*' subsequent reputation: he calls it 'a unique and timeless album' and 'strong and serious stuff', observing that it is not rock and roll, but rather, in a moment of insight signposting his later works, 'it is music that is intelligible to us because of rock and roll'. Equally revealing are his frequent allusions to the work of Bob Dylan, a critical commonplace which would tail Morrison henceforward.[8] Back to Bangs:

> Van Morrison is interested, obsessed with how much musical or verbal information he can compress into a small space, and, almost, conversely, how far he can spread one note, word, sound, or picture. To capture one moment, be it a caress or a twitch. He repeats certain phrases to extremes that from anybody else would seem ridiculous, because he's waiting for a vision to unfold, trying as unobtrusively as possible to nudge it along. Sometimes he gives it to you through silence, by choking off the song in midflight: 'It's too late to stop now!' It's the great search, fuelled by the belief that through these musical and mental processes illumination is attainable. Or may at least be glimpsed.[9]

This is superb and insightful writing, as well as being proof of Morrison's point when he said 'It's all in *your* head' about the album's charmed reputation,[10] which is a smart technique for separating out what was personal for him in the songs and the impact that those same songs have upon the listener. He thereby opened the songs up, with some generosity as well as track-covering, to connect with the unique and individual experiences of each listener. The sound of the jazz players came close to anticipating, duplicating and then developing the sound Morrison had in his head – the fact that no other Morrison album sounds quite like *Astral Weeks* is not because subsequent attempts have failed, it's rather that this is where he was at that time, and once stated, why repeat? This is the root of the jazz methodology, or philosophy, and it is doubtless a hard one to fully adhere to. Any genuinely creative artist faces this dilemma – whether to repeat a winning or well-regarded formula and make further artistic and financial capital of it, or simply abandon it and move on to the next set of ideas and methods which present themselves. Van Morrison has usually followed the latter course. So the move from 'Gloria' to 'Brown Eyed Girl' to 'Slim Slow Slider' in three years illustrates this process to be in train right from the outset in his recorded work.

What, then, characterises the sound world of *Astral Weeks*? First, a voice. With it, double bass, vibes, a drum set, brushed for the most part, acoustic guitar which is often almost flamenco in its dramatic and sensual twists, a handful of percussive effects, brass, flute and soprano sax at specific points, while strings and harpsichord were overdubbed later. There is a delicate buoyancy to the guitar and bass and the determinedly non-standardised rhythmic patterns of the drums unites the tracks. It is a sound which gives the impression of being one beat behind itself – the sound always seems to be just about to grasp a more firmly grounded version of itself but never quite attains that stability, instead always seeming to be a breath away from falling apart. It is this very high-end shambolic sound that allows the songs to apparently take shape before our eyes and ears, almost as if the musicians themselves aren't quite sure of what is coming next. This isn't entirely rhetorical illusion: enough of the jazz philosophy is at work, and put to work by supremely skilled practitioners of it, for that knife-edge between discovery and collapse which characterises the record to be sustained and not to simply disperse in the air. Unlike the free jazz experiments of late Coltrane (*Ascension* (1965) or *Interstellar Space* (1967), for example), or the earlier and sorely under-rated British sax player Joe Harriott (the self-explanatory *Free Form* (1960) and *Abstract* (1962)[11]), the musical construction of *Astral Weeks* marries the values of improvisation to those of acknowledged structures – Morrison's own songwriting pedigree, and that which Nick Logan missed from his hearing of the record – and incorporates the values and virtues of both methodologies. So the splendid paradox is that the formative example of through-composition in Morrison's work to some extent ignores the formal rules of 'well-made' composition altogether – it certainly reimagines them, and challenges the perceived limits of such techniques and approaches to the musical work. Bangs took a more fevered view:

> The whole ensemble – Larry Fallon's string section, Jay Berliner's guitar (he played on Mingus's 'Black Saint and the Sinner Lady'), Connie Kay's drumming – is like that: they and Van sound like they're not just reading but dwelling inside of each other's minds.[12]

There is certainly a degree of telepathy in successful moments of writing and recording music like this. Of such matters, Morrison would later say in an interview:

> VM: Well you need the groove, and you need compatibility, you need to get people on the same wavelength . . . it's almost like telepathy.
>
> [Candy Dulfer]: We always want you to be happy because we know when you are happy and relaxed these magical things happen in the music. What are the ideal circumstances for you?
>
> VM: Well . . . a group of musicians that are on some kind of wavelength, that have some kind of rapport, not only with me but with themselves . . . a rhythm section

with some rapport . . . a piano player who can work off the vocal . . . I need somebody in there who can work off the vocal . . . to lead it . . . but I work with musicians who have a rapport with me, and with themselves, that's ideal.[13]

The aural evidence is that a community of a kind did emerge in the swift sessions for this album. Yet they are also an index of loneliness, for these are songs of exile: they were for the most part written in Belfast, but recorded in New York with this small jazz group. So *Astral Weeks* is a truly transatlantic record but also one which in some ways transcends time and space altogether. It is Morrison's first and, some would argue, most complete sound world, an almost physical space into which you can pass and dwell until the record ends, when you can carry away from that place memories as surely as you would had you made a 'real' journey to a location situated in real time, and real space. The through-composition here is of mood, instrumentation, and of the *sound* of Morrison's voice. This we can call the *Astral Weeks* voice in that we do not hear him sing quite like this again anywhere, and it feels like the sound of change itself. So many of the songs are to do with memory, loss and leaving something behind that the tone of the voice, a kind of troubadour's keening mixed with a blues-serrated rasp, is itself a central instrument within the composition of this mood and this ensemble of emotion and memory.

It seemed to me that the day would inevitably come that Morrison would play the album straight through in concert as, say, half of a live show, and in late 2008 and early 2009 he played a run of shows where he did exactly that. Having resisted the lure of the 'heritage' concert before, it was a way of him reasserting control over these songs, which Warners still own, and the issue of the live album and DVD of the Hollywood Bowl shows on his own label illustrate the financial as well as the artistic motive.[14] This acknowledgement of the integrity of the collection begs the question: how do songs from this most unified of works survive and function on their own? No singles were issued from the album, and it has always seemed to me that 'Sweet Thing' seemed lonely and somewhat stranded on 1990's *Best Of* compilation. Morrison told Jeremy Marre that a lot of his material written after Them and around the Bang era was 'suppressed', by 'the producer' (Bert Berns), who wanted either his own songs or guaranteed hits, 'like "Brown Eyed Girl" . . . he liked that one 'cos he knew that was a hit! . . . If it wasn't a hit, he didn't wanna know'. Marre asked him if he could cite any examples of this 'suppression':

'Well a lot of the stuff that came out later, called *Astral Weeks*, a lot of the songs on that I was doing then but that was completely suppressed; I actually recorded a lot of those songs, but the session was sabotaged. The engineer on the session sabotaged the thing . . . tapes were lost and all this kind of stuff . . . so I actually recorded *Astral Weeks* three times and the third time I recorded it was for Warner Brothers, but all the material on that [the earlier sessions] was suppressed because it wasn't commercial . . . it wasn't pop music, so . . .'[15]

Bert Berns was quite right in that: *Astral Weeks* is not pop music. The lyrical mode of the record is that of elliptical evocations of a primal landscape, green thoughts in exile. It is not lyrically repetitious like the blues but is informed by the cyclic discourses of the blues – the lonely places in which life passes; the loved one placed and perceived at some distance from the singer; the places once inhabited, reimagined in exile, their meanings reconfigured forever in the act. The blues is about the personal moment and feeling made universal. This sensitivity to these places is a key part of Morrison's gift: did Dylan ever write about Hibbing? Lennon about Woolton? Only obliquely, perhaps. The language of *Astral Weeks* is local and universal, contemporary and ancient, temporal and timeless.

Side One: 'In The Beginning'

The album starts with a moment of pure rhythm as an acoustic guitar, double bass and a shaker set up the very distinctive jazz-skewed, folk Bo Diddley rhythm which propels the song (and which would be born again on 1986's 'A Town Called Paradise'). As that little snowdrift of adjectives used to describe the first ten seconds of the song shows, this is music that evades, even ignores categorisation. Not deliberately, in a mimetic, nose-thumbing way – it is just how it is, and what it is. Richard Davis noted that he recalled the recording process as nothing out of the ordinary, and he'll be right: what we find in the music is greater than the sum of its parts. Davis observed that

'Some people are disillusioned when I tell them about making the record. People say: "He must have talked to you about the record and created the magic feeling . . ." To tell you the truth, I don't remember any conversations with him. He kept to himself. He didn't make any suggestions about what to play, how to play, how to stylize what we were doing. We were into what we were doing, and he was into what he was doing, and it coagulated.'[16]

Flautist John Payne told Thomas C. Palmer, Jr.:

JP: I believe 'Astral Weeks', the title one, was not particularly one they were going to do. They just threw it in as the last – it was the first one I played on, myself, the end of the first session. He said, well, let's do one more, and then he – I'd been yelling 'let me play, let me play' because I was young and foolish and didn't know my place. But I'm glad I was, because if I hadn't been young and foolish and didn't know my place I would have never made it on that album. So it helps sometimes. The other guy played great, you know. But I just said I can play as well as he did – I can do what he's doing.

W: And they replaced him with you?

JP: After that, for that one song. And the next two sessions they just used me. Just to save money on the budget. They thought I did fine on that song. And they named me as the person on the album, so I must have.[17]

The 'other guy' is on 'Beside You' and 'Cyprus Avenue'.

The song slowly builds a musical setting for Morrison's voice, which comes in at 0.10; at first the effect is disorientating. The first time I brought a copy of the album home, bought one foggy Tuesday morning from a long-gone Liverpool record shop, Penny Lane Records, I thought there was something wrong with my turntable – I had never heard anything like it before. This is a feeling perhaps shared by many readers of this page – the apparently shambolic arrangement, the playing which seemed out of synch with itself: where are the choruses? What are these strange instruments doing seemingly jammed together like this? What on earth is he singing about? I was happy to discover that these feelings were not exclusive to me – the leader of Dexy's Midnight Runners, Kevin Rowland, wrote about his first encounter with the album:

It was during the boiling hot summer of 1976 that I first heard it. Punk was about to happen, but this album, showed me something really different. Before that, Van Morrison had been, in my perception, some American type singer . . . songwriter; long hair, jeans, country rock kinda thing. No thank you very much sir, not my cup of tea. Then I heard *Astral Weeks*. What was it? I couldn't understand it, it sounded bizarre and tuneless at first, as if he was making it up as he was going along. Oddly, it happened that I heard the whole album three times that same evening.

The circumstances were: I was in a wine bar in Birmingham my girlfriend. It was a lovely hot night and we spent the whole evening there. The woman running the bar, was clearly very into the album, she had it on an 8 Track cartridge machine [popular in the 70s] and instead of stopping when it came to the end of the record, she let it go around and around. The process in my head went something like this; the first time I heard it; I thought, it sounds like he is just making up the words and the tune, as he goes along, crazy. The second time, I thought, there's more to it than I first realized. I was starting to hear some melody in it, by the third time, I knew there was something powerful going on.

> That was how I got into *Astral Weeks*, Van Morrison's first masterpiece. The long term effect it had on me, is something else entirely.[18]

Rowland's emotions, moving from confusion, through outrage and into obsession, reflect the processes via which music can change the listener – Rowland was by his own admission a different person after hearing the album, while *Astral Weeks* remained the same. It's like falling in love: you are changed within from without.

The title track introduces us to this sound world, and requires from the unprepared listener something unusual in the sphere of pop: close and attentive listening. It builds with graded gradual grace, like a flower, slowly opening. The strings come in as an autumnal shiver at 0.28 and then drop back at 0.46; the flute's first tentative toot is at 0.56, and stays in the mix until the strings hustle back in at 1.14. Both string segments are frosted with three notes on the vibes, lending more to this autumnal hue. At 1.42, the song changes up a gear as Morrison begins the verse with 'There you go . . .' This is a verbal formula that also appears in 'Friday's Child' as an observational gambit which is also one of desire. Here there is more intimacy and fond observation than formerly in the phrase and, to match this, the acoustic rhythm is suddenly more urgent, and the steps of the flute more substantial, as the music begins to gather its own momentum. The bass playing remains in the high end, and at the low neck of the instrument, the shortened strings emitting a strange atonal pulse which is at once running parallel to the mood and contrary to the rhythm, yet is in harmony with both. This 'verse', if we can apply conventional terminologies to such an unconventionally structured song, lasts 1.42–3.32 and it is this compositional technique – where the music flows from and into itself as much as it moves forward – which is a key part of the through-compositional mode we find on this album. At 3.33 we can hear the change; the acoustic rhythm guitar part is modified, breaking the tension which has built up over the two-minute build to this shift. A rhythmic curlicue is added and the 'strum' of the earlier part of the song is broken down into tonally distinct segments – listen to the guitar from 3.33 on. This is the musical equivalent of the lyrical mood, with its reference at 3.18 to the subject of 'There you go' finally 'coming through', breaking free of something. The release offered by the shift in the rhythm and tonality of the acoustic guitar from 3.33 infuses the song with the reality of this break. Tellingly, after this shift, Morrison returns to the opening lyric of the song – this is what I mean by the through-compositional mode here being orbital and spiral as well as linear. The beginning returns in order to survey what has been achieved – a kind of peak, or crest of the song – and also to herald the gradual spinning down of the song, down to its sparse yet intense finale, like the matter of a collapsed star falling in on itself. The shimmering strings over the songs coda deliver a feeling both of freedom and weightlessness ('Way up in the heaven') and also knowledge of the body, referring forward to the album's borrowing from 'All Shook Up' on 'Cyprus Avenue': 'And my insides shake just like a leaf on a tree'.

The metaphysical boldness of Morrison's repeated assertion that he belongs 'In another time / And another place . . . And another face' again anticipates a discovery he would make further down the road, that the likes of W. B. Yeats had worked at the same seam of creativity and ideas before him, and that he was in some ways as much a successor to that tradition as to that of the blues, indexed immediately in this song by the reference to Leadbelly. Indeed we recall that Morrison recorded one of Yeats's 'Mask' poems twice over with different arrangements; once in 1983 under a new title, 'Your Original Face', and once under Yeats's title 'Before the World Was Made' for *Too Long In Exile*. The immediate response to the thought of 'another face' (sung only once, unlike time and place which are repeated twice each) is the lead acoustic guitar arresting the slow drift of the song's conclusion and, via a blues-flamenco twist of notes, reins it in; it's time to conclude.

Morrison's final *sotto voce* 'Yeah' at 6.56 feels entirely spontaneous, almost uttered to himself, in an acknowledgement of what had gone before, and that it's now over. It concludes in a curious and hitherto uncommented upon deep wheeze of bass harmonica. This introduces a whole other discourse into the song, linking back to the blues pulses of the central verse and how it escalates to the shift in the guitar pattern at 3.33. The reference to Huddie Ledbetter and the blues landscape of the opening verse evoke a place where things end and where they begin, born again where the ditch and the back roads stop.[19]

The mood, set by the title song (which we should note is unique on the album in not featuring the title in its lyrics), is picked up and confirmed by the ear-pricked inquisitiveness of the opening notes of 'Beside You', again picked out on a Spanish acoustic. This is a song which, although new to anyone listening to *Astral Weeks* in 1969, had already been attempted in the studio by its author, having been recorded in a very different guise as part of the Bang recordings.[20] By the time Morrison re-recorded the song for *Astral Weeks*, it had been musically transformed, although lyrically it remained remarkably unchanged. Picking out notes around the song's root chord, Jay Berliner establishes a mood of evening time, of light beginning to fade, and of sight falling behind it. Warren Smith again drops vibe notes like dewdrops onto the melody. You do need to turn to Spanish or Portuguese music for the closest kin to this and here is where Nick Logan probably heard his Feliciano. 'Beside You', in its evocation of heat and dust, is proof positive of Morrison's assertion that this album has nothing to do with pop or rock at all; it seems connected to much older and more deeply embedded cultural traditions of expression, welling up together to make something new. The lyric opens at 0.23 with an evocation of an absence, via a motif which we now read as central to Morrison's lyrical methodologies: 'Little Jimmy's gone, way out on the back street'. But we soon discover that 'Beside You' is the album's greatest challenge to the idea of the 'well-made song'; in those terms it barely exists. The song and the instruments that play it function in a continuous jostle for position, a sound both unsettled and unsettling. In terms of its structure, it is powerfully linear, like a road stretching out to the horizon.

Lyrically there are some moments to which it returns, even providing an internal rhyme ('And you roam from your retreating view . . . Ev'ry scrapbook stuck with glue / And I'll stand beside you'), but the arrival of the title in the lyric signals a shift back to another open-ended, free-flowing verse. The emotional and dramatic centre of the song is not provided by the title but by the brace of repetitions Morrison works into the lyric with 'You breathe in, you breathe out . . .', in particular recalling the visceral impact of his vocal in the previous year's 'TB Sheets', and the auto-descriptive vocal revolutions of 'You turn around, you turn around, you turn around' anticipating the dizzying repetitions of the word 'love' in the other Bang remake on this album, 'Madame George'. The song is in my view the most challenging listen on the album: I remember 'Beside You' actually frightened me at first hearing – I'd been delighted, bored, moved, provoked and indifferent to songs before, but never frightened. It seems to open up a whole new window on the world that *Astral Weeks* both inhabits and creates.

The lyrics, when transcribed, fail to make much 'sense' in the literal meaning of that word but when matched with the gloaming of the musical environment they light up like burning coals. The meaning is in the unity of sound and word, of music and lyric and, I'd argue, this meaning is both infinitely fluid and also definitive to this performance of it. As Morrison said, 'It's all in *your* head'. The scraps of images that fly together for the song are individually memorable – I like the scrapbooks, the tipping trucks and the Sunday six bells, the window with your lantern lit – and conjure up glimpses of a world of dusk and half-light. The vigorous restatement and forceful assertion of the title and the desire behind it reveal this to be a song about being with someone in the spiritual sense on a journey, rather than being always in their physical presence, and this is emphasised with a cacophonous finale. It is by far the least performed song on the album, testament perhaps to its singularity and the debt it owes to the time and place at which it was recorded.

Who doesn't feel the spirit lift when the welcoming, opening chords of 'Sweet Thing' start up after the troubling angularities of 'Beside You'? Or happy as Richard Davis's bass cleaves to the harmonic climb of the guitar, delivering that sense of sweet return we get from the opening moments of 'Sweet Thing'? This is morning again, after the troubled twilight and vexed nightfall of 'Beside You'. Where that song had something of the haunted about it, 'Sweet Thing' is a song of love and dedicated to a feeling one finds located in another, as much as it is actually about that other person. It is the reward. The bass affirms an inner wholeness after the fragmentary seeking of it in 'Beside You', and warmly, generously encircles the chorus, urging it forward into the light. Meanwhile the sibilant hi-hat of Connie Kay adds to the powerful, gentle acoustic swing, describing the key rhythmic pulse of the whole album, heard on the title track and now felt here as a unifying element of through-composition, and evidence of the record's integrity. The sense of sparkling dew dawn is accentuated by the use of a triangle at 0.07 and then, at slightly increasing intervals up to the arrival of the hi-hat at 0.39, at which moment it chimes for the last time independently before being absorbed into the joyful swing of the track. This may well have been an accidental conjunction, but it is a moving and affecting one.

The meaning of the song is encoded into its structure, for what it sounds like is what it is: a gradual growing perception of a feeling of joy and delight in simply being alive, which wells up throughout the song and just keeps on growing. It's a young man's song, for sure, but has a message for everyone – borrowing ever so slightly from Bob Dylan's tricksy sense inversions, the central lyric is 'And I will never grow so old again'.[21] This suggests time can be arrested, contemplated and made to run backwards – while still running forward. Descartes, in his *Meditations*, proposed that the nature of time and our understanding of it are one and the same thing – so the apparent anti-logic of Morrison's lyrical twist has some resonance for us here: how one feels and experiences time influences the impact it has upon us.[22] Life may feel short or it may feel long and tedious but it is best lived with an awareness of its passing. Blake advised us to kiss the joy as it flies, and the carpe diem school of poetry runs on this idea. Yet while Andrew Marvell used the idea as a sly seduction technique in his 'To His Coy Mistress', this song is more concerned with the fullness of the moment and of living fully in the *now*. Thus this song is doing just that: it kisses the joy as it flies. Morrison would later look for ways to go beyond even this realisation, as we discovered in our consideration of 'Coney Island', which dares to imagine being able to capture and dwell in an idyllic moment.

From its opening, strummed acoustic opening, 'Sweet Thing' lifts its face to the light, and the lyric reinforces this sense of renewal and of optimism. The 'merry way' which seemed somewhat melancholic in 'Beside You' is here shown to be an enlightened and enlightening one; the whole perspective shifts, as 'Go on your merry way' seems to infer some loss and regret and here 'I will stroll the merry way' swings the emotional polarities around, standing as evidence of renewal and refreshment. I am particularly fond of the line 'It's me, I'm dynamite, and I don't know why', in which the lack of cunning or of self-consciousness is key to the mood of the whole album. The song's meaning is somehow emphasised by its defiant fade, and its unwillingness to conclude and to *stop growing*. As the song disappears, it continues to climb, with Larry Fallon's string arrangements here being particularly, intuitively sympathetic to the whole mood of the song. These overdubs, added a week later at Century Sound under the guidance of engineer Brooks Arthur (whose studio it was, and who had engineered much of the Bang material), add much to the record as a whole: strings, horns, harpsichord. Morrison apparently seemed to have become more confident at these sessions, adding and suggesting more than at the time of the initial recording, Payne recalled.[23]

The last track on the first vinyl side, or 'In The Beginning', is 'Cyprus Avenue'. This is the first and perhaps still most celebrated of Van Morrison's evocations of the Belfast in which he grew up, making use of the power of the name to evoke, create and thereby modify the meaning of place. Barely a day can go by now on Cyprus Avenue in Belfast 5 without someone either thinking of the song as they pass along the avenue of trees, or someone visiting it specifically because of the song. There are resonances of this further on up the road in Morrison's recordings, with his take on Patrick Kavanagh's poem 'On Raglan Road', recorded with the Chieftains for 1988's *Irish Heartbeat*; again a place that has an individually perceived sense of magic or 'aliveness' which informs a piece of work and then goes back out into the world, connects with people and changes that place thereby. Morrison spoke about this in the BBC TV programme *Arena: One Irish Rover* in 1990:

> 'I *must* be an Irish writer . . . we're preoccupied with the past because we're trying to transcend the mundane existence . . . that there IS something else, never mind "must be" . . . there is something else and in Ireland, it's *there* . . . this preoccupation with the past, it's not sentimental . . . as with Raglan Road, it's an ordinary street with rows of houses, but you go away thinking this is an incredible place, it must be, has to be . . . it's out of this world . . . I mean the lives that have been lived in this place, the things that have happened . . .'[24]

'Cyprus Avenue' then is a powerful evocation of place which does indeed try to transcend the mundane existence of the ordinary street with rows of houses, by seeking out and illuminating the lives that have been lived. It opens with the now familiar strummed guitar, but the atmosphere takes an unexpected leap into the baroque with the first notes of a harpsichord, following a light melodic counterpoint. The harpsichord itself lends an air of stateliness, of order – it is a very precise instrument – but also brings confusion of time; it is a sound that, though not unfamiliar to the modern ear, is nonetheless associated with a former era. The names of the great harpsichordists are evocative not only of the high classical era but also of a vanished cultural order: William Byrd, Henry Purcell, George Frideric Handel, J. S. Bach and, the capo of them all, Domenico Scarlatti. The harpsichord is used in cinema or television to evoke an era of courtliness but also one of a sense of moral unease, of certainties under threat, and about to be shaken. Harpsichord music, for all its gentility, is part of the music of social and personal negotiation of change.

It wasn't new to 'pop' either by late 1968; as part of 1967's expansion of the instrumental palette of popular music it had been co-opted by psychedelia, which was very interested in these breakdowns of time and place using musical means. Putting apparently seventeenth-century and freshly made sounds together was part of the impact – it even turns up briefly on the Beatles' *Sgt. Pepper's Lonely Hearts Club Band*, right at the opening of 'Fixing A Hole', as well as on various tracks by the Monkees, including Michael Nesmith's sublime 'The Girl I Knew Somewhere', where the solo is played superbly by ace harpsichordist Peter Tork. So if both the Fab and 'Prefab' Fours were using them, the harpsichord was well within the range of pop in 1968. What is unusual is the manner in which it is used here, not to add a textural gloss to a pop sound, but to deliver something of the cultural resonance associated with the instrument – the sense of longing, of vexation, and of the courtliness which concealed the passion. Scarlatti wrote his harpsichord dances for men and women to be close to each other; to negotiate intimacies within a fixed system of social and sexual codes.[25]

The harpsichord on 'Cyprus Avenue' brings some of this to the song, accidentally or by design, no matter. This is another of the shared strands of through-composition on the album; emotional negotiation made feasible by reaching back into the past, to create the future via the fully realized 'now' of the present. The narrator of the song is 'caught', and not for the first time, in the 'now' of the moment on Cyprus Avenue, and is simply having to live it: 'Nothing that I can do'.[26] The harpsichord arrives at 0.14, only just ahead of the vocal, which enters at 0.15, drawing the two textures together. The harpsichord is somehow synonymous with and analogous to the emotional drive of the lyric. At 1.00 the strings are added, very deep in the mix, and the flute starts to toot equally discreetly.

The first line of the song is a confession, not only of the current circumstance, but of it being part of a wider pattern: caught one more time. Adhering to the blues model, the verses throughout the song are structured so that the first two lines are repeated to become the third and fourth lines, with the fifth and sixth delivering the lyrical payoff. Musically the chord changes after the fourth line and we get a different perspective, in the first verse via an allusion to an encounter in a car which may be rhapsodic, or sleazy, or perhaps both. Whichever way, there is an air of fatalistic acceptance about it: 'Nothing that I can do'. Thus established, the scene brings the song up to the minute mark – a reined-back ripple on Davis's bass, the strings start to murmur and the flute tentatively starts to dab around the melody before the new verse begins. We learn no more about the moment in the car seat; the song's perspective swings around to the world without. Borrowing an image from Hank Williams, the lyric cites a mansion on the hill: in Williams's song of that title the narrator is looking up at a mansion in which the woman he loves dwells unhappily, with a rich husband but a loveless marriage. Morrison's lyric is, as we might expect, far more elusive in its specifics – why it calls upon his attention and causes him anxiety is not spelt out. We feel it rather than see it. The bass snakes round like smoke-rings while the harpsichord keeps to its chordal blocks, freeing the fiddle, flute and bass to weave up and around the melody.

The third verse at 3.16 is heralded by a change in the bass and harpsichord. Davis tugs on the bass in order to propel the melody forward as Morrison sings of walking by the railroad – the physical movement is accommodated musically here – and the harpsichord begins to compress its chords into single, rhythmic and loping strides. This is difficult for the instrument as the note of a harpsichord is not 'clean' like that of a single string, it involves much peripheral vibration, thus adding a dreamlike, not entirely focused element to the sense of urgency. The otherworldly quality which the song develops over its seven minutes is due in no small way to this effect. The overdub more than once comes in just a fraction behind the beat, a little off the beat, a half-pulse late (listen to 3.37–39), and this too adds something of this ambience of mesmerised urgency. This verse is quite unlike the other sections of the song and subsequently has acquired an almost independent existence of its own. This became far more apparent in the live version developed in the early 70s live shows (captured on *It's Too Late To Stop Now*) when Morrison's own onstage direction 'Railroad!' acted as a cue to the band to go into this section. It still turns up as an independent element within 'workshop' sessions in the live show up into the early twenty-first century.

So at 3.52, at the close of the 'Railroad' section, the harpsichord takes off into an ornate and stunningly beautiful set of runs until 4.01 where, under the weight of a guitar crescendo, it is edited out, returning at 4.15, to reinforce the image of the woman by the railroad. The song then begins to find its way back to its source, with the appearance of the narrator's 'lady' fantastically bedecked with rainbow ribbons in her hair, transported like a princess via six white horses and a carriage, back from the fair. The harpsichord is dropped again at 4.22 until it returns at 4.30 and remains until the final fade. Morrison borrows this from Leadbelly: the 'Yonder come Miss Rosey' of 'Midnight Special' becoming the 'Yonder come my lady' of this 'Railroad' section of 'Cyprus Avenue'. The 'Midnight Special' is, of course, a railway train, too. We note that neither she nor the image presented to us is coloured with any further detail or brought closer to us, but we do notice that this transcendent vision ('transcending the mundane existence . . . it IS there', as Morrison put it) gives way to the song's final verse, which is the same as the first. This device of locating the source in the destination is a poetic convention, we might argue ('In my end is my beginning' as T. S. Eliot wrote in the *Four Quartets*), and of course James Joyce's *Finnegans Wake* is similarly bluesy in its circularity.[27] Here, however, the movement is not linear or cyclic but spiral, and an upward one at that: we arrive back in the same place, but all is changed utterly.

The close of the first of Morrison's 'Two Quartets' on this album refers us back to the spirit of place that runs through the songs on the side, from the opening line of 'Astral Weeks', 'If I ventured in the slipstream', to the encounter with the girl, by the railroad (note the country-blues terminology: not 'railway'), and way up on the avenue of trees. That Morrison does not identify the street by name a third time in the exquisite coda assists our drift away from demanding times, names and places. Indeed the coda is it seems expressly designed to avoid that sense of being fixed by such detail – the place we enter into at that point is one only partly situated in time and space; what seems most compelling about it is the way such restrictions and co-ordinates of existence sublimate into the single, deeply lived present moment. Listen to the difference between the vocal performance of the first verse and this last one, with its urgency and discovery and purposeful wildness, and its important final twist: 'I'm looking straight at you'. This ties the fantastical down to the real, and changes the power dynamic too: 'Nothing that I can do' becomes 'I'm looking straight at you', revealing a boldness and directness, an active as opposed to a passive being. That's the change; from being conquered to being connected. The return to the first and last verse at 4.45 is prefixed by a climactic 'Babybabybabybabybabybaby', and the climbing back into the melody and chord structure of the song's opening, now transformed by what has taken place in the meantime.

This vocal performance is a resource upon which Morrison has drawn for much of his subsequent recording career. The images of the leaves in the autumn, the image of the railroad, the image of the woman seen but not approached, and the image of the intimate, heated sexual encounter, the 'wait a minute' rhetoric, the country fair, the dazzling vocal extrapolations of vowel sounds – 'Raiiiinnnbow ribbons', the repetitions ('Wayuponwayuponwayupon'), the technique of the slow dissolve of a song (as opposed to a well-made number concluding with, in the grand tradition, 'ad lib to fade', which of course he can, has and does do, like everyone else does – the very last seconds of 'Cypress Avenue' are an enigma in themselves ('Roo me'?, 'Woo me'?, 'Ooh-ee'?) – leading to the refusal to deliver pat conclusion and musical closure (the song fades on inconclusive notes, repeated over and again).

Morrison's vocalisations on this song seem at their most sinuous and deft, going down low ('And I'm conquered'), and up to the top (and some way beyond it) of his range on 'Rainbow ribbons'. He uses the blues throat on 'I may go crazy . . .', from the chest and from the nose ('All the little girls rhyme somethinnnnng'), the stuttering and the vibrated note on 'Tongue gets tied . . . Every time I try to speak', both of which were further developed, often with humorous intent, in the live shows of the early 1970s. The coda begins at 5.30 ('Wayupon') and the sound picture starts to relax, with spaces opening up again between the instruments, whereas in the final verses it had become a tight, focused knot of sound. This has the air of an aftermath of some sorts, which perhaps prepares for the 'Afterwards' of Side Two.

Side Two: 'Afterwards'

Why don't people like 'Young Lovers Do'? It is, I think, a song in need of some advocacy. Even in 1973 Bob Sarlin was writing that 'it is the album's only bad song . . . it is such a lapse of taste that it would be futile to try to explain why it occurred . . . it is a song easy to forget'.[28] Its crime may well be its placement between two giants of Morrison's reputation and arguably the twin poles of the album as a whole, 'Cyprus Avenue' and 'Madame George'. Yet if it does nothing else it illustrates that those two songs are not simply two expressions on the same face; furthermore it sets up the arrival of its illustriously annotated neighbour by providing some light and shade between the two similarly constructed 'epics'. This is another aspect of through-composition – not that everything 'sounds the same' but that a sound can flourish, grow, and develop in intriguing and unexpected directions while remaining integral and faithful to itself. This is true, I'd argue, of 'Young Lovers Do'. It is also, along with 'Sweet Thing', the most approachable and covered cut on the record, with Jeff Buckley being an interpreter of both tunes on his *Live at Sin-E*, alongside Maria McKee's nicely primed alt. country version of 1993. Greil Marcus's review of the album set the tone for how the song has been viewed and heard ever since, and also sets out a rule which Marcus himself has, to his credit, proceeded to break in just about everything he has since written: 'It is pointless to discuss this album in terms of each particular track; with the exception of "Young Lovers Do," a poor jazz-flavoured cut that, is uncomfortably out of place on this record, it's all one song, very much "A Day in the Life".'[29]

It puzzles me why this little number has come in for such a critical mauling.

It is even denied a definitive title: being referred to sometimes as 'Young Lovers Do', or 'The Way Young Lovers Do', and even, on the label of my vinyl copy, 'Way Young Lovers Do'. The song itself is kin to 'Sweet Thing' in that it describes the experience of love, and of the feelings of love, and despite spending much of its time in the stars it is the most 'grounded' of the songs on *Astral Weeks*. It is also closest to what Morrison would be doing over the next three years. Beneath the wildness and benign, ramshackle quality, the arrangement hints at some anxiety as well as bliss. The lyrical insistence on just how young lovers should behave suggests some perceived discrepancy with how the couple in the song conduct their affair, and the tension underlying the brightness of the music reflects this. The togetherness in the song seems to take place in a fantastical realm, with the couple sitting on their own star, dreaming of the way they are and how they want to be; there seems to be some vexation at the difference between the imagined and the real. There's a link back here too, to 'The Smile You Smile (I Love You)' from the Bang sessions, where Van had sung '[S]itting between two stars / And say that's my point of view'. There's togetherness here, but defended singularity too.[30]

This is one of the key themes of the album, and in their expression of both energy and vexation, of desire and frustration, the music and lyrics of this song deliver as powerfully as any other of the songs gathered together here. Taking the opportunity to quote from a track featured on his beloved *Ray Charles At Newport*, Morrison delivers a nice internal rhyme with 'The night-time, that's the right time'. The connection between this jazzy number and Ray Charles's debuting of his harder jazz sound at Newport in 1959 is an intriguing point of contact. Mixing musical styles while retaining integrity and unity is something that Morrison picked up from Ray Charles and 'Young Lovers Do' shows the pupil has learned much from the teacher, in terms of its internal dynamics and also how it relates and lends meaning to the material which surrounds it.

Maria McKee's 1993 album *You Gotta Sin To Get Saved* contains versions of both 'Young Lovers Do' and the Them number 'My Lonely Sad Eyes'. I asked her about her interest:

> PM: So when you came to record *You Got To Sin To Get Saved*, why did you choose to cover 'Young Lovers Do'?
>
> MM: Well by that stage I knew Van a little, I'd been living in Dublin for a few years and I wanted to do something from him, maybe that not everybody knew . . . it's hard to take a song out of *Astral Weeks* and get it alone, y'know? But 'Young Lovers Do' I adored, then and now, it's a delight and a challenge to sing. And the way he sings it too . . . oh I just love the feel on that, it's so all out there.[31]

Her take on 'Young Lovers Do' is risky, getting the song alone, but it yields some great rewards. It begins with a skirl of semi-acoustic, and accentuates the dance pulse at the centre of the song; the brass is here, but mixed lower than on the original. McKee is one of the best female vocalists of the post-punk era yet the vocal line tests her limits and her technique – her performance is wild and scatty, as the song permits, but equally it observes the constraints that such freedoms demand as well as offer. This reminds us what a remarkable thing Morrison's voice is on *Astral Weeks*, holding together the wildness and the chaos alongside the technique and the measured deployment of the performance – the freedom and the control being explored and exerted in the single moment. This is one of 'Young Lovers Do''s gifts to its parent album and, I'd argue, it functions perfectly harmoniously with the thematic and compositional strands running through the record as a whole. It also links the climax of Side One's emotional accumulation to the more melancholic and measured comedown on Side Two by mixing desire and frustration so potently in musical and lyrical discourses. It is bold, vigorous and certainly, as Maria McKee said, 'all out there'.[32]

'Madame George' must be hard to live next door to. Morrison mentioned that 'I actually recorded *Astral Weeks* three times'[33] and we have evidence of the first or second time, via the Bang sessions version, recorded in November of 1967 under the production of Bert Berns at Century Sound, the same place at which *Astral Weeks* as we know it would be recorded less than a year later. As with the lyric to its companion piece, 'Cyprus Avenue', the words to 'Madame George' are both evocative of the spirit of place while being almost completely free of specific detail. They are a series of cinematic tableaux that cumulatively come to 'mean', according to the tendencies of each individual listener, and indeed perhaps each individual listen. *Astral Weeks* is not fixed; it is free. That is the point.

So the Bang 'Madame George', though it struggles against the 'forty or so people' that Bert Berns brought to the session (it sounds like it, too), shares with its younger self a vocal melody which is remarkably unchanged between the two versions. All else changes though: it is initially unrecognisable, opening with Morrison's voice delivering the unlikely command 'Put yer fur boots on' in an accent pure East Belfast – hear that 'fur'! Some rather stilted party-time banter ensues before the track lurches to its feet, and the lead vocal, with a few lewd exceptions, maps out the form we hear on *Astral Weeks*, albeit struggling to make itself heard above the deliberately ragged and shambolic arrangement. That 'deliberately' means fake, in this case. We also get a tambourine, an upturned bucket drum sound, a rambling guitar line and the rock solid Sweet Inspirations, featuring Cissy Houston, Sylvia Shernwell, Myrna Smith and Estelle Brown. They keep on track while the track purposefully falls raggedly about. While not without virtue, one would not listen to this recording and hear a song one rearrangement away from classic status.[34] It's curious that a track which strives so hard to sound 'live' ends up sounding utterly theatrical and stagey, while the *Astral Weeks* version sounds so complex and texturally rich that we might assume hours of labour spent. However, Morrison noted later that 'Madame George' was 'recorded live . . . the vocal was live and the rhythm section and the flute too and the strings were the only overdub . . . The song is basically about a spiritual feeling'.[35]

It begins, in the *Astral Weeks* way, with strummed acoustic but not-quite-folk guitar; it has a muted quality that suggests an overcast ambiguity, something poised between hope and despair. Anyone not picking up the correspondence between 'Cyprus Avenue' and this in terms of atmospheres is directed to the opening lines: 'Down the Cyprus Avenue / With the childlike visions leaping into view'. We note that they are, whatever their nature, 'childlike' and not childish – this is not a renunciation of the younger self, but rather what Morrison would later call 'a sense of wonder'. It also alerts us to how art might both preserve and permit access to such feelings even when age or experience has made the ordinary life more stale. Think of the moving finale to 2002's 'The Beauty Of The Days Gone By', when he asks for the memory of that beauty and the wisdom it brought to 'keep me young as I grow old'.[36]

So it is testament to the 'Afterwards' version of 'Madame George' that the blues structure is abandoned – both 'Astral Weeks' and 'Cyprus Avenue' use a cyclic model, where their structures return to their opening verses and then proceed to their conclusions via free-form codas. 'Madame George' only repeats a single musical line that changes yet remains the same:

> Ford and Fitzroy, Madame George . . .
> Happy taking Madame George . . .
> Into the eyes of Madame George . . .
> The one and only Madame George . . .[37]

and a grouped set of rhymes at the far end of the song, 'Wonder why . . . Dry your eye . . . say goodbye'. It is this line around which the song is constructed, so that the linear becomes cyclic. Lester Bangs wrote of the song that:

> [I]t is the album's whirlpool. Possibly one of the most compassionate pieces of music ever made, it asks us, no, arranges that we see the plight of what I'll be brutal and call a lovelorn drag queen with such intense empathy that when the singer hurts him, we do too . . . Morrison has said in at least one interview that the song has nothing to do with any kind of transvestite – at least as far as he knows, he is quick to add – but that's bullshit.[38]

I wouldn't necessarily call the song the album's whirlpool but I do like the feel of that phrase. Bangs perhaps means that all the rest of the record is dragged down and absorbed into it, and this tallies with his assertion that the whole of the album sounds like its maker was in great pain, and that this song is somehow the centre which pulls all other activity into itself and the song has certainly often been the central feature of the writing about the record, often eliciting the dramatic mode that Bangs characteristically employs here.

Gerald Dawe's view was somewhat broader and pan-culturally based: while calling it 'the key lyric in *Astral Weeks*', he also cites it as a cultural ever-present in the Belfast he knew of 1969–70, and how that period corresponded to a break-up of the world that he and Morrison had grown up with. 'Madame George captured that feeling, and still does. It was the strange quiet before the storm', he wrote. Dawe describes the song as an 'ashling', that is, a term from Old Irish, the aislinge, a dream or vision. In doing so he deliberately connects Morrison's work with a much older tradition of creativity and a specifically Irish tradition of ways of seeing and feeling.[39] Dawe's contribution to thinking about the song is at its best in his connection of the 'old' Belfast to Morrison's evocation of it on the cusp of its disappearance. That Morrison could not have known or anticipated what was to happen simply deepens and widens the song's resonances from a lost world of childhood – 'Throwing pennies at the bridges down below / In the rain hail sleet and snow' – to a wider sense of loss that the entire community was about to suffer. According to Gerald Dawe:

> 'Madame George' is a portrait of a society about to withdraw from public view at the same time as the voice which describes it is also leaving the scene. Memories shift and coalesce. The site of the poem blurs and moves in and out of focus. It is the Belfast of Cypress Avenue; there is a Fitzroy Avenue too. The rituals of collecting bottle-tops/Going for cigarettes and matches in the shops are identifiably Belfast. But the journey is on a train from Dublin up to Sandy Row. Parsing the song in this fashion does not take us far. What is constant is the voice and the connections which the accent makes between raps, cops, drops and gots.[40]

Dawe is right to draw attention to the role of Morrison's accent – in the Bang version we heard it unmistakably, in 'Put yer fur boots on!' – and some of the song's enduring ability to speak of the city even to those who do not know it is encoded within that accent. Dawe wrote about hearing a particular line:

> The shock of hearing the phrase, 'On a train from Dublin up to Sandy Row' has never quite left me. An inexplicable connection, coded beneath the words themselves, identified for the first time the actual city in which I lived.[41]

Yet the song touches and connects with people who have never been to, never mind lived, in Belfast, so that cannot wholly explain the impact the song has made. We might find the connection in his allusion to something which is 'coded beneath the words themselves' – something which transcends the local frames of reference, just as we might listen to some Roma or Portuguese or Inuit music and be moved by it without necessarily 'understanding' the lyrics, or even the cultural use to which any given song might be fit or put. We do not need to have lived in these places or know the social rituals in order to feel their significance or their power. These things reside in the music, informed as it may be by these ideas and places, but nonetheless the music must stand independent of them in order to endure.

So the song opens with a double-back to the avenue of trees: 'Down the Cyprus Avenue / With the childlike visions leaping into view', from whence stemmed Gerald Dawe's 'ashling'. This is followed by the sound of the female footfall ('The clicking-clacking of the high-heel shoe'), linking the figure to that of Madame Joy (a song considered later in this section) on her way up to the university and the signifier of the high-heeled shoe, an image of sophistication and perhaps decadence, on the cobbles is in itself an image of cultural juxtaposition but also of a unity. Dawe writes rather beautifully of East Belfast being 'a scallop-shell of class segregation' in this era, where the working-class district would face the waters of Lough Erne following the crescent of the shore, so that working- and middle-class districts were arranged like layers of an onion away from the Loughside but thus had long areas of cheek-by-jowl contact.[42] At 0.36 we are given some co-ordinates: 'Ford and Fitzroy, Madame George'. The reference to the soldier boy at 0.44 of course now carries a resonance for us that Morrison could not possibly have anticipated in 1966/67 when he first wrote this song. Northern Ireland was on the brink of being in the grip of soldier boys, both British and Irish, for a generation. The song is an unconscious lament for the passing of this old Belfast, the Belfast of the free movement between Dublin and Sandy Row, one that was yet to come. This elegiac quality is part of its enduring potency and capacity to move. In the lyric, the boy is 'much older now, with hat on, drinking wine', all signifiers and assertions of his having changed – the hat, the wine, instead of the bareheaded boy in the rain, hail, sleet and snow going for matches in the shops. The introduction of very low-level, loose-limbed marching drums and fife behind the images of the soldier emphasise both the fullness of the moment and also the deeper and wider cultural resonance for the contemporary listener.

An allusion to 'sweet perfume' on the cool night air intrigues – it is exact ('*that* sweet perfume'), as if it could not be any other, but then becomes only '*like* Shalimar', the brand name of a perfume made by perfumier Guerlain that was very popular in the mid-1950s, evocative of the first stirrings of normal life returning after the end of rationing in the UK. It took its name (as did a 1980s pop-soul group) from the Shalimar Gardens, built in Lahore by Moghul Shah Jahan in the mid-1600s and still in existence in modern Pakistan with UNESCO World Heritage Site status. The gardens were famed for their heady and intoxicating scents, and the musky heaviness and extravagant exoticism of the Guerlain perfume lent the product a dangerous and memorable presence. Morrison's evocation of perfume both natural and man-made and associated with a deep and enduring mythology appeals to and satisfies both the senses in the present moment and the encoded eternal within that present 'now'.

The camera gaze then moves outside, to the world of the street and of childhood, with the trams stopping, the kids collecting bottle tops, being sent to the shops for cigarettes and matches – all moving details of ordinary life being lived ordinarily, unconsciously even, but with a sense of melancholy by the narrator who is outside looking in. The word 'fall' is key here in understanding the narrator's relationship to his material: 'Oh that's when you fall / Oh that's when you fall', the repetition harking back to blues structures, and also pointing forward to the unexpected second half of this apparently complete and moral assertion. Morrison uses the biblical term for the original sin, 'Fall', but it is also one with impeccable existential credentials, with *The Fall* being the English title of Albert Camus' last novel, published in 1956, its French title being *La Chute*. The lyric flows on: 'And you fall into a trance'. So that's *where*, as well as *when* we fall. The verse which comes closest to recapturing the sleazy mood of the Bang version makes reference to the arrival of the cops and 'immediately drops everything she got / Down into the street below', which, if multiple interpreters are to be believed, represents a rare Morrison reference to a scene involving narcotics. I'm not convinced that the 'everything' necessarily refers to, say, a stash of dope, but it is clearly something that needs to be hidden, a secret – and we all have plenty of those.

At the close of this section of the song, Morrison serves up a quintet of end rhymes ('below', 'go', 'Row', 'below', 'snow') which spin the song around, dizzying the senses, and adding to the perceived potency of the lines about Sandy Row which Gerald Dawe highlighted. Part of their power is of course the framework and structure in which they appear but also in *how they are sung*. That last line, 'In the rain, hail, sleet and snow' (3.50–54), encompasses the poetry of ordinary life in its rhythm, its lilt and its discovery of the marvellous in the ordinary. Morrison's ability to do this – to move from the mundane to the miraculous simply by gesturing towards it – is a key element of his methodology and his gift.

The coda of the song, by which I mean, broadly, the portion of the recording from 5.55 to the end, incorporating as it does the gulp for air that occurs at

7.06–59 when the song surges up again, follows. Like those of 'Cyprus Avenue' and 'Astral Weeks', it slowly spins away from us and has an enduring presence in his live set, with the 'Way down home in the backstreet' section turning up in live versions of other related works such as 'The Healing Game' and 'Celtic New Year', right up to the present. For songs concerned with identifying the eternal in the passing moment this is entirely fitting. Like the other songs here we get the sense of these songs not quite having a beginning or an end in the traditional sense, that these songs may be simply excerpts from a music which is playing all the time, and that these few minutes of it that we have on and as *Astral Weeks* are merely examples of where we or the players have been able to tune into it. The song exercises all the senses: the childlike vision, the clicking-clacking of the high-heeled shoe (as opposed to the fur boots of the Bang take), the sweet perfume, the touch in the glove, and taste, in the entwined sensual swirling of the tongue in the central 'love that loves' motif. It fully engages and tests all the senses.

As Dawe says, a kind of 'prac. crit.' on the lyrics reveals only part of what happens when we hear 'Madame George' or indeed any of these songs: it is the sound which lends much of the meaning and/or significance to them. Look for example at the lines 'And as you leave the room is filled with music / Laughing music, dancing music all around the room'. Until sitting down to write about it I had never even wondered what these lines actually were, although I have heard the song times without number. They are delivered as a continuous slur of sound, tight, loose, loud, soft, harsh, gentle – pure creativity in sound. In order to understand it, you have to hear it. But I need to write about it. The swirling of the 'love to love' section is that of desire, of sensuality, of tongues moving together so that it is impossible to tell where one person begins and the other ends; it is love in sound. The song contains strange snapshots of claustrophobic interiors where curious figures skulk, and also sweeping images of the island of Ireland. It presents an image of the place on both the micro and macro scale. Lest we forget, too, George is Morrison's Christian name, and was his father's too.

The song also records the ecstasy and melancholia of parting: it is a break from the world which has been and an embrace of the world as it might be. Howsoever eager that enfolding of a new reality is, the lingering farewell to the old is felt deeply in the slow lingering coda of 'Madame George' ('Say goodbye, goodbye, goodbye . . .') and the parting soul kiss ('the love that loves . . .') that connects and disconnects in a single moment. This is the fracture that Gerald Dawe alludes to when he calls the song 'a portrait of a society about to withdraw from public view'. This particular image and section has proven one of Morrison's most enduring pieces of work, and one need only to listen to, say, Maria McKee's 'Panic Beach' or David Gray's cover of Soft Cell's 'Say Hello Wave Goodbye' to hear how its mood and feeling have been passed on.[43] We can compare this lingering parting with, say, 'Goodbye Baby (Baby Goodbye)', one of Bert Berns's songs Morrison was obliged to record for *Blowin' Your Mind!*, and its payoff line: 'I'm gonna kiss you one more time and then I'm going away'. This was perhaps in Morrison's mind when he reimagined that farewell as something of significance rather than such a kiss-off. This song is remarkably similar in its constituent elements to 'Cyprus Avenue' and 'Madame George', with its references to one more kiss, one more touch, an ambiguous goodbye, the train coming down the track and the like. There is perhaps even an unacknowledged influence on it: Morrison even uses the phrase 'I'll be on my merry way', which turns up on both 'Beside You' and 'Sweet Thing', and is surely a contribution of Morrison's own coinage to the song.[44]

There is also a shadow at George's elbow: 'Madame Joy', the supposed companion piece to this song. As Morrison told Richie Yorke:

> 'The original title was 'Madame Joy' but the way I wrote it down was 'Madame George'. Don't ask me why I do this because I just don't know. The song is just a stream-of consciousness thing, as is 'Cyprus Avenue' . . . It may have something to do with my great aunt whose name was Joy . . . Apparently she was clairvoyant, that may have something to do with it . . . [she] lived in a street just off Fitzroy Street which is quite near to Cyprus Avenue.'[45]

While the biographical derivations need not detain us, the central status of 'Madame George' was gilded still further when the 'answer song', 'Madame Joy' was issued in 1998. Recorded in 1973, this curious chamber piece describes a woman who works at a university (possibly Queens in Belfast, possibly not) and how her charisma and poise affected 'those men' who watched her walk to work. It was recorded at Morrison's own Caledonia Studios, in Fairfax California with the *It's Too Late To Stop Now* band, a long, long way away from 1960s Belfast. The reference in 'Madame George' to folded arms and history books is a point of connection between the two songs, with Madame Joy walking down to the university 'With her books in her hand . . . to teach them . . . To help them understand'. This curio, although perhaps a somewhat unexceptional song in itself, signposts out to other aspects of the world *of Astral Weeks*, with lyrical references to 'Cyprus Avenue' ('She just kept on walking down the street'), 'Slim Slow Slider' ('looking for her boy') and 'Ballerina' ('Steppin' lightly').[46]

It is the light step of the ballerina which replaces the clicking and clacking of the high-heeled shoe. As Buzacott and Ford note, the move to 'Ballerina' represents the first through-flow of tempo on the album; they also note that some find this unconvincing.[47] It convinces me. The move from 'Madame George' to an image as culturally fully fixed as feminine (as opposed to the embedded ambiguities of the nature and character of Madame George him/herself) as a ballerina traces the shift from the Old World to a New World in which every move is expressive of the inner self, and consciously so. The life lived unconsciously in 'Madame George' is now a focused attention upon the vocabularies of the body, expressing them via a system of techniques and gestures which both celebrate and develop the body, via the unity of music and movement. Surprisingly, the song may pre-date even the Bang era – Them guitarist Jim Armstrong recalled working the song up in the last live days of Morrison's tenure with Them, on their American tour of 1966:

> 'A lot of the stuff we rehearsed was the guts of *Astral Weeks*, like 'Ballerina'. Alan [Henderson], Ray [Elliott] and I sat acoustically with flutes and stuff playing that into a tape recorder. And we used to do 'Ballerina' on that tour, so the band was creative.'[48]

This is perfectly likely – songs don't come from nowhere, and Them were a superb, fully musical outfit – but the sound on this recording is pure, through-composition *Astral Weeks* and as such exemplifies why Morrison had to 'spread his wings', away from Them, and from Belfast.

On its genesis, he observed:

> 'I was in San Francisco one time in 1966 and I was attracted to the city. It was the first time I had been there, and I was sitting in this hotel and all these things were going through my head, and I had a flash about an actress in an opera house appearing in a ballet, and I think that's where the song came from.'[49]

The performative aspect of this source is present in the finished tune. The opening line of 'Ballerina' is 'Spread your wings' – a command to go out into the world and surely a build on the sense of departure at the close of 'Madame George' – we then hear of a '22-storey block' rather than the streets of East Belfast, emphasising the new setting. Morrison's vocal performance here (e.g. at 2.06 or 3.46) makes leaps and unexpected twists and turns which we think at first he will surely not be able to accomplish, yet he does – these are in themselves balletic, the song striving to make real the title via such leaps of sustained faith and daring. The song also has something approaching a chorus, and the repetitions of the title each time provide a cue for some change to be accommodated into the song. It is perhaps his strongest and most assertive vocal on the album: listen to his 'Alright' which calls time on Richard Davis's pulsating single-note solo at 3.36: confident, assertive, calmly in charge of what is happening. His vocal is pitched between this new confidence and the delight of discovering where and how the song can lead them. The 'subject' of the song is freedom itself: 'Grab it, catch it, fly it, sigh it, die it', that is, to live like this is hard and takes discipline but it is worth it. Yet it appears effortless and, in Milan Kundera's phrase, an unbearable lightness of being – 'Stepping lightly' just like a ballerina, which actually requires a profound focus of mind and body in unison. This is what it is to be sentient, and alive, and awake: 'Just like a ballerina'.[50]

This ecstatic state has deliquesced into something darker by the time we reach 'Slim Slow Slider': Morrison described it thus:

> '[The song] is about a person who is caught up in a big city like London or maybe is on dope, I'm not sure. A lot of these songs are not really personal and that's why I have to try to interpret them. A lot of them are just speculations on a subject. I think that's what most of the songs on *Astral Weeks* are, speculation on a given theme.'[51]

We note that Morrison uses the idea of 'a big city like London' and 'is on dope' as distinct, if related conditions – but not synonymous. Transition and change are permanent states, rather than a successful jump from one world to another, as the sweet optimism of 'Ballerina' – look! It's easy! Take off your shoes! – suggested; instead the change, the move forward may feel like a slide backward, away from the light, and the lightness of being that 'Ballerina' describes. The song itself is an exercise in minimal technique, but in the way that Samuel Beckett's work is – that is, in little we discern much. The title of the song provides little more than a sibilant, alliterative opening line; the song concerns someone who may fit the description, but is left otherwise unidentified. The musical evocation is of a wide-open strand at dawn, and a figure moving in the half-light; yet the lyric mentions Ladbroke Grove in inner West London, and its more famous parent district Notting Hill, which also turned up in 'Friday's Child'. Indeed I'd suggest that this song is the dark obverse of the daring if fatalistic optimism of 'Friday's Child'. That brightness has now burned down to a jaded urban languor. The instrumentation comprises acoustic, double bass, flute, soprano sax. The reference to Ladbroke Grove (mistranscribed as 'that brick road' in Yorke's book) evokes a place where unlike in Belfast one cannot be both in the city and on some sandy beach at one and the same time. Thus the beach that the figure in the song stands on must be in the mind, held simultaneously with what the eye sees.

At 3.06 comes the infamous edit, where the song suddenly cuts, and, according to John Payne, we lose 'five to ten minutes of instrumental jamming, semi-baroque and jazz stuff'[52] memorably described by Buzacott and Ford as 'like a piece of paper caught up in a whirlwind',[53] an insightful image reflecting the condition of being carried by events, and of the risks of freedom. Certainties that seem established are suddenly and without warning swept away and the world is revealed as other than how it seemed. 'Slim Slow Slider' itself seems attuned to this kind of disruption, as a kind of sentinel and also advanced notice of it, a sort of symbolic annunciation which can only be understood in retrospect. John Payne's flute and soprano sax on this track sound, in Payne's own words, 'as if they were coming from across a lake', and this is in part how this tale of inner-city desolation of the soul evokes images of open land by water. Davis's bass part adds both top and bottom to the guitar and vocal, and it is interesting to note that live performances of this song have stuck closely to this arrangement. Unlikely as it seems, this song was the subject of a strange and beautiful cover version very shortly after the album's release. Johnny Rivers called his 1970 album *Slim Slo Slider* and included two versions of the song, alongside a version of 'Into The Mystic'. Some critics sniffed, but Morrison liked the covers, saying that the main reason he 'dug' it was that Rivers 'does it like himself and he doesn't try to do it like anybody else'.[54]

Indeed, through-composition seems to me to be an aspect of that methodology, that way of trying to '[do] it like himself', which absorbs influence from without by processing them from within, so that, as he said about Ray Charles:

> 'You can't really explain Ray Charles, you know, it's . . . *everything* . . . just such a range of emotions, music, everything . . . he could do anything, but whatever he did was still Ray Charles, whatever it was. If he sang 'Mary Had A Little Lamb', it'd still be Ray Charles . . . he's his own genre. It's all Ray Charles music now.'[55]

We can conclude that Morrison's music, too, is its own genre and *Astral Weeks* is a central part of that; it's all Van Morrison music now.

VEEDON FLEECE (1974)

Although Morrison would hint at a return to the kind of methodologies employed on *Astral Weeks* in *Saint Dominic's Preview*'s two sprawling acoustic side-closers, and the 'Green' second side of *Hard Nose The Highway*, it wasn't until *Veedon Fleece* in 1974 that the idea of through-composition returned to fully inform an album's worth of material. It is also his least-explained album, with his most extended comments on the record occupying little more than a single page of Ritchie Yorke's book.[56]

The consequence of a trip around Southern Ireland in the autumn of 1973, this ten-track collection was initially greeted with confusion, frustration or indifference. Surely his next move would have been to take his all-conquering Caledonia Soul Orchestra live band into the studio? Yet this record is so unlike the high drama of the live album that preceded it that most reviews were vexed; even the most sympathetic qualified their praise. 'Van's back on form alright and I don't even care if I can't understand any of it', wrote a young Nick Kent.[57] It was recorded in two blocks, the bulk at Morrison's own Caledonia Studios in Fairfax in November 1973, then, at Warners' request, a brace of songs were cut at New York's Mercury Sound in early spring 1974. Warners, in Tom Petty's phrase, didn't hear a single, and so Morrison gave them 'Bulbs', a cast off from sessions in 1972, and a new song, 'Cul de Sac'.

The album seems to revisit some aspects of the sound world of *Astral Weeks*, but with substantial differences: aside from anything else, he was now the senior partner in the deal. No another day, another dollar for the players on these sessions. Checking the credits list we have twinned players for the most part. We can read the first name as player on the Fairfax recordings, the second as player on 'Bulbs' and 'Cul de Sac'. To remind ourselves, Morrison was also wearing a new vocal hat. Instead of singing from the gut, as he had previously done after the manner of the blues singers he so admired, this album, at least in its opening volleys, presented a voice located somewhere further up the chest, a voice produced at the back of the throat, and in the case of the wholly unexpected falsetto, in the head. Like *Astral Weeks*, *Veedon Fleece* possesses a sound that belongs wholly to itself. It doesn't sound a bit 'like' the 1968 record yet it is clearly related to it. This wasn't unprecedented: *Astral Weeks* displayed a variety of aspects of the voice, and *Moondance* too had a range, from 'Crazy Love' to 'Caravan', but here, on the far side of his arrival as a global player on the music scene, the deconstruction of his sound and vocal style was unexpected to say the least.

Where *Astral Weeks* was an exploration of Belfast roots, *Veedon Fleece* draws from Ireland from an outside perspective: witness how the streets of Arklow are not named as they are on *Astral Weeks* (Cyprus Avenue, Ford and Fitzroy, Sandy Row and the rest). He is a visitor, a guest in his own country. It is an album of exile on local and global scales: back from many years across the Atlantic, and across the American landmass itself, out on the West Coast, but he is also a Northern Irishman in the Republic. The intimacy and propinquities of *Astral Weeks* are supplanted by a complex hybrid of Irish and American cross-currents which reflect back upon both place and Morrison's relationship with it. The cyclic return to both the acoustic jazz modes of *Astral Weeks* and Ireland as subject matter both feed into this through-composition.

The album opens with 'Fair Play', a combination of acoustic, hi-hat, acoustic double bass and voice – as I said, it has much in common with *Astral Weeks* without sounding anything like it. Here the lyrics, though pleasingly runic, set his stall out by making a direct reference to Ireland – but not to Belfast – in part by catching the rhythms and commonplace usages of everyday speech. In the song's title he alludes to a distinctively Irish phrase, 'Fair play to you', meaning 'well done', or 'to be fair with you', even if you don't approve of the person or what they have done. The song also refers to Killarney's lakes, a reference which is easy to miss at first as he swallows the first half of the place name (0.22). The tempo, a kind of early-hours last waltz, allows both singer and musicians to wander through the song with some room for manoeuvre; the lyric accumulates like found fragments of a travel journal, spinning from Killarney's lakes to references to paperback books of Oscar Wilde, Henry David Thoreau and Edgar Allen Poe (his reading, perhaps, on the Irish trip). These segue into the chorus of sorts which makes reference to 'Geronimo' and 'Hi Ho Silver', the Lone Ranger's admonishment to his horse on the 50s TV show – a mythic allusion which is picked up in another title on this record. So the two strains of influence – Irishness and American popular culture in the shape of films, TV, literature and music – quietly sublimate here. As such this represents a significant moment in his artistic development. The song observes the *Astral Weeks* through-compositional model in returning to its first verse for its last and then allowing the song to find its own way home via an elliptical, slow winding down.[58]

'Fair Play' also sets the tone for how this record is going to *sound* – the great slabs of sound, the breathtaking surges and ebbs and flows of the musical dynamics of the Caledonia Soul Orchestra era are set aside and instead we have this spare, low-lit acoustic Irish folk-jazz,which murmurs of intimacy rather than the public platform. This is perhaps the reason that despite its apparent simplicity the music proved difficult to reproduce onstage. *Veedon Fleece* is still the least represented album in terms of live performances of its songs in Morrison's catalogue, with the concluding quartet of 'C' songs ('Cul de Sac', 'Comfort You', 'Come Here My Love' and 'Country Fair') having only three dozen outings between them, and the middle two have never been played live by Morrison at all. 'Streets Of Arklow' is the most played cut but even this is very rarely heard and the album's single, and last track to be added, 'Bulbs', only saw a few outings around the time of the album, just before he slipped into the so-called 'period of transition' in the mid-70s.

The mix of complexity and directness is further focused in the way an epic moral fable such as 'Linden Arden Stole The Highlights' is related simply by piano, Jeff Labes's overdubbed strings and, as explored in the Chapter Five of this book, a vocal which redefines Morrison's capacity as a vocal stylist. It is powerful, and recognisably Morrison, but comes from the back of the throat rather than deep in the chest. As we discovered, he has here found another voice, and this voice is one of the key elements of the through-composition of this record. Putting aside some of the blues rasp, it is smoother and somehow more haunting and haunted sounding – the atmosphere of this song is that of the parlour room recital, after the style of the great Irish tenor Count John McCormack, the singer standing stock-still beside the piano, declaiming the song.

The song is a torch ballad about a kind of Irish-Californian samurai and places great emphasis upon the burdens of the body, in contrast to the 'light' lightness of 'Ballerina' and the 'dark' lightness of the 'Slim Slow Slider'. Linden Arden's tale is one of corporeal burden, with references to him being able to fight with one hand behind his back, the whiskey pulsing through his veins, and, most dreadfully, to him beheading his rivals outside the place in which they were drinking, when they come from San Francisco to confront him. As the narrative details mount, Morrison's vocal delivery remains steady, refusing to deviate from the narrative mode until Jeff Labes's string overdub slithers into the mix at 1.45 and unlocks a remarkable escalation in the vocal, already hinted at by Morrison's remarkably graphic, even onomatopoeic pronunciation of 'cleave' at 1.23–24. This corporeal emphasis enforces material realities. Morrison sings of how Linden Arden 'took the law into his own hands': this is a purely physical world, red in tooth and claw, and this realisation sends the song soaring into a kind of hybrid of horror and lament, a kind of refined keening which carries both sentiments simultaneously, and thereby sets both free. Linden Arden had listened to the stories and the answers to his questions but needed to resort to real physical action in order to survive. The control the players exert over their material is exemplified by how Morrison evokes the eruptive moment for this brutal, most physical of characters, and the crime he felt forced to commit: he put his fingers through his glass. It is such a delicate image, which is taken up by the tinkling shards of the piano's answering five-note run (1.55–58), one for each finger Linden Arden puts through that symbolic glass.

This song and narrative feel rooted in the pulp cowboy fiction of Morrison's youth – the Wild West as a frontier between law and lawlessness, between old and new worlds. This grittily idealised vision of the West is a subtheme of the opening of the album, with the Lone Ranger references in 'Fair Play', in this song, and particularly the next. Yet 'Linden Arden' references the brutal realities of such a life, as opposed to the rounded homilies of Hollywood or the cowboy novel. The moral ambiguities of some of Zane Grey's work, most notably *Riders of the Purple Sage*,[59] inform this take on life at the frontier, but it stands as a fable from which it is hard to draw a clear and simple moral. 'Linden Arden' is in my view among Morrison's finest songs and performances.[60] Making plain the narrative link and the importance of through-composition to this album, the last line of the second song becomes the first line of the third.

'Who Was That Masked Man?' clearly takes its title from the cry of the villain or townsfolk in the Lone Ranger stories, and the phrase has a cultural resonance both comic and profound. Morrison was an artist on the cusp of effecting a disappearing act, and one who was well aware of the risks of revealing one's identity in public too readily. So the title is humorous, but it's not a joke. Likewise, this cut debuts Morrison's full-on falsetto; indeed the song opens with it, taking the first line a cappella before the band drops in on the word 'lonely', with again an acoustic guitar playing a sticky, The Band-style lead role and the metronomic tick of a rimshot providing the rhythm. A blusier piano than the grand neo-recital style of 'Linden Arden' tugs away under the vocal with dramatic minor chords. Morrison's vocal is a surprise to hear, a very high and accomplished falsetto. Where 'Linden Arden' starts with a rendition of its unwieldy title, this song shuns any mention of its title anywhere in the lyric, locking instead on a psychological sketch of a wanted man – it could be part two of the previous narrative in some ways but, of course, everyone knew who 'Linden Arden' was: he hid nothing. In this song, the subject is lonely and on the run, 'living with a gun'. The musical setting is appropriately lean, and shot through with a steady yet fraught anxiety. The lyric has a self-justifying rationale; it includes a reference to being 'well protected by the glass', the screen which we have just seen breaking down. The lyrics are the thoughts of a fugitive in the wee small hours, fevered and meditative at one and the same moment; this narrator clings to the idea that good and evil are not moral absolutes, and that all men are capable of both: 'the hand does fit the glove'. This delivers some resolve to the confusion. Morrison said that the song was 'about what it's like when you absolutely cannot trust anybody. Not in some paranoia, but in reality . . . The guy is just stuck in a house with a gun and that's it period'.[61] That block on further interpretation is a familiar reflex of course.

Sinéad O'Connor had another response to this unexpected theme of deep dark violence in the butchery of 'Linden Arden' and the safe-house purgatory of 'Who Was That Masked Man?', discussing the album with Dave Fanning on Irish radio:

> 'I think this [*Veedon Fleece*] is far superior to *Astral Weeks*, and I love *Astral Weeks*, but this is to me the most definitive Van album altogether . . . the finest song of Van's is 'Who Was That Masked Man?' It's a supreme piece of songwriting; I've never heard him sing in falsetto either, apart from anything else . . . it's a kind of Curtis Mayfield type of voice.
>
> He managed to avert [*sic*] ever dealing with the political situation but I think

> this ['Who Was That Masked Man?'] does deal with a lot of the political situation . . . politically he's never approached Ireland, except for me in this one song which I think is an incredible insight into what was going on in those times in his country as such, y'know?
>
> Linden Arden is . . . a gangster type character [Dave Fanning: 'Very violent, unusual for Van.'] and the song is a very subtle comment on what was going on between Ireland and America in terms of assisting what was going on.'[62]

Sinéad O'Connor's high praise for the song and its parent album stems in part from her admiration of Morrison's art ('it's a supreme piece of songwriting'), and also his ability to allude and elude in reference to 'what was going on in those times in his country'. She identifies a connection between the iconographies of 50s popular culture, evident in this song's title, with the realities of the 1970s in 'his country'. This is part of the connective strand that runs through the songs on this record – the regarding of the homeland as a place which in itself is a cultural composite. In order to see this one needs to leave and then return as a stranger, even if that return is purely one conducted via the creative imagination informed by memory. Thus we see how a record like *Veedon Fleece* is connected to the body of work made by Irish artists in exile – Joyce's Dublin, reinvented in Zurich, Paris and Trieste, Sean O'Casey's Ireland, coined in London and rural Devon, the Irish landscape felt as much as seen by Samuel Beckett in Paris – all unimaginable, in every sense, had they been writing within the island of Ireland itself. This culture of exile, later explicitly developed as an idea by Morrison, is strong and is absolutely central to the mingling of aching fondness and slow-chilling of the blood which runs through the songs on *Veedon Fleece*.

This sense of exile in one's own land is further pursued in 'Streets Of Arklow'. It delves deeper again into the established mood, opening with lugubrious, ominous rhythms and acoustic guitar picking. Given this beginning, we might not expect a lyric of refreshment and willing abandonment to the moment, yet that is to some extent what we get, despite the music and the lyrics not duplicating each other's mood exactly. This is at one level a song of joy coming out of darkness – 'And the morning, coming on to dawn' – but it does not necessarily sound like it. The slow, thoughtful tread of the music matches the cautious mood of the lyric as the song develops, and the light slowly illuminates the scene, the flooding of the land with light mirrored in their own internal awakening of a kind: 'And our souls were cleaned, and the grass did grow'. This duality, being aware of the physical and the metaphysical realms, sees both benefiting from the return of the light, and furthermore demystifies both, placing them on a plane of natural order.

Drifting through the song is a Morrison perennial, the figure of the wandering gypsy. He focuses more fully on these figures in 'Caravan' or 'Gypsy' but here they simply stand as ghostly yet material representative figures of freedom: 'We love to wander . . . we love to roam'. They do not belong in the fixed topographies of the town (the mapped, named, fixed streets of Arklow), yet their presence there introduces another type of balance to the song (joining the light/dark, human/non-human, physical/metaphysical pairings), between the free and the fixed, the wandering and the rooted. Morrison and his party (the 'we') of the song are pitched somewhere between the two here, not quite belonging to either side of the equation, being in transit but not perpetually so. The gypsies – a nation without a territory – represent another way of understanding place, nationhood and belonging which sets aside what Sinéad O'Connor described as 'what was going on in those times in his country'.

It is not so much that Ireland is a place of mystery, imagination and dreams (a kind of tourist-brochure view) but rather that the place, and the idea of it, unlocks these elements within Morrison's own creativity. The song itself employs certain rhetoric of the folk song – the title relates to the strain of 'street' songs, such as 'Streets of Laredo', the second cousin of 'Saint James Infirmary', or even Ralph McTell's busker's favourite 'Streets Of London'. Unlike those songs, Morrison's song does not deliver a full and coherent narrative – like much of the rest of this record it achieves its aims by alluding and suggesting rather than unravelling a tale *in toto*. The instrumentation is, again, close to that familiar from *Astral Weeks* but the structures are at once more fully realized and less expansive. with the upright bass, the piano, the acoustic snapping out anxious strips of notes, the vocal starting low and climbing as the song progresses, all wreathed around by the ambiguous half-light cast by Jim Rothermel's flute, sounding fully like a one-take performance. It is never less than a brooding meditation upon the nature of place; despite it seeming a pleasurable experience, the sound of that experience is troubled, as if the revelation sought has brought not only illumination.[63]

Why Arklow? Well, firstly, he was there. The town is south of Dublin on the County Wicklow coast, and was once a centre for boatbuilding and a destination for itinerant mariners. It is thus an industrial centre that faces out to sea, and this combination of the grounded and exile may have appealed to Morrison; of course he may just have found a mood unlocked during his time there. The Tom Collins photograph of him with two Irish wolfhounds which graces the album cover of *Veedon Fleece* was taken at Shelton Abbey, the ancestral home of the Howard family, Earls of Wicklow, just North of Arklow, and the dogs supposedly belonged to Irish-American writer J. P. Donleavy, whom Morrison had visited on this 1973 holiday.[64]

The song concludes dramatically and in real time, as do all the songs recorded in California for this album; only 'Cul de Sac', from the New York sessions, fades. The songs are performed as set pieces, which observe the Aristotelian mode having a beginning, a middle and an end – even the gorgeously light-headed slow waltz of 'Fair Play', which drifts towards its conclusion that comes with a repetition of the title and a ringing piano triad. So the streets of Arklow, referenced so intensely here, are a route map of another sort – to a kind of internal discovery, made manifest in the material world: 'Our souls were cleaned, and the grass did grow'. As Morrison said, 'I wrote a song about what I was feeling while we checked it [Arklow] out'.[65] The town illuminates the natural world and thereby the soul.

This is a road travelled even further in the concluding track on Side One of the vinyl album, and, I'd suggest, has to stand where it does. The streets of Arklow lead to the threshold of 'You Don't Pull No Punches But You Don't Push the River'. Morrison's mood was clearly expansive and open to discovery and is reflected as such in the song titles on this record. When on 26 November 1922 Lord Carnavon asked Howard Carter what he could see on peering into the gloom of the newly opened tomb of Tutankhamen, he supposedly said that he could see 'Things . . . wonderful things'. This is a way of seeing into 'You Don't Pull No Punches But You Don't Push the River': it is hard to know where to look first, so abundant and startling are its contents. The final, orchestrated note at 8.41 is the drawing to a halt of an extraordinary journey. Where have we arrived, and where have we been? All is the same, yet everything seems changed – this is the power of art. Furthermore, the song takes more than its title from gestalt therapy; central to that thought is the idea that there is a circle of emotional wholeness, in Brian Hinton's phrase, and this album makes that journey both in itself and in its description of that journey having been taken out in the 'real' world of streets, lakes and rivers.

This title, as Johnny Rogan points out, possibly came in part from a book title, *Don't Push the River (It Flows by Itself)*, Barry Stevens's record of experiences of gestalt therapy in Canada in the late 60s, published in 1970. Stevens described herself thus: a 'High School drop-out, 1918, because what she wanted to know, she couldn't learn in school',[66] which, entirely coincidentally but intriguingly, echoes Morrison's comment about his relationship with formal education: 'There was no school for people like me'.[67] Very briefly, gestalt therapy is a technique via which the subject learns, or at least strives to learn, how to distinguish between actually feeling and perceiving something and quantifying and seeking to explain or interpret that same experience. It is also a shedding of habits of such culturally dictated understandings and so illuminates the difference between feeling something and thinking about feeling something. D. H. Lawrence wrote about a similar need to keep distinct the appetites of the body and the contemplation of them, a condition he called 'sex in the head'. This he found almost a crime against human nature itself, and it informs the 'natural' sex of *Lady Chatterley's Lover*. Lawrence's resistance to cure-alls and 'isms' would have made him suspicious of gestalt but there is some natural overlap between the two ideas. The therapeutic element of gestalt is supposed to 'teach' this technique to the subject, so they can change their learned habits of understanding their own experience, becoming aware of what they are doing psychologically and how they can change it. The payoff, and what might have interested Morrison, is the idea that by acquiring the method one might be more fully able to experience the perpetual 'now', while allowing the past to be present but not guide the mood or direction of the moment. This earns the mood we find in 1991's 'On Hyndford Street', here 'it's always being now'.[68]

For an artist so drawn to the meaning, if not the baggage of the past, a method which would reconcile that with living fully in the now would undoubtedly strike a chord with Morrison. Yet it is characteristic of the creative soul that no single set of guidelines or explanations will suffice or answer all its possible questions, and it is so with Morrison. Indeed, just within the realm of this song, he cites Baba, William Blake ('and the Eternals', figures from his *The Book of Urizen*), the Sisters of Mercy and the pleasures of the body as ways of breaking through and finding some kind of 'answer'. Not untypically, the mythological or symbolic models he cites are not those borrowed from any of these cultures or even his own Irish culture, steeped in mythological figures as it is, as Yeats knew well. Instead, he coins his own: the Veedon Fleece. To Ritchie Yorke, he suggested it was 'actually a person's name. I have a whole set of characters in my head that I'm trying to fit into things' and 'I just started singing it in one of the songs as a stream-of-consciousness thing'.[69] Certainly it seems to have had no specific meaning preceding Morrison's use of it – although it has now been borrowed for the name of a textile company in the UK.[70]

Part of the value of Morrison's work is to see how he identifies the 'otherness' of the world shadowing the world we see: as he asks, via Peter Handke's verse in 'Song Of Being A Child', 'Isn't what I see and hear and smell / Just the appearance of the world in front of the world?'[71] In the phrase 'Veedon Fleece', Morrison thus coins a language to describe this otherness: here is the '*IT*' that Sal Paradise and Dean Moriarty were after in *On the Road*. The song provides a summative climax to the first side of the record and supplies the emotional wholeness which seems central to at least part of what we understand as gestalt, arriving at a moment poised between going forward and looking back – and just being, in the here and now. This approach to interpreting and processing experience provides another of the strands of through-composition of this record, directing its tone and mood in a sense as fully and warmly as does the musical soundscape, the instrumentation and arrangements.

Keeping up with the names and images as they flash by us in this song is an experience not unlike watching the astronaut as he is propelled on through time and space at the climax of Stanley Kubrick's *2001: A Space Odyssey.* We see and hear details but they are really merely part of the whole that is at the limit of perception; it simply *is*. So for all the good it does us we can say, for sure, that the Sisters of Mercy, in the words of their own mission statement, are

> women who commit their lives to serving God's people, especially those who are sick, poor and uneducated. In the spirit of the Gospel, our mission is to help people to overcome the obstacles that keep them from living full and dignified lives. A life of prayer and community animates and supports us in our mission.[72]

What enlightenment does this bring in terms of the song and beyond? Perhaps that they too are searching for the 'Veedon Fleece', being the key that unlocks everything but which can only be found by living according to the principles of your mode of enquiry – be that tender mercies, contemplation, philosophy or song. Likewise Blake's 'Eternals' were figures which represented human instincts or habits unleashed from the corporeal frame and so come closer to allegorical figures, resembling that which they represent. They feature in a number of William Blake's longer prophetic works, such as *The Book of Urizen*:

> Eternals I hear your call gladly,
> Dictate swift winged words, & fear not
> To unfold your dark visions of torment.[73]

It's not too fanciful, I'm saying, to connect Blake's idea here with the long strange journey into darkness and light that is 'You Don't Pull No Punches, But You Don't Push the River', with its dictated, swift-winged words' ('a stream-of-consciousness thing') and the 'dark visions of torment' unfolded in its tortured course, like a river flowing to the ocean, with the final, slow note at its resolution (8.41) being that dispersal into the greater body of water. The motif of the wandering spirit is central but also one which moves on in the spirit of enquiry and pursuit of wisdom. The swiftness of cross-reference always puts me in mind of Derek Bell's great, grounding analysis of Morrison's pursuit of what he here called the Veedon Fleece: 'Van wants answers and he wants them now and if you haven't got them you can fuck off.'[74]

The song opens with acoustic guitar, joined at 0.10 by a five-note cycle on the piano and a shaker. Morrison's vocal starts at 0.19 and he scats, making great capital from the simplest of sounds, 'da-da-da'. The lyric arrives, flowing up and out of this sound at 0.42 and to see the words transcribed does little justice to the effect of hearing them sung – of course. Music is experienced via feeling first and reason second, and it's our job to try to somehow connect the two. The *Veedon Fleece* model of performance allows Morrison to expand and extemporise upon and around the sound of the words as he is singing them so that their emotional and dynamic impact is less to do with what he's saying than how he is shaping the sounds. The lyric offers little in the way of coherent, progressive narrative; rather it is a stained-glass array of fragments of thoughts and ideas which, though irregular, in themselves seem to fit organically together to forge a unified whole of remarkable cohesion, integrity and unity.

We can describe the lyrics, so we probably should: the opening section relates a Hardyesque, unspecified encounter between a young man and a girl on some shady lane. Such matters are quickly set aside as the plan to set out and search for whatever is out there is detailed – where they are going to go, and how, and in whose company. It is auspicious company, too: William Blake and the Eternals, the Sisters of Mercy, and 'Baba' or the teacher. The journey is the performance itself, as Morrison voice sweeps up and down the register, often in the space of a single line. Listen to his singing of the title in full for the penultimate time at 8.08–14. The presence of mind on show in the accomplishment, like gently folding wings, of the last seconds, 8.28–41 is in itself pure experient poetry, like the return home of a friend thought lost, or the settling of a bird at dusk.

Jeff Labes introduces shivering strings as Morrison riffs around the title at 4.20–44 and 6.00–38; they fall into pizzicato briefly before resuming their vibrating buzz behind the flute part of Jon Rothermel. They deliver a skewed nod to Hollywood programme music's idea of 'Native American style' music, familiar from Western movies, at 6.54, surely a musical allusion to the earlier references to childhood visions of the Wild West. Indeed the lyric briefly alludes to 'the West', which is taken to mean the west coast of Ireland, via the biographical context, but it need not necessarily be. It might just as easily be the American west, with its beaches and cathedrals in San Francisco and Los Angeles, or indeed anywhere: everywhere has a west. This is a specific model with a universal reach. Likewise at 7.19, he mentions 'contemplating Baba' and I would suggest that here the term is used in its most general sense of 'teacher', and not a specific 'celebrity' guru.

Labes's string arrangement in this final quarter of the cut is worthy of special mention, as it echoes the ebb and flow of the movement of the river, and in its final seconds concludes the song with a resolution both deeply satisfying and spiritually ambiguous enough to suggest that full conclusion may still be tantalisingly out of reach. The title, in itself nonsensical, when repeated in the four sections of the song, takes on (like the idea of the Veedon Fleece itself) a kind of logic and accrues layers of meaning firstly through repetition but also, in Seamus Heaney's phrase, via the force of assertion.[75] 'Veedon Fleece' is the name this moment, feeling or place is given and, although the mythological terms of reference are intensely, even eccentrically personal, its representative status as the goal and focus of concentrated human activity down through the ages renders it a universal object of curiosity and desire. The tentative suggestion of resolution at the song's close leaves just enough room for the listener to find a way into that search. We are neither excluded nor spoon-fed; we are by implication among all these figures 'Searching for the Veedon Fleece'.[76]

Opening the album's second side, and one of the two non-Fairfax cuts on *Veedon Fleece*, 'Bulbs' was added to the record when Warner Bros. wanted the album to be longer, and to have a single to promote it with – so Morrison, with perhaps some heaviness of heart, went into New York's Mercury Sound studios in March 1974 and recorded the song for a second time. It had previously been recorded in 1972 during sessions which resulted in *Hard Nose The Highway*, so was by no stretch of the imagination a new song. It has a harmonic similarity to Joe South's 'Games People Play' hit of 1970, and probably stretches back almost that far, and a very FM radio-friendly sheen which the rest of the album eschews. Opening with some broad strokes on the acoustic guitar, the bass folds in at 0.11, with the vocal following at 0.13, and it is clear from the outset that this is a completely *American* song. The opening verse alludes to a football game as an uneasy sort of metaphor for the music business, and in doing so uses the American vernacular as easily as 'Fair Play' does the Irish. The band tips in at 0.34, initially via an open hi-hat, and then a country-rock rhythm is picked up by rimshots on the snare, alongside the electric guitar, wearing its best pedal-steel effect, and the album's signature blues piano. After the first run through the verse/chorus structure, the rhythm picks up another notch and the snare is worked over by brushes. While the track explicitly resists the thud of a rock track, we suddenly notice that Side One has been completely free of electric instrumentation.

Morrison's vocal on 'Bulbs' is something of a revelation in itself, despite the circumstances of the recording. If this album does anything, it allows Morrison to experiment with vocal techniques in the way that he had not done so readily on his previous post-*Astral Weeks* studio albums. On this single track he wails high, delivers some basso-Satchmo scat and draws out the power of the extended vowel sound ('screamiiiing' at 3.28–29). In fact, the song swings very nicely, and despite being anomalous in terms of recording and writing, it does not digress substantially from the through-composition nature of the album. It is, however, the first time we hear an electric guitar on the album, and this is a

New York feature – only 'Cul de Sac' also has it. The middle section is divided into two parts: the 'Joe South' section (1.38–2.00), with the 'la-la's' being very close kin to 'Games People Play', gives way to a deep section I can best describe as meditative scat, borrowing from Louis Armstrong, King Pleasure and Paul Robeson in equal measure (2.01–23). The lyrics of this song are light: it is the sound of the song as a whole which is its virtue, and marks it out as a hidden pleasure in his repertoire. However, we can note that the bulbs of the title are electric ones, and not those of Wordsworth's daffodils. The song begins to really cook at 2.44, with the line 'It was outside . . .', and the final lyric is a kind of self-admonishment, from the singer to himself: 'All you gotta remember, is after all, it's all showbiz'. A return to the 'Joe South' section follows, leading up to the final vocal section from 3.26, with some impressive open-throated extrapolation of syllables on 'screaming' and 'hear'; it has very precise and satisfying resolution. So, a minor work, but one which is a showcase for his experiments with vocalising techniques at this time.[77]

It is followed by its New York neighbour, 'Cul de Sac', a song also recorded in California but finished at Mercury Sound. Although recognisably from a different session, I'd argue that this song with its steady, stepping piano part, rhythmically marking out the sections of the song, deserves its place here, and contributes fully to both the mood and the flow of the record overall, as part of the 'C' songs which dominate Side Two, and the dual mood of transit and contemplation. This tone is there from the outset, with its intro which traces steps down via piano, bass and drum. Morrison comes in at 0.14 with the title phrase, and in his elongated pronunciation of 'Be' he invests energy as a singer (he leans on the sound for four seconds) and lends emphatic meaning to the word. The business end of this song is what we might call the chorus, although it isn't really such a formally constructed thing. Beginning at 1.15, it introduces another level of melody to the song, with its gorgeous image of travel to the nearest star, and gives this a truncated rhyme with 'Palomar'. The change from the muted rimshots of the intro to the deliciously crisp snap of the snare in this section, particularly under the word 'star' at 1.21, elevates the whole enterprise, and the minute-long section reaches a controlled crisis at 2.18 as he sings 'You will double back . . . to a cul de sac'. He punctuates the line with an aside of 'And this is it', a superb example of one of his vocal techniques which in a sense are as influential to his inheritors as are his more obvious virtues; listen to David Gray, Kevin Rowland or even Marti Pellow for evidence of this and how it has been brought into the commercial mainstream.

The theme of movement which precipitates return is made plain here: every road turns out to be a cul-de-sac, 'not as far as a country mile', because every road leads back to its own beginning. This is the lesson of Side One, via the likes of 'Punches', 'Fair Play', and most obviously 'Streets Of Arklow'. That 'And this is it' is the most important moment in the song though, spoken as much to himself as to anyone else; it is the sound of someone finding the right shape and sound to express what they wanted, or needed, to express. For another example of the same phenomenon, listen to the last seconds of 'Astral Weeks', and the hushed 'Yeah' there signifying the job done. Being in a cul-de-sac, we can also remind ourselves of the question after the close of 'You're My Woman' on *Tupelo Honey*: 'How's that?' It was not an entirely rhetorical enquiry; lost in the moment, maybe it sounded good or maybe it sounded less than good and he needs to know – how's that? Having a vision is not the same as knowing exactly what is going to happen when and where, and the room for improvisation – space for the music to breathe and for something to *happen* – is a key creative element common to all Morrison's most thoroughly through-composition collections, though by no means unique to them, either. So his 'And this is it', I'd suggest, was not scripted or rehearsed, but just a response to where the song was and where it was taking him at that particular time and place. It is the room he has to dig around in freshly discovered areas of his voice which offers final proof of 'Cul de Sac''s place at the table. The scatting from 5.25 right through to the fade picks up the growling debuted in 'Bulbs' and is some of his deepest vocalising on record, in every sense, drawing on the pure sonic experiments on *Astral Weeks* and pointing forward to the outer limits of *Common One*.[78]

'Comfort You' is one of Morrison's unsung love songs; it seems to me to be one of the relatively few grown-up love songs that we have. Alongside it I'd put Paul McCartney's 'Maybe I'm Amazed', XTC's 'I Can't Own Her', Bob Dylan's 'You're A Big Girl Now' or ABBA's 'Like An Angel Passing Through My Room',[79] all bittersweet mixes of desire, loss, frustration and the quiet acceptance that the object of desire cannot be possessed, only reached and connected with, somehow. Morrison spoke about the song in the following way:

> 'I Wanna Comfort You' [the song's pre-release title] is a song about just letting somebody put the weight on you [here we note that he is duplicating, not decoding or 'explaining' the lyric]. Like when things becomes too much for one person to handle . . . having somebody to lean on. The end is like the reverse situation, of you leaning on them.[80]

The dynamics of a relationship are sketched feelingly here, the ebb and flow, the mutual support, the changing polarities, the give and take – a balance which is difficult to maintain but somehow ever-present. Again I need to cite Kevin Rowland, whose devastatingly powerful 'Plan B' from 1981 coins it this way: 'Bill Withers was good to me / Pretend I'm Bill, and lean on me'. The reference to Bill Withers's 1972 hit 'Lean On Me' enables Rowland to evoke the same two-way flow of support and emotional connection.[81] The images of empathy in this song are strong, direct and most moving. As ever on *Veedon Fleece*, the string arrangements of Jeff Labes unify and add greatly to this effect, circling above the song yet pulsing deep in its veins at one and the same time. This image of the inner and outer realms being unified via song matches the lyrical mood very closely, with its emphasis on togetherness and love as tenderness and care, reciprocated. The duality not as part of a deal but as an acknowledgment of a shared vulnerability and humanity. It's remarkable to me that this song is as little known as it is, so mature and uncommon are its articulations of love and fellow feeling.[82]

The continuities between the mood and feel of 'Comfort You' and the opening of 'Come Here My Love' make the songs belong to each other, as the opening trio of songs on Side One do. It is the next stage of comfort and closeness: come here, my love. The ancient green shade of *Astral Weeks* is felt here once more, and the song is unusual in being just guitar and voice, an arrangement not often found in Morrison's catalogue. The song however does not sound like a typical singer-songwriter strum. The guitar resists chords, instead picking its winding way through a complex set of notes, creating a mood poised between the slow Spanish style of the troubadour and the rhythms of a troubling dream. Morrison told Ritchie Yorke that it was 'just a love song', and sidestepped a later enquiry on the subject equally deftly:

> Jonathan Cott: In 'Come Here My Love,' you sing: 'In fathoms of my inner mind/I'm mystified by this mood,/This melancholy feeling that just don't do no good.'
>
> VM: That's it, that says it right there, that's what I'm talking about: I am 'mystified'.
>
> JC: The song continues: 'Come here my love and I will lift my spirits high for you,/I'd like to fly away and spend a day or two/Just contemplating fields and leaves and talking about nothing.'
>
> VM: That's it. Talking about absolutely nothing.[83]

The delight with which he settles on that 'Talking about absolutely nothing' is mischievous – why should he explain anything? This is fair enough – he's given us plenty with the song. But 'nothing' is not an absence – Samuel Beckett was very fond of quoting the aphorism attributed to Democritus, 'Nothing is more real than nothing', and this paradox beats at the heart of Morrison's best work too. Talking about nothing is perhaps 'more real' than talking about 'something' if that something is standing in the way of the truth. 'Nothing' is in touch with deep realities in a way that the confetti of 'somethings' which distract us perhaps are not; thus are love and truth connected. All he would say about it to Yorke was 'it's just a love song'. Morrison would play again with these ideas more directly, if less satisfyingly, on 2008's 'No Thing'.[84]

The existential dimension to this song, so small, brief and yet so cavernous, was picked up in the cover version by This Mortal Coil on their 1986 album *Filigree And Shadow*. On Side Two of the double album, between songs by Judy Collins, Gene Clark and Tim Buckley, the song is barely recognisable from the *Veedon Fleece* original but succeeds in capturing, and building upon, some of the haunted quality of the Morrison album in its mix of textures ancient and modern. The cover cleaves only partly to the melody and is delivered as a kind of Gothic drone, the vocal (credited to 'Jean') mixed far back in the space of the song, as if it were the voice of a ghost or an unborn child, calling the song's subject over to 'the other side'. The phrase 'Come here my love' here possesses a different, dangerous kind of intimacy. In this, the cover points out perhaps unsuspected links between Tim Buckley's 'Song To The Siren' (This Mortal Coil's most famous cover, sung by Elizabeth Fraser of the Cocteau Twins) and 'Come Here My Love' itself.[85] Morrison's vocal, in common with the rest of this record, seeks out corners which it previously has left unexplored. There's a kind of warm weariness in the leaf-edge rasp of his tone which suggests a desire to set aside ceremony and speak directly of desire but also the need for connection: come here, my love.[86]

This gloaming, twilit mood gives way with a seeming natural inevitability to the song cycle's final turn of the wheel, 'Country Fair'. Morrison referred to this song as a revisiting of an emotional space recognisable from *Astral Weeks* and also *Moondance*'s lead-off track, 'And It Stoned Me', but a visitation transformed.

> '"Country Fair" is just about things that you remember happening to you when you were a kid. You could say it's a bit like "And It Stoned Me", it has the same kind of feeling anyway. It's the same kind of idea but it's not fishing.'[87]

Quite. But the evocation of an idyll, now remembered as the dews of night arise, seems by accident or design an apposite place to draw the day of this album to a close. The idyllic moment detailed in 'And It Stoned Me', 'Redwood Tree' and even 'Coney Island' is reflected back upon the song here, where the younger selves were 'too young to really know', and time was like sand slipping through their hands, an image of children at careless play in the sweet summertime which is remarkably affecting. The river flows, reflecting the passage of time back at the narrator: same river, different moment. Always the same, always different. Morrison would make this traditional connection between the flow of the river and the flow of time more directly in 1983's 'River Of Time', but here the whole landscape seems allegorical, as if seen in a medieval painting.

As in 'Country Fair', 'And It Stoned Me' seems to strongly evoke atmospheres within the outside world which reflect the internal life, so that the happiness and joyousness of life felt by the boys in the song somehow brings about the events of the song. The kindness of the old man who gives them the bottles of drink from his great big gallon jar, the good fortune of the pick-up truck being hailed, and stopping, at the last minute, the wish that it won't rain all day, followed by 'Then the rain let up, and the sun came up' – there is an atmosphere of harmoniousness and correspondence between desire and experience which is free and uncluttered, undenied and undeniable. These moments may be mistaken as the natural order but are also celebrated and noticed as rare and special: 'And it stoned me to my soul'. They are not like other special events we notice, but just like Jelly Roll (i.e. analogous to the joy of listening to music) and just like going home (a key desire of the blues idiom, and certainly of Morrison's own repertoire). Thus the everyday, the easily overlooked, the oft-repeated experience is revealed as a continuously flowing source of something marvellous.

Beyond the heat of the day, and the heat of experience, lies 'Country Fair'. Where the former song is concerned with quicksilver movement, intense awareness of the body and its relationship to the world and the elemental forces that surround it, 'Country Fair' is a phase of reflection, of absolute stillness, stunningly realized in song and in sound. The heat and motion of 'And It Stoned Me' has coalesced into a Vishnu-pool of contemplation; limbs grown heavy and tired, like Blake's evocations of children in the moment between waking and sleeping in 'The Echoing Green'. The motion is now the river of time: 'We stood and watched the river flow / We were too young to really know / In the country fair'. The battle between sun and rain has ceased 'In the cool night air', and they are now allies 'On an old rainshine open day'. The term 'open day' has double resonance here – there is an openness of the spirit, and 'open day' is a euphemism for a fair or a carnival, some kind of communal celebration within a locality of town or village, which by its annual nature serves as a marker of another year of our mortal spin having passed. It is likewise an acknowledgement of the season cycle, an enduring source of inspiration and image for Morrison, and something towards which he is acutely and intuitively sensitive – consider Side Two of *Hard Nose The Highway*, 'High Summer', 'A Sense Of Wonder', 'Snow In San Anselmo', 'Fire In The Belly' and so on.

Where 'And It Stoned Me' is a report fresh from the instant of experience and discovery, here there is reflection, looking back on such a moment and thereby reading it differently; the state of Experience looking back at the state of Innocence. By definition, the state of Innocence excludes self-consciousness of its fleeting nature – 'We laid out in the long green grass / And never thought that it would pass' – and this observation infers that it has, indeed, passed into memory. The objects which surround the 'We' of the song now seem loaded with significance of a different kind – the grass, the pine cones, the pebbles: 'We counted pebbles in the sand / Sand like time slippin' through our hand'. This brings to the song a sense of great timelessness, almost geological and therefore philosophical (how else to seek to understand infinity?) in nature, and this precipitates a shift in the timescale of the song itself. The pebbles on the sand one day will become the sand, and this shift of understanding in the timescale, away from the instant, present moment at hand to an image which gives a flash of insight into the nature of time itself, as well as our own brief yet eternal acquaintance with it make for a remarkable shift of perspective in this song.[88]

What of the internal unity of this album? Nowhere does Morrison refer to the songs on *Veedon Fleece* in terms of each other as opposed to in themselves, which, given the obvious links between Tracks One, Two and Three, is in itself noteworthy. Likewise, the last three tracks on the album flow one into another with a unity of deepening immersion into a mood which is blue, but radiant. The wind-down of Side Two of *Veedon Fleece* is like the stages of a meditation which leave the listener rested but also somehow coming out of it refreshed and more aware than before. 'Country Fair' is a reflection upon the former self, but in the same place: it's the same kind of feeling. There's the recorder of Jim Rothermel, and an acoustic guitar are played, recorded and mixed in such a way as to suggest a kind of sitar-style drone rather than a succession of recognisable notes. A second guitar follows the vocal line for the first half of the verses, adding emphasis and urgency to these notes, swinging in and then sweeping away again, giving the track its feeling of stillness and poise. Summarising the themes of the record, it attests to how much the 'we' of the song have changed since last they contemplated this time and place, stood in this place. It is the theme of change and also of eternal return. The recorder, floating around and across the arrangement, and foregrounded for much of it, adds this feeling of the ancient to the present moment, as though some form of portal to the past has opened up, uniting past, present and future selves in a moment of resolution represented by the satisfying concluding note on which the song ends.

It is fitting that the album ends on a note that feels to me like the moment of falling asleep, of perfect rest, and like the moment of awareness before one fades into restful slumber. Or perhaps even the reverse – the album begins with a falling into dream, and the end of 'Country Fair' represents the close of that mood, the clicked finger and thumb that brings re-entry into the 'real', waking world. It seems to me entirely appropriate and related that the opening of *Common One* begins in a very similar way to the manner in which *Veedon Fleece* closes, in a haunt of ancient peace, and in the space between dreaming and waking. But first we have to get to that place. How? By going into the music.

INTO THE MUSIC (1979)

Listening to the pure FM-radio, endless summer music of *Wavelength*, Morrison's most substantial love letter to America, it seems remarkable that the intensity of his preoccupation was the prelude to a goodbye – think of Richard Thompson's salty phrase in 'I Misunderstood': 'I thought she was saying good luck, she was saying goodbye'.[89] The deep entanglement of *Wavelength* was indeed a kind of conclusion: although Morrison would still record in the US, the American phase of his art was over.

Where did his muse take him? With remarkable speed (*Wavelength* was recorded and issued in 1978, its follow-up a year later) he delivered *Into The Music*. Morrison has observed that this album was where he really got back into the mood again, and the evidence for this is plain. Borrowing its title from Ritchie Yorke's superb book (itself a twist on the title of 'Into The Mystic'), its direct annunciation of the state of Morrison's art is unmistakable. Looking at the cover art we see this captured too: a close-up shot of Morrison's face, shot from his left, guitar strap over his left shoulder suggesting he is in the middle of a song, his eyes closed in a kind of rapture or transportation, oblivious to the camera and lost in music, in the words of the song. This unposed moment could not be less like the staged cover shot of *Wavelength*, yet both album covers were shot by Norman Seeff, and clearly Morrison felt both were truthful (or at least appropriate) images to accompany the music within. The muted reaction to *A Period Of Transition* had perhaps spurred Morrison back towards the mainstream, to reassert and rediscover whether his credentials as a writer of great popular songs were still intact. Indeed, perhaps whether he could still do it at all – whether he was still on the wavelength, able to 'tune in' to the music, and then take it to market. *Wavelength* represents that point of connection between what had gone before and what was to come: it was a welcome back and also a valedictory performance. After it, everything changed.

Into The Music, while being recorded in Sausalito and mixed in Hollywood, is, curiously, a European record, and one made in, and from, exile. It was issued in August 1979, in the same week as Bob Dylan's *Slow Train Coming*; this is relevant in a number of ways, not least that the shockwaves of Dylan's embrace of a fundamentalist Christianity were still convulsing the post-punk landscape. The certainties of the rock era (1970–76) had been pitchforked into the skip by punk's iconoclasm and likewise here, by Dylan's apparent betrayal (if no-one called him 'Judas' at this time then a good opportunity was missed) of the ideals of the counterculture. Yet Dylan understood how those hippie ideals had proved a sham; how the dreams of material and social reorganisation through secular means had been appropriated by the culture industries and sold back as entertainment, either by Hollywood or via hippie entrepreneurs who had slid very easily into their seats at the top table. Dylan's personal sense of drift (and his tendency towards absolutes) led him to register in a Bible Studies class, but the burden of expectation was something he was keen (not for the first time) to get out from under of, and to slough off. In the swirl of all this, the release of a new Morrison record was not such a great event; this freed the music from the glare of centre-stage scrutiny, and makes the record an under-exposed delight.

In the long tale of Morrison's work, *Into The Music* is the album that changed everything. In terms of through-composition, it matches its lyrical concerns to a musical unity which is a sheer delight and a mysteriously under-celebrated one. The very distinctive sound, which is both acoustic and *loud*, has its multiple roots in the sublime voice of Katie Kissoon, the arrival of the great Pee Wee Ellis, and the forceful fiddle playing of Talia Toni Marcus. Morrison thus had around him a very strong group of players, both live and in the studio, and the arrival of this band signalled the dawn of strongest run of live and studio work of his career. The Caledonia Soul Orchestra can be seen in some ways as an under-realized ensemble in comparison. Morrison really delivered with this band, and took the inspiration and insight somewhere, while the perfected live shows that made *It's To Late To Stop Now* seemed not to offer their leader a way past them. Interestingly, the studio albums that that line-up contributed to have none of the force of the live record, even by their own author's estimation – consider Morrison's retrospective view of *His Band And The Street Choir* and *Tupelo Honey* as makeweight albums, telling Ritchie Yorke they were made 'when someone was on my back to get something cranked out'.[90]

An irony of the album's relative obscurity is that it opens with one of his most famous songs. The unfailingly cheering 'Bright Side Of The Road' connects the upbeat pop mood of *Wavelength* to this album, but in its arrangement and performance points forward into a new mood. The song is both a rejoinder to, and a companion piece for, Chips Moman and Dan Penn's 'Dark End Of The Street'. That country-soul standard is evoked in Morrison's first line, and as such is a declaration of intent – moving into the music is a movement into the light; the glass is more than half-full on this record. Both songs imagine a togetherness in the future ('We'll steal away to the dark end of the street / Just you and me' and 'We'll be lovers once again / On the bright side of the road') but the emotional emphases are skewed in favour of the upswing in Morrison's case, a corrective to the downswing of Moman and Penn's darker mood. It's no wonder

Richard and Linda Thompson covered this song during their Sufi period, given its articulation of love as protection and shelter. In Morrison's song, love, or the feeling of it, opens the self up to the world, and to happenstance.

The opening snare skip ushers in a jaunty, unexpected alliance between tablas (sounding remarkably like a banjo), mandolin and harmonica – a combination not unlike the music you might hear in folk-sessions in pubs in East Belfast, the Isle of Man and North Liverpool. A shout of brass cues in his vocal. The 'other' version of this song, issued on *The Philosopher's Stone*, was recorded at the same sessions but is quite a different thing: opening on a circular harmonica riff which is absent from the *Into The Music* version and upping the rhythmic pace into a performance more breathless and urgent. The easier pace of the album version seems to suit the natural philosophy of the lyric, however. The 'bright side' is a hope for tomorrow, and not necessarily a metaphor for the next or another world – he sings directly about this world and about mortality, via the span of time we are given. As a piece of carpe diem it is not as fatalistic as 'Precious Time' (itself a kind of bluebeat rewrite of 'Bright Side Of The Road'), but is more optimistic about the need to get stuck into that life, to indeed seize the day, than Moman and Penn's song. The joy in 'Bright Side' is one of physically 'being' rather than 'having', and there is a very strong sense of crossing over, of transcendence in the song – consider the opening two lines: 'From the dark end of the street / To the bright side of the road'. The song is both the burden and the freedom from it: 'Help me share my load/help me sing my song.'

The song benefits greatly, as does the album as a whole, from the contributions of Katie Kissoon, and here she provides an echo of Morrison's lead vocal, a fore-echo of a technique which would come to the fore in the early/mid-90s, during Brian Kennedy's tenure. Kissoon lobs each line back to its author and this togetherness assists the build of a sense of strength and positivity that drives the song forward. This socialisation of the feeling also expands the emotional remit of the tune, and the 'we' of the song is open to the world, rather than closed off from it, as is the case in 'Dark End Of The Street', where the promised end-state is 'Just you and me'. The 'Satchmo' section at the song's end is both silly and gorgeous; in it there is such pleasure in the singing and in the reconnection with early inspiration and feeling. A question: does he say 'Cricket!' at 1.35?[91]

The album then tips into its deeper waters and themes, leaning on an open door and falling into 'Full Force Gale'. The sound swoops and flies like a bird, and in some ways delivers the true start of the album – this is a mercurial gospel song. This aspect was foregrounded by Elvis Costello's a cappella performance on *No Prima Donna*, in a superb arrangement by Phil Coulter, who recalled hoping that matching Costello with Dublin folk choir the Voice Squad 'would make a powerful sound. Elvis was unsure at first, but we made a believer of him!' That album unexpectedly centralizes *Into The Music*, giving it three out of ten tracks.[92] There is an undeniable propinquity between *Into The Music*'s atmospheres of a kind of renewed faith and energy connected to Christianity and Bob Dylan's *Slow Train Coming*, released, as we have noted, the same week in 1979. Morrison is far less ready to yield to totalities – his 'faith' or otherwise is his own business and it only informs (directly, at least) two of the songs here, this and 'Rolling Hills'. 'Full Force Gale' features the guitar work of Ry Cooder and despite Wim Wenders' working with, and enthusiasm for the work of, both men, this is their only recorded collaboration to date; he contributes a typically loose-stringed slide-guitar solo. The lyric, sung with directness and visceral palpability by Morrison, 'describes' the feeling of encounters with 'the Lord'. It is a physical effect – he is 'lifted up again' as if by a natural force, the full-force gale being a simile for this: '*Like* a full force gale'.[93] So *Into The Music* is an album with religious elements, but it is not a religious album in the sense of *Slow Train Coming* or *Saved*. If we employ biblical terms, *Slow Train Coming* is what we might call an Old Testament record, concerned with vengeance, judgement and punishment; *Into The Music* is New Testament, dealing with forgiveness, love and kindness. In this it is closer to a supposedly 'secular' Dylan song from 1976, 'Oh, Sister': 'And is our purpose not the same on this earth / To love and follow his direction'.[94]

'Full Force Gale' describes a pastoral idyll, far from the city or the beach of Venice, USA, a place where inner and outer modes harmonise, and the landscape is expressive of his inner emotion: this is of course a technique familiar from and important to the whole body of Morrison's work. The language is of repose and Biblical in its evocation of place and the spirit: 'gentle', 'sanctuary', 'shady', 'whispering', and, like King Belshazzar[95] he 'saw the writing on the wall'. In the latter case he reclaims the phrase from the banality of secular colloquialism and reconnects it to this original biblical context. The song is unambiguous in its assertions, but wholly non-judgemental of others, and it is in this that *Into The Music*'s 'Christian' songs are quite different to those of *Slow Train Coming*. *Into The Music* is an album which has a sole and single purpose – that is, to pursue and describe Morrison's new convictions, while Dylan's album, for all its power and beauty, brims with what he once renounced as 'fingerpointing songs': what is 'When You Gonna Wake Up?' but a finger-pointing song, even if he is looking in a mirror while pointing.[96]

As if to illustrate the key difference between *Into The Music* and *Slow Train Coming*, 'Steppin' Out Queen' is a generous, open-hearted song which skips along with a Motown snap; the horns and Toni Marcus's fiddle sublimate here. The lyric describes a girl getting ready for a wild night out, and how the night goes – it is the description of a party girl ('Oh you know you make the scene') but there is none of the misogyny typical of rock music. Here the girls are not rebuked for 'dressing up for each other', as in 'Wild Night'. The song is an act of fond observation, and a celebration of the life force at work in their busyness, and contains very generous wisdom about life: 'Well you go through the drama'. This is focused in the gorgeous and unexpected coda (4.30–5.29) where Katie Kissoon's backing vocal waltzes around with Morrison's scatting; the song picks up in the very depth of the fade, tantalisingly suggesting the possibility of what lies beyond. This is the first of the songs to explore the key mood of *Into The Music*, of being unafraid of life, and of love, embracing both, and showing a willingness to go through the drama – a theme which is picked up in the album's climactic double of 'It's All In The Game'/'You Know What They're Writing About'.[97]

'Troubadours' employs a 'period' horn arrangement to evoke the time of the troubadours themselves; this is roughly the early middle ages, from the late twelfth to the late fourteenth century, and they were primarily in France. The word is probably from Old French and while the etymology of the term is somewhat disputed (between Old French and medieval Arabic), what is clear is that it referred to travelling poet-musicians whose stock in trade was the song of love and wit, who would travel from town to town, and sing, play and carouse, and then move on. In this here-today-gone-tomorrow existence they seemed enchanted: the romance of this existence later informed the pleasure of the circus coming to town and of course still thrives today, in the idea of a band being on the road hitting town for one night only and then being gone in the morning. As such, we can understand the appeal of the troubadour to Morrison as both symbol and subject within a song. If we are looking at Morrison's habit of, and interest in, connecting with tradition and refreshing it and building upon it, then this song is an unusually clear example of that process. The lyric describes the world inhabited by the troubadours as well as the effect that they had upon it. The emphasis is on the *sound* of the musicians in the lyric and that is reflected in the melody and arrangement of the piece, which seeks to 'tune in' to that sound – indeed the lyric asks if we can hear and 'dig that sound', while we recall how in the Montreux 1980 DVD performance Morrison commands us three times to 'Listen!' as Pee Wee Ellis delivers a trio of scorching sax solos. The trumpet of Mark Isham follows a determinedly medieval pattern, a style which would re-emerge later on 'Dweller On The Threshold', the descending intervals of which are anticipated by the more languid, romantic horn chart used here by Isham and his fellow arranger Ellis.[98]

Developing this theme of the slow, even wilfully 'acoustic' life, 'Rolling Hills' is a superb exercise in experimental vocal technique, with the continual slurring of syllables providing the extraordinary setting for a lyric Christian in acclamation yet also one with a whiff of pagan pantheism in its celebration of being. This is similar to the kind of Christianity espoused by Blake in the final etching for his *Songs of Innocence and Experience* and borrowed from 1 Corinthians 15.44: 'it is raised a spiritual body'. The lyric revolves around these lines:

1) Among the rolling hills, I'll live my life in Him
2) I'll take out my pen and write my song among the rolling hills
3) I will do my jig and live among the rolling hills

The lyric is set to a pastoral jig which again suggests a song of innocence achieved through loss and rediscovery of that state through body and spirit. This simplicity is no fey pastorale. It is more like, as Morrison says, borrowing from D. H. Lawrence in the 1985 song 'A New Kind Of Man', a song of a man who has 'come through'.[99] This simplicity brings with it some toughness and directness. Marcus's fiddle leads this song from the front, and, especially as it follows directly upon 'Troubadours', there is a sense of this song as being an organic part of the landscape that he describes. The allegorical landscape of the lyric is akin to that of the medieval poet or painter, the topography being expressive of the character, and indeed of the existence of a creative, guiding hand, and of the link between God and Man. It is again instructive to compare this vision of God at work in Man with Bob Dylan's exactly contemporary work. The line in the latter's 'Precious Angel' – 'You either got faith or unbelief, and they're ain't no neutral ground' – speaks of a simplicity of a very different shade, and 'Rolling Hills' attests to this integrated openness and generosity of interpretative mood in spiritual matters as 'Steppin' Out Queen' does for more worldly ones.[100]

'You Make Me Feel So Free' connects this spiritual mood with a very human one, drawing together the feeling of affection we pick up in 'Steppin' Out Queen' and the joyous mood of 'Rolling Hills', mixing spiritual and physical ecstasies. This song features a superb vocal performance with one of Morrison's wittiest and most humane lyrics, being wise and also laugh-out-loud funny on at least one occasion: 'I heard them say that you could have your cake and eat it / But all I wanted was one free lunch'. On any other album this tune would be a stand out in both the quality of the song and the performance of it, but so high is the standard on *Into The Music* that it is frequently overlooked. It has, however, received a healthy number of performances in concert, though not always by its composer – see the version on *A Night In San Francisco*, for example, where it is sung in a close facsimile of the *Into The Music* version by Brian Kennedy. It also turned up as the opener on *No Prima Donna*, sung by Sinéad O'Connor, arranged in a much deeper, 50s slow-jazz swing, while her vocal hovers above the music like a hummingbird tentatively testing and touching upon the melody. Morrison's original is more mercurial and fleet of wing-heeled foot, harmonising with the theme of freedom.

The lyric is enlightening and enlightened and, if you're ready for it, a real lesson in how to live. The song accepts the randomness of existence and embraces chance, and does so in great good humour and, again, real wisdom – not in a sage-like sense but one borne out of both experience and observation. Morrison's vocal is in complete concord with his meaning – listen to the scatting in the final section 3.28 to the close at 4.07 (incorporating a remarkable plosive burst at 3.43–49) – perfectly expressive of this pleasing and rich mix of a wisdom drawn from experience and a natural intelligence via which that experience is processed, into a form of understanding.

> I'm gonna throw my cards there right down on the table
> Spin a wheel and roll the dice
> And we'll live the way it turns up and we'll live the way it comes up
> Baby you know that's the price

The first side concludes on this fully ecstatic note, promising a kind of completeness which pulls together the spiritual and physical realms into a single (we might say Blakean and bluesy) unity: 'I'm so doggone *free*'.[101]

What was originally Side Two of the album constitutes 25 minutes of a sustained and slowly developing mood and state of mind explored through sound. There are four songs on the side, and while only the final two are linked in their performance, all four form an indivisible quartet. The first track, 'Angeliou', opens with an elegant and decidedly Old World flourish, redolent of dance steps and tea houses and old town squares; this is European music. The first strokes of Toni Marcus's fiddle build on this High Romantic feel, and the melody is waltzed around four times before, at 0.30, the more recognisably blues-based main body of the song slides into place – but the intro has done its work; this is a song of the Old World. Morrison's first vocal contributions are of approbation, two *sotto voce* 'Yeah's affirming that something is right here. The 'official' vocal begins at 0.41 and consists at first of the title repeated 13 times over 14 possible repetitions in 45 seconds (0.41–1.26: on the penultimate repetition Morrison replaces the name with 'Things you do'). After the first time around the structure he mutters to the band 'One more time again' (1.04), and round they go once more. Whether we view this kind of detail as truly spontaneous and 'authentic' (to employ that loaded term) or as planned and theatrical, the impact is very strongly one of 'liveness' of performance and emotion, and of the possibilities of creativity that move and drive this music forward – something is *happening* behind those mikes.

The arrangement is powerful and also somehow dainty; the blend of the piano, the fiddle, the muted horns and the discreet toe-tap of the rhythm tipping back and forth between rimshot and tight hi-hat lends the melody a quiet force. In the Montreux 1980 DVD performance the title phrase is buoyed up by a momentary upsurge in the horns which blasts upward in a manner which resembles the shift from verse to chorus during 'Spirit' from *Common One*, a version of which was recorded during the *Into The Music* sessions. It was, I'd suggest, these explorations into internal dynamics that provided the springboard for Morrison's great works in the 1980s.

The song 'proper' begins at 1.29, evoking the month of May in the city of Paris, chiming perfectly with the Old World evocation of the melody and arrangement – it is a romantic view of Europe, almost a pre-Great War one, but one coloured by composition in exile. Morrison may have never lived in Paris but many of the great Irish writers with whom Morrison was beginning to discern a link did – James Joyce found solace, and a publisher, there for his *Ulysses* when he was banned and reviled in his home country and when no-one else would go near the book. Sylvia Beech published Joyce via her Shakespeare and Company press and bookshop, still to be found on Rue de la Bûcherie. Joyce's ardent friend, admirer and student, Samuel Beckett went to Paris in the 1930s, moving there permanently in 1939 at the outbreak of the Second World War, preferring, he said, 'France at war to Ireland at peace',[102] and stayed until his death in 1989. So the city has enormous resonance as an evocative image – the city of romance of travel brochure lore, and also of intellectual liberty, of freedom of the body and of the mind. Morrison lets these evocations do the work for him, and for the song, mentioning only bells ringing in May in Paris, yet with these few sketchy details a whole set of emotional connections are made.[103]

A key element of this quartet of songs is that they all feature spoken-word interludes. In 'Angeliou' there is one from 2.50 to 4.24, where the return to singing is cued by a firm crack on the snare – a very typical Morrison rhetorical detail familiar from live performance here employed in the studio to capture the 'liveness' within the recorded and repeatable moment. The matter of the spoken section is of a realisation of connection between people and the realities of chance, as described in 'You Make Me Feel So Free'. These interludes proved to be forerunners of the growing importance of the spoken word in Morrison's work over the next ten years or so. Sinéad O'Connor described Morrison's singing style as sometimes being 'animated speaking',[104] and this section illustrates her point perfectly, as his delivery ebbs and flows between a singing and a speaking voice, delivering the spoken lines with a rhythmic musicality that is redolent of Blake and the song poets (such as Yeats, Joseph Campbell and Patrick Kavanagh) with whom he was later to discover a kinship. The repetitions of 'Hey' (4.12–16) are meaningless in the dictionary sense but saturated with empathy in his use and delivery of them here. Katie Kissoon's contribution is as vital as ever, via two high, plaintive swooning swoops of sound behind the monologue, signifying moments of responsive otherness which bring the narrative back to the idea of an emotional dialogue or conversation. Indeed, the song, like the album it is from, is about connection, about making connections between the like and the unalike, between opposites and between concordances. These connections are of feeling, and go beyond rational or intellectual discourse ('It wasn't *what you said* it was just *the way that it felt to me*' (my italics)), and in that sense it is about love: 'Will you be my baby?' The album finishes on a double song which is directly about 'a thing called love'. Yet this isn't the love of 'She Loves You' or even of 'Gloria': this is a connection which draws into itself every aspect of an individual and makes it both heavy and light – the search and the journey, the heavy connection translates as pure feeling which frees and makes light the soul: 'Will you be my baby?'

After the spoken interlude and six repetitions of 'Will you be my baby?', we are back to the restatement of the title, sung three times and then echoed by 'Yes I will' in happy answer to the question. We might expect this to conclude the track, but there is a final twist that is a vital moment in the emotional flow of the record and also the development of Morrison's own expressive vocabulary. At 5.37 he shushes the band and confides: 'Yeah . . . I got a story too . . . but my story . . . ain't got no words . . . it goes something like this.' Here again the natural emphasis is on feeling expressed in sound, articulated via the non-verbal vocal expression, on pure feeling as opposed to rationalised response: the story has no words. So what then does it sound like? It sounds like how it feels. Morrison riffs vocally around, above, beside and beneath the word 'Angeliou' in a series of remarkable, breathtakingly beautiful extrapolations which speak deeply of the emotional meaning of the act of speaking the name of a loved one. This runs from 5.58 to the moment the song disappears at 6.43 where, like 'Steppin' Out Queen', it concludes with an unexpected acceleration at the point of the final fade, directing us to the next track in a gesture of continuity.

At this point this immaculately sequenced record steps up again, to a song which has become a kind of standard of Morrison's better nights onstage, 'And The Healing Has Begun'. The clang of this track is perhaps the most complete realisation of the *Into The Music* sound – the fiddle, the acoustic guitars, the drums loud and friendly, the piano rich and textured, representative of a harmonic unity across the songs, exploring a unique mood. This is the very definition of through-composition. The song itself feels elastic, with the loose tightness of Morrison's technique of studio improvisation really coming to the fore. It might ebb and flow, it might surge and fall away, Morrison's voice might soar and rasp, or drop down into the spoken interlude which connects it to the other songs in the second half of this album.

It also feels as though it could last two minutes or two days and its duration seems entirely natural and uncrafted, like the shape and length of a bough of a tree, combining rough and smooth surfaces and textures. The lyric enters with a reference to walking down the avenue again, one of his key images which function as a kind of connective shorthand linking songs across time and space, yet here this ecstatic mood is one which is projected into the future. The 'now' in which the song dwells may be dark but the future is going to be better, and it is music that both promises and, in a kind of self-fulfilling prophecy, delivers the healing it sings of. In a way this is the reverse of Cole Porter's 'Let's Face The Music And Dance', where the future is screened out via a hedonistic insistence on the present moment: music there doesn't heal, it simply offers a stoical way of ignoring reality. That mood is as equally true as Morrison's, I'd say, but offers less in the sense of music's power to transform anything other than the present moment. This is the 'foreground' Morrison spoke about to Chris Welch ('All this is just the foreground, but the background is something else'), whereas 'And The Healing Has Begun' explores the background, the 'something else' that is going on.[105]

The song starts out in the spirit of a post-gig jam, something which has grown out of music itself, matching a live looseness with a studio clarity and in this way the record both concludes and introduces important sets of ideas and methodologies in Morrison's lyrical and musical vocabulary. This song embodies this sense of something good getting going, even in its title. It opens up slowly yet directly, like something suddenly becoming clear over the horizon where once vision was obscure: it achieves this by returning to source. It makes a direct connection between place and felling, locale and experience – 'the avenue' provides not only the context for all that will happen, but is also somehow both cause and effect of its own processes. It sounds fantastic; the textures of each instrument rich and direct, finding their place in the mix, and the track acquires an entirely naturalised atmospheric. The ensemble has discovered a sound and they are going to explore it.

Morrison employs the rhetorical strategies that distinguish his best work onstage right here in the studio – listen to his instruction to drummer Peter Van Hooke at 4.45 ('Wait a minute, Pete . . . listenlistenlisten'), and the drums' break down at 4.49. The track flows, like a tributary into a delta, into the curiously humorous spoken interlude, detailing stage by stage what at first seems to be an attempted seduction, making (as in 'Gloria') the move from the meeting on the street via going 'Behind this door here' to the private space of a room. This suggests they make themselves comfortable, noting the somewhat refined drinks on offer – sherry, port – and then he sidles up towards her on the settee, talking about Muddy Waters and the backstreet jelly roll (a euphemism for sex, of course). But then comes the biggest surprise of all: instead of pursuing this to its conclusion (as in 'Gloria'), the song suddenly explodes into a dazzling musical ejaculation of the sheer joy of being alive in the here and now, and a refusal to step back from this realisation. At 6.28, just at the moment where we are sure the seduction will be complete, the song surges up: 'We gonna stay out, all night long! / And then we're gonna go out / And run across the fields!' The band follow him, feeling his every move in an echo of the sensual intimacy hinted at in the scene on the settee.

This blast of sheer life-energy is not simply adolescent, rather it is in the spirit of both confronting and embracing what in 'Mr Thomas' Robyn Hitchcock called 'the charge of life'; indeed Morrison chose this song to cover a couple of years later. The spirit of Dylan Thomas's best work infuses much of Morrison's, via a vigorous embrace of the 'now' alongside a celebration of the life force itself (see 'The Force That through the Green Fuse Drives the Flower'), as well as a cocky jaw-jutting come-on to the alternative. Thomas's poem 'Do Not Go Gentle into That Good Night', with its admonishment to the old and the young of the importance of living fully, or as Thomas puts it, raging 'against the dying of the light', echoes through Morrison's cry 'We gonna stay out . . . all night long!' Both men share a magnetic attraction to the power of memory and reminiscence; much of Thomas's most poetic writing on memory was actually written as prose, in works such as 'Reminiscences of Childhood' or 'Holiday Memory'.[106]

At the musical heart of all this is the kick of Peter Van Hooke's drums, the heartbeat around which the dynamics of the song wind and unwind themselves. Rhythm – the beating of the heart – is at the heart of all. This realisation is informed by, created by, and made real by, the song, by the sound of Morrison's voice, by the way he brings the band down at 4.45, and how it swings up again at 6.49, by the completeness of the realisation of a feeling made song. This is the image and experience of 'the healing', a response to 'the charge of life'. Of course this is a theme which then develops and flows into the album's finale, the medley of 'It's All In The Game' and 'You Know What They're Writing About'; outrageously I'd also suggest that the seed of Morrison's post-1979 working methodology is contained in the moments 1.51–55, as he calls out 'You know what they're . . .!', cueing in and giving way to a Peter Van Hooke drum crash. It's all in there.

So in some ways 'And The Healing Has Begun' is the summative moment of *Into The Music*, and the medley of 'It's All In The Game' and 'You Know What

They're Writing About' that follows it is as much an exploration of that summative mood as a development of it. Morrison's version of 'Game' has become another live favourite, of which much is frequently expected, in that it has become the site for what are known as 'workshop' sessions, where Morrison, if he is so minded, lets the song drift into the open spaces offered by 'You Know What They're Writing About' and explores a space which is about as close to a physical one that music can reach – it is almost palpable. The version here is slow, quiet and restrained, hushed almost – live it has spanked along at a brassy volume (as on *A Night In San Francisco*) and been set aside briskly, but most frequently it has proved the way into some scintillating, daring musical explorations which are almost entirely unique to Morrison's own methodologies.

The importance of the backward glance, which is simultaneously the sound of a soul pressing forward, and the arrival of overt nostalgia in his work via song comes with 'It's All In The Game'. The melody of this song was written by Charles Dawes in 1912, as 'Melody In A Major' and lyrics were put to it in 1951 by Carl Sigman. It then became a hit for many singers, and thereafter a 'standard'. As Morrison explained at Malvern on 25 November 2003, in a concert for the BBC:

> 'This is a song from the 50s, the kind of thing you used to hear on Radio Luxembourg, about '58 . . . am I allowed to say that? . . . [laughs] . . . said it anyway! . . . anyway, this has been recorded by many many many many many people, including . . . Johnny Mathis, Nat King Cole . . . the Four Tops . . . there's a great version by Jimmy Witherspoon but he didn't do it like this . . .'[107]

He then slipped back into his own 'You Know What They're Writing About', without mentioning the best-known version in the UK, by his old collaborator Sir Cliff Richard. The song, with its mix of innocence and experience, romance and its bitter counterpoints of unrequited rejection – breaking up and making up – is in some ways absolute standard pop song fare, and, as he says, not untypical of 'the kind of thing you used to hear on Radio Luxembourg, about '58'. But if we believe in the ability of the popular song to capture and transmit the common experience, then this needs must be read as a virtue. Furthermore, its directness allows Morrison room to manoeuvre musically and vocally within the song; the multitude of covers testifies to the adaptability of the song, and the free translation and movement of the emotions which it evokes.

What's remarkable about the song as Morrison records it is how it fits into the sonic landscape of *Into The Music* and how central it became in his live sets during the remarkably creative decade which followed this album. The song became the site of some of his finest live work, affording a space for him to stretch the song, the band and himself according to local conditions. In 25 years of concert going, I have only once seen him play the song straight, without the suffix of the 'workshop' section, so much so that when the arm came down after the last verse in Harrogate, 2005, the audience let out a collective gasp of startlement. For our purposes in exploring the lead-up to the lofty heights of *Common One*, what the version on *Into The Music* shows is his thinking and desire for his music to express something above and beyond the confines traditionally associated with the structures of the well-made popular song. You could listen to Sir Cliff's perfectly executed version for some time before you were put in mind of it flowing into a meditation upon the nature of love and of the popular song itself. 'You Know What They're Writing About' is a growing bud from the main stem of 'Game', developing into something entire of itself while remaining firmly grounded in the older song (a method which would come to feed some of his best live work in years to come). But, more pertinently, it is a reflection back upon that song – the song contains within itself its own critique. From a performance of a standard, Morrison leans towards the listener and draws them into the process – '*You* know what they're writing about' – turning the performance into a reflection on the nature of song itself, and the eternal recurrence of themes within art: 'Down through the ages, it's a thing called love'.

This connection of the apparently fleeting emotion or cultural moment, as embodied in a pop song, and the grand themes of antiquity, is a remarkable one, and like all moments of innate wisdom, seems to be the stuff of common sense once made. Morrison steps back from the narrative of the song while simultaneously digging deeper into it – using the vocabulary of the song, the universal, 'Ain't it a wonderful game / Ain't it a marvellous game', and then adapting it to the local and particular: 'Meet me down by the river . . . down by the pylons'. Ally to this the intimate whispering down to fade, the use of the dynamic between sound and its tonic counterpoint silence, and the focus moves from the image (the popular song *about* love) to the thing itself (the feeling itself). Traditionally sound connotes meaning and significance, silence the absence of it, but music functions in the space between these two. If you care to, turn the volume right up to the maximum your player will allow and follow the song down to its last stirrings deep in the groove, deep into the fade. There's no sweary adolescent abruptness as in the case of a much older and hard-to-find fade, but a hushed satisfaction in his tone in this virtually hidden conclusion, which suggests an arrival at the riverside, at the foot of the pylon.

The two songs are like two sides of a hinge opening this door for the singer: the older standard being an archetype of the well-made love song, his own number being an example of the lost art of the answer song, reflecting upon the nature of writing about love in popular song. The latter leans forward out of the speaker and addresses the listener directly: 'we' are the 'You' of the title and we are left in no doubt that we are 'You . . . you . . . *you know*! You know what they're writing about!' Thus the particular and intensely personal becomes the shared and the universal; we are drawn into the emotional ebb and flow of the song and our own lives are implicated in the songs. We are sent back to the beginning of the album to reappraise its content and its connection to our own lives in the light of this mutual discovery. If we're *listening* to the music.

Laura Barton wrote about these songs:

> When I first left home, my dad gave me a copy of this album [*Into The Music*], and ever since these three songs have been my private crib-notes on love. I generally only play them in succession, and their peculiar pitch and trough of joy and sadness and gruff wisdom make me feel as if my heart has inflated like a giant red balloon, bobbing on the surface of something far bigger than me.[108]

Barton's observation of the interconnectedness of the songs and their emotionally cumulative effect is original, candid and funny, and the high point of this process and creative turning point of the whole album comes, I'd argue, when Morrison finally abandons the lexicon of love available in the romantic song altogether and pushes beyond the limits of such ideas of the well-made song: 'And when there's no more words to say about love I go . . .' He then issues a keening sound, inarticulate in lexical and linguistic terms but deeply expressive in emotional and auditory ones (2.37–3.00) which finally resolves itself into the songtitle at 3.03. We know what it means; we know how it feels. The whole point of 'You Know What They're Writing About' is a reflection on the conventions, range and limits of the love song as understood within popular culture. It is preceded of course by a standard of just that repertoire in 'It's All In The Game'; as Morrison said in Malvern, listing other acts who had performed the song, 'but he didn't do it like this'. He is being matter of fact, but is also expressing a deeper truth. His version is unself-consciously reflexive, scrutinising the form and matter of the song at the same moment at which it is sung for real, and this contemplation blooms in its own meditation on the subject, 'You know . . .' itself. This is a remarkable achievement, and one that opened the door into a new era of creativity and musical vocabularies for Morrison – it's no coincidence that the closing section of 'You Know' is the first reference to meeting down by the pylons, which would become a key landmark in the emotional topography of live performances in the 80s.[109] The willingness of these songs to take a musical idea and extrapolate and explore it points towards the 'workshop' ethic of the live sets and, with their dropouts into murmured interior dialogues, anticipates the arrival of the spoken word as a key feature of his style in the 1980s. What follows?

The slowly dissolving certainties of the well-made song as detailed in the dazzling scrutiny of 'You Know What They're Writing About' paved the way for Morrison's great experiment in testing just what, how much and how little could be accommodated within the confines of a song, in the shape of *Into The Music*'s symbiotic other, *Common One*.

O, MY *COMMON ONE* (1980)

At the turn of the decade, Morrison was clearly considering not only the limits of the popular song as a means to express what he was interested in expressing, but also his own relationship to song itself. How might the shape and order of a song be expanded, developed and reconfigured in order to allow it to acquire a new expressive vocabulary? That is what he was starting to investigate on the run of songs in the second half of *Into The Music*, and which reaches a first full bloom on *Common One*. The album didn't, as some reviewers seemed to feel way back in 1980, just fall unannounced and unexpected from the tree – as we have seen, on his previous two albums there were signs that the Van Morrison of the 1970s was about to slough a skin.

Common One was recorded *in situ* in France, at the Super Bear Studios at Miraval, which sits in the Alpes Maritimes, above Nice in the South of France, over a straight run of eight days (11–19 February 1980). The studio was well used at the time, as a kind of alternative for those who did not wish to trek to Martinique to use George Martin's studio there, and it numbered Queen, Paul McCartney and Ringo Starr alongside myriad jazz acts among its late 70s clientele. The year before *Common One* was recorded, Pink Floyd had annexed the studio, recording that monument to bleak socio-cultural prognoses, *The Wall*. Their reason for choosing the studio was one of tax economies – they had to be out of the UK from 6 April 1979 to 5 April 1980 – and they stayed at Super Bear from April to November 1979. They had moved to Culver City Studios in the US by the time Morrison and band arrived. Morrison's reasons for choosing Super Bear for this project might be at least in part connected with Mick Cox's observation that in rehearsal or in London studios, the musicians likely as not disperse at the end of the session. Here, living in, the atmosphere must have been far more concentrated and intense. This was perhaps what Morrison was looking for, and this focus fed into and communicated itself to the recording itself. Pee Wee Ellis spoke about the circumstances of the recording:

Why did Van decide to take you to France to record the album?

PWE: Isolation – to make it special and it really was . . .

> *One of the songs which has returned to the most recent live show is 'Haunts Of Ancient Peace'. How did that song evolve in the studio?*
>
> PWE: Van had the structure of the song. I put the horns down and the dynamics and variation of the song came from Van's direction, basically. It feels different every time we play it . . . The spirit was definitely in that album – it was taking the music in a different direction . . . going to France, that was like a residency, really. We'd had a couple of days of rehearsals and then ten days or so in France . . . it was a performance, it's documented and it won't change . . . some day, sooner or later, they'll get it.[110]

The sound of the record is rich and singular, a deep well of cool stone, full of motion but also an image of perfect stillness. Each instrument is clearly defined – listen to the first 52 seconds of 'Haunts Of Ancient Peace', before the vocal comes in: each element is clearly distinguishable from its surroundings, yet all are part of the same whole. We might also note a very strong similarity to the textures of Miles Davis's 'In A Silent Way' in the sound of this track. The instruments have a muted quality: David Hayes's bass is diamond clear but adds a mid-tone rather than a felt, deep note, while Mick Cox's guitar is a muted semi-acoustic; the drums are brushed or gently struck with a light stick, and add to the sense of meditative restraint and contemplative reflection. The rhythms seem to be those of the natural world and the turn of the seasons, rather than those of the city or of rock and roll. After all, the line 'At night we rest and go to sleep' is antithetical to the usual rock lyric's idea of what the night is for. The languid openness and the space available to the instruments forms part of the remarkable fluidity of the sound here, yet it is one which retains its internal structures and unity of purpose. There is a slow-dripping coherence, as the landscape is opened up to the listener with a far-sighted vista 'Across the countryside and towns'. Morrison is interested in stillness, and in digging in – as he says in an ad lib, 'Sing the song'. Lyrically this is a song celebrating staying put, and contemplating one's surroundings and connecting with the spirit of place: 'Be still'. It is a deep-green, rich-brown sound, the colours of nature and of earth. Something had happened to Morrison's singing in the two years since *Wavelength* too, and this would prove to be the dominant voice he would use for the next decade and a half. He is digging deeper into the trick of extrapolating sound, phoneticising and more consciously making vocal capital out of delivering the *sound* as well as the lyric itself. Hear 'Oh, when I can't ffffffind my feet' at 6.02–06, a line which indirectly found its way into the title of a book of poems.[111]

Mark Isham's trumpet/flugelhorn sets the emotional tone, that this is a place that moves slowly, the notes stretching out with languid native intelligence, in the rays of the dawn – it is a kind of waking up, by slowing down. 'At night we rest and go to sleep' suggests John Ruskin's emphasis on observing and acknowledging the natural rhythms of day and night, the seasons, and the earth. 'A song of harmony and rhyme' and 'the countryside and towns' emphasise this balance and unity, matching apparently opposed elements and making of them a satisfyingly unified, harmonised whole. Pee Wee Ellis's sax solo is modular for him but this only reinforces the still-point nature of this moment being captured. The song is definite in its evocation of the mythologies of Englishness, with lyrics like 'The Holy Grail we seek . . . We see the New Jerusalem' drawing in connected ideas of Glastonbury and of Blake's reimagination of England, like Woody Guthrie's invitation to reimagine the meaning of America in 'This Land Is Your Land'. The deep creative paradox in this song is caught by the final line, 'Be still in haunts of ancient peace': this song evokes something moving forward, which describes, evokes, and distils stillness; it is the opening salvo in process of meditation.[112]

As has often been the case, Morrison found the title of the song from a book; in a chatty moment he remarked onstage in Torquay in 2002 as he introduced the song, 'I got the title of this song from a book by Alfred Austin . . . if anybody's interested'.[113] We're interested. *Haunts of Ancient Peace* by Alfred Austin was published in 1902, during Austin's tenure as Poet Laureate. Though he succeeded Lord Alfred Tennyson as Poet Laureate in 1896 (Tennyson died in 1892, but his successor's arrival was delayed for four years as no suitable candidate was deemed to be available. Austin was appointed in 1896 and was succeeded by Robert Bridges more directly upon his death at the age of 78 in 1913. Austin is an overlooked figure, almost to the point of critical oblivion. In deference to his illustrious predecessor, Austin's volume takes its title from a line in a Tennyson poem 'The Palace of Art', one which is reproduced on the book's front papers:

> And one, and English home – gray twilight pour'd
> On dewy pastures, dewy trees,
> Softer than sleep – all things in order stored,
> A haunt of ancient peace.[114]

Haunts of Ancient Peace is not, however, a book of poetry, but rather the record of a tour Austin undertook with a female companion who loved only her garden. The trip's purpose was to divine a kind of English spirit of place in wilder places beyond the well-tended confines of the garden, and of identifying places in which this spirit of the 'haunt of ancient peace' resided. Austin refers to the book as 'this discursive volume',[115] a citation which suits *Common One*'s spirit as well as it does Austin's book. By wild coincidence, an offhand remark on the same page reveals that the date of departure from the cherished garden and out among the regions took place on 31 August, Morrison's birthday. This can be no more than simple serendipity (can it?), but it is nonetheless noteworthy, given Morrison's creative response to the book.

Austin's poetry displays a consciousness of life lived outdoors and he is very aware of the subtle changes in the landscape and the world that moves in harmony with it, of the turn of the seasons. This is well displayed by the inclusion of the poem, 'If Time Would Halt', in which he is looking for connections between how things were, and how things are, in order to proceed to how things might be.[116] This is a habit of mind Morrison shares, of course, and his work is strewn with references to such spots of time – just think of the car seat in 'Cyprus Avenue' or the last line of 'Coney Island' – and Austin uncannily anticipates another Morrison title, by referring to 'those supposed equinoctial gales that have an untimely trick of sometimes blowing cold for three days in the very middle of August'.[117]

The book doesn't feel as influential in its content as in its evocation and suggestion of possible ambient textures, of ways of perceiving atmospheres, of how artistic evocations of time and place might actually unlock time itself and allow the participant to slip through apparently fixed structures of time and place via a kind of formalised meditation or concentration. That's why the last lines of 'Haunts Of Ancient Peace' and 'Summertime In England' are instructive: 'Be still, in haunts of ancient peace' and 'Can you feel the silence?' respectively. We are asked to hear and feel something which is considered an absence. Yet as Democritus said, 'Nothing is more real than nothing'.

As Poet Laureate, Austin was required to be creative in a very public way, and had something to say about the nature of fame, too, including a discourse on fame as a restrictive and reductive phenomenon:

> A man's reputation, if he deserves one, is invariably made for him by his enemies . . . he is decried into consideration, and belittled into fame . . . I shall owe nothing to any of you, eulogise me as industriously as you may. I shall owe my reputation wholly to myself, my own best enemy . . . The day after Petrach was crowned with the laurel wreath, he was attacked by ruffians under the very walls of Rome . . . [he quotes Petrach's letter to Bocaccio] 'it was necessary to be constantly on the alert . . . for jealousy had made enemies of even my friends . . . the laurel made me known, only to be tormented. Without it, I should have led the best of lives, a life of obscurity and peace'.[118]

This illustrates that Morrison's ideas on the nature of fame are not unique to him and his circumstances. Indeed there are strange flashes of the 'fame blues' portion of Morrison's catalogue here, such as 'Professional Jealousy' ('for jealousy had made enemies of even my friends'), and his determination not to be seduced by public praise ('I shall owe nothing to any of you, eulogise me as industriously as you may'), and the wish for anonymity found in 'This Weight' ('Anonymity is all I want, you see' echoes 'I should have led the best of lives, a life of obscurity and peace'). It is not necessarily the artist's intention to make the aesthetically pleasing object, because 'I shall owe my reputation to myself, my own best enemy', a nicely piquant twist on the process. As Morrison says in 'Satisfied', 'You got to change it on the inside first'. So it feels like Austin's book influences *Common One* in that it determinedly seeks out the non-metropolitan places, the better to see into and connect up to the spirit of place and thereby discern the essential nature of England, which, as we have noted, is perhaps unusually a central theme of this album, recorded by an Irishman in a studio in France.

Leaving 'Summertime In England' for later, Side One of the vinyl album closed with 'Satisfied', a quietly funky number which became the second most frequently played song from the album in Morrison's live set. Opening with something like a soft parachuted landing after the final free-falling moments of 'Summertime In England', 'Satisfied' is a quietly tumultuous piece, and a very funky track. Jackie Leven once observed about Morrison's lyrics that he'll often take you by surprise as to where the lyric goes, and that's what happens here, particularly after the first verse and the pastoral scene that is built up, where we might expect more of the same. Yet suddenly the book he invokes is not a work praising nature, but J. D. Salinger's *Catcher in the Rye* – there is a link here of course with the generation of the Beats. Salinger, had he continued to write, would have been seen as kin, and perhaps even successor, to Kerouac. Instead, excepting a selection of short stories and a short novella, Salinger has spent the rest of his life trying to avoid the fame that the book's success had brought him, seeking to block the publication of a biography and memoirs. Morrison may well recognise Salinger's refusal to 'be a writer' and be defined by his work, and his ability to keep the publicity machine at bay. Yet to avoid the spotlight is easier for a writer, you might think, than a singer in an industry predicated almost as much on the coining of the image as it is on the selling and distribution of music. As far as 'Satisfied' goes, this is another example of what the detractors call his namedropping tendency – yet he notes that he *doesn't* want to 'change his name' and write a book 'Just like *Catcher in the Rye*'. It's a strong observation – it's a book he clearly admires but why would he write a book 'just like' it, when it already exists?

His frank admission of vexation – 'Sometimes I think I know how it is / Other times I'm completely in the dark' – looks forward to his similarly candid estimation of just how far all the philosophical speculation and explorations have taken him in 1990's *Enlightenment*, where on the title track he notes, with prosaic directness, 'Enlightenment, don't know what it is'. This is a refreshing acknowledgement of the ineffable, and puts us in mind of the question 'What's it all about?' from Bacharach and David's 'Alfie', which Morrison quoted in live performances of 'In The Afternoon' in 2002. 'Satisfied' also inhabits a kind of duality of location familiar from pastoral literary models seen most famously in Shakespearean comedy, where there is vacillation between the wildness and freedom of pastoral life and the intrigue of life in the court, where the rules of the latter do not apply in the former – 'Go to the mountain / Come back to the city'. Of course we need to recall that growing up in Belfast he saw how both the city and the mountains form a backdrop to life, and that movement between the two was not a globe-girdling leap; the two co-existed. The music is a slow but sure-footed shuffle, on a solid foundation of Hammond organ supplied by John Allair and some choice, fat brass. It makes for a very satisfying sound, and one which in its sense of completeness echoes the song's title and provides a correspondence to the rock and roll idea of needing more, more, more, as enshrined in Jagger and Richards's '(I Can't Get No) Satisfaction'. The tune's measured conclusion, ending on a note both high and attainable, further suggests that this is a realistic proposal, and not a momentary ecstasy. At the close of the remarkable sojourn of the album's first side it is like the putting down of a book, and a walking back out into the light.[119]

Side Two of the vinyl album opens with 'Wild Honey', a tune Morrison has never played in concert. Curiously, Pee Wee Ellis mentioned this song as a potential in-concert favourite in a 1997 interview but it didn't make the cut:

> [Toni Schiavone]: Are you aware of how the audience is reacting while you are playing?
>
> PWE: Oh yeah! Sure – you've got to be in touch with the audience. 'Wild Honey' is another of the songs which is likely to feature in the live set in the near future.[120]

It opens with a stately if less-than-strident horn fanfare, although the song is led more fully by the airy, drifting string arrangement. It is a direct love song, with a sweeping, serene melody. The wild honey of the title is unrelated to the tupelo variety nor is it that sort offered by the Beach Boys a decade or so earlier; it is actually a reference to the quickening pulse in the proximity of the loved one: 'Can't you hear my heart beat, just for you? / It's beating so wild, honey'.

This is set in a familiar Morrison moment: 'in the early morning / When the light comes shining through'. The music evoked in the song is being played live in the here and now by a band, but it is also known and strongly rooted: 'the music is tried and true'. This connects the song to the album's tendency towards the ancient. The song's bridge section also employs the archaic terminology characteristic of the album as a whole, referring to the song's subject as 'thee'. This sense of rootedness and the co-presence of the ancient in the present is expressed musically and lyrically on this album, and this holding together of disparate elements is a key feature of *Common One*'s through-composition.

'Wild Honey' is a gorgeous, smooth and romantic song – honeyed, even – and a butterfly-light interlude on an album of towering audacity. In its easy warmth and tight looseness it employs and frees the integrity of the *Common One* sound; Pee Wee Ellis's sax stretches out its limbs like a lizard basking on a hot rock. Morrison's vocal curls around the melody, with a benign confidentiality of tone. The sublime slow upslide of the horn section (0.16–18, for example) emphasises this sensuality. The song's central, romantic question ('Can't you hear my heart beat?') is effectively the 'body' equivalent to the 'mind' question which closes 'Summertime In England': 'Can you feel the silence?' This serves to discern in the local and the intimate the universal and expansive themes of the album's wider canvas; the personal and the universal echo and reflect each other – the world is seen in the grain of sand. And you can slow dance to it, too.[121]

The shared lyrical devices found in 'Satisfied' and 'Wild Honey', such as the light and darkness, the land and the sea, and the mountain and the city, connect these songs to each other but also to a specifically Northern Irish song tradition. So although there is no stylised 'Irishness' in this music, the tradition of a song like 'The Mountains Of Mourne' is evoked, where such oppositions co-exist:

> Oh, Mary, this London's a wonderful sight,
> With people all working by day and by night.
> Sure they don't sow potatoes, nor barley, nor wheat,
> But there's gangs of them digging for gold in the street.
> At least when I asked them that's what I was told,
> So I just took a hand at this digging for gold,
> But for all that I found there I might as well be
> Where the Mountains of Mourne sweep down to the sea.[122]

Here, in Percy French's evocation of it, the Northern Irish landscape becomes representative not only of belonging and the symbol of the urge to return, but is also held in the mind during times in the town – the mountain and the city two are symbols of states of mind, and of being. Thus the landscapes of *Common*

One are recognisable but also deeply, rootedly, ancient in their symbolic nature. This is an album with very, very deep roots indeed.

'Spirit' picks up on this connection between ancient and modern. It is a remarkable song which employs a powerful dynamic – the verses tick along quite metronomically until the chorus bursts almost volcanically from them, breaking free from the constraints of the instrumentation. The structure is the kind of simplicity that seems absolute and effortless but is hard-won – the quiet/loud/quiet/loud dynamic supposedly pioneered by the Pixies in the late 80s and taken up by their acolytes Nirvana in the 90s is here, in a different form, but also *in excelsis*. The horns that punctuate the dark wood-panelled enclosure of the lyric suggest the long road outside, and the chorus, in the vernacular, takes the roof off. This ebb and flow, this surge and settling back, does not merely mimic the rise and fall of desire and moments of enlightenment and illumination – it actually offers a way into that state of mind, and gives us a powerful aphorism: 'Oh no, never let spirit die'. The ensemble is fully in control of the mood here.

The lyric itself is uncomplicated; it is how it is sung, and how the music lifts and falls around it which lends it its incandescent power. Morrison's voice comes down to something just above a strong, steady whisper in the verse and hollers out the single line four times over in each chorus. The song misbehaves in terms of the expected dynamics of recorded pop or rock music, behaving more like a classical piece that will reduce to almost nothing and then well up with an almost physical presence. The chorus comes blazing up out of the verses, like something suddenly catching alight; listen to it at 0.55 and 3.02. It demonstrates musically the periodic nature of enlightenment, and how 'Spirit' itself comes when it is needed – within the confines of this well-measured song, it's every 16 bars, but then that's when it's needed. In the first instance, the change is bridged by a vocal cue ('Say help me angel' (0.54)) but, by the time of the second, the horn blast has acquired an organic force of its own – the song breaks here simply because it *has to*. The tune is also a showcase for the trumpet playing of Mark Isham, and the solo between 1.30–2.18 is a brightly glimmering point of light in the distance on this song's horizon as it 'keep[s] walkin' on', and it is brought back to the present and immediate moment by a smart snap on the snare at 2.18. The Hammond organ churns away under this, evocative of the arduousness of the journey. A choppier, punchier horn part closer to the 'Satisfied' arrangement suggests a more directed sense of purpose from 4.08–32, where endurance is once more needed in the 'you keep walkin' on' segment.

The lyric and the vocal are focused on strategies of survival, while the rhythms of the verses are those of labour, endurance, and of quiet persistence ('When you've given up hope and you're down in despair . . . And you sit in your room and you're alone . . . And you follow the road . . . And you keep walkin' on . . .'[123]) which are redeemed and elevated by the updraft of the chorus. The journey, and the soul making it, is sustained by the periodic upsurges of the chorus, providing inspiration and momentum – the final adjustment to the lyric locates 'Spirit in your soul', therefore establishing a kind of unity which has been achieved through this process, and the two are no longer distinct entities. The process has changed a situation which apparently had no prospect of resolution into one which is now an image of metaphysical sublimation and transcendence – 'Spirit in your soul'. Tellingly, in the last line of the song, Morrison repeats the chorus line once only, and in a voice poised between that he uses for the verses and the chorus. Likewise, the music rises commensurately just for that moment. The contrary states are held together inside, internalising the duality and it becomes a unity. The two are brought together. This sense of completeness at the song's end is satisfying in itself, and it sets the table for the next step, which we uncover in 'When Heart Is Open', the album's closer.

While of a similarly ambitious scale, this number is far less structured than 'Summertime In England'; it is a single musical piece, without tempo changes, and without disruption of the slow-dripping trip to nowhere, which, paradoxically, leads somewhere. A single musical mood is fully explored, on to the breathtaking moment where the silence at the centre of all music is touched, just for a moment. Its appearances in live sets have always been by necessity minimal and in the form of brief glimpses: the song is easier to précis than to perform, and that can be done in a few bars. Live 'performances' have therefore been closer to an acknowledgement of it than a recreation of it. A weightless weave of voice, guitar, flute and trumpet opens it, with guitar notes rolling out of the darkness; the song is open-ended, and feels like it could actually go on forever. As Paul McCartney said of the piano riff to Ray Charles's 'What'd I Say', 'that's the riff of the universe . . . that goes on forever'.[124] 'When Heart Is Open' is as far as one could imagine, musically, from Ray Charles's definitive r'n'b, but shares common ground with it in this sense – it is wholly open-ended and defies conclusion. It is less a formally composed song than a slice of the music of the spheres that has somehow leaked onto tape at Big Bear.

Pee Wee Ellis recalled the making of this particular song:

> 'I remember that song, 'When Heart Is Open', we were just taking a break from recording and sitting in this cafe and we just decided to go straight back into the studio and put the song down straight away. Somehow, by the time we got back we'd lost the drummer so we carried on without him! Van told them to turn on the tape recorder – and that was it – we hadn't worked it out before hand or anything – we just played. He stood there in the middle and we followed him.'[125]

Here is the end-point of Morrison's interest in and experiments with improvisation, usually the province of the live stage, transposed into the studio. 'When Heart Is Open' in all its depth and resonance is a completely improvised, unscored, organic piece of music, demonstrating Morrison's skill for directing the ensemble familiar from onstage performance, but here we see it at work in the studio – 'He stood there in the middle and we followed him.' So the far end of this extraordinary record stirs into life almost imperceptibly. It's hard to identify quite when and what the first note is, it seems to suddenly appear, like a figure moving imperceptibly closer to an observing eye. As a 'song', in the manner of the work of a 'songwriter', it barely exists, being a free-flowing agreement of guitar, voice, flute and bass. The absence of any rhythmic insistence is certainly key to the atmospherics of the track; it flows, like water, and apparently just as unconsciously. Periodic glissandi and crescendos are led by the voice: hear how the instruments follow the voice in increasing the collective volume at 4.06–28 for real evidence of Pee Wee Ellis's assertions about following the singer.

The Wagnerian hunting horn part from 0.18–28 evokes the slow-dawn stillness of the mood, but also keys into the timelessness of the sound – it is a simple two-note lift which lasts a languorous time, and is a fore-echo of the more urgent call we hear in the opening riff of 1983's 'Cry For Home'. It comes back round at 0.35, building via a third, even more Wagnerian note (0.41) and then takes flight into a dappled Miles Davis ripple of tones, *à la* 'In A Silent Way'. This overlaps with the arrival of Morrison's wordless vocal at 1.14, at first a kind of muscular keening above and around the notes, with a rare example of him employing melisma (1.28–30), and then returning to the root of the bass, via the tune's home note from 1.41–2.02. He will return to this bass home note at the song's close. The vocal 'proper' comes in on this note at 2.16. The voice leads the music forward; there is an organic pulse within the sound, the instruments being led and hauled back by the voice. Morrison's vocal performance on this track is pure innovation, from the low, stirring-from-dreams growl under the first section right down to the only solo a cappella singing Morrison has committed to disc.

The repetition of the title phrase becomes the emotional as well as the performative centre of the track. While not formally mantric in its use (the other lyrics are both generated by and seem to gather around the phrase 'And when heart is open'), all the other lyrics are generated by this phrase. It doesn't appear shorn of its 'And', thus suggesting an unending array of consequences, domino style, of the heart being open – the heart of the song is open to perpetual addition – we are back to Paul McCartney's 'riff of the universe' that 'just goes forever', but here the central, even Buddhist paradox, is that there *is* no riff. The phrase 'And when heart is open' is self-sustaining, and effectively 'is' the circular riff, which seems to have no beginning and no end, and, in the words of another song on this record, 'just *is*'. The lyric reflects this, by accident or design, or something of both: 'When there's no coming / And there's no going'. This stillness is at the centre of this song, and of the whole of the album; the final whispered moment of the album's opener, 'Haunts Of Ancient Peace' admonishes us to 'Be still'.

An anecdote: I used to listen to *Common One*, on vinyl, through headphones in bed in my student digs. I rarely made it through to the end of 'When Heart Is Open' without falling asleep, sometimes waking for a moment when Morrison's voice is completely unaccompanied (14.00–32), or stirred by the fathoms-deep bass note that comes in at 14.33, but I was most frequently woken by the needle ticking off the revolutions in the run out groove, in the dark. I cite this as a compliment, by the way. I had never heard music so deep and so restful and 25 years later there hasn't been much to supersede it in this sense.[126]

The references in 'When Heart Is Open' to meeting 'your lover' hark back to the root of this album, a root found in the second side of *Into The Music*, and specifically its last two songs – we recall the invitation to 'Meet me down by the pylons' in 'You Know What They're Writing About'. Here Morrison deliberately uses pastoral/archaic language ('You will tarry'), and the references to a life lived out of doors (the greatcoat, the big boots, the walking in the woods – all of which he would don again for 'A Sense Of Wonder') and thus being subject to the seasons and the rhythms of nature (the meadow, the waterfall, the deer, the woods) are employed to naturally but powerfully evoke a feeling of timelessness – this could be yesterday or the fifteenth century. The central lyrical motif, of the 'flower, slowly opening', is evocative of and possibly borrowed from Buddhist mythologies about the nature of experience and consequent enlightenment of the self. The 'meeting' with the lover, that is, the beloved outside the self and the effective evidence of one's own existence within Buddhist teaching, is arrived at at the moment where worldly business is set aside, in the self given over to stillness ('When there's no coming / And there's no going / You will meet / You will meet your lover').

Unlike 'Summertime In England', with its manifold structure and sizzling internal dynamics, 'When Heart Is Open' has never dominated his live performances, yet in its own quiet way, it is just as influential on Morrison's subsequent work, partly as evidence that he had come to the end of a line of enquiry. Just as *Into The Music* gave way to the towering, Miltonic audacity of *Common One*, the close of that album yielded up not further tunnelling into dark sound but instead the new morning, and the fresh, crisp economies of form which are the very stuff of *Beautiful Vision*, perhaps best summed up in the first few bars of *that* album's opener, 'Celtic Ray'. His bold experiment of through-composition on *Common One* is at its most remarkable in how it succeeds in pulling together strands of his technique and making the vocabulary of the pop song speak directly to, and of, his unwillingness to restrict his work to given shapes and scales. This was to prove to be the central strand of his work through his remarkable run of records in the decade that followed; in those successes we feel always at their centre the consequences of *Into The Music* and *Common One*. Morrison had found his way from America back to Europe and, furthermore, to the places and people and sounds he had left behind 15 years previously. So through-composition affected not only what *Common One* was but also what preceded it, and what flowed from it. The apparent dead stop of 'When Heart Is Open' was then actually a new bud, a growing point which begat the sound that dominated his work for the next five years or so, wholly unlike it in its surface details, but utterly indebted to it for its conciseness, compaction and emotional economies.

GETTING TO THE TOP OF THE MOUNTAIN: 'SUMMERTIME IN ENGLAND'

Where *Astral Weeks* and to a lesser extent *Veedon Fleece* were 'Irish' records, and *Into The Music* a very European one, *Common One* is that relatively rare thing, a consideration of England by an Irish artist. It is the mythical, magical properties of the English landscape that attract him, and furthermore, it is the regions, very determinedly so, which are explored in 'Summertime In England'. We are not in the metropolis, the old haunts of 'Friday's Child' and the 'Slim Slow Slider'; the focus is on the so-called 'provinces', the places Alfred Austin went to look for the deep hidden soul of England. Morrison's lyric name checks Kendal and Bristol, towns which are remote from each other, but which share space with an older 'mythic' version of English space. Bristol is 'down by Avalon', and Kendal is on the cusp of the Lake District, famously the source of inspiration for the Lake Poets, who included Wordsworth and Coleridge, both of whom are cited in the song.[127] We move seamlessly into the mystic, by passing from the 'real' England to that of the insightful imagination. As with 'Coney Island', if one were to try and use the song's place names as a kind of gazetteer, and follow the journey for oneself, you would soon be lost. For example, Kendal has no lakeside, being some ten miles south-east of the southernmost lake of the Lake District.

Geographical accuracy is hardly the point, of course: this is a journey of the imagination and of the spirit, just as in 'Coney Island' or 'Streets Of Arklow'. But here the ambition of 'You Don't Pull No Punches' and the real-world observations of Arklow are audaciously combined into a single epic tone poem where landscape and soul are held together and as a consequence change each other.

This echoes 'And our souls were cleaned / And the grass did grow', from 'Streets Of Arklow', but it is a development of that idea in both the scale of the piece and also the depth into which that increased scale allows the song to explore and experience, as well as summarize and comment upon the process. 'Punches', for all its proto-epic structure is in some ways facing backward to the 'Cyprus Avenue' or 'Madame George' model, where the lengthy song is a slow build within a single mood. Here, what dazzles about 'Summertime In England' is the way its tempo, lyrical focus and musical dynamics shift gear with an inner logic, like the light on a hillside as the sun is covered then revealed by fast-shifting clouds, and feeling just as natural, unforced and unstoppable.

In this way the song reflects a tradition much older than popular song as we recognise it, and one curiously anomalous within it – the pastoral. This, historically speaking, is a tradition of a kind of poetic writing which evokes life lived in the open, reflecting the seasons, the rhythms of nature and the natural world more strongly than those of man-made chronologies which were themselves a kind of nineteenth-century invention, 'railway time' and all. The nineteenth-century hortatory writers such as John Ruskin, that great aesthete, moralist and one of the first advocates of the mystical qualities of the English Lake District, were concerned that the industrial revolution and the shift to the cities by great numbers of the population meant that they lived their lives enclosed, away from the light, and that they would therefore lose touch with the rhythms of the seasons and an understanding of natural rather than man-made time. We note that the last lines of 'Summertime In England' ask as whether we can 'feel the light in England' as well as 'the silence'; it is this kind of consciousness which infuses *Common One* as a through-composition collection and 'Summertime In England' in particular as its absolute centrepiece.

Throughout his repertoire, Morrison has been very attentive to the calendar and the rhythms of the turning year. The references to months (see 'Fire In The Belly'), seasons (see 'Autumn Song'), and weather (see 'Snow In San Anselmo') are profuse and in this his work undoubtedly has a strong strain of the pastoral running right through it, and it surfaces most strongly on *Common One*. Thus we can link this strange record to ancient folk traditions as well as bold innovations in the sense of what can be attempted and accomplished within the structures of twentieth-century popular song. While Shakespeare borrowed from the pastoral tradition in order to satirise contemporary mores in plays such as *A Midsummer Night's Dream* (1596) and *As You Like It* (1599), one of the most famous examples of the pastoral in English poetry lies in his 'rival' Christopher Marlowe's *The Passionate Shepherd to his Love* (1599) while Edmund Spenser's *The Shepherd's Calendar* (1579) is effectively an early piece of folk-music collecting, stitching and adapting aspects of 'collected' oral poetry concerning the turning of the seasons together into well-made verse. 'Summertime In England' particularly reflects Marlowe's poem in the paradoxical emphasis on the uniqueness and the commonplace nature of the song's object of desire, with the song's subject being addressed passionately as 'O my common one', both special and unnoticeable. This mood is not unlike that of another famed example of English pastoral, Thomas Gray's 'Elegy in a Country Churchyard'(1751), with its reference to beauty going unnoticed:

> Full many a gem of purest ray serene,
> The dark unfathomed caves of ocean bear:
> Full many a flower is born to blush unseen,
> And waste its sweetness on the desert air.
> Some village-Hampden, that with dauntless breast
> The little tyrant of his fields withstood;
> Some mute inglorious Milton here may rest,
> Some Cromwell, guiltless of his country's blood.

But it is beauty not unnoticed by him; this poem also provided the title for Thomas Hardy's novel *Far from the Madding Crowd* (1874):

> Far from the madding crowd's ignoble strife,
> Their sober wishes never learn'd to stray;
> Along the cool sequester'd vale of life
> They kept the noiseless tenour of their way.[128]

Hardy also alluded to, or sampled, the poem in his epic novel of the life of a 'common one', *Tess of the D'Urbervilles: A Pure Woman* (1891), referring to graves in the churchyard at Marlot, 'some mutely Miltonic, some potentially Cromwellian'.[129]

These themes harmonise closely with the spirit of *Common One* overall and 'Summertime In England' in particular: first in its willingness to focus on the provincial life, 'among the regions', as he would later put it in the live version; secondly it dwells thereby on the unseen life, or the common one, and at its emotional centre is a figure in a red robe, the colour of desire, who has always in my mind been a Tess figure – the great beauty, wronged and unseen by the world but stoical and accepting of it: 'Oh my high in the art of suffering one'. Hardy's Wessex, as a powerfully felt but wholly imaginative territory in Dorset and the west, is like Avalon: a secret, other identity for a part of England which both reveals and transforms the places it describes. Neither 'exists' materially, but thrives as an idea, as testament to the spirit of place. Hardy reinvented the land and places he knew and was born into, calling forth their magical qualities by remaking them through art – we must surely see a connection in ambition and methodology between this and Morrison's evocations of place both real and imaginatively transformed.[130]

So 'Summertime In England' has a complex, multi-layered structure yet one which feels quite seamless and unforced – like the movements of clouds or water in a river course. It divides into six main sections, and within these sections we can discern ebbs and flows, pulses, pauses, surges and settlings back. In terms of structural tabulation we have:

0.00–08: drums

0.08–2.38: initial set up of themes, 'meet me in the country' section, introduction of song title

2.38–4.28: first 'gospel' section: 'The voice of Mahalia Jackson', 'It ain't why . . .'

4.28–6.58: return to opening theme and tempo, incorporating spoken section 5.04–23

7.48–13.35: return to gospel mood/tempo, church organ, slow build to climax at 11.50–13.35

13.35–15.32: slow wind-down of track: 'And you listen to the silence' becomes 'Can you feel the silence?' at 15.24

15.32–15.37: silence

The juxtapositions are simple in one sense. The two fleet-footed rhythmic sections, given their cue by the sibilant beat of the eight-second drum intro, are laid next to a brace of gospel-paced, less musically 'busy' sections, the latter of which floods the plain of the song and finally leads it down to the place where it meets the ocean of silence at the song's end. This duality, which finally achieves a kind of sublimated unity, is of course complicated by the internal dynamics of each section, which relate to each of the other sections as well as their own. 'Spirit', from the same album, utilises this quiet/loud structure more obviously, with the chorus erupting in a brassy blast from the contemplative, even-paced verses. Here the distinctions are more subtle and complex.

The shuffling, skittering beat that opens the song sets the rhythmic template for one of the key parts of this extraordinary piece of music, one which is massive and sprawling yet utterly precise and without ornament – every note that is here is here because it needs to be. The irony of writing at length about a song the central lyrical tenet of which is 'It ain't why, it just is' is not lost on me, but of course the flinty and direct wisdom of that observation is both end-point and opener for philosophical debate and consideration. The squeezed gasp of sound from Van Hooke's cymbals at the start of the track set the wheels in motion, around a forceful yet reserved drum motif. Few Morrison tracks begin with drums – there is a reason for this one doing so. It is the sound of the album gathering itself together and setting out on the road, having roused itself from restful slumber in 'Haunts Of Ancient Peace'. Morrison's understanding of the role of vocal dynamics is made plain as his vocal comes in at 0.08, almost timidly at first, with his suggestion that he'd like to meet someone, in the country, in the summertime in England. Mick Cox's acoustic takes up the shuffle of the drums, which themselves step up again at 0.26 when the folk-funky electric guitar enters, chugging the urgent, nagging riff, and pushing the song forward. This dynamic prelude sets the track up for the journey it is about to embark upon.

Up to 2.38, the first section evolves out of the drumbeat which opens the track and does so by gradually layering more and more atop the rhythm, with organ, strings and horns joining Morrison's vocal, alongside the swooping bass line (which would become far more important to the piece in its subsequent development as a central feature of Morrison's live sets for the next decade) and the acoustic and electric guitars, emphasising and developing the chunky but fleet-footed rhythmic undertow upon which this section runs. Jeff Labes's string arrangement for this track is in itself a paradox. It is absolutely essential, or so it feels, to the mood and the meaning of the track as recorded here, yet in its innumerable live incarnations, it was never granted a string arrangement in concert, even at the famous 25 July 1986 concert at the Greek Theatre in Berkeley. That concert featured a string quartet led by Terri Adams, with arrangement duties again met by Labes. The version of the song that night was stunning, but made no use of the strings. So Labes's strings are central to the moment as caught in France, early 1980. Indeed the strings provide the bridge from the up-tempo section to the first 'gospel' segment of the song, in which the lyrical mood as well as the musical one shifts, making reference to 'The voice of Mahalia Jackson' coming 'through the ether'. This delivers another of the radio references which we have seen lace Morrison's work, working as a kind of telepathy, a picking up of something on his own particular wavelength.

The dominant element here is slow, forceful repetition. In the phrase 'It ain't whywhywhywhy . . .' the interrogative is repeated nine times, and this will be expanded later. His voice here starts to explore the possibilities opened up to it by this song. Listen to how he sings 'And you wore it down through the ages' for an example of how his delivery communicates the emotional meaning of the line (2.55–3.03) and how his voice becomes a central (although not necessarily *the* central) texture of the through-compositional element of this album. The 'suffering' that shows in the eyes of his companion is paired with a reference to the voice of Mahalia Jackson: the sense of sight and the sense of hearing unify in a feeling. Furthermore, music is by association connected with the possibility of healing, of making that suffering better, or more bearable, by transforming it into something noble and bringing dignity: 'O my high in the art of suffering one'. 'It ain't why, it just is' stands for good and for ill, and rising above such binaries is one of the gifts this song gives us.

At 4.28, after the 'Why why why', we tip back into the opening mood again, but here it is somewhat changed, freer, picking up speed, like a stone rolling down a hill, until he arrests it at 4.49 with 'Wait a minute'. This is musically echoed by Labes's arrangement at this point, the strings pausing and pawing the ground, eager to take off again – the internal dynamics here are breathtaking. He leans into the infamous spoken section which has polarised opinion in the past but is fine by me. It sits perfectly well within the ever-changing mood of the song overall and earns its place, introducing some fellow travellers: Yeats, Lady Gregory, T. S. Eliot, James Joyce. These were all products of the very late nineteenth century and key figures in the development of an aestheticising of the shock of the early twentieth century who transformed the breakdown of what we might characterise as Victorian certainties (and continuities with the ancient landscapes into which *Common One* taps) via the destruction of that solid ground in the Great War and incorporated this fragmentation into their work. Eliot's *The Wasteland* is the prime example of this; indeed the fragmentary coherence of works like *The Wasteland* and James Joyce's *Ulysses* (both 1922) find more than a faint echo in the complex unities of 'Summertime In England' itself. Of course none of these figures were English: Yeats and Lady Gregory were Anglo-Irish aristocracy, Joyce was Dublin Irish and Eliot an Anglophile American born in St. Louis, Missouri, who became naturalised as English – hence the song's 'T.S. Eliot chose England'. Ever aware of drifting too far in any one direction, watch Morrison change this line on the Montreux 1980 DVD to the biographically correct if contextually incongruous 'T.S. Eliot joined Lloyds Bank', to the amusement of John Platania. Towards the close of this section the momentum returns, and his finger-clicks ground the number again and this perkiness of mood begins to lead down to the epic latter section, with a reference to Blake in its allusion to 'Jesus walking down by Avalon'. It is this landscape and its transformative powers which interests Morrison on this record. The section spins down with an question: 'Can you feel the light in

England?', introducing the theme of sensory mingling – we don't see the light, we *feel* it.

At 7.48 the strings form a bridge between this faster segment and the start of the lengthy build to the emotional climax of the song. The busyness and bustle of the earlier sections is set aside for clarity and focus. A crisp on-beat snare follows the church organ which ushers in this section, and the album's title is foregrounded in the line 'O my common one / With the light in the head'. Light is the central motif, as the 'common one', whomsoever we imagine her to be, is associated throughout with light, and illumination ('my illuminated one'). The unmistakable, undeniable sax of Pee Wee Ellis enters the song, and makes its arrival like a positive thought whisper-pushing itself into the consciousness of the song at 8.07, a key moment in the development of this song. This section builds from here, slowly, inexorably, to the emotional climax which I would place in the section running from 11.45 to 14.00, particularly around the crashed cymbal at 11.55 on the 'old' in 'O my common one with the coat so old'. This seems a moment of radical unity, where the fast and slow, the inner and outer, elements come together definitively. Here at this moment we see and feel the common one pure and fully revealed, here she is 'in all her revelation'. Where 'Cyprus Avenue' in its live incarnation alluded to such a vision, 'Summertime In England' earns and wins such a vision, finding the musical and lyrical and emotional vocabulary to render her up. This urge is at the heart of the song and the album, and is close to the central pursuit of Morrison's work overall.

From this climactic point, the song spirals slowly down like sparks dying in dark air, down to the incandescent slow fade which begins around 13.35. It is light rather than sound which Morrison is seeking to explore and invoke here ('can you feel the light in your soul?'), locating the illumination as being one found within rather than without. In these last few moments we feel as if all senses are working hard, and thereby transcending themselves – we 'feel' the visible (light), we 'feel' the silence (sound, or its afterglow), we are all perception. The song ends at 15.32 with Morrison half-singing half-whispering 'Can you feel the silence?' and his solo voice is the last we hear of the song. We are granted, on CD at least, 5 seconds of silence to contemplate before the next song kicks in. It's just enough to 'feel the silence', but not enough to become distracted from it. The silence hangs, in the way it is used by Wordsworth in *The Prelude*, for our consideration and exploration – which is where we began, by the lakeside.[131]

'IF YOU DON'T KNOW WHAT I'M TALKING ABOUT, WHY ARE YOU HERE?': THE 'LIVENESS' OF 'SUMMERTIME IN ENGLAND'

Listening to the complexities, the lyrical audacity, the musical dynamism, the sheer risk-taking which guides 'Summertime In England', one might not have predicted a substantial live presence for this song, especially bearing in mind the frugal infrequency of similarly minded pieces from *Veedon Fleece* and *Astral Weeks*. Yet, remarkably, something stunning emerged in live performance. Indeed I'd argue that this song proved to be a great turning point for Morrison's stagecraft and his understanding of what could be achieved live on stage and in performance in a public space. If you have enjoyed 'It's All In The Game' or 'In The Afternoon' or 'Celtic New Year' in all their extrapolated revelations live, you have 'Summertime In England' to thank for it. My view is that of all Morrison's compositions, this is the song that has exerted most influence over its author, that is, it cleaves most closely to the metaphysical idea of the song teaching the singer. Yet frustratingly, very few of these performances were captured on tape or film and, alas, the version on the Beacon Theatre 1989 show issued on sell-through video is a dud – Morrison's voice is shot (he had flu, apparently) and furthermore the high point of the song in concert had been passed by this point. We see this in how, as in the 1994 live album's version of 'In The Garden', the song is pelted through at such a pace that the sections, and thus the space in which the song could breathe and develop, have been compressed and condensed to such an extent that the performance functions as a kind of cipher of itself, a sort of summary, or a medley of one. It's good, but much is lost.

In contrast, the only commercially issued live take of 'Summertime In England', tucked away on the B-side of a single ('Cry For Home') in spring 1983, catches the song just at the moment of its first blossoming, from being a live performance of the album cut (as seen and heard in the Montreux 1980 DVD) to something which developed a life and a shape entirely worked out and grown on stage. This recording, made at the Usher Hall, Belfast, in June 1982, is the track to which I always direct people when they ask me what is so great about Van Morrison. It fades in and the take is at great speed, but not in great haste. This is the sound of a band well drilled, mercurial but also very robust, with the sizzling keyboard stabs of Phil Coulter and downward pull of David Hayes's bass coming to the fore. The sections are all in place yet it has accelerated from the album's 15.37 running time to a punchy 6.59, and is somehow undiminished by this. The spoken word section contains a development of the album version, including references to W. H. Auden and Christopher Isherwood. Their escape from pre-war Europe to the US via Iceland is described with a factually correct yet somehow censoriously plosive description of how they 'spppplitt!' He also quotes, not entirely accurately, from Beckett: '... and Samuel Beckett said, I can't go on ... but I'll go on'. The source of this is Beckett's novel *The Unnameable*, the final line of which is 'I can't go on, I'll go on'.[132]

This recording preserves an early version of the echo-vocal technique between Morrison and Pee Wee Ellis. Ellis was asked about this:

> [Tony Schiavone]: The call and response routine in Summertime In England remains a powerful highlight of the live shows and it appears to have made its first appearance in May 1981. How did that develop?
>
> PWE: Van had the idea during a rehearsal in San Francisco. He asked us who wanted to answer him in the song and I said I would do it. I still enjoy it ... it's fun ... you never know what he's going to come up with when we do it ... if things are going well for Van it can become an amazing performance.[133]

In this section the song also refers to D. H. Lawrence ('Mr Lawrence!') and, indirectly, his poem 'Song of a Man Who Has Come Through', a phrase which seemed to hold some appeal for Morrison, as it turns up strongly in 'A New Kind Of Man'. Deep into the 'Mr Lawrence' section, something happens and the audience start laughing and applauding, Morrison and Pee Wee Ellis break up and the song suddenly comes out of itself – it's over, and it's right that it is. Something has happened, and the song comes through. It's a remarkable thing to hear.[134]

The title of Lawrence's poem is perhaps what appealed most to Morrison, a song of having survived, of having endured the changes, the embattlement, and come out the other side – the same but changed. So the litany of names in 'Summertime In England' is not 'namedropping' (as some critics have claimed) but an exploration of connections between what has gone before and what has been thought and felt before, via works of the imagination and via shared mythological frameworks of interpretation, and what is here and now. The mythological is the way to get to the real. As Morrison said in 2008, 'behind the ritual, you'll find the spiritual'.[135] Indeed, the lyric's place names mix the mythological and the topographical. Avalon co-exists with Kendal and Bristol, a superb sweep from, as the song later was to reflect in its live performances, North to South, the mythological, secret or hidden England hard by the 'real' place; the sweep being accentuated by riding *up* to Kendal and going *down* by Bristol, and then to Avalon. What is important about the psychological territory mapped out in 'Summertime In England' is that it is defiantly non-metropolitan. It emphasises the provinces or, as Morrison calls it in his call and response with Pee Wee Ellis on the Belfast recording, being 'among the regions'.

Their vocal exchanges riffing on that phrase assist the sense of a previously overlooked or bypassed sense of mystery and richness – 'We're gonna go right through the middle of the land' – that is, the heart of the country, the essence of it. It is, in Seamus Heaney's term, digging.

In his famous poem of that name Heaney compares his father's and grandfather's work and craft with his own, drawing out the differences and likenesses between pen and spade in a way that echoes with Morrison's insistence on his own artisan status. Heaney's poem concludes with this thought:

> Between my finger and my thumb
> The squat pen rests.
> I'll dig with it.[136]

Morrison, like Heaney, is acutely aware of the differences between how he and previous generations made their livings (made plain in 'Choppin' Wood'), but he also establishes connections between what he does and artisan labour. Heaney says he'll dig with his pen, that is, the tool of his trade, and Morrison uses the sharp edge of his music to illuminate what he sees, and that is his tool: 'It's just a job, you know', as he reminds us in 'Why Must I Always Explain?' How does this fit into 'Summertime In England'? 'Can you feel the light in England?' is a question both paradoxical, deliberately blurring realms of perception (as he will do later with the almost gnomic question, 'Can you feel the silence?'), and also a real, non-rhetorical enquiry, earned by the work which has preceded his asking of it. Morrison sees a link between his work and that of previous generations. So there is in the live version's central call-and-response section a real sense of enquiry, embodied in the bridging phrase 'Let's take a look'.

Seamus Heaney crops up in this section, alongside D. H. Lawrence and Dylan Thomas. Heaney's *Preoccupations*, a collection of his essays and think pieces from 1968–78, was published in 1981 and clearly Morrison had armed himself with a copy.[137] The book impacted upon his thinking, his art, and his own relationship with it: 'Mr Heaney! I read your book . . . preoccupations . . . among the regions'. The key detail here harks back to Hardy, Austin, Yeats and Gray: it is in 'the regions', the non-metropolitan centres, that what he is 'looking for' might most richly be found. Heaney's book did not influence Morrison's work as directly as, say, the language of Alice Bailey's theosophical propositions, which swayed the lyrical mood of *Beautiful Vision*. But the spirit of these ideas, of the real meaning of a place/landscape, of a land being hidden and something that needs to be consciously sought out ('Let's take a look'), and indeed the scale of the endeavour ('We're gonna got from north to south . . . east to west . . . right through the middle of the land'), perhaps come via Heaney. Like his English contemporary Ted Hughes, he read the landscape as a kind of manuscript, seeing and decoding a meaning and a life within the land that was obscure or opaque to the casual glance. He took a look. John Montague, later to appear with Morrison in *A Coney Island of the Mind*, wrote in a review of Heaney's book that 'We should feel privileged when a poet admits us to his workshop, as Seamus Heaney seems to do in *Preoccupations*.'[138] Here Montague coincidentally uses the term which would be later used to describe the performance technique through which some of Morrison's greatest stage work would emerge, the 'workshop' versions of certain songs. Indeed this live take of 'Summertime In England' is a prime example of one such workshop.

Next in the litany comes Dylan Thomas, or as he calls him, 'Mr Thomas!'. Morrison notes that 'we lost a few', referring to how Swansea-born poet and writer Dylan Marlais Thomas died in New York City in 1953 at the age of 38, just a year older than Morrison was in 1982. This has resonance for the artistic connections between the two 'Celtic' artists, and Morrison was soon to record a sparkling cover of Robin Williamson's 'Mr Thomas' that would emerge as a B-side and then 15 years later in an unedited version on *The Philosopher's Stone*. On his mind is a connection; so he calls him up. Then before moving onto 'Mr [D. H.] Lawrence', he brings the band down with 'But wait a minute', a superb recorded example of how Morrison moves and guides and directs his band in live performance, and how keenly the musicians attend to his gestures. He begins to whisper, with some wonder in his voice, 'Mr Lawrence', which is echoed by Pee Wee Ellis, following his lead, and they repeat this nine times, sometimes right up close to the mike and sometimes far, far back from it, creating an enthralling sense of suspense and ebb and flow. After the ninth iteration, the performance steps aside from itself as the perspective changes *à la* the rhetorical shift of 'You Know What They're Writing About', as Morrison leans into the mike and issues a decidedly non-rhetorical question to the audience:

VM: If you don't know
PWE: If you don't know
VM: What I'm talking' bout
PWE What I'm talking' bout
VM: Then why are you here?
PWE: Why are you here?

The band surges back in as the crowd, both moved by this 'liveness' of address and also of course wishing to show that they *do* know what he's talking (as opposed to writing) about, roars its approval. Yet what *is* he talking about? I'd suggest that he is considering the unseen connections between ideas and emotions over time and space and place, and by radically normalising these links – 'If you don't know what I'm talking about, then why are you here?' – he hauls these ideas into the mainstream of cultural exchange. As he would say later, this is not rock and roll. 'Mr Lawrence' is invoked five more times at great, passionate volume, before Morrison admits 'a man come through' twice and Ellis leads the band via a skyscraping solo into the final section. Morrison, job done, introduces the band, begins to sing 'Put your head on my shoulder' and then, frustratingly, the track is given a vertiginous fade and we lose the last few moments of this thrilling example of Morrison, in John Montague's phrase, admitting us to his 'workshop'. For all these reasons and more, this seems to me to be one of the very best Morrison recordings, live or studio, that has been made commercially available.[139] It also represents the dynamic breakthrough facilitated by the sublime wholeness expressed via through-composition. That's what these four albums, our three-cornered quartet, have in common, and they reveal deeply rooted and absolutely fundamental core details of Morrison's work and creativity. Late in 2008, an unexpected acknowledgement of the centrality of this creative technique led to a late flowering of an early bloom.

Postscript

Make It Real One More Time Again: *Astral Weeks* Live

In late 2008, an announcement was made which placed even the most focused of Morrison watchers on the back foot – he was to play *Astral Weeks*, in full, live in concert, for the first time. Initially there were just two shows scheduled, at the Hollywood Bowl on 7 and 8 November. Both were recorded, and the set performed on the 7th was issued in early 2009 on Morrison's own label. Having refused the idea of music as heritage so firmly for years, what moved him to decide that this was a good idea? The heritage concert is a contemporary performance phenomenon with artists from the late, great John Martyn to the original, devastatingly powerful line-up of Leeds' Gang of Four playing favoured albums in full. It is an odd idea – after all, we can listen to these albums whenever we like, via disc, tape or sound file. The recreation of albums this way responds to two apparently opposed desires – to hear the music, played live, right now, indexing the uncapturable significance of 'liveness', and also to acknowledge groups of songs – *albums* – as having an internal logic and integrity all of their own. Furthermore, we listen differently to different albums, and some require more active listening than others – that's why some music is called 'easy listening'.

The issue of listening as an active rather than passive activity is meet to the case of *Astral Weeks*. As we have suggested, that album in some ways requires the hearer to develop a new way of listening, just as the record shows Morrison to have found a new way of singing, alongside the blending of disparate musical elements into a new and radical unity. Yet as we have noted, these are songs which have had limited exposure on the live stage – indeed the stats tell us that songs from *Astral Weeks* are as underperformed live as material from, say, *A Period Of Transition*. So when it was announced in Autumn 2008 that Morrison was going to give concerts in which he would perform the whole of the album there was great anticipation, more so when it became known that he was aiming to reunite as many of the musicians who played on the original album as possible. For one reason and another it was only guitar player Jay Berliner who made the stage in Hollywood, but what was the thinking behind this policy? In part, it was an acknowledgement of the specialness of that album and combination of players, but equally it was an experiment – can such moments be recaptured? This is consistent with his periodic interest in the nature of memory and the power of art to aid reconnection with moments past – musical performance as a kind of time travel, or even a defeat of time itself, as Morrison's tone poem of a sleeve note infers ('I've transcended . . . time'[1]). Less metaphysically, Morrison was also asserting his ownership of these songs – the original album remains the property of Warner Bros. – and the shows gave him a chance to reclaim the cultural capital of these songs, alongside an acknowledgement of their market value. It worked: ticket prices for the Hollywood Bowl and New York shows, and the UK shows of 2009 were among the highest ever seen for single shows by an artist of the 'rock' era – all shows sold out smartly. The shows also seemed to offer the possibility of reaching a rapprochement with these songs, drawing them fully into the Morrison repertoire.

So how did the reality match up to the burden of expectation coming from the audience and, just maybe, the artist, of such an unexpected reunion, of such a deliberate and integrated return to the time and place of *Astral Weeks*? While certain songs were not entirely unperformed – see 'Cyprus Avenue''s starring role on *It's Too Late To Stop Now* – the difference in this case was of course that all eight songs were to be presented together. It is noteworthy that although in the past Morrison has said that the division of the sides of the original album into 'In The Beginning' and 'Afterwards' was relatively insignificant, it is retained here as a listing device on the sleeve, while the encore material is categorised, curiously as 'Bonus'.

Morrison's voice is remarkably unfazed by the 40-year gap between then and now, which suggests that there is a specific voice which is necessarily brought to bear upon a certain set of songs, one that is both required and called out by those particular tunes. Likewise, Morrison was unambiguous in his estimation of these shows: 'There was magic on that stage. I felt it. We had only one rehearsal after forty years and took to the stage and brought it. I hope that comes through to the listener. It did for me and the players.'[2] The natural flow of the performance seems to correspond with the music's charmed reputation. As listeners, we hear what the audience in Hollywood heard, with the album being introduced (not by Morrison) as a whole: 'Ladies and gentlemen, we present to you . . . *Astral Weeks*'.[3] The title track arrives, that unmistakable rhythmic pulse tugging away at the tune's root, with the little shivers of strings glistening upon the surfaces. The vocal is strong and free, drawing on both the head notes of the young man and the deeper, chest resonance of the mature voice. It is quite moving to hear the two registers lock together in the way that they do on these performances. The performance does not then offer a 'heritage' version of the well-known album track – for example, the fiddle interlude after 'come through' at 2.48 is a contemporary touch, showing how integral is the fit between his new music and where his music came from as it melds with the wisps of flute which dance around the rhythm. David Hayes's intuitive downward reach on the double bass cues in the 'home on high' coda at 5.44. This section reveals how Morrison's ability to extend and extemporise at the unbound end of a song in concert goes right back to *Astral Weeks* itself, as he pulls down the section credited as 'I Believe I've Transcended', the initial central feature of which is a riffing on the word 'Caledonia', initially as a conversation with the flute of Richie Buckley. The latter part is a reworking of the 'Mountainside' lyric heard on the epic live 'Burning Ground', drawing together the threads of his earliest work with the running stream of his creativity via one of his most powerful and startling live performances. Under all this the strings hover, awaiting resolution.

'Beside You', one of the very least performed numbers from the original album, is fresh and as uncanny as its original – listen to the note he reaches on 'dogs' at 1.27–28. The diamond-studded highway is rediscovered as an image of the dream of the road as framed by Kerouac and Hank Williams, alluring, endless, but lost and dark. Yet someone is there, too, beside you. This song is much harder to realize live than, say, the title track, because of the absence of a delineated melodic or rhythmic centre, but of course that is precisely what lends the song its unsettling quality, emphasised by the flamenco flourish that closes the tune.

Surprising the audience and undoing the heritage nature of the performance by straying from the original song order, 'Slim Slow Slider' arrives, restored to its extended form (on the album it was truncated by the infamous edit before the spiralling outro). This is a song Morrison has played not too often live but often enough for him to be more confident of the shapes his voice needs to assume to deliver its troubled mix of resignation and anxious hope in a live setting. The real pleasure in this begins after the main body of the song, from 3.25 where he begins to explore the sound and feeling of the notes and the flow of the notes through the voice. This leads into the song's spur, credited as 'I Start Breaking Down', which is punctuated by a stunning and abrasive guitar figure – effectively a desiccation of the strings' tone, making the instrument one of pure percussion – in a little storm which runs from 4.50, the band following him and building up behind him until it subsides again at 6.20. The effect is not unlike the remarkable moment in 'Almost Independence Day' analysed in Chapter Six, and demonstrates how this song not only admits the chaos described in the lyric as a musical texture but somehow requires it to fully converse with that lyric.

Following on, 'Sweet Thing' provides new, dear light after such brooding darkness as it does on the original album, where it follows 'Beside You'. Morrison swoops up and over and around the vocal melody, yet it is the instrumental section, rolling and tumbling from 2.27–3.00, which is the emotional centre of this performance, with Tony Fitzgibbon's viola fully expressing the freshness and natural ecstasies of the song. Morrison's harmonica snuffles unexpectedly in the last minute-and-a-half, from 4.14 on, provide a bluesy earthing of this abundant, celestial energy in an unmistakable run, drawing in his superb technique of breathing, singing and speaking through the instrument, Little Walter-style, but utterly himself.

'The Way Young Lovers Do' reveals itself unexpectedly to be balancing on the ball of a two-note jazz turnaround, picked out here by the guitar of Jay Berliner. This expresses the giddy heart of this song, perpetually finding its balance through forward movement, seeking steadiness but pursuing change. The song is discharged quickly, and is by far the shortest tune here, but it is one of the best ensemble performances on this album. As Morrison told the *Los Angeles Times* on the eve of the Hollywood shows, 'the song 'The Way Young Lovers Do'. What is it? I don't know – I made it up. Anyway, what 90-year-old does not want to feel like young lovers do? Most probably would – it's as simple as that'.[4] It is remarkable that a 64-year-old would connect the ideas of a 23-year-old to the desires of a 90-year-old, and in doing so Morrison centralizes the importance of living fully in the here and now. The tune is taken straight, and is close to the original.

Where this song was followed by 'Madame George' on the original album, here it leads to 'Cyprus Avenue' – this tune has form in the Van Morrison live catalogue, providing the unforgettable performances which closed his set right up to the issue of *It's Too Late To Stop Now*. Morrison's vocal references this collective memory with his onomatopoeic stuttering over his tongue getting tied, just as he did in the early 1970s shows, referencing again the underlying humour which sits quietly with the emotional intensity. Yet the performance also finds room for the fresh element too: it is a joy to hear Paul Moran's harpsichord reprising the late Larry Fallon's original overdubs, surely the first time these have been attempted onstage. The coda to the tune is now credited as 'You Came Walking Down' and is brief – there is no attempt to repeat the famous dramatics of the early 70s version and it is all the better for that. As we noted earlier, he ain't gonna fake it, like Johnnie Ray. Instead we get a gentle, reflective, tough melancholia and the sometime-heard dream vision of the street in the winter, and the vision of the windfall of apples – the girl in the song suddenly thereby being connected to the charmed figure in 'Steppin' Out Queen', just a windfall away. The song is less open to renewal in some ways, from being so firmly fixed in the collective memory as it was in 1973, but this version brings something new to the table and in doing so the bloom on its cheek is still in bud.

'Ballerina' is another of the tunes on the album which has tended to be overshadowed by the two epic tracks, and this version is so sweetly in agreement with the 1968 version that just the sound of it is very moving. Time is indeed somehow transcended here, as Morrison's tone poem of a sleeve note suggests, and this song's fidelity to something which we don't necessarily hear out loud on either version seems to me to open a door into a kind of metaphysical timelessness and eternal moment available only through the portal of the music itself. We step lightly where otherwise our steps and bodies are heavy. The lengthy repetitions of 'very' and 'the light' work against the restlessness of the crowd from 5.00–18, and indeed he shushes the crowd twice in this short section, illustrating a rare dynamic between stage and audience and also how proprietorial a crowd can be about the songs that move them. The tune kicks up its heels, quite unexpectedly, at 5.44, where the song had been looking like it was heading for a long, misty wind-down. It suddenly surges up with an almost hoedown energy, the curlicues of fiddle emphasising this. Almost as soon as it starts, this is then brought back down and by 5.54 we are back to the suspended elegance of the original – this short, sharp change is perhaps a reference to the enforced show business of the lyric at this point ('Here comes the man, and he says the show must go on'), and Morrison is never happy to concur with this showbiz maxim. Indeed he laughs directly after this, clearly having fun with the tune, the band, and himself. He delivers some nice, extended unison singing from 6.48 in the spur credited as 'Move On Up', itself a reference to Curtis Mayfield and James Brown, a connection made plain in the ad libs here. The tune moves toward to its close as the seven-note motif studied in Chapter Five appears from 9.01–06, and is very briefly picked up and echoed at 9.05 by the sax of Richie Buckley, his experience and long track record with Morrison showing here in that he is supremely attentive to what the singer is doing, even if only for a fleeting moment.

The *Astral Weeks* section of the CD closes with 'Madame George'. Never heard before on a live album, it cleaves closely to the 1968 recording, including the shuffle of military drums behind the soldier boy, for example. Despite its renown, this song has been rarely heard live and while in terms of numbers of performances it is not so far behind 'Cyprus Avenue', the latter feels much more familiar thanks to its crucial place in the set caught on *It's Too Late To Stop Now* – such is the power of the live recording. Again, the blues root of the tune becomes discernible, revealed through the shimmering beauty of its meditative still point, slowly, sensually seesawing between two chords, pushing forward and pulling away. Here Morrison does not list the song's coda as a separate piece, instead he uses the image of the train to take over and lets the mood do the work toward the tune's close, and he is back-announced at 7.38–48, while he is still singing. The band spread and loosen a little as he goes, as they always do, the focus less intently held, until the final breakdown at 8.36.

The 'encore' section features 'Listen To The Lion' and, curiously, a piece entitled 'Common One' which is a segment of 'Summertime In England'. 'Listen To The Lion' lends its name to his new record label, taking over from Exile, it seems, and provides the encore on this album. It is a fine, free and supple version, making great use of the harmonica technique briefly heard on 'Slim Slow Slider', and which was also heard on the BBC show from Malvern in 2003. This arrangement lacks the gorgeous horn motif that graced that version but is still a pleasure to hear – the final segment powered by the suck-and-blow harmonica is dubbed 'The Lion Speaks', making plain the connection between the invitation to listen and the actual sound we are being directed toward. The harmonica takes the role of the vocal experiments we explored in the Chapter Five.

'Common One' turns out to be the gospel section from 'Summertime In England', with the famed echo technique between Morrison and Buckley picking up from the 1982 version. This version also incorporates a verse from 'A Town Called Paradise', and the 'squealing feeling' section worked up live in the late 80s. I certainly never thought I'd hear Morrison return to this way of working and it shows that he can do it, most directly, whenever the spirit moves him. It also features, once again, the seven-note motif, briefly heard on 'Ballerina' but exchanged fully this time with Buckley's sax, from 2.50–3.26. From 4.27 we head for the close, with the question 'Can you feel the silence . . . in the mystic church?', which dwindles forcefully as we hear Morrison and Buckley retreat from the mikes and is pulled right down to the tick of the snare before winding up with the band in full accord at 6.12. It provided the final tune in the evening's first set and is transplanted to this final position with a purpose. It is a resonant précis of the mood not only of 'Summertime In England' but of Morrison's post-*Astral Weeks* output as a whole, and confirms that it is from this song, and this mood, that Morrison found a substantial, rich and mature musical and lyrical vocabulary via which to express, create and explore his hymns to the silence.

Appendix One

Case Study – On the Road: The 2006 Shows

The year 2006 was one of both consolidation and change for Van Morrison. He played 92 shows over the 12-month period, in the following countries:

- The UK (39)
- The US (23)
- Spain (14)
- Ireland (2 (+ 1 private show))
- Canada (2)
- Germany (3)
- Austria (1)
- Switzerland (3)
- The Netherlands (2)
- Norway (2)

Total: 92 shows

It is not only the number of shows he played that is revealing, but the geographical spread. Quite sensibly, he spent some of the winter months of January and February (as identified in 'Fire In The Belly') playing in sunnier southern European climes, specifically Spain. He opened the year's account with a brace of shows in Tenerife, the main island of the Canary Islands, then moved to the mainland with two shows in Madrid, and then a run of shows in the southern region of Andalucía, in the cities of Malaga, Almeria and Granada. This Hispanic sojourn was interrupted only by his near-traditional two-night return to the Waterfront Hall in Belfast in the first days of February. The light and warmth of Almeria will no doubt have felt all the more pleasant when he flew back out to Spain the following week. What these shows did enable him to do was to give the new country material a gradual run-in, and they were 'officially' debuted at the Waterfront on 3 and 4 February, both shows featuring five of the tracks from the soon-to-be issued *Pay The Devil*. This was done by expanding the relatively compact band which had played the Spanish shows, introducing Paul Godden on pedal steel, Bob Loveday on fiddle and, most crucially, Crawford Bell on guitar, trumpet and vocals, replacing Matt Holland. This signalled the very definite arrival of the crisp, 'Northern Irish country' sound which would come to dominate Morrison's live sound until the *Astral Weeks* revival in late 2008.

By the time he went back to Spain the country material was integrated enough to occupy seven slots in the 90-minute, 23-song set in Almeria, and this included a central block of four running consecutively. He brought the show back to the UK in mid-February for two nights in Brighton – this effectively represented the public debut in Britain of this material and the new album again supplied up to a third of the set on both nights. During this trip to the South Coast Morrison stepped aboard the promotional merry-go-round via an interview with Nick Barraclough for BBC Radio 2's country music show, which was broadcast free to air as a one-hour special to promote the release of *Pay The Devil* on 15 March. The schedule then took him to Zurich, Switzerland for two nights (22–23 February), for a more muscular and funky 'Central European' set – he always funks up for shows in Switzerland, an example of how attentive he is to place in his performance. The shows featured Candy Dulfer aiding and abetting Teena Lyle, and were particularly notable for the fact that the first night went almost ten minutes over the infamous 90-minute mark, thanks to an almighty version of 'And The Healing Has Begun', with which the evening closed.

Making his way over to the US for a show on 2 March, Morrison stepped up the promotional drive for *Pay The Devil*, opening the run of shows with effectively a 'secret' warm-up show at Rancho Nicasio, a storied roadhouse at West Marin, California. Owned by Bob Brown, former manager of Huey Lewis and the News, the venue provided a welcoming and conducive atmosphere for the show. Tickets went for $150 and up, and very quickly. Morrison had played here before, albeit in much looser times and circumstances, doing the vocal chores for a band put together by David Hayes for a party for a local, supportive radio station in 1979. The venue had obviously stuck in his mind, and it was an appropriate place for the warm-up show. The show was also notable for a 4 p.m. start, designed to combat jet lag for the band. The area is a kind of home from home for Morrison and local girl Shana Morrison guested on 'More And More'. Here also we saw the debut of pedal steel player Cindy Cashdollar and fiddle player Jason Roberts, both full-on country/rock players and veterans of Asleep At The Wheel. Duly warmed up and de-lagged, 3 March saw the tour get back to the traditional venues, in San Francisco and Los Angeles, and then on to Texas, which, to borrow from 'Snow In San Anselmo', hadn't happened in nearly thirty years – Morrison had lasted played in the state in October 1979, at Austin. By contrast, Morrison had played California well over a hundred times over the same period. This is a good example of the concentrated patterns of his live work, which see him a frequent visitor to some locales and a virtual stranger to others. These patterns operate on a micro-scale too – for example, he rarely plays shows in the east of England, while visiting the north, south and west frequently. Quite remarkably, until November 2007, he had never played in Norwich, the beautiful and distinguished county town of Norfolk, and he has played in Cambridge only five times.

These US shows served as a limbering up for the 'Big One' as far as this tour was concerned: the Ryman Auditorium in Nashville on 7 March. This show was filmed and parts of it were issued on the DVD included in later, limited edition copies of *Pay The Devil*, alongside interview footage. An edited version of this was shown in the UK on BBC Four on 9 June. The Ryman is an unusual venue in that it is arranged in a kind of semi-circle, with pew-style seating, for the very good reason that it was originally a gospel tabernacle in downtown Nashville. It was built in the 1890s and was the home of the Grand Ole Opry from 1943 to 1974. This detail and 'change of use' exemplifies the deep link between country and gospel musics and their connections with religious ritual. The Ryman was, and is, famed for its intimacy. Indeed the 'new' venue for the Grand Ole Opry, 'Opryland', built in 1974 to seat a bigger audience and be better suited to broadcasting, was designed to replicate the style and shape of the Ryman in order to retain that sense of community and closeness. They did this in part by removing the old stage from the Ryman and using it as the stage at Opryland. So the stage Morrison stood upon on 7 March 2006 was not the same one trodden by Hank Williams, Kitty Wells or the Carter Family, although everything else in the Ryman is as it was in their day.

While the Ryman set included only six of the *Pay The Devil* tracks, thus not deferring absolutely to the occasion, Morrison's appearance at the Ryman conferred 'authenticity' upon his recordings of these songs, and his right to tread the boards went undisputed. Of course to country music aficionados the majority of the songs on *Pay The Devil* are very familiar – like Elvis Costello's Nashville-recorded, Billy Sherrill-produced *Almost Blue* from 1981, the album spread knowledge of these songs beyond the usual niche market and showed up links between what the market expects of Morrison and these songs, which are less well known to his general audience. In the interview footage on the

DVD Morrison emphasised this, speaking as warmly of Ray Charles's country recordings as, say, Hank Williams or Webb Pierce's work. He seeks to break down these boundaries because that's how he feels the music to be working, as opposed to how it is understood commercially through genre-based marketing. Just as Costello added Gram Parsons songs to the country canon on *Almost Blue*, Morrison slipped Rodney Crowell's 70s country-rock cult classic 'Til I Gain Control Again' onto the album and also gave it its live debut at the Ryman. This was the highlight of a determined set, Morrison reaching deep down into the gut for a superb, caustic finale to the song. For the last number, however, we were back in the Belfast backstreet, with the 'Celtic New Year/Healing Game' double.

A show in Boston and the whole operation, *sans* Cindy Cashdollar and Jason Roberts, swung back over to Europe, first a run of four shows in England and a TV promo appearance. Morrison played 'Big Blue Diamonds' on the legendary prime time Parkinson chat show – no chat ensued, however – and it was then over to Norway for two shows in Stavanger in early April. All shows focused on the new album, mixed with a rotating selection of material, and all being around 22 songs in length. The set varied little in local terms in this run of shows – no repeat of his flirtations with the flourishing Norwegian jazz scene, for example, which produced such marvels at Voss in 1988 – but the material was bedded in very well by this stage.

Three nights at the Pigalle Club in London in mid-April, with sky-high ticket prices, were cancelled at short notice, and his next show was at the famous-for-golf Gleneagles Hotel in Killarney in the Irish Republic. This was not as it first might seem a corporate event – although Morrison would play a golf-friendly private show in Dublin later in the year – and this outing was distinguished by the rare live appearances of 'Warm Love' and, appropriate for a show deep in *Veedon Fleece* country, 'Streets Of Arklow/You Don't Pull No Punches'. Swerving back west over the ocean from Ireland's Atlantic coast, his next show was at the legendary Hollywood Bowl, the first of a four-date trip to the US. The last of these shows was at another iconic venue, New York's Madison Square Garden was followed by a break in live work from April 24 to May 18, after which he played two shows in Germany, in Duisberg and Berlin. Both shows included 'Irish Heartbeat', a big favourite with his German audiences, and a song he often plays in that country.

From here he next played in Perth, Scotland, followed by four solid-ground shows in Northern Ireland, doubling up at both Warrenpoint and Londonderry, as part of the 'Blues on the Bay' festival. These signalled the start of Morrison's summer schedule, as the festival season kicked off. The next few weeks saw him yo-yoing across Europe, playing Valencia in Spain, London (a single Pigalle show), Hampton Court Palace for two nights, then back to Spain and the great

Basque city of Bilbao. Early July found him at the 2006 Montreux Jazz Festival at the legendary Casino Barriere, linking up with his old friend Claude Nobs, before a two-week break. Into high summer, a string of shows took in seven in the UK (of which five were outdoor, with two nights at a favoured venue, the Princess Theatre in Torquay), three in the US (which saw him reunited with Cindy Cashdollar – the European shows post-April had been without pedal steel), one in Canada (Toronto), one in Austria (Vienna) on his sixty-first birthday, and one in Leipzig, his first trip to the former East Germany.

By the time he visited the Greek Theatre in Berkeley on 12 September, *Pay The Devil* was contributing only two of the 19 songs, but the sound of it was becoming increasingly that of the set. In part this is due to the full complement of the Crawford Bell Singers adding their distinctively Nashville-meets-Ulster vocal style, alongside the third link-up with Cindy Cashdollar. The corporate event mentioned earlier took place on 20 September at Dublin's City West Hotel, being the Ryder Cup Gala Dinner, and the invitation-only guest list was groaning with VIPs, including his auld sweat Bill Clinton, 'New Biography' fan George Bush, Michael Douglas and his wife Catherine Zeta-Jones, alongside multitudes of sportspeople from Arnold Palmer to English cricketing legend Ian Botham. Though musically this event seems unpromising, it was significant in that it marked the arrival of the answer to Morrison's European pedal steel problem, in the shape of prodigiously gifted Yorkshire-born pedal steel and dobro player, Sarah Jory, scion of the celebratedly musical Jory family of West Yorkshire. Diving back into the deep end, the next two shows were an early/late double at Ronnie Scott's in Soho. With interesting, if not typical perversity, Morrison's finally having found his own pedal steel player coincided with the minimising of the *Pay The Devil* material in the set – these two shows featured only 'Playhouse' (both sets) and 'There Stands The Glass' (early). A pre-Halloween ramble across the UK took the show to Blackpool, giving two shows as part of Liverpool's 'Irish Festival' and a strong show in York, which I was able to see. These all really integrated the new sound – the Crawford Bell Singers, Sarah Jory – into Morrison's musical vocabulary, as opposed to the schism between the 'country' and the 'non-country' repertoires.

The remarkable live year for Morrison took another wholly unexpected turn in early November, when he appeared as support act in North America for the Rolling Stones on their *Bigger Bang* tour for three nights in the first week of November, delivering somewhat abbreviated sets. The first night of this stint in Vancouver he did not make due to illness, but played the shows at Seattle and Oakland. These curious events were the first 'support gigs' Morrison had ever played post-*Astral Weeks*, the likes of his tours with Ray Charles and Bob Dylan being 'co-billed'. Following these incongruous money-spinners,

Morrison returned to Spain, for two shows in Zaragoza, the second night of which (18 November) yielded an unexpected resurgence in the *Pay The Devil* material, featuring four of the album's songs (including rare outings for 'Til I Gain Control Again' and 'Things Have Gone To Pieces') in a superb and varied set that included 'Foggy Mountain Top', 'Into The Mystic', the self-descriptively rare 'Once In A Blue Moon' and 'Meet Me In The Indian Summer'.

A two-week break took the year into December, and a five-show run up to Christmas took the show to Edinburgh's Usher Hall, the Sage at Gateshead, Malvern's Festival Theatre (another favourite venue), Bristol's much-visited Colston Hall, and back up north for a show at Glasgow's Clyde Auditorium. The sets included a core of material and a variety of songs that appeared as one-offs. For example, at the Malvern show, his fondness for the venue perhaps led him to dust down 'Enlightenment' and 'A Shot Of Rhythm And Blues', bringing his 'country year' to a close by going back to a country-blues number he cut on a previous foray into the area, 2000's *You Win Again*. Two conducive shows between Christmas and New Year in the US brought 2006 to an end. The final shows of the year were in San Francisco and, for the first time, Las Vegas – where he did indeed play the 'Las Vegas' version of 'Have I Told You Lately'. Thus his year closed in the home of a certain kind of showbiz, and following the steps of Presley, Sinatra and the Rat Pack.

As an example of Van Morrison's schedule as a working musician, 2006 is particularly illuminating. Early on the promotional round influenced the set by degrees and then came to dominate at a certain opportune time, before being gradually sublimated into the overall musical vocabulary and performative repertoire. Then there were the corporate gigs; the money-spinning supports; the warm-up gigs; the shows scattered far and wide; the shows right down the road at home; shows in York and New York, Malvern and Las Vegas; the festival shows for the picnickers and the shows at the legendary jazz clubs.

This is just one year on the road. Morrison has been touring and playing professionally for nearly 50 years. The road does indeed go on forever; little wonder he calls it 'going up that mountainside'. At the centre of it all, the cause and the reason for it all, is still the music.

Appendix Two

Recording Studios/ Concert Venues Used By Van Morrison For Albums

Blowin' Your Mind!: Century Sound Studios, New York.
Astral Weeks: Century Sound Studios, New York.
Moondance: A&R Recording Studios, 46th Street, New York.
His Band And The Street Choir: A&R Recording Studios, 46th Street, New York.
Tupelo Honey: Wally Heider Studio, San Francisco/Columbia Studios, San Francisco.
Saint Dominic's Preview: Wally Heider, Pacific High Studios, San Francisco/The Church, San Anselmo, California.
Hard Nose The Highway: Caledonia Studio, Fairfax, California.
It's Too Late To Stop Now: Rainbow Theatre, London/Troubadour, Los Angeles/ Santa Monica Civic Auditorium, Los Angeles.
Veedon Fleece: Caledonia Studio, Fairfax, California/Mercury Studios, New York.
A Period Of Transition: Caledonia Studio, Fairfax, California.
Wavelength: Shangri-La Studios, Malibu, California.
Into The Music: Record Plant, Sausalito, California.
Common One: Super Bear Studios, France.
Beautiful Vision: Record Plant, Sausalito, California.
Inarticulate Speech Of The Heart: Harbour Sound, Sausalito, California/Tres Virgos, San Rafael, California/Record Plant, Sausalito, California/Townhouse, London.
Live At the Grand Opera House, Belfast: Grand Opera House, Belfast.
A Sense Of Wonder: Record Plant, Sausalito, California.

No Guru, No Method, No Teacher: Studio D, Sausalito, California/Record Plant, Sausalito, California.
Poetic Champions Compose: Wool Hall, Beckington.
Irish Heartbeat: Windmill Lane Studios, Dublin.
Avalon Sunset: Eden Studios, London/Townhouse Studios, London.
Enlightenment: Wool Hall, Beckington/Townhouse Studios, London/The Kirk, Rode.
Hymns To The Silence: Wool Hall, Beckington/Pavilion Studios, London.
Too Long In Exile: Wool Hall, Beckington/The Plant, Sausalito, California.
A Night In San Francisco: Masonic Auditorium, San Francisco/Mystic Theatre, Petaluma.
Days Like This: Windmill Lane Studios, Dublin/Realworld, Bath.
How Long Has This Been Going On?: Ronnie Scott's, London.
Tell Me Something: Wool Hall, Beckington.
The Healing Game: Windmill Lane Studios, Dublin.
Back On Top: Wool Hall, Beckington.
The Skiffle Sessions: Whitla Hall, Belfast.
You Win Again: Wool Hall, Beckington.
Down The Road: Wool Hall, Beckington.
What's Wrong With This Picture?: Wool Hall, Beckington/Kilmurray House, Dublin/Westland Studios, Dublin.
Magic Time: Wool Hall, Beckington/Windmill Lane Studios, Dublin.
Pay The Devil: Windmill Lane Studios, Dublin.
Live At Austin City Limits Festival: Zilker Park, Austin, Texas.
Keep It Simple: Windmill Lane Studios, Dublin.
Astral Weeks Live At The Hollywood Bowl: Hollywood Bowl, California.

Notes

Chapter One: Imagining America: Jazz, Blues, Country and the Mythologies of the West

1 See, for example, L. Cooper and B. Cooper: 'The pendulum of Cultural Imperialism - Popular Music Interchanges between the US and Britain 1943–1967', in G. Crnkovic and S. Ramet (eds): *Kazaaam! Splat! Ploof! The American Impact on European Popular Culture Since 1945* (Oxford: Rowman and Littlefield, 2003), pp. 69–82.
2 See Mo Foster: *Play Like Elvis! How British Musicians Bought the American Dream* (Sanctuary, 2000).
3 *Red, White and Blues*, dir. Mike Figgis, 2003.
4 Ritchie Yorke: *Van Morrison: Into the Music* (London: Charisma Books, 1975), p. 20.
5 Stephen G. Smith: 'Blues and Our Mind-Body Problem', *Popular Music*, Vol. 11, No. 1, January 1992, pp. 41–52.
6 Big Joe Turner: 'Oke-She-Moke-She-Pop', *Flip, Flop And Fly 1951–1955* (Rev-Ola/Cherry Red, 2006); Robert Johnson: 'Crossroads', *The Complete Recordings* (Sony, 1991).
7 Alan Lomax: *The Land Where the Blues Began* (London: Minerva, 1993); John Lomax: *Adventures of a Ballad Hunter* (New York: Macmillan, 1947); John Lomax (ed.): *Folk Songs as Sung by Leadbelly* (New York: Macmillan, 1936). See also the discography at http://culturalequity.org/alanlomax/ce_alanlomax_discography.php
8 Van Morrison interviewed on *Soul Britannia*, dir. Jeremy Marre, BBC, 2007.
9 Van Morrison interviewed by Paul Sexton in *Billboard*, 18 March 2006.
10 Van Morrison: 'John Henry' and 'Western Plain', *The Philosopher's Stone* (Exile, 1998).

11 *So Hard to Beat*, dir. Stuart Bailie, BBC Northern Ireland, 2007.

12 H. Barker and Y. Taylor: *Faking It: The Quest for Authenticity In Popular Music* (London: Faber and Faber, 2007), pp. 1–23. See also ibid., p. 60 (variant versions), p. 88 (comparison between Ledbetter and Mississippi John Hurt) and p. 298 (discussion of Ry Cooder's versions of Leadbelly songs). For further background on this, see Marybeth Hamilton: *In Search of the Blues: Black Voices, White Visions* (London: Jonathan Cape, 2007), Chapter Four, 'Sound Photographs of Negroes', pp. 79–124.

13 Van Morrison interviewed on *Soul Britannia*, dir. Jeremy Marre, BBC, 2007. Online at: http://www.vanmorrison.com

14 Morrison discusses the possible connection between fado and the blues with Michelle Rocca on the promotional VHS video tape for the *Days Like This* album, 1995.

15 Van Morrison: 'Sometimes I Feel Like A Motherless Child', *Poetic Champions Compose* (Mercury, 1987).

16 Jackson C. Frank: 'Blues Run The Game', *Jackson C. Frank* (Columbia, 1965/ Sanctuary, 2008); Simon and Garfunkel: 'Blues Run The Game', *Old Friends* (Sony, 1998).

17 Samuel Floyd: 'The Power of Black Music', *Black Music Research Journal*, Vol. 21, No. 2, Autumn 2001, p. 218.

18 Ibid.

19 Van Morrison interviewed by Ben Greenman in *The New Yorker*, 9 March 2009.

20 Them: 'Mystic Eyes', *The Story Of Them* (Deram, 1997).

21 Ray Charles: *Live At Newport* (Atlantic, 1959) (the intro to 'Fool For You').

22 Paul Oliver: *Blues Fell This Morning: Meaning in the Blues* (Cambridge University Press, 1969). Morrison made this remark at the Barbican Theatre, York, on 7 October 2006.

23 Van Morrison interviewed by John Kelly in the *Irish Times*, 11 April 1998.

24 Ben Sidran to the author, March 2008.

25 Van Morrison: 'Moondance', *Moondance* (Warner Bros., 1970).

26 Modern Jazz Quartet: *Sundance* (Atlantic, 1964).

27 Yorke, p. 73.

28 Van Morrison: 'Moondance/My Funny Valentine', *A Night In San Francisco* (Exile/Polydor, 1994).

29 Van Morrison: 'I Will Be There', *Saint Dominic's Preview* (Warner Bros., 1972).

30 Van Morrison with the Caledonia Soul Express: 'Caledonia'/'What's Up, Crazy Pup?', (Warner Bros., 1974) (single); Louis Jordan and His Tympany Five: 'Caldonia' (aka 'Caldonia Boogie'), *Louis Jordan And His Tympany Five* (JSP, 2001) (1945 recording).

31 Peter Wolf in *Rolling Stone*, 12 November 1998.

32 Van Morrison, Georgie Fame and Friends: *How Long Has This Been Going On?* (Verve, 1995).

33 Chet Baker: 'Almost Blue', *Let's Get Lost* (RCA, 1989).
34 Van Morrison, Georgie Fame and Friends: 'Heathrow Shuffle', *How Long Has This Been Going On?* (Verve, 1995).
35 Ben Sidran: *Black Talk: How the Music of Black America Created a Radical Alternative to the Values of Western Literary Tradition* (New York: Holt, Rinehart & Winston, 1970; London: DaCapo, 1980); Ben Sidran: *Talking Jazz Conversations with Great American Musicians: An Illustrated Oral History* (London: Da Capo, 1994); Ben Sidran: *Ben Sidran: A Life in the Music* (New York: Taylor Trade Publishing, 2003).
36 Ben Sidran to the author, April 2008.
37 Van Morrison, Mose Allison, Ben Sidran and Georgie Fame: *Tell Me Something* (Verve, 1996).
38 Waylon Jennings: 'Are You Sure Hank Done It This Way?', *The Essential Waylon Jennings* (Sony, 2007).
39 Ryman Theatre documentary DVD issued with later versions of *Pay The Devil* (Exile, 2006).
40 Elvis Presley: 'Milk Cow Blues', *The Sun Recordings* (RCA, 1979).
41 Dick Weissman: *Blues: The Basics* (London: Routledge, 2004), p. 66.
42 Ryman Theatre documentary DVD issued with later versions of *Pay The Devil* (Exile, 2006).
43 Van Morrison: 'Foggy Mountain Top', *The Philosopher's Stone* (Exile, 1998).
44 Yorke, p. 91.
45 Van Morrison: 'I Wanna Roo You', *Tupelo Honey* (Warner Bros., 1971).
46 Martin Buzacott and Andrew Ford: *Speaking in Tongues: The Songs of Van Morrison* (Sydney: ABC Books, 2005), p. 249.
47 Van Morrison: 'Tupelo Honey', *Tupelo Honey* (Warner Bros, 1971); Van Morrison and Bobby 'Blue' Bland: 'Tupelo Honey', *The Best Of Van Morrison Vol. 3* (Exile, 2007).
48 Van Morrison and Linda Gail Lewis: *You Win Again* (Exile, 2000).
49 Jools Holland, sleeve note to *You Win Again* (Exile, 2000).
50 These comments can be found online at: http://www.lindagaillewis.com
51 Van Morrison: *Pay The Devil* (Exile, 2006).
52 Van Morrison: 'In The Afternoon' on 'Meet Me In The Indian Summer' (Exile, 2002) (single).
53 Nathaniel Hawthorne (1850): *The Scarlet Letter* (London: Penguin, 2005); Jeannie C. Riley: 'Harper Valley PTA' (Plantation Records, 1968); Kitty Wells: 'Paying For That Back Street Affair' (female version) written by Billy Wallace and Jimmy Rule (RCA Victor, 1953). The first verse runs thus:

> Yes, I thought that you were true when I fell in love with you
> For you told me you always would play square
> Then I learned you had a home that your wife had done gone wrong
> And our love was just a back street affair.

54 Van Morrison: 'Back Street Affair', *Pay The Devil* (Exile 2006).
55 Ibid., 'Till I Gain Control Again'.
56 Greil Marcus: *Mystery Train: Images of America in Rock 'n' Roll Music* (London: Penguin, 2002); *O Brother, Where Art Thou?*, dir. Joel Coen, 1999.
57 Ryman Theatre documentary DVD issued with later versions of *Pay The Devil* (Exile, 2006).
58 Van Morrison: 'Philosopher's Stone', *Back On Top* (Exile, 1999).
59 Van Morrison interviewed by Ivan Martin in *Sunday World*, 2 January 2000.
60 Ibid.
61 John Ingham, *National Rockstar*, 21 September 1976.
62 George Melly: *Revolt into Style: The Pop Arts in Britain* (London: Penguin, 1970), pp. 28–30.
63 Lonnie Donegan: *Talking Guitar Blues Anthology* (Sanctuary, 1999).
64 Lonnie Donegan: *Muleskinner Blues* (BMG, 1998).
65 Van Morrison, Lonnie Donegan and Chris Barber: *The Skiffle Sessions* (Exile, 1999). Sleeve note by Van Morrison.
66 *Van Morrison in Ireland*, dir. Mike Radford, 1980.
67 Van Morrison, Lonnie Donegan and Chris Barber: *The Skiffle Sessions* (Exile, 1999). Sleeve note by Van Morrison.
68 Ibid.
69 Van Morrison in *Red, White and Blues*, dir. Mike Figgis, 2003.
70 Van Morrison, Lonnie Donegan and Chris Barber: *The Skiffle Sessions* (Exile, 1999). Sleeve note by Lonnie Donegan.
71 Lonnie Donegan in *Red, White and Blues*, dir. Mike Figgis, 2003.
72 Van Morrison, Lonnie Donegan and Chris Barber: *The Skiffle Sessions* (Exile, 1999). Sleeve note by Lonnie Donegan.
73 Oliver, p. 234.
74 See Norm Cohen: *Long Steel Rail: The Railroad in American Folksong* (University of Illinois Press, 2000).
75 Yorke, p. 52.
76 Van Morrison: 'Crazy Face', *His Band And the Street Choir* (Warner Bros., 1971).
77 Van Morrison and Lonnie Donegan: 'Muleskinner Blues', *The Skiffle Sessions* (Exile, 1999); Van Morrison: 'Muleskinner Blues', *Songs Of Jimmie Rodgers: A Tribute* (Sony, 1997).
78 Lonnie Donegan: 'I Wanna Go Home', *Talking Guitar Blues* (Sequel, 1999); see also the Beach Boys: *Pet Sounds*, (Capitol 1966/1990), and Alan Lomax: *Bahamas 1935: Chanteys And Anthems From Andros And Cat Island* (Folkways, 1955).
79 Lonnie Donegan in *Red, White and Blues*, dir. Mike Figgis, 2003.
80 Van Morrison: *His Band And The Street Choir* (Warner Bros., 1970).
81 See http://www.geocities.com/tracybjazz/hayward/van-the-man.info/discography/index.html and also 'The Clouds Have Lifted', *Los Angeles Times*, 17 November 98; *Wavelength*, No. 18.

82 Yorke, p. 89.
83 The Beach Boys: *Sunflower* (Brother, 1970/Capitol, 2000); Johnny Rivers, *Slim Slo Slider* (Liberty, 1970/BGO, 1998).
84 Yorke, p. 89.
85 Van Morrison: 'Give Me A Kiss', on 'Precious Time'/'Naked In The Jungle'/'Give Me A Kiss' (Virgin/Exile, 1999).
86 See http://www.geocities.com/tracybjazz/hayward/van-the-man.info/discography/index.html and also 'The Clouds Have Lifted', *Los Angeles Times*, 17 November 98; *Wavelength*, No. 18.
87 Van Morrison interviewed on *Soul Britannia*, dir. Jeremy Marre, BBC, 2007. Online at: http://www.vanmorrison.com
88 *Candy Meets . . . Van Morrison* (Candy Dulfer series in which she interviews fellow musicians), NPS (Dutch public service TV), recorded in Cardiff, 14 April 2007 and broadcast 28 October and 11 November 2007.
89 Van Morrison: *Wavelength* (Warner Bros., 1978).
90 Van Morrison interviewed by Jonathan Cott in *Rolling Stone*, 30 November 1978.
91 Johnny Rivers: *L.A. Reggae* (United Artists, 1974). This album includes his reggae cover of 'Brown Eyed Girl'.
92 See Jackie DeShannon: *Jackie* (Atlantic, 1972/2003). The album features her exquisite versions of 'I Wanna Roo You', 'Flamingos Fly' and 'Santa Fe' alongside 'Sweet Sixteen' and 'The Wonder Of You', the last two written by Morrison but never issued. He also produced these five tracks.
93 *Candy Meets . . . Van Morrison*, NPS (Dutch public service TV), recorded in Cardiff, 14 April 2007 and broadcast 28 October and 11 November 2007.

Chapter Two: What Makes the Irish Heart Beat?: The Irishness of Van Morrison

1 Van Morrison interviewed on *Soul Britannia*, dir. Jeremy Marre, BBC, 2007. Online at: http://www.vanmorrison.com
2 See, for example, Rob Strachan and Marion Leonard: 'A Musical Nation: Protection, Investment and Branding in the Irish Music Industry', in *Irish Studies Review*, Vol. 12, No. 1, April 2004, pp. 39–49.
3 Van Morrison: 'Celtic Ray', *Beautiful Vision* (Phonogram, 1982).
4 Van Morrison: 'Cleaning Windows', *Beautiful Vision* (Phonogram, 1982).
5 Van Morrison interviewed by Chris Michie in *Wavelength*, No. 22.
6 The Gospel According to Mark 15.39 (King James Bible).
7 Jerry Lee Lewis: 'What Makes The Irish Heart Beat', *Last Man Standing* (Artful, 2006).
8 Van Morrison: 'What Makes The Irish Heart Beat', *Down The Road* (Exile, 2002).
9 C. S. Lewis: *Surprised by Joy* (London: Fount, [1955] 1998), p. 25.
10 Van Morrison in *A Coney Island of the Mind*, dir. Peter Lynden and Tom

Tyrwhitt, Channel Four, broadcast 12 March 1991.

11 C. S. Lewis: *The Lion, the Witch and the Wardrobe* (London: Collins, 2001).

12 Van Morrison: 'So Quiet In Here', *Enlightenment* (Polydor/Exile, 1990).

13 Van Morrison: 'Into The Mystic', *Moondance* (Warner Bros., 1970).

14 Van Morrison: 'Saint Dominic's Preview', *Saint Dominic's Preview* (Warner Bros., 1972).

15 Van Morrison interviewed by Donal Corvyn in *Hot Press*, conducted 1974 and published 1977.

16 John Buchan (ed.): *The Northern Muse: An Anthology of Scots Vernacular Poetry* (London and Edinburgh: Thomas Nelson, 1924).

17 Bob Dylan: 'If You See Her, Say Hello', *Blood On The Tracks* (CBS, 1974).

18 Van Morrison: 'Northern Muse (Solid Ground)', *Beautiful Vision* (Phonogram, 1982).

19 Van Morrison: 'Crazy Jane On God', *The Philosopher's Stone* (Exile, 1997); 'Before The World Was Made', *Too Long In Exile* (Exile, 1993); W. B. Yeats: 'Before the World Was Made' and 'Crazy Jane on God', *Selected Poems* (Penguin, 2000).

20 Van Morrison interviewed by Niall Stokes in *Hot Press*, March 2000; Van Morrison: *Irish Heartbeat* (Phonogram, 1988).

21 Bill Clinton: St Patrick's Day speech, 17 March 1999; *Wavelength* No. 21, September 1999, p. 32.

22 John Glatt: *The Chieftains: The Authorised Biography* (Century, 1997), p. 222.

23 Ibid., p. 217.

24 Ibid., pp. 215–16.

25 Van Morrison in *Van the Man: In Conversation and Concert*, Ulster TV, recorded at the Riverside Theatre University of Coleraine, 20 April 1988.

26 See, for example, Alan Stivell: *Renaissance Of The Celtic Harp* (Phonogram, 1973).

27 Glatt, p. 220.

28 Van Morrison interviewed by Donal Corvyn in *Hot Press*, conducted 1974 and published 1977.

29 Count John McCormack: 'Star Of The County Down', *The Voice Of Ireland* (Platinum, 2003); see also W. B. Yeats: *The Celtic Twilight* (Prism Press, 1990).

30 *The Roots Of Van Morrison* (Catfish, 2002); *Van Morrison's Jukebox* (Chrome Dreams, 2007).

31 Van Morrison and the Chieftains: 'Raglan Road', *Irish Heartbeat* (Mercury, 1988); a live version of the song appeared on *The Chieftains St Patrick's Day Special*, BBC Northern Ireland, 17 March 1988.

32 *On Raglan Road* documentary, RTE, 1994, archived online at: http://www.rte.ie/laweb/ll/ll_t03i.html

33 Benedict Kiely, ibid.

34 Van Morrison in *Van the Man: In Conversation and Concert*, Ulster TV, recorded at the Riverside Theatre University of Coleraine, 20 April 1988.

35 Van Morrison interviewed by Bob Geldof on *The South Bank Show: Cool Clear Crystal Streams*, ITV, 21 October 1990.
36 The song was first collected in Donegal by Padraic Colum and Herbert Hughes and published by Boosey & Hawkes in London in a work entitled *Irish Country Songs* in 1909.
37 Glatt, p. 220.
38 Maurice Leyden (ed.): *Belfast: City of Song* (Brandon Books: Dingle, Co. Kerry, 1989), p. 81.
39 *A Coney Island of the Mind*, dir. Peter Lynden and Tom Tyrwhitt, Channel Four, broadcast 12 March 1991.
40 Gerald Dawe: *The Rest Is History* (Newry: Abbey Press, 1998), pp. 29–30.
41 Louis Macneice on Carrickfergus in a BBC Northern Ireland documentary broadcast in 2001 and archived online at: http://www.bbc.co.uk/northern ireland/learning/getwritingni/wh_macneice.shtml. Macneice also wrote a poem, 'Carrickfergus', published in his *Selected Poems* (Penguin, 2005).
42 Dominic Behan with Steve Benbow: 'The Kerry Boatman', *The Irish Rover* (Folklore, 1963).
43 Van Morrison and the Chieftains: 'Carrickfergus', *Irish Heartbeat* (Mercury, 1988).
44 Glatt, p. 215.
45 Ibid., p. 213.
46 See, for example, *En Passant Par . . . La Bretagne: La Routes Des Celtes* (Cassettes Regionales Hachette CRH 05, 1978).
47 Joseph Campbell: *As I Was among the Captives: Joseph Campbell's Prison Diary, 1922–1923*, ed. Eiléan Ní Chuilleanáin (Cork: Cork University Press, 2001). See also S. Larsen and R. Larsen: *A Fire in the Mind: The Life of Joseph Campbell* (London: Doubleday, 1991).
48 Mary O'Hara's book *A Song for Ireland* (Dublin: Michael Joseph, 1982) is an invaluable resource for this kind of folk terminology and how it appears in Irish traditional song. Morrison made an unlikely live appearance on Mary O'Hara's Sunday afternoon television programme of hymns and religious songs in August 1984, performing 'Northern Muse (Solid Ground)'.
49 Glatt, p. 220.
50 Van Morrison and the Chieftains: 'My Lagan Love', *Irish Heartbeat* (Mercury, 1988).
51 Stephen Houston: 'Step We Gaily on We Go, This IS Mairi's Wedding. Now It's All for Mairi's Birthday! She'll Still Be Singing at 90', *Daily Record* (Scotland), Saturday, 5 May 2004.
52 Van Morrison and the Chieftains: 'High Spirits', *The Philosopher's Stone: The Unreleased Tapes Volume One* (Exile, 1998); Van Morrison and the Chieftains: 'Shenandoah', *The Long Journey Home* (RCA Victor, 1998)/*The Best Of Van Morrison Vol. 3* (EMI/Exile, 2007).
53 See http://www.moles.co.uk

54 Van Morrison (with Fay Howard and Ben Norman): *Scenes From The Ancient Irish Saga Of Cuchulainn* (SULIS Music, 1990) (cassette only).

55 Lady Augusta Gregory: *Cuchulain of Muirthemne* (Dublin: Colin Smythe, 1973); W. B. Yeats: *Fairy and Folk Tales of Ireland* (London: Pan Books 1979). The Cuchulain plays are: *On Baile's Strand* (1899/1903), *The Green Helmet* (aka *The Golden Helmet*: 1908/1910), *At The Hawk's Well* (a 'noh' play, 1916), *The Only Jealousy of Emer* (1919) and *The Death of Cuchulain* (1939, finished shortly before his death on 28 January 1939). See also *Early Irish Myths and Sagas*, trans. Jeffrey Gantz (London: Penguin, 2001), pp. 134–47.

56 *A Coney Island of the Mind*, dir. Peter Lynden and Tom Tyrwhitt, Channel Four, broadcast 12 March 1991.

57 Ibid.

Chapter Three: Get the Words on the Page: Van Morrison as Writer

1 Van Morrison interviewed in *The Word*, August 2007.

2 Paul McCartney on the BBC Ray Charles tribute show *What'd I Say*, BBC, 24 July 2004.

3 See Ken Lieck: 'Dancing about Architecture', *Austin Chronicle*, 29 July 1999.

4 Lester Bangs: 'Spawn of the Dublin Pubs: Them Creatures and a Wight Named Van', sleeve note to *Them Featuring Van Morrison* (Decca, 1972).

5 Paul Williams: *Rock and Roll: The 100 Best Singles* (San Francisco: Entwhistle Books, 1993).

6 Dave Marsh: *The Heart of Rock and Soul: The 1001 Greatest Singles Ever Made* (New York: New American Library, 1989).

7 Them: 'Gloria', *The Story Of Them* (Decca, 1997).

8 Eddie and the Hot Rods: 'Gloria', *Live At The Marquee EP* (Island, 1976) (hear this version on the Simon Gee-curated *The Van Morrison Songbook* (Connoisseur, 1997)); Patti Smith: 'Gloria', *Horses* (Arista, 1976). See also Mike Daley: 'Patti Smith's 'Gloria': Intertextual Play in a Rock Vocal Performance', *Popular Music*, Vol. 16, No. 3, 1998, p. 235.

9 Van Morrison interviewed by Victoria Clarke in *Q*, No. 83, August 1993, p. 64.

10 Van Morrison: 'Gloria', *Too Long In Exile* (Exile, 1993); John Lee Hooker: 'I Cover The Waterfront', *Mr. Lucky* (Virgin, 1991).

11 Kate St. John to the author, June 2007.

12 Van Morrison: 'Gloria', *A Night In San Francisco* (Exile, 1994).

13 Van Morrison interviewed by Edna Gundersen for musiCentral (http://www.musicentral.com), 1997.

14 The Sweet Inspirations were Cissy Houston (Whitney Houston's mother), Dee Dee Warwick (Whitney Houston's aunt), Myrna Smith and Jeff Berry. Dee Dee Warwick is also Dionne Warwick's sister, and made some incredibly soulful recordings for Atlantic in the early 1970s.

15 Yorke, pp. 42–43.

16 John Collis: *Inarticulate Speech of the Heart* (London: Warner Books, 1996), p. 81.
17 Van Morrison interviewed in 1971 by Happy Traum in *The Rolling Stone Interviews 1967–1980: The Classic Oral History of Rock and Roll* (London: St. Martin's Press, 1981), p. 122.
18 Colin Harper and Trevor Hodgett (eds): *Irish Folk Trad and Blues: A Secret History* (London: Cherry Red Books, 2004), p. 67.
19 Lester Bangs: 'Astral Weeks', in Greil Marcus (ed.): *Stranded* (London: Da Capo, 2007).
20 Charlie Gillett: *Sound of the City* (London: Souvenir Press, 1970), p. 88.
21 Van Morrison interviewed on *Soul Britannia*, dir. Jeremy Marre, BBC, 2007. Online at: http://www.vanmorrison.com
22 The KLF: *The Manual: How to Have a Number One the Easy Way* (Glasgow: KLF Communications, 1988).
23 Theodor Adorno: 'On Popular Music', in R. Leppert (ed.): *Essays on Music* (University of California, 2002), pp. 437–38.
24 Van Morrison interviewed in 1971 by Happy Traum in *The Rolling Stone Interviews 1967–1980: The Classic Oral History of Rock and Roll* (London: St. Martin's Press, 1981).
25 Van Morrison: 'Thirty Two', *Bang Sessions* (Black Box, 2005).
26 Robert Bruce and Abner Silver: *How to Write a Hit Song and Sell It* (New York Lexington Press, 1945), p. xii.
27 Ibid., p.32
28 Adorno, p. 442.
29 Bill Flanagan, sleeve notes to *Bang Masters* (Sony, 1991).
30 Ibid.
31 Van Morrison: 'Brown Eyed Girl', both versions on *Bang Masters* (Sony, 1991).
32 Van Morrison: 'Jackie Wilson Said (I'm In Heaven When You Smile)', *St. Dominic's Preview* (Warner Bros., 1972).
33 Kevin Rowland to the author March 2008. The Dexy's Midnight Runners version is on *Too Rye Aye* (Phonogram, 1982/2000).
34 *Candy Meets . . . Van Morrison*, NPS (Dutch public service TV), recorded in Cardiff, 14 April 2007 and broadcast 28 October and 11 November 2007; Van Morrison: 'Songwriter', *Days Like This* (Exile, 1995).
35 Ibid.
36 Smokey Robinson, BBC radio interview, April 2007.
37 Adorno, p. 446.
38 Yorke, p. 23.
39 Bob Dylan: 'All The Tired Horses', *Self Portrait* (CBS, 1970); Van Morrison: 'Tore Down a la Rimbaud', *A Sense Of Wonder* (Phonogram, 1985); 'I'd Love To Write Another Song', *Avalon Sunset* (Polydor, 1989).
40 Scotty Wiseman and Lulu Belle: 'Have I Told You Lately That I Loved You?' (Columbia, 1945).
41 Buzacott and Ford, p. 234.

42 Van Morrison: 'Have I Told You Lately', *Avalon Sunset* (Polydor, 1989).
43 Van Morrison: 'Someone Like You', *Poetic Champions Compose* (Phonogram, 1987).
44 Fiachra Trench to the author, August 2005.
45 Van Morrison: 'Come Running', *Moondance* (Warner Bros., 1970).
46 Van Morrison: 'Queen Of The Slipstream', *Poetic Champions Compose* (Mercury, 1987).
47 *Moondance*, dir. Dagmar Hirtz, 1994. The song appears as an instrumental theme and as a vocal version sung by Brian Kennedy, issued on *No Prima Donna* (Exile, 1994).
48 Sam Cooke to Dick Clark on *American Bandstand*, 4 April 1964 [VHS] (Columbia/Eagle); see also Peter Guralnick: *Dream Boogie: The Triumph of Sam Cooke* (London: Abacus, 2006), p. 565.
49 Van Morrison: 'Crazy Love', *Moondance* (Warner Bros., 1970).
50 Ray Charles and Van Morrison: 'Crazy Love', *Genius Loves Company* (Concord, 2004); also appears on *The Best Of Van Morrison Vol. 3* (EMI/Exile, 2007).
51 Van Morrison: 'Hungry For Your Love', *Wavelength* (Warner Bros., 1978).
52 Gene Vincent: 'Be-Bop-A-Lula', *Blue Jean Bop* (Capitol 1957/EMI 2003); *The Girl Can't Help It*, dir. Frank Tashlin, 1956. See also Derek Henderson: *Gene Vincent: A Companion* (London: Spent Brothers, 2005).
53 Van Morrison: 'She's My Baby', *Enlightenment* (Polydor, 1990).
54 Van Morrison: 'Reminds Me Of You', *Back On Top* (Exile, 1999).
55 The Beach Boys: 'All Summer Long', *All Summer Long* (Capitol, 1964); Jerry Keller: 'Here Comes Summer' (Capitol, 1959).
56 Van Morrison: 'Lover Come Back', *Keep It Simple* (Exile, 2008).

Chapter Four: Caught One More Time: Themes and Thematics

1 Van Morrison: 'Sweet Thing', *Astral Weeks* (Warner Bros., 1968).
2 Genesis 2.8-9; 2.22-24 (King James Bible).
3 John Milton: *Paradise Lost*, Book XII (London: Penguin Classics, 2003), p. 279.
4 Andrew Marvell: 'The Garden', in *Selected Poems* (London: Penguin, 1982), p. 54.
5 Bob Dylan: 'In The Garden', *Saved* (Columbia, 1980).
6 Van Morrison interviewed by Mick Brown on *The Interview Album* (Phonogram, 1986).
7 Van Morrison: 'In The Garden', *No Guru, No Method, No Teacher* (Phonogram, 1986).
8 Van Morrison: 'Thanks For The Information', *No Guru, No Method, No Teacher* (Phonogram, 1986).
9 Derek Bell in *Van the Man: In Conversation and Concert*, Ulster TV, recorded at the Riverside Theatre University of Coleraine, 20 April 1988.

10 Van Morrison: 'Alan Watts Blues', *Poetic Champions Compose* (Mercury, 1987).
11 Johnny Mercer, Joseph Kosma and Jacques Prévert: 'Autumn Leaves'. Recorded by many artists, including Nat King Cole for the film of the same name, in 1956.
12 Van Morrison: 'I Need Your Kind Of Loving', *Hymns To the Silence* (Exile, 1991).
13 Yorke, p. 109; Van Morrison: 'Autumn Song', *Hard Nose The Highway* (Warner Bros., 1973).
14 Van Morrison: 'A Sense Of Wonder', *A Sense Of Wonder* (Mercury, 1985).
15 John Keats: 'To Autumn', in *Complete Poems* (London: Penguin, 2007), p. 434.
16 Van Morrison: 'Wild Children', *Hard Nose The Highway* (Warner Bros., 1973).
17 Van Morrison: 'Autumn Song', *Hard Nose The Highway* (Warner Bros., 1973); sleeve note to *Astral Weeks Live* (Listen to the Lion Records, 2009).
18 Van Morrison: 'A Sense Of Wonder', *A Sense Of Wonder* (Mercury, 1985).
19 Van Morrison: 'When The Leaves Come Falling Down', *Back On Top* (Exile 1999).
20 Samuel Beckett: *The Unnameable* in *The Beckett Trilogy* (Picador, 1979), p. 453.
21 Ecclesiastes 3.3 (King James Bible); The Byrds: 'Turn! Turn! Turn!', *Turn! Turn! Turn!* (CBS, 1966).
22 Morrison is thought to have read and been interested in David Tame's book, *The Secret Power of Music* (Northampton: Turnstone Press 1984) and Cyril Scott's jazz-baiting *Music: Its Secret Influence through the Ages* (Northampton: Aquarian Press, 1982; originally published in 1958).
23 Van Morrison interviewed by Chris Welch in *Melody Maker*, 3 March 1979.
24 Van Morrison: 'And The Healing Has Begun', *Into the Music* (Phonogram, 1979).
25 Van Morrison: 'Did Ye Get Healed?', *Poetic Champions Compose* (Mercury, 1987).
26 Van Morrison: 'Till We Get The Healing Done', *Too Long In Exile* (Exile, 1993).
27 Van Morrison: 'The Healing Game', *The Healing Game* (Exile, 1997).
28 John Lee Hooker: 'The Healing Game', *Don't Look Back* (Point Blank/Virgin, 1999); Van Morrison and the Chieftains: 'The Healing Game', *Omagh: Across The Bridge Of Hope* (White Label, 2002).
29 Van Morrison: 'Tir Na Nog', *No Guru, No Method, No Teacher* (Phonogram, 1986).
30 Van Morrison: 'Orangefield', *Avalon Sunset* (Phonogram, 1989).
31 Van Morrison: 'Get On With The Show', *What's Wrong With This Picture?* (Verve, 2003).
32 Fiachra Trench to the author, August 2005.
33 Van Morrison: 'Golden Autumn Day', *Back On Top* (Exile, 1999).
34 Bert Berns, sleeve note to Van Morrison: *Blowin' Your Mind!* (Bang, 1967).
35 See, for example, Winslow Anderson: *Ancient Highways* (Journal Register Co., 2000).

36 Promotional video interview with Michelle Rocca for the *Days Like This* album, 1995; Guy Peellaert, *Rock Dreams* (San Francisco: Popular Library, 1982).
37 Van Morrison: 'A Town Called Paradise', *No Guru, No Method, No Teacher* (Mercury, 1986).
38 Van Morrison: 'Ancient Highway', *Days Like This* (Exile, 1995).
39 William Shakespeare, *Macbeth* (London: Penguin Playtext, 1996), Act III, Sc. 1.
40 Alice Bailey: *Glamour: A World Problem* (London: Lucis Trust Press, 1950), p. 25.
41 Adorno, p. 365.
42 Foster, p. 152.
43 Ibid.
44 Van Morrison: 'Wavelength', *Wavelength* (Warner Bros., 1978).
45 Joni Mitchell: 'You Turn Me On, I'm A Radio', *For The Roses* (Asylum, 1972).
46 Olaf Stapledon: *Star Maker* (London: Penguin, 1973), p. 126.
47 See Paul Durcan: *Endsville* (Limerick: Brian Lynch New Writers Press, 1967); *Going Home To Russia* (Dublin: Blackstaff Press, 1987); and *Daddy Daddy* (Dublin: Blackstaff Press, 1990).
48 Paul Durcan: 'The Drumshanbo Hustler: A Celebration of Van Morrison', *Magill*, May 1988, p. 56.
49 Ibid.
50 T. S. Eliot, set of six 78 rpm discs (HMV 1947 C.3598–3603).
51 Van Morrison: 'In The Days Before Rock And Roll', *Enlightenment* (Polydor/Exile, 1990).
52 John Montague: 'The Hill of Silence', in *Mount Eagle* (Bloodaxe, 1989).
53 Read by Montague *A Coney Island of the Mind*, dir. Peter Lynden and Tom Tyrwhitt, Channel Four, broadcast 12 March 1991.
54 Van Morrison in *A Coney Island of the Mind*, dir. Peter Lynden and Tom Tyrwhitt, Channel Four, broadcast 12 March 1991.
55 Van Morrison: 'Just A Closer Walk With Thee (See Me Through Part II)', *Hymns To The Silence* (Exile/Polydor, 1991).
56 Quoted in Mary Bryden (ed.): *Samuel Beckett and Music* (Oxford University Press, 1998), p. 27. Debussy is cited as part of the weave of perception presented in Morrison's 'On Hyndford Street'.
57 John Cage: *4'33"* (1952) (Hungaroton, 1993); John Cage: *Silence: Lectures and Writings* (Boston MA: MIT Press, 1961); Cockney Rebel: 'Make Me Smile (Come Up And See Me)' (1975), on *Best Of* (EMI, 2008); The Beach Boys: 'The Little Girl I Once Knew' (1965), *Today/Summer Days (And Summer Nights!)* (Capitol, 1990); Talk Talk: *Laughing Stock* (Verve, 1991).
58 See James Knowlson: *Samuel Beckett: Damned to Fame* (London: Bloomsbury, 1997).
59 Samuel Beckett: *Proust and Three Dialogues with Georges Duthuit* (London: Calder and Boyars, 1965), p. 103.
60 Van Morrison: 'So Quiet In Here', *Enlightenment* (Exile/Polydor, 1990); Slade:

'Cum On Feel the Noize' (1973), *The Very Best Of Slade* (Polydor/UMTV, 2006).

61 Van Morrison: 'Astral Weeks', *Astral Weeks* (Warner Bros., 1968).

62 Samuel Beckett: *Waiting for Godot* in *The Complete Dramatic Works* (Faber and Faber, 2006), p. 11.

63 Van Morrison: 'Why Must I Always Explain?', 'Village Idiot', *Hymns To The Silence* (Exile, 1991); Paul Robeson: 'Old Man River', *Best Of Paul Robeson* (Digital Music, 2003). (This CD also contains 'Sometimes I Feel Like A Motherless Child' and 'Shenandoah', both later recorded by Morrison, and 'Mighty Like A Rose', a title he borrowed for a song recorded by Them in 1966.)

64 See Note 55. The author of 'Just A Closer Walk With Thee' is unknown, but it has been recorded by many artists in addition to its use in church music. Jimmie Rodgers, Cliff Richard, Ella Fitzgerald and Little Richard all issued recordings of the song, while the Bob Dylan and Johnny Cash duet recorded around the time of *Nashville Skyline* remains in the vaults.

65 Van Morrison: 'Hymns To the Silence', *Hymns To The Silence* (Exile, 1991).

66 Van Morrison: 'On Hyndford Street', *Hymns To The Silence* (Exile, 1991).

67 David Steindl-Rast: *The Music of Silence* (London: HarperCollins, 1995), p. 147.

68 Ibid.

69 Miles Davis: *In A Silent Way* (Columbia, 1969).

70 Van Morrison: 'In The Afternoon' on 'Meet Me In The Indian Summer' (Exile, 2002).

71 Van Morrison: 'Sometimes We Cry', *The Healing Game* (Exile, 1997).

72 Van Morrison: 'Little Village', *What's Wrong With This Picture?* (Blue Note, 2003). Sonny Boy Williamson: 'Little Village' (1957), *Bummer Road* (Chess, 1969).

73 Van Morrison: 'I'm Tired Joey Boy', *Avalon Sunset* (Phonogram, 1989).

74 Stéphane Mallarmé in Jean C. Harris: 'A Little-known Essay on Manet by Stéphane Mallarmé', in *The Art Bulletin*, Vol. 46, No. 4, December 1964, pp. 559–63.

75 *The Wind in the Willows*, dir. Terry Jones, 1996. This is the most recent cinematic adaptation of Kenneth Grahame's 1908 novel.

76 Van Morrison: 'Piper At The Gates Of Dawn', *The Healing Game* (Exile, 1997).

77 Knowlson, p. 165.

Chapter Five: Listening to the Lion: Van Morrison as Singer and Musician

1 'Van Morrison in Conversation with R.D. Laing', in Bob Mullan (ed.): *Memories of R.D. Laing* (London: Cassell, 1997), p. 33.

2 Van Morrison: 'Don't Start Cryin' Now', *Live At Austin City Limits Festival* (Exile, 2006).

3 Them: 'Don't Start Cryin' Now', *Them* (Decca, 1965)/*The Story Of Them*

(Decca, 1997); sessionography in Clinton Heylin: *Can You Feel the Silence?: A New Biography* (London: Penguin Viking, 2003), p. 515.

4 See Gordon Thompson: *Please Please Me: Sixties British Pop, Inside Out* (Oxford University Press, 2008), pp. 210–11.

5 Them: 'My Lonely Sad Eyes', *Them Again* (Decca, 1966)/*The Story Of Them* (Decca, 1997).

6 Maria McKee to the author, February 2008.

7 Maria McKee: 'My Lonely Sad Eyes', *You Got To Sin To Get Saved* (MCA, 1992).

8 Van Morrison, Lonnie Donegan and Chris Barber: *The Skiffle Sessions* (Exile, 1998), sleeve notes.

9 Yorke, p. 66.

10 Paddy Moloney interviewed in *Q*, August 1991.

11 Kevin Rowland to the author, April 2007; Maria McKee to the author, February 2008; B.B. King in *La Vanguardia* (Barcelona newspaper), 27 November 1997.

12 James Gavin: *Deep in a Dream: The Long Night of Chet Baker* (London: Vintage, 2003), p. 284.

13 Greil Marcus: review of *Self Portrait* (1970) in *Rolling Stone*, republished in B. Hedin (ed.): *Studio A: The Bob Dylan Reader* (London: W. W. Norton, 2005), p. 74.

14 Van Morrison interviewed by Chris Neal in *Performing Songwriter*, Vol. 16, No. 116, March/April 2009, p. 48.

15 Van Morrison interviewed on *Soul Britannia*, dir. Jeremy Marre, BBC, 2007. Online at: http://www.vanmorrison.com; Van Morrison: 'Whinin' Boy Moan', *What's Wrong With This Picture?* (Exile, 2003); 'That Old Black Magic' on 'Days Like This' (Exile/Virgin, 1995).

16 Alyn Shipton: *A New History of Jazz* (London: Continuum, 2007), pp. 677–79.

17 Van Morrison: 'Moody's Mood For Love', *Too Long In Exile* (Exile/Virgin, 1993).

18 Shipton, p. 421.

19 Roland Barthes: 'The Grain of the Voice', in Simon Frith and Andrew Goodwin (eds): *On Record: Rock, Pop and the Written Word* (London: Routledge, 1990), p. 296.

20 'Troubadours' on *Van Morrison Live In Montreux 1980/1974* [DVD] (Exile/ Eagle Vision, 2006).

21 All the following quotes are from Van Morrison: *Veedon Fleece* (Warner Bros., 1974/Exile, 2008).

22 Barthes, p. 269.

23 L. A. C. Strong: *John McCormack – The Story of a Singer* (New York: Macmillan, 1941), p. 77.

24 See David Gray: *White Ladder* (EastWest, 1999). *White Ladder* features 'Nightblindness' and 'Say Hello Wave Goodbye', the latter quoting extensively from 'Madame George'.

25 Van Morrison: 'Hey Where Are You?' (unissued song recorded under Lewis Merenstein, 1968).
26 D. H. Lawrence: *Women in Love* (London: Penguin, 1982), p. 132.
27 Dante Alighieri: *The Divine Comedy* (Oxford World Classics, 1998); Stapledon: *Star Maker.*
28 'Van Morrison in Conversation with R.D. Laing', in Bob Mullan (ed.): *Memories of R.D. Laing* (London: Cassell, 1997), p. 39.
29 Them: 'Friday's Child' (originally issued on a Decca Netherlands EP, 1967); *Them: Rock Roots* (Decca, 1976); *The Story Of Them* (Deram/Decca, 1997).
30 See Iona Opie and Peter Opie (eds): *The Oxford Dictionary of Nursery Rhymes* (Oxford University Press, 1997); Nancy Sinatra: 'Friday's Child' (Reprise, 1966).
31 Van Morrison: 'Summertime In England (Live)', B-side of 'Cry For Home' (Phonogram, 1983).
32 See Mary Bryden and Peter Mills: *Beckett at Reading* (Reading: Whiteknights Press, 1999), p. 43.
33 Herbie Armstrong: 'Friday's Child', *Back Against The Wall* (MMC, 1983); Lisa Stansfield: 'Friday's Child', *No Prima Donna: The Songs Of Van Morrison* (Exile, 1994).
34 Van Morrison: 'TB Sheets', *Bang Masters* (Sony, 1991).
35 Randy Newman in *Mojo*, No. 178, September 2008, p. 48.
36 See the PRONI website: http://www.proni.gov.uk/
37 Spike Milligan interviewed in *Q*, No. 35, August 1989.
38 Bill Flanagan, sleeve notes for Van Morrison: *Bang Masters* (Sony, 1991).
39 Van Morrison: 'You've Got The Power', B-side of 'Jackie Wilson Said' (Warner Bros, 1972).
40 Van Morrison radio interviewed by Tom Donohue, November 1974.
41 Van Morrison: 'Twilight Zone', *The Philosopher's Stone* (Exile, 1997); 'Twilight Zone' on *Van Morrison Live In Montreux 1980/1974* [DVD] (Exile/Eagle Vision, 2006).
42 *Wings of Desire*, dir. Wim Wenders, 1986.
43 Sinéad O'Connor on *The Dave Fanning Show*, RTE Radio 2, 28 November 2007.
44 Van Morrison: 'Song Of Being A Child', *The Philosopher's Stone* (Exile, 1998).
45 Phil Everly in Roger White: *The Everly Brothers: Walk Right Back* (London: Plexus, 1998), p. 114.
46 Van Morrison with James Hunter: 'I Don't Want To Go On Without You' on 'Days Like This' (Exile, 1995); also on *The Best Of Van Morrison Vol. 3* (Exile/EMI, 2007).
47 C. S. Lewis: *The Lion, the Witch and the Wardrobe* (Oxford University Press, 2005).
48 Respectively: Johnny Rogan, *Van Morrison: No Surrender* (London: Vintage, 2005), p. 276; Heylin, p. 258; Buzacott and Ford, p. 132.
49 Van Morrison: 'Angeliou', *Into The Music* (Phonogram, 1979).

50 Yorke, p. 96.
51 Van Morrison: 'Listen To The Lion', *Saint Dominic's Preview* (Warner Bros., 1972).
52 *Candy Meets . . . Van Morrison*, NPS (Dutch public service TV), recorded in Cardiff, 14 April 2007 and broadcast 28 October and 11 November 2007.
53 Van Morrison: 'Listen To The Lion', *It's Too Late To Stop Now* (Warner Bros., 1973).
54 Van Morrison interviewed in the *Los Angeles Times*, 9 January 2009.
55 Quoted in Rogan, *No Surrender*, p. 634.
56 Ibid.
57 Van Morrison: 'No Religion', *Days Like This* (Exile, 1995).
58 Ben Sidran to the author, May 2008.
59 Van Morrison interviewed by Chris Neal in *Performing Songwriter*, Vol. 16, No. 116, March/April 2009, p. 48.
60 *Candy Meets . . . Van Morrison*, NPS (Dutch public service TV), recorded in Cardiff, 14 April 2007 and broadcast 28 October and 11 November 2007.
61 See the sleeve notes to Elvis Costello and the Attractions: *Imperial Bedroom* (F-Beat, 1982).
62 Bill Bruford in *Prog Britannia*, BBC 4, broadcast 9 January 2009.
63 Van Morrison interviewed on *Soul Britannia*, dir. Jeremy Marre, BBC, 2007. Online at: http://www.vanmorrison.com
64 Joachim Berendt: *The Jazz Book* (New York: Lawrence Hill Books, 1992), p. 153.
65 Heard to best advantage on 'Irish Heartbeat', *Inarticulate Speech Of The Heart* (Mercury, 1983).
66 Mick Cox, Wavelength Convention, Manchester, September 1998.
67 Van Morrison interviewed by Steven Davis: 'The Mystic', in *New Age*, August 1985 (interview conducted 17 May 1985).
68 Vladimir Jankelevitch: *Music and the Ineffable*, trans. Carolyn Abbate (Princeton University Press, 1961), p.137. Also quoted in Mary Bryden (ed.): *Samuel Beckett and Music* (Oxford University Press, 1998), p. 16.
69 William Blake: 'The Echoing Green', in *Songs of Innocence and Experience* (London: Tate Publishing London, 2006).
70 Van Morrison: 'Celtic Swing', *Inarticulate Speech Of The Heart* (Phonogram, 1983).
71 Van Morrison: *Poetic Champions Compose* (Phonogram, 1987).
72 Sir George Trevelyan: 'Meditation and its Purpose'. Online: http://www.sirgeorgetrevelyan.org.uk
73 Van Morrison: 'I'll Take Care Of You', 'Instrumental/Tell Me What You Want' and 'Close Enough For Jazz', *Too Long In Exile* (Virgin/Exile, 1993).
74 Van Morrison interviewed by Al Jones, Danish radio, 1985; transcribed in *Wavelength*, No. 29.
75 Van Morrison interviewed by Nigel Williamson about *Magic Time*, 2005.
76 Barbican Theatre, York, 10 March 2004.

77 Van Morrison interviewed by Niall Stokes, *Hot Press*, 28 October 2003.
78 Humphrey Lyttelton: *It Just Occurred to Me* (London: Robson Books, 2007), p. 166.
79 Rob Walker: *Letters from New Orleans* (New Orleans: Garrett County Press, 2006), pp. 175–94. See also Rob Walker's excellent website: http://nonotes.wordpress.com
80 Van Morrison: 'See Me Through Part Two (Just A Closer Walk With Thee)', *Hymns To The Silence* (Exile, 1991).
81 Van Morrison: 'Magic Time', *Magic Time* (Exile, 2005).
82 Louis Armstrong: 'Saint James Infirmary' (1928), *Best Of The Hot Five And Hot Seven* (Sony, 2008).
83 Van Morrison: 'Saint James Infirmary', *What's Wrong With This Picture?* (Verve, 2003).
84 Van Morrison interviewed by Niall Stokes, *Hot Press*, 28 October 2003.
85 Van Morrison: 'Saint James Infirmary', *Live At Austin City Limits Festival* (Exile, 2006).
86 Official online interview for *What's Wrong With This Picture?*, 2003. Online at: http://www.vanmorrison.com
87 Van Morrison interviewed by Donal Corvin in *Hot Press*, No. 3, 7 July 1977 (conducted in 1974).
88 Ibid.
89 *As I Roved Out* was a weekly programme showcasing folk music of the British Isles on the BBC Home Service, running from 1951 to 1958. This programme was conceived, presented and compiled by uilleann piper and folk-song collector Seamus Ennis (1919–82). An episode in June 1957 featured the McPeakes, just when Morrison would be hearing them in Belfast, and their wider reputation – and that of 'Wild Mountain Thyme', which they performed on this show – grew from this exposure.
90 The quote is from Captain Simon Fraser: *Collection of Melodies of the Highlands and Islands of Scotland* (Sydney, Nova Scotia: Cranford Press, 1982). 'No. 77, Bochuiddar/Balquidder' in that collection was applied to Tannahill's lyric, with small variants. See also R. A. Smith: *Scottish Minstrel: A Selection of Vocal Melodies of Scotland Ancient and Modern Arranged for the Pianoforte, Vols I–VI* (Edinburgh: Robert Purdie Press, 1825). 'Balquidder' is found therein in Vol. I, p. 49. The earliest version which is clearly attributed to Tannahill comes from George Farquar Graham (ed.): *The Popular Songs of Scotland with Their Appropriate Melodies* (Edinburgh: Muirwood, 1850). There are many subsequent reprints with other editors.
91 Fraser.
92 Maurice Leyden (ed.): *Belfast: City of Song* (Dingle, Co. Kerry: Brandon Books, 1989), p. xi.
93 Anonymous sleeve notes for *The McPeake Family Of Belfast* (Xtra, 1958).
94 The Byrds: 'Wild Mountain Thyme', *Fifth Dimension* (CBS/Sony, 1966).
95 Gary Shearston: 'Wild Mountain Thyme'/'Billa Bong' (Magnet UK, 1978).

96 Correspondence between Gary Shearston and the author, May 2008.
97 Correspondence between Kate Rusby and the author, March 2008.
98 Yorke, p. 110.
99 Ibid., p. 112.
100 Van Morrison: 'Purple Heather', *Hard Nose The Highway* (Warner Bros., 1973).

Chapter Six: On the Burning Ground: 'Liveness' and the Recording Studio

1 Van Morrison interviewed by Rick McGrath in *Georgia Straight*, May 1971.
2 Ben Sidran to the author, February 2008.
3 *Candy Meets . . . Van Morrison*, NPS (Dutch public service TV), recorded in Cardiff, 14 April 2007 and broadcast 28 October and 11 November 2007.
4 *NME Poll Winners Concert 1965* [DVD] (Video Beat Productions).
5 Maria McKee in conversation with the author, February 2008.
6 *Them!*, dir. Gordon Douglas, 1954. The film's poster tagline read: 'A Horde So Horrifying No Word Could Describe . . . THEM!'
7 Them: 'The Story Of Them', *The Story Of Them* (Decca/Deram, 1997).
8 Heylin, p. 68.
9 'Caravan', in *The Last Waltz*, dir. Martin Scorsese, 1976. The performance also appears on *Van Morrison At The Movies* (Exile, 2008) and The Band: *The Last Waltz* (EMI, 1976).
10 Van Morrison: 'Behind The Ritual', *Keep It Simple* (Exile, 2008).
11 William Shakespeare: *The Tempest* (London: Penguin, 2005), Act V, Sc. I, lines 38–62, p. 177.
12 Claude Nobs, sleeve notes to *Van Morrison Live At Montreux 1980/1974* (Exile/Eagle Vision, 2006).
13 Pink Floyd: *The Wall* (EMI, 1979); Sid Vicious: 'My Way' in *The Great Rock 'n' Roll Swindle*, dir. Julien Temple, 1979.
14 Yorke, p. 114.
15 Ibid., p. 11.
16 Phil Coulter in Rogan: *No Surrender*, p. 292.
17 Kevin Rowland to the author, February 2007.
18 Kevin Rowland to Andres Lokko, 2006. In 'Interview in-DEX' section of www.dexys.co.uk
19 Kevin Rowland to the author, February 2007.
20 Van Morrison: *It's Too Late To Stop Now* (Warner Bros., 1973).
21 Kevin Rowland did something similar in his live versions of 'Respect' with Dexy's Midnight Runners, singing 'Do I make any sense over there? Do I make any sense over there?' as he strode from left to right on the stage. Rowland denied explicit reference but told me that 'like I said, he showed that intimacy was possible'. Listen to 'Respect' on the reissue of *Too Rye Aye* (Phonogram, 2000).
22 Van Morrison interviewed by Michelle Rocca in *Vox*, January 1995.

23 Van Morrison: *Live At The Grand Opera House, Belfast* (Phonogram, 1984).
24 Van Morrison: 'Caravan', *Moondance* (Warner Bros., 1970).
25 Van Morrison: *A Night In San Francisco* (Exile, 1994).
26 'Sooner Or Later' by Mike Vernon, Bob Ross and Gary Shaw.
27 Ray Charles: *Live At Newport* (Atlantic, 1959); Kraftwerk: *Trans-Europe Express* (EMI, 1977).
28 Van Morrison: *Live At The Austin City Limits Festival* (Exile, 2006).
29 *Candy Meets . . . Van Morrison*, NPS (Dutch public service TV), recorded in Cardiff, 14 April 2007 and broadcast 28 October and 11 November 2007.
30 Van Morrison: 'Melancholia' and 'In The Afternoon', *Days Like This* (Exile, 1995).
31 Van Morrison: 'In The Afternoon' on 'Meet Me In The Indian Summer' (Exile, 2002).
32 Ibid., 'Joe Turner Sings' section.
33 Big Joe Turner: 'Don't You Get Me High', *Flip, Flop And Fly 1951–1955* (Rev-Ola/Cherry Red, 2006).
34 Van Morrison interviewed in *Uncut*, No. 98, p. 56.
35 Fiachra Trench to the author, August 2005.
36 Ted Templeman in Heylin, pp. 248–49.
37 Mick Glossop videocast for Recordproduction.com and *Resolution* magazine. Online at: http://www.mickglossop.com
38 Fiachra Trench to the author, August 2005.
39 Bob Dylan: *Chronicles, Volume One* (London: Simon and Schuster, 2004), p. 159.
40 Fiachra Trench to the author, August 2005.
41 Ibid.
42 Ibid.
43 Walter Samuel interviewed by Tim Goodyer. Archived online at: http://www.prostudio.com/studiosound (accessed 5 September 2008).
44 Van Morrison interviewed on *Soul Britannia*, dir. Jeremy Marre, BBC, 2007. Online at: http://www.vanmorrison.com
45 Walter Samuel interviewed by Tim Goodyer. Archived online at: http://www.prostudio.com/studiosound (accessed 5 September 2008).
46 Heylin, p. 256.
47 *Rolling Stone*, 22 June 1972.
48 Yorke, p. 97.
49 Van Morrison: 'Almost Independence Day', *Saint Dominic's Preview* (Warner Bros., 1972); Pink Floyd: 'Wish You Were Here', *Wish You Were Here* (EMI, 1975).
50 Yorke, p. 97.
51 Van Morrison to R. D. Laing in Bob Mullan (ed.): *Memories of R.D. Laing* (London: Cassell, 1997), p. 37.
52 Peter Van Hooke in Heylin, p. 378.
53 David Hayes, ibid.

54 Van Morrison to R. D. Laing, in Mullan, (ed.): *Memories of R. D. Laing* (London: Cassell 1997) p. 37.
55 W. B. Yeats: 'The Lake Isle of Innisfree', in *Collected Poems* (London: Wordsworth Library, 2000), p. 31.
56 Van Morrison: 'Rave On John Donne', *Inarticulate Speech Of The Heart* (Phonogram, 1983).
57 Buddy Holly: 'Rave On' (Coral, 1958).
58 W. B. Yeats: *A Vision* (London: Papermac/Macmillan, 1981), p. 14.
59 Wool Hall was initially set up for the use of its owners, pop band Tears For Fears, in the wake of the great success of their first two albums, but after their struggles with the very expensive and commercially damp third album, *The Seeds Of Love*, they opened the studio for commercial use in early 1987. Van Morrison was one of their first customers, following the Smiths, using the studio to arrange, plan and record *Poetic Champions Compose* over a few weeks in the summer of 1987. Morrison bought the studio in 1994, selling it a decade later. It is now closed. See information archived online at: http://www.recordproduction.com/wool_hall_studios.htm
60 Van Morrison in *Van the Man: In Conversation and Concert*, Ulster TV, recorded at the Riverside Theatre University of Coleraine, 20 April 1988.
61 Heylin, p. 412.
62 Ibid., p. 411.
63 Yorke, p. 103.
64 Samuel Beckett: *Endgame*, in *The Complete Dramatic Works* (Faber and Faber, 2006), p. 119.
65 Dick Hebdige: 'Even unto Death: Improvisation, Edging and Enframement', *Critical Enquiry*, Vol. 27, No. 2, 2001.
66 Ibid.
67 Van Morrison interviewed on *Soul Britannia*, dir. Jeremy Marre, BBC, 2007. Online at: http://www.vanmorrison.com
68 Samuel Beckett: *Endgame*, in *The Complete Dramatic Works* (Faber and Faber, 2006), p. 119.
69 Van Morrison: 'Alan Watts Blues', *Poetic Champions Compose* (Mercury, 1987).
70 Alan Watts: *Cloud Hidden, Whereabouts Unknown: A Mountain Journal* (London: Vintage, 1974), front papers, 'Searching for the hermit in vain'.
71 Listen to Bob Andrews's solo on Nick Lowe: 'I Love The Sound Of Breaking Glass', *Jesus Of Cool* (Radar, 1978/2008).
72 Fiachra Trench to the author, August 2005.
73 Van Morrison: 'Meet Me In The Indian Summer', *Down The Road* (Exile, 2002) and 'Meet Me In The Indian Summer' (Exile, 2002); the latter is included as a remix on *The Best Of Van Morrison Vol. 3* (Exile, 2007).

Chapter Seven: Down the Road: Exile, Place and the Idea of Eternal Movement

1 *Candy Meets . . . Van Morrison*, NPS (Dutch public service TV), recorded in Cardiff, 14 April 2007 and broadcast 28 October and 11 November 2007.
2 Van Morrison: 'Stranded', *Magic Time* (Exile, 2005).
3 *Oxford English Dictionary* (Oxford University Press, 2004).
4 See the sleeve notes to Karoly Cserpes and Marta Sebestyen: *Kivandorlas [Emigration]* (Hungaraton, 1988).
5 Van Morrison: 'Astral Weeks', *Astral Weeks* (Warner Bros., 1968).
6 *A Coney Island of the Mind*, dir. Peter Lynden and Tom Tyrwhitt, Channel Four, broadcast 12 March 1991.
7 Van Morrison: 'Too Long In Exile', *Too Long In Exile* (Exile/Virgin, 1993).
8 Van Morrison: 'Whatever Happened To PJ Proby?', *Down The Road* (Exile, 2002).
9 Nick Lowe: 'Endless Grey Ribbon', *Labour Of Lust* (Radar, 1979).
10 Jack Kerouac: *On the Road* (London: Penguin, 1972), p. 128.
11 Van Morrison interviewed by Niall Stokes in *Hot Press*, 28 October 2003.
12 William Burroughs quoted in the introduction by Ann Charters to Kerouac: *On the Road*, p. xxvii.
13 Kerouac: *On the Road*, p. 20.
14 Van Morrison: 'Cleaning Windows', *Beautiful Vision* (Mercury, 1982).
15 Kerouac: *On the Road*, p. 185; Van Morrison: 'Real Real Gone', *Enlightenment* (Polydor/Exile, 1990); Nellie Lutcher: 'He's A Real Gone Guy' (Capitol, 1947).
16 Van Morrison: 'On Hyndford Street', *Hymns To The Silence* (Exile, 1991).
17 Simon and Garfunkel: 'America', *Bookends* (CBS, 1968); Bruce Springsteen: 'Born In The U.S.A', *Born In The U.S.A* (CBS, 1984).
18 Them: 'Route 66', *Them* (Decca, 1966)/*The Story Of Them* (Decca, 1997).
19 Nat King Cole Trio: 'Route 66', *Best Of The Nat King Cole Trio* (Compendia, 1996). See also, for example, Tom Snyder: *Route 66: Traveler's Guide and Roadside Companion* (London: St. Martin's Press, 2000) and Michael Wallis: *Route 66: The Mother Road* (New Orleans: St. Michael's Press, 2008).
20 Van Morrison: 'Caravan', *Moondance* (Warner Bros., 1970); Van Morrison: 'Gypsy', *Saint Dominic's Preview* (Warner Bros., 1972); Van Morrison: 'Gypsy In My Soul', *Magic Time* (Exile, 2005).
21 Van Morrison: 'Going Down Geneva', *Back On Top* (Exile, 1999). See also Vince Taylor: *Alias Vince Taylor: Le Survivant* (Paris: Editions Delville, 1976) and listen to Golden Earring: 'Just Like Vince Taylor', B-side of 'Radar Love' (Track, 1973).
22 Van Morrison: 'Whatever Happened To PJ Proby?', *Down The Road* (Exile, 2002).
23 Van Morrison: 'Philosopher's Stone', *Back On Top* (Exile, 1999).
24 *Candy Meets . . . Van Morrison*, NPS (Dutch public service TV), recorded in Cardiff, 14 April 2007 and broadcast 28 October and 11 November 2007.
25 Peter Marshall: *The Philosopher's Stone: A Quest for the Secrets of Alchemy*

(London: Macmillan, 2001), p. 13.

26 Van Morrison: 'Haunts Of Ancient Peace', *Common One* (Phonogram, 1980); 'You Don't Pull No Punches (But You Don't Push The River)', *Veedon Fleece* (Warner Bros., 1974).

27 Louis Armstrong and His All Stars: 'Didn't He Ramble', *Pasadena Civic Auditorium June 20, 1956* (Giants of Jazz, 1990).

28 Van Morrison: 'Foreign Window', *No Guru, No Method, No Teacher* (Phonogram, 1986).

29 Kate St. John to the author, June 2008.

30 Van Morrison: 'Down The Road', *Down The Road* (Exile, 2002).

31 Van Morrison 'Stranded', *Magic Time* (Exile, 2005).

32 Van Morrison: 'Song Of Home'; 'End Of The Land', *Keep It Simple* (Exile, 2008).

33 D. H. Lawrence: 'The Spirit of Place', in D. H. Lawrence: *Studies in Classic American Literature* (London: Penguin, 1982). See also Merlin Coverley: *Psychogeography* (London: Pocket Essentials, 2007).

34 Guy Debord: 'Introduction to a Critique of Urban Geography', *Le Livre Nues*, No. 6, 1955.

35 Them: 'Mystic Eyes', *Them* (Decca, 1965).

36 *Dick Clark's American Bandstand* [VHS] (Vitrona, 1985).

37 Guy Debord: 'Introduction to a Critique of Urban Geography'.

38 Seamus Heaney: *Preoccupations: Selected Prose 1968–1978* (London: Faber and Faber, 1980) *A Coney Island of the Mind*, dir. Peter Lynden and Tom Tyrwhitt, Channel Four, broadcast 12 March 1991.

39 Van Morrison: 'Orangefield', *Avalon Sunset* (Polydor, 1989).

40 Fiachra Trench to the author, August 2005.

41 *A Coney Island of the Mind*, dir. Peter Lynden and Tom Tyrwhitt, Channel Four, broadcast 12 March 1991.

42 See, for example, George Wingfield: *Glastonbury: Isle of Avalon* (London: Wooden Books, 2007) and also http://www.glastonbury.co.uk; Mississippi John Hurt: *Avalon Blues* (Rounder, 1995).

43 See Jeremy Dibble: *C. Hubert H. Parry: His Life and Music* (Oxford University Press, 1992).

44 Van Morrison: 'Somerset', *What's Wrong With This Picture?* (Verve, 2003).

45 Van Morrison: 'When Will I Ever Learn To Live In God?', *Avalon Sunset* (Polydor, 1989).

46 Van Morrison: 'Avalon Of The Heart', *Enlightenment* (Polydor, 1990).

47 *Belfast Sunday Telegraph*, 8 July 2007.

48 Lou Reed: *Coney Island Baby* (RCA, 1975); Lawrence Ferlinghetti: *A Coney Island of the Mind* (New Directions Publishing Corporation, 1958).

49 Fiachra Trench to the author, August 2005.

50 Van Morrison: 'Coney Island', *Avalon Sunset* (Polydor, 1989).

51 Van Morrison: 'I'm Tired Joey Boy', *Avalon Sunset* (Polydor, 1989).

Chapter Eight: A Three-cornered Quartet: Van Morrison and the Art of Through-composition

1 Van Morrison interviewed in *Uncut*, No. 98, July 2005, pp. 64–65.
2 Yorke, p. 52.
3 John Payne in *Wavelength*, No. 23, p. 11.
4 Dylan Thomas: 'Vision and Prayer', in *Collected Poems 1934–1952* (London: J.M. Dent, 1973), pp. 129–40.
5 Nick Logan in *New Musical Express*, 27 September 1969.
6 José Feliciano: 'Light My Fire' *Light My Fire* RCA 1967
7 Lester Bangs: 'Astral Weeks', in Greil Marcus (ed.): *Stranded* (London: Da Capo Press, 2007)pp. 178–88.
8 Greil Marcus, review of *Astral Weeks* in *Rolling Stone*, 1 March 1969.
9 Bangs: 'Astral Weeks', p. 185.
10 Yorke, p. 53.
11 John Coltrane: *Ascension* (Impulse!, 1965); John Coltrane: *Interstellar Space* (Impulse!, 1967/1972); Joe Harriott Quintet: *Free Form* (1960) (Gott Discs, 2007); *Abstract* (1962) (Gott Discs, 2007).
12 Bangs: 'Astral Weeks', p. 187.
13 *Candy Meets . . . Van Morrison*, NPS (Dutch public service TV), recorded in Cardiff, 14 April 2007 and broadcast 28 October and 11 November 2007.
14 The shows were at the Hollywood Bowl and in New York. The Hollywood shows were edited for release as *Astral Weeks Live* (Listen to the Lion, 2009).
15 Van Morrison interviewed on *Soul Britannia*, dir. Jeremy Marre, BBC, 2007. Online at: http://www.vanmorrison.com
16 Richard Davis in *Wavelength*, No. 23, p. 11.
17 Ibid., p. 12.
18 Kevin Rowland: Blog entry No. 5, 'Van Morrison'. Online at: http://profile.myspace.com/index.cfm?fuseaction=user.viewprofile&friendid=135573349
19 Van Morrison: 'Astral Weeks', *Astral Weeks*, (Warner Bros., 1968).
20 Van Morrison: 'Beside You', *Bang Masters* (Sony, 1991); Van Morrison: 'Beside You', *Astral Weeks* (Warner Bros., 1968).
21 Van Morrison: 'Sweet Thing', *Astral Weeks* (Warner Bros., 1968).
22 René Descartes: *Discourse on the Meditations* (Stanford University Press, 1979), pp. 39–41.
23 John Payne in *Wavelength*, No. 23.
24 *Arena: One Irish Rover*, BBC, broadcast 16 February 1991.
25 Domenico Scarlatti: *Harpsichord Sonatas Vol. One*, played by Pieter-Jan Belder (Brilliant Classics, 2001); The Beatles: 'Fixing A Hole', *Sgt. Pepper's Lonely Hearts Club Band* (Parlophone, 1967); The Monkees: 'The Girl I Knew Somewhere', *Headquarters* (RCA, 1967).
26 Van Morrison: 'Cyprus Avenue', *Astral Weeks* (Warner Bros., 1968).
27 T. S. Eliot: 'Burnt Coker' in *Four Quartets* (Faber and Faber, 1986), p.27; James Joyce: *Finnegan's Wake* (Faber and Faber, 1982).

28 Bob Sarlin: *Turn It Up (I Can't Hear the Words)* (New York: Simon and Schuster, 1973), p. 9.
29 Greil Marcus, *Rolling Stone*, 1 March 1969.
30 Van Morrison: 'The Way Young Lovers Do', *Astral Weeks* (Warner Bros., 1968).
31 Maria McKee to the author, February 2008.
32 Maria McKee: 'The Way Young Lovers Do', *You've Got To Sin To Get Saved* (Geffen, 1993).
33 Van Morrison interviewed on *Soul Britannia*, dir. Jeremy Marre, BBC, 2007. Online at: http://www.vanmorrison.com
34 Van Morrison: 'Madame George', *Bang Masters* (Sony, 1991).
35 Yorke, pp. 60–61.
36 Van Morrison: 'The Beauty Of The Days Gone By', *Down The Road* (Exile, 2002).
37 Van Morrison: 'Madame George', *Astral Weeks* (Warner Bros., 1968).
38 Bangs: 'Astral Weeks', *Stranded*, p. 179.
39 Gerald Dawe: 'The Burning Ground: Belfast and Van Morrison', in Gerald Dawe: *The Rest Is History* (Newry: Abbey Press, 1998), p. 57.
40 Ibid.
41 Ibid., p. 56.
42 Ibid., p. 54.
43 Maria McKee: 'Panic Beach', *Maria McKee* (Geffen, 1990); David Gray: 'Say Hello Wave Goodbye', *White Ladder* (EastWest, 2000).
44 Van Morrison: 'Goodbye Baby (Baby Goodbye)', *Bang Masters* (Sony, 1991).
45 Yorke, p. 61.
46 Van Morrison: 'Madame Joy', *The Philosopher's Stone* (Exile, 1998).
47 Buzacott and Ford, pp. 96–97.
48 Jim Armstrong in Colin Harper and Trevor Hodgett: *Irish Trad Folk and Blues: A Secret History* (London: Cherry Red Books, 2004), p. 94.
49 Yorke, pp. 62–63.
50 Van Morrison: 'Ballerina', *Astral Weeks* (Warner Bros., 1968).
51 Yorke, p. 63.
52 John Payne in *Wavelength*, No. 23, p. 12.
53 Buzacott and Ford, p. 97.
54 Johnny Rivers: 'Slim Slo Slider', *Slim Slo Slider* (Liberty/UA, 1970/BGO, 2001 (with *Homegrown*)). See also http://www.johnnyrivers.com; this comprehensive site contains sound files of Rivers discussing aspects of his career, including the *Slim Slo Slider* album.
55 Ryman Theatre show DVD issued with *Pay The Devil* (Exile, 2006).
56 Yorke, pp. 16–18.
57 Nick Kent: review of *Veedon Fleece*, *NME*, 12 October 1974.
58 Van Morrison: 'Fair Play', *Veedon Fleece* (Warner Bros., 1974).
59 Zane Grey: *Riders of the Purple Sage* (Dover Books, 2003). First published in 1912.

60 Van Morrison: 'Linden Arden Stole The Highlights', *Veedon Fleece* (Warner Bros., 1974).
61 Yorke, p. 18.
62 Sinead O'Connor on *The Dave Fanning Show*, RTE Radio One, 27 November 2007.
63 Van Morrison: 'Streets Of Arklow', *Veedon Fleece* (Warner Bros., 1974).
64 *Wavelength*, No. 15, March 1998, p. 24.
65 Yorke, p. 18.
66 Barry Stevens: *Don't Push the River (It Flows By Itself)* (Toronto: The Real People Press, 1970), p. xi.
67 Yorke, p. 21.
68 For further reading, see the founding work of Gestalt by Frederick Perls, et al.: *Gestalt Therapy: Excitement and Growth in the Human Personality* (London: Souvenir Press, 1994); Sergio Sinay: *Gestalt for Beginners* (San Francisco: Writers and Readers Press, 1997); and Ansel Woldt and Sarah Toman (eds): *Gestalt Therapy: History, Theory, and Practice* (London: Sage Books, 2005).
69 Yorke, p. 17.
70 See http://www.veedonfleece.com
71 Van Morrison: 'Song Of Being A Child', *The Philosopher's Stone* (Exile, 1998).
72 See the Sisters of Mercy website: http://www.sistersofmercy.org
73 William Blake: *The Book of Urizen* (New York: Dover Editions, 1998).
74 John Glatt: *The Chieftains: The Authorized Biography* (London: St. Martin's Press, 1997), p. 216.
75 Seamus Heaney: *Preoccupations* (London: Faber and Faber, 1981), p. 13.
76 Van Morrison: 'You Don't Pull No Punches But You Don't Push The River', *Veedon Fleece* (Warner Bros., 1974).
77 Van Morrison: 'Bulbs', *Veedon Fleece* (Warner Bros., 1974).
78 Van Morrison: 'Cul de Sac', *Veedon Fleece* (Warner Bros., 1974).
79 Paul McCartney: 'Maybe I'm Amazed', *McCartney* (Apple, 1970); XTC: 'I Can't Own Her', *Apple Venus Vol. One* (Cooking Vinyl, 1998); Bob Dylan: 'You're A Big Girl Now', *Blood On The Tracks* (CBS, 1974); ABBA 'Like An Angel Passing Through My Room' *The Visitors* (Epic/Sony, 1981).
80 Yorke, p. 18.
81 Dexy's Midnight Runners: 'Plan B' (single, EMI, 1981).
82 Van Morrison: 'Comfort You', *Veedon Fleece* (Warner Bros., 1974).
83 Van Morrison interviewed by Jonathan Cott in *Rolling Stone*, 30 November 1978, pp. 50–53.
84 Van Morrison: 'No Thing', *Keep It Simple* (Exile, 2008); Yorke, p. 18.
85 This Mortal Coil: 'Come Here My Love', *Filigree And Shadow* (4AD, 1986).
86 Van Morrison: 'Come Here My Love', *Veedon Fleece* (Warner Bros., 1974).
87 Yorke, p. 18.
88 Van Morrison: 'Country Fair', *Veedon Fleece* (Warner Bros., 1974); Van Morrison: 'And It Stoned Me', *Moondance* (Warner Bros., 1970).
89 Richard Thompson: 'I Misunderstood', *Rumor and Sigh* (EMI, 1992).

90 Yorke, p. 89.
91 Van Morrison: 'Bright Side Of The Road', *Into The Music* (Phonogram, 1979).
92 Elvis Costello and the Voice Squad: 'Full Force Gale' on *No Prima Donna* (Exile, 1994); Phil Coulter to the author July 2008.
93 Van Morrison: 'Full Force Gale', *Into The Music* (Phonogram, 1979).
94 Bob Dylan: 'Oh, Sister', *Desire* (Columbia, 1976).
95 See Daniel 5 (King James Bible).
96 Bob Dylan: 'When You Gonna Wake Up?', *Slow Train Coming* (Columbia, 1979).
97 Van Morrison: 'Steppin' Out Queen', *Into The Music* (Phonogram, 1979).
98 Van Morrison: 'Troubadours', *Into The Music* (Phonogram, 1979).
99 Van Morrison: 'Rolling Hills', *Into The Music* (Phonogram, 1979);Van Morrison: 'A New Kind Of Man' *A Sense of Wonder* (Phonogram, 1985); D. H. Lawrence: 'The Song Of A Man Who Has Come Through' in *The Complete Poems of D. H. Lawrence* (London: Wordsworth Editions, 1994) p.112.
100 Bob Dylan: 'Precious Angel', *Slow Train Coming* (Columbia, 1979).
101 Van Morrison: 'You Make Me Feel So Free', *Into The Music* (Phonogram, 1979).
102 Israel Shenker: 'Beckett: Moody Man of Letters', *The New York Times*, 5 May 1956.
103 Van Morrison: 'Angeliou', *Into The Music* (Phonogram, 1979).
104 Sinead O'Connor on *The Dave Fanning Show*, RTE Radio One, 28 November 2007.
105 Van Morrison to Chris Welch *Melody Maker*, 3 March 1979: see also Note 23, Chapter Four.
106 Thomas, Dylan: *Collected Poems 1934–1952* (London: Dent, 1982); *Collected Stories* Phoenix Books 2000; Van Morrison: 'For Mr.Thomas', *The Philosopher's Stone: The Unreleased Tapes Volume One* (Exile/Polydor, 1998).
107 Van Morrison, during the BBC Radio Two broadcast of a concert performed at the Malvern Theatre, 25 November 2003.
108 Laura Barton: 'Hail, Hail Rock and Roll', *Guardian*, 9 February 2007.
109 Van Morrison: 'It's All In The Game/You Know What They're Writing About', *Into The Music* (Phonogram, 1979).
110 Pee Wee Ellis to Toni Schiavone in *Wavelength*, No. 12, July 1997, p. 22.
111 Leonard Gontarek: *Van Morrison Can't Find His Feet* (Chicago: My Pretty Jane Press, 1996).
112 Van Morrison: 'Haunts Of Ancient Peace', *Common One* (Phonogram, 1980).
113 Van Morrison, introducing 'Haunts Of Ancient Peace' at the Princess Theatre, Torquay, 30 August 2002.
114 An excerpt from Tennyson's poem, 'The Palace of Art' (1832, revised 1842), Stanza 22, in the front papers of Alfred Austin: *Haunts of Ancient Peace* (London: Macmillan, 1902).
115 Ibid., p. 11.
116 Ibid., p. 16.

117 Ibid., pp. 103–4; Van Morrison: 'Cold Wind In August', *A Period Of Transition* (Warner Bros., 1977).
118 Austin, pp. 133–34.
119 Van Morrison: 'Satisfied', *Common One* (Phonogram, 1980).
120 Pee Wee Ellis to Toni Schiavone in *Wavelength*, No. 12, July 1997, p. 23.
121 Van Morrison: 'Wild Honey', *Common One* (Phonogram, 1980).
122 'The Mountains of Mourne' was written by Percy French in 1896. It has become a standard of the Irish folk repertoire. There is a monument to French, featuring the words of his song, by the shore in Newcastle, County Down, where the mountains of Mourne do indeed sweep down to the sea.
123 Van Morrison: 'Spirit', *Common One* (Phonogram, 1980).
124 Paul McCartney on the Ray Charles tribute TV show *What'd I Say*, BBC, 24 July 2004.
125 Pee Wee Ellis to Toni Schiavone in *Wavelength*, No. 12, July 1997, p. 22.
126 Van Morrison: 'When Heart Is Open', *Common One* (Phonogram, 1980).
127 Van Morrison: 'Summertime In England', *Common One* (Phonogram, 1980).
128 Thomas Gray: 'Elegy In A Country Churchyard'(1751) *Poetical Works of Thomas Gray* (Oxford University Press, 2008), p. 94. See also Christopher Marlowe: *Collected Poems*, Chaney and Striar (eds), (Oxford University Press, 2005). Spenser, Edmund: *The Shephard's Calendar and Other Poems* (London: Dent, 1965).
129 Thomas Hardy: *Tess of the D'Urbervilles* (London: Penguin, 1984). First published 1891; Thomas Hardy: *The Dynasts* (London: Macmillan, 1984). First published 1908.
130 See, for example, Simon Gatrell: *Thomas Hardy's Vision Of Wessex* (London: Palgrave Macmillan, 2003).
131 William Wordsworth: *The Prelude* (London: Penguin Classics, 2005), p. 45.
132 Samuel Beckett: *The Unnameable* in *Three Novels* (London: Picador, 1984), p. 324.
133 Pee Wee Ellis to Toni Schiavone in *Wavelength*, No. 12, July 1997, p. 22.
134 D. H. Lawrence: 'The Song of a Man Who Has Come Through', in *The Complete Poems of D.H. Lawrence* (London: Wordsworth Editions, 1994), p. 112.
135 Van Morrison: 'Behind The Ritual', *Keep It Simple* (Exile, 2008).
136 Seamus Heaney: 'Digging' in *New Selected Poems* 1966–1987 (London: Faber and Faber, 2002).
137 Seamus Heaney: *Preoccupations: Selected Prose 1968–1978* (London: Faber and Faber, 1981).
138 John Montague, *Guardian*, 5 September 1988.
139 Van Morrison: 'Summertime In England', recorded at Usher Hall, Belfast, June 1982 and issued as the B-side of 'Cry For Home' (Phonogram, 1983). (Available as a 45 rpm 12", and, an oddity, a 7" with 'Cry For Home' at 45 rpm and 'Summertime In England' on the flip at 33-and-a-third rpm.)

Postscript: Make It Real One More Time Again: Astral Weeks Live

1 Sleeve note, Van Morrison: *Astral Weeks Live* (Listen to the Lion Records, 2009).
2 Van Morrison interviewed by Chris Neal in *Performing Songwriter*, Vol. 16, No. 116, March/April, 2009, p. 47.
3 Van Morrison: *Astral Weeks Live* (Listen to the Lion Records, 2009).
4 *Los Angeles Times*, 8 November 2008.

Bibliography

PRIMARY

Brooks, Ken (1999): *In Search of Van Morrison* (Andover: Agenda).

Buzacott, Martin and Ford, Andrew (2005): *Speaking in Tongues: The Songs of Van Morrison* (Sydney: ABC Books).

Collis, John (1996): *Van Morrison: Inarticulate Speech of the Heart* (London: Little, Brown/Warner Books).

Cruickshank, Ben (1996): *Into the Sunset: The Music of Van Morrison* (Andover: Agenda).

Daley, Michael (1998): 'Patti Smith's "Gloria": Intertextual Play in a Rock Vocal Performance', *Popular Music*, Vol. 16, No. 3, pp. 235–53.

Dawe, Gerald (1998): *The Rest Is History* (Belfast/Newry: Abbey Press).

Dewitt, Howard A. (2005): *Van Morrison: Them and the Bang Era* (Fremont, CA: Horizon Books).

Dunne, Michael (2000): '"Tore Down a la Rimbaud": Van Morrison's References and Allusions', *Popular Music and Society*, Vol. 24, No. 4, Winter, pp. 15–24.

Glatt, John: *The Chieftains* (1997): *The Authorized Biography* (London: St. Martin's Press).

Hebdige, Dick (2001): 'Even unto Death: Improvisation, Edging and Enframement', *Critical Enquiry*, Vol. 27, No. 2, Winter, pp. 333–53.

Heylin, Clinton (2002): *Can You Feel the Silence?: Van Morrison: A New Biography* (London: Viking Books).

Hinton, Brian (1997): *Celtic Crossroads: The Art of Van Morrison* (London: Sanctuary).

Humphries, Patrick (1997): *The Complete Guide to the Music of Van Morrison* (London: Omnibus).

Kelly, Pat (1993): *More Than a Song to Sing: Mystical Ideas and the Lyrics of Van Morrison* (Darlington: Rowan Press).

Lobert, Anja (2008): 'Cliff Richard's Self-Presentation as a Redeemer', *Popular Music*, Vol. 27, No. 1, January, pp. 77–97.
Mills, Peter (1994): 'Into the Mystic: The Aural Poetry of Van Morrison', *Popular Music*, Vol. 13, No. 1, January, pp. 91–103.
——(2008): 'Van Morrison and Irish Cinematic Lyricism', in Richard C. Allen and Stephen Regan (eds): *Irelands of the Mind: Memory and Identity in Modern Irish Culture* (Newcastle: Cambridge Scholars Publishing).
Onkey, Lauren (2006): 'Ray Charles on Hyndford Street', in Diane Negra (ed.): *The Irish in Us: Irishness, Performativity and Popular Culture* (Durham USA/ London: Duke University Press).
Pietzonka, Katrin (2002): *In the Age of Uncertainty the Search Goes On: Van Morrison's Musical and Spiritual Journey* (Marburg, Germany: Teetum Verlag).
Rogan, Johnny (1984): *Van Morrison: A Portrait of the Artist* (London: Elm Tree Books).
——(2005): *Van Morrison: No Surrender* (London: Vintage).
Sarlin, Bob (1973): *Turn It Up (I Can't Hear the Words)* (New York: Simon and Schuster).
Smith, Joe (1988): *Off the Record: An Oral History of Popular Music*, ed. Mitchell Fink (London: Pan).
Smith, Stephen G. (1992): 'Blues and Our Mind-Body Problem', *Popular Music*, Vol. 11, No. 1, January, pp. 41–52.
Turner, Steve (1988): *Hungry for Heaven: Rock and Roll and the Search for Redemption* (London: Viking).
——(1993): *Van Morrison: Too Late to Stop Now* (London: Viking).
Yorke, Ritchie (1975): *Van Morrison: Into the Music* (London: Charisma Books).

SECONDARY

Adorno, Theodor W. (2002): *Adorno: Essays on Music*, ed. R. Leppert (Berkeley/ London: University of California Press).
Adorno, Theodor W. and Horkheimer, Max (2002): *The Dialectic of Enlightenment*, ed. and trans. Edmund Jephcott (Stanford University Press).
Alighieri, Dante [1472] (1998): *The Divine Comedy* (Oxford World Classics).
Anderson, Iain (2007): *This Is Our Music: Free Jazz, the Sixties and American Culture* (Philadelphia: University of Pennsylvania).
Anonymous (1996): *Pearl, Cleanness and Sir Gawain*, ed. J. J. Anderson (London: Everyman Classics).
Auslander, Philip (1999): *Liveness: Performance in a Mediatized Culture* (London: Routledge).
Austin, Alfred (1902): *Haunts of Ancient Peace* (London: Macmillan).
Bailey, Alice [1936] (1972): *A Treatise on the Seven Rays: Volume One: Esoteric Psychology* (New York/London Lucis Press).
——(1950): *Glamour: A World Problem* (New York/London: Lucis Trust Press).

Barker, Taylor (2007): *Faking It: The Quest for Authenticity in Popular Music* (London: Faber and Faber).
Barnes, Jonathan (1982): *The Presocratic Philosophers* (London: Routledge).
Barthes, Roland [1964] (1977): 'The Grain of the Voice', in *Image, Music, Text*, ed. and trans. Stephen Heath (New York: Hill and Wang).
Beadle, Jeremy J. (1993): *Will Pop Eat Itself? Pop Music in the Soundbite Era* (London: Faber and Faber).
Beckett, Samuel [1934] (1976): *More Pricks than Kicks* (London: John Calder).
——(1965): *Proust and Three Dialogues with Georges Duthuit* (London: Calder).
——(1975): *Mirlitonnades* (Paris: Editions de Minuit Paris).
——(1984): *Collected Poems 1930–1978* (London: John Calder).
——(1984): *Three Novels* (London: Picador).
——(1989): *Nohow On* (London: Calder).
——(2006): *The Complete Dramatic Works* (London: Faber and Faber).
Benjamin, Walter [1936] (1999): 'The Work of Art in the Age of Mechanical Reproduction', in Benjamin Walter: *Illuminations* (London: Pimlico).
Berendt, Joachim (1992): *The Jazz Book: From Ragtime to Fusion and Beyond* (New York/Lawrence Hill Books).
Bible, The (Authorised King James version) ed. Carroll, Prickett (Oxford University Press 2008 edition).
Blake, William (1979): *Complete Poems* (University of Minnesota Press).
——(2001): *Selected Poems* (Oxford University Press).
——[1790–3](2004): *The Marriage of Heaven and Hell* (Dover Books).
——[1789] (2006): *Songs of Innocence and Experience* (London: Tate Publishing, facsimile edition).
Bourdieu, Pierre (1986): *Distinction: A Social Critique of the Judgement of Taste* (London: Routledge).
Braudy, Leo (1997): *The Frenzy of Renown: Fame and its History* (New York: Vintage).
Bridge, Ursula (ed.) (1953): *W.B. Yeats and T. Sturgeon Moore Correspondence 1901–1937* (Oxford University Press).
Brocken, Michael (2003): *The British Folk Revival 1944–2002* (Aldershot: Ashgate).
Bruce, Robert, Silver, Abner (1945): *How to Write and Sell a Song Hit* (New York: Lexington Press).
Bruce, Robert, (1946): *How to Write a Hit Song and Sell It* (New York: Lexington Press).
Bryden, Mary (ed.) (1998): *Samuel Beckett and Music* (Oxford University Press).
Bryden, Mary and Mills, Peter (1998): *Beckett at Reading* (Reading: Whiteknights Press).
Buchan, John (ed.) (1924): *The Northern Muse: An Anthology of Scots Vernacular Poetry* (Edinburgh/London: Thomas Nelson).
Cage, John (1961): *Silence: Lectures and Writings* (Boston, MA: MIT Press).

Campbell, Joseph (2001): *As I Was among the Captives: Joseph Campbell's Prison Diary, 1922–1923*, ed. Eiléan Ní Chuilleanáin (Cork: Cork University Press).
Camus, Albert [1956] (2006): *The Fall [La Chute]* (London: Penguin).
Charles, Ray and Ritz, David [1978](2004): *Brother Ray* (New York: Da Capo).
Charters, Samuel B. [1959] (1975): *The Country Blues* (New York: Da Capo).
Chatwin, Bruce (1987): *Songlines* (London: Jonathan Cape).
Cohen, Norm (2000): *Long Steel Rail: The Railroad in American Folksong* (University of Illinois Press).
Colyer, Ken [1989](2009): *When Dreams Are In The Dust* (London: Ken Colyer Trust).
Cooper, David E. (2008): *A Philosophy of Gardens* (London: Oxford University Press).
Courrier, Kevin (2005): *Randy Newman's American Dreams* (Toronto: ECW Press).
Coverley, Merlin (2007): *Psychogeography* (London: Pocket Essentials).
Croft, Barbara L. (1987): *'Stylistic Arrangements': A Study of William Butler Yeats's 'A Vision'* (Bucknell University Press).
Crotty, Patrick (1996): *Modern Irish Poetry: An Anthology* (Dublin: Blackstaff Press).
Davis, Michael (1978): *William Blake: A New Kind of Man* (New York: Paul Elek).
Dawidoff, Nicholas (2005): *In the Country of Country* (London: Faber and Faber).
Dawson and Propes (1992): *What Was the First Rock 'n' Roll Record?* (London: Faber and Faber).
Day, Steve (1998): *Two Full Ears: Listening to Improvised Music* (Chelmsford: Soundworld).
Debord, Guy (1997): *Theory of the Derive* (Barcelona: Museum of Contemporary Art).
Descartes, René [1637] (1979): *Discourse on the Method*, trans. F. E. Suttcliffe (Stanford University Press).
Dewe, Mike (1998): *The Skiffle Craze* (London: Planet).
Dibble, Jeremy (1992) *C. Hubert H. Parry: His Life and Music* (Oxford University Press).
Doggett, Peter (2001): *Are You Ready for the Country?* (London: Penguin).
Donne, John (1998): *Selected Poems of John Donne* (Oxford University Press).
Durcan, Paul and Brian Lynch (1967): *Endsville* (Dublin: New Writers Press).
——(1987): *Going Home to Russia* (Dublin: Blackstaff Press).
——(1990): *Daddy Daddy* (Dublin: Blackstaff Press).
Dyer, Richard (with supplementary material by Paul McDonald) (1999): *Stars* (London: BFI Publishing).
Dylan, Bob [1966] (1971): *Tarantula* (London: Panther).
——(2004): *Chronicles, Volume One* (London: Simon and Schuster).
Eisenberg, Evan (1987): *The Recording Angel: Music Records and Culture from Aristotle to Zappa* (New York: McGraw Hill/London: Picador).
Eliot, Thomas Stearns [1922](1982): *The Wasteland and Other Poems* (London: Faber and Faber).
——[1945](1986): *Four Quartets* (London: Faber and Faber).

Evans, Andrew and Wilson, Glenn D. (1999): *Fame: The Psychology of Stardom* (London: Vision Books).
Ferlinghetti, Lawrence (1958): *A Coney Island of the Mind* (New Directions Publishing Corporation).
Ferry, David (ed.) (1998): *The Odes of Horace* (London: Farrar Strauss).
Fonseca, Isobel (1996): *Bury Me Standing: The Gypsies and Their Journey* (London: Vintage).
Foster, Mo (2000): *Play Like Elvis! How British Musicians Bought the American Dream* (London: Sanctuary).
Fraser, Captain Simon [1816] (1982): *Collection of Melodies of the Highlands and Islands of Scotland* (Sydney, Nova Scotia: Cranford Press).
Friedland, Roger and Boden, Deirdre (eds) (1994): *NowHere: Space, Time and Modernity* (Berkeley/London: University of California Press).
Friel, Brian (1980): *Dancing at Lughnasa* (London: Faber and Faber).
Frith, Simon and Goodwin, Andrew (eds) (1990): *On Record: Rock, Pop and the Written Word* (London: Routledge).
Gantz, Jeffrey (trans.) (1981): *Early Irish Myths and Sagas* (London: Penguin).
Gavin, James (2003): *Deep in a Dream: The Long Night of Chet Baker* (London: Vintage).
Gillett, Charlie (1970): *Sound of the City* (London: Souvenir Press).
Gioia, Ted (1997): *The History of Jazz* (New York/Oxford: Oxford University Press).
Gittins, Ian (2007): *Top of the Pops: Mishaps Miming and Music* (London: BBC Books).
Gontarek, Leonard (1996): *Van Morrison Can't Find His Feet* (New York: My Pretty Jane Press).
Gorski, William T. (1996): *Yeats and Alchemy* (New York: SUNY Press).
Graham, George Farquar (ed.) (1850): *The Popular Songs of Scotland with Their Appropriate Melodies* (Edinburgh: Muirwood).
Gray, Michael (2006): *The Bob Dylan Encyclopaedia* (London: Continuum).
Gray, Thomas (2008): *Poetical Works of Thomas Gray* (London: Oxford University Press).
Gregory, Lady Augusta [1902] (1973): *Cuchulain of Muirthemne* (Dublin: Colin Smythe).
Grey, Zane [1912] (2003): *Riders of the Purple Sage* (New York: Dover Books).
Gurlanick, Peter (1995): *Searching for Robert Johnson* (London: Penguin).
——(2006): *Dream Boogie: The Triumph of Sam Cooke* (London: Abacus).
Guralnick, Peter, et al. (eds) (2003): *Martin Scorsese Presents the Blues* (London: Amistad/HarperCollins).
Guthrie, Woody [1943] (1974): *Bound for Glory* (London: Picador).
Hamilton, Marybeth (2007): *In Search of the Blues: Black Voices, White Visions* (London: Jonathan Cape).
Hardy, Thomas [1891] (1984): *Tess of the D'Urbervilles* (London: Penguin).
——[1908] (1984): *The Dynasts* (London: Macmillan).
——(1982): *Collected Poems* (London: Macmillan).

Harker, Dave (1980): *One for the Money: Politics and Popular Song* (London: Hutchinson Press).

Harper, Colin and Hodgett, Trevor (2004): *Irish Trad Folk and Blues: A Secret History* (London: Cherry Red Books).

Hawthorne, Nathaniel [1850] (2005): *The Scarlet Letter* (London: Penguin).

Heaney, Seamus (1981): *Preoccupations: Selected Prose 1968–1978* (London: Faber and Faber).

——(2002): *New Selected Poems 1966–1987* (London: Faber and Faber).

Henderson, Derek (2005): *Gene Vincent: A Companion* (London: Spent Brothers).

Hengelaar-Rookmaaker, Marleen (2002): *New Orleans Jazz, Mahalia Jackson and the Philosophy of Art: Vol. 2 (The Complete Works of Hans R. Rookmaaker)* (New York: Piquant Editions).

Herbst, Peter (ed.) (1981): *The Rolling Stone Interviews 1967–1980: The Classic Oral History of Rock and Roll* (London: St. Martin's Press).

Hewett, Ivan (2003) *Music: Healing the Rift* (London: Continuum).

Hoare, Ian, Anderson, Clive, Cummings, Tony and Frith, Simon (1975): *The Soul Book* (London: Methuen).

Hoggart, Richard (1957): *The Uses of Literacy: Aspects of Working Class Life* (London: Chatto and Windus).

Houston, Cissy (with Jonathan Singer) (1998): *How Sweet the Sound: My Life with God and Gospel* (New York: Doubleday).

Hughes, Hubert and Colum, Padraic (eds) (1909): *Irish Country Songs Sung by Count John McCormack* (London: Boosey & Hawkes).

Jankelevitch, Vladimir [1961] (2003): *Music and the Ineffable*, trans. Carolyn Abbate (Princeton University Press).

Joyce, James [1914] (2007): *Dubliners* (London: Penguin).

——[1916) (2007): *Portrait of the Artist as a Young Man* (London: Penguin).

——[1918) (2007): *Exiles* (London: Penguin).

——[1922] (2007): *Ulysses* (London: Penguin).

——[1939] (2007): *Finnegans Wake* (London: Penguin).

Kavanagh, Patrick (2005): *Collected Poems* (London: Penguin).

Keats, John (2007) *Complete Poems* (London: Penguin).

Kerouac, Jack [1957] (1988): *Dharma Bums* (London: Penguin).

——[1957] (1988): *On the Road* (London: Penguin).

KLF, The [Bill Drummond and Jimmy Cauty] (1988): *The Manual: How to Have a Number One the Easy Way* (Glasgow: KLF Communications).

Knowlson, James (1998): *Damned to Fame* (London: Bloomsbury).

Knowlson, James and Knowlson, Elizabeth (eds) (2006): *Beckett Remembering, Remembering Beckett* (London: Bloomsbury).

Lahr, Jane (ed.) (2000): *The Celtic Quest in Art and Literature* (New York: Welcome Books).

Laird, Tracey E.W. (2005): *Louisiana Hayride: Radio and Roots Music Along the Red River* (New York: Oxford University Press USA).

Larkin, Philip (1976): *All What Jazz* (London: Faber and Faber).
Larsen, S. and Larsen, R. (1991): *A Fire in the Mind: The Life of Joseph Campbell* (London: Doubleday).
Lawrence, D. H. [1920] (1982): *Women in Love* (London: Penguin).
——[1923] (1982): *Studies in Classic American Literature* (London: Penguin).
——(1994): *The Complete Poems of D.H. Lawrence* (London: Wordsworth Editions).
Lewis, Clive Staples [1950] (2005): *The Lion, the Witch and the Wardrobe* (Oxford University Press).
——[1955] (1998): *Surprised by Joy* (London: Fount).
Leyden, Maurice (1989): *Belfast: City of Song* (Dingle, Co. Kerry: Brandon).
Lomax, Alan (1993): *The Land Where the Blues Began* (London: Minerva).
——(2003) *Alan Lomax: Selected Writings 1934–1997*, ed. R. Cohen (London: Routledge).
Lomax, John (1947): *Adventures of a Ballad Hunter* (New York: Macmillan).
——(ed.) (1959): *The Leadbelly Legend* (New York: Folkways).
Lomax, John and Lomax, Alan (1936): *Negro Folk Songs as Sung by Leadbelly* (New York: Macmillan).
Lyttelton, Humphrey (2006): *It Just Occurred to Me* (London: Robson Books).
Macneice, Louis (2006): *Selected Poems* (London: Penguin).
Macpherson, James (2006): *The Poems of Ossian and Related Works* (Edinburgh University Press).
Marcus, Greil [1975] (2002): *Mystery Train: Images of America in Rock 'n' Roll Music* (Penguin).
——(1991): *Dead Elvis: Chronicles of a Cultural Obsession* (London: Penguin).
——(1997): *Invisible Republic* (London: Picador).
Marcus, Greil (ed.) (2007): *Stranded* (London: Da Capo Press).
Margolick, David (2001): *Strange Fruit: Billie Holiday, Café Society and an Early Cry for Civil Rights* (London: Canongate).
Marlowe, Christopher (2005): *Tamburlaine the Great Parts One and Two*, ed. Anthony B. Dawson (New Mermaids Series: London: A&C Black).
——*Collected Poems* (2005): ed. Striar Chaney (London: Oxford University Press).
Marsh, Dave (1989): *The Heart of Rock and Soul: The 1001 Greatest Singles Ever Made* (London: New American Library).
Marshall, Peter (2001): *The Philosopher's Stone: A Quest for the Secrets of Alchemy* (London: Macmillan).
Marshall, P. D. (1997): *Celebrity and Power: Fame in Contemporary Culture* (Minnesota/London: University of Minnesota).
Marvell, Andrew (1982): *Selected Poems* (London: Penguin).
McCarthy, John and Morrell, Jill (1993): *Some Other Rainbow* (London: Bantam Press).
McLaverty, Michael (1978): *Collected Short Stories* (Dublin: Poolbeg Press).
Melly, George (1970): *Revolt into Style: The Pop Arts in Britain* (London: Penguin).

Methodist Church (1993): *Hymns and Psalms Hymnbook* (Peterborough: Methodist Publishing House).
Mezzrow, Mezz [1946] (1997): *Really the Blues* (London: Flamingo).
Middleton, Richard (ed.) (2000): *Reading Pop* (Oxford University Press).
Milligan, Spike (1963): *Puckoon* (London: Penguin).
Milton, John [1667] (2003): *Paradise Lost* (Penguin Classics).
Montague, John (1989): *Mount Eagle* (Newcastle: Bloodaxe).
Morris, Jan (2002): *Trieste and the Meaning of Nowhere* (London: Faber and Faber).
Mullan, Bob (ed.) (1997): *Memories of R.D. Laing* (London: Cassell).
Nietzsche, F. [1886] (2003): *Beyond Good and Evil* (Penguin Classics).
O'Brien, Flann [1939] (1978): *At Swim-Two-Birds* (London: Picador).
O'Casey, Sean (2001): *Three Plays* (London: Faber and Faber).
O'Connor, John (2003): *Shakespearean Afterlives: Ten Characters with a Life of Their Own* (Cambridge: Icon).
O'Hara, Mary (1982): *A Song for Ireland* (Dublin: Michael Joseph).
Oliver, Paul [1960] (1990): *Blues Fell This Morning: Meaning in the Blues* (Cambridge University Press).
Oliver, Paul, et al. (1970): *Yonder Come the Blues* (Cambridge University Press).
Opie, Iona and Opie, Peter (eds) (1997): *The Oxford Dictionary of Nursery Rhymes* (Oxford University Press).
Peellaert, Guy [1973] (1982): *Rock Dreams* (San Francisco: Popular Library).
Perls, Frederick, et al. [1951] (1994): *Gestalt Therapy: Excitement and Growth in the Human Personality* (Chicago: Souvenir Press).
Peterson, Richard (2000): *Creating Country Music: Fabricating Authenticity* (University of Chicago Press).
Phelan, Peggy (1993): *Unmarked: The Politics of Performance* (London: Routledge).
Plato (2007): *The Republic* (London: Penguin Classics).
Pope, Alexander [1743] (2009): *The Dunciad*, ed. Valerie Rumbold (Edinburgh: Longman/Pearson).
Ramet, Sabrina (ed.) (2003): *Kazaaam! Splat! Ploof! The American Impact on European Popular Culture since 1945* (Oxford: Rowman and Littlefield).
Raine, Kathleen (1979): *From Blake to 'A Vision'* (Dublin: Dolmen Press).
Reeves, James (ed.) (1961): *John Donne: Selected Poems* (London: Heinemann).
Resiman, David (1953): *The Lonely Crowd* (London: Doubleday).
Richard, Cliff (with Penny Junor) (2008): *My Life, My Way* (London: Headline).
Rojek, Chris (2001): *Celebrity* (London: Reaktion Books).
Ruskin, John [1899] (1981): *Praeterita* (Oxford University Press).
Said, Edward [1978] (2003): *Orientalism: Western Conceptions of the Orient* (London: Penguin).
Scott, Cyril [1958] (1982): *Music: Its Secret Influence throughout the Ages* (Wellingborough, Northamptonshire: The Aquarian Press).
Shakespeare, William [1591/first folio 1623] (1974): *The Tragedy of Richard III*, ed. Wells, S. (London: Penguin Playtext).

Shakespeare, William [c.1603–07/first folio 1623](2005): *Macbeth*, ed. C. Rutter (London: Penguin Playtext).
Shakespeare, William [c.1610/first folio 1623] (2007): *The Tempest*, ed. M. Butler (London: Penguin Playtext).
Shipton, Alyn (2007): *A New History of Jazz* (London: Continuum).
Sidran, Ben [1971] (1995): *Black Talk* (London: Payback Press).
——(1995): *Talking Jazz: An Oral History* (Petaluma, California: Da Capo press).
——(2003): *Ben Sidran: A Life in the Music* (New York: Taylor Trade Publishing).
Sinay, Sergio (1997): *Gestalt for Beginners* (San Francisco: Writers and Readers Press).
Skene, Reg (1974): *The Cuchulain Plays of WB Yeats* (London: Macmillan).
Smith, R. A. (1825): *Scottish Minstrel: A Selection of Vocal Melodies of Scotland Ancient and Modern Arranged for the Pianoforte, Vols I–VI* (Edinburgh: Robert Purdie Press, 1825).
Snyder, Tom (2000): *Route 66: Traveler's Guide and Roadside Companion* (New York: St. Martin's Press).
Spenser, Edmund [1579](1965): *The Shepherd's Calendar and Other Poems*, ed. Henderson (London: Everyman).
Stapledon, Olaf [1936] (1973): *Star Maker* (London: Methuen/Penguin).
Steindl-Rast, David (1995): *The Music of Silence* (London: HarperCollins).
Stevens, Barry (1970): *Don't Push the River (It Flows by Itself)* (Toronto: The Real People Press).
Swami, Purohit (trans.) [1935] (2004): *The Geeta: The Gospel of the Lord Shri Krishna* (London: Faber and Faber).
Tame, David (1984): *The Secret Power of Music* (Wellingborough, Northamptonshire: Turnstone Press Ltd).
Tassin, Myron (1975): *Fifty Years at the Grand Ole Opry* (London: Pelican).
Taylor, Vince (1976): *Alias Vince Taylor: Le Survivant* (Paris: Editions Delville).
Thomas, Dylan (1973): *Collected Poems 1934–1952* (London: J.M. Dent).
Thompson, Gordon (2008): *Please Please Me: Sixties British Pop, Inside Out* (Oxford University Press).
Thoreau, Henry David [1854] (1982): *Walden, or, Life In The Woods* (London: Penguin Classics).
Wald, Elijah (2004): *Escaping the Delta: Robert Johnson and the Invention of the Blues* (New York/London: Amistad/HarperCollins).
——(2002) *Josh White: Society Blues* (New York: Routledge).
Walker, B. M. and Dixon, H. (1984): *No Mean City: Belfast 1880–1914* (Belfast: Friar's Bush Press).
Walker, Rob (2005): *Letters from New Orleans* (New Orleans: Garrett County Press).
Wallis, Michael (2008): *Route 66: The Mother Road* (Gordonsville, VA: St. Michael's Press).
Warhol, Andy (2007): *The Philosophy of Andy Warhol: From A to B and Back Again* (London: Penguin).

Waters, John (1994): *Race of Angels: Ireland and the Genesis of U2* (Dublin: Blackstaff Press).
Watts, Alan (1974): *Cloud Hidden, Whereabouts Unknown – A Mountain Journal* (London: Vintage).
Weissman, Dick (2006): *Blues: The Basics* (London/New York: Routledge).
Wenders, Wim (1989): *Emotion Pictures: Reflections on the Cinema* (London: Faber and Faber).
Whitcomb, Ian (1973): *After the Ball* (London: Penguin).
White, Roger (1998): *The Everly Brothers: Walk Right Back* (London: Plexus).
Whitman, Walt (1995): *The Complete Poems of Walt Whitman* (London: Wordsworth).
Wilcher, Robert (ed.) (1986): *Andrew Marvell: Selected Poetry and Prose* (London: Penguin).
Williams, Paul (1993): *Rock and Roll: The 100 Best Singles* (San Francisco: Entwhistle Books).
Wingfield, George (2007): *Glastonbury: Isle of Avalon* (London: Wooden Books).
Woldt, Ansel and Toman, Sarah (eds) (2005): *Gestalt Therapy: History, Theory, and Practice* (London: Sage Books).
Wolfe, Charles K. (1977): *Tennessee Strings* (University of Tennessee Press).
Wolfe, Charles, K. (ed.) (1985): *Songs of the Mountains* (Philadelphia: Woodhead Books).
Wordsworth, William [1850](2005): *The Prelude* (London: Penguin Classics).
——[1802] (2006): *The Lyrical Ballads* (London: Penguin Classics).
XTC with Farmer, Neville (1998): *XTC: Songs and Stories* (London: Helter Skelter).
Yeats W. B. [1888] (1979): *Fairy and Folk Tales of Ireland* (London: Pan Books).
——[1925/1937] (1981): *A Vision* (London: Macmillan).
——[1938] (1996): *Autobiographies* (London: Macmillan).
——(1997): *Collected Plays* (London: Penguin).
——(2000): *Collected Poems* (London: Wordsworth Library/Penguin).

WEBSITES

An excellent enterprise seeking to catalogue every show given by Van Morrison, particularly helpful in the composition of Appendix One:
http://ivan.vanomatic.de/
A brilliant labour of love and an essential resource:
http://www.geocities.com/tracybjazz/hayward/van-the-man.info/index-2.html
The official website:
www.vanmorrison.com

Discography

PRIMARY

Them (Decca, 1965).
Them Again (Decca, 1966).
Them: Rock Roots (Decca, 1975).
Blowin' Your Mind! (Bang, 1967).
The Bang Masters (Epic/Legacy, 1990).
Astral Weeks (Warner Bros., 1968).
Moondance (Warner Bros., 1970).
His Band And The Street Choir (Warner Bros., 1970).
Tupelo Honey (Warner Bros., 1971).
Saint Dominic's Preview (Warner Bros., 1972).
Hard Nose The Highway (Warner Bros., 1973).
It's Too Late To Stop Now (Warner Bros., 1974).
Veedon Fleece (Warner Bros., 1974).
A Period Of Transition (Warner Bros., 1977).
Wavelength (Warner Bros., 1978).
Into the Music (Warner Bros., 1979).
Common One (Mercury, 1980).
Beautiful Vision (Mercury, 1982).
Inarticulate Speech Of The Heart (Mercury, 1983).
Live At The Grand Opera House Belfast (Mercury, 1984).
A Sense Of Wonder (Mercury, 1985).
No Guru, No Method, No Teacher (Mercury, 1986).
Poetic Champions Compose (Mercury, 1987).
Irish Heartbeat (Mercury, 1988).
Avalon Sunset (Polydor, 1989).
Enlightenment (Polydor, 1990).

Hymns To The Silence (Polydor, 1991).
Too Long In Exile (Polydor, 1993).
A Night In San Francisco (Polydor, 1994).
Days Like This (Polydor, 1995).
How Long Has This Been Going On? (Verve/Exile, 1995).
Tell Me Something (Verve/Exile, 1996).
The Healing Game (Polydor/Exile, 1997).
Back On Top (Virgin/Exile, 1999).
The Skiffle Sessions (Virgin/Exile, 2000).
You Win Again (Virgin/Exile, 2000).
Down The Road (Polydor/Exile, 2002).
What's Wrong With This Picture? (Blue Note/Exile, 2003).
Magic Time (Polydor/Exile, 2005).
Pay The Devil (Polydor/Exile, 2006).
Live At Austin City Limits Festival (Exile, 2006).
Keep It Simple (Polydor/Exile, 2008).
Astral Weeks Live (Listen To The Lion Records, 2009).

Spoken Word Contribution

Cuchulainn with Fay Howard and Ben Norman (SULIS Music, 1990) (cassette only).

Compilations

The Best Of Van Morrison (Polydor, 1990).
The Best Of Van Morrison Vol. 2 (Polydor, 1993).
The Story Of Them (Deram, 1997).
The Best Of Van Morrison Vol. 3 (Exile/EMI, 2007).
At The Movies (Exile/EMI, 2007).
Still On Top (Exile/EMI, 2007).
The Philosopher's Stone: The Unreleased Tapes Volume One (Polydor/Exile, 1998).
No Prima Donna: The Songs Of Van Morrison (Polydor/Exile, 1994).
Now And In Time To Be: A Musical Celebration Of The Works Of W. B. Yeats (Grapevine, 1997).

Singles

'Jackie Wilson Said'/'You've Got The Power' (Warner Bros., 1972).
'Caledonia'/'What's Up, Crazy Pup?' (Warner Bros., 1974).
'Joyous Sound'/'Mechanical Bliss' (Warner Bros., 1977).
'Gloria'/'It Must Be You'/'And The Healing Has Begun'/'See Me Through'/'Whenever God Shines His Light'/'It Fills You Up'/'Star Of The County Down' (VANCD 11) (Polydor/Exile, 1993).
'Days Like This'/'I Don't Want To Go On Without You'/'That Old Black Magic'/'Yo' (Polydor/Exile, 1995).

'The Healing Game'/'Full Force Gale '96'/'Look What The Good People Done'/'Celtic Spring' (Polydor/Exile, 1997).
'Rough God Goes Riding'/'At The End Of The Day'/'The Healing Game (Alternative Version)' (Polydor/Exile, 1997).
'Precious Time'/'Naked In The Jungle'/'Give Me A Kiss' (Virgin/Exile, 1999).
'Back On Top'/'Tell Me'/'Sax Instrumental No.1'/'John Brown's Body'/'I'm Ready' (Virgin/Exile, 1999).
'Philosopher's Stone'/'These Dreams Of You'/'Raincheck' (Virgin/Exile, 1999).
'I Wanna Go Home'/'New Burying Ground'/'Midnight Special (Alternative Take)' (Virgin/Exile, 2000).
'Let's Talk About Us'/'Singing The Blues'/'The Ballad Of Jesse James' (Virgin/Exile, 2000).
'Meet Me In The Indian Summer'/'In The Afternoon'/'In The Midnight' (Virgin/Exile, 2002).

SECONDARY

ABBA: *The Visitors* (Epic/Sony 1981).
Allison, Mose: *Back Country Suite* (Prestige, 1957).
——*Autumn Song* (Prestige, 1959).
——*I Don't Worry About A Thing* (Atlantic, 1962).
——*Allison Wonderland Anthology* (Rhino, 1994).
Armstrong, Herbie: 'Real Real Gone' (Real Records, 1982).
——*Back Against The Wall* (Avatar/MMC, 1983).
Armstrong, Louis and His All Stars: *Pasadena Civic Auditorium June 20, 1956* (Giants of Jazz, 1990).
Baker, Chet: *Live At Ronnie Scott's* (DRG, 1984).
——*Let's Get Lost* (RCA, 1989).
Band, The: *Cahoots* (Capitol/EMI, 1971).
Barber, Chris: *The Pye Jazz Anthology* (Sanctuary, 2008).
Beach Boys, The: *All Summer Long* (Capitol, 1964).
——*Sunflower* (EMI, 1970).
——*Surf's Up* (Brother, 1971).
——*Pet Sounds Sessions* (Capitol, 1997).
Beatles, The: *Sgt Pepper's Lonely Hearts Club Band* (Parlophone, 1967).
——*The Beatles* [aka 'The White Album'] (Apple, 1968).
——*Abbey Road* (Apple, 1969).
Behan, Dominic (with Steve Benbow): *The Irish Rover* (Folklore, 1963).
Bell, Crawford: *The Master's Hand* (Cross Rhythms, 1993) (cassette only).
Benson, George: *Greatest Hits* (WEA, 2004).
Berry, Chuck: *The Collection* (Chess, 2003).
Berry, Heidi: *Love* (4AD, 1990).

Bowie, David: *Young Americans* (RCA, 1975).
Brown, James: *Live At The Apollo* (Polydor 1963).
—— *Sex Machine* (Polydor 1970).
Buckley, Jeff: *Complete Live At Sin-E* (Sony, 2003).
Byrds, The: *Fifth Dimension* (CBS, 1966).
——*Turn! Turn! Turn!* (CBS, 1966).
——*Sweetheart Of The Rodeo* (CBS, 1967).
Carter Family, The: *Keep On The Sunny Side* (Proper, 2004).
Charles, Ray: *Golden Hits* (SPA, 1988).
——*Genius Loves Company* (Geffen, 2004).
——*Live At Newport* (Atlantic, 1958).
——*Modern Sounds in Country and Western Music* (HMV, 1962).
——*Modern Sounds in Country and Western Music Vol. Two* (HMV, 1962).
Chieftains, The: *A Celebration* (RCA Victor, 1995).
Clash, The: *The Singles* (Sony, 2001).
Coltrane, John: *My Favourite Things* (Atlantic, 1961).
——*Ascension* (Impulse!, 1965).
——*Meditations* (Impulse!, 1966).
Colyer, Ken: *Just About As Good As It Gets* (Smith and Co., 2007).
Cooke, Sam: *Complete Recordings of Sam Cooke* (Speciality, 2002).
Costello, Elvis: *Almost Blue* (F-Beat, 1981).
——*Imperial Bedroom* (F-Beat, 1982).
——*Mighty Like A Rose* (Warner Bros., 1991).
Cserpes, Karoly and Sebestyen, Marta: *Kivandorlas [Emigration]* (Hungaraton, 1988).
Davis, Miles: *Kind Of Blue* (Columbia: 1959).
——*In A Silent Way* (CBS/Columbia/Sony, 1969).
Debussy, Claude: *Complete Works for Piano*, played by Aldo Ciccolini (EMI Classics, 2001).
DeShannon, Jackie: *Jackie* (Atlantic, 1972/2003).
Dexy's Midnight Runners: *Searching For the Young Soul Rebels* (EMI, 1980).
——*Too Rye Aye* (Phonogram, 1982).
——*Don't Stand Me Down* (Phonogram, 1985).
Donegan, Lonnie: *Lonnie* (Pye, 1957).
——*Putting On The Style* (Chrysalis, 1978).
——*Muleskinner Blues* (RCA, 1999).
——*Talking Guitar Blues* (Sequel, 1999).
Drake, Nick: *Bryter Later* (Island, 1970).
Dylan, Bob: *The Times They Are A Changing* (CBS, 1963).
——*Blood On The Tracks* (CBS, 1974).
——*Nashville Skyline* (CBS, 1969).
——*Self Portrait* (CBS, 1970).
——*Desire* (CBS, 1976).
——*Oh Mercy* (Columbia, 1989).

——*Modern Times* (Sony, 2006).
Eddie and the Hot Rods: *Live At The Marquee EP* (Island, 1976).
Edmunds, Dave: *Anthology 1968–90* (Rhino, 1993).
Elliott, Ron: *The Candlestickmaker* (Collectors Choice, 2003) (1970 recording).
Fame, Georgie: *Cool Cat Blues* (Go Jazz, 2004).
——*Georgie Fame and the Blue Flames* (Commercial, 1998).
——*Funny How Time Slips Away* (Castle, 2001).
Fairport Convention: *Liege and Lief* (Island, 1969).
Feliciano, José: *Light My Fire* (RCA, 1967).
Forbert, Steve: *More Young, Guitar Days* (Southbound, 2003).
Formby, George: *The Best Of* (Music For Pleasure, 1969).
Frank, Jackson C.: *Jackson C. Frank* (Columbia, 1965/Sanctuary, 2008).
Gray, David: *White Ladder* (EastWest, 1999).
Guthrie, Woody: *The Very Best Of* (Music Club, 1992).
——*Dustbowl Ballads* (Camden, 1998).
Joe Harriott Quintet: *Free Form* (Gott Discs, 2007) (1960 recording).
——*Abstract* (Gott Discs, 2007) (1962 recording).
Hayes, Tubby: *Tubbs* (Fontana, 1961).
——*Mexican Green* (Fontana/Mercury, 1968).
Holly, Buddy: *The Best Of Buddy Holly* (MCA, 2002).
Holst, Gustav: *The Planets Suite*, Philharmonia Orchestra, London, conducted by Leonard Slatkin (RCA, 2001).
Hooker, John Lee: *The Country Blues of John Lee Hooker* (Riverside, 1959).
——*It Serves You Right To Suffer* (Impulse, 1966).
——*That's Where It's At!* (Stax, 1969) (1961 recording).
——*Never Get Out Of These Blues Alive* (ABC, 1972).
——*The Healer* (Chameleon/Virgin, 1989).
——*The Hot Spot* (OST Virgin, 1990).
——*Mr. Lucky* (Virgin/Pointblank, 1991).
——*Don't Look Back* (Virgin/Pointblank, 1997).
—— *John Lee Hooker Anthology: 50 Years* (Shout!/Factory, 1948–98).
——*Boogie Man* (Spectrum, 2001).
——*The Boogie Man 1948–1955* (Charly, 2006).
Hunter, James: *People Gonna Talk* (Go/Rounder, 2006).
Hurt, Mississippi John: *Avalon Blues* (Rounder, 1963).
Innocents Abroad: *Quaker City* (Stormfield, 1987).
——*Eleven* (Stormfield, 1989).
Jackson, Mahalia: *Queen Of Gospel* (Music Club, 1993).
Johnson, Robert: *The Complete Recordings* (Sony, 1990).
Jones, Tom: *Carrying A Torch* (Dover, 1991).
——*Reload* (Gut, 1999).
Jordan, Louis: *Louis Jordan and His Tympany Five* (JSP, 2001).
Kennedy, Brian: *On Song* (Curb, 2003).
King, B.B.: *Live At The Regal* (ABC/MCA, 1965).

——*80* (Geffen, 2005).
Kissoon, Mac and Kissoon, Katie: *Love Will Keep Us Together* (Disky, 2002).
KLF, The: *1987: What The Fuck Is Going On?* (The Sound of Mu(sic), 1987).
Kraftwerk: *Trans Europe Express* (KlingKlang, 1977).
Leadbelly: *The Very Best Of Leadbelly* (Music Club, 1993).
Lewis, Jerry Lee: *High School Confidential* (MCA, 1958).
——*Sings The Country Music Hall Of Fame Hits Vols One and Two* (BGO, 2002).
——*The Best Of Jerry Lee Lewis* (Music Club, 1998).
——*Last Man Standing* (Artful, 2006).
Lewis, Linda Gail: *I'll Take Memphis* (Fox Records, 1992).
——*Out Of The Shadows* (Ritz, 2002).
Little Richard: *Here's Little Richard* (Speciality, 1957).
——*Little Richard's Greatest Hits* (Vee-Jay, 1965).
——*The Original British Hit Singles* (Ace, 1999).
Lowe, Nick: *Labour Of Lust* (Radar, 1979).
MacGowran, Jack: *MacGowran Speaking Beckett* (Claddagh, 1966).
McCormack, Count John: *The Voice Of Ireland* (Platinum, 2003).
——*Come Back To Erin Original Recordings Vol. Two, 1910–1921* (Naxos, 2004).
McKee, Maria: *Maria McKee* (Geffen, 1990).
——*You Gotta Sin To Get Saved* (Geffen, 1993).
McPeakes, The: *The McPeake Family Of Belfast* (Xtra, 1958).
Memphis Minnie: *All The Published Sides, 1929–1937* (JSP, 2008).
Modern Jazz Quartet: *Sundance* (Atlantic, 1964).
Monkees, The: *Headquarters* (RCA, 1967).
Morrissey: *Kill Uncle* (EMI, 1992).
Nat King Cole Trio: *Best Of The Nat King Cole Trio* (Compendia, 1996).
Newman, Randy: *Good Old Boys* (Reprise, 1974).
Penn, Dan and Oldham, Spooner: *Moments From This Theatre* (Proper American, 1999).
Pierce, Webb: *More and More* (Decca, 2009).
Pink Floyd: *Wish You Were Here* (EMI, 1975).
Pogues, The: *Red Roses For Me* (Stiff Records, 1984).
Presley, Elvis: *The Sun Recordings* (RCA, 1979).
Prima, Louis: *The Louis Prima Collection* (HMV, 2000).
Rivers, Johnny: *Slim Slo Slider* (Liberty/UA, 1970).
——*L.A. Reggae* (Liberty/UA, 1972).
Robeson, Paul: *Best Of* (Digital Music, 2003).
Rodgers, Jimmie: *The Best Of Jimmie Rodgers* (Xtra, 2004).
Rowland, Kevin: *The Wanderer* (Phonogram, 1988).
Rusby, Kate: *Sleepless* (Pure, 1999).
——*10* (Pure, 2002).
——*The Girl Who Couldn't Fly* (Pure, 2005).
——*Awkward Annie* (Pure, 2008).
St. John, Kate: *Indescribable Night* (All Saints, 1995).

——*Second Sight* (All Saints, 1999).
Scarlatti, Domenico: *Harpsichord Sonatas Vol. One*, played by Pieter-Jan Belder (Brilliant Classics, 2001).
Sex Pistols: *Never Mind The Bollocks Here's The Sex Pistols* (Virgin, 1977).
Shearston, Gary: *Dingo* (Charisma, 1974).
——'Wild Mountain Thyme' (Magnet, 1978) (single).
Siberry, Jane: *Summer In The Yukon* (Reprise, 1992).
Sidran, Ben: *Live At Montreux* (Arista, 1979).
——*Live With Richard Davis* (Go Jazz, 1984).
——*The Essential* (SAM Productions, 2008).
——*Dylan Different* (Nardis, 2010).
Simon, Paul: *Hearts And Bones* (Warner Bros., 1983).
Simon and Garfunkel: *Bookends* (CBS, 1968).
——*Old Friends* (Sony, 1998).
Slade: *The Very Best Of* (Polydor/UMTV, 2006).
Sly and the Family Stone: *Greatest Hits* (CBS/Sony, 2002).
Smith, Bessie: *Blues Queen* (Sony, 2007).
Smith, Patti: *Horses* (Arista, 1976).
Smiths, The: *The Queen Is Dead* (Rough Trade, 1986).
Spivey, Victoria: *Victoria Spivey Volume III, 1929–1936* (Document Records, 1995).
Springsteen, Bruce: *Born In The U.S.A* (CBS, 1984).
Stivell, Alan: *Renaissance Of The Celtic Harp* (Phonogram, 1973).
Strauss, Johann: *Strauss Waltzes*, Vienna Philharmonic, conducted by Willi Boskovsky (Decca, 2000).
Strawbs, The: *Bursting At The Seams* (A&M, 1973/2004 CD reissue).
Talk Talk: *The Colour of Spring* (EMI, 1986).
——*Spirit Of Eden* (EMI, 1988).
——*Laughing Stock* (Verve, 1991).
Them: *Now And Them* (Deram/Rev-Ola, 1967).
This Mortal Coil: *It'll End In Tears* (4AD, 1984).
——*Filigree And Shadow* (4AD, 1986).
Turner, Big Joe: *Flip Flop And Fly 1951–1955* (Rev-Ola/Cherry Red, 2006).
Turtles, The: *Battle Of The Bands* (White Whale, 1967).
U2: *October* (Island, 1981).
Vincent, Gene: *Blue Jean Bop* (Capitol, 1957).
Waterboys, The: *This Is The Sea* (Ensign, 1985).
——*Fisherman's Blues* (Ensign, 1988).
Waters, Muddy: *At Newport* (Chess, 1960).
——*Electric Mud* (MCA/Chess, 1968).
——*Hard Again* (Blue Sky, 1977).
Westbrook, Mike: *The Westbrook Blake: Bright As Fire* (Impetus, 1998) (1980 recording).
White, Josh: *Chain Gang Songs* (Elektra, 1958).
——*Spirituals and Blues* (Bounty, 1960).

——*Live At The Royal Festival Hall, London* (EMI, 1960).
——*Good Morning Blues* (MFP, 1961).
——*Empty Bed Blues* (Pye Golden Guinea, 1962).
Williams, Hank: *My Home, The Highway* (Newsound, 1999).
——*40 Greatest Hits* (MGM, 1976/1992).
Wilson, Brian: *Smile* (Nonesuch, 2004).
Wilson, Jackie: *The Original Soul Brother* (Music Club, 2006).
XTC: *Apple Venus Volume One* (Cooking Vinyl, 1999).

Various Artists

Beauty An Oilean (Claddagh, 1978) (Blasket Islands folk music).
En Passant Par . . . La Bretagne: La Routes Des Celtes (Cassettes Regionales Hachette CRH 05, 1978) (Breton folk music).
Omagh: Across The Bridge Of Hope (White Label, 2002).
The Roots Of Van Morrison (Catfish, 2002).
Two Weeks In The Real World (Real World, 1998).
Van Morrison's Jukebox (Chrome Dreams, 2007).
Vanthology (Evidence, 2003).

FILMOGRAPHY

Astral Weeks Live at the Hollywood Bowl: The Concert Film, dir. Darren Doane and Van Morrison, 2009.
Beyond the Clouds, dir. Michelangelo Antonioni, 1994.
Cal, dir. Pat O'Connor, 1984.
Chet Baker Live at Ronnie Scott's (Umbrella Entertainment, 1986/2002 reissue).
The Departed, dir. Martin Scorsese, 2006.
Drei Amerikanische Albumen, dir. Wim Wenders, 1968.
Lamb, dir. Colin Gregg, 1986.
The Last Waltz, dir. Martin Scorsese, 1977.
The Long Journey Home, dir. Thomas Lennon, 1988.
Moondance, dir. Dagmar Hirtz, 1995.
NME Poll Winners Concert Wembley Empire Pool 1965 [DVD] (Video Beat Productions, 2002).
Out of Ireland, dir. David Heffernan, 2000.
Red, White and Blues, dir. Mike Figgis, 2003.
The Schooner, dir. Bill Miskelly, 1983.
Slipstream, dir. David Acomba, 1973.
Someone Like You, dir. Tony Goldman, 2001.
Them! Gordon Douglas, 1954.
Van Morrison in Ireland, dir. Michael Radford, 1978.
Van Morrison: The Concert, dir. Jon Small, 1990.
Van Morrison Live in Montreux 1980/1974, dir. Dick Carruthers, 2006.

Wings of Desire [Der Himmel Uber Berlin], dir. Wim Wenders, 1987.

ESSENTIAL FREE TO AIR TV

Arena: One Irish Rover, BBC, broadcast 16 February 1991.
Back on the Corner, BBC Northern Ireland, recorded at Waterfront Hall, 2 and 3 February 1997.
Candy Meets . . . Van Morrison [Candy Dulfer series in which she interviews fellow musicians], NPS [Dutch public service TV], recorded in Cardiff, 14 April 2007 and broadcast 28 October and 11 November 2007.
A Coney Island of the Mind, dir., Peter Lynden and Tom Tyrwhitt, broadcast 12 March 1991.
Old Grey Whistle Test: Van Morrison Live at the Rainbow, BBC, recorded 24 July 1973 and broadcast 27 May 1974; repeated 1975/1976/1980.
So Hard to Beat, BBC Ulster, dir. Stuart Bailie, 2008.
Songs of Innocence: Van Morrison and the Chieftains, Channel 4, recorded at the Ulster Hall Belfast 15 September 1988 and broadcast 17 March 1989.
Soul Britannia, BBC Four, dir. Jeremy Marre, 2007.
Talk about Pop, RTE Dublin, recorded 2 November 1973, broadcast 11 November 1973.
Van the Man: In Conversation and Concert, Ulster TV, recorded at the Riverside Theatre University of Coleraine, 20 April 1988.

Index

Entries in **bold** refer to case studies or lengthy references to the subject